THE CHOICE

ZHANG PING

Translated by
James Trapp

SINOIST

Published by Sinoist Books (an imprint of ACA Publishing Ltd)
London - Beijing
info@alaincharlesasia.com ☎ +44 20 3289 3885
www.sinoistbooks.com

Published by Sinoist Books (an imprint of ACA Publishing Ltd)
in association with China Translation and Publishing House

Author: Zhang Ping **Translator:** James Trapp
Editor: Matthew Keeler.

Original Chinese Text © 抉择 *(jue ze)* 2005
People's Literature Publishing House, Beijing, China

ALL RIGHTS RESERVED. NO PART OF THIS PUBLICATION MAY BE REPRODUCED IN MATERIAL FORM, BY ANY MEANS, WHETHER GRAPHIC, ELECTRONIC, MECHANICAL OR OTHER, INCLUDING PHOTOCOPYING OR INFORMATION STORAGE, IN WHOLE OR IN PART, AND MAY NOT BE USED TO PREPARE OTHER PUBLICATIONS WITHOUT WRITTEN PERMISSION FROM THE PUBLISHER.

English Translation text © 2023 ACA Publishing Ltd, London, UK.
A catalogue record for *The Choice* is available from the National Bibliographic Service of the British Library.

This novel is entirely a work of fiction. The names, characters and incidents portrayed in it are the work of the author's imagination. Any resemblance to actual persons, living or dead, events or localities is entirely coincidental.

Paperback ISBN: 978-1-83890-549-1
eBook ISBN: 978-1-83890-550-7

Sinoist Books is honoured to be supported using public funding by Arts Council England.

CHAPTER ONE

IT WAS FOUR O'CLOCK IN THE MORNING when Mayor Li Gaocheng heard that the trouble with the workers at the Zhongyang Textile Group was about to kick off. The general manager, Guo Zhongyao, told him on the phone that they had been hard at it all night but had not been able to talk the workers round and two deputy general managers were almost beaten up in the process. Even Party Secretary Fan Ligang, who was already retired from the company, had his home besieged by the workers, and two hooligans took the opportunity to smash the glass in his porch. The company's security department completely failed to deal with the incident, and even a hundred or more men sent in by the Economic Crimes Unit of the Public Security Bureau proved unable to stop the situation degenerating into chaos. There were at least three or four thousand people gathered in the company's dormitory compound at that time, and some of their leaders had said that they were going, as a group, to the gates of the Municipal Party Committee's office early the next morning to present a petition. There were more than twenty coaches at the head office to collect the workers, and it was being reported that people were still contacting other work units for more transport. If that wasn't forthcoming, they would use the forty or more trucks that were at the factory! If so many people really were allowed to go, needless to say, those sixty or seventy vehicles gathered at the gates of the Municipal Party Committee could cause chaos across the whole city.

Mayor Li Gaocheng, who had just spent the last two hours failing to go to sleep, gave up on the idea completely for the time being. He had thrown on some clothes and was sitting dazedly on the edge of his bed, completely at a loss what to do next. The Zhongyang Textile Group was a big company with more than twenty thousand workers. In its previous incarnation as the Zhongyang Textile Factory, it had been one of the largest textile mills in North China and it was more than twice as old as the People's Republic itself. Its construction was said to have been on the orders of the Empress Dowager Cixi herself, and it was reckoned to have been the largest, most modern textile mill of that era. Over several decades of fluctuating fortunes, be it during the turbulent fighting of the Warlord Era, the War of Resistance against Japanese Aggression or the War of Liberation, and no matter whether it was in the hands of the Qing Government, the warlords or the Japanese, the factory was always flourishing, well-managed, well-run, well-funded and profitable. It was a key industry of whichever government was in power at the time. Even if, sometimes, it did not quite live up to people's expectations, it always pulled through, and it had never experienced any strikes or industrial unrest.

After the Liberation, the Zhongyang Textile Factory was finally taken over by the government in a public-private partnership and underwent a large-scale technological revamp, which returned it at a stroke to its former glory, making it one of the great success stories of the early industrial construction of the People's Republic of China, particularly for the local economy. In 1958, during the Great Leap Forward, the Zhongyang Textile Factory put huge effort into expansion, almost doubling the number of workers at the time, from around eight thousand to more than fifteen thousand. The provincial leadership gave explicit instructions that it should be the number one textile factory in the north of China, not only in scale but also in growth and size of workforce. As a result, the Zhongyang Textile Factory was plunged into a predicament unprecedented in its history. Because of the lack of money and technology and especially because of the breakdown in diplomatic relations with the Soviet Union, there was an extreme shortage of the machine parts previously supplied by the Soviets, which led to the almost complete paralysis and collapse of the factory's production. These difficulties persisted for three years, and it wasn't until 1964 that the factory was finally able to regain its strength. But, within a matter of days of its resurgence, the Cultural Revolution began, and it was only after 1978 that a complete reorganisation began and updating of technical knowledge and manufacturing equipment was resumed, so that the order and scale of production could be fully restored.

In 1985, the Zhongyang Textile Mill was officially renamed the Zhongyang Textile Group, with more than twenty branches under it. At the same time, in an ambitious move, the group also merged three factories that were about to close down and saved two enterprises that were on the verge of bankruptcy. These actions were unparalleled at any other stage in the history of the Zhongyang Textile Factory, and its contribution to the country as a whole was undeniable.

After 1985, the Zhongyang Textile Group began a downward spiral, moving from profit into loss after 1986. The deepening reform of the national tax system, the full liberalisation of grain and cotton prices, the rapid rise of township enterprises, the further establishment of a market economy, the mismanagement of large state-run enterprises and the growing weight of its own financial burdens all combined to drag the Zhongyang Textile Group into an increasingly untenable position. By the end of 1995, excluding external debts, the accumulated losses and liabilities of the group had reached 450 million yuan. The most recent figures had still not been included and the total external debt was expected to be close to 600 million yuan. The company had not been able to pay a single salary since February that year, and by July 1995 the monthly subsistence allowance of 200 yuan for each retired worker and cadre had also been suspended. By January 1993, some of the company's branch factories had already begun to cease production. By the end of 1994, most of the branch factories were essentially out of production, and in October 1995 the faltering Zhongyang Textile Group finally collapsed, and the entire company ceased production, marking the demise of the once mighty Zhongyang Factory.

There was bound to be trouble when a major state enterprise stopped all production and ceased work completely. It had its pensioners and almost thirty thousand workers and cadres with the year coming to an end and the Spring Festival almost upon them; the workers hadn't been paid for more than ten months, the weather was freezing, they had neither food nor drink, and prices were skyrocketing. Of course there was bound to be trouble.

The municipal authorities wasted no time in making the rescue of the Zhongyang Textile Group the focus of their work for 1996. The Municipal Standing Committee convened several meetings to study the matter and decided that Mayor Li Gaocheng should personally take charge with a steering group to be formed by the Municipal Bank, the Municipal Economic Committee, the Municipal Planning Committee and the Municipal Finance Committee. Together they would find solutions to the catalogue of problems that beset the Zhongyang Textile Group. It was already October 1995 by the time the committee was established. Although they started work immediately and had already submitted several reports to the Municipal Government, as the end of the year approached they were beset by all kinds of different problems. These kept them so busy that they were unable to come up with a final decision on how to handle the Zhongyang Textile Group. In January 1996, the municipal authorities readdressed the problem, and this time they made it a matter of policy that, by Spring Festival without fail, a way should be found of paying the entire Zhongyang workforce between one and two months' backpay. Everything else could wait until after the holiday. It had never occurred to the authorities that the workers would start anything at this critical juncture, and when they did, it was on such a dramatic scale, it inevitably caused consternation.

Mayor Li Gaocheng cudgelled his brains but could not come up with a failsafe plan. Truth be told, over the last few years, the gates of the Municipal Government had seen plenty of petitions and noisy protests, to the extent that the office workers going in and out of the government buildings scarcely raised an eyebrow at them or paid them any heed at all. They seemed to be just another everyday occurrence, and these unconnected, trivial incidents really had little or no effect. After all, it doesn't matter how many frogs croak at the same time, they are never going to bring the sky tumbling down. But this was different. For one thing, there were already three or four thousand workers involved, and who knew when more might not join them? Not to mention the sixty or seventy coaches. That many people and coaches on the road outside the gates of the government offices would make the traffic grind to a halt in no time flat. The road on which the government offices stood ran east-west through the centre of the city for more than five kilometres. Even in a normal rush hour at the beginning or end of the working day, it became blocked by people and cars, so the effect of several thousand protesting workers could easily be imagined. Secondly, this was the most volatile time of the year. With the year-end approaching, commodity prices were rising steadily, and, although the Municipal Government had put certain measures into effect, these had failed to steady or stem the inflation. Not long before, the authorities had taken the important decision to use a variety of measures to make it easier for farmers to bring their vegetables directly into the city to sell, and had set up an open market in the city centre for this purpose. Contrary to expectation, however, not only had prices not dropped, they had actually continued to rise even further. There were some people who said that letting the farmers sell their vegetables at will inside the city was like inviting a wolf into your house. And once the farmers found themselves in the city, their eyes were suddenly opened: they had never imagined their vegetables could command such prices! And who, they thought, would be such a fucking idiot as not to take advantage? Their own produce was much fresher than the stuff that came to market through middlemen, so why on earth should they sell it any cheaper? Thus, not only did the price of vegetables not fall, it actually began to rocket upwards, and, as it did so, it dragged the price of other goods up with it. This also served to kill stone dead any chance the wageless strikers and other laid-off workers had of setting up their own little businesses selling vegetables. In a situation so rife with seething grievance and resentment, it was hardly surprising if other people decided to hitch their own wagons to the protest. Thirdly, the Provincial Government offices were in a street not far from the Municipal Government, and if the protest spread there, its effect would be greatly increased, especially since, for the last couple of days, a delegation from a western European country had been in discussions with the Provincial Government over an investment project. If, by any chance...

Not daring to think about the matter any further, Li Gaocheng massaged his eyes and temples, trying to restore a little feeling. He knew he had to come up with a plan as soon as possible but he had run out of time. He looked at his watch and saw it was 4.25, still maybe a couple of hours before dawn. The Zhongyang Textile Group was located in the suburbs, fifteen or so kilometres from the city centre, and, if the workers really were coming into town by coach, it wouldn't take them much more than half an hour to get there.

He thought about phoning Municipal Secretary Yang Cheng but hung up before he had even finished dialling the number.

Municipal Secretary Yang and he had a few differences of opinion over matters concerning the Zhongyang Textile Group. Yang Cheng had always advocated major surgery on the company, including at the management level. Li Gaocheng was opposed to this idea and found it fundamentally unacceptable. This was not just because the leadership of the Municipal Government held the Zhongyang management in very high regard, with some of the very top brass believing they had shown supreme resilience and trustworthiness; the main reason was that Li himself was too friendly with the Zhongyang management and too emotionally invested in them. You could pretty much say that he had personally nurtured and earmarked for promotion the entire current management team of the Zhongyang Textile Group. He knew each and every one of them inside out and upside down, and completely understood their individual characters and temperaments. Of course, the municipal secretary's viewpoint also had its logic, as the current tense relations between the Zhongyang Textile Group and the cadres and workers were the direct responsibility of this same management team. But the difficulties the company found itself in were the same difficulties faced by other large and medium-sized companies across the country, so was it either fair or realistic to pile all the grievances and responsibility for the situation solely on the shoulders of these few men? Everyone has their shortcomings, and if you get rid of one group, lock stock and barrel, won't the replacements you bring in have their own set of failings? Besides, sacking an entire management team was neither seemly nor practical. Was changing teams when a problem arose any guarantee that the new team was going to solve the problem? Could anyone taking on the work say for sure that no problems would arise? Moreover, given the size and structure of the Zhongyang Group, what person of experience, ability, determination and responsibility was going to want to take that on? So, when it came down to it, what purpose was a wholesale change of management going to serve? Was it to get to the root of the problem or was it in fact a serious dereliction of duty? How could it be explained to both the people and the leadership? If the situation wasn't resolved after repeated changes, how would it be possible to face the people? How would it be possible to face the leadership?

On this occasion, he didn't go through with the phone call because he couldn't give the impression of passing the buck as soon as a problem arose. At this point, he had not taken any action to resolve the problem but nor had he reached the point where he was obliged to make a report to the municipal secretary.

After a moment's thought, he first telephoned his personal secretary, Wu Xingang, telling him to instruct his driver to rush the two of them to the Zhongyang Textile Group in fifteen minutes' time. Then he called the mobile number of the general manager of the Zhongyang Group, asking him immediately to do the following things:

First, he was to investigate exactly who all the leaders of the current protest were and, as soon as possible, find a way of gathering them all together to tell them that the mayor wanted to talk things over with them face to face. He needed to make a good job of convincing them that they could discuss all of their demands and conditions directly with the mayor.

Second, he was to withdraw all the company security men, not leaving a single one at the scene. None of the company cadres, nor the security men, were to retaliate in any way, neither physically nor verbally. They would be recompensed by the Municipal Government for any damage or any harm inflicted upon them. Any injury to a worker or any other incident would be closely investigated and the culprits severely punished.

Third, nothing was to be said or done that was against the interests of the cadres and the people; in particular, there was to be absolutely no bandying about of irresponsible threats or other loose talk. Anyone who did or said anything of the kind and was found out could expect no leniency and would be dealt with severely.

Fourth, immediately to start using the company's broadcast and cable TV to keep emphasising to the mass of workers that they shouldn't participate in the protests, and, in particular, they most certainly should not come into the city to present any kind of petition. The Municipal Government was deeply concerned for the Zhongyang Textile Group and would certainly make sure that the whole workforce, both current and retired, would be properly looked after before the Spring Festival. Moreover, for anyone, be they management or anyone else, and particularly anyone who participated in the current protest, for whatever reason, the Municipal Government guaranteed that they would not be held to account later, nor would they suffer any kind of ongoing persecution or petty settling of scores. It was vital to free the mass of workers from any fears about future consequences, and they must absolutely not be made to think they were being forced into any kind of "outlaw" status so they felt they had nothing to lose now in taking their protest further.

Fifth, he himself would be at the company before 5.20 that morning and would meet with the workers at the Old Cadre Activity Centre in the company dormitory compound. He didn't want any official reception committee or any personal protection detail.

CHAPTER TWO

ALTHOUGH LI GAOCHENG SOUNDED VERY CALM and methodical on the telephone, he was actually wracked by doubt. Things were not the same as they had been only a few years ago when even a casual remark from management reverberated like a clap of thunder. Now, official documents could cascade down incessantly, and no matter how stern and solemn they were, and how many times they were repeated, the ordinary folk on the receiving end never took them to heart. A single mouse-dropping can spoil a whole pot of soup and a single act of rank corruption is enough to break the hearts of the whole people. No matter with how many repetitions, yearly, monthly or daily, no matter how grand or lowly the audience, no matter how much effort was put in, firm decisions could be taken to impose strict laws and severe punishments, to crack down hard on corruption, to rectify Party conduct, showing no trace of tolerance or leniency, but in the end it was always the same old situation, with tigers prowling the land, and bluebottles filling the sky. Kill one tiger and another bounded along; swat one swarm and another roiled up. In such unchanging circumstances, who was going to take seriously any document you issued, any meeting you held or management orders you gave?

Li Gaocheng was fifty-four years old, which was still considered young for the mayor of a top-level provincial city. Even so, his hair was already streaked with grey at the temples, and his face was creased with wrinkles. He had always been thin but was getting thinner with age and was completely unlike some mayors who were always smiley, sleek, plump and shiny. His appearance was generally pleasing to his subordinates, and the ordinary people, in particular, found that it inspired affection and trust. He often joked about this at the dining table with his leadership colleagues and peers, saying: "With my appearance, however the people look at me, what they see is an upright and honest official, but when they see your plump faces and fat bellies, they immediately know you are corrupt."

Li Gaocheng truly believed it when he called himself an honest and upright official, and he had a completely clear conscience when he looked back at his decades as a cadre.

The reason for his enduring and affectionate relationship with Zhongyang Textiles was that the company had served as his springboard since he had spent several years as the Party secretary and director of the Zhongyang Textile Factory. He was one of the first students after the founding of the People's Republic to graduate from a textile industry technical middle school, and it could be said that he had spent half his life in the industry. He was originally from the south, but because, at that time, all the major textile industry was concentrated in the northern interior of the country, after he graduated from technical middle school, he was posted to the loess plain of northern China. First, he worked for nearly ten years as a technician, deputy workshop director and workshop director in the Xinhua Textile Factory, and then he moved on to the provincial textile factory where he spent nearly eight years, during which time he was a workshop director, Party secretary of the workshop, chief engineer and deputy factory director. In 1980 he transferred again to become deputy secretary of the Party Committee and deputy director of the Zhongyang Textile Factory, and in 1982 he was appointed to the joint post of secretary of the Party Committee and director of production for the factory. Holding these two posts when he had just turned forty, Li Gaocheng became the de facto boss of the twenty thousand workers of a large-scale manufacturing company and was also the youngest cadre of a top-level government department in the province.

The Li Gaocheng of that time was smug and superior about his exalted status and he vowed that, in his hands, the Zhongyang Textile

Factory would become the number one modernised industry in the whole country. That period was a golden age for the state-run textile industry; there was a steady stream of raw materials and no cause at all for any concern, as farmers rushed to sell their produce to the factory through the back door. Demand in the market outstripped supply, and goods lorries snaked in a constant stream in and out of the province, with the queue usually stretching several kilometres back from the factory gates. All the staff, junior and senior, in the supply and distribution department were as spoiled as little lords, and the other workers cursed them behind their backs, complaining how fucking fat those bastards in marketing were!

In fact, it was the same for everyone at the time: how fashionable it was to be a worker at the Zhongyang Factory and how famous was the company brand! To have the factory emblem on your jacket made you the envy of all the other lads and lasses. How much ink was spilt and how many phone calls were made by officials, great and small, trying to get a job at the Zhongyang Textile Factory out of Li Gaocheng!

During this time, it was Li Gaocheng who completed the first technical overhaul of the Zhongyang Factory after the Cultural Revolution. Financing the project was no problem at the time as all it took was one telephone call to access tens of millions of capital. No one could have imagined then that an enterprise like Zhongyang Textiles could show a loss, let alone not be able to repay its loans. It was unthinkable that an evergreen money tree like that could ever wither.

In 1983, Sino-US relations were strained and China's textile exports were restricted. Zhongyang Textiles also felt the pressure, and their products were soon backlogged, with all the warehouses in the factory overflowing. What should be done to react to such pressure? Even the provincial and municipal leaders were uncertain. Li Gaocheng gave the matter some thought and finally decided that they would not stop production, not even for a minute! At the time, all the employees of the factory shared his conviction that Zhongyang Textiles' products would never go unsold.

No one felt pessimistic or discouraged, and certainly no one had lost hope. Inside the factory, the atmosphere was as noisy and enthusiastic as ever, and everything was as orderly as usual with no hint of discord or loss of discipline. The workers were all following their normal routines, and morale was high. The only one who felt the enormous pressure was Li Gaocheng, and there was no knowing how many peaceful nights' sleep he actually managed to get during this period. Often, he would be woken halfway through the night by a sudden shiver of fear which kept him awake until morning.

The factory had already completed its technical renovation and doubled its output. There was a backlog of more than ten months' worth of product and the factory's inventory was at the highest it had been in several years. More than twenty warehouses temporarily rented in the city were already completely full, as were thirty or so similar units in the suburbs and more than sixty in nearby county towns. The value of stock in these warehouses was already almost 200 million yuan, and the company's loans and external funding liabilities had reached 450 million yuan!

How could Li Gaocheng possibly sleep at a time like that? During the day, his spirit felt as though it was suspended in mid-air, and physically he felt as though he was walking on cotton wool. At night, he seemed to be lying on a bed of clouds. It was now that the grey began to appear in his hair, the wrinkles began to spread across his face and he aged considerably.

But the whole workforce was united and of one mind. The current management team of the Zhongyang Textile Group were all, in fact, survivors of that original workforce. They were a cohort that had undergone a rigorous examination, had stood by each other through thick and thin, and were united in will. Perhaps without such a cohort, Li Gaocheng might not be the man he now was!

At the time, he was a pioneer among medium and large-scale industries in establishing the rule that management personnel should not travel to and from work by car. He himself was living in the urban area so the journey to and from work was almost forty kilometres, which he did by bicycle, come rain or shine. He had a simple lunch in the factory canteen with the workers, and he never got home from work before ten o'clock at night. One evening it was midnight before he returned, and public security officers stopped and detained him for ages as he crossed a bridge in the city, because they thought he looked dodgy. They didn't believe he could be the director of the Zhongyang Textile Factory and were only convinced after they had telephoned the factory security office. This incident caused a sensation when it was reported in the newspapers. It was still big news that a cadre from a top-flight industry actually cycled to and from work every day. The workers in his own factory and in others were all impressed by this: where else could you find a cadre with such integrity and self-discipline?

The crisis then only lasted ten months or so, and perhaps shouldn't even be called a crisis; compared to what was going on currently, it really only ranked as a temporary embarrassment. After ten months, the sales path was freed up again and the re-opened marketplace swallowed up everything it was offered as voraciously as a man who hadn't eaten in a hundred years. In little more than a year, both the goods that came off the production line and all the reserve stock were completely sold out. At that time, with the price of all cotton fabrics rising, the products of the Zhongyang Textile Factory were sold at prices so high they would, in other circumstances, have seemed like profiteering!

Zhongyang Textiles was awash with money then! It had gold coming out of its ears and cash sweating from its pores. The only problem was how to spend it all!

In February 1986, as an outstanding national entrepreneur, winner of the national May 1st Labour Medal and a national model worker, Li Gaocheng was elected as deputy mayor of the city and member of the Standing Committee of the Municipal Party Committee.

As deputy mayor, Li Gaocheng was in charge of both standard industry and light industry, and, as he was an alumnus of the Zhongyang Textile Factory management team, it was only natural that he was particularly interested in and protective of that business; the Municipal Government leadership were also very comfortable with him handling anything to do with Zhongyang Textiles. In 1986, under his guidance and with the subsequent approval and ratification of the Municipal Party Committee, the Zhongyang Textile Factory management team carried out a complete overhaul of itself. Under the prevailing system of factory manager's responsibilities, he instructed the 59-year-old former factory manager Yuan Mingliang, the 57-year-old chief engineer and deputy factory manager Zhang Huabin, and the 54-year-old female deputy factory manager Li Suzhi all to retire and act as advisers to the factory. He then appointed his most capable staff member, the then deputy manager, 48-year-old Guo Zhongyao, as manager; he made 47-year-old deputy secretary, Chen Yongming, Party secretary; 45-year-old deputy secretary, Wu Mingde, deputy factory production manager; and 44-year-old general supply and distribution manager, Feng Minjie, deputy factory supply and distribution manager.

Li Gaocheng didn't give up control all at once at that time, and for a long time he continued simultaneously to hold the posts of factory general manager and secretary of the Party Committee. It was only when he was absolutely convinced he could safely let go and relax that he relinquished his duties first as factory manager and then as Party secretary.

He was very satisfied with the new management team, and the Municipal Government leadership were equally pleased. To begin with, this was a rejuvenated management team, and it was also a tried and tested, bold and able team. The average age of its members was only just over forty-five which made it the youngest management team of any state-owned medium or large-scale industry in the province. In particular, it was no small thing that they had all worked at the factory for between fifteen and twenty years. At the very least, this showed that they had been tried and tested by both the workforce and the management. Equally, the fact that they had worked in the same factory for so long, and made their way, rung by rung, up the ladder, demonstrated that they had both ability and a popular base. That too was no small thing.

Of course, there was some resistance.

The old factory manager, Yuan Mingliang, and the deputy manager, Li Suzhi, regarded this new team rather differently, and the chief engineer and deputy manager, Zhang Huabin, was particularly vehement in his opposition.

Their principal objections focused on Factory Manager Guo Zhongyao and Deputy Supply and Distribution Manager Feng Minjie.

In Guo Zhongyao's case, they reckoned that he was not sufficiently able and believed that, in such a large state-owned industry, any deficiency in high-level awareness and advanced academic learning was a handicap to the smooth running of the business. They felt that Guo Zhongyao clearly displayed just such a deficiency. In the same way, they did not greatly value the so-called "boldness" that Li Gaocheng so prized: a manager who lacked ability but displayed great "boldness" was the sort of manager who needed careful consideration and could sometimes be a manager to be feared. Chief Engineer Zhang Huabin even went so far as to raise doubts about some of Li Gaocheng's original actions at the factory, pointing out that Li's insistence on increasing production, regardless of the surplus already in the warehouses, had actually been very risky, and could even be viewed as an abrogation of his responsibilities. If the same circumstances arose at present, it would be extremely dangerous: it would be gambling with the fate of the entire factory and its twenty thousand workers, and it would not be in line with the norms and standards of a modern enterprise. Moreover, the impact and implications of this behaviour on the current team were equally profound. If this was what was meant by "boldness", then such "boldness" was very definitely a cause for concern. And for another thing, they felt that there was something both suspicious and untrustworthy about Guo Zhongyao's show of moral virtue. They were even less satisfied with the style and conduct of the deputy factory manager in charge of supply and distribution, Feng Minjie: there seemed to be a lot of holes in his strategies for selling the product surplus, and many people had blown the whistle on problems they had encountered. Putting a man like him into such an important position could only serve greatly to diminish people's trust in the company.

Of course, Li Gaocheng didn't agree with any of this.

Although Guo Zhongyao had graduated from technical middle school, he had also, some time ago, put himself through technical college. Besides, education is not the same as ability, nor is knowledge the same as drive. Li Gaocheng had watched the man for himself over many years as he grew up. When Li first arrived at the Zhongyang Textile Factory, Guo Zhongyao was a workshop boss in charge of the best workshop in the whole factory and had been a technical standard bearer and advanced practitioner with many years' experience. His innovatory abilities and spirit of initiative impressed everyone in the factory, especially after he was promoted to deputy factory manager and deputy secretary; in the most difficult and critical period of the factory's history, he showed extraordinary skills and remarkable perseverance with the kind of untiring spirit that left a deep impression on Li Gaocheng. In order to sell the factory's backlog of stock back then, Guo Zhongyao did not go home once in the first half of the year, and he seemed to have visited every region of the country. He pretty much sold half of all the stock on his own in those six months. However, he fell seriously ill after he got home and lost almost ten kilos in weight. He was delirious for four days and nights and stayed lying in a hospital bed for a whole month before he recovered. How could such a model worker be accused of lacking ability or courage? And how could his way of thinking be questioned? The problem his detractors saw in his moral ethos lay in the fact that he and his wife had divorced. It was because he was always on the move and seldom had time for his family that his wife fought and argued with him all day long, and this eventually led to the breakdown of the marriage. Wasn't it too petty and small-minded to question his ethos just because of that? Li Gaocheng had also long been generally aware of the various complaints and denunciations regarding Factory Supply and Distribution Manager Feng Minjie's views and of supposed problems with him. In fact, the supply and distribution department of the Zhongyang Factory had always been a black-or-white kind of place and there probably wasn't a single person who had worked there against whom some kind of complaint or accusation hadn't been made! Everyone who worked at the factory reckoned that the whole department was dripping with cash. Of course, it is a widely held prejudice that anyone who works in marketing is bound to be flush with money. Are you not really just talking about yourself when you talk about other people like this? Is this any proper approach to problems? Feng Minjie had worked in the supply and distribution department for more than ten years, and no significant problems had ever come to light. The set of strict and well-thought-out rules and regulations formulated by the Zhongyang Factory supply and distribution department had been promoted nationally in the textile industry and had been commended by the leadership of the Ministry of Textiles. Feng Minjie's strict management of the department could even be said to verge on the harsh. Once he discovered a problem, he always acted according to the rules and showed no mercy. Just over the last few years, he had dealt severely with seven individuals, two of whom had been expelled from the factory. Among them there was also one for whom Li Gaocheng himself had put in a good word with Feng Minjie, but, even so, the man was severely dealt with in the end. In truth, most of the people who complained about Feng and informed against him were those who Feng had disciplined. Isn't that really all you need to know?

Even those old comrades who were opposed to the new management team had never expressed dissatisfaction with Li Gaocheng since he became mayor. Nor did the fact that he had ordered these men to take a step back from the front line have anything to do with their views, which Li thought were completely understandable at the time. It was all for the good of the factory, otherwise why would they have risked offending people by making their harsh comments?

Notwithstanding all that, on this particular night, Li Gaocheng was feeling angry because a number of those same old comrades were among the protestors! This was not something he had anticipated! What was the reason for it? What was it really all about?

I can understand the reasons for the workers to be protesting, he thought. But you are all old cadres, old Party members. Where is your organisation and discipline? Are you still upset about what happened back then?

If that was really what was behind it, it was completely outrageous!

CHAPTER THREE

Mayor Li Gaocheng could hear the noise of the protest before he even went through the gates of the dormitory compound.

As his car drove in, he found himself confronted by the dark mass of people. At a rough reckoning, there were at least seven or eight thousand of them, probably more! At a loss what to do, he sat in his car, unable to move, for a long time. He had never expected there to be so many! What was really going on here? Was it only because they had no wages and no money?

How was this possible?

He suddenly felt the gravity of the situation; supposing all these people spilt out onto the street? The consequences would be unthinkable.

With this huge crowd in front of him, he knew he couldn't go charging into the compound in the car. He would have to get out and walk in, right in among all the workers. His chest tightened and his legs shook so much that he almost couldn't get out of the car. His secretary, Wu Xingang, gave him some timely support and gently helped him out.

He could feel his secretary's hands shaking too and, glancing at him, saw that his face had gone rather pale. His mind suddenly went blank. He felt how weak and powerless, isolated and helpless he was. Even on an ordinary day, he often felt secretly amazed by the power and influence he wielded and had trouble understanding how it was possible. But this night, as he faced that crowd of people, he also felt how weak and fragile that power and influence really was.

Was he really capable of talking round this great crowd of people? How could he get them all to trust and believe him? Could he do it? Was it really possible? He felt more and more lost.

"Are we still going in, Mr Mayor?" his secretary whispered anxiously in his ear.

He stared blankly for a moment, then quickly came back to his senses. He asked himself: What's the matter with you? When did you become so timid? Didn't you work for years in that place you're staring at now? Aren't these workers in front of you now the same workers you spent all your time with over so many days and nights? You've only been away from here a few years, so what has made you so timid and hesitant? What has made you feel so estranged from the place? Is it you who has changed or the workers? If your conscience is clear, why are you like this?

"What do you mean? What do you think we're here for? Of course we're going in!" Li Gaocheng suddenly pulled himself together and said with some anger: "Come on! Follow me!"

It was not clear who first spotted the mayor, but someone shouted out, then many others joined in, and after a thunderous clamour had passed through the crowd, the thousands of people present suddenly fell silent. The only noise left was the sound of breathing and of the biting, early morning wind.

He looked silently at the crowd in front of him, and the countless eyes of the crowd looked silently back at him.

The harsh light of the streetlamps was turning the factory square a deathly white. He felt a sudden, indescribable thrill, and saw in the people's eyes a sense of trust and expectation, even of respect and gratitude. There was no resentment, no anger, no hatred or hostility. All the tension and anxiety of a moment ago seemed to disappear.

"Hello everyone! I am Li Gaocheng. I've heard that there's something going on here in our factory, so I've come out to see you all!"

An old, grey-haired employee standing at the front called out in a trembling voice: "Factory Manager Li, is that you? Is it really you? Why are you here?"

The words "factory manager" almost brought tears to Li Gaocheng's eyes. The old worker looked very familiar, but he could not even remember what job he had done, let alone what his name was. He hurried over to the old man and took his hand, saying in a shaky voice: "It is me, old comrade! I am Li Gaocheng and I heard that you were coming into the city to see the municipal leaders. I thought it would be best if I came to meet you first."

"It is so good that you're here, so good that you're here." The old man's eyes were suddenly moist with tears. "Now you are mayor, Manager Li, it is very difficult for us to get to see you. We have tried many times, but we can't even get into City Hall, let alone your office."

"Well, I'm here now, aren't I? From now on, if anything happens, you can come straight to me. My secretary is here too, so you can take my word on it. You can stop worrying now." Li Gaocheng spoke sincerely and his whole demeanour was very honest and open.

"You can stop trying to fucking sweet-talk us! If we weren't up in arms, do you really think you'd be here, Mister Mayor?" a voice in the crowd shouted out, apparently in a deliberate attempt to be provocative.

"That's right! He's still bullshitting us now!"

"Give him a chance to speak. Let's hear what he wants here today, what he's up to! Is he just trying to stop us going into the city, or has he really come to talk things through?"

"If you want to know the truth, we weren't coming to see you today. We want to see the Municipal Party secretary and the Provincial Party secretary! You're hand in glove with them and we've never trusted you anyway!"

Li Gaocheng stood rooted to the spot, and it was as if a bomb had gone off in his brain. He had been mayor for some time now, and no one had ever dared curse him to his face and berate him in front of such a crowd. His chest, which had just relaxed, suddenly constricted again, and he found himself unable to speak for a moment. He hurriedly recapped to himself what he had said and whether he had just misspoken somehow. If not, why had the mood of the crowd changed so suddenly after just a couple of sentences?

"Stop yelling! Stop yelling! Everybody stop yelling! Let's listen to what Mayor Li has to say. You can all have your say when he has finished!" A tall old man with the look of a cadre, standing at the front, turned round and shouted at the crowd, in an apparent attempt to keep order.

The crowd immediately fell silent.

"Listen everyone! Even though it is the middle of the night, Mayor Li has come here to listen to everyone's opinions and requests," Li's secretary, Wu Xingang, shouted to the crowd in explanation. "If he had any other intentions, do you think he would have come here with just me? Before he came here, he told your company's management over and over again that anyone, no matter what views they held or problems they had, could talk directly to him as mayor. He also ordered them to stand down all the company security men and not to have any kind of confrontation with you all..."

Before he had even finished talking, a clamour of voices rose from the crowd and confusion reigned again.

"You're lying! It's all bullshit! You lot are always saying one thing and doing another so you can go on cheating ordinary people!"

"Let the mayor talk to us for himself! What did he actually say to the management?"

"The company bosses have just been on the loudspeaker saying that the municipal leaders are on their way out here. They said that we will be severely fined and punished if we keep going about things the wrong way, that things won't go well for the leaders of the protest, that it won't matter who they are if they are found out! If you are saying one thing to the officials and another thing to us ordinary people, how can you expect us to trust you?"

"Just look around you! Can you see any security men? If there aren't any, then we can all go home!"

"We don't believe a single word you say. You officials are all the same these days – none of you are any good!"

"Make that smarmy secretary shut up! We want to hear from the mayor himself!"

"Mayor Li! In front of all of us, tell us exactly what is going on!"

"Let the mayor speak!"

Once again, Li Gaocheng found himself rooted to the spot, unable to speak. But then an indescribable anger shot through him. So that's how things stood, was it!? It had never occurred to him that the company management might talk to the workers like that, doing completely the opposite of what he had wanted! This was all simply unbelievable!

But you have to believe it! Several thousand people are all saying the same thing! Is it possible that so many of them could all have agreed to lie to you? But this had all happened in the space of less than twenty minutes! Who had the power to organise that? Who had that kind of influence and motivation? Was it even possible?

And if that really was what the management were saying, what were they up to? Were they putting on a great show of being fierce to scare the people away? Or were they taking the opportunity to show certain people in a bad light? Either way, it was just plain outrageous! Stupid and unconscionable too!

What was up with this manager, Guo Zhongyao, anyway? What had brought him to this? Could it be he was afraid? Or confused? Or had he misunderstood his, the mayor's, intentions? Perhaps he had misheard what had been said on the telephone. But how could that be?

What really shocked and pained him was that relations between cadres and workers at the Zhongyang Textile Group could have become so strained. It was hard to believe that the company management could still function in such an environment. How could they keep their authority? In a company that size, how many people actually still listened to them?

He couldn't help but remember what the secretary of the Municipal Party Committee, Yang Cheng, had said to him not long ago. When discussing the problems of the team at Zhongyang Textiles with him, Yang had twice told him that the company's workers had a lot of complaints about the current management, and that the team should consider making some changes.

"Let the mayor speak!"

"Why isn't the mayor saying anything?"

"He can't! He doesn't dare say to our faces what he has been saying behind our backs!"

"They're all in it together!"

"Tell us exactly what you are going to do, if you dare, Mayor Li!"

This burst of impassioned shouting from the crowd immediately brought Li Gaocheng back to his senses.

He suddenly realised that now was not the time to try to look into all these matters; the vital thing now was to repeat to the crowd, word for word, his original intentions. Whatever he had said at first, he had to say again now, precisely, without ambiguity. Even if it caused trouble later, he couldn't hide a thing.

But then, almost at the same time, there was a violent disruption in the crowd. Amidst a storm of yelling and shouting, a group of people came hurtling out, almost as if a bloody path had been cut through the mass of workers. Out of breath and in a panic, General Manager Guo Zhongyao, Party Secretary Chen Yongming, Deputy General Managers Wu Mingde and Feng Minjie and several other key members of the management team, escorted by almost a hundred security guards, came running towards Li Gaocheng. When Guo Zhongyao saw him, he almost burst into tears.

"We did as you told us to, Mayor Li, and were waiting in the Old Cadre Activity Centre. We never expected them to stop you here and surround you like this!" As Guo Zhongyao was speaking, he wiped the sweat from his face and the tears from his eyes. "You've already seen for yourself that this lot are hell bent on causing trouble. We..."

"Comrades! Fellow workers! Everyone should stay calm! Everyone must stay calm!" At this point, Chen Yongming, secretary of the company Party committee, addressed the crowd in a loud voice. "Listen, everyone, Mayor Li came here tonight to solve our company's problems. We all know that Mayor Li is a very busy man, and his health is not good. Everyone must stay calm and quiet..."

The crowd was noisy and chaotic; it seemed that no one was listening to him, and no one cared what he had to say. In fact, no one could even hear him and there were a lot of them who were actually trying to shout him off the stage.

"Go away! See him off! We don't want to listen to him!"

"We've heard enough from you! Who do you think you are? Go away! There's no place for you here!"

"We must listen to the mayor! Mayor Li, please stand up and talk to us!"

As if he couldn't control himself anymore, Deputy General Manager Feng Minjie, who had been standing to one side, suddenly leapt up some nearby stairs and shouted at the crowd: "What do you mean by behaving like this in front of the mayor? Have you no organisation, no discipline? Do you know what it means to attack and insult the mayor like this? Have you thought about the consequences? What kind of behaviour...?"

His speech was immediately met by a barrage of catcalls and curses.

"Get the fuck down from there! Who the fuck do you think you are anyway?"

"How have you got the nerve to stand up there, Feng Minjie?"

"Pull that corrupt bastard down from there! Tell him to fuck off!"

"Fuck you!"

"Fuck off!"

In the face of the crowd's angry cursing, Li Gaocheng became more and more soberly aware that if he, as mayor, sided with these managers now, or the mob thought that he was hand in glove with them, then this current unrest could turn into something really big and might even become unmanageable. He had to step forward immediately and tell them the truth, be straight with them. In particular, it was essential that he clarified the facts and dealt with the workers' misconceptions.

First, he ordered all the company security men to leave the scene immediately and not to hang around anywhere in the vicinity. He also told all the management team except for Guo Zhongyao to leave too and go home to wait for news. He had come here today to talk to the workers not the management. Him telling the managers to leave meant the workers would know they could say whatever they had to say without having to worry. If they had problems, they could raise them; if they had opinions, they could voice them. Even if it was a case of making a report against someone, laying a complaint or raising a petition, they could speak safely. And if there was any question of someone trying to retaliate, then no matter who it was, they would be taken straight to the Municipal Government to be questioned by the mayor.

Lastly, he gave an honest account of what had been said on his recent telephone call with Guo Zhongyao, concealing or omitting nothing. When he had finished, he told Guo to confirm the accuracy of his account.

Guo Zhongyao promptly did so. He went on to explain that much of what had been said in the company broadcast just now had been added on the spot by the announcer as the script was being put together. How that came about, and who ordered it on what basis, would be investigated immediately on his return to the office and a satisfactory explanation would be provided for everyone.

As soon as Guo Zhongyao had finished, Li Gaocheng ordered him to leave.

The crowd in front of Li Gaocheng had been growing fast all this time, and there were now almost ten thousand workers in the dormitory compound, which was only a middle-sized space.

That huge mass of people had suddenly gone unusually quiet, but it wasn't clear whether the mayor's words had moved everyone or whether his actions had regained their trust. Close-on ten thousand pairs of eyes were silently fixed on the slight figure of Mayor Li Gaocheng; no one spoke and no one stirred.

His eyes suddenly filled with tears.

These people were putting their complete trust in Li Gaocheng, in the government and in the nation.

He suddenly remembered the oath he had taken when he first joined the Party: in this life and in this world, I must work wholeheartedly for the welfare of the people, always be loyal to the Party and to the people, never fail to live up to their expectations, and always speak the truth and work to the practical benefit of the people... forever...

CHAPTER FOUR

AT 5.20 THAT MORNING, the workers finally chose their representatives to talk to the mayor; or, to be more precise, chose their delegation, which consisted of thirty-five representatives with twelve nominated spokespeople, and another almost one hundred observers.

A small conference room in the Old Cadres' Activity Centre was filled to overflowing.

Outside the Centre, not only had not a single one of the original crowd of almost ten thousand workers left, as daylight came, the number swiftly increased even further. They filled to bursting the little courtyard of the small three-storey building, itself no more than three hundred square metres in size. There was no idle chatter and no unnecessary shuffling or jostling. The whole dormitory compound was silent, as if time itself had frozen.

Quite possibly the entire workforce of the factory was gathered there, waiting in total silence, waiting for the outcome of a negotiation that would decide their fate.

It was the coldest time of the day at the coldest time of the year. The oppressive cold air caused many of the old former workers to cough ferociously and incessantly as the choking smoke of cheap cigarettes filled the air and the pinpricks of light from those cigarettes flared in the crowd, fed by the constant biting wind...

It felt like the eve of a decisive battle, and the atmosphere and emotion disquieted everyone and set them on edge.

The person who felt all this most keenly was Mayor Li Gaocheng.

He had just told the workers: "If you want to go to the Municipal Government to present a petition or lay a complaint, you want to see the top brass, don't you? Well, I am the mayor, so is it not good enough to come to me and talk to me directly? Here I am now, so talk freely to me and see if I can't resolve things. If there is anything I can't solve, if anything is left unfinished, then it is not too late for you to go and see some other municipal leader or even take it up to the provincial leadership. Why did you feel you had to take to the streets today? Wasn't it for just the same reason? To resolve your problems? Nor should you have any misgivings or other distressing thoughts about my intentions towards you all. Is that enough for you?"

At this point, the mayor felt a lump in his throat. In all honesty, did he, as mayor, truly have no responsibility for the situation at the factory and the circumstances the workers found themselves in? When you really came down to it, wasn't blaming everything on the market economy and on the deepening reforms in itself a corrupt abrogation of responsibility? For decades, these workers here in front of him had believed in the country and the government, doing whatever the Party told them to do; running without hesitation to wherever the leaders pointed; not fearing hardship and hard work; willing to sacrifice whatever was necessary; never considering the cost; not caring about gains and losses; all with little income but great dedication, and the only reward being the country's continued progress and long-term stability. Now, the Party and the government had called on the people to carry out unprecedented reforms, for which the workers had paid the greatest price, putting their country before their families. But, as it stood, when workers could not even get paid, when it was a problem to maintain the most basic standard of living even during the New Year holidays, could all this be blamed on the reforms? Could he, as mayor, say that it had nothing to do with him? The workers had listened to the state, and so now how could it be said it had nothing to do with the state?

From the day the Communist Party was born, workers had given it their all; they had always been loyal to the Party and full of confidence in it, hoping that the cause of reform led by it would bring wealth and prosperity to the country and, in a small way, to themselves. Even today, they still hoped that the Party would solve their problems and that the factory and the company would thrive again...

Could he really accuse them of troublemaking? He suddenly felt a twinge of guilty conscience about his own thoughts and feelings. Could he justify himself to them? Could he clear it with his own conscience?

There was no heating in the conference room. The representatives had insisted that, since the company was broke, even with the onset of winter, central heating should not be used anywhere, so it was like an icebox in the room. The lighting was also very dim and that made it seem even colder. Even though there were more than a hundred people crammed into the room, they were still shivering with the cold. Li Gaocheng particularly felt it because he hadn't put on an overcoat when he went out, as, with the heating and air conditioning in his home, office and limousine, he never put on many layers. So now the cold chilled his body to the marrow, and, without the benefit of padded boots, his feet were almost completely numb. Luckily for him, one of the old workers gave him an army greatcoat, and he gradually warmed up a little.

How could it be so cold? It was enough to freeze your intestines!

He silently looked at the faces in front of him, all staring anxiously at him, and suddenly felt how simultaneously familiar and strange they were. How many meetings of this kind had he already had over the years? Hadn't he always drawn strength and confidence from the smoke-filled atmosphere? Back then, how many ideas had the cadres and workers given him? How many countermeasures had they thought up? And how many sleepless nights had they endured in order to sell the backlog of thousands of bolts of cloth that had accumulated? Back then, although the work had been hard and tiring, his relationship with the workers and cadres was very deep and cordial! So now, why had they become so distant all of a sudden? Was it because his status had been elevated, or because he cared less about the factory? Or was it because the workers' perception of themselves had changed?

He could see the feelings of distance and unfamiliarity In the eyes of the workers. It was usually said that when an old factory manager like himself returned to the factory where he had put his heart and soul into unstinting effort, he should still feel a kinship with the workers and cadres that he used to be so close to. And what friendly and affectionate conversations they should have! So now, how could it be like this, with all their eyes looking at him as though they had never seen him before, as if he was some kind of monster!?

What was going on? How had this problem arisen?

Was it just because the company had stopped their work and the workers were receiving no pay?

No, that wasn't it! That couldn't be the only reason they were looking at him like that!

It was perhaps only then that he gradually began to realise things weren't as straightforward as he had thought.

Over many years, he had presided over countless meetings, large and small, and had never had the feeling of impotence he was experiencing today or been at a loss for words.

There was nothing to say, no way to talk about it, but, even so, something had to be said. He really hadn't expected it to be so difficult. He couldn't help thinking how incompetent he was as a mayor, how lacking in what was needed.

As his silence stretched out, the atmosphere became more and more tense, and the room fell into a deathly hush, as if the air was being sucked out of it.

There was no one to help him out, no one to chair the meeting for him, and no pre-written script to read from. Everything was down to him, and he alone had the solution. This was what he had asked for. If you don't answer the knock at the door for yourself, whatever it is won't go away but will come back and end up knocking on your head. Whether he chose to be active or passive, it all came down to him as mayor.

He quickly tried to focus his disorganised thoughts on what he should say to the delegates first.

Just then, the people in the crowd outside started chanting: "Set up the loudspeakers! We want to hear the mayor too!"

"Find an amp! Find an amp! Like the boss of the company uses. Get the mayor to use an amp. We all want to hear him."

"We've been fooled enough already! We're not happy with this!"

Li Gaocheng thought for a moment then quickly said to the delegates in front of him in the conference room: "By all means do what the workers are asking for and set up an amplifier and a loudspeaker immediately. Then the people outside will be able to hear whatever we say in here."

With surprising speed and efficiency, seven electricians arrived, and in less than a quarter of an hour, everything was installed. The effect was also surprisingly good, almost as good as a live radio broadcast, with even the coughing of the delegates and the scraping of tables and chairs in the conference room clearly audible outside.

The speed of the operation helped calm Li Gaocheng's nerves. Someone also handed him a nice hot cup of tea, which drove the cold from his body and even dispelled the numbness in his feet.

At around six o'clock, as the sky was gradually getting light, the discussions finally began.

Naturally, Li Gaocheng spoke first, making a few introductory remarks in which he re-emphasised his sincerity and expressed his deep sadness at the state the company currently found itself in. If anyone had anything to say, they should say it, as it was precisely in order to hear everyone's opinions that he had come there. No matter how uncomfortable their questions, everyone should ask them, and if there was even the slightest suggestion of any kind of retribution being taken by the company, the Municipal Government would take it extremely seriously. What it came down to was that the company belonged to everybody and could only survive if everybody took an interest in it. So, what needed to be said should be said and what needed to be discussed should be discussed. If everybody wasn't concerned about the company, didn't cherish the company, they wouldn't be braving the freezing cold to go and see the leadership of the Municipal Government, would they?

Then, it was the delegates' turn to speak.

In his wildest imaginings, Li Gaocheng had not expected the first person to speak to be Ding Jincun, the highest ranking, oldest and most prestigious old Red Army man in the factory and the first person to hold the post of company Party secretary.

Perhaps because the lighting in the room was so gloomy, Li Gaocheng hadn't been able to make out that the man right in front of him was Ding Jincun. To be honest, having a senior figure like

Ding Jincun sitting in front of him in this capacity really put him on edge, and he was ashamed of himself. When the old man stood up to speak, and he finally recognised who he was, he was so surprised that he hurried down from the stage and apologised to the old man as he tried to persuade him to sit down. He really hadn't recognised him, truly he hadn't, and he was really sorry that at his age he had had his rest disturbed by having to come out, especially on such a cold night...

Ding Jincun insisted on remaining standing to speak, saying that it was easier for him that way. He went on to say: "I share your sadness that the company has come to this, and I find it very hard to take. Did you really think I would be able to sleep tonight with all this going on?"

Ding Jincun was already eighty-four years old but he was hale and hearty, clear-thinking, showing no sign of being affected by old age. He spoke at a moderate pace, his voice neither too high nor too low, and his words carried a lot of weight.

The old man said that he must first state that he was firmly opposed to what the workers were doing tonight. How could they do it?

"At the drop of a hat, we send delegations to the Municipal or Provincial Party Committees to discuss complaints with the leaders, but is that really any way to solve our problems? Should we be treating the Communist Party in the same way as we treated the Kuomintang? We are forgetting our roots! When was our Party ever not committed to the workers? When did we stop relying on our working class? Some people are already saying that the Communist Party is now reliant on money and not on the working class. That's bullshit! If the Communist Party doesn't rely on the working class, can it still call itself the Communist Party? Just now, the national government is having a few troubles and difficulties, so, I say we should just grit our teeth, tighten our belts and endure it as long as it takes to get through it. Once we get over this hurdle, won't everything come together? Is it really so difficult to get by at the moment? Is it worse than during the Cultural Revolution? Is it worse than those years of natural disasters? To be really brutal, is it worse than living under the Kuomintang? Are we really worse off than under the old society? So, people are making all this fuss, just because they want the state to give us two months' wages? Even if they pay us that, what real difference will it make in the great scheme of things? Of course, some people are really struggling because the whole family works in this factory and they are finding it really hard to make it through without wages! But look how many people have gathered here together today! Are we really saying that, pulling together, we can't all make it through? I don't believe it now and I will never believe it! So, even with the size of the protest here today, I still have to say I don't agree with this approach, and I will always be firmly opposed to it!"

At this point, Ding Jincun suddenly changed the subject and raised his voice to a noticeably higher pitch. "Just because I'm against the workers making a scene doesn't mean that I don't have my own opinions or that I think there's nothing wrong in the company. Some of the leaders nowadays defy description! What a disgrace they are! Always drunk! Up to their necks in corruption! Were any of our old leaders like that? The company has reached this crisis, but they don't seem to take it seriously! They eat, drink and play around just as they like! They even go off abroad whenever they like! They say that is the way of things nowadays, that nothing can be achieved without wining and dining and a bit of fun. What a load of crap! Is that how the Communist Party achieved its great deeds of daring? By eating and drinking and having a bit of fun? When the Communist Party fought for the new world, it fought with its bare hands! What were the foundations of the new China? Did eating and drinking and having a bit of fun make people bleed for the Party and die for the Party to fight for a new world? These people are not even a little bit communist! This one says he is going abroad on a fact-finding mission – he says it's for a joint venture with Niger or Nigeria or some such. If that's the case, what is he doing in Russia? In the United States, the United Kingdom or France? Why does he go to Hong Kong, Thailand, Malaysia and Singapore? If it is a fact-finding trip, why does he take his wife with him? He spends millions of dollars for two to three years, and what 'facts' does he have to show for it? Fuck all! Millions and millions of yuan! Millions and millions of yuan! That money is the sweat of the workers! If it was your company, would you act like that? Wouldn't your family tear you apart and eat you? Wouldn't your subordinates cut you to pieces?

Would tens of thousands of workers put up with a bunch of profligate bastards like that? Spendthrifts, the lot of them! Just a bunch of spendthrifts...!"

At this point, Ding Jincun's eyes filled with tears, and he sobbed uncontrollably, unable to say another word.

There was a deathly hush inside the conference room, and the dense crowd outside fell just as silent.

Many people wept silently too and wiped the tears from their faces, over and over again.

Li Gaocheng stood there in a daze. He had never thought that this highly respected old Red Army man, a former manager, could hold such an opinion of the current team. It was so shocking that he was lost for words.

What was wrong with this company? Could the management really be as bad as the old man had said?

The next speaker was Ma Decheng, a sixty-seven-year-old worker.

His hair was grey and his face heavily wrinkled. Unlike Ding Jincun, he looked and acted his age, with a stooped back and a faint, wavery voice.

Ma Decheng said that he had never wanted to make trouble, but all fourteen members of his family worked for Zhongyang Textiles and they were really struggling to get by. So he just wanted to go with everyone to the Municipal Party Committee and the Provincial Party Committee to get some help from the leaders and to find some work for his children. Ma Decheng could not stop crying as he spoke. His sobs were as hoarse and weak as his voice, and they deeply moved everyone who heard them. Through his tears, he said: "The factory management told us we had to fend for ourselves, and everyone had to find their own way of coping, but there is no way for my family, no way at all! Generations of my family rely on this factory. I came here when I was seventeen, and my wife was fifteen when she joined. My two sons and two daughters came to work here as soon as they graduated from junior high school, and so did my grandson and granddaughter. We are all, every generation, just one step from the grave, living from day to day. We can't even get a pension now, so if we die soon we will be less of a burden on our children and grandchildren. What else should we think of doing? My sons and daughters are now in their forties. They are old and weighed down and their health is not good. If even the youngsters can't find work, who will want them in that state? If you want to start a business, you don't have the capital, and there is nowhere to borrow money. Who would want to lend us anything anyway, the position we are in? Besides, what kind of business could we do? I'm not going to lie, I'm almost seventy years old and I've never even ridden in a taxi. As for my grandchildren, the youngsters are a little better off. If they can't find a good job, there's always something they can do. My grandson works every day, hauling coal or something else, earning whatever he can so he can put some money into the household. I've reached the point where I don't care if you jeer when I say my two granddaughters are hostesses who sing and dance for customers in a club. They cry till their eyes are red when they get home. They say, 'I'm never going to get married, never going to get married. Those men who spend all day in the club are all bastards.' Life holds nothing for them, nothing at all, and as their grandparents it breaks our hearts, my wife and me..."

At one point, the old man was crying so hard he could barely breathe. The meeting room was filled with sobs.

After a long time, the old man cried almost in a frenzy: "Mayor Li, Mayor Li! We don't want anything, we really don't want anything! They can eat, drink and play around, spend all that money! Even if they are corrupt, we can accept it. Let them be corrupt. No one can control them, so we really do not care. It doesn't matter how corrupt they are – as long as they can keep the factory open, as long as they can get us work, that's all that matters! We workers aren't good at anything else. We don't know how to steal or rob. We don't cheat. We just work and we work hard! Don't let the company shut down again! Don't let the company shut down again! If it does, the company really will collapse for good! If that day comes, who have we workers got to turn to...?"

The old man began sobbing again and many of the people in the room couldn't help joining in. For the crowd outside, the sound of the crying was clearly audible!

Li Gaocheng could not stop himself crying either. He never thought that this old worker, who had given his whole life to the factory, could say such things. Regardless of the truth of the old man's words, the sincerity of his feelings towards the company was enough to make everyone feel emotional. Could there be a better worker anywhere in the world? And if workers of that calibre could not restore the company, how could they, as leaders, still have the nerve to face the world?

Another thing that cut him to the quick was the attitude of the old workers towards the company management! He believed that what they said was true, but what he found so hard to take on board was how the management team he had promoted could really be so corrupt, and how the workers could really be so helpless.

The next to speak was the former chief engineer, Zhang Huabin.

The old engineer truly looked his age. He had graduated from the textile department of the top-flight university, the Northwest College of Engineering, during the Kuomintang period and had been considered a man of exceptional talent and promise in his youth. When the Kuomintang retreated in defeat, they continued to favour him and urged him to set up a large-scale textile production operation in Taiwan. Even though they had already bought him his plane ticket, he kept thinking the matter over and eventually found a way of staying behind. From that point on he remained continuously in the Chinese textile industry for almost fifty years. He worked as an engineer at several different major textile factories, and he left his mark on the Shaanxi Textile Factory, the Shanxi Textile Factory, the Jilin Textile Factory and the Jinhua Textile Factory, and their stories bore witness to the blood, sweat and tears he had put into them. He was a genuine patriarch of the textile industry of the new China. Once he arrived at the Zhongyang Textile Factory, he spent uninterrupted decades there until his retirement. He was originally from Jiangsu, the land of fish and rice, but spent most of his life eating sorghum and corn on the loess plateau. Even now, he still lived in the dormitory compound of the Zhongyang Textile Group, where he and the next generations of his family would probably continue to live forever.

When Li Gaocheng arrived that night, the news that Zhang Huabin was there had a considerable effect on his thinking. However you looked at it, it should simply never happen that a former member of management, an engineer who had decades of experience in the textile industry, a veteran of the trials and tribulations of that industry, should join in the protests of the workers. What was more, he had been bitterly opposed to the current management team when it was appointed, so didn't his espousal of the workers' cause now rather smack of revenge? In the current circumstances, even if the management had acted wrongly or made mistakes, he should have avoided any trace of suspicion and should certainly not have attended that night. He must have known all this, and, no matter what, he should not be aligning himself with the masses.

Even so, when he actually saw the old engineer, he could not say why, but his heart softened. He hadn't realised how much the man had aged since he last saw him. His hair was completely white, his complexion was much darker, his previously bright eyes now looked dull and cloudy. An intellectual like Zhang Huabin should never be reduced to looking like that. To Li Gaocheng's way of thinking, Zhang's declining years should be ones of richness and joy. He was a highly honoured and respected member of the company. The workers all valued and respected him and he was inseparable from the company, where he was consulted on all matters and his ideas and solutions were eagerly sought. He should not be left lonely and abandoned but should live in a comfortable environment and a happy atmosphere. As a southerner, with a southern wife, he would know how to enjoy life. He would also know how to maintain his health and take care of himself. He should feel younger the longer he lived, and the better life he should lead. He should look pink-cheeked, fit, radiant and cheerful. So how could Zhang Huabin have been reduced to the state he saw him in now? He was struck by a growing sorrow – after all, couldn't this man be considered the very backbone of the Zhongyang Textile Factory and couldn't it reasonably be said that without the hard work of a group of intellectuals such as Zhang Huabin, the company would not exist on its current scale nor have enjoyed its past glories. As mayor, as a colleague of those men and as a former manager who had enjoyed so much help and support from them, he should really have shown them much more warmth and support. Just for a moment he couldn't help feeling a stab of shame and remorse.

Despite his ageing appearance, when Zhang Huabin began to speak it was immediately obvious to everyone that he had something different from the others to say. He might be an old man, but there was nothing aged about his intellect. His words were brief and to the point and extremely well thought out. They went straight to the heart of the matter and convinced with simple reason.

"No matter whether the Zhongyang Textile Group has come to its current state through the actions of individuals, because of circumstances beyond its control or a combination of the two, we are now at the point where we have to come up with countermeasures without delay. If people continue to be so laissez-faire, to pass the buck, to be indecisive, to ignore the facts, to close their eyes and ears, to leave everyone to their own devices, then, no matter who they are or what position they hold, they will be committing the greatest crime against the state and the people! This is also an illustration of deep-level corruption, and the disastrous consequences of that corruption are going to be enormous, frightening, harsh and long-lasting! If there are still people who disagree, then they should just look at what is happening to the company's factories. Some of them have already been shut down for more than ten months, and if they are out of action for another ten months, or even more, they will never be able to start up again. This is not me being alarmist or speaking just for effect. Anyone with the least bit of common sense can see that, if a factory does not operate for two or three years, that factory effectively no longer exists as a factory. Machines rust, parts get lost, equipment corrodes, and everything ceases to function. If you want to start it up again, it would be almost the same as building a new factory! If a company such as ours is quietly to disappear with no one taking responsibility, won't that be the greatest corruption of all? In no country, in no period of history, would such a shocking act have ever been tolerated! This is the blood and sweat of the people, Mayor Li! You are a former manager here at Zhongyang Textiles, so I know how well you understand this! How can we be so irresponsible as to push all these workers, twenty or thirty thousand of them, out into society? Can we allow this to happen and not care? Look what the Zhongyang Textile Group has become! A slum! Crime is breeding here, riots are breaking out, organisations are breaking down and morality is declining! We want stability in society but how can there be any stability in a slum like this? It is heartbreaking to watch! The question of slum eradication was raised by the Americans at the beginning of the twentieth century, when they pointed out that if such slums were ignored and left to grow, it would not be long before they would wipe us all out. But not only are we paying no attention to these problems, we are even creating new slums with our own actions! People who parrot things like 'the survival of the fittest' and 'everyone should rely on their own ability and find their own way' are, if not political hooligans, then, at least, accomplices in crime! How, in all conscience, can we treat the workers like this when they have devoted their lives to this country, to the Party and to the people, and today are left penniless and truly unable to help themselves? How can you tell them it is 'natural selection' and say they have to 'find their own way out'? Is that either fair or just?"

The whole conference room and courtyard were silent, and Zhang Huabin's speech seemed to have shaken everyone present to the core.

Once again, Li Gaocheng was deeply moved. To be honest, his own thinking had not been as far-sighted and profound as Zhang Huabin's. He had, on occasion, been vaguely aware of some problems, but he had never applied such a high degree of rationality in considering them. So, when Zhang Huabin unflinchingly described all these issues, the shock was like nothing he had felt before. He keenly felt his dereliction of duty, just as he did when some of the workers had rebuked him, saying: "If we weren't all set to take action, would you have come here, Mr Mayor?" If he was honest with himself, what had he actually done since he took up office? If it wasn't documents and meetings, it was meetings and documents, meeting and greeting, tied up in red tape, and always floating on the froth of official life with no escape from it. Even if you did escape, you were still always surrounded by a gaggle of senior cadres. You listened to reports, watched presentations, let yourself be led to a few carefully chosen sites for a cursory tour; then the food and the drinks, the boasting and the flattery, and that was it. That's all there was. Where was the time to think about issues properly, ferret them out, examine them and resolve them? You didn't even give the nation's problems the same amount of thought and attention as an ordinary person or a run-of-the-mill intellectual; far less, in fact. Your critical thinking got lost in the mountains of documents and the oceans of meetings; your real self drowned in lakes of wine and stumbled through forests of food. The more exalted you were, the more minions you had. They sat with you when you ate, followed you wherever you walked and waited while you slept. Where was the time to exercise your brain cells and consider the best strategies?

Sometimes, as a mayor, he felt he was worse off than an ordinary member of the public. What words did he have to offer these workers standing in front of him, their expressions full of longing and earnest expectation? Just a few days ago, he had signed off on a document that required laid-off workers to be self-reliant, to constantly strive to improve themselves, to update their knowledge, to sharpen their sense of competition, and to actively participate in training in order to adapt to the needs of the new situation so that they could rejoin the workforce as soon as possible. At the time, he thought this was a good document, so he gave instructions to the relevant units, asking that it be distributed to all factories and mines for discussion and study. However, when he arrived at the Zhongyang Factory that night and faced these workers and cadres, he suddenly felt how superficial and irresponsible his instructions and ideas were! It was just the same for Zhongyang Textiles, and for these workers who had spent their whole life working there: they too were the products of the planned economy, they had been working for the Party and the country all their lives, they had been reliant on the Party and the nation all their lives. A lifetime of wiring terminals, a lifetime of carrying cotton bales. For many years, they had been asking them to be dedicated and loyal to their work, to love their work and to act as small cogs in the great machine. Now, faced with so many workers who had left their jobs and had no special skills, could he just push them out onto the market without taking any responsibility for them? Could he, in all conscience, still ask them to show self-sufficiency, self-respect and self-worth?

Thinking about it, Li Gaocheng suddenly remembered something someone had once said: "You can't take a man who has been chained up for years, release him, bring him to the starting line and say, 'Now you're free to compete with everyone else', and still feel confident that you've done a perfectly fair job."

Could you really do that? Could you bear to do it?

Normally, whenever a meeting was held, no matter who was speaking, he would always be interrupting and voicing his own feelings and experiences. But now, for some reason, he couldn't interject a single word. He really didn't know what to say; he really didn't have anything he could say.

He could only listen silently and remember.

The old chief engineer continued to speak in a loud, resonant, thoughtful voice. "...today, there are still many people who worry about our company and who are concerned about its future. But, when the day comes when the company really does collapse, and the workers are left without hope, who will there be left, on that bleak day, to go and talk to the leadership? When the wind is twenty degrees below zero, who will be left to stand in it and report the situation? By then, what can we expect from the workers? As their passion is gradually extinguished, will they still have the same love for the company as before? Will they still have the same love for the country? Will they still follow the Party with the same fervour in deepening the reforms? It's not just a waste of a company, it's also a waste of the patriotic hearts of the workers! I am not exaggerating about them – just look for yourselves at what these so-called managers have done over the last few years! In 1990, the state loaned them 80 million yuan, resulting in a loss of 12 million. In 1991, the state loaned them 60 million yuan, resulting in a loss of 14 million. In 1992, the state loaned 50 million yuan, resulting in a loss of 8 million. In 1993, the state loaned them 100 million yuan, resulting in a loss of almost 20 million. In 1994, the state loaned them 80 million yuan, resulting in a loss of 16 million. In 1995, despite the extreme financial difficulties the country was in, the state still loaned them 60 million yuan, resulting in an expected loss of 20 million. It was a weird, unbreakable cycle – the more loans were made, the more the losses accumulated! Why? How on earth did these losses come about? It makes no sense, and, what is more, it doesn't comply with the law. It really makes you think. Over the past few years, excluding the external monies owed to us, a large part of which can never be recovered, our total external debt, plus interest, has reached 580 million yuan! In fact, the real figure is much more than that! When it comes down to it, how and why did these debts come about? These are questions we need to ask and matters that we need to investigate. Yes, there are also problems with our state-owned enterprise system – the burden is too heavy, the costs are too high, the organisation is too big, the management mechanism is too rigid, the competition between individual and township enterprises and ourselves is weighted against us, and so on. But can this be the only reason? There are many, many other large-scale textile factories whose circumstances are essentially the same as ours – in Shaanxi, Shanxi, Jilin and Shandong for example – so why are those other large-scale enterprises getting more and more active and more and more successful? And why are we, a textile factory actually situated in the cotton-producing area of the country, going steadily downhill until we have reached the point where we have to stop production with nearly 600 million of debt? Is our technology not working? Is there something wrong with it? There are more than two thousand graduates from technical school, more than fifteen hundred technicians, more than eight hundred engineers and more than twenty international students in the Zhongyang Textile Group, numbers unmatched by any township or individual enterprise. Is our equipment not good enough? Since the 1980s, our company's equipment renovation project has continued almost non-stop. In 1993, the state loaned us more than 100 million yuan to complete the project. Even today, some of our equipment is still top-of-the-range and will remain competitive for another three to five years, or maybe even eight to ten. No individual or township enterprise can compare with that. Do we not have the markets? There is always a shortage of our plain cotton broadcloth on the domestic market, and it is in constant demand. The same is true internationally where our products are highly competitive and we can't supply enough of them. There is no problem with quality, as our products have always had a very high reputation and people trust them. Again, no individual or township enterprise can compete with us in these respects. So when we say the burden is too heavy, we can find ways to reduce it. If the cost is too high, our quality advantage can offset it. The organisation may be too big, but we can streamline it, can't we? If the management mechanism is too rigid, isn't it the preferred state policy to tear down all barriers and revitalise state-owned enterprises? As long as you are committed to public service, as long as you really are an official committed to the people, what difficulties cannot be overcome and what problems cannot be solved? The truth is, the biggest problem lies here, in the management of the Zhongyang Textile Group. What exactly have they been thinking about all day, and what have they actually been doing?"

At this point, Zhang Huabin's voice suddenly rose much higher, and his emotions became more intense.

"In 1989, hospitality expenses were 1.2 million. In 1990, 1.7 million. In 1991, 2.4 million. In 1992, 3.6 million. In 1993, 4.3 million. And in 1994, 4.7 million. In 1995, just after the suspension of production, the hospitality expenses were still over 4 million! If you add in the branch factories and subsidiaries, the annual hospitality expenses for all purposes are almost 10 million! Ten million! Think about it, everyone! What can this figure mean? It means that it will almost eat up the annual salaries of more than twenty thousand workers! And one-eighth of the total fixed assets of Zhongyang Textiles! It will swallow up two or three branch factories and subsidiaries! Twenty of our dormitory buildings! Fifty to sixty thousand bolts of our cotton cloth! It is more than enough to swallow up the five schools for our children! In 1994, the state loaned us 80 million yuan, and in the first half of the year, we falsely reported a profit of 5.4 million yuan. We even staged a grand celebration for the Municipal Party Committee and the Municipal Government. They little knew that the annual hospitality expenses were more than twice that figure!

"But that's enough about food and drink. Let's talk about another kind of greed. In 1995, the nation's finances were tight and the banks were very strict with loans. But even in such a difficult situation, the government moved heaven and earth to give Zhongyang Textiles a loan of 60 million yuan because the state still wanted to keep such a large enterprise alive and successful. And what did the company do with that money? Let me give you just one example. They sent a deputy general manager, a deputy secretary, three managers and deputy managers of the supply and distribution department, and two cotton inspectors to buy more than two thousand tonnes of cotton from a remote county in Jiangxi, which is not even a cotton-producing area! The price per tonne for first- and second-grade cotton was more than 18,000 yuan, but less than a tonne of what they brought back was first- or second-grade! Less than ten per cent was third-grade! More than fifty per cent was actually fifth- and sixth-grade, and thirty per cent was completely unusable! The average market price for cotton of that kind at the time was never more than 12,000 yuan a tonne! That's a difference of 6,000 yuan per tonne! On over two thousand tonnes of cotton, where did all that difference go? Even if the difference was only half of the price actually paid, that is still several million yuan! Even if not a cent went into their own pockets, what were they doing spending so much money buying so much rotten cotton at such high prices? Did they not understand? There were deputy general managers with many years' experience in marketing and distribution, there was a director of supply and distribution who had worked in the department for decades, and there were top-level cotton inspectors, who couldn't be fooled about any grade of cotton! Were they all being duped? The management could have taken immediate legal action over these tens of millions of yuan worth of cotton. There was a contract and legal representatives, the vendor was an old contact they had dealt with for many years, and there were witnesses and physical evidence, so how could anyone wriggle out of it? They had brought the cotton back more than six months ago, and with it sitting rotting away in the warehouses, why hadn't they sued the supplier? What is hardest to understand is why, with so much completely unusable, rotten cotton already, and all the company's workers complaining angrily, had they actually gone back to the same place and bought another four hundred and fifty tonnes of cotton? And forty per cent of that consignment was unusable too! We simply don't understand how they could do this! How could they dare to do it? Why did they have such little regard for the law and for morality? Even though the workers reacted so angrily when they bought such useless cotton, they made no attempt to explain the problem to them, they did not even admit there was a problem, and they made no attempt to investigate who was responsible. Instead, they closed ranks within the company. There were repeated threats and intimidation on the company television, and they even threatened that anyone who said there was a problem with the cotton, or made a fuss about the affair, would be severely investigated! Retired workers had their pensions suspended, and current workers were dismissed. Their actions turned ordinary people into criminals! Who gave them the right to do that kind of thing? Now we've talked about their greed for food and money, let's talk about their greed for territorial control..."

Zhang Huabin talked for an hour, until the sky was fully light, and then stopped, although he clearly had more he could say.

Li Gaocheng had been making continuous notes in a little book. He hadn't said a word, nor, indeed, had he wanted to. He hadn't even had time to think, let alone ask any questions. The only thing he was aware of was a violent assault on his emotions that had shaken him in a way he had never experienced before. He simply couldn't bring himself to believe that everything Zhang Huabin had said was true, but he couldn't not believe that all the events described had indeed happened. He knew that an intellectual like Zhang would never invent such things in front of such a large crowd of workers, nor would he pile blame on the management for events that had never happened. But, in order fully to understand the situation, he couldn't just hear one side of the story – he had to hear the other side too. That is to say, he had to hear what the management had to say and what their explanation of events was. It is, after all, sometimes difficult for an outsider to understand what is truly at the bottom of an affair. However, what had really shaken him was not only that such major issues as hospitality expenditure and the buying of cotton, especially the purchase of several million yuan worth of rubbish cotton unfit for use in production, could have been kept hidden until now from the Municipal Government – and that included him, as mayor – but also that the ordinary workers had been prevented from reporting it. That was both astonishing and outrageous!

Starting from five in the morning and ending at two in the afternoon, in addition to the twelve representatives who had the right to speak, another seven also had their say.

No one in the conference room left halfway through, and the crowd outside the room continued to grow throughout the event. By eight or nine in the morning, there were more than twenty thousand employees present!

Breakfast and lunch were both taken on the spot, in the form of instant noodles with a sachet of pickled vegetables and took up only a few minutes. In fact, the representatives even kept on talking through the meal.

The main issues raised by the delegates concentrated on the following aspects:

First, economic issues. There were many economic issues that should be considered major, such as buying cotton, problems in technical renovation projects, and problems in the development of the so-called tertiary sector. In 1993, the state solved many of their difficulties with a loan of 100 million yuan, intended to carry out a comprehensive transformation of the company's outdated equipment. However, in the circumstances, some people took advantage of this to make a lot of money, fraudulently using substandard equipment and materials, and stealing from the company. What was particularly shocking was that, under the guise of selling scrap, they secretly sold the obsolete machinery to a township enterprise specialising in textile machines, who refurbished, repainted and relabelled them, without actually making any technical improvements, and then sold them back to the company at an inflated price! In 1994, against all odds, the state continued to support the Zhongyang Textile Group with a further loan of 80 million yuan. In response to this unprecedented windfall, the company management made a decision that no one had expected, and indeed, that no one had even dared imagine possible. They used 22 million of it to establish Xinchao Co. Ltd and set up almost a hundred businesses in more than twenty cities inside and outside the province, which included restaurants, hotels, dance halls, business centres, clothing companies, assorted processing industries and coal mines. The managers and directors of these businesses were almost exclusively children and other relatives of the Zhongyang Textiles management. So, what had the business situation of this Xinchao Co Ltd been like over the last two years? How much profit had it paid to the parent company? What state was it in now? Only the management knew; the employees had been told nothing. Because state money had been used to establish a limited company, this meant that the management were not responsible for any deficits, losses, collapses, bankruptcies or even the total loss of all the funds. Who told them they could do this? Did the top brass know about it? The company owed its employees an explanation.

Second, the question of conduct. For example, visiting all the country's most famous scenic spots on the pretext of arranging supply and distribution issues; or taking families on foreign holidays on the pretext of inspecting joint ventures; or spending all day eating and drinking on the pretext of providing hospitality to foster connections; arranging year-round accommodation for mistresses on the pretext of public relations negotiations; even going so far as to gamble with public money, falsely describing it as a disguised gift and then, on return to the company, writing off the whole, huge sum with an informal IOU. One particularly shocking example was that of Feng Minjie, deputy manager in charge of supply and distribution, who was caught by the Public Security Bureau frequenting prostitutes while on a buying trip. He was locked up for a couple of weeks before being bailed by the company. He was not punished in any way and even had his twenty thousand yuan fine reimbursed from company funds. There was the case of General Manager Guo Zhongyao. He was divorced and had never remarried, and had a constant succession of young, female secretaries. One by one, they were reassigned to important posts and, whereas old staff members who had spent decades at the company had no access to new housing, these young secretaries in their early twenties were all assigned new accommodation. They had generally only been at the company a couple of years and none of them were married! Many employees had reported issues like this to the relevant managers on multiple occasions but had never elicited any interest. Some people said that such things were just par for the course in the business world. But the workers simply did not understand: if these issues were not considered to be problems, what was? Was this still a state-owned enterprise or not? Was the Communist Party in charge or not?

Third, issues of organisation. Among the twenty thousand employees of the Zhongyang Textile Group, there were more than two thousand full-time cadres not engaged in production! There were more than twenty at deputy departmental director level, more than five hundred at departmental level, and more than fourteen hundred at section level. Particularly in recent years, they had promoted whoever they wanted to promote, and found jobs for whoever they wanted to find jobs for. Anyone at all could suddenly, for no apparent reason, be made a section leader or department director, regardless of their status, their skills and abilities, or their technical know-how and academic qualifications. The workers said that nowadays all over society, people were buying official posts, and that was certainly true of this company. If you wanted to be a manager somewhere, a director somewhere, or a contractor somewhere, all you had to do was hand over the money. The more you sent, the better your position and the greater your chances of making money for yourself. This company might have ceased production and shut down, but the small factories, industries and companies all around it were flourishing like never before. As long as you could get yourself into a position where you could keep the leaders comfortable and show them due consideration, you could make as much money as you liked. And if you had money and status, wealth and position, was that really going to stop you trampling others underfoot and scrabbling for more? If all the management in the company were behaving like that, how could the company possibly thrive? If one profligate raises a brood of profligates, and that brood of profligates is followed by a whole host of profligates, it is sheer fantasy to think that family is ever going to be anything except profligate!

Fourth, the issue of the company's security department. The Zhongyang Textile Group's security department was currently the biggest of its kind in any city-level state-owned enterprise. There were more than two hundred and thirty actual company personnel in the main department, and one hundred and twenty or so more from the Economic Crimes Unit of the Public Security Police. Each principal member of the company management team had two or three personal security officers on revolving shifts, day and night; the workers called them their minders and referred to the security department as the Kempeitai.[1] Even now, when the pensions of retired cadres were not being paid, these "minders" were still getting their pay and their bonuses. As early as 1992, the state had already ordered large and medium-sized state-owned enterprises to disband their security services and similar departments. However, the Zhongyang Textile Group had not only not disbanded its security service but had actually continued to expand both its size and scope of operations. The representatives believed that the Zhongyang Textile Group's location did not merit such a large security department. The company was based in the suburbs, and for many years it had nurtured very good relations with the local residents and there had never been any problems with theft or looting. Security was very tight around the company's internal and external facilities, but there wasn't really very much valuable enough to be worth stealing, and no one was going to take the risk for some bits of cotton cloth or yarn and some machine parts. Before the Zhongyang Textile Factory became the Zhongyang Textile Group, the security department only consisted of sixty or so staff, divided into three teams of twenty plus. Even then, they had nothing to do all day except rattle the handles of the main gates and stroll round the warehouses, and the other workers were not reticent in their opinion of them. So what about now, with the company idle and this new three- or four-hundred-strong security department still in place? What was the company doing still providing for that many security personnel? What was the real reason? A large number of these security men were migrant workers and temporary staff brought in from outside the area and had no connection with the local area. They didn't listen to anyone else, only the company management, and would do anything at a word from them. If anyone was thought to be a problem, they could not only be arrested, handcuffed and questioned, they could also be locked up. All it took was for someone to make a casual accusation or put in a report upstairs, and that was it. As for the content of the report, that didn't matter to them. If it was false, the fault lay with the bosses upstairs, and it really had nothing to do with them. This power was frightening and very unsettling, so the workers called them all sorts of terrible names behind their backs, even going as far as to refer to them as a pack of wild dogs kept by gangsters.

Fifth, the management were now spraying around a lot of extraordinarily irresponsible comments, causing great confusion and putting a lot of mental pressure on their employees. It was being said that the best way to solve the company's current predicament was to file for bankruptcy. It was being said that there were unskilled, incompetent people hanging around the main gates waiting to start work. It was being said that in the market economy that now prevailed, nobody cared about anybody else and anyone who tried to take control of this company would be the first to find themselves starving to death in the future. It was being said that after two or three years of studies and reports costing several million yuan, it was decided that the company was not even going to be a joint venture, and the responsibility for it was going to be shuffled off onto the nation and the government. It was being said that this was because if it became a joint venture, hundreds of millions worth of loans the management had made would never be repaid... As a result, the company was in a constant state of panic and the workers had no idea what to do for the best. The more the employees thought about it, the more disgruntled and angrier they felt. The workers had been with the company all their lives, and now the management had brought ruin upon it. The leadership had all made themselves rich, but they still wanted to bankrupt the company. Did they really think they could escape the blame?

Sixth, the issue of the powers of the management...

Seventh, the issue of how responsible the management was for the current state of the company...

Eighth, what was the company actually going to do?...

Ninth...

Tenth...

CHAPTER FIVE

It was after four o'clock in the afternoon by the time they had finished having their say. Li Gaocheng massaged his throbbing temples, his mind a blank.

He had more than half-filled his little book with notes, and the fingers on his writing hand were numb. He had certainly not expected to have so much evidence to record, nor for the workers to have had so many complaints.

More than a hundred issues, large and small, had been raised, and there was a complete list of twenty-one criminal charges! This was completely unexpected and worse than anything he could have dreamt of. Supposing there were indeed that many issues with the company management, let alone any more, even if only a tenth of them, a hundredth of them, were true, it would be enough to have the whole team expelled from the Party, arrested and taken to court.

What especially bewildered him was that these criticisms were not just aimed at one or two management cadres but at the whole team! The whole organisation! They didn't just encompass management boardroom-level cadres, but section-level cadres too. That was to say that there were issues with the vast majority of the management cadres, the most important ones in particular, and very serious issues at that.

Corporate corruption!

For some reason, the phrase leapt into his mind, but he couldn't say where it had sprung from.

He could not believe it, but there was no way of denying it. How could the whole team have turned bad? Was that even possible? At the outset, when he was at Zhongyang Textiles himself, they had all been such excellent cadres! In such a difficult environment back then, during those arduous days, they had all proved themselves. That experience had shown them to be good cadres, in terms of quality at least. But then, in the time since he had left the company, which really was only a matter of a few years, how could they all have gone bad? And not just bad, but this bad! Very seriously bad!

But there it was! Faced by twenty thousand workers outside and a hundred-plus employee representatives inside the conference room, he felt it was not possible for so many people to be lying to him, to be speaking out of anger and to be making groundless, false accusations without any reason or evidence!

Of course, he hadn't yet checked out any of the issues, nor heard the management team's explanations. There certainly wasn't just one side to this affair.

However, one thing was absolutely certain – these things had happened and the facts were there to see. What remained to be seen was how they could be explained and how to understand where the truth actually lay.

So, his next task, that had to be completed within one or two days, was to hear the management team's report and explanation. The very least he should get, as mayor, was a clear account of these issues.

But for now, faced as he was by all these people inside and outside the conference room, eagerly expecting him to say something, he had to make a clear and unequivocal statement of his position. If he did not give the crowd a proper explanation, he would not be able to leave without a disastrous loss of face. Consequently, he made four points.

First, the Municipal Party Committee and the Municipal Government alike had always been very concerned about the current situation at the Zhongyang Textile Group and were as anxious as everyone else. Even in those busiest days after the end of 1995, leading up to the New Year, the leaders had devoted themselves to the consideration of Zhongyang Textiles for several days in a row. It was essential to have confidence in this, and to trust the government. It would never forget about the company or neglect its workers. The government of the Communist Party had always relied on the workers in the past; it did so now and would always do so in the future. As long as the Party was in control, this principle was unshakeable.

Second, he understood how they all felt, but he didn't agree with what they were doing. What kind of impression would they be giving society by going to the Municipal Committee or the Provincial Committee in different groups? This would damage not only the image of the government but also the image of Zhongyang Textiles and even the image of the working class itself. It was not that the government couldn't solve the problems at the company; the question was how best to solve them. Collective petitioning and hundreds of people gathering in front of the Provincial and Municipal Governments was actually a sign of lack of confidence in them. It was not his intention to criticise everyone by what he said, nor to criticise their own intentions. But he did hope that everyone would now change their thoughts and actions for the future. Everyone has difficulties, and this was true of government as well. In the current situation, it was necessary to work together, with one heart and one mind. Only in that way could everyone help each other to get through these difficulties.

Third, as mayor, he felt very guilty and ashamed of what had happened at Zhongyang Textiles that day, and he himself bore a great deal of responsibility. To be honest, over the last few years, especially since becoming mayor, he had lost interest in the company and become somewhat indifferent to it. But when he came to Zhongyang Textiles today, he was both shocked and stirred to hear so many heartfelt words. He hadn't expected everyone to have such a deep affection for the company and to be so concerned for its future. For decades, so many workers and cadres had cherished the company as if it were their own home, and they loved it so much that they could not afford to lose it. That was quite amazing and no small thing! He believed it was an illustration of the real and most precious wealth of the nation! As long as they had that wealth, there were no difficulties that they could not overcome, and there would be no problems that they could not solve. On that point alone, he, as mayor, was far inferior to everyone there! By this measure too, the staff and cadres who had come to the company that day were all good people! For this, he paid tribute to everyone, and offered them his deepest bow!

A burst of warm applause came from the representatives in the conference room, and he simultaneously heard the sound of similar clapping from outside. He continued on to his final point.

"Fourthly, I have made a full note of every issue raised by you all today. I am going to take it back and make a full and detailed report to the Municipal Government and the members of the Municipal Committee..."

At this point, he suddenly discovered that he could not continue to speak. He heard a roar like a tsunami rushing in from outside the conference room. He stood stunned for a moment, not understanding what the noise was. But when he saw that the representatives in front of him were all standing and applauding, he immediately understood that it was the cheering and applause of twenty thousand employees! It was the kind of joyful applause and cheering that truly came from the heart.

He had seldom heard such cheering in recent years, and, once again, it stirred him to his core. Of everything that he had said, it was perhaps only these last words that convinced them that he was being honest with them and speaking the truth!

The clapping and cheering went on for more than ten minutes, and the avalanche of noise filled the whole dormitory compound.

Li Gaocheng's spirits were inevitably elevated by all this and he continued in impassioned tones. "You should know that some of the municipal leaders may have already heard about these issues of yours, but they have come as news to others, myself included. Of course we must take them further, understand them and investigate them properly. No matter how things stand, no matter what the truth of the matter, as long as questions remain, I will definitely consult with the Municipal Government leaders as soon as possible, so that they can make a rapid decision to send a working group, an investigation team, to conduct a serious, thorough and comprehensive enquiry into all the problems of the Zhongyang Textile Group! They will find out exactly what the issues are and who did what. They will show no indulgence or leniency..."

Once again, Li Gaocheng was unable to continue as another thunderous round of cheering and applause interrupted him. It lasted for seven or eight minutes before he could go on to say: "However, I do want to make it clear to everyone that, so far, I have only heard your side of things and have not yet had a chance to hear the management's explanation of these issues. When I have finished listening to you, I still have to hear them out too. I want to hear what they have to say, and find out what their thinking is. All I say to you is that I hope you will trust me and not have any misgivings about me. I have already heard from what you have told me that many of you think I handpicked the Zhongyang Textiles management team and that they are all my people. Because of this, many of you also think that I will be biased towards them and shield them, that I might even find some way out for them and exonerate them. I promise everyone on my honour, on my conscience and on my Party membership, that I will not do so. Absolutely not! It is not something I have done in the past, it is not something I will do now, and it is not something I will ever do in the future! I may have many failings, but I think that you all know that I, Li Gaocheng, am not that kind of person. No matter who I may have promoted and no matter what relationship they may have with me, if they go to the bad and become corrupt, that is the end to any connection between them and me. I will not let my lifelong reputation be sullied by any corrupt element. If I were to have an association with someone who was corrupt, if I was to stick by them regardless, would that not make me corrupt too? Let me tell you all very clearly that I, Li Gaocheng, may make mistakes and commit errors, but I will never become corrupt myself! In this day and age, no matter what position I am in or what I do, I have to square myself with my conscience! I have to be worthy of the people who gave me life…"

He finally finished his speech to shouting and cheering as loud as spring thunder. It may be that many of his final words were lost in the tumult of applause, but that did not matter to anyone, as what they were interested in was his mood, his attitude, his stance and his tone. Words were not important; his meaning was. That was what the hearts and minds of the people wanted.

The cheering and applause seemed to revive his affection for Zhongyang Textiles, and it also settled his resolve. He could no longer drag his feet over the issues at the Zhongyang Textile Group; he had to sweep aside any interference and seriously take charge of the matter again himself. If such a large enterprise, with so many employees and cadres, continued to drag on like this, the collapse would not just be of the company; the chain reaction and social impact would be long-lasting and significant.

With such employees, with such people, what issues could not be harmoniously resolved? With just a few words, and with a promise that was not yet fully defined and still far from being fulfilled, he could stir up thousands, no tens of thousands of workers, with so much emotion and expectation in their cheers and applause! But they must be absolutely sure not to let the hearts of the workers cool off again as, if the people's enthusiasm was allowed to die down and congeal, would he ever hear such cheers and applause again? If they only woke up to what was going on at that stage, it would almost certainly be too late and the price to be paid would likely be very heavy. Ten times, a hundred times, no, a thousand times what it might be now.

That was right – it was still not too late. There was still time for everything, and it could all turn out well. As he left the conference room, the cheering and applause from the crowd standing in the winter sun swelled to a roar again. Not a single one of the onlookers had left. Despite being buffeted by the icy wind all night and day, there was not the slightest trace of fatigue or drowsiness in their expressions. Their dust-streaked red faces were filled with excitement and eagerness. Many of the former workers had tears in their eyes as they stared at him as if he was a long-lost relative. Many people seemed to want to come forward to shake hands with him and say a few words to him, but it was as if there was an invisible barrier between them, holding them back...

CHAPTER SIX

LI GAOCHENG DID INDEED STAY BEHIND, as he simply did not feel he could just go when he was so deeply moved by the sincerity of the workers. His position as mayor meant that if he was at all perfunctory or insincere in what he said, the next time he came he would almost certainly get the same scornful reception given to the company management team the night before and be jeered off the stage.

Of course, he could have just walked away from the matter, placating everybody and telling them what they wanted to hear in big, empty words. Then he could go back and report on everything he had heard to the other leaders on the Municipal Party Committee and in the Municipal Government. That way he could wash his hands of the matter. So, what, in the end, should he do? Everybody was watching. The problem of state-owned industries was a nationwide, universal one. The nation's leaders were agitated about it, so what was the point of him, a small-time mayor, playing the big shot? Even if something happened, it was a collective issue, and wouldn't reflect on him alone as mayor. That's the way things were nowadays: when there was something good and meritorious, there would always be people fighting over it. Anything bad, wrong or unacceptable got brushed aside as if it had nothing to do with anyone. If it went wrong, it would be a collective wrong; if there were problems, they would be collective problems. As long as something became a collective issue, no matter how big it was, it would not be considered a real problem, and it would be treated as something trivial and minor. Bad things were only done by individuals, as what reason could there be behind collective wrongdoing? Corruption was only the corruption of the individual; how could a whole group be corrupt?

At this point in his thought process, he stopped dead, stunned, as though he had been hit by a cosh. Was this not what the management of Zhongyang Textiles themselves were thinking and acting upon? Even if the problems reported by the masses were all true, so what? As long as it was everyone's fault, then what was the problem? If the whole team was broken and rotten, and all of them were corrupt, wouldn't that then be a problem for their superiors? A group of companies at the departmental level, a large enterprise with more than twenty thousand workers, and the entire leadership team, or the majority of the key members of the leadership team, are corrupt!? What, exactly, are you, as municipal leaders, going to do?! How do you supervise and manage the situation? How do you take responsibility? If one person is corrupt, you can deal with it; if the whole team is corrupt, the responsibility is that much greater, and how can you handle it successfully? To deal with them, you have to deal with yourselves first! What's more, wasn't the leadership team of this company hand-picked and built by you!?

A shudder that came from deep inside shook him again. If this really was what those people were thinking and doing, the prospect was terrifying. They could do anything they liked under the pretext of collective decision-making, collective management and collective operation without taking any responsibility at all. Moreover, it was a case of "if one prospers, they all prosper; if one is hurt, they are all hurt", and if anything happened, they would all close ranks. They would be thinking: you want to investigate us, that's fine – if you come alone we can bury you! Besides, if the poison doesn't kill the rat, isn't it only because it's not strong enough, and won't they think you are just trying to soft-soap them? After all, this is a loss-making company we are talking about, with hundreds of millions of debt. Who was actually going to come to such a loss-making enterprise to find out what the problem was? That's why the ordinary people were sayin: the bigger the losses, the bigger the problem; the bigger the losses, the more people dare take their share; and the bigger the losses, the more money those people dare take out. Many corrupt people were raking in the cash under the cover of loss-making enterprises, making a fortune out of the state. It was in this way that national property was being eaten up and lost, bit by bit, without anyone taking any notice or trying to stop it.

He knew quite well that was what they were up to, but there was nothing he could do about it, especially as the management's own leaders could say to them that their hands were tied and there was nothing to be done. At most, if there was absolutely no alternative, one or two of them might be removed, but then everything would just go back to the way it was and nothing would change. They would go on doing what they had been doing, with no repercussions, and he would be like a dog trying to bite a hedgehog, with no way of getting at them. This might well be the deepest form of corruption, and the most frightening.

Was that really the state that the Zhongyang Textile Group was in? Was its whole management team like that? If so, how was he going to confront them?

He couldn't think about it any further but at the very least there was no way he could believe that this was how things were; even less could he believe that every one of these people he had promoted himself could have gone to the bad like this.

After a short break, he ordered his secretary, Wu Xingang, immediately to inform the whole management team that they were to be in the conference room at the company's head office within an hour and that they should be prepared to give a detailed report and explanation of the main issues reported by the staff. During his break, he had called a few numbers in the city and made a few necessary arrangements. Last of all, he had called the Municipal Party Committee secretary, Yang Cheng, and given him a succinct explanation of what had just happened and the current state of affairs. Yang didn't say anything on the phone except that he would wait for Li's return and then they could consider things further. His parting words were full of unspoken meaning when he said that there were two sides to everything and when you focus on one side, you tend to neglect the other. The workers could have their say and the management theirs, but, in the end, what mattered were the facts.

Li Gaocheng thought about Yang Cheng's words for a long time but couldn't work out why he had said that or what he meant by it. Was it a warning to him not to take sides in how he listened and what he believed? Was he expressing the hope that Li wouldn't waste time banging his head against a brick wall? Or was he worried that he might go off half-cock and do something troublesome?

No matter what lay behind the secretary's words, they did serve to calm him down a lot. That was right – the situation was still far from demanding any kind of showdown or settlement. Absolutely everything was just in its early stages.

He drank some water and rested in his chair for ten minutes or so. When he saw the time had come, he took his car to the company office. In no time flat, no more than eight or nine minutes, he was at the main gates.

Once through the gates, Li Gaocheng got out of the car. It was still a little way from the gates to the office building itself but he did not want to be driven.

An ominous feeling suddenly enveloped him with great force.

It took him a while to realise that the ominous feeling emanated from the dead silence that shrouded the company compound.

A major enterprise with more than twenty thousand employees, especially at around four o'clock in the afternoon, should be a scene of bustling activity, with an endless stream of traffic going in and coming out, and the whole place alive with voices. Particularly in a large textile-based enterprise, the rumbling of machines and the ear-splitting sound of the looms should make it feel as if the sky was trembling and the earth shaking, even at a distance from the workshops.

An old technician and factory manager who had worked in the textile industry for decades would have a warm, comfortable familiar feeling inside him whenever he heard that kind of sound and saw that kind of scene.

Of course, excessive noise is harmful to people, especially in the textile industry, and a great deal of effort had been put into finding technical improvements to minimise that noise. But for some reason, as soon as Li Gaocheng heard that kind of noise, harmful as it was, he immediately felt much more secure and at ease. Without that noise, he felt uneasy and unsettled, as if something important was missing.

But now, this place he was so familiar with and missed so much; this place of chaos, smoke and dust which he even saw in his dreams; this place was like a deserted wilderness! There was no roar of machines, no clutter of people, no busy vehicles, no dust clouds, no voices shouting at each other. There were not even any of the sparrows they had tried so hard but unsuccessfully to eliminate – not a single one!

In the cold wind, those tall factories looked so dark, so empty and so lifeless. Every one of the workshop doors was tightly closed, and some of them had seals on them. So much time had passed that some of the seals had turned a yellowish black. As a result, the entire factory looked as if it was dying, with no bells tolling to mark its passing. It was gloomy and desolate! The sight cut Li Gaocheng to the quick and he felt as if a thousand arrows had pierced his heart. How could such a large enterprise that had been so flourishing come to this in just a few years? Profligacy was profligacy, but surely it was impossible for everything to be gone so quickly!

He looked in silence at the scene of decay in the company compound, and his heart wept. As he approached a nearby spinning workshop, the largest of them all, and one that he knew well, he felt an irresistible urge to open the doors and look inside.

He stood silently beside the door for a while, and his secretary, Wu Xingang, realising what he was thinking, asked: "Shall I find someone to open the door, Mayor Li?"

There was a long pause before Li Gaocheng replied, rather listlessly: "Yes, go and see if you can find anyone. If you can't, it doesn't matter if I can't have a look."

Wu Xingang looked at him in astonishment. He had never heard the mayor sound so sad. He stood there for a moment, then hurried off to find someone.

"…if a factory does not operate for two years or three years, anyone with a little common sense will understand that it effectively doesn't exist anymore… Mayor Li, you are also a former manager of Zhongyang Textile, so I think you will understand this better than others!" He didn't quite understand why, but the words of the old chief engineer, Zhang Huabin, rang in Li Gaocheng's ears again. Yes, he really did understand the truth of those words. If these workshop doors were sealed up like this, then the whole factory meant nothing; it really didn't exist anymore.

So, how could you start it up again now? Its debts were nearly 600 million! Nearly 600 million! What did that actually mean? A large enterprise like the Zhongyang Textile Group could have reconstructed itself two or three times over with that much money! It was no joking matter.

But now, how much more money and talent would it need to start up again?

No wonder some people said the best thing it could do was declare bankruptcy. As soon as it did that, the debt would be gone, the burden would be removed, responsibility would disappear, and the management team would disperse. The workers could find their own way, the cadres would be transferred; there might be lots of noisy moaning and whining, but everything would come up smelling of roses, the clouds would scatter, the sky would clear, and after a while, there would be nothing to look at.

Who was to blame? Reform! That was the simple answer. If the people want to berate anything, they could berate reform, and if they want to blame anything, they could blame the market economy. Socialism was dead; the collective economy had collapsed. The only reform was the return to capitalism, and the market economy was now the private economy. Look how prosperous and vigorous the private enterprises and joint ventures were! They were new, strong, thriving and constantly changing with the times! They couldn't be squeezed or crushed. How could state enterprises possibly compete with them? Sooner or later, state enterprise would be dead in the water.

So, let the common people put all their resentment on reform and opening up, while our cadres remain unchanged, still doing nothing and relying on others, still lying comfortably in the embrace of the state, indifferent to the reform and future of the country, ignoring their own responsibilities, insensitive, just letting things happen, carefree and complacent, or should that be drunk and sleepy? Spraying money around drinking themselves silly, all the time deceiving themselves and others. If they were not corrupt or degenerate, then they were certainly destroying themselves and digging their own graves. It was suicide!

If you showed no responsibility towards the people, they would show none towards you. You could abandon the people, but the people would then abandon you. There was an ancient saying that water can carry a boat, but it can also capsize it. Could it be that we are not as wise as the ancients?

If market stalls are scattered, they can easily be reassembled; with people, it is not so easy.

The sound of hurried footsteps dragged Li Gaocheng back from the depths of his contemplations. His secretary Wu Xingang had brought a gaggle of men and women with him to open one of the workshop doors. There were watchmen, admin staff, team leaders, workshop bosses, machinists, electricians, loom operators, more than a dozen of them, young and old.

It was probably a rule that if anyone wanted to open a workshop door after the factory had been shut down, it could only be done if there were people there to supervise each other, otherwise it was not permitted. The door was hard to open, probably because it hadn't been touched for such a long time. The two top locks alone took a considerable time. The three bolts were rusted closed, and it seemed as though they were never going to open.

When the door finally rumbled open, a rush of cold air and an overwhelming musty smell flooded out, almost suffocating them.

There was no electricity, and although the electrician fiddled with them for a while, he couldn't get the lights in the workshop to turn on. It was dark and gloomy inside, but after a while, eyes adjusted and the rows of dusty looms and lathes began to appear. The dust on the floor was half an inch thick, and a few clumps of discarded, grey cotton yarn were scattered across the floor.

Was this the place to which he had devoted most of his life and talents? Was this the place that he had been dreaming about, that he had been thinking about, that he could never forget? Was that bunch of boring grey objects really the looms and lathes that he could never see enough of, that he could never forget? Where were the clean floors, the shiny blue enamel, the dazzling lights, the nimble weavers, the exhilarating clamour, the hustle and bustle... where had all that old splendour and enthusiasm gone?

He suddenly felt a lump in his throat and something clutched at his heart. What was going on here? What was at the bottom of all this? How could a perfectly good factory, a perfectly good workshop, suddenly turn into this?

Without a word, he went over to one of the machines, slowly stretched out his hand, and patted it gently. His hand was covered in dust but now a sliver of brighter metal glinted dully on the body of the machine. He could tell at a glance this was still a good machine. But this newly upgraded machine was sitting silently there in the dark and might well be obsolete again before it even had a chance to start work.

Surely to abandon so many valuable pieces of state machinery was tantamount to a criminal waste of public resources and oppression of the people!

If these machines were privately owned, would they be treated like this?

A low sobbing noise came from behind him, and when he turned round, he found himself rooted to the spot.

It seemed that every one of the dozen or so people standing behind him was sobbing and weeping!

His own eyes filled with tears, and, although he resisted for a moment, in the end he couldn't stop them from flowing.

The sight of the mayor's tears spurred the others on to further wailing.

The cries of sorrow immediately filled the workshop.

The old worker who had brought the keys could hardly stand for weeping and he said, in a shattered voice: "Mayor Li! Mayor Li! You have to find a way for us to go back to work! We don't have any demands, we don't want any reward, even if we don't get a cent in pay, that's OK, as long as we have enough to live on, as long as we are allowed to start the machines up again, as long as there is noise in the workshops again, we will endure exhaustion and hardship... Mayor Li, we are all nearing retirement and have only a few days left to work, so let us do our best for this factory... Mayor Li, we have worked here all our lives and if we have to retire when it is in this state, it will really be too much for us, really too much! It has been more than a year now, and every day our hearts have felt crushed – we can't abandon this factory, we simply can't..."

Li Gaocheng's own eyes were flooded with tears, and it was a long time before he could speak.

These were true Chinese workers; they had given their whole lives without complaint or regret, and still had nothing. Even when their wages were not being paid, they were still concerned for the factory and were still protecting the factory every minute of the day!

This was what made the situation so grievous and heartbreaking.

CHAPTER SEVEN

When Li Gaocheng entered the meeting room at the company head office, the dozen or so members of the management team had already been waiting there for him for more than half an hour.

The meeting room was very rudimentary and sparsely furnished. There were a few old-fashioned sofas on their last legs, a few old tables and chairs from the 1950s and 1960s, no coffee tables, no flower pots, no decorations, and the lighting was still the old-style bare fluorescent tubes. No one smoked, so there were no ashtrays. This had been a rule in Zhongyang Textiles for decades – no employees or cadres who entered the factory, regardless of their position or job, were allowed to smoke. Smoking was not allowed even in the bathhouse and toilets, and there was no smoking room in the entire factory.

This was completely different from those meeting rooms, large and small, that Li Gaocheng was used to now. Whatever the atmosphere – serious, enthusiastic, nervous or relaxed – those rooms were always full of smoke, coupled with the sound of water being poured and whispering voices. But the feeling in this room was entirely unfamiliar; people were sitting in silence, all with grim faces, no one was drinking, no one was smoking, no one was even moving around. Nonetheless, every face looked so familiar and so real to him.

It was as if he was suddenly transported back to the fondly

remembered days of the past. This was how the meeting room had looked when he took over at Zhongyang Textiles, and how it had still looked when he left. So many years had passed since then, but the meeting room was still the same! How many meetings had been held here in this so familiar room, during those long, sleepless nights? How many issues had been discussed? How many decisions made? How much toil and effort had these people put into the rise and fall of this textile business?

His heart softened again at once. The anger that had been building up seemed mostly to have dissipated. Look at this simple meeting room, and then look at these straightforward faces! How angry could he still be? He had promoted these people, and he had, to say the least, put them to the test in many different ways. Besides, even if there were some mistakes in decision making, some mismanagement, it certainly wasn't likely that their motive was to bring down the company. What kind of a manager of a company, a department or a factory would want to destroy the place he or she was in charge of, so that they could take the blame and leave the place in disgrace? Did that make any kind of sense? Would anyone do that? Only a psychopath!

General Manager Guo Zhongyao was fifty-eight years old this year, four years older than Li Gaocheng. Just one look at his grey temples, at the wrinkles on his face, at his hunched back, and you could immediately feel the weight of the burden he was carrying. Such a heavy burden! When a man reached such an age and occupied such a position, was it really likely that he would initiate such mistakes? In just a few years he would be leaving his post and withdrawing forever from the company stage. Would he choose a peaceful retirement and a quiet old age, or would he gamble his life away for the sake of something that was really not his concern? Even an ordinary person, a person with a moderately level head would never choose the latter, let alone a department-level cadre.

So, what would Deputy General Manager Feng Minjie choose to do? What about Wu Mingde? And Party secretary Chen Yongming, what would he do? They were all now in their fifties and would be in their retirement years in the blink of an eye. It was hard to imagine that they would do something like that. Even if people do change, it takes time. How could anyone become a dyed-in-the-wool villain overnight?

Back then, when Li Gaocheng left the company, these men were still in their forties. That was the most precious age: an age of maturity, sophistication, and charm – a golden age. At that time, Li Gaocheng was still the vice mayor in charge of industry. His great idea then was to use Zhongyang Textiles as a spearhead to drive the improvement of the city's economy as a whole and to promote the reform of state-owned enterprises. He was very concerned about Zhongyang Textiles' every move, and he took a hand in every decision they took. The managers came running to him almost every day and he had them give detailed reports and explanations of everything. Li Gaocheng was an expert: nothing could be hidden from him, and nothing escaped him. One look and he could tell if you were up to no good or not.

It was pretty much a cast iron guarantee that, for those few years at least, Zhongyang Textiles was not going to have any major issues or make any big mistakes. These people were surely not going to become corrupt at that time, because, even if you want to, you have to have the right conditions to do so. With a young and dynamic team, and with a mayor who had just left the company still keeping an eye on it at all times, there were not going to be many loopholes or opportunities that escaped notice.

After that, Li Gaocheng studied at the Central Party School for a year. But even when he was there, he never completely lost touch with what was going on at Zhongyang Textiles. The situation there was no longer so rosy, and things were fast becoming very serious. However, he still had a hold on the general situation, and he still knew exactly where the problem lay. During that year, the various principal figures in the Zhongyang management would make sure to come to see him whenever they were in Beijing and would report to him about the company's situation. Although there were ups and downs, they remained full of confidence and felt that the problems could be solved, and the difficulties overcome. Indeed, when all was said and done, it had only been a year, so what major problems could have arisen?

Shortly after returning from the Central Party School, he was chosen as a mayoral candidate and was elected mayor at the Municipal People's Congress. In the following couple of years, because of the large-scale movement of members of the Municipal Party Committee and the Municipal Government, the specific responsibilities of many of them had not been settled, and charge of the city's industrial affairs rested directly with Li Gaocheng, who did not relax his vigilance over the affairs of Zhongyang Textiles. He personally issued instructions on many issues regarding Zhongyang Textiles, particularly on how to improve operations for an enterprise on that scale. He also specifically maintained communications with the leaders of the Municipal Economic Commission, the Municipal Planning Commission, the Municipal Finance Commission, the Municipal Bank and the Municipal Industrial Office, and held discussions and consultations with them. Although he was extraordinarily busy, he made sure he was well abreast of the fundamental situation at Zhongyang Textiles, and there were no problems sufficient to cause concern there at that time.

So, up until 1992, at least, the management team at Zhongyang Textiles was sound and trustworthy.

Did that mean, then, that the problems all began after 1992?

The truth of the matter was that, after he became deputy mayor with responsibility for industry, he became rather less connected to affairs at Zhongyang Textiles. It wasn't that he didn't want to keep abreast and be involved, rather that he actually had no way of doing so. As the deputy mayor in overall charge of industry, it would have seemed very out of place for him to intervene in one particular company. That really was not his job. In the few years that marked his move from an active business to a government administrative department, he had come to realise more and more clearly that management and management methods were very different things in those two sectors. In a business, you can yell and shout and make a lot of noise, and when cadres get together, they can sometimes fight ferociously over work-related matters. Status and age are irrelevant as long as you are acting in the interests of the company, and if you argue or quarrel, you never take it to heart, and once the argument is over, it is over. No one will care, and no one will harbour any resentment. But in a government administrative department, it is a completely different matter. On the surface it may be all peace and harmony, but look underneath and you'll see a seething mass of dragons and tigers fighting tooth and nail. If you are used to a job just handling business and find yourself in a new job where you have to handle people, you can find it exhausting, stifling and exasperating. Even so, there were still people who said that Li Gaocheng was still reliant on and closely attached to Zhongyang Textiles. Zhongyang Textiles' cadres were dangerous people to provoke, and only Li Gaocheng knew how to handle them. The only reason the Zhongyang management dared reach so high was because they knew Li Gaocheng was holding them firmly by the waist. With him in the background, no one else thought to interfere in the affairs of the company. As long as he was there, the Zhongyang Textile Group was as solid as a rock and as invulnerable as cast iron. However, the matter of reorganising the management team there did give him a particular headache. In the ordinary course of events, members like General Manager Guo Zhongyao and Party Secretary Chen Yongming, who had been in post for many years, were due to be moved on and replaced. However you looked at it, even a man of steel could only last so long working in that kind of exhausting job, where there was no rest day or night, and you were always living off your nerves. Besides, staying one place for too long, is always likely to cause problems. Movement and change are not just a necessity of work but also an aspect of human nature. But because he, the mayor, had himself come out of Zhongyang Textiles, whenever discussions turned to that company and its management team, his presence seemed to stifle debate. Very few people offered any ideas, let alone suggested what should be done. He often thought to himself that if one day something really did happen at Zhongyang Textiles and the company actually collapsed, however you looked at it, the greatest responsibility would lie with him. It would be him who brought harm on the company and its cadres!

This was why he always had feelings of guilt and self-reproach about the management of Zhongyang Textiles and felt more than a little sorry for them. Maybe if it wasn't for him, or if he wasn't mayor of this city, these people might have left long ago and their lives would be much more peaceful and stable.

Looking at it another way, was it not for the same reasons that, over the last several years, these people had undergone a fundamental change in attitude which made them more willing to take risks and open themselves up to corruption? Was it not because their old boss was now mayor, because they had such a special relationship with him, because he was such a firm defence for them, such a solid backstop, that, in the shade of his spreading branches, they felt free to act like foxes exploiting the might of the tiger and ruthlessly exploit every advantage of his patronage? It was hardly surprising that Yang Cheng, the newly appointed secretary of the Municipal Party Committee, said that the management of the Zhongyang Textile Group should have been changed long ago.

For a long time, he said nothing, just sitting in silence on the chairman's dais.

Looking at the dozen or so familiar faces in front of him, he really couldn't believe that they were capable of so many mind-boggling, unbelievable things.

How was it possible? Over the past few years, although to outward appearances he had not been giving a thought to Zhongyang Textiles, of course, in secret, he had never given up on them. Whenever the opportunity arose, he always asked about the situation there and these leading cadres of Zhongyang Textile often came to him to discuss issues, big and small, and to make reports. No matter whether they were in the city for a meeting or were celebrating the New Year or other holidays, they always came to his office or his home to sit and talk. When it came down to it, he still knew all about the affairs of Zhongyang Textiles, or at least he had a pretty good idea, so it was not as if this group of people had all suddenly become corrupt and he was still in the dark and didn't know anything about it!

The truth was, he was not usually a soft-hearted person, nor was he a weak and indecisive senior cadre. His reputation was well-known in the city government. But for some unknown reason, whenever Zhongyang Textiles were involved, he always felt lost and confused. He had absolutely no idea what to do for the best!

Was it just an emotional connection? Or was it, as other people said, because he had promoted all these people in front of him and they were all colleagues and comrades who had shared both joys and sorrows with him, who had been through thick and thin together? Had he, thereby, unconsciously, become their backstop and protector, and somehow strengthened their presumptuousness and greed?

Or was it because they had decided for themselves that they were never going to be promoted or transferred, they weren't getting any younger, the company's situation was deteriorating and any prospect of leaving it was getting more and more distant; so, if there was nothing in it for them as they were, why not make the best of it and go over to the other side and see what that had to offer. Because of the mayor, their careers were completely hopeless; but also because of the mayor, they could do whatever they liked there and no one would dare stop them or ask questions. So why not just get on with it and take whatever you want? With a mayor in the background to give you support, whether you tried it or not you had nothing to lose either way, so you would be a fucking idiot not to try!

Is that what they were thinking? Is that what they were doing? Li Gaocheng stared silently at them and they returned his stare in equal silence. There was something like a silent prayer in his heart as he considered the situation.

It all depended on what they said in explanation.

Because, no matter what, they were elbow deep in this mess and the state the company was in was down to them.

They had to give an account of themselves, and they had to come up with some kind of statement.

CHAPTER EIGHT

THE DEBRIEFING OF THE COMPANY LEADERS began at precisely 5.20pm. Li Gaocheng's opening remarks were brief, as he knew that they had heard everything he had said to the workers at the Old Cadre Activity Centre, and that they knew exactly what the staff representatives had said and asked for. In fact, there was no need to say anything else – all he wanted at this point was an explanation and an answer.

"The first thing is for you to tell me the truth. The second thing is for you to tell me the truth. And the third thing is for you to tell me the truth. If you are straight with me now, I will be straight with you."

Guo Zhongyao asked cautiously whether, as it was getting late, should they not have something to eat first and then report when they had finished.

Li Gaocheng waved the suggestion away without even looking at him. "How can you think of eating at a time like this? If the workers see me going out for dinner with you, do you think they will ever let me out of the gates again?"

Li Gaocheng was in a completely different frame of mind from when he had just been addressing the workers. What he was facing now was the bosses, the heart of the company, a blazing fire, a social group over which he had no direct control and which had no fear of him. This group's actions and feelings were directly linked to his own honour and advancement; they could affect both his status and his official career. Facing this group, he could not be free and easy, not even a little relaxed; he could not laugh or be angry. Every action had to be thought through and every word had to be fully weighed and carefully checked. For here, now, he was the real boss; he was the heart of the company; he, too, was a blazing fire. The people before him were all subordinates; he had control over them all and they were all terrified of him. In particular, his own likes and dislikes had a direct bearing on their honour and promotion, their positions and their careers. Here, he could say whatever he wanted to say and do whatever he wanted to do, and he didn't have to care about anything at all. Whatever else happened, these were people that he himself had promoted, and, whatever else happened, he was still the mayor and their former boss, and he could do what he liked with them.

When they saw how Li Gaocheng was behaving, they looked nervously at each other. After a few minutes, Guo Zhongyao opened a notebook, put on his glasses with trembling hands, glanced cautiously at Li Gaocheng and said: "Then let me make my report first."

Just this sentence pained Li Gaocheng. Guo Zhongyao was an old man now, but he was still just the same as before, respectful but frank. This illustrated what is probably a kind of interpersonal relationship unique to Chinese people: as long as you were someone's superior at one time, you would always be his superior. Even if his status changed, even if he had become your superior, in his heart, he still regarded you as his superior. Even if someone is your teacher for only one day, you should regard him like your father for the rest of your life. It is no wonder that many leaders, once in office, always try to find ways to promote their own people. So such subordinates will always be grateful to you from the bottom of their hearts, and will never forget to show that gratitude for the rest of their life. Otherwise, they would be considered unkind, unrighteous, unfaithful, unfilial; a true gentleman clearly differentiates between gratitude and grievance, and only a small person recognises a debt but does not repay it. If someone comes into conflict with their old superiors or rebels against the person who promoted them, their integrity is destroyed forever and they will never be able to stand tall in front of others for the rest of their life. And was it this special interpersonal relationship that was at the root of all the ills in our cadre class? A new chief brings in new aides and the number of cadres was getting bigger and bigger; there were more and more gangs and cliques forming round the bosses, and, no matter how important the problem was, as long as it involved this kind of special relationship, people would be daunted and deterred, and things would all of a sudden become complicated and difficult. Li Gaocheng suddenly felt that he, too, was trapped in this kind of relationship and could not extricate himself from it. They had only just started and already he was thinking and acting soft. Could it be that his own feelings were already biased and he had already edged over to their side? If that was so, then how could he really get to the heart of the problem and resolve it? How could he win the hearts and minds of all the workers and cadres of the factory so they respected authority and embraced virtue?

He must be cold as iron, strict but fair and he must not neglect the hearts of tens of thousands of workers for the sake of the few people in front of him. If there was a problem, he could not be soft-hearted, let alone soft-handed.

Guo Zhongyao's report was very serious and meticulous. Although he refuted every point, one by one, and turned them back on the other side, he managed to remain so correct and focused. There were no fierce words, no intemperate complaints, no bitter grievances and no fiery emotions. Presumably, he had had his arguments ready long ago, and every one of them was full and complete, well-founded and methodical.

Guo Zhongyao's report and explanation apparently represented the views and opinions of the entire upper management team. Firstly, he said he believed that the company management was responsible for the losses and liabilities of Zhongyang Textile Group over the last few years, that management thinking had become more and more old-fashioned and rigid in recent years, that market awareness had been weak and limited, and that they had been too slow in embracing change. Everything was still done according to the old rules and regulations, and this was true of both systems and management alike. They wanted to change, but they did not dare, and they were simultaneously advancing and retrenching. They were always looking for orders and instructions from above and waiting for the leaders to speak. In the absence of any such thing, they did not know what to rely on. So when it came to transforming planning into action in the marketplace, they were not just half a beat off the pace, they were a long way from catching up, and indeed might never catch up. Guo Zhongyao said that all that the company's managers, himself included, had wanted over many years was to be cherished and protected like a child by its mother. All they ever did was wait for the state's support, funding and investment; they relied on the leadership, the state and the government; if they lacked something, they asked for it; if it didn't come, they waited; if they couldn't wait, they went looking for it. You couldn't go wrong if you obeyed the Party, and you couldn't go wrong if you obeyed the government. They always thought that, since the company was owned by the Party and the state, and the workers also belonged to the Party and the state, how could the Party and the state not concern themselves with such a big factory, so many workers, and such a large scale of operations? If they didn't, what was the use of socialism? What would have happened to the principle of the leadership of the workers? When the state and the government really did wash their hands of the company and the buck stopped with them, they were dumbfounded. But by then it was too late, it was all too late and there was nothing to be done. These kinds of old thinking and old ideas really harmed themselves and others, harmed the factory, harmed the nation, and harmed tens of thousands of company workers. It was really sad to think about it now. If they had had these experiences and learned these lessons five or ten years ago, and had completely changed their ideas and ways of thinking, as they had now, he didn't believe the company would have collapsed into the state it was now in. In the space of five years, they had accrued almost 600 million yuan in foreign debts! Even they had not imagined they could owe so much...

At this point, Guo Zhongyao's eyes filled with tears and his voice choked with sobs, so he was unable to continue for quite a while. The whole meeting room filled with the sound of sobbing as many of those present also found themselves unable to hold back their tears.

Truth be told, Li Gaocheng had his own strong opinion about whether this speech of Guo's was just whining or whether it constituted a proper report on the issues. It was true that the mindset of waiting for state intervention was a very significant barrier to changing attitudes in the inland provinces, and that included the factory managers of medium and large-scale industries and the senior cadres of government departments. It was fair to say that many people shared the same idea, and bringing about any fundamental change in it was extremely difficult. But could he, Li Gaocheng, therefore draw the conclusion that, because the state had washed its hands of such matters, all those medium and large-scale industries that relied on the expectation of state aid were therefore doomed to total ruin? How could the management of such a large-scale enterprise so casually shuffle off any responsibility? When before had the state ever walked away from medium and large-scale state-owned industries? Quite apart from anything else, hadn't those hundreds of millions of loans come from state funds? Even when the state and the government were in straitened financial circumstances, hadn't they still given a company like this an average of 100 million a year in loans? How could that, in any way, be described as them washing their hands and walking away? Did that sound like anything the management of a major enterprise should be saying? But, faced with Guo Zhongyao's tear-choked silence, how could Li Gaocheng bring himself to say any of this? If he stopped to think about it, and this really was what Guo genuinely believed, could he actually say it was unreasonable? Especially after they had faithfully and wholeheartedly followed the instructions of state and government for so many years! Whatever the Party ordered them to do, they did; whatever policies the state came up with, they followed. So now, how were they supposed to change completely overnight when the Party and the state suddenly ordered them to take everything on their own shoulders, to find their own markets and to arrange their own sales paths and outlets? Could they really be expected to have that kind of grit and determination? The plain truth was that they had always played the role of children to the Party and the government, so how were they supposed to cope when they were suddenly snatched out of their mother's embrace? It was no easy task! He held back what he wanted to say, knowing that if he were to spill out, unthinkingly, everything that he actually felt, it would just sound like an outpouring of bitterness and spite.

After a seemingly endless silence, Guo Zhongyao continued:

"Let us turn to the purchase of cotton. The cotton we bought was no good. This is undoubtedly true and we are indeed responsible. We have never tried to conceal this. We explained all the circumstances in detail on many occasions at cadre meetings, and we also gave repeated explanations to the staff. The workers all complained, and even some of the cadres shared the mood of discontent. It is also true that some people were bitterly resentful about the affair. We can all fully understand that, but we really have had no way to tell the cadres and workers the real cause of the problem. Can we really deny responsibility? To tell the truth, Mayor Li, we didn't even want you to know about it because if you did, although we could accept your criticism and censure, if we were to have to inform on others, then that would be the end to the fortunes of this company. We couldn't tell you. We simply couldn't...!"

At this point, Guo Zhongyao couldn't stop himself choking up again. Li Gaocheng was very sensitive to the various possibilities of the situation: they could be deliberately keeping him in suspense or laying a trap or trying to fool him. Or they could be genuinely holding back some shameful secret, and if that was the case, it must involve some important government departments. Those could be planning committees or economic committees; they could be commerce or tax agencies; they could be departments of finance or industry; they could even be banks. There had been far too many instances of this kind of thing in the industrial world over the last few years and this mentality was very widespread. It was said that manufacturing companies were getting more and more powerful and more and more numerous, and that they were getting more and more independent. In fact, the truth was that they were beset by increasing numbers of "interfering mothers-in-law" who were making them more and more fearful. There is an old saying that the smaller a temple is, or the shallower a pond, the more you notice the evil influences; also that the harder a temple is to get into, the more the monks there want a piece of you. However, you must also be sure not to offend those you can least afford to. If you do end up offending one of them, you are caught between a rock and a hard place and will never have a day's peace again.

At this point, Feng Minjie, the deputy general manager in charge of supply and distribution, couldn't stop himself interjecting: "Let me report on this matter, Mayor Li. I was directly responsible for it. Clearly, I think I should have a say."

Li Gaocheng was silent for a long time before agreeing. For some reason, he felt a little uncomfortable with Feng Minjie's eagerness. Why was he in such a hurry? The general manager was in mid-report and, before he could finish talking about a particular issue, Feng had hurriedly interrupted. Was he panicking because he didn't think there was enough time for him to make his own report?

As soon as Feng Minjie started speaking, Li Gaocheng's suspicious mood gradually disappeared. Feng Minjie was just as eloquent as he had always been and just as quick-witted. His speciality and strength lay in his public relations skills which was one of the most important reasons Li Gaocheng had used him back then. No matter when or in what difficult circumstances, his fluency never deserted him, and he could be eloquent, long-winded or short and pithy as required. If he needed to arouse your sympathy, the words flowed out of him like a river; if he needed to persuade you, one word of his had the weight of a hundred. Back at that difficult time when the factory had a major backlog of merchandise, his public relations skills made a contribution that no other employee could possibly match. Back then, no matter how many troubles and worries Li Gaocheng had, as long as he heard Feng Minjie's slightly hoarse voice, he would feel happy and carefree, and it gave him self-confidence and encouragement. Now, the familiar voice and familiar words seemed to take him back to the old days, and they suddenly seemed to have been brought much closer together.

Feng Minjie spoke clearly, succinctly and convincingly, and it seemed that as soon as he spoke, the feeling of panic and unease completely disappeared. He first made it clear that he was speaking only for himself and not for the organisation. He said that, from start to finish in 1995, it was he who had undertaken all the cotton purchases. If there was any responsibility to be apportioned, then it rested entirely on him and had nothing to do with the general manager. He went on to explain that the state loan in 1995 was decided in April, and the loan procedures were all completed in June. But with the arrangements fully in in place, it had been delayed until late November. To get these funds transferred as soon as possible, the company still had to run for almost eight months without them, but the contract between them and the vendor of the cotton was drawn up in July. That contract would only be signed and entered into, with all legal guarantees, once an advance payment of 3 million yuan was made.

But the company didn't have that money to hand at the time as it couldn't even pay the workers' wages or its electricity and water bills. Although the state had agreed the loan of 60 million yuan in April, despite the most strenuous efforts, the company had been unable to raise the money for the down payment on this crucial contract. So time was money, and that contract was life or death to the company. No matter how good a deal it was, if both parties did not sign it, it would just be so much scrap paper. Ordinarily speaking, to an outsider, a company their size should have no problem raising 3 million yuan. But the truth can be cruel, and, size notwithstanding, the company was completely unable to find the money. Nowhere in the whole, large city was there anyone willing to lend the company 3 million yuan. Who was going to throw that kind of money into a company with a foreign debt of several hundred million? They could only wait impatiently for the loan from the state, and all they could do was run around anywhere they could think of, lobbying for support. In the July contract, the average price of grade 1, 2 and 3 cotton was set at 14,000 yuan per tonne, but in late August, it suddenly rose to 16,500. In September, it rose again to 18,000 yuan, and in October, it rose to nearly 19,000. By the time they got the loan in November, even the price of grade 4, grade 5 and grade 6 cotton exceeded 18,000 yuan per tonne. The loan came to them seven months late, and it cost them more than 8 million! Besides, in late November, it was the middle of the winter season, and they were obliged to go out and buy cotton! They had dozens of buyers, all over the place. Out of all the cotton-producing areas, it was a cotton and hemp company in a county in Jiangxi that provided the two thousand tonnes of cotton that the company needed.

Feng Minjie continued sorrowfully: "That province is not a cotton producer and we were well aware that their cotton was not good quality. In fact, this company's cotton was second hand, bought in from somewhere else and was someone else's future order. The bottom line was that this company was well-funded and was in no rush to sell its cotton, whereas we desperately needed the cotton and just had to watch them raise the price of the raw material. We had no option but to buy from them, inflated price or no. We held seven or eight rounds of negotiations with them trying to get the price of the cotton down and in the end we spent an average of 18,000 yuan per tonne on two thousand tonnes of cotton. That was roughly 300 yuan per tonne lower than the price elsewhere. Yes, it wasn't great quality but it wasn't as bad as some people are saying. Something over fifteen per cent was grade 2, up to twenty per cent was grade 3, ten per cent was grade 4, and roughly twenty-five per cent each was grades 5 and 6. Before finally signing the contract, we called in the company's best engineers and cotton inspectors, and we talked the deal over and over with them and inspected and reinspected the goods. The quality wasn't good, but we had to buy it because who knew how high the price of cotton might rocket. Besides, if we didn't buy it, the company's own raw materials were already exhausted, and without raw materials a year's work by the company would have come to nothing. What were tens of thousands of workers going to do and how were they going to eat? The individual quality of cotton was not ideal, but it could be used in combination, and it was better than having no work at all. Some people said that since we knew that cotton was no good, why did we go back and buy a second batch of several hundred tonnes from the same place? Those people really didn't stop to think before they opened their mouths. If we really had been playing games, would we really have gone back a second time? Could we really have been either that dishonest or that stupid? What really happened was that the other company said they still had another one hundred tonnes or so on top of what we had already taken off them, and if we wanted it they would let us have it rather cheaper than the first load. We were well aware of the nationwide state of the cotton market, and we were certainly not going to find anything cheaper elsewhere. After we got back, on the one hand we stabilised the situation for everyone, and on the other, we set about using the cotton. In fact, we found that the quality was OK, so we bit the bullet, went for broke and bought another four hundred and fifty tonnes. However wretched we thought it was, there was nothing else we could do – nothing. Thanks to the actions of others, or, rather, their inaction, we simply didn't have the money! Our buyer wept when he saw us. He had lost count of how many times he had agreed a price with someone then had to watch helplessly as some other factory made off with the cotton because the money wasn't there. Time and time again he urged the company and cajoled people. We are in a market economy now – you can go anywhere with money but nowhere without it. What use is a top brand name when people only recognise money? In recent years, the reputation of large and medium-sized enterprises has not been good. The bigger the brand, the more they're afraid of you and the more they avoid you. On the other hand, we too have reason to feel guilty – on the face of it, we are all office cadres and general managers of a large company, but, in fact, we are far worse than the small-time bosses of individual and township companies. You can't live in a house, you can't invite guests, you can't give gifts, you can't ride in a car, and you can't even wear clothes that are far worse than other people's. When they see your shabby appearance, they already think less of you, so how can you possibly compete with anyone?"

The small meeting room was silent, and everyone seemed to have been deeply moved by Feng Minjie's words. Li Gaocheng too was caught up in the mood and atmosphere they had wrought. He wanted to interrupt and say something, but he didn't seem to get the chance. This appeared to be intentional on the part of Feng Minjie who didn't want any interruptions; he just wanted Li to listen, to hear his confession. He wanted to make an impression and completely reverse how Li felt about things.

Feng Minjie continued: "After so many years, I really didn't think it would be so difficult to get anything done now. When you go out you are kowtowing left, right and centre, and even back at home you spend all your time bowing and scraping. Whenever you go out, you look up and see the weight of everybody else and their business pressing down on you. Everybody else seems to be controlling you and they are all telling you that industry should be decentralised, free and autonomous. But, whatever the truth of the current situation, you can't help feeling more and more encircled and constricted, more and more controlled and oppressed, and beset by more and more interfering "mothers-in-law". Just as an example, take that loan in 1995. The state and the government had determined to give us the money, the bank was not short of cash, so why did it take so long to get to us? We simply couldn't understand why. Would they act the same if it was their own company? Would they put up with it? When they could see our company was losing money, hand over fist, why didn't they feel even just a little concern? We ran ourselves off our feet, talked ourselves hoarse, paid for countless meals, and, to put it bluntly, how much food did they stuff in their mouths at our expense and how much money did they take out of us? We could not understand how some people could be so black-hearted in the way they dragged you down and didn't offer any kind of help. With things the way they are, Mayor Li, the only thing to do is tell the truth. The fact is that it was the same every year and every loan was the same story. If they hadn't dragged us down and oppressed us and if there hadn't been so many old women constantly getting in our way, do you think that Zhongyang Textiles would be in the state you see it in now? So now, the workers are rioting, and the company is about to go bankrupt. You would think they might show some urgency now, but not a bit of it. Is this how they treat all companies like ours? When did they ever do anything to help or support them? Yes, there are problems in our systems, flaws in our management, and our ideas are a bit outdated, but can that be the only explanation for everything that goes on? If we genuinely had authority, if we really were our own masters, if this company would absolutely let us have the final word, do you think we would be in this state today? Mayor Li, in speaking to you like this today, our intention is absolutely not to take the opportunity to moan about our leaders. To be honest, we have talked this through many times, and if you were not our old boss, Mr Mayor, we might well have given up long ago. Why should we go on suffering here if nothing we try actually works? If things go on like this, we will inevitably have to take the blame. The only thing we are afraid of is that we will end up labelled as the bad elements in the company. We have worked hard here all our lives, and that is all we will get out of it, the badge of corruption…"

In conclusion, Feng Minjie gave Li Gaocheng an unequivocal guarantee that if there were any inaccuracies in what he had said today, he would take full legal responsibility. He added that he welcomed any supervisory and judicial departments to come in to conduct strict audits and investigations. He would do everything in his power to actively assist and cooperate with them. If any serious corruption was found, he would immediately accept the blame and resign, and he was willing to accept any judicial punishment no matter how severe.

It must be said that Li Gaocheng was deeply moved by Feng Minjie's speech. As well as giving him much to think about, he had also found it inexplicably touching. Although there had been a degree of acrimony and resentment in what he had to say, Li Gaocheng believed in the truth of his account and he had not indulged in any mendacity, boasting or other nonsense. Indeed, when Feng Minjie had finished talking, Li Gaocheng's doubts seemed gradually to have dissolved. In particular, there now seemed to be a fairly reasonable explanation of the affair of the cotton, which was the thing he had found most worrying and unacceptable. It was his belief that the bosses of these companies would never dump such an unspeakable mess on him, an economic mess involving millions, if not tens of millions of yuan. It might not just be more than their jobs were worth – it could be more than their lives were worth. He trusted his intuition, even though he also understood that it basically came from an intractable affection for, and belief in, his old subordinates.

He was often very adamant in his assertion that, on many occasions, emotion and reason ought to go hand in hand.

CHAPTER NINE

THE MANAGEMENT REPORT of the company's leaders continued until midnight with hardly a break. They didn't even leave the conference room for dinner, but just had a pack of instant noodles and a sausage per person. The meal took less than a quarter of an hour in total, and after they had finished eating they went on with the report.

Although it was an extremely simple dinner, it served greatly to relax the tension in the conference room. It also caused great hilarity when Party Committee Secretary Chen Yongming found he could not bite through the skin of the sausage. Even Li Gaocheng laughed uproariously.

With the mood eased, the report continued much more easily.

Secretary Chen Yongming then talked about promotion and appointment of cadres within the company and the organisational work of the Party Committee in recent years.

Chen Yongming said he acknowledged that the proportion of cadres in the company was too large but said that this was a universal situation caused by the official economic system and not a problem solely of the Zhongyang Textile Group. Compared with the whole province and the whole country, the proportion of cadres in the company was still relatively low, and the comparative youth of those cadres was noteworthy. In recent years, Zhongyang Textiles had indeed promoted a large number of cadres, eighty per cent of whom were young and middle-aged. They had formulated very strict rules and regulations regarding the issue of promoting cadres and had consciously enhanced the transparency and openness of their selection, and done their very best to achieve genuine fairness and democracy on the basis of equal competition.

"These measures of ours have been carefully examined by the organisational departments of the Provincial Party Committee and Municipal Party Committee. They have been recommended as an advanced model for the city and the whole province and have received many awards and commendations from higher-level departments. However, it would not be objectively truthful to say that there have been no problems at all with cadres we have promoted over the past few years. As has already been stated, if any problem has arisen amongst the recently promoted cadres, we have dismissed those who should be dismissed, investigated those who merited investigation, and dealt with those who needed to be dealt with. In doing so, we have shown no excessive leniency or tolerance. In addition, we investigated anyone selected for promotion with equal thoroughness. In this latter respect, from 1990 onwards, we investigated more than twenty newly promoted young cadres. The crux of the matter is that, over the last few years, our reserve of cadres has continuously diminished, and the loss of managerial and technical talent has become more and more serious. Those talents we value we are never able to keep hold of. Indeed we don't have the conditions to retain them – we can't raise salaries, we can't improve status, we can't offer housing and we can't promise better prospects. What young person would want to stay under those circumstances? I certainly wouldn't! So, in recent years, the biggest problems we have encountered in promoting cadres are simply that they cannot be found, selected or used. So, when people say that we have been corrupt in promoting cadres in recent years, it really is laughable. Last year, we had our eye on a young college student on the staff, but even after all our blandishments he refused the post. Later, he told people that he came here only for some training and experience and had no intention of staying any length of time. It was annoying to hear that at the time, but not so much after we thought about it. Could we really blame the young man? Could we really question his dedication on this basis? In this company, with several hundred million in foreign debt and its inability even to pay wages, even if you offered a general manager's post, he wouldn't have taken it. When it takes so much persuasion and so much hard work just to promote a cadre, how could anyone be corrupt even if they wanted to?"

At this point, Secretary Chen Yongming could not keep a note of resentment out of his voice as he continued:

"There are also some people who say that some of us managers are not just corrupt in our actions but are morally corrupt in our overall attitude too. They are saying that some of us are setting our mistresses up in senior posts in the company and even swapping our secretaries for younger girls. We really can't imagine how these people can be so irresponsible in what they say! To put it bluntly, all they want to do is spread gossip in an attempt to bring down our team and smear the management's reputation. It is public knowledge that General Manager Guo Zhongyao is divorced. Everyone knows that things weren't right in his household and that his wife had an evil temper. Even his own son and daughter urged him to get divorced, believing there was no value to anyone in prolonging a marriage like that. Before the divorce, everyone seemed to be in agreement, but once it had happened, that agreement turned to suspicion. In the past it would have been the widow who had all the trouble, but now it seemed to land at the general manager's door. Could it be that a divorced man is destined only to have abnormal relationships in his dealings with women? Is it always going to be an issue when a divorced general manager promotes a woman to a management post? Since more than seventy per cent of the staff at the Zhongyang Textile Group are women, however you look at it, how can the management just get on with their work? Yes, it is true that in the past two years we have employed a number of female cadres to do public relations work at the company, but what is wrong with that? It is a fact of the job nowadays and the way society is going. It's always better to have a smart and capable woman, whether she is involved in purchasing or marketing, or whether she is working on a project or signing a contract, than to have a man. If you go about your job in the same straightforward way you always used to, no one's going to buy it anymore. And if that's the way society is, what can we do to change it? Of course, it's not that our critics don't understand this, they just want to use it against us. That's how it is in our country today – if you want to break someone, you start by smearing him. So you say Manager Guo, or whoever, keeps changing secretaries, giving them houses and setting them up in jobs, no matter that it is nonsense, it's still going to have an effect, isn't it? What kind of a person is it who talks like that?"

If Guo Zhongyao hadn't stopped him, Chen Yongming might have gone on and on. To be honest, understandable as Chen Yongming's words were, they were actually quite offensive, not because of their content, but because of the man's attitude and emotion as he spoke. Apart from anything else, as a Party secretary of a company, he should not have been talking about this issue in such an antagonistic and judgemental way. This was what the people thought, or at least a part of them did, so it really shouldn't have been treated with this kind of hostility and contempt. When something is wrong, some people are always going to put the worst interpretation on it. You can say they are under a misapprehension or have a one-sided point of view, but you certainly can't accuse them of running a smear campaign or conspiracy to achieve some aim or other. If that kind of talk got out, could the tensions with the masses ever be eased? Really, Chen Yongming should never have spoken the way he did. Did he think that he, Li Gaocheng, was any less aware of Guo Zhongyao's marital difficulties, or any less understanding of them? No matter what your opinion of the masses, you couldn't talk like that, just because you were a leading cadre, and these people were front-line workers. It was a fundamental right of the masses and one of the most sacred rights that the Party had bestowed on them from the very start. No one had the right to deprive them of it or denigrate it!

Next, Wu Mingde, the deputy general manager in charge of finance, talked about the company's general economic situation.

He said he recognised that some people were saying that the company's finances were in a chaotic and unregulated state, but such talk was completely groundless and extremely irresponsible. This was the principal cause of the tension between the cadres and the workers and the main reason for the emotional instability that was evident amongst the workers at that time. Once this kind of scepticism and distrust became entrenched, nothing you could say would shift it, and no reports you made would change it. Wu Mingde believed, therefore, that the key to calming the inflamed emotions of the masses was to hope that the leadership would send a financial working group as soon as possible to review and verify all the accounts and give a satisfactory account of them to the masses. He told Li Gaocheng that he should not think they were afraid of this process, rather they were looking forward to it. As long as the accounts were verified and the conclusions were made public, the pressure would be relieved and the masses would be reassured.

Wu Mingde continued: "Now the opinions of the masses are at their most vehement, we also need to explain two other issues. One is the question of inviting clients to dinner, and the other is the question of going abroad on fact-finding missions. Treating clients to dinner is a difficult thing to explain. It is true that there has been a great deal of expenditure in this area over the years, but none of it is unaccounted for or unjustified, and the amount is by no means as much as some people are making it out to be. When people say that it must cost millions a year just to take clients to dinner alone, that is just plucking figures from the air. The company has hundreds of salespeople and buyers and purchase personnel who live and eat away from the company all year round, and that is a huge expense in itself. Including the travel expenses and subsidies of all the company's business travellers, plus all the company's entertainment expenditure, the annual amount is over 2 million yuan, but even in 1992, the most expensive year, the total amount did not exceed 3 million yuan. All these accounts can be checked, and, as long as they are verified, everything will be fine. The real question is whether some of the dinners should actually have been held, and whether some clients were appropriate guests. Of course, all this has long been an open secret – something that is well understood but not talked about, something that is not done openly but goes on all the time under the counter. You have to do it. If you're looking for someone to get something done, it's not going to happen if you only talk about it in the office. In business today, you can take someone to dinner, take them to a dance hall, send gifts to their home, and that's all quite all right, quite all right. Nowadays, if you want to evaluate some individual's competence and abilities, right from the outset the process relies on whether you can take certain bosses and other key people out to dinner. You know quite well it is against the rules, but you can't not do it. But let's just focus on the loans we've taken out over the last few years. Do you think there was a single one of those years when we didn't have to go begging to the high-ups over and over again before we could actually get the money in place? Do you really believe we wanted to spend so much time at the dinner table with those people? Do you know how awful we felt sitting there, biting our tongues and holding our tempers in check? But that money represented the blood and sweat of the workers and was the company's only lifeline.

"As for the fact-finding trips abroad, we already know that the people have strong opinions about them, and they are not so easy to explain away. The workers are going without pay and bonuses and we go off spending all that money on trips abroad! Of course, feelings are running high and the people have their own opinions about it. All the more so because, recently, there have been a number of work units going on completely unnecessary trips and they are being widely discussed all over society. The workers' suspicions and opposition are quite understandable, but in the current circumstances, our workers are particularly up in arms because our trips haven't actually resulted in anything. Once we have something to show for them and can launch a new project, all the ill feeling will disappear. The question that faces us now is whether, given the situation the Zhongyang Textile Group currently finds itself in, just how necessary is it to go on fact-finding trips and bring in foreign investment and technology? I personally think that it is not only necessary but essential in order to turn around the situation and get out of the current predicament as soon as possible. This is one of our most promising and effective strategic decisions so it is absolutely necessary to spend the money on these foreign trips. Some people are saying that we are visiting too many different places, that we are taking our wives in the guise of researchers and that these trips are really just vacations. But if we want to attract foreign investment and find suitable partners in the company's current circumstances, how can we be expected to succeed in just one or two trips? Yes, we have been to America and Russia and France. America is a wealthy nation and we were the guests of our potential contact. Russia may be poor, but it has very advanced technology and equipment, and it is right next door to China. They both offer us potential opportunities. As far as France and the UK are concerned, we have existing contacts there and we felt it was only right to go. And there is absolutely no truth in the stories about us taking our wives on fact-finding trips. The only member of the management team who did do that was our chief engineer, Gao Shuangliang, and that was simply because his wife is a highly qualified engineer too. For a loss-making company with heavy debts like ours, if we don't put ourselves around and go looking, foreign investment and partners aren't just going to come to us, are they? After two years of hard work, our fact-finding trips have borne fruit – we have already signed an MOA with Nigeria, and our agreement with Niger will soon be finalised as their representatives have already carried out their own on-the-spot inspection here. Those two countries are both cotton producers, so they can provide the raw materials and we manufacture the final product. We are currently negotiating a specific plan. One of the biggest obstacles we are facing now is our foreign debt problem. People are quite willing to cooperate with us, but they are worried by the size of our debt, and it gives them pause for thought. Even though these debts have nothing to do with them, they are still apprehensive, as the way they see it, a company like ours is effectively bankrupt and there is no reason it should survive. With so many foreign debts, how can it continue to produce anything? If we do not cooperate with them, are we not trying to cheat them out of their cotton? Even if it is not cheating, when the year-end settlement comes and all the profits go to the bank, how is that different? So, no matter how much we explain to them the difference between our two countries, no matter how favourable the terms we offer them, they are still too concerned about the situation to come to a final decision."

At this point, Wu Mingde threw a cautious look at Li Gaocheng and continued, with equal circumspection:

"Mayor Li, both these countries have the same request. They believe that since what is being proposed is a partnership of equals, our debt should be excluded from consideration in the deal, or, at the very least, we should get our bank to give them a certificate of guarantee making it clear that their new tranche of investment has no connection with our existing debt. If this can indeed be guaranteed and settled, then a bi-lateral can be signed immediately. We have already discussed this with our bank on numerous occasions, Mayor Li, and also had extensive talks with the Municipal Department of

Industry and the Municipal Economics Committee. However, none of them are willing to give a clear answer, and all they will say is that a detailed report on the matter must be made to the Municipal Party Committee and the Municipal Government, and they can only give us an answer after they have obtained the consent of top-level officials and their relevant departments. We too are sensitive to the gravity of this matter, but it is the one thing that will decide whether we get out of our current difficulties and whether the Zhongyang Textile Group succeeds or fails. We have made detailed studies and done all the calculations, and, if we agree to the stipulation that our debt is excluded and removed from the new deals, the whole company will be completely reinvigorated. Our main problem in recent years has been the shortage of funds and the inability to buy high-quality raw materials, which obviously directly impacts our sales. This vicious circle has led to the burden on Zhongyang Textiles becoming heavier and heavier, to the point that production has been stopped. Now, once we get these joint ventures with foreign countries, all our problems can easily be solved. Our partners are countries that produce high-quality cotton, which can provide us with our raw materials. This solves not only our capital shortfall problem but also our problems with sourcing raw material, the more so since most of our products will be sold back to the partner countries. This, in turn, is equivalent to solving our sales problem, and at the same time, it can also bring much-needed foreign exchange into the country. It really does kill all these birds with one stone, so why don't we just do it? As long as Zhongyang Textiles is up and running, and everything is moving in the right direction, shouldn't any money earned go to the state? Doesn't this business belong to the state anyway? In fact, it is simply not reasonable or even possible for a joint venture party to take on hundreds of millions of debt before they have even formed an agreement with us. We are going to have to repay these foreign debts to the state sooner or later, and if we get stuck on this point, we are never ever going to find a partner. Even the stupidest of the stupid are not going to saddle themselves with responsibility for hundreds of millions of our debt and then sign an agreement with us. From a business ethics point of view, we could simply never do this anyway. We are not telling you all this, Mayor Li, because we want an answer from you. We are just reporting the situation, but of course we'll listen to any suggestions you may have about what we should do."

  As Wu Mingde was talking, Li Gaocheng found himself being drawn, almost without knowing it, into a state of deep contemplation, in which he remained, even after Wu had finished. He was very satisfied with both Wu's actual words and with his train of thought, and he found the speech very persuasive. It was right for him to say that if the management had economic problems, then people should be sent in to carry out an audit; this is what they hoped would happen and they would actively welcome it. He had admitted that a lot of money was being spent on entertaining clients, but he had explained very clearly why this was reasonable and necessary and he could not be faulted on this. His response to the accusations that members of the management team were taking foreign holidays under the guise of fact-finding trips was completely reasonable. Li was particularly moved by the man's exposition of the problems and obstacles in the way of foreign cooperation and how he passed the matter over to him. For Wu was quite right that it was surely a pipe dream to think they might get someone to take on more than 500 million yuan and still enter into a partnership; that had to be an unrealistic condition. But he had also said that this condition was in fact an illusion and was irrelevant. And, if you thought about it, that was true. The company was owned by the state, and the responsibility was the state's, so it was a simple fact that, sooner or later the state would meet the state's debt. If the condition was met in this way, then the company, which was on the verge of extinction, could be pulled back from the brink; if the company could survive, the workers would be pacified and the state would be relieved of the burden. Was there any reason not to do this? And as long as the enterprise survived and made a profit, at least the debt would be reduced a little; even if it was not paid off, at least the country would no longer be pouring money into this bottomless pit; and if it became a joint venture, at least the country would be relieved of the burden. This issue merited serious study, and they should be asked to come up with a report and a feasible plan to be submitted to the Municipal Party Committee and Municipal Government for consultation and study as soon as possible.

With his thinking at this stage, all Li Gaocheng did was ask Guo Zhongyao: "How do you see this affair, Lao Guo?"

Guo Zhongyao's mind appeared to be elsewhere and he jumped, as if startled, and stared blankly for a moment.

"What affair?" he asked confusedly.

Li Gaocheng was surprised by his distraction, as, by the look of it, he hadn't heard a word that was being said for quite a while. The real question was, what had he actually been thinking about all that time? But Li swiftly forgave him: he was probably just too tired and sleepy. He was almost sixty after all, and even a youngster's attention could drift away after so many hours of nervous tension. He looked at Guo Zhongyao's wrinkled face, the heavy bags under his eyes, his drooping eye bags, his haggard and bewildered expression, and couldn't help feeling a little distressed. It is no easy thing to be a manager in a company like this. Finally, he said softly: "With the company in this state, what do you think the next step should be? What should we do to get the business up and running as quickly as possible?"

Guo Zhongyao gave Li Gaocheng a long hard look, before saying slowly: "Do you really want my honest opinion, Mayor Li?"

Li Gaocheng looked at him in surprise, not expecting this kind of question from him. He held himself in, but there was still a lot of anger in his voice when he said: "With the company in the position it is, you can say anything you like!"

"I don't want to cause you any trouble, Mayor Li." His eyes a little downcast and not looking directly at Li Gaocheng, Guo Zhongyao shook his head vigorously and said: "There's no way out, no way out at all. Everything that's just been said is false – there's not a single reliable strategy. We already owe more than 500 million and, no matter how clever they are, no one can pay off that kind of sum! How much is one year's interest alone? Even with all our factories running and our order books full, the annual profit won't be anywhere close to enough to cover the interest. Look how heavy the burden we're carrying is! Tens of thousands of active employees, thousands of retired ones, all depend on this enterprise for the necessities of life. How much money does that take every year? Even now, the entire company has stopped production and is lying idle but the monthly management costs are still millions of yuan. How can anyone come up with a solution to that, the state we are in now? There is no way out, really no way out!"

Li Gaocheng looked at him in amazement again. He had never even considered the possibility that General Manager Guo Zhongyao could have such a bleak and hopeless view of the company. He couldn't keep the irritation out of his voice when he said: "So, according to you, this company is already finished and we should just shut up shop and be done with it. Is that right?"

"I'm just telling the truth, Mayor Li. Even if you sack me, I'll still say the same," Guo Zhongyao said, and burst into tears. "This company is surely done for and the only thing it can do is go bankrupt..."

The words Li Gaocheng most feared and least wanted to hear had finally come out. He stood there dumbfounded for a moment, his mind a blank.

At this point, he heard Deputy General Manager Feng Minjie break in: "There were some things we didn't dare to tell you, Mayor Li. At this moment, it is impossible to start the factory up again. The workers have stolen everything in the workshops, and have even dismantled the machines for parts. If you sell the company, it will throw the people into chaos, and they will go to the bad. If you declare bankruptcy now, the debts can still be offset, but if you drag it out, you will really go broke, and I'm afraid everything will be one big mess..."

Party Secretary Chen Yongming also broke in: "There is another thing we originally weren't going to tell you about. Despite the number of workers who came out last night, in fact, not many of them really made any trouble. At most, they just stood by and joined in the fun. They came to see us in secret first, saying that when they came out to kick up a fuss, they were actually trying to help the management speak out. The company belonged to the state, the workers belonged to the state, so why wasn't the state taking control? If they came out and made trouble, it would lift some of the responsibility from us managers and our burden would be lighter. If they made enough noise for the state to take proper notice, investment would come in, loans would be made, and wouldn't everything be much easier for us?"

Deputy General Manager Wu Mingde joined in again: "Mayor

Li, the majority of the real troublemakers in the company were people who had something against the management or who had been disciplined by them. To put it bluntly, most of those who started the trouble were in fact gangsters, thugs and hoodlums, and very few honest workers and cadres were actually involved. For example, one of those who started the trouble was the deputy director of the finance department who had been put on probation for two years. When his son was running an outside company and needed money urgently, he used his position to embezzle a large sum of money. After the incident, the company took serious action against him and informed the parent company. The deputy director was very unhappy about this and repeatedly picked fights with the management. Now, the company his son runs has become a major player and is so wealthy and powerful that he has found many backers in the province and the city, and many Zhongyang Textiles workers now work for him. This father and son are the most active pair in these troubles. The deputy director has been spreading the word everywhere that they want to take revenge and give the management something to think about. They also say that they have the money, people and backing, and this time they will put these bastards of managers in prison..."

Li Gaocheng was still sitting in stunned silence. For some reason, the words of Yang Cheng, the secretary of the Municipal Party Committee, suddenly popped into his head again:

"The problem for the Zhongyang Textile Company is that it should have made up its mind a long time ago..."

CHAPTER TEN

It was after one o'clock the next morning before Li Gaocheng returned home. He hadn't slept for almost forty hours. Although he had a splitting headache and was so tired that he was almost in pieces, he didn't feel sleepy at all. After taking a quick shower and pouring himself a glass of hot water, he wrapped himself in a warm quilt, kept his eyes wide open and let his thoughts roam free.

What to do? After he had finished listening to the management report at Zhongyang Textiles, he hadn't intended to say any more, but found that he couldn't stop himself venting his anger.

That whole long, long report seemed to boil down to one thing, which was that the management team had done nothing wrong and did not bear any responsibility. The workers were all speculating that any complaints had been made for ulterior motives, that the current situation of Zhongyang Textiles was the fault of the system, and, as for what was the best way to get the company out of its current predicament, there were only two answers. One was through joint ventures with foreign countries, provided that all debts were written off; the other was to declare bankruptcy and make this huge company with tens of thousands of employees completely disappear from the earth.

It was ridiculous! If that's how things really were, what were all you management cadres actually doing? When you had money and power and benefits, you were all living it up with the best food and wine, going everywhere by car and taking a big salary, but as soon as things started going wrong at the company, clouds of gloom descended, everyone went around with long faces and sighing, and your only thought was to scatter to the four winds. Is that all your so-called talents and abilities are good for? If you are looking for managers who are only any use when things are in their favour, you can find them anywhere, but what kind of real leadership is that? If the management of all state-owned industries were at the same level and of the same quality as you, sooner or later the whole of the medium and large-scale industrial sector in China would be doomed! If that is how things stand, the best thing you lot can do for me is to go back to your villages and start growing crops, though given the way you are, I don't suppose you will even be very good farmers!

But scolding is scolding, and solving problems is solving problems. The predicament of Zhongyang Textiles couldn't be completely solved just by reprimands, investigation and serious discipline. Even if they were all removed from office and punished, that didn't mean that the company would get out of its predicament anytime soon.

The key question was what to do now? How to come up with a practical plan to get the heavy machinery of Zhongyang Textiles up and running as soon as possible, instead of sitting around waiting for it to rust and fall apart. This was the first thing that had to be done, and other problems could be solved later.

But, when he really thought about it, he gradually began to feel that what the managers had said just now was not unreasonable. Large-scale operations, heavy burdens, poor turnover and shortage of funds were the common fatal problems of state-owned enterprises. If you order them to run around and dance when they are weighted down with chains and shackles, are they really going to run around and dance? But those individual enterprises can do whatever they want in their own interests, using any means they like, fair or foul, like evading tax, docking wages, speculating and taking kickbacks, offering heavy bribes, and straightforward theft, open or opportunistic, all without any scruples and, more importantly, without having to answer to the state or to employees. Can any state-owned enterprises do that? Although most individual businesses were law-abiding, they had far more freedom, fewer burdens and less pressure, and much more power to decide things for themselves. Moreover, the kind of recklessness and brazen rule-bending employed by some individual enterprises were all completely illegal and heavily censured for state-owned businesses. With such unfair competition, how much more time and effort did state-owned enterprises have to put in to stay on top? How could even the most capable managers and entrepreneurs achieve anything in such circumstances? Wasn't it unreasonable they should meet such difficulties? Didn't they deserve some understanding?

For so many years, we have been talking about the separation of government and enterprise, but when have they ever truly been separate? Not to mention the randomness of our appointment and dismissal of corporate cadres, which keeps managers and factory directors of all kinds permanently nervous and on edge. Then there are the arbitrary seizure of funds from state-owned enterprises and the ordering of products purely on spec without a definite market, which can plunge a business into crisis at any time. In 1990, when the Municipal Party Committee built an office building, it took 8 million yuan from the Zhongyang Textile Group in one fell swoop, which was almost all the remaining company profit for the year! A year later, Li Gaocheng was promoted from deputy mayor to mayor by election, and many of the ordinary folk, including the staff and cadres of Zhongyang Textiles, bad-mouthed him behind his back saying he had bought his way to the mayorship. In fact, what none of them knew was that, at that time, it was Li Gaocheng who had been most strongly opposed to the whole affair of all the members of the Municipal Party Committee. During those years, especially during the boom years, Zhongyang Textiles received demands for returns to the state of millions of yuan every year. This, coupled with unreasonable tax rates, left Zhongyang Textiles with little respite and no ability to expand production. It was generally the case that if some member of the top brass happened to take admiring notice of your success, he would insist that you further expand your production, even if it meant scraping the bottom of the barrel, thereby forcing you to misrepresent your production and make something out of nothing; you could even be obliged to pay taxes and hand over profits when you were barely in the black! If state-owned enterprises were always to be run like that, how could they ever prosper? If you force them into bad actions all the time, how can they be expected to act well? How can they be expected not to go to the bad?

Can we really blindly put all the blame on them personally? How can we really hold them responsible? And now they are being forced to come up with a solution. Isn't this like asking someone else to take the medicine for a disease you have?

You are currently the mayor of the city, and you are also the former factory manager of Zhongyang Textiles. You were an excellent entrepreneur for many years. Before you became mayor, you were a model vice mayor and were in charge of the company for many years, so isn't it really you who should be having the ideas, you who should be coming up with the plans? You! Nobody else! You!

So, given the current situation at Zhongyang Textiles, what do you think should be done? Li Gaocheng's mind suddenly went blank again.

The door of the bedroom opened quietly and his wife, Wu Aizhen, stood silently in the doorway.

There were two bedrooms in the house and, since Li Gaocheng had become mayor, he and his wife had more and more frequently slept in separate rooms so as not to disturb each other and make it impossible to get a good night's sleep. In truth, his wife's workload wasn't much lighter than his own. She was the deputy procurator general and director of the Anti-Corruption Bureau of the city's Dongcheng District Prosecutor's Office and was often incredibly busy. They each had their own telephone in their bedroom, and it seemed as though Wu Aizhen's one was constantly in use; sometimes the calls were still coming in right into the small hours. She also had a pager and a mobile phone and often received calls even during meal times. When she had a lot of cases on, she seldom got home before eleven o'clock at night. On top of that, she was the mayor's wife, which gave her even more to do. Normally, the two of them saw each other most often at breakfast time and after dinner. Particularly over the last two years, the nights they spent in the same bedroom had become fewer and fewer.

Wu Aizhen was eleven years younger than her husband and had recently celebrated her forty-third birthday. He was already thirty-one when they got married and she was only nineteen. He had graduated from a technical school, but she was a teacher training vocational high school graduate. The only real difference was that he had graduated before the Cultural Revolution but she was one of the worker-peasant-soldier students from that event at its height. When they got married, he was just an ordinary technician who had recently been made deputy workshop director, but just as Wu Aizhen graduated, because there was a staff shortage when the public prosecutor's office was reorganised, that was where she was posted. Li Gaocheng was quite ordinary looking, but his wife was really quite a beauty. So, no matter how you looked at it, they were an unlikely couple. So much so that, even now, when they walked down the street together, few people took them for husband and wife. The fifty-four-year-old Li Gaocheng looked like he was in his sixties, and the forty-three-year-old Wu Aizhen could be taken for someone in her thirties. People who didn't know them thought they must be father and daughter, and, even so, they attracted quite a few ribald comments. With others, the belief persisted that Li Gaocheng must have been married before and divorced and that Wu Aizhen had to be his second wife. In fact, their first meeting had been quite accidental and not at all romantic. When Wu Aizhen was still at her teacher training studies, her school had arranged an engineering and agriculture work-study activity and she had been assigned to Li Gaocheng's workshop; the stars were aligned and the two became a couple. Three months later, when Li Gaocheng sponsored Wu Aizhen's membership of the Communist Party, the two were apparently already lovers. A year and a half later, they were married in a very simple ceremony.

For many years after the marriage, Wu Aizhen liked to ask, from time to time: "How could I have fallen in love with you at that time!?" She was still asking the same question even now, and also had a favourite mantra: "You're only here today because of my good fortune!"

He never argued about this, as, for one thing, it was just his wife's little joke, and, for another, it was also true that since they got married, his status had positively surged upwards. No matter what hurdles presented themselves, they were always crossed smoothly and easily.

Whenever he was promoted or transferred it was never because he had gone running to someone to exploit a connection. He sometimes couldn't help feeling that it was a little strange that his wife brought him not only her fragrant warmth but also good luck and opportunities.

Twenty years after their wedding, he not only loved his wife dearly, from time to time he also defended her resolutely. Usually, whatever earth-shaking events might be going on in the outside world, once back home he deferred to his wife in everything. Of course, there had never been, nor was there then, any major issue of principle between them; their different occupations, the difference in their status, coupled with his eleven-year seniority and the loving tenderness of his wife meant that they never argued nor experienced any awkwardness about anything. In the soft lamplight, his wife still looked so young, pretty and charming. They had two children, a boy and a girl, both of whom were now at university. In the prevailing circumstances, this amounted to good family planning. Perhaps because she had had her children early or perhaps because of the good care she took of herself, his wife's physical appearance had hardly changed at all. He sometimes wondered to himself how his wife had managed to avoid the signs of ageing in spite of how hard she worked, how little rest she got and how much pressure she was sometimes under.

Every time their daughter, who was in her first year at university, came home, she would tease him occasionally, saying: "You need to watch your figure, Dad! You're looking less and less of a match for Mummy!"

Fortunately, both children had inherited their mother's good points and had grown up very like her. Moreover, they were both exceptionally intelligent and they had never needed any help at high school or in getting into university. His wife was given to remarking that it seemed that she was just as intelligent as him. On weekdays, no matter how busy or tired he was, as soon as he got home to this warm and happy atmosphere, all his troubles and worries would immediately disappear. In the past two years, both children had gone to college one after another and, apart from the nanny, they were the only people left in the family home. Now both of them seemed to have reached the most illustrious but burdensome period of their careers. Although there were only the two of them, the chances of meeting each other were getting fewer and fewer. In the past, the children were always there, and no matter how busy the two of them were, they had to rush back to eat at home. Now the children were not there, all they had to do was make a phone call if they weren't going home for the meal, so, most of the time, the nanny ate at home alone.

This kind of thing seems to be inevitable if both parties are leadership cadres. One was the mayor and the other was the head of the Anti-Corruption Bureau, and both were as busy as it was possible to be, with nowhere to hide.

He looked silently at his wife, and to his surprise on this occasion, she came on into his bedroom. She lay down quietly beside him, and asked, as she looked at him with some concern: "Is it all over?"

"Ha! If only it was that simple!" He pulled back the quilt and gently settled it over her.

"Is it really tricky?" she asked, her large eyes sweeping over his face.

"It doesn't matter how difficult it is, it still has to be done. We can't delay dealing with Zhongyang Textiles any longer."

"Are the workers really making a big fuss?"

"If I'd got there two hours later, there might have been real trouble."

"Are Guo Zhongyao and the others really out of control of the situation?"

"It's not that they can't control it, it's that they've just had enough. And the workers won't listen to them at all."

"How can that be? Doesn't Guo Zhongyao carry a lot of weight?" His wife's face was full of worry. She knew all the leaders of Zhongyang Textiles intimately, because they had been frequent guests in her home.

"It seems that he has crumpled completely, and I think he has given up hope himself." For some reason, at the sight of his wife's worried face, he suddenly felt deep sympathy and regret for Guo Zhongyao.

"It really is that serious? People have been spreading rumours about Zhongyang Textiles. They are also saying that you were besieged by the workers for seven or eight hours. There are even some whispers that you were almost beaten up and the city riot squad sent several hundred men to save you from the crowd."

"What nonsense! If it really was as bad as that, how could I ever have the face still to be mayor?" Li Gaocheng thought the idea was quite funny, but he wasn't laughing.

"I was really frightened at the time. I tried to call Xiao Wu several times, but he didn't call me back. What's up with that secretary of yours that means he can't even return a phone call?" Wu Aizhen looked really angry.

"There wasn't a telephone. There is only one switchboard left in the whole of Zhongyang Textiles, and the others have been cut off because the bills haven't been paid. Xiao Wu had nowhere to call you back from."

"How is that possible?" The expression on his wife's face was becoming more and more serious. After a long time, she went on to ask: "What are you going to do next? Just let it collapse?"

"I haven't come up with a proper solution yet. The company owes more than five hundred million yuan."

"What do the workers who are causing the trouble say?"

"You can work it out for yourself – they want work to start up again, they want their wages, they want the company audited, they want accountability, and they want severe punishment for any corrupt elements in the company."

"You agreed to all that?"

"Of course I had to agree – they are not unreasonable requests."

"So are you getting ready to investigate it all?"

"You're the anti-corruption chief. What would you do?"

"I would say don't investigate if you don't have to. It's really better not to investigate."

"...Why is that?" He couldn't help being a little surprised, as he hadn't expected his wife to say that.

"You are going to find problems in this whole affair, no matter who you investigate. If you do go ahead, the management team is finished. If that happens, you won't be able to save the company. If you want to investigate such a big company, you can't be sure that you won't pull up all the dirt when you pluck a single radish, and that will mean a whole lot of trouble. In that case, I am afraid that even your position won't be safe. This is no joke. I have worked in the Anti-Corruption Bureau for a long time and I understand these things better than you."

"...Oh!" He was momentarily stunned. He had considered all this, but didn't think it was as serious as his wife was making out.

"It's really better not to investigate. You're better off sacking one or two of them than investigating. Zhongyang Textiles is where you started out, and in investigating the company, you are actually investigating yourself. Once you look into Zhongyang Textiles, even if you can't find any problems, your reputation in the city will still be greatly damaged. Once you find out what's really wrong, you are all done for. You don't have any wiggle room on this. You have to fight back."

"What if the problems are really serious? What then? Deny all responsibility? Turn a blind eye? Just try and muddle through? How can we explain it all to the workers?"

"You are the mayor, and it's not your responsibility to explain. You should let others take on the responsibility, not you. Even if there is responsibility, it can only be a collective responsibility. It is the responsibility of the entire Municipal Party Committee and the Municipal Government – it has nothing to do with you. In such an important matter, you should always let the whole administrative body make a decision and take responsibility."

So that's what his wife actually thought! "Do you mean that you should always shuffle off responsibility and never take any on yourself?"

"There is no question of shirking responsibility in a matter like Zhongyang Textiles. What personal responsibility do you have, in fact? And what responsibility do Guo Zhongyao and the others have that cannot be shrugged off? Does our government have no responsibility? Does the state have no responsibility? Is it reasonable to let an individual bear all of this? Is it right? Yang Cheng, the secretary of the Municipal Party Committee, has repeatedly demanded a complete solution to Zhongyang Textiles' problems, precisely because he can shirk all responsibilities. He has only recently arrived in the city, so he doesn't really have anything to do with it. So, you must make sure you don't let him put all the responsibility on you alone."

His wife's eyes were clear and bright, like she was standing in front of a child. Looking at him, she said: "You and I have been together for more than twenty years, and I still don't understand you. You have a strong sense of responsibility, which is both your strength and your fatal weakness. You are the mayor now, and you need to keep your wits about you. You need to take advantage of your comparative youth and think of ways to climb further up the ladder. Don't get bogged down thinking about so-and-so or such-and-such. You need to grow up!"

He looked at his wife as if he didn't know her and was lost for words.

He never thought that his wife could talk like this, let alone that she could change so much.

It seemed he had a lot to learn about her.

His wife cuddled up beside him as usual and soon fell into a gentle sleep, but her faint snoring kept him awake for a long time.

He spent the whole night thinking about what his wife had said. Wouldn't it be terrible if the current leaders all thought and acted like that? If you were talking about corruption, wasn't this also a kind of corrupt thinking? If personal, leadership and social responsibilities were all thought about and calculated like economic activities, what hope was there for this nation and this government? What? How could you win the trust of the people and of society? It was the height of corruption to equate doing economic work with correcting the behaviour of the people. If that was what she meant by "growing up", then that was really quite terrifying.

When had this change in his wife begun? She had even begun to take on herself the task of "correcting" and "guiding", and this household expression of those two processes was at the same time frightening and seductive. It is the same wherever it takes place: you start "correcting" and "guiding" someone else, and they want to do the same back to you?

CHAPTER ELEVEN

AT SIX O'CLOCK IN THE MORNING, Li Gaocheng was startled awake by the telephone.

It was his secretary, Wu Xingang, telling him that several staff representatives from Zhongyang Textiles had been waiting from early at the doors of the mayor's office, hoping to talk some more about the company's affairs. They said that there were too many people the day before, the situation was too strange, it had all happened too quickly and there were still a number of things that hadn't been clarified. They thought that the mayor was likely to be reporting on the Zhongyang Textiles situation to the Municipal Party Committee and the Municipal Government today, and they wanted to get to the bottom of a few things before that happened, to ensure that the mayor's report wasn't biased or unbalanced in any way.

Li Gaocheng had not actually been thinking of reporting to the Municipal Party Committee and the Municipal Government that day, as he felt that what had happened the day before had been too rushed, and there were a number of things he needed to go into more deeply. Only when the key problems of Zhongyang Textile were identified or the crux of the problem was fully understood would it be possible to report on Zhongyang Textiles to the leaders of the Municipal Party Committee, the Municipal Government and the Standing Committee of the Municipal Party Committee. Today, he just wanted to exchange opinions with the secretary of the Municipal Party Committee and the head of the Bureau of Industry, or maybe explore their thinking about Zhongyang Textiles before deciding on his next move. How could they think it was all so simple that, after just one visit yesterday, he would be in a position to make a formal report? Wouldn't that be just too sloppy, casual and irresponsible?

Still, their arrival was very convenient because he needed to settle his own thinking before exchanging opinions with the Municipal Party Committee secretary. This was especially true because Secretary Yang Cheng had always had his own ideas about Zhongyang Textiles, and he, Li Gaocheng, could not afford to be ambiguous in his own views. No matter what the issue, he had first to come up with his own convincing arguments and reasoning. So, before any meeting with the Party Committee secretary, he really needed a frank discussion with these staff representatives. With this kind of thing, it certainly didn't do to go into battle unprepared.

"Don't get bogged down thinking about so-and-so or such-and-such. You need to grow up!" He couldn't help suddenly recalling his wife's words of the night before. He hadn't expected them to have had so profound an effect and it made him realise that from time to time he needed to think about and analyse issues that arose from what his wife said. He found this thought very disturbing.

He glanced at his wife, sound asleep beside him, but didn't disturb her. There were a number of things he realised he needed to talk to her about, and, at this rate, it was quite possible a degree of estrangement might arise between them.

He had a hurried bite of breakfast and reached the government office before it was even seven o'clock. That gave him at least two hours to talk to the workers' representatives.

There were six of them altogether and, in addition to the old factory manager, Yuan Mingliang, and the former chief engineer, Zhang Huabin, both of whom had spoken at yesterday's meeting of staff representatives, there were also the current chief engineer, Gao Shuangliang, an accountant from Zhongyang Textiles' tertiary enterprise, Xinchao Co. Ltd, and two other staff representatives.

The expressions and atmosphere were completely different from the day before, perhaps because the crowds were gone, or perhaps because of the solemnity of the mayor's office. There were faint but discernible smiles on some faces, rather than angry scowls, and the language and deportment had become more polite.

The first words the old factory director spoke were: "I know we are really inconveniencing you, Mayor Li."

This made Li Gaocheng feel an indescribable but very real sadness about where he now found himself. This was an affair that he absolutely should be taking charge of as part of his job, that people should be at his door asking about, but when they did, they apologised for inconveniencing him. Sadly, people were already treating this kind of topsy-turvy attitude as the norm.

He didn't say anything more about it at this point, but casually told them to sit down and said: "Your timing is perfect. I really wanted to talk this over with you properly. You can talk openly today. Once that door is closed, everything is just between us. You can say whatever you want and there will be no repercussions if you make any mistakes."

The first person to speak was the old chief engineer, Zhang Huabin. "Mayor Li, I heard from the staff that the management were making their report to you until after midnight, and everyone wants to know what they were saying to you. Once we know what they said in their report, then we'll be able to talk things through with you properly."

Li Gaocheng was taken aback for a moment, as he hadn't expected Zhang Huabin to ask such a thing. When he talked with the management, he had told them too that they should speak openly without any constraint. If he told the people in front of him now what had been said, would it be considered a violation both of the principles of good management and of his original promise? If he told them, might it not create even more serious antagonism between workers and management? It was no trivial matter, and looking at it from the larger perspective, he really should not reveal the contents of the report willy-nilly.

Probably guessing his qualms, Zhang Huabin said: "Even if you don't tell us, Mayor Li, we still have a good idea of what they said. How about this? We will work out what we think they said, put it together with what we know they have already said, and form our opinion from that. If we are right, or we are on the right lines, you can tell us so and if we are wrong, you do the same. Do you think that will be all right?"

Without waiting for Li Gaocheng to reply, Zhang Huabin continued: "They will have said that the business of buying that cotton wasn't their fault. Because of relations with the bank and other agencies, the payment of the loan was delayed so they had to buy inferior quality at a high price. But, despite this, they took a lot of remedial measures that ensured losses were minimised. Thus, things are really in not too bad a state, not too bad a state at all, and if they hadn't taken their countermeasures in time, the results would have been disastrous."

At this point, Zhang Huabin didn't stop to ask if he was right or not, but went straight on to refute these claims. "Nothing of the sort happened. It is a complete fabrication. They have been spreading this story since last year, and all they are trying to do is divert the responsibility for the problem and the anger of the workers elsewhere – it is not our fault, it is the corrupt financial system and related departments that have caused our losses. They were forced to give these people gifts, to treat them to dinners, and if they did that for one set of people, they had to do it for another, and so on. They will have said that us workers couldn't possibly understand this kind of thing, nor could we imagine how rotten today's society had become. They didn't dare offend any of these people and departments, let alone report them, or even mention them to anyone. If any of them took offence, the company would have no hope for the future. In a nutshell, none of it was their fault – it was all down to corruption."

At this point, Li Gaocheng couldn't stop himself from jumping to his feet. Zhang Huabin had not raised his voice, and his tone remained very mild throughout, but once again, Li felt a powerful tremor pass through him deep inside. Zhang's words were just too rational and too universally recognisable. Nowadays, everybody was talking about corrupt this and corrupt that. Corruption was like terminal cancer: if you don't treat it, you may still live a few more years, but once you start treating it, the treatment never seems to end. You have to send money and gifts to do anything, to go to school, to get assigned a job, to get medical treatment, to get housing, to get a transfer, to get involved in lawsuits and especially to get a promotion! It seemed that corruption itself couldn't get any more corrupt, and with even the roots now rotten there was no hope at all. You couldn't deny the existence of corruption, nor its seriousness in some areas, but just how serious was it overall? Was it as pervasive and severe as some rumours had it? And where did those rumours come from? And how did the ordinary people get to know about them? The truth was, with things like the promotion of officials, or the liquidity of large and medium-sized enterprises, the only people who knew the details were the leaders. They were the ones who created and incited hatred in society! Some of these so-called leaders were lower than scum, more destructive than moths in a closet, and every one of them should be punished!

Apparently oblivious to Li Gaocheng's changing mood, Zhang Huabin continued calmly: "Actually, this is all pure invention on their part, and none of it's true. All it needs is a little investigation, and everything will become clear immediately. The loan in 1995 was life-saver funding for the Zhongyang Textile Group and was allocated by the state to meet the most difficult of situations. The governor and the secretary of the Provincial Party Committee all gave their strongest instructions that it should be approved. You know all this, Mr Mayor, and you also gave your approval. In particular, the loan was approved by the state Bank, and this was absolutely in line with state policy at the time. Who would have dared to delay the granting of such a loan for several months? As far as we know, the loan was approved on 25 August 1995 and was actually in place, with the company already having the right to use it, on 10 September 1995, when the new cotton was not yet available nationwide. So there was no question of the funds not being available and the contract being voided. We can say with one hundred per cent certainty right now that they are lying to you. In fact, there is no need for me to say any more, as everything will be quite clear once the matter is investigated. There is another thing of which you may not be aware – in the two months after the loan was received, that is, in the most critical two months for the Zhongyang Textile Group, the management of the company was in the hands of Deputy General Manager Feng Minjie. Of the other principal members of the management team, one went to Xinjiang to attend a seminar on market theory for large enterprises, but the trip took nearly a month all told. After his return, he went to Dunhuang and Lanzhou, taking his wife with him. As for the others, one group, led by the general manager, Guo Zhongyao, went to the United States, while the rest, led by the secretary of the Party Committee, went to Hong Kong, Thailand, Malaysia and Singapore. And they all took the opportunity to bring their wives along with them. Except for Guo Zhongyao who is unmarried, there wasn't a manager's wife who didn't go abroad. They may have reported to you that they have never travelled abroad with their wives, but they are just tricking you. Yes, it is quite true that they have never taken their own wives abroad because what really happened was that they took each other's wives. For example, when Chen Yongming and his lot went abroad, Deputy General Manager Wu Mingde's wife was among the staff, and Chen Yongming's wife went with Guo Zhongyao and Wu Mingde. They have deceived their superiors and deceived the ordinary people. They have acted with particular irresponsibility towards a huge state-owned enterprise, and now they are all blaming everyone except themselves. Did you ask them where they all went in September and October 1995? Did they go to buy cotton from all over the country as they said? In fact, they delayed the cotton-buying process until they had all come back from their travels, one by one, and then they made a hasty decision for the rush purchase of raw materials. But by then the price of cotton had risen sharply, and cotton was sold out all over the country. The only person who can say that he has ever purchased cotton is Feng Minjie, the deputy general manager in charge of supply and distribution. He did not go abroad at the time, but nor did he take any steps to order cotton. According to what he told others, he couldn't take that responsibility. It was too big an issue and he couldn't make a decision by himself. Was this the real reason? Some people said that Feng Minjie's issue was even bigger. First, he was the deputy general manager in charge of supply and distribution. Second, he was the highest-ranking leader left behind. Third, he had full power to make decisions at that time, but he did nothing. All he ended up doing was to let the team collectively make a decision to buy in more than two thousand tonnes of low-quality cotton from a county in Jiangxi that hardly produced any in the first place. Maybe all of this was a trap that Feng Minjie set on purpose. He wanted this result, so that no one could say anything about him personally. 'It was you who went abroad,' he was saying. 'Why are you blaming me?' In fact, there was only one person who actually went abroad on a genuine fact-finding trip and that was Gao Shuangliang, the current chief engineer of the company."

Li Gaocheng had been pacing back and forth across the office, but when he heard this, he gradually came to a halt.

How could this be? This matter should be investigated properly and cleared up once and for all. He didn't believe that Zhang Huabin could be lying to him about something as big as this. If he was, indeed, telling the truth, or, rather, if an investigation proved that he was, then everything he had felt yesterday was wrong, and there could only be one conclusion: that the management of Zhongyang Textiles had been lying to him from beginning to end and from top to bottom! No wonder it was Feng Minjie who had made the report on all this yesterday. All the others, including General Manager Guo Zhongyao, had kept quiet. Although it was still too early to draw conclusions, one thing could probably be confirmed immediately, and that was that, in September and October of 1995, most of the company's leaders were abroad, travelling and sightseeing! They had gone all round the houses to get their wives out of the country, but every one of them swore blind that they had never taken their wives with them. They really knew how to do things!

His mood, which had previously been a bit more relaxed than before, began to get more serious again. The management report he had heard yesterday had allowed him to breathe a sigh of relief, and his principal feeling had been that at least the management of Zhongyang Textiles were not going to have any great problems economically speaking. If the economics were OK, then any other problems they had would be of a different order. In other words, they would not and could not fall foul of the government's ongoing crackdown, and the contradictions in attitude between them and the workers would not become antagonistic and based on enmity. In the market economy, the most difficult hurdle for people is precisely that of economics and finance.

At this point, Gao Shuangliang, the current chief engineer, said softly: "Mayor Li, there is another thing you must not believe them about."

"What's that?" Li Gaocheng asked, almost automatically.

Gao Shuangliang was a shortish man, with quite small eyes, and he wore a pair of wide, thick-lensed glasses for his short sight. He spoke in a low voice, and his face did not show any expression. You could tell at a glance that he was an extremely cautious person. When he heard Li Gaocheng's question, he hurried to reply but remained very cautious.

"All this talk of joint ventures, in my personal opinion, is just imaginary. Up to now, they have been going on about cooperations with Niger and Nigeria, both of which I know are non-starters. You could go so far as to call it a scam. I think their aim is just to use this to reassure people, to give them an excuse to go on foreign jaunts, or at least to convince the leadership and the ordinary people that those jaunts really are on company business. It means they can also use it as a way to shuffle off responsibilities Zhongyang Textiles can't get out of, onto the bank. In fact, they really did talk to the bank about these foreign joint ventures, but the bank did not agree to their plan. That was just the result they wanted – they could say that it wasn't because they didn't have a way out of the situation, or that they were not capable, it was because the bank didn't agree. The truth is, those so-called joint ventures did not exist. When they went to America, they went to New York and Chicago. When they went to England and France, they went to London and Paris. When they went to Australia, they went to Sydney. What do you think they were looking for there? Foreign investment? Who was going to hand over their money to people like them? Who was going to chuck cash down a bottomless pit? There was no hope at all of that, but they still went rushing off abroad on trip after trip. Public opinion against them was growing and growing, and they were spending more and more foreign currency, to the point where they couldn't explain it away anymore, so, in the end, they packed me and my wife and some others off to Niger and Nigeria. Before they sent me, the company had welcomed a black businessman who was said to be the agent of a company in Niger that was looking for a partner in a joint venture in the cotton-processing field. We investigated this agent very carefully and found that he was indeed from Niger, that he was the agent for a company, and he was genuinely looking for a Chinese partner in a joint venture. Zhongyang Textiles received this guest with great ceremony, put him up in a high-end hotel and treated him to banquets every day. After almost a month of research, he said he wanted to go back to Niger to report to his chairman before getting back in touch with our company. But after he left, there was no serious follow-up at all. We received a few telexes, but they did not amount to anything. In view of this situation, the company decided to send us to Niger. We found the address, and the company did actually exist, but what the company bosses told us was very different from what the agent had claimed. They said that they had sent their agent to ask us to build a cotton mill in their area. All the investment would come from our side, and they would only guarantee the future supply of cotton. There were no concessions, no guarantees and no promises. There was nothing for it but for us to try going on to Nigeria, but we came away empty-handed from there too. Not only was there no sign of any project, there wasn't even the faintest hint of anything. Even so, the management were putting it about everywhere that they had already found a foreign company that was going to go into partnership with us and that a letter of intent had already been signed. None of it was true. I know the whole story from beginning to end, and the so-called letter of intent was just some introductory written materials shared between the two sides. Nonetheless, they kept boasting about it, over and over, and even entered into several sets of negotiations with the bank, hoping that the bank would agree to their terms."

"So what you are saying is that they made all those foreign trips but the only genuine one was this one that you went on?" Li Gaocheng asked him with some incredulity.

"That's about the size of it." Gao Shuangliang thought for a moment, then continued: "That's not to say that they didn't think about the company at all on those foreign trips. I think, to be fair, they really did want to find a partner company. If they had been successful in forming a joint venture, it would have let them off the hook. But that was really only one of their reasons for going, or you could call it just an excuse. And it's not just me – I don't think anyone, them included, thought it was feasible. No foreign company anywhere was going to want to go into business with a loss-making enterprise that already owed close on 600 million yuan. Unless, of course, as they were hoping might happen, the state and the bank took on all the debt. Then they might be able to attract a foreign partner with some foreign capital. But would the state ever agree to it? Would the bank? I certainly wouldn't! A company established by the state that is also in debt to the state now wants to take that state-owned company into a foreign joint venture? Even in their own terms, shuffling off the debt like that is an irrelevant and impossible proposition. It's simply absurd! What do I mean by irrelevant and impossible? Once a joint venture is established, it means that the property rights of the company are shared between the two parties or will be shared, come a certain point. That means in turn that while the state assets have lost almost half of their value, the debt will still be passed on to the state in full. Who would agree to such a thing? Who would dare to agree to such a thing?"

Li Gaocheng could feel sweat starting out on his forehead. It seemed to him that the words of this unremarkable-looking chief engineer were aimed directly at him. He had got it all wrong yesterday: he had felt that everything they had said was completely reasonable, even to the extent that he had thought he ought to fall in with their way of thinking. He had thought he had it all pat, but he hadn't even thought through to this level; he simply hadn't gone deep enough into it. Even the people below him had got there but he hadn't, and he was the mayor. Supposing his emotional attachments had got the better of him, did that mean he should forfeit his position? He was in a position of national leadership, but when the nation found itself under threat, there he was trapped by his own subconscious and wrapped up in some psychological complex that he wouldn't admit to but couldn't break free from. It even seemed he had lost all sense of responsibility and reason. It looked as though he needed to take a long, hard look at himself. He was a mayor and that is no minor position, nor one to be taken lightly; it was quite possible that, with a moment's negligence or a fleeting emotional impulse, he could lose the state tens of millions, hundreds of millions of yuan. The most lamentable aspect of all this was that, as he became a traitor to the state, or, at least, performed a traitorous action, he hadn't even realised he was doing it.

Li Gaocheng strove to control his emotions, reminding himself that, whatever was being said, this was just one, unverified view of the affair, and he rather feared that it would be a very long time before any definite conclusions could be formed. He couldn't help recalling the feeling he had had when listening to the report that had been delivered the day before in that small meeting room; hadn't he also been deeply moved by the hard work and effort the management team had put in? Hadn't he shown understanding and approval of everything they had done? How had he changed his mind so completely now he had heard the other side? Was that what happened to all leaders? Or was it true for everyone that you believed the last thing you heard? That you could be convinced by one side's story and then find the other side's version equally believable? Since the whole affair was so complicated, with each side having their own different versions and rationales, perhaps the best thing would be to gloss things over and blame them both equally. Basically, don't make trouble and don't argue; things weren't easy for anybody nowadays and everyone had their own reasons. They were all in a market economy now, so what was the point of fighting and arguing? Even if things weren't as messed up as they are now, what was the point in people laying complaints against and persecuting each other? So, even if he came down hard on those who deserved it and talked to those who needed to be talked to, in the end nothing would come of it and everything would stay the same. What did it matter whether the masses believed anything or not, or whether the workers were satisfied or not? Just let them get on with it! If this really was how things stood, as time went on would there still be any standards of right and wrong? How could anyone evaluate the merits and faults, or distinguish the correct from the incorrect? If even people like him were so muddled and confused, how could the nation possibly be well governed? If a leader, especially a senior leader of a government department, lost his judgment on this issue, he would be digging his own grave! He suddenly thought of what he had encountered at the company the night before, when he had been extremely unhappy with the management situation, and how it had led to such a tense relationship between the cadres and the people! In fact, if things went on like that, it wouldn't be long before he would be in exactly the same position as them, until, one day, he would find himself surrounded by workers and other ordinary folk every time he went in and out of his office, and he might, in fact, find himself in an even worse situation than the Zhongyang management!

He didn't know why he was allowing himself to get distracted, thinking about these abstruse problems, when he was listening to a report on such a weighty matter.

Perhaps because he had remained silent for so long, the whole office went quiet too. When he suddenly returned to his senses, he said hurriedly: "Speak up, speak up! Go on talking! Say what you have to say and just go on the way you have been. That will be fine. Go on, speak up! Speak up!"

"I will speak now, Mayor Li." It was former factory manager Yuan Mingliang who piped up very cautiously and carefully, very respectfully too. He was a completely different man from the grand and imposing factory manager of the day before. The all-powerful, indomitable manner and bearing had gone, to be replaced by goodness, benevolence, serenity and compliance. Li Gaocheng suddenly found himself deeply and inexpressibly moved by the change in the man's attitude. The old factory manager's demeanour yesterday was probably down to the fact that, deep down, he didn't properly recognise Li Gaocheng's status as a mayor. Even though he had been a mayor for a while and had enjoyed the status corresponding to the position all that time, he hadn't reached that status in the eyes of this old factory manager. Despite the actuality of his mayoralty, the old man neither recognised it nor acknowledged him in it. Thus, from one point of view, his title had no legitimacy for him, but perhaps the reason for the old man's change in attitude today was because he, Li, had now adopted a stance and made a commitment; he had expressed himself and taken action. So, now the old man had a new understanding of him and new expectations, and that explained his complete reversal of behaviour and attitude. Because he, as mayor, had shown himself ready really to solve the company's problems, to go with the will of the people and look after the company's affairs well, the old factory manager and, of course, all the workers in the company had turned their opposition into support, their indignation into respect, and they had become the respectful and receptive group they now presented themselves as. What people are willing to obey from the bottom of their hearts is not status, power and prestige, but values, intentions and attitude. If someone wholeheartedly serves the interests of the common people and the future of the nation, they will recognise and admire you. On the other hand, if he is not dedicated to the people and to the nation, no matter how powerful he is, no matter how prominent, in their hearts, the people will despise him, hate him and see him as their enemy!

This was the simplest of truths and a mantra repeated every hour of the day, but how many people genuinely applied it in their daily lives, especially on critical issues, and, indeed, even on issues of great importance that concerned the fate of the nation and society? How many people showed it the same concern as they had for their own future, fate and interests?

Take this former factory manager for example, who was nearly seventy years old; yesterday he seemed to hate you to your very bones, but today he was professing undying loyalty to you again. So, why was he doing it? Was it just for himself? Was it just for his own individual interests? What, for that matter, were the interests of all the others? What exactly had they actually got from this factory where they had worked all their lives, the place on which they had spilt their blood, sweat and tears? Or what had they once had? Nothing! That was the honest answer. Nothing at all! Even today, at a time when they should be enjoying a carefree and peaceful old age, they still had nothing; not even the most basic pension was guaranteed! If they were angry, resentful, filled with hatred and hostility, that was perfectly understandable. It was even just as it should be! That was their right, the only right they still had in this society!

Li Gaocheng wanted to smile reassuringly to express his sympathy and respect for the old factory manager, but, for some reason he found he couldn't. In the end, he just said softly: "You should always think of me as your subordinate, Manager Yuan. For heaven's sake, don't always treat me as the mayor. Just say whatever there is to say and tell me whatever you are thinking. There's absolutely no need for you to stand on ceremony and treat me like an outsider."

As soon as the words were out of his mouth, he regretted them. He realised how false and contrived they must sound. Were they really going to be enough to stop them treating him like an outsider? He wouldn't even talk to his close friends or family like that, would he? Or to those managers of the Zhongyang Textile Group, for that matter. Whatever his emotions might be telling him, he really was still an outsider.

However, when the old factory manager heard this, he did seem to be deeply moved:

"I am greatly relieved to hear you say that, Mayor Li, and so is everybody else. After what you said to us yesterday, we already regarded you as family. We haven't come here today with any new ideas and certainly not with any new concerns. We just want you to be more prepared, so your thinking about this matter will be more complete and you will be able to give even more consideration to it. In fact, you already know what kind of man I am – I'm not a man to go behind someone's back to stir things up and plot and scheme, even less to harm anyone or make false accusations. As for Guo Zhongyao and Feng Minjie, I have no grudge against them, nor do I have any fundamental conflict of interest. I am already old and will not live much longer and, as for my children, they are all grown up now and, even if the company collapses or goes bankrupt, they will still be able to find work somewhere else; they're not afraid of not being able to find a job. They are all telling me that at my age, I shouldn't still be slaving away for the company, and the truth is that, as an old man, I really don't want to get on the wrong side of them. If it was just down to me, I wouldn't be acting as a workers' representative like this, and I certainly wouldn't have come here today. It's just that I feel sorry for this company and this factory, Mayor Li, and the company really can't let these people trample it into the dirt like this.

"You don't have to go into anything else, Mayor Li – just talk about how they set up the Xinchao Company. They used tens of millions of state loans for investments, but three years later, how much return on the money has there been for the factory? There are dozens of subsidiaries of Xinchao, all over the province and the country, and, essentially, all their managers and bosses are relatives and cronies of the Zhongyang management. They hijacked the company name and used state funds, but they are making a huge amount of money just for themselves. The state took the losses and they pocketed all the profits whilst at the same time taking a salary from the state, using the title of 'cadre' given to them by the state, riding in the state-owned cars, and enjoying the state's welfare benefits. But all the time they have been acting only for themselves. No capital, no risk, no danger! Do you think the workers aren't furious about all this? Mayor Li, I need you to listen to me when I say that people change. Think about it! When our generation retired, we handed back what had to be handed back, paid back what needed to be paid back, then we had a farewell party and the company patted us on our backsides and sent us on our way. It's all different nowadays. In the year before last when Guo Zhongyao let the company's chief accountant retire, and last year when he let the company's deputy general manager and deputy secretary of the Party Committee retire, each of them was given an investment fund equivalent to one million yuan so they could set up in the tertiary sector. Nominally, of course, they are doing it on behalf of the company, but in fact this is really quite a common arrangement in today's society. The company's management have been working all their lives, and they can't just leave – they have to find something to do. In other words, although they may appear to have retired, they really haven't at all.

"This would be fine in a better organisation, but not in our company, Zhongyang Textiles. Here it's a crime. How can we tolerate them taking the money we need to survive so they can set up businesses for themselves? You must know that when we retired, Mayor Li, we didn't set up any businesses. It didn't even occur to us! But the whole ethos has changed now and if you don't meet their conditions when someone is about to retire, they simply don't retire. Even if they do retire and you still don't deliver for them, they may well cause you trouble at every turn and even sue you. They believe they can hold you to ransom because they think they know all your secrets and you wouldn't dare not give them something to do. Are they really expected to retire with nothing to show for it? That's why Xinchao Co. Ltd has kept growing and growing. The workers' opinion is that if a skinny horse is infested with fat lice, the horse has no chance of survival. I am speaking from the bottom of my heart now, Mayor Li. I have worked at Zhongyang Textiles all my life, and I have seen it all. In a country like ours, and especially in a system like ours, the key lies in the leadership, and the most important issue is the issue of cadres.

"An organisation must take the lead in pushing its cadres hard because if there is a problem with the cadres, the whole organisation is done for. This is because there is quite simply no one else to control them. Over the last few years, we have been talking continuously about the need to separate enterprise and government, about the need to decentralise control of enterprise and to give real power to factory directors and managers. All that is quite correct, but, in our country, it needs very careful consideration and close attention. If you give that kind of power to the directors and managers, who is going to control and supervise them? They have had the power delegated to them, but those beneath them have no kind of control over them, so don't they have complete control over everything that goes on both in the company and in the factory? They can do what they like, employ who they like and spend the state's and the company's money how they like. If they are good men in themselves and hard-working leadership cadres, then there is nothing serious to be afraid of, but if you run into incompetent cadres with no ability and selfish motives, who no one has any control over, don't you think that is something to be truly terrified of? If you put the company and the factory into the hands of people like that, you are just handing them over to a bunch of profligates.

"Supposing all of a manufacturing company's leadership cadres are completely unselfish and exceptionally honest, but have no ability, no drive, no instinct for innovation and are always clinging to the past, then is the company not bound to fail in their hands, sooner or later? It's exactly the same thing – simply because these leaders and cadres are appointed from above and are not really acknowledged by any of the workers, so as long as the people at the top do not care, there is nothing that the people below can do about it. Mayor Li, I am not saying any of this to complain about anyone or blame them, let alone to take the opportunity just to whine about things. But with the company in the state it is now, can you really have any pride in yourself if you still cling to this kind of thinking? I have been saying for a long time that there is only one way of viewing this – the problem with Zhongyang Textiles is multi-faceted, but far and away the most important is with the leadership cadres.

"As long as we make up our minds to solve the problem of the leadership cadres at the company, everything else can be readily managed or, at least, we can set about managing it. It is the key issue, but it is a very challenging one. What we are most worried about is that the top leadership are too soft and credulous, and they will just accept whatever our management says and not give any more thought to it. If we keep putting things off and putting things off, and everything just stays the same as before, as we wait for the factory to be dragged under and all the workers dispersed, then it will be too late. Since both sides, staff and management, want an investigation, arrange for a team to come in and do just that. As long as it is all thorough, conscientious and even-handed, even if it doesn't uncover any problems, everyone will be reassured and there won't be any worries or doubts left…"

Li Gaocheng listened in silence. He had originally intended to add something himself, but, after the old factory manager had finished, he felt he had nothing to say. Yuan Mingliang's words had made the whole thing even clearer: even if there weren't any financial question marks over these people, and they hadn't been bending the law for their own profit, and it turned out they were just a bunch of very mediocre people, it really wasn't any better than if they had been real profligates. Although the old factory manager had said that nothing else lay behind his words, Li Gaocheng couldn't help feeling that they were aimed at him personally. Truth be told, from the outset, all these leadership cadres at the Zhongyang Textile Group owed their positions to his support and patronage. Yes, of course many opinions on them had been sought from other people, but that was really just for show. Who was actually going to want to or be able to object to a team that he himself had put together? The old factory manager and the old chief engineer had both voiced their opposition at the time, but hadn't he dismissed their objections? Didn't he feel uneasy about it all, even now? If it hadn't been for the major problems at Zhongyang Textiles, he might have been left fretting over this matter for the rest of his life! When you got down to it, weren't his intimate relations with the management team the real reason he had been vacillating so much over the company's situation today? Was that not the cause of all his worries and concerns? Could he deny it, however much he would like to?

Perhaps because the meeting had already been going on so long, or perhaps because they could sense the mayor's low mood, none of the other representatives said anything more. As they left, some of them left behind a petition signed by more than ten thousand workers demanding a thorough investigation of corruption in the management team. In addition, the chief accountant of the

Zhongyang Textiles subsidiary company, Xinchao Co. Ltd, left him the itemised company accounts for the last few years.

They were both very thick documents and they weighed heavy in his hands.

CHAPTER TWELVE

Li Gaocheng's heart sank as he looked at the two weighty documents in front of him. The signatures of more than ten thousand workers were enough to fill more than a hundred pages. As he leafed through the pages, it became apparent that there were no proxy signatures and all ten thousand had indeed signed in person. More than ten thousand signatures! He had never seen such a large petition in his life! The format and content of the document were both also very meticulous and had clearly been subjected to much scrutiny and discussion. There was a short summary of the content of the petition at the front; it was only one page long, in large characters, no more than a thousand of them, and written with great emotion, verve and energy. Its presence was probably in consideration of how busy senior figures were known to be and it was, of course, designed to attract attention and consideration. Such requests and petitions were commonplaces of leadership life and nothing to be surprised about in general. If it wasn't concerning a particularly serious, important or headline-grabbing issue, normally such things would not attract the leadership's attention. If you wanted to shock them into noticing or create a deep impression, not only did you have to give the problem colour and resonance and emphasise its profound ramifications, you also had to make its wording and physical presentation eye-catching and arresting. Not only did you have to grab the leadership's attention immediately, you also had to elevate their concern and make them think that it demanded immediate action and couldn't be pushed to one side. The thousand words at the front of this document certainly seemed to meet those specifications. The current state of affairs of the Zhongyang Textile Group, the appalling corruption of the company's management, the serious tension between the company's cadres and the people, the strong and insuppressible resentment of the staff, the potential chain reaction all this could set off and the possible negative impact on society were all highlighted in those thousand words. They were shocking without making you feel they were either alarmist or fanciful.

What followed this opening summary was a petition of about ten thousand words which gave a lot more detail and presented a large body of evidence. This material had to be a detailed and comprehensive interpretation of the initial presentation, listing, with justifications, the ten major complaints of corruption in the Zhongyang Textile Group and the dozens of disciplinary violations by the company's management. At the end of this material were the signatures of more than ten thousand staff and cadres. Li Gaocheng looked at the number of pages, and there were a whole hundred and thirty-six of them! The other document was the itemised accounts of the Zhongyang Textiles' tertiary enterprise, Xinchao Co. Ltd. He flipped through it, and it was three hundred pages long! His jaw dropped and he felt very uneasy. He was amazed how many family members and children of the leaders of the Zhongyang Textile Group, both retired and still working, were involved in this so-called "tertiary enterprise"! Xinchao Co. Ltd was almost like a home-from-home for the sons and daughters of the leading cadres of the Zhongyang Textile Group! At the front of this three-hundred-page list of accounts, there was first a list of the members of the management of Xinchao as well as the management teams of all its subsidiary branches. After the name of each manager, deputy manager, plant manager, deputy plant manager and principal financial officer, there was a bracketed note clearly indicating his or her family connections: for example, "nephew of the secretary", "son of the deputy general manager", "nephew of the director of the second branch", "wife of the director of the eighth workshop" and so on. Moreover, the financial situation of each branch and the flow of funds in and out, all the methods and instances of the secret transfer of state assets to personal assets, detailing losses to the state and profits to the individual, were also clearly recorded. He really wondered how all this information had been dug out and, in particular, how the detailed list of accounts had been reproduced. It was not just the accounts of one branch, it was the financial and personnel information of dozens of branches. It must have been no easy task to get everything in such detail. How much work must it have taken? How much patience and tenacity must it have required? The old saying was true: "If you want people to know something, you have to do it yourself." What particularly shocked Li Gaocheng was that these two huge documents had been copied! That meant that the copies the staff representatives had given him were certainly not the only ones and it was more than likely that they had sent others to other leaders including those higher up the chain of command.

It shocked him and, at the same time, gave him a feeling of indescribable exasperation. What had come over people today? At the drop of a hat, they would produce a document and make dozens or even hundreds of copies of it, spreading it all over the place. With the spread of computers and photocopiers, even complaints seemed to have been modernised, so you couldn't guard against them, and you couldn't cover them up even if you wanted to. However, there were also advantages to all this: since everybody knew, everybody shared the responsibility. There would be meetings, discussions, studies and there would be no need for so many explanations and reports. If everybody knew the substance of the complaint, they also knew the seriousness of the problem, and the discussion could go straight to the point. The flip side of that, however, was that if everybody knew about it and had seen it, then responsibility was shared around; that was just the same as saying nobody took responsibility and people could just say, if you're not going to take control of the situation, nor am I.

However, the more he thought about the two documents in front of him, the more weighed down he felt and the more he felt that there was no way to get rid of them.

He knew that people would inevitably only have one way of viewing all this: the Zhongyang Textile Group was his, Li Gaocheng's, affair; the management team had been handpicked by him, and from the very beginning the model of the Zhongyang Textile Group was a model that he himself had established. Therefore, any problems and changes in the Zhongyang Textile Group would be inextricably linked with him, and there was no escape for him, no matter what.

It seemed to him that the arrangements he had come up with the day before had been completely disrupted by these uninvited guests.

He had originally wanted to have a good talk with Yang Cheng, secretary of the Municipal Party Committee, and tell him, in a detailed but down-to-earth manner, about the situation at Zhongyang Textiles and the problems that had occurred there. Although the issue of state-owned enterprises was an agenda item that came up for study again and again in almost every meeting of the Standing Committee of the Municipal Party Committee, this time the problem was fundamentally different from before. This time, the Zhongyang Textile Group, one of the largest enterprises in the city, had encountered a serious and unusual problem. A vicious incident, unprecedented since the founding of the People's Republic of China, had occurred. It had even developed to the point of impacting on the Municipal Party Committee and the Municipal Government, on up to the Provincial Party Committee and the Provincial Government! In those few municipal state-owned large and medium-sized enterprises that went into a slump, if decisive measures were not taken and great attention was not paid to them, it was likely to cause a chain reaction, and the consequences could be disastrous! Therefore, it was essential that he brought it to the serious attention of the Party Committee secretary first and, before any meeting of the Municipal Committee, it would be best, if possible, to report to and ask for instructions from the relevant comrades of the Provincial Party Committee and Provincial Government. This was by no means a trivial matter, as it not only related to the reform of the city's state-owned enterprises, but also affected the stability of society and the people's morale. There was no room for sloppiness or excuses.

But the arrival of these few people had completely overturned all his previous plans.

The truth was that what had been overturned was not just his plans, but his whole standpoint, attitude and way of framing the problem. To be honest, after listening to the reports and explanations of the management the day before, his feelings and views about the company had indeed changed a lot. In particular, he had found that many of the views of the senior management were diametrically opposed to those of the workers. In the course of the night, he had thought through the matter over and over, repeatedly warning himself that he must be objective, he must be realistic, and he must not be emotional. The views of the two sides should be analysed objectively; each had its own shortcomings and areas where it went too far, and the feelings of both sides had to be taken into account. In a word, both sides should be treated correctly, but the treatment of the factory workers should come from a perspective of love and care and be aimed at solving their practical difficulties. At the same time, great efforts had to be made to do more ideological work with them and to give them emotional guidance, especially for those who were dissatisfied with the way reforms were shattering the old tradition of the "iron rice bowl". Their emotions should be engaged through reasoning and through serious and patient persuasion. Over the years, due to China's unique national conditions, the employees of state-owned enterprises, who were known as "iron rice bowls" because of their fixed wages, preferential treatment and various kinds of special status, had actually come to be regarded as a higher class than other workers.

It could be argued that this feeling of nostalgia for the "iron rice bowl" was likely to develop into something that hindered reform. It was not difficult to see that many problems would become apparent if the dissatisfaction of employees of state-owned enterprise were to be analysed from this point of view. Of course, such an analysis and viewpoint could only be tacitly acknowledged and understood but not openly expressed. The key to getting it right with the workers and to fully engaging their emotions was to consider all sides. Indeed, it can probably be taken as a basic guiding principle that there are two sides to every problem. Thus, the management too needed to be treated correctly and their views understood. Of course, this did not mean that any of them who demonstrated corrupt or illegal conduct should be shown any tolerance or leniency. Whatever needed investigation should be investigated, and whatever needed to be dealt with should be dealt with. If problems were discovered, it should not matter who the culprit was or at what level they were operating. Anyone breaking company policy should be disciplined and anyone breaking the law should be imprisoned. Expulsion from the Party, dismissal from post and other severe punishments should all be used to set an example. But on the other hand, every effort should also be made fully to understand the managers of state-owned enterprises, especially those with whom the employees were particularly dissatisfied, and to treat them fairly. The heavy burdens, backward technology, lack of funds and poor management of state-owned enterprises were ongoing problems left over from the time the country was run under the planned economic system; none of these had any real or fundamental connection with the existing management of those enterprises. It would be neither fair nor of material benefit to heap all the problems and difficulties found in state-owned enterprises on these managers, nor would it be in any way realistic. There was no reason to blame them for the problems of history and of the unique economic phase the country currently found itself in. These included the usual complaints such as slowness in adapting to new concepts, lack of awareness of new advances, lack of leadership, too deep an attachment to traditional thinking, and so on.

All that was easy to talk about but how easy was it actually to do something about it? Private enterprises did not have the rules and regulations of state-owned businesses and they could act as they pleased, without worrying about their methods. Could the bosses of state-owned enterprises do the same? Sometimes there were things that needed to be done, that had to be done, and you just had to harden your heart and get on with them. In similar circumstances, private enterprise had nothing to scruple over, nothing to worry about, but as soon as a complaint was made against a manager in a state-owned company or someone informed on him or her, the high-ups would send someone to investigate, and they could end up in prison in no time flat. *The people don't sue and officials never investigate.* This sentence was often heard now to the extent that it had pretty much become a truism, tried and tested and not to be questioned. In exactly the same circumstances, if no one sued, there was no problem, but as soon as a suit was brought, the game was up. In modern state-owned work units and enterprises, all manner of things might come to light, but, as long as you kept your own head down, no matter what problems might be uncovered, in the end, it all depended on how deeply senior leaders wanted to investigate them and to what extent they were able to control them.

The night before, Li Gaocheng's plan had been to discuss with Party Committee Secretary Yang Cheng how to interpret the situation and then what to do about it. His premise was that there could be two correct interpretations, and the principle, therefore, was that there could be two correct ways of dealing with it. On that basis, the next step was to send out an investigation team both to regulate the mood of the people and to stabilise the cadres; it was only under those conditions that he could proceed to the next step, and it was only at that point that he could properly consider how to get the company back on its feet and how to bring it back to life.

He felt that, at this time, this was the most secure strategy and the most reliable method; at the very least it wouldn't cause any major problems, nor would it lead to any serious miscarriage of justice that might lead to mockery and end up by keeping the spotlight on him.

But now he had been confronted by the workers' representative a second time and he had these two thick files of complaints in front of him, the theoretical basis of the ideas and opinions he had gone over and over in his head the day before had been shaken to pieces in front of his eyes.

Faced with this huge petition of more than ten thousand signatures, faced with these hard-come-by investigation results and lists of accounts that were the fruits of the labours of countless people, faced with the demands and expectations of so many workers, faced with such shocking corruption and such blatantly scandalous behaviour, although none of it had been properly investigated and nothing could be definitively proved yet, was it really going to be so easy for him to casually come up with two accurate judgements and two correct solutions for such serious and intense confrontations? Was it all as straightforward as he had been saying? Would each side shoulder their responsibilities, undergo criticism and self-criticism, and distribute the blame equally so that the affair would be over, the problem would be solved and the dark clouds would all be dispersed? Would all the difficulties at Zhongyang Textiles thus be resolved? Was it all really that easy? Or was he working from selfish, ulterior motives and deceiving himself over the whole affair? Or was he being too indifferent and insensitive?

At the time, he had made such solemn pledges and promises in front of all those cadres and all those workers; he had been so passionate and enthusiastic! But now, when he turned around and saw all those former subordinates, who he had personally promoted, once again sitting oh-so respectfully in front of him, all those pledges and promises, all that passion and enthusiasm, they suddenly seemed to have changed their tune and gone cold. Confronted by these people, however cold-hearted and unforgiving he might appear, deep down inside him, the bond was still too strong to break.

To put it bluntly, there was nothing he could do about the problems with Zhongyang Textiles and he didn't have the heart to tackle them anyway. All he wanted to do was smooth things over, make peace and work around things. It was so hard for everyone these days, and nothing was easy, so, in the light of the overall situation, resolving the problems without harming anyone was the best policy to maintain stability. They were in a time of peace, so why turn internal contradictions within the people as a whole into adversarial conflict in the company? Besides, if any individual made a complaint, or if there was a collective petition, then all conditions should simply be agreed to. Whatever methods came up from below, the government should adopt them; whatever suggestions on how to manage things came from the lower levels, the government should act upon them; whoever their subordinates named as corrupt, those in charge should make a great show of investigating them. The essential principle was: if there is no trouble, do nothing, but if there is trouble, take total control; if there is no trouble, don't make any concessions, but if there is trouble, concede everything. If the government were to set this example, then all companies, large and small, would follow suit. However, if that was actually what happened, eventually the government would have no peace and that would in no way be conducive to deepening reform and reinforcing social stability.

Li Gaocheng felt that all his thoughts on the affair were entirely reasonable and that, by taking the overall situation as his starting point, he had been able properly to make it his focus. However, now he had been confronted by the haggard, concerned faces of the staff and cadre representatives, now he had seen those two thick documents containing all the serious material of the petition, he suddenly felt too ashamed of his conclusions to look any of these people in the eye.

He couldn't understand how his judgement had become so self-contradictory. One day he would see things one way and he would become aggressive and emotional; the next day he would see them completely differently and make a 180-degree turn.

Was he lacking in the necessary ability, or was he just too reliant on his emotions? What had happened to his customary rationality? Suppose all the cadres in China were like him – wouldn't the government find itself in total chaos?

He gave himself a moment to calm down, then picked up the phone to call Zhongyang Textiles. He ordered General Manager Guo Zhongyao and Party Committee Secretary Chen Yongming to come over to his office immediately.

Whatever else, he still wanted to see these two men again. He wanted to reconfirm his feeling that, in fact, either he was wrong or someone was lying to him.

Within half an hour, the two men arrived simultaneously at his office.

The two of them still looked scared, submissive and wary, and spoke so softly that he barely heard their greetings. They came in quietly, sat down quietly and looked at him quietly. Their expressions made them look like two children in front of a stern father.

His heart lurched. He suddenly realised that his own feelings and emotions as he looked at them were exactly like that; he felt like a father looking at his sons.

He couldn't help asking himself why, when he saw the management team of Zhongyang Textiles, the first thought that came into his head was whether they could really change. Were they really as bad as people had reported them to be? Could they be that rotten?

He had always felt that things had not been easy for them, that they were still the same as they had been in the past and that they were fundamentally good people. From the bottom of his heart, he had always wanted to protect them and keep them from any harm. The fellow-feeling between comrades-in-arms is very difficult to break and is something that is always with you.

Perhaps he really should recuse himself from handling the problems of the Zhongyang Textile Group. As the management team were all his protégés, he really should avoid the whole thing. Otherwise, it was very likely that he would become entangled in a very tricky dilemma which would just draw him in deeper and deeper until he was left with no way out.

But would recusing himself actually get him out of such a difficult situation? The more he was seen to do so, the more other people's suspicions might be roused about where he stood and the more they might read into his equivocation. Moreover, if, as mayor, he didn't take up a clear and firm position, this might encourage others not to either. Ambiguity and vagueness in him would simply cause more of the same and worse. This was where a mayor had to show leadership and, if he didn't take a clear stand, he would become a laughing stock. If it went well, it would be to his credit, but if it went badly, he would have to shoulder all the blame. In the end, it was his business, and if he wasn't willing to take control of it, why should anyone else want to get their hands dirty?

This was a dilemma for him.

In the end, it seemed to him that he was going to have to take control himself, and that it was better to do so earlier rather than later, and that it was better to be proactive rather than reactive. What it came down to was that he was a mayor, so, with such an important matter, it was down to him to call the shots and make the decisions. There was nowhere for him to hide and nowhere for him to run to.

When nothing was going on, it seemed that anyone could be an official; there was even a popular saying that if you weren't good enough to be a leadership cadre, what were you good for? Basically, it was because that was the way things were in peacetime. Once there was any kind of incident, any kind of major incident, that was when leadership cadres had to prove themselves. Just as true gold reveals itself in fire, it was at such times that it instantly became apparent whether you were competent or incompetent, talented or mediocre, the genuine article or a fake.

With all this in mind, Li Gaocheng stared at the two men for a long time before saying something that surprised even himself:

"All right then, since this is where we are, let's cut to the chase and not keep going all round the houses. I have called you here urgently today because there is one thing I want to ask you. It is something genuine, something from the bottom of my heart, something pure and unadulterated. Each of you must give your own answer and there is no room for deliberation, no room for discussion and no question of blame. I just want to ask you if there is a problem at Zhongyang Textiles or not. Is there a problem with you? Is there a problem with the management team? Put it how you will, my question is basically, is there a problem or not? If there is, how big is it? Has internal discipline been broken or has the law been broken? As I said, don't try to explain, don't try to justify, just keep it simple. If there is a problem, say so. If there isn't, tell me there isn't."

The office went silent for a long moment, so silent it might as well have been empty of people. Party Committee Secretary Chen Yongming looked at General Manager Guo Zhongyao and then looked again, as Guo seemed to have fallen into a deep reverie. For a long time, he looked neither at Li Gaocheng nor at Chen Yongming. His expression was completely impassive, giving absolutely nothing away. He looked neither nervous nor under pressure and, least of all, did he look as though he was, in any way, panicked or afraid. The reverie that Guo Zhongyao was immersed in seemed to be a kind of deep meditative trance that was oblivious to everyone and everything. All that was evident was a slight sadness, a slight heaviness, a slight frustration, a slight despair. However, faint as these were, these manifestations were enough to make Li Gaocheng feel extremely uncomfortable.

Li asked himself whether his own words had been too harsh or too upsetting. Or was it too humiliating, too difficult for them to answer?

Was it really a difficult question to answer?

For anyone with a clear conscience, a few simple words would suffice: there is no problem.

"I have not pocketed the state's money, I have not taken advantage of the state or the enterprise in any way, and nor have I turned public property into private property or appropriated collective property for myself."

What was difficult about that as an answer? As a national cadre, as a manager of a state-owned enterprise, as a person with some prestige in the country and among the ordinary people of this country – in short, as a communist – this should be an easy question to answer, unless you really had done something disgraceful, something that would bring shame to that name and that status.

Or was there an answer that falls somewhere in between? That is to say, on the one hand, I have not done anything unreasonably greedy or self-serving, but, on the other, I have done things that are shameful and are beneath this name and status. So, perhaps this seemingly simple question was indeed very difficult to answer, or to know how to answer.

Would that be a viable answer? Or a viable solution?

Li Gaocheng looked silently at these two important senior figures in the company and didn't say a word for a very long time. He felt that, just at this moment, there was nothing he could say and nothing he should say. He felt that if he did speak, or even allowed his face to show any kind of emotion, the solemn, awe-inspiring atmosphere in the office would be broken. He felt that it was not these two subordinates in front of him who could not take the psychological pressure, but he himself who was likely to crack. What right did he have to demand selflessness and incorruptibility from the manager of a state-owned enterprise cast adrift on the tides of the market economy?

Could he do such a thing himself? Had he done such a thing himself? How easy would he find it to turn down a sumptuous banquet? How easy would he find it to refuse all the money and gifts that came at him from every direction? Could he distance himself from cadres and superiors who he knew were corrupt but couldn't prove it, and have no dealings with them? Could he ignore and refuse to get involved with the pet projects and requests of people with special status or crucial roles?

He should count for himself just how many bribes in the form of gifts and presents he approved for distribution every month of the year! If he wanted, he could be invited to a banquet under a variety of pretexts almost all the time! Last year's trade fair had not been a large-scale affair, but the hospitality, entertainment, sightseeing and gift expenses for those Hong Kong, Taiwan and foreign businessmen amounted to tens of millions!

If some high-up were to ask him the same kind of question that he was asking, would he be able to answer in just a few words as he was expecting these men to do?

He couldn't help remembering what his wife had said the night before: "Gaocheng, everyone has responsibility for this situation, both the state and the government. There is no reason to make the management of Zhongyang Textiles carry it alone, and there is no reason for you to take it on personally either. It is a collective responsibility, not an individual responsibility."

He didn't know why he had suddenly remembered his wife's words just at that moment. The office remained as quiet as the grave.

In contrast to General Manager Guo Zhongyao's expression and demeanour, Party Committee Secretary Chen Yongming appeared to be looking about him without any sense of purpose. He looked nervously at Guo Zhongyao and then at Li Gaocheng, as if he wanted to see the answer, or at least some clue as to how to answer, on one of their faces, before he committed himself.

It was no great surprise really. Although Chen Yongming was the Party Committee secretary at the Zhongyang Textile Group, Guo Zhongyao was his superior in terms of qualifications, in terms of age, and, indeed, in terms of ability. What was more, under the current factory manager responsibility system, it was Guo Zhongyao who had the senior legal status at Zhongyang Textiles. If the Party secretary of a company didn't position himself correctly, or didn't know how to manage his position, he would often naturally find himself in a subservient situation. So, as Party Committee secretary, perhaps Chen Yongming had already given himself the secondary role, or perhaps he realised that, according to his own criteria, at this moment he should let Guo Zhongyao speak first, and only after he had ascertained Guo's ideas and intentions, could he decide how he himself should reply.

The seconds ticked away, and the office was still deathly silent. Guo Zhongyao was still sitting there expressionlessly, and Chen Yongming was still looking around vacantly.

Then the telephone on the desk rang, making all three men jump.

To Li Gaocheng's surprise, it was his wife, Wu Aizhen. In normal circumstances, she seldom called at this hour, even if it was something very important, as she knew it was his busiest time. Mostly, she would ring his secretary and get him to pass on a message if he, Li, was busy. This was, in fact, a kind of rule or tacit understanding that had grown up between husband and wife over the years to try and make sure neither was disturbed when they were busy. What particularly puzzled him was that his wife knew that he was going to see Party Committee Secretary Yang Cheng this morning, so why was she calling his office now?

His wife was being particularly gentle and soothing that morning and it irritated Li Gaocheng rather that she didn't seem to have anything important to tell him. They talked about this and that for quite a while without her getting to any kind of point. He didn't get too annoyed with her, however, as it suited him to drag things out a little, and he let her prattle on. Finally, however, his suspicions were aroused and he gradually became aware of the real purpose of his wife's call.

"I hear that some of the troublemakers from Zhongyang Textiles came charging into your office early this morning. Is that right?" she asked casually.

"Oh, you know about that, do you?"

"Good news stays indoors, bad news travels a thousand *li*! Don't you know how many pairs of eyes are always on you as an important municipal figure?" There seemed to be a veiled warning in her words.

"How did you get to hear about it? Someone must have tipped you off – otherwise how would you know they were here before they've even left?" There was more to Li Gaocheng's words too, but he didn't let on what it was.

"It's not necessarily a bad thing to have so many people concerned about you and watching you." His wife's tone suddenly became grave. "Seriously now, Gaocheng, are those troublemakers still with you?"

Li Gaocheng was at a loss for words; he didn't know how to answer.

"If they're still there, I'll keep it short." His wife grew more serious and lowered her voice even more. "The Devil is on the loose now! It's coming whether you like it or not! When you went to Zhongyang Textiles just recently, didn't they heap everything on you? Can't you see they're trying to make you take responsibility for it all? Just answer me this – has Yang Cheng called you at all so far?"

"...no." It was true, he hadn't.

"Have any of the other municipal leaders called you?" His wife followed up her first question.

"No." It was true, they hadn't. "But I told Wu Xingang yesterday to call and agree a meeting with Yang Cheng first thing this morning."

"Forget about Wu Xingang – he's just a minor secretary. Yang Cheng is a municipal secretary, a real player. Do you think he's going to take any notice of a minor secretary when this is such a big deal? A whole day and a whole night have passed, and he hasn't even phoned to ask you about it, has he? Can't you see he is shovelling the whole stupid mess over onto you!?"

Li Gaocheng noticed that this was the second time his wife had used the phrase "Can't you see?"

"Stop over-complicating things! If you keep second-guessing something, you never get anything done! All right then, if there's nothing else, we'll talk about all this when we get home. I've still got people here." Li Gaocheng was really unhappy with his wife for talking about this kind of thing so openly on the telephone and he wanted to hang up.

"I haven't finished yet, so keep listening!" His wife was unrepentant. "You know I've never talked about your work before, but this is different. It's obvious the whole thing is coming down on your head. Just think about it! Do you think it's got nothing to do with you that the workers are kicking up a fuss? Do you think it's got nothing to do with you that not a single one of the other municipal leaders has asked you about it? And do you still think it's got nothing to do with you when these people come looking for you in your office first thing in the morning today? Slice it how you will, it's all about getting you to send someone to investigate and it's all about getting rid of the Zhongyang Textiles management team, lock, stock and barrel. If things have got that far, can you still say it's not coming crashing down on you? Can you still insist it's nothing to do with you? Can you still say I'm over-complicating it? Didn't I tell you yesterday that any investigation of Zhongyang Textiles is an investigation of you? Getting rid of the management team means they want to get rid of you too! If you take that threat lightly, if you don't take notice of it, when the time comes it will be too late for regrets. If you want my advice, since they've already come looking for you, tell them to go looking for Yang Cheng and the others too! No matter who comes to see you, treat them as your colleagues and don't let them isolate you. There is no need for you to pull all the responsibility down on your own shoulders – you left Zhongyang Textiles a long time ago and you don't have any connection with the company anymore. With what's going on now, the more they make it an individual responsibility, the more it lands on you. The more you can make it a collective responsibility, the less of it comes your way. The more it is made an individual responsibility, the bigger and more complicated it becomes. The more you can make it a collective responsibility, the more it will just go away. If an investigation is directed at everyone, there won't be any problem. If it is directed at an individual, it will never go away and if you can't take it, you'll just have to pack up and go. Once you've seen Yang Cheng you can leave it up to others to decide whether to investigate or not and whether to regulate the situation or not. You must know that it's the same anywhere when something is out of control – it becomes the responsibility of whoever steps up to try and manage it. State-owned enterprises are a headache even for central government, so how do you think we're going to find a way of handling it? Suppose you do get to the bottom of what's going on at Zhongyang Textiles and suppose you do get rid of the whole management team there, do you think you will have solved the whole problem? How could it be that simple?"

Li Gaocheng kept repeating "OK, OK, OK" over and over before finally managing to stop his wife talking.

For a long time after he had hung up, his wife's words still rang in his ears. He hadn't given much thought to how reasonable her opinions were, but what had startled him was the depth of her "official experience" and "political principles"; he had trouble understanding just when she had acquired such things. This both scared and dumbfounded him.

If this was what was being said at his wife's Anti-Corruption Bureau, then there really was big trouble.

When he lifted his head to look at the two men in question, he realised that they had been watching him in silence for what seemed like an eternity. The atmosphere in the office had changed completely after that telephone call. He suddenly realised how opportune the timing of the call had been for the two men in front of him; it was almost as if it had come to their rescue. He couldn't help wondering how his wife had known they were coming to see him so very early in the morning. She had given every appearance of being fast asleep when he left. Someone must have reported it to her.

So, who could it have been? And why had they done it? Why had his wife made that telephone call? Was it just a question of not wanting him to get involved with this business on his own? It really couldn't be that simple.

Just at that moment, the telephone rang again. It was the secretary of the Municipal Committee, Yang Cheng.

"I've been waiting for you, Lao Li. Weren't you supposed to be coming to see me this morning?"

"Yesterday's representatives from the workers at Zhongyang Textiles came to see me again, and there were a few details I wanted to go over." Li Gaocheng looked at his watch and continued: "I'll come over in twenty minutes. Is that all right?"

"In that case, I think we'd be better leaving it until this afternoon. It is already almost eleven o'clock and this isn't something we can talk through in a hurry. As it happens, some staff representatives from the company have come to see me too. I might as well hear what they have to say first. How about we talk it all through at two this afternoon?" Yang Cheng's tone was very gentle and open to negotiation.

"All right, I'll come over once we're back to work this afternoon."

Li Gaocheng's heart seemed to settle back into its proper rhythm as he put down the telephone. So, they had gone to see Yang Cheng, had they? And they were sitting in his office at this very moment! He suddenly felt a weight come off him and he began to relax. Then, his wife's words rang in his ear again: "…with what's going on now, the more they make it an individual responsibility, the more it lands on you. The more you can make it a collective responsibility, the less it comes your way. The more it is made an individual responsibility, the bigger and more complicated it becomes. The more you can make it a collective responsibility, the more it will just go away…"

He couldn't help but be a little alarmed by and ashamed of his recent feelings. He had felt that such actions were disgusting and hateful when his wife put them into words just now, but when his own everyday words and actions were just the same as she described, he felt nothing at all. Wasn't the latter even more terrible than the former?

He fell silent again, looking at the two men in front of him, and they looked silently back at him.

After a long time, he gestured at them and said, rather helplessly: "If you don't think there's any more to be said, you'd better go away. Come back and we'll talk again whenever you have thought it through."

Party Committee Secretary Chen Yongming finally showed some agitation as he said: "It is not easy to give an answer to what you have asked, Mayor Li. If it was just directed at me, of course I would dare to guarantee that there is no problem with me – there hasn't been in the past, there isn't now and there won't be in the future. But if you are asking me to say that there is no problem with the Zhongyang Textiles management team or that there is no problem with the company as a whole, then there is no way I can give a proper reply. With so many cadres and such a huge organisation, I simply can't say for certain there are no problems."

Looking at the frustration that showed on Secretary Chen Yongming's face, Li Gaocheng suddenly realised how big his question really was. His starting point at the time was, in fact, the same thing he had been most worried about when he first got involved with the issue of Zhongyang Textiles; he was afraid that there was a problem with the whole management team, a problem of collective corruption. How he was to view the whole issue depended on whether this was the case or not. This was probably the key to the whole problem and the most important element in finding a solution. That's why he had told these two important staff members to come and see him and asked them his question. He was following his intuition. In this way, he just wanted to batter his way to the truth without causing any more major problems. As to whether they could actually find a reply or not, he simply didn't give it any more thought.

Looked at from another point of view, it might turn out to be no bad thing if they couldn't come up with an acceptable reply or couldn't reply at all.

At last, Li Gaocheng turned to look at the general manager, Guo Zhongyao. "What about you? Do you feel you can't answer either?"

Guo Zhongyao looked up at Li Gaocheng, put his head in his

hands and said, without emotion: "Do you really want me to tell the truth, Mayor?"

Li Gaocheng couldn't help staring at him in amazement; previously, Guo Zhongyao and the rest of the management team had always called him Mayor Li, and he had never heard them address him just as "Mayor". He couldn't quite put his finger on it, but it seemed to him there was something hard and unyielding in Guo Zhongyao's words.

"Does that mean that everything you've told me before is false?" He found himself more than a little annoyed at Guo Zhongyao's attitude. "What's going on now to make you act so mysterious with me?"

"Since we are where we are, I will tell you the truth. The fact is, the situation at Zhongyang Textiles is no different from anywhere else. If you really do look into it properly, then you really will find problems, and if you don't, you won't. If it's only a little investigation, you'll only find little problems. If it's a big investigation, you'll find big problems."

Li Gaocheng was dumbstruck again. He had never expected Guo Zhongyao to say anything like that! Chen Yongming was wide-eyed in amazement too; it seemed he hadn't expected it either!

A deathly hush fell over the office.

CHAPTER THIRTEEN

NEITHER TOO LATE NOR TOO EARLY, it was the ideal time. The habit of taking a noonday nap in China is directly connected to the management system, and it is particularly indispensable for busy, hard-working senior cadres. They take their lunch in the work unit then have a quiet lie down in their office; this kind of midday rest is essential not only for adjusting the mind, but also for replenishing physical strength. That is why most important leaders in China have a simple but very necessary daybed or sofa in their office, on which they can have a lie-down. Taking a nap in your office is not just a quiet and restful experience, it is also a time when you can avoid the unwanted intrusion and nagging of family and visitors. So, for a leading cadre with a hectic and punishing schedule, it is both precious and essential. People who are aware of this never disturb their bosses at this time unless it is a matter of life or death.

Work begins again at two o'clock, so arriving at ten past is perfect timing. It gives someone time to wake up properly, wash their face and make a cup of tea. When you do go in, you can start talking straight away and you don't have to waste a whole lot of time waiting for them to catch up with themselves.

However, when Li Gaocheng entered Yang Cheng's office, it became evident to him that Yang had not taken a midday nap. The man had all his attention fixed on something which, when Li approached the desk, he saw were the two thick volumes of the petition and its supporting evidence.

So that's what he was looking at!

Li Gaocheng's heart lurched.

Yang Cheng gestured at him to sit down on the sofa, made two cups of tea and came over to sit with him.

The two men sat very close together.

Yang Cheng was nearly ten years younger than Li Gaocheng and had been in the last cohort to graduate from university before the Cultural Revolution. He belonged to that lucky group who had academic qualifications and experience; they had both ideology and culture but had not been impacted by too much persecution. When the talents that the country desperately needed were in short supply because of the faults of the Cultural Revolution, they turned out to be the mainstay of the nation. With the country focused on economic construction and urgently needing a group of intellectuals to serve as leading cadres, they were brought in from all corners of the nation, put into the most critical and important positions, and promoted and promoted until they reached heights that they had never dreamed they could attain. At that time, promotion was much easier than it had since become – the promotion of cadres did not seem to have as many rules and regulations, and those promoted did not seem to have to dance as much attendance on their superiors. The nation was in dire need, and there was no new talent coming through; people sat having discussions and conducting studies on who to promote, but the person being promoted had no idea what was going on. It would come as such a surprise when he was told by word of mouth that he would often sit there dumbstruck for hours before it sank in. Then, by the time the official notification was sent out, he was already a celebrated leadership cadre. Learning on the job, he worked while he studied and studied while he worked, and there was no trial period or probation. He was never asked if he had any grassroots experience, and it was no problem if he wasn't a Party member; he could join immediately and that would be that. Many of the country's leading cadres, who now had important jobs and occupied high-level positions, were promoted at that time and, of course, Yang Cheng was one of them.

Deep down, Li Gaocheng regarded these cadres very highly.

They had mostly been promoted at a time when there were few rules and regulations, so they themselves were not sticklers for such things. Their positions had been comparatively easily come by, so they were not so worried about keeping or losing them. They had real talent and they also had real social and political experience; although they themselves had not been affected too badly by past events, they could see and feel clearly what China now needed, and what the biggest threats to the country and the people now were. As intellectuals themselves, they knew how to respect knowledge. As they themselves were the products of reform, they in turn were the most loyal supporters, participants and promoters of reform.

Although Yang Cheng had not been transferred into this post very long ago, Li Gaocheng's intuition gave him a good feeling about this secretary of the Municipal Party Committee, comparatively young as he was. What particularly attracted and reassured him was that Yang Cheng, who was also already a member of the Standing Committee of the Provincial Party Committee, like Li himself did not have much of an official background behind him. That alone made him feel much closer to Yang, both emotionally and in terms of status. People said that the current system inherently brought governors and secretaries, mayors and secretaries, prefects and secretaries, and village chiefs and secretaries into conflict; generally speaking, there were indeed very few Party and government departments that were not in conflict with each other. The secretary managed the cadres, and the mayor managed the economy; one managed people, and the other managed money. Thinking about it, there was nothing in principle to bring them into conflict, but in practice, there were points of contradiction everywhere, and conflicts arose from time to time. For example, if the mayor was to focus on the economy and business management, the primary challenge was to have a group of business leaders who understood the economy, knew management, and were market aware. But the decision on how to employ these corporate talents rested with the secretary not the mayor. It was this fundamental contradiction that determined the permanence, acuteness and extent of the conflict between the two. However, in Li Gaocheng's many years as mayor, he had seldom felt this way. For one thing, he was a man who rarely gave much thought to this area, and, as his wife always said, he only knew how to plan things, not people. Secondly, it may also have had something to do with the several secretaries with whom he had worked. The last secretary, for example, was fifty-eight years old when Li became mayor, and the fact that he was nearing retirement age meant that he discussed everything with Li and seldom disagreed with him. But now, there was Yang Cheng, only forty-six or forty-seven years old, almost ten years younger than Li Gaocheng, who was very well aware that, before he was transferred in as Municipal Party secretary, many people had fancied Li for the job. So, over this recent period, the two men had worked very well together. As mayor, Li Gaocheng recognised in particular that Yang Cheng had shown great respect for his opinions on many matters, and that he had been very open and fair in the democratic manner with which he had handled several quite major personnel decisions. There had certainly been nothing he had done that would raise any eyebrows. Additionally, Li Gaocheng felt that in a myriad of very important matters, he himself had always given priority to the work, to the bigger picture and to his career. He hadn't done anything questionable, no one had anything to say against him, nor had there been any conflicts or contradictions that had proved hard to resolve.

All in all, he felt very good about having Yang Cheng as Party secretary – at least for now.

Yang Cheng was a very direct and decisive person. He seldom went in for "polite talk" or non-committal language. He always got straight to the point without beating about the bush. As soon as the two of them sat down, Yang Cheng started out with: "I hear that the workers kicked up a real fuss last night. Did you see it all?"

"You're not wrong. It was almost as bad as the Cultural Revolution. If I'd got there any later, who knows how much worse it would have been. You didn't even see it, and I can tell it has you rattled just thinking about it." Li Gaocheng was equally direct.

"I heard Wu Xingang say there were almost twenty thousand of them."

"That's about right. At any rate, everyone from the company who could get there was there. It was freezing cold all night and there was snow on the ground but that didn't put anyone off, young or old. They were all wide awake and full of energy. It seemed there was a lot of tension between the crowd and the cadres, and everyone was on edge." Li Gaocheng seemed to be reliving the atmosphere and emotion of the night before, and it was really affecting him.

"Is it really serious, Lao Li?" Yang Cheng's face was right up close to Li Gaocheng.

"Yes, really serious!" he replied, very directly.

"Have we reached the point where the problems at the company are beyond any control the management team can exert?" Yang Cheng followed up his first question.

"As things stand, I'm afraid so." This was genuinely what Li Gaocheng thought.

"In your opinion, can the reputation and prestige of the company's leading cadres be restored?" Yang Cheng's question went absolutely to the crux of the matter.

"Probably only with the greatest difficulty." Li Gaocheng thought that was all he could say.

"I think our feelings about all this are pretty much the same, Lao Li, and I've been thinking about nothing else for the last two days. It has not been a short process for the contradictions of this business to get to this point. All this shows that in big state-owned companies like Zhongyang Textiles, these irreconcilable contradictions exist and build up over a very long period of time. So, what I think is that if we really want to resolve the problems at Zhongyang Textiles, the first thing we have to sort out is what the irreconcilable contradictions actually are and what it is that causes them and allows them to persist. I think this matter can be solved as long as we can get to the crux of the problem. More importantly, this is likely to have serious wider implications for the reform of state-owned large and medium-sized enterprises."

At these words from Yang Cheng, Li Gaocheng fell silent for a long time. He hadn't expected that Yang Cheng would have thought the matter through so thoroughly and so deeply. Questions that seemed, in the normal course of things, easy to answer, became much less easy when you were put on the spot for an answer. When you came down to it, what actually was the most important problem at Zhongyang Textiles? What was the essence of this intensified and now very serious conflict? Li Gaocheng had taken note of the words Yang Cheng had used: irreconcilable contradiction. If that really was how he saw things, it meant that Yang Cheng, as the secretary of the

Municipal Party Committee, already had a settled view or at least a more mature view on the problems at Zhongyang Textiles. And if the contradiction was indeed irreconcilable, that meant it had, in essence, become antagonistic. It was just this antagonism that, in turn, made it irreconcilable. Was this really how Yang Cheng saw things?

After some thought, Li Gaocheng said tentatively: "To be honest, I've been completely tied up with superficialities for the last two days, and I've only had five or six hours sleep in that time. Just this morning I've had two lots of representatives from the company come to see me, and all I've done is listen to them talking about the problems and giving their opinions. Of course, with so much going on, they all have their own versions and ideas about them. I really haven't yet been able to give any profound thought to how exactly I should be looking at this whole business with Zhongyang Textiles. You have listened to them too, Secretary Yang, and I would like to know your initial impressions and approach."

"I don't know all the specifics yet. I've listened to the feedback from those people this morning, and I've looked at the materials they sent just now, and, especially in the light of what you have told me about the numbers involved in the disturbance, and about how antagonistic the relationship between the cadres and the masses is, it seems that the problem is a great deal more severe than we had imagined. The way I see it, given how things have developed, the essence of the problem, the real sticking point, is that the cadres have made the ordinary people their opponents, and the people view the cadres as their most hated, most unforgivable enemies."

Yang Cheng appeared to be completely immersed in deep contemplation and seemed not to have either noticed or to care about Li Gaocheng's tentative words.

"I haven't fully thought this through, Lao Li, but I feel that if a company's management and employees are in irreconcilable opposition, philosophically and emotionally, it is a serious dereliction of duty and failure in office on the part of the management cadres, even if no direct fault can be found with them. In other words, there is no longer any value in the existence of such a management team and it has lost all its relevance. The vast majority of workers no longer listen to their orders and have joined ranks in opposing them. If we have any illusions about such a management team, or even want to maintain it, the final result can only be like locking the stable door after the horse has bolted. Not only would we lose the team, we would also lose the hearts and minds of the people. So, Lao Li, what do you think we should decide?"

Intellectually speaking, it had to be said that Yang Cheng's opinion was certainly valid, and from one point of view, at least, it hit the nail squarely on the head. But, emotionally speaking, and he could not say exactly why, Li Gaocheng found himself unable to accept it. In any case, however heinous the management of Zhongyang Textiles might be, wasn't it too harsh and premature to come to such a conclusion before any investigation had taken place or any evidence had been found? Also, Yang Cheng had only heard one side of the story so far and had not yet had any contact with the management cadres. Under such circumstances, how could he come to such a hasty decision to sideline the whole management team? Additionally, they had still not really clarified the real reason for the disruption caused by the workers and anything else that lay behind it, so how could they draw such a conclusion? What Li Gaocheng found so hard to accept in emotional terms was that he was personally undertaking the investigation of the problems at Zhongyang Textiles, and he should be the person on the Municipal Party Committee and Municipal Government leadership team best informed on the subject. He was also very familiar with the fundamental circumstances of the Zhongyang management team, so he should be the person with the most say about the problems at the company, and he should also be the lead in deciding how a decision should be reached. At the very least, his opinion should be sought first. How could Yang Cheng, the Municipal Party Committee secretary, rush to make a judgement without hearing his report first?

Li Gaocheng thought for a while and then said: "And did you come to the conclusion that there was no hope for the management team at Zhongyang Textiles after listening to the feedback from those workers' representatives this morning, Secretary Yang?"

As soon as the words were out of his mouth, he immediately regretted them. He could hear the sneering disapproval in his own voice and he couldn't help feeling secretly surprised at his own sudden change of position. Before coming here, he had been thinking about how to persuade the secretary of the Municipal Party Committee to resolve the problems at Zhongyang Textiles and, in particular, how to convince him that a good-sized special investigation team should be put together as soon as possible and immediately sent into the company to conduct a comprehensive review and inventory. At the same time, a temporary work team would be formed to take over the total management of Zhongyang Textiles. But now, within fifteen minutes of arriving in Yang Cheng's office, his attitude had changed completely. Was it because Yang Cheng's words had piqued his pride, or did he simply feel unable to step down? He suddenly felt, deep down in his heart, that he could never tolerate any attack from others either on his feelings or his work. Because of this, his subconscious told him, he was the more obliged to cherish and protect the management team at Zhongyang Textiles. How was it that he was thinking like this? At this point, he hurriedly tried to make up lost ground by saying: "Actually, the same would be true of anyone who has heard the workers' report and seen the evidence they have put together – anyone would feel the same, and that includes me!"

"No, Lao Li, I think that this way of looking at things is wrong, particularly in relation to Zhongyang Textiles." Yang Cheng was still caught in a kind of weighty reverie and didn't seem to have noticed or understood in the slightest the change in what Li Gaocheng was feeling and saying. "This is definitely not something just for feelings – relying on emotion in such a serious conflict and contradiction would be too one-sided. I don't know why, Lao Li, but I always had a hunch that we might not see eye to eye over Zhongyang Textiles. I have already told you that what I have said represents my personal views and opinions, and the reason I am telling you this is that I want to share them with you first. But they are only my personal views and opinions. I think we should first reach a basic agreement on how to deal with the issue of Zhongyang Textiles, and that's what we should do right now. If we can't agree, that's fine, as long as we are both clear about each other's views and opinions. If we have a mutual understanding, we don't have to second-guess each other. After this, you will go back to the Municipal Party Committee, where you will make a comprehensive and detailed report, let everyone brainstorm the affair, and in the end, you will come up with an appropriate and workable solution. However, Lao Li, you must remember one thing – when solving the problem of Zhongyang Textiles, in the end, it is the bigger picture that you have to be concerned with. There is one thing that I have to say no matter how much it may irritate or annoy you, and no matter whether you understand it or not – it is all down to you. How the question of Zhongyang Textiles is settled, whether it is settled quickly or not, whether it is settled satisfactorily or not, whether the workers are satisfied or not, whether they cause trouble again, whether there are any consequences or not, the key to the whole thing rests with you."

CHAPTER FOURTEEN

It was already after eight in the evening when Li Gaocheng and Yang Cheng left the office together.

In the course of those more than five hours, the two men's conversation was generally quite congenial. The time together had given Li Gaocheng another opportunity to fully appreciate the younger man's way of thinking and style of leadership. It was the first time since Yang Cheng's appointment that the two of them had had such a long time with each other to exchange information and discuss issues. The first surprise for Li Gaocheng was the way Yang Cheng explained to him his view of and thinking on the Zhongyang Textiles situation before he had heard the report. This was something he certainly had not anticipated. He thought it was a strange way for a municipal secretary to behave and wondered whether it might not have implications he could not yet see. When he took this together with some of the opinions Yang Cheng had expressed earlier, he found he was gradually getting a sense of the municipal secretary's tough and hard-nosed style. It was a style he had seldom encountered in his previous several decades of work, and he wasn't at all sure how to deal with it. He was young and energetic, but wasn't he also a bit too domineering and arrogant? Was it not ill-considered and disrespectful to employ this tone and manner in his dealings with an experienced mayor almost ten years his senior and who should himself have been secretary of the Municipal Party Committee?

But, looked at another way, there was nothing strange, exceptional or hard to understand about it. Yang Cheng's views on Zhongyang Textiles had been formed a long time ago. Back in 1995, not long after he had taken office, Yang Cheng had not minced his words about the company when addressing a leadership meeting on the reform of state-owned enterprises held by the Municipal Party Committee and the Municipal Government. He had said that with an enterprise that size, which public opinion had so much to say about, and which was carrying such big losses, serious consideration should be given to changing its whole management team. It must be said that, at the time, Li Gaocheng had a very low opinion of these remarks. Without a proper investigation, Yang Cheng had no right to speak out on the matter, yet there he was, a Municipal Party Committee secretary, fresh on the scene, shooting his mouth off and delivering his opinion. It amounted to not just a criticism but also an accusation, implying that, up until then, almost nothing had been done correctly in this important provincial capital. In all honesty, this was the most unpromising and incompetent kind of leadership; it was also simple-minded and a manifestation of ignorance. Even if the previous government and the previous secretary had made some mistakes or taken some misguided decisions, the new secretary should never have criticised them so openly and so offhandedly when he had only just taken up office himself. It was not just a matter of manners, it raised questions about his essential quality too. This affair stuck in Li Gaocheng's mind for a long time after. Whatever else, the Municipal Party Committee secretary of a provincial capital and a senior Party cadre was not supposed to be so crass. Later on, his views on Yang Cheng changed for several reasons: one, because Yang Cheng proved to be a very practical and capable person; two, because he showed himself to be a very consistent person; and three, because his behaviour ultimately demonstrated that he was also very open and democratic. Nor was he alone in this opinion of Yang Cheng. The man didn't hold grudges, didn't work behind people's backs, didn't go in for cliques and factions and, in particular, didn't behave in a dictatorial manner and presume that he had the last word on anything. For example, in the case of Zhongyang Textiles, back then he was consistently in favour of radical surgery on the management team and had said so in meetings on many occasions. But later on, in the face of Li Gaocheng's disagreement with and opposition to wholesale action, although he didn't waver from his own thinking, he listened to what Li had to say and still decided to let the mayor take personal charge of the reform of state-owned enterprises, which naturally included the Zhongyang Textile Group.

Many people told Li Gaocheng afterwards that they thought he had been the winner in this first public contest between mayor and Municipal Party Committee secretary, but Li Gaocheng never saw it that way, nor felt any sense of victory. On the contrary, he often thought that, although he had the upper hand on the surface, in fact, he had put a noose around his own neck and handed the real initiative to the other side.

Sometimes, Li Gaocheng also secretly wondered to himself what state Zhongyang Textiles would have currently found itself in if Yang Cheng's advice had been followed. Even if it hadn't worked out – and this was what Li didn't want to admit, even to himself – it would never have been as bad as it was now, no matter what. It was also true that if a new management team had been formed, wouldn't it inevitably have been better than the current one? At the very least it wouldn't have made the public so angry and discontented.

This tended to make Li Gaocheng feel more and more stressed the more he thought about it, and the more worried he became, the more trouble he had eating and sleeping. This was why, when a really serious situation developed at Zhongyang Textiles, he did not inform Secretary Yang Cheng, but went straight to the company and took the huge risk of trying to solve the problem at the scene of the trouble.

Was he not now caught in a trap of his own devising and suffering self-inflicted damage?

Maybe the truth really was so cruel: if you wanted to defend someone, or protect the interests of a certain group, then there was a price to be paid and sacrifices to be made in the process, and, at any time, you might find yourself implicated and found guilty by association. Right or wrong, it always came back to you, and you were responsible for any problems!

In a nutshell, that was the Chinese way, and it was also the way of Chinese politics.

This was probably one of the most important constraints of

Chinese politics: if it's your responsibility, you have to accept that responsibility for good or for bad!

One thing that reassured Li Gaocheng was that, in the course of his many contacts with Yang Cheng, including today's long meeting, he felt that the secretary was a trustworthy person. He actually found himself deeply moved by the thought that Yang Cheng was such an unsophisticated, unworldly, straightforward character that he was almost too naïve and trusting to be the Municipal Party Committee secretary. But, then again, he also often felt that Yang Cheng was not to be underestimated. His kind of simplicity and truthfulness could often embarrass you and put you in an awkward position. If he thought something was wrong, once he found out about it, he would step forward and say so; and if he was certain of the correctness of something, he would stand firm on it, even if he had to offend a lot of people.

He was not over-cautious, but he was meticulous, and he was often better informed than anyone on things people thought he was unaware of.

Thus, there were several aspects of this afternoon's report that had secretly surprised and alarmed him. He had not expected Yang Cheng to have a clearer picture of the goings-on at Zhongyang Textiles than he did himself. In particular, the secretary had not just known what the management had said but had known in exact detail what they had discussed on specific topics. He knew more than Li did himself about the personal experience and family circumstances of the principal managers. He knew, for example, what makes of car the general manager, Guo Zhongyao, and the Party secretary, Chen Yongming, drove. And he knew that, although the deputy general manager, Feng Minjie, drove a Santana, the interior finish of that Santana had cost 200,000 yuan! None of this information was in the petition materials, and Li had simply no idea how he had obtained it.

That conversation he had had with Yang Cheng still made him shiver uneasily.

"I have a feeling, Lao Li, but I don't know whether it is true or not. I have always felt that you have a clearer picture of the problems at Zhongyang Textiles and a better understanding of their seriousness. You probably want to extend your investigation a bit and take another look, in the hope that the situation there may improve."

Li Gaocheng was so taken aback he couldn't speak. He hadn't given this any thought, and didn't even know himself whether, deep down inside, it really was what he was thinking. One part of it, however, was a hundred per cent true, and that was that he did indeed dream of the situation improving at Zhongyang Textiles. It would be to the benefit of the workers, the management and himself. Or, rather, most of all, it would be to his benefit.

Why to his benefit? To free himself of the worry? To enhance his reputation? Or was it purely emotional? Probably, most of all it was to free himself of the worry. He was exhausted by Zhongyang Textiles. Exhausted both emotionally and physically.

When Li Gaocheng didn't reply, Yang Cheng went on relentlessly to say something even more thought-provoking:

"For you as mayor, and me as secretary of the Municipal Party Committee, the most worrying thing about Zhongyang Textiles is not whether there is a problem with the current management, nor how big that might be. If there is a problem with the management team, just change the team. If there is a problem with the leadership cadres, those that merit dismissal should be dismissed, and those that merit punishment should be punished. That is all easy to handle, and there is nothing to worry about there. The only thing I worry about, Lao Li, is that the problems at Zhongyang Textiles may be just the tip of the iceberg. When the whole iceberg is exposed, we may face the most severe of tests as mayor and secretary. When that happens, I don't know if you and I will be able to withstand it, whether you and I will still be able to sit together like this..."

Li Gaocheng was surprised that, as Yang Cheng said this, the secretary of the Municipal Party Committee, who always gave a strong and decisive impression, seemed so sad and melancholy. This sadness and melancholy instantly transmitted itself and he suddenly felt how serious, profound and thought-provoking the man's words were.

"The tip of the iceberg": what an intimidating expression that was! What was lurking beneath that tip? If they were about to face the most severe test, what exactly was that test going to be? And then there were those words which Yang Cheng had repeated so often and which really got through to Li Gaocheng:

"...how the question of Zhongyang Textiles is settled, whether it is settled quickly or not, whether it is settled satisfactorily or not, whether the workers are satisfied or not, whether they cause trouble again, whether there are any consequences or not, the key to the whole thing rests with you."

Was it because he couldn't make up his mind? Or was it because, in his heart of hearts, he wanted to protect these former protégés of his? In other words, was it simply his own existence that made the problems of Zhongyang Textiles insoluble, however much he wanted to solve them?

But if that was the case, why did Yang Cheng keep telling him, over and over, that he, Li, had to take responsibility for solving the problems at Zhongyang Textiles and that he, and no one else, could solve them? Whoever tied the bell on the tiger should be the one to take it off: was that it? Could that really be what Yang meant? He refused to believe it.

But Yang Cheng seemed to be certain of his opinion, and his expression was one of absolute sincerity without a trace of deceit or hypocrisy. His eyes were full of emotion, trustworthy and impossible to deny.

But what was the reason for this?

"He is very young, but he is a slippery customer." This was his wife's immediate reaction to the question. She had not spoken very loudly, but her words went right through him.

"How can you say that? Yang Cheng is not the kind of person you think he is!" He was appalled by his wife's opinion.

"I know there is no such thing as a bad person in your eyes!" His wife kept her temper, and her tone was still mild and gentle. This was his wife's greatest and most appreciated strength: the angrier he became, the calmer she was.

She had got home earlier than him that day, and the food was particularly delicious, including two dishes she had cooked herself.

As he slowly ate his meal, his wife looked at him happily, as though he had just been promoted or had done something astonishingly important. In truth, she was fundamentally very satisfied with his conversation with Yang Cheng, and felt that he had struck the right tone.

"Look at it this way – Zhongyang Textiles is where you set up home, and other people look on it as your backyard. If there is a fire in that backyard then they will just have a good laugh at your expense. I can say anything I like about Zhongyang Textiles and that's fine, but if other people start pointing the finger, that is very definitely not OK. Only its master should beat a dog. Do you think I would let people say what they please about the cadres that I promoted, and investigate them when it takes their fancy? If it was left to them, what kind of prestige do you think you would have among the municipal cadres? When the time comes, who will still stay loyal to you? Who will protect you? If you don't look after your own people, or can't look after them, who will still look to you for anything?"

"Where did all that come from?" Li Gaocheng frowned at his wife.

"People are constantly moving forward. How many do you think are as constant and unchanging as you?" She was still smiling as she replied. "Do you think Yang Cheng is as foolish as you? Since he takes the problem of Zhongyang Textiles so seriously, and says that the management team is so useless, why is he still letting you find the solution? He has even said that only you hold the key to whether the problem can be solved and how well it can be solved! It is an incredibly serious problem, but he is putting all the responsibility on you, and you still say that he is not a slippery customer? That he's not that kind of person?"

"All right then, tell me! Whose responsibility is it? Who else is there in the city who can take control of this whole Zhongyang affair? Who else can take that responsibility?"

"Of course it's down to you! No one else is going to stick their oar in!"

"So why are you having a go at Yang Cheng for telling me to take control of it? It doesn't make sense!"

"I'll tell you the real reason, but it can't be put like this out loud." His wife still sounded completely reasonable. "It's not his place to make accusations and criticisms, and it's not his job to decide who should be in charge of Zhongyang Textiles. It's up to you to decide, not up to him."

He felt as though his wife was nudging him along in the direction she wanted and he even began to think there might be some sense in what she was saying. He chewed his food in silence, without tasting it, and didn't say anything else.

Sitting beside him, she chattered on. "Do you really reckon Yang Cheng is as simple as you think? If he was like you say, do you think he could really be such an important figure in a provincial capital? When he was in his forties, he became a member of the Standing Committee of the Provincial Party Committee, and soon he was a member of the Central Committee, a deputy secretary of the Provincial Party Committee. Now he's in his fifties, he's close to becoming the secretary and he might even go on to join the Political Bureau of the Central Committee. He is young and promising, a secretary of the Municipal Party Committee who everybody thinks is going places. Do you think he is bothered about you? Do you think he values you? Even if he does respect you at the moment, all he really respects is your influence, the fact that you are not in conflict with him and that you are not going to have any effect on his future career. He particularly needs you now because he's a newcomer. He hasn't got a firm foothold yet and his wings aren't fully fledged. Besides, you're not a bad person – you're honest, you get on with your work and don't play games. Where else is he going to find someone like that to work with? But if you think that means he'll be straight with you and not play any tricks, then you're as wrong as you can be. When the critical moment comes, he'll only think about protecting himself. Just look at the trouble with the workers at Zhongyang Textiles! Everyone knows that this is no trivial matter, that it is so serious it is going to have major repercussions and its impact will be profound. Not to mention there is no way of explaining it to the Provincial Party Committee and the Provincial Government. Today, the whole country is extremely sensitive to the reform of state-owned enterprises and there's no recovering for anyone who fails in an affair like this. Think about it! How was he ever going to take the responsibility on himself? He goes on about how serious the problem is, but he takes no responsibility. Even so he makes you think he trusts and respects you. Is that the behaviour of a simple man? But just because he is so slick, that doesn't mean you have to follow him up the greasy pole. Wait for the meeting of the Standing Committee tomorrow morning, and then your aim should be to make sure that all the decisions are collective decisions, all the responsibilities are collective responsibilities, but that all the exercise of power over specific issues is in your hands..."

Out of the blue, he suddenly wondered what it would be like if his wife was mayor and not him. What would the situation with Zhongyang Textiles be like then? It turned out that he really didn't think much of his wife. Suddenly, as if just realising something, he asked dazedly: "How do you know about the Standing Committee meeting tomorrow morning? Who told you so quickly? And what about this morning..."

"Aiya! The whole city is in an uproar and you still think you can hide things from people?" His wife was beginning to sound a little exasperated. "You still think you can keep secrets these days? You lot spend all your time talking about being open with the people, so how can you keep a meeting of the Standing Committee a deadly secret?"

Once again, he looked at his wife as if he hardly knew her. Ever since the trouble started at Zhongyang Textiles, his wife's temperament seemed to have changed completely, as had her words, actions and thinking. He was beginning to feel that the Zhongyang affair was gradually taking over his whole household.

What he was having increasing trouble understanding was how his wife had changed in the way she had over the situation at Zhongyang Textiles. What was up with her? What was behind it all?

Li Gaocheng took several phone calls, one after the other, during his meal. Almost all the calls were from top-level members of the Municipal Standing Committee and the Municipal Government.

"Mayor Li, are you going to be discussing the situation at Zhongyang Textiles at the Standing Committee meeting tomorrow?"

"Yes, but how did you know that?" Once again Li Gaocheng was puzzled. How did these people get their information so fast that they already knew the content of tomorrow's meeting?

"It's such an important matter, of course I know. Is there anything you want to say before the meeting, Mayor Li?"

"No, I'll say everything I have to say there."

"Understood. I'll know what to do at the meeting then."

Basically, they all used the same tone of voice, and they all said the same thing. What really upset him and what he least understood was how these people all seemed to understand his position and thinking on the subject, and how they all seemed to know everything about his views and opinions as well! And they all understood what they were supposed to do at the meeting!

What was it that they understood?

What were they basing that understanding on? How was it possible?

What on earth was going on?

He suddenly felt as if he had fallen into a muddy bog, unable to extricate himself, and no one could help him. All he could do was, inch by inch, sink deeper and deeper into it.

CHAPTER FIFTEEN

Li Gaocheng could never have imagined that the Standing Committee meeting would open the way it did. There was no discussion. No one made a statement. No one even said a word!

There was a brief speech by Yang Cheng, secretary of the Municipal Party Committee, followed by his own report that lasted nearly two hours. He talked about not only the views and feelings of the workers but also the views and feelings of the management of Zhongyang Textiles. The rest of the time was meant for everyone to discuss the matter and express their own opinions and ideas.

The result was a long, long silence in the room.

Secretary Yang Cheng urged people to contribute several times, and Li Gaocheng repeatedly asked everyone to let go and speak freely. But no one did.

Even their faces remained expressionless!

However, when a different subject was introduced, the room immediately came to life. The warmth of the atmosphere made it seem as though the committee members had just been released from a lengthy confinement.

The problem of Zhongyang Textiles was apparently a bottomless well that no one either dared or wanted to enter.

Was it because of him? Li Gaocheng stared at the familiar yet unfamiliar faces ranged in front of him and he suddenly recalled all those phone calls of the evening before. They had all said that everything was clear, that they understood and that they knew what to do at the meeting.

So, what exactly had they done? They hadn't said a word or made a sound. They hadn't even looked him in the eye.

What were they so worried about? What had made them like this?

He had a vague feeling that all those telephone calls of the night before could equally well have been made to Municipal Party Committee Secretary Yang Cheng.

In other words, they had probably said the same thing to both Yang Cheng, secretary of the Municipal Party Committee, and Li Gaocheng, the mayor. The result was that now they were in the meeting, none of them wanted openly to express their own opinion and they were all pretending to be deaf mutes. Obviously, the only reason for this was that they were afraid of offending one or other of the city's two principal leaders.

Why was this? Obviously again, there could only be one reason. They were actively aware, or had guessed, that there were still unresolved differences and contradictions between him and Yang Cheng on the issue of Zhongyang Textiles.

Obviously, since the mayor and the secretary of the Municipal Party Committee were in conflict on this matter, no one else at the meeting was going to put their foot in it by stirring up trouble between those two on this issue. Besides, wasn't it just a problem with a state-owned enterprise? No matter how big the problem, no matter how broad the impact, no matter how serious the situation, it didn't really have much to do with them. Wasn't that what the mayor and the secretary were there for? What were they themselves expected to do about it? It seemed that some people were only concerned with matters that involved their own interests, their careers and their personal relationships, and were quite happy to turn a blind eye and a deaf ear to things that affected the nation and the great mass of ordinary people.

But was he, Li Gaocheng, in any position to say such things about them and pass judgement on them like this?

Shouldn't he first reflect on himself and examine himself before analysing the motives of others and judging them? If the topmost beam is crooked, so will all the ones below it be, and do not subordinates always follow the example set by their superiors? If he didn't have a mature and serious position on the issue of Zhongyang Textiles, how could he expect others to express their own views and opinions without any bias or fear?

Shouldn't he be the first to express an opinion? Shouldn't he sincerely and openly express his own views and opinions without reservation, and then let everyone else have their say in order to decide what should be done?

Looking at the calm and solemn expression on the face of Yang Cheng, the secretary of the Municipal Party Committee, Li Gaocheng experienced a flash of unexpected understanding: if Yang Cheng was a good person, then he was likely to be an exceptionally good person, but if he had gone to the bad, he was equally likely to be so bad he would be impossible to control.

Yang Cheng had remained essentially silent since the beginning of the meeting; except for a few simple opening remarks, he had hardly said a thing. His expression too had remained so impassive that the other people present scarcely even looked at him. This greatly puzzled and surprised Li Gaocheng, since, based on his previous experience of the man, he rarely remained so silent at meetings like this. Indeed, at the last meeting of the Standing Committee of the Municipal Party Committee, under his influence, the atmosphere had been remarkably cordial, and the speeches had been exceptionally enthusiastic. That meeting had been called to discuss the expansion project for the main streets of the city, so it involved many serious and sensitive issues such as demolition and land use. Even so, everyone had been very open and to the point in expressing their views and opinions, and there were no constraints or taboo subjects at all. So how could the same people have changed all of a sudden today? It seemed to have a lot to do with Yang Cheng's attitude.

If Yang Cheng wanted to put stumbling blocks in his way on this issue, or if he had bad intentions towards him, then Li Gaocheng felt that it was very likely that all his own ideas and goals would come to nothing. As the situation in the current meeting made clear, Yang Cheng could embarrass and hinder him just as much as he chose to. The final result could only go one way and that was that everything would be done the way he wanted it.

But if Yang Cheng did not have any bad intentions towards him, then one way of looking at his silence quite possibly was that he was fully behind Li Gaocheng's actions and giving him his support. Or, to put it another way, Yang Cheng actually wanted to hear the real thoughts and opinions of the other members of the Standing Committee. In fact, he wanted actively to help Li Gaocheng come up with a more mature way of thinking and decision-making. This was why he had secretly told Li Gaocheng in advance his own views and opinions so that once they were in the meeting, he wouldn't give any indication of them as a sign to the others that he was fully behind the mayor's thinking on the matter of Zhongyang Textiles and that any decision taken would naturally be based on the mayor's own opinions.

If that was what Yang Cheng was thinking and what he was actually doing, then the main responsibility for how things went at the meeting rested with him, Li Gaocheng.

Yang Cheng had already clearly demonstrated his attitude to the Standing Committee as secretary of the Municipal Party Committee and that was that he was not, at the outset, going to express any opinion of his own. But his own silence as mayor, on the other hand, gave people the opposite impression: that, in an affair where emotions were rising and different opinions and conflicts were being bandied about, an affair which he should be taking control of and which no one else wanted to get involved with, what were they supposed to think when he didn't say a word? What they would inevitably think was that he was keeping quiet because he was in conflict with the Municipal Party Committee secretary.

If that was the case, then it was clear that only he could turn round the atmosphere in the meeting room. First, he had to clarify his own standpoint, and, in particular, he had to be firm on one issue – that was to let the members of the Standing Committee know that there was no room for any more delay in dealing with the problems at Zhongyang Textiles. Those problems had reached a critical juncture, and if they weren't settled once and for all, it would be a serious and irreversible mistake. This was not a matter for one person alone but something on which the whole Municipal Committee and Municipal Government must take the lead. If there really were to be bad repercussions and awful consequences, then every person there in the meeting had a responsibility that could not be shirked.

The situation was indeed serious and the problems severe, so their attitude must be resolute, and their actions decisive. That was the thinking he had to express; otherwise, it would be very difficult for the meeting to continue, and the only possible result would be that the problem of Zhongyang Textiles would just drag on meaninglessly.

Even if Yang Cheng did have ulterior motives, this was the only way to go now. All Li Gaocheng could do was assume that Yang was a genuinely good man, as that was the only way he could solve the current urgent and immediate problem.

It was at this moment that Yang Cheng was summoned to take a telephone call.

Li Gaocheng couldn't help feeling there was something odd about this, and he intuitively knew that this was no ordinary call. Anyone who could summon the secretary of the Municipal Party Committee out of a meeting of the Standing Committee over the telephone was no ordinary person.

Unless something really bad and unexpected had happened, like an accident at home or something involving his wife and children... but the chances of anything like that were very slim.

Most likely he had been summoned by the top brass. Of course, it still might be something else.

But if it wasn't something else, who could it be?

He tried guessing for himself.

He realised the rest of the committee were doing the same.

After about ten minutes, Yang Cheng returned to the committee room.

His face still gave nothing away and he didn't look at anyone. Once he had resumed his seat, he turned his head to Li Gaocheng and whispered: "Telephone call for you, in the office next door."

"Who is it?" Li Gaocheng was taken aback.

"Go and find out." Yang Cheng didn't even look at him.

Yang Cheng's secretary, Xiao Li, was waiting for him outside the committee room and led him to the office with the telephone. Then he shut the door and went quietly away.

"Hello, who's there?" Li Gaocheng asked cautiously.

"Is that Lao Li? This is Yan Zhen."

"Ai! Secretary Yan! Yes, this is Li Gaocheng speaking." It was Yan Zhen, the deputy secretary of the Provincial Standing Committee on the line! No wonder he had no scruples about calling the secretary of the Municipal Party Committee out of a meeting of the Standing Committee.

"You're in a meeting, aren't you?" Yan Zhen asked directly.

"Yes, the Standing Committee, Secretary Yan," Li Gaocheng replied, all the time trying to guess why this man might be calling. "Is there some kind of emergency?"

"There's been a lot of pressure over the last two days, hasn't there?" There seemed to be genuine kindness and concern in Yan Zhen's tone.

"...pressure?" Li Gaocheng struggled to reply for a moment. "Secretary Yan, do you mean..."

"Stop pretending you're not worried. Do you think I don't know what's being discussed in your meeting? You've always been the same, bottling up the important stuff and keeping it to yourself!" Yan Zhen was clearly speaking to him in the tone of an older man, but he was actually a year younger than Li Gaocheng.

However, Li Gaocheng had long grown accustomed to Yan Zhen's way of speaking to him. High-up officials are always trying to keep their juniors down, and in any case, it was pretty much true that Yan Zhen had been single-handedly responsible for Li Gaocheng's rise through the ranks. When Li was factory manager at Zhongyang Textiles, Yan Zhen was the mayor. If it hadn't been for Mayor Yan's support and recommendation, Li would never have got to be deputy mayor. After Li had not long been in that post, Yan Zhen was appointed head of the Organisation Department of the Provincial Party Committee and became a member of the Standing Committee of the Provincial Party Committee. It was at that point that people began to comment on what a great blessing it was for Li to have Yan Zhen behind him and that his was a lucky star that gave him such a springboard and green light to a smooth and successful career. Moreover, everyone who followed Li Gaocheng similarly seemed to enjoy dazzling success, benefitting like people enjoying the cool shade of a great tree; equally, for anyone Li Gaocheng approved of, or who he thought he could promote or redeploy, their future was pretty much assured. So, during the time Li Gaocheng was deputy mayor and Yan Zhen was head of the Provincial Party Committee Organisational Department, a large number of cadres were appointed on Li's recommendation, not to mention many of Li's subordinates, like the great majority of the senior management at the Zhongyang Textile Group, who were selected for promotion. Later still, when Li Gaocheng was recommended for the post of mayor, most people believed this also was mainly down to the part played by the head of the Provincial Party Committee Organisational Department, Yan Zhen. Without Yan Zhen's trust and support, it would have been impossible for an enterprise cadre to rise from grassroots level to become the deputy mayor, let alone the mayor, of a provincial capital city.

Everyone who knew anything about Li Gaocheng reckoned that without Yan Zhen's support, firstly he would never have become deputy mayor; secondly, he would never have become mayor; and thirdly, he would never have been able to select and appoint so many cadres.

Later on, people also said that it was because of Yan Zhen that Li Gaocheng was defeated in the competition for the post of secretary of the Municipal Party Committee, as it happened that Yan was studying at the Central Party School when the Provincial Committee was considering candidates for the Municipal Committee. Additionally, the strengthening of the push for younger cadres and the unstable economic situation in the city made it desirable that Li Gaocheng continued uninterrupted as mayor. That was why even Li Gaocheng's wife complained at every opportunity: "If you've got your support at court, then you get to do whatever it is, whether you've got the ability or not, but if your support is absent, you don't get to do anything regardless of your ability. Without Yan Zhen, did you really think a little man like you could become Municipal Party Committee secretary?"

Li Gaocheng himself had never even thought about complaining about this, and he had always greatly respected Yan Zhen. He felt that Yan was nothing like what those other people were saying and that these questions of promotion and employment were very trivial ones. He felt that Yan Zhen was decent, genuine, serious, meticulous, prudent in words and deeds, strict and upright, and he was a very shrewd judge of people. When it came to himself, Li always expressed his gratitude to and admiration for Yan Zhen from the bottom of his heart. Before Li Gaocheng became deputy mayor, he had no direct relationship with Yan Zhen as mayor, and it could even be asserted that they had scarcely any dealing of any kind with each other. His contacts with Yan at that time were mainly through work and he felt that it was principally because of his work record that he had eventually been promoted. The Zhongyang Textile Factory was very famous at the time, with a lot of powerful influence and a very prominent reputation. How aloof, how indifferent to favour or disgrace, how reliable in a crisis the Li Gaocheng of those days was, and all those qualities stemmed from his own efforts and abilities. He had no thought of giving up his current work to become any kind of government leader, nor did he ever consider, at that time, what kind of contacts, backing and support he might one day need or how much energy and material resources he would have to devote to that aspect. Before he became deputy mayor, he had never once visited Yan Zhen's home in private, rarely even went to Yan Zhen's office, and Yan Zhen had never smoked a single one of his cigarettes. This was the main reason why he still so deeply appreciated and respected him right up to the present day. Perhaps because of this, people viewed their relationship as particularly tight and mysterious. Later, when Yan Zhen returned from studying at the Central Party School, he was quickly appointed deputy secretary of the Provincial Party Committee in charge of organisation and went on to become a leading light of the committee who everyone valued and respected. Particularly recently, Yan Zhen's future prospects had become clearer and clearer, and his position had become more and more prominent and more and more secure. Not long ago, he was appointed as the executive deputy secretary of the Provincial Party Committee, not only in charge of organisation, but also of industry, economy and public security law. In addition, the provincial governor was over sixty years old, and the provincial Party secretary had been in post for nearly six years. There were rumours from time to time that he would soon be transferred to the central government or some other important position. So, people began to pay more and more attention to the measure of the Executive Deputy Secretary. What's more, except under exceptional circumstances, very few people in a province were in a position to be appointed executive deputy secretary, so

Yan Zhen's influence continued to grow. All this naturally involved Li Gaocheng, so his personal influence, whether on the Municipal Party Committee or in the Municipal Government, had also quietly increased a great deal. This was probably the main reason why the Standing Committee was currently so oppressive. One of the principal parties was a young Municipal Party Committee secretary and the other was a mayor, not yet considered old, with powerful backing who might well be in a position to remount a challenge. It was only natural that anyone would be very careful and think twice about some sensitive issues in the context of the relationship between those two players.

Li Gaocheng was more than a little puzzled by this sudden telephone call. How did Yan Zhen know there was a meeting of the Standing Committee today? He also knew the content of the meeting and the atmosphere in the room!

It suddenly struck him that Yan Zhen must have something to say to him about the Zhongyang Textiles affair.

"Secretary Yan, I know originally the first thing I should have done was to give you a briefing, but then I thought about it and decided it would be better to work out a plan before reporting back to you," Li Gaocheng said, desperately trying to work out what Yan Zhen was thinking. "You are always so busy and have so many things on your plate. The fact is, we didn't do our job properly and almost landed you with a big mess."

"Look at you getting ahead of yourself again!" Yan Zhen said with undercurrents of both benevolence and authority in his words. "Do you think this is a minor matter now that you and I are in the middle of such a tense situation? I'm telling you, some of the staff representatives from Zhongyang Textiles have already gone to Secretary Wan and Governor Wei, and I've heard that they want to take things even further. Do you know what that means?"

"Uh..." Li Gaocheng immediately froze. Secretary Wan was Wan Yongnian, the current secretary of the Provincial Party Committee, and Governor Wei was Wei Zhengguo, the current provincial governor. That meant that the representatives of the workers at Zhongyang Textiles had approached not only the most important men in the city but also the most important men in the province, right up to the top! This was something that Li Gaocheng had not expected at all. He hadn't thought those people would make such a big fuss and refuse to give up. What did it all mean? The first thing it meant was that they didn't trust him. It meant that the pressure on him was growing and growing. It meant that if the problem was not solved as soon as possible, it was likely to keep growing and growing too. Li Gaocheng tried to keep calm as he spoke into the receiver: "Did they come looking for you too, Secretary Yan?"

"What do you think? I'm the deputy secretary in charge of industry and the economy! Of course they came! Did you really think you could handle such a big problem on your own? If you had come and seen me earlier, I could have prepared myself mentally too. Do you think you can decide this kind of thing by yourself?" There was a clear sense of resentment and discontent under Yan Zhen's gentle tone. "All right, all right, I'm not really criticising your thinking. We'll talk about this again later. At this point, I just want to leave this thought with you – this issue with Zhongyang Textiles is completely within your purview. Moreover, you are familiar with the situation there, so I think it is best for you to solve their problems. It is up to you to decide how to do it, and in doing so, the main purpose is to avoid it developing any side issues or detours. Especially with something like this, you mustn't let people who are dissatisfied with the status quo and have opinions on reform take advantage of it. We are not opposed to petitioning, complaining, reporting and informing, but when it comes to petitioning and reporting, we need to separate the two issues and analyse each of them. These days, some people have access to a whole heap of information, and they seem to know absolutely everything there is to know about their work unit. How acceptable do you think that is? In addition, there are some people who are taking the opportunity of the downturn in state-owned enterprises to push liberalisation and democratisation. You need to pay attention to these issues, be wary of them, and not let people use them. I suggest that the Standing Committee considers things some more from this point of view and researches how to manage them. It is up to you to come up with ideas and not end up just going round the houses with these digressive issues. I've just explained all this to Yang Cheng, and he basically agrees with my point of view. If you have any differences of opinion that can't be reconciled, come straight to me. After the Standing Committee meeting is over, come and see me to tell me how things stand. Right, that's how I see things. Do you have any other ideas?"

"Is that what you told Yang Cheng too, Secretary Yan?" It seemed to Li Gaocheng there were some points perhaps he hadn't fully understood.

"I know you have some concerns, but what should be said, must be said. Taking into account the overall situation doesn't mean that you can't take a stand and maintain your principles. You have to be clear when you should be clear. When it is time to show your colours, you must show your colours. Yang Cheng has the advantage over you in this respect." Yan Zhen was very outspoken, and he gave the firm impression he knew everything there was to know about Li Gaocheng and Yang Cheng's views. "I made it very clear to him that these are my personal views and opinions and that I hadn't discussed them with you; otherwise, I wouldn't have called him first and then you."

For a while after hanging up, Li Gaocheng just stood there, dumbfounded. He had never expected that Yan Zhen would tell both of them the same thing at the same time! He couldn't imagine what would have gone through Yang Cheng's mind when he heard those words. What left him deeply disturbed was the thought that, after listening to what Yan Zhen had to say, Yang Cheng might think that it had all actually come from him, Li Gaocheng.

If Yang Cheng thought that or believed it might be so, then he would necessarily think that he was using Yan Zhen to put pressure on him and letting Yan Zhen say the things for him that he didn't want to or couldn't say for himself. He might also then conclude that he, Li Gaocheng, was hiding some shameful thoughts and deeds to do with the problems at Zhongyang Textiles. Otherwise, why would he get the deputy secretary of the Provincial Party Committee, Yan Zhen, to telephone him and do so with such urgency that he interrupted a meeting of the Standing Committee?

It was hardly surprising that Yang Cheng did not even look at him when he came back in the room after taking the telephone call.

It was hard to see how to explain it. If no one had tipped Yan Zhen off, why would he have called them out of the Standing Committee meeting so urgently? And why was he so agitated? There was a bit of a rumpus at one of the city's businesses, but it hadn't developed into anything. What could that possibly have to do with the deputy secretary of the Provincial Standing Committee, and why was he so excited about it?

Was it because the Provincial Government were taking the affair particularly seriously? Or was it because the provincial governor and the Provincial Party Committee secretary had both taken an interest? Or could it be because Yan Zhen's future prospects would be affected if the disturbance grew too big and began to affect his superiors?

Of course, there could be other explanations: he could have been tipped off, or someone connected with the affair could have gone to see him, or someone higher up the chain of command could have rung him...

Of course there was no way of being sure that Yan Zhen's own affairs weren't linked with it all somehow...

"...the tip of the iceberg!" The phrase leapt unbidden into Li Gaocheng's head.

He couldn't help feeling as though he was walking on thin ice across a yawning abyss.

A vague shadowy thought had been haunting him for the last few days, and now it gradually began to take shape: suppose only a fifth, even a tenth of the problems at Zhongyang Textiles were reflected in the petition materials.

With those kinds of numbers, it was no longer just a question of investigation, dismissal and punishment, but a question of sentencing, imprisonment and even execution!

If Yang Cheng's words had been frightening, General Manager Guo Zhongyao's were even more so: "...If you really look into it properly, then you really will find problems, and if you don't, you won't. If it's only a little investigation, you'll only find little problems. If it's a big investigation, you'll find big problems."

Checks or no checks, life or death, problems or no problems, responsibility or no responsibility, investigation or imprisonment, disciplinary action or execution; it seemed that all these questions were focused down here! And the very crux of the crux of the whole matter was the management!

Looking at how things stood at the moment, it could very well be that the crux of the crux of the matter was he himself!

Everlasting glory or everlasting stigma; genuine goods at fair prices or a load of tat; dragging out an ignominious existence or living a life of honour and glory; an object of scorn or a majestic presence. All this was at stake!

Either way, there was no choice. There was absolutely no middle way on this issue.

No wonder people trembled with fear at the mere mention of this affair and no wonder that an honest and upright Standing Committee meeting could be broken up by it.

Li Gaocheng pondered on all this as he silently made his way back to the meeting room.

Once he was squarely back in his seat, he looked up and realised that the whole room had gone silent. Then he saw that everyone was silently looking at him.

He suddenly came back to his senses.

He understood that now was the time he must make his position clear; now was the time to make sure everyone absolutely understood his views and opinions. First, the problems at Zhongyang Textiles were very serious ones. Second, the problems at Zhongyang Textiles could not be pushed to one side anymore. Third, the problems at Zhongyang Textiles had to be identified and investigated. Fourth, the workers at the company must be told as soon as possible how the problems at Zhongyang Textiles were going to be resolved.

CHAPTER SIXTEEN

THE MEETING ENDED at around 1.40 in the afternoon.

There was no rest break, no meal break, and no one proposed one either. Li Gaocheng's statement of his position only lasted ten minutes, but it had an enormous effect on the atmosphere of the meeting.

As soon as Li Gaocheng finished speaking, Yang Cheng immediately expressed his complete agreement with Li's views and opinions. As soon as the two men were seen to be in agreement, the atmosphere in the room immediately became much more enthusiastic. People competed to speak. Some were fierce, some were conservative; some were extreme, some were restrained. But the major sentiments were basically the same: we must use the utmost determination to solve the problems at Zhongyang Textiles as soon as possible. Most of the speeches were in the same vein: problems with state-owned enterprises were commonplace and they should use Zhongyang Textiles as a test case for finding the fundamental rules for solving the underlying problem of state-owned enterprises; all workers see things from a worker's point of view, and management has a management standpoint so it is necessary to treat both sides correctly and understand them fully; in solving problems, our fundamental purpose should be to develop the enterprise and reverse any difficulties; we should not adopt the big stick approach and order all the cadres to stand down at once or make assumptions about what the problems with them are; we must mobilise the enthusiasm of the workers, but also protect the legitimate rights and interests of business leaders... so, in one way or another, everyone showed themselves to be extremely active, extremely concerned and extremely responsible.

Li Gaocheng was amazed by the extraordinary change in mood of the meeting. He gradually began to understand that this total turnaround was the result of that telephone call. The fact that he took his stand as soon as he came back from taking the call, and that the Municipal Party Committee secretary had, just as urgently, done exactly the same thing, almost certainly resulted directly from that call and that led everyone at the meeting to understand that it was no ordinary person at the other end of the line. They were convinced that some important leadership figure had given his instructions, and that was what had brought about the change in Li Gaocheng and Yang Cheng.

This change in the two key figures and the new unity between them relieved everyone of their concerns. Now their leaders' intentions were clear, everyone believed they could speak their mind, and the atmosphere in the meeting room became a great deal warmer.

Watching what was happening in front of him, Li Gaocheng remained deeply saddened, and could not raise the least bit of enthusiasm. What was wrong with these people? Where was their sense of responsibility and concern? A company with tens of thousands of employees was unable even to pay their wages, and these people hadn't found that something to worry about? Yet all it took was just a word or a suggestion from some leader or other and they immediately took it to heart and would not dare to relax or slack off for an instant. They seemed fundamentally unconcerned about the lives and deaths of tens of thousands of people, but the attitude of some leader or other could determine all their own thoughts and actions. What gave them their real purpose in life? Was it their leaders? Was it the nation? Was it the Party? Was it the ordinary people of the country? They seemed to have lost their awareness of any of those and they had become desensitised and numb to the reality of everything that was going on around them.

If they were this topsy-turvy, if they were so undiscriminating, so insensitive, so insouciant, what was the meaning of the existence of these management cadres? What meaning was there to what they did?

Li Gaocheng suddenly realised how difficult it was for a country and a government truly to achieve democracy, justice, morality, equality, openness, transparency, integrity and righteousness.

The words of Yuan Mingliang, the old factory director of Zhongyang Textiles, came unbidden to his mind: "I have worked at Zhongyang Textiles all my life, and I have seen it all. In a country like ours, and especially in a system like ours, the key lies in the leadership, and the most important issue is the issue of cadres. An organisation must take the lead in pushing its cadres hard because if there is a problem with the cadres, the whole organisation is done for. This is quite simply because there is no one else to control them... as long as the people at the top do not care, there is nothing that the people below can do about it..."

What about themselves then?

If there was a problem with an important figure at the top level of government, if they had the support of their own superiors, what could the people below them do about it? But if there really was a problem at the top of government, what kind of desperate danger did that put the government in?

For many years now, their relationship with society had always been that the leadership cadres had been able to rely totally on the inner qualities and charisma of the individual to regulate society, as well as on those individuals' self-discipline. This meant that it often happened that a virtuous cadre could ensure the prosperity and happiness of the area of society they controlled and a rotten cadre could equally ensure the misery and devastation of his subordinates...

Now, tens of thousands of workers were crying out with hunger and cold, while they, the leadership cadres, were preoccupied with personal gain and loss and career advancement. As time passed, what ability to lead did that mean they would have, and who exactly would they be leading?

He really didn't understand why he was devoting so much thought to this. Maybe it was because the workers the night before yesterday had impressed him so deeply, so strongly, and so unforgettably. Maybe that was what had prompted him into so much fretful contemplation.

Nor could he understand why his thinking and his stance were so frequently contradicting themselves, and how the difference between the opinions he found himself holding at different times was so great. Every time he saw the tears in the workers' eyes and heard their grievances, he couldn't help but steadfastly take their part and pledge to fight constantly for their interests; but, on the other hand, when he heard the management report on their difficulties, he couldn't help putting himself in their place and feeling great sympathy with them. He felt that they were in an impossible position and that he should show them as much tolerance and understanding as possible. Faced with such conflicting opinions, he couldn't decide whether there was a problem with the position he had adopted or whether it was his emotions leading him astray.

It seemed he had a lot of thinking to do about himself.

In particular, though, it would be completely wrong and a big mistake to shuffle off all the responsibility onto these members of the Standing Committee seated in front of him now.

If he behaved correctly and honestly himself, they would act even without his orders, but if he didn't, they wouldn't obey him even if he ordered them. If he showed himself still to be confused and hesitant, he had no hope at all of anyone taking his side and speaking in support of him!

Since everyone seemed to think this was all his problem, then it was down to him to do something about it. To be honest, he really was the only person who could, and he didn't have any choice in the matter.

He proposed a complete plan of action. The first thing was to determine the policy and overall plan for solving the problems at Zhongyang Textiles. He would immediately send a working group into the company to start a comprehensive audit and investigation of the Zhongyang Textiles problem, with explicit instructions to try to resume production and let nothing get in its way. The second thing was to determine the essential nature of the problems and the starting point for conducting a comprehensive audit and investigation of them. The investigation was intended to solve the problems, not to attempt to correct individuals, let alone start any kind of correctional campaign. At the same time the format and principles of the audit and investigation were established: the audit should be focused on business affairs, not personnel, and if the problems were not finally resolved, the content of the investigation should be kept strictly confidential, so as not to trigger or increase instabilities among the workers. In addition, the composition and structure of the personnel appointed to the Zhongyang Textiles Working Group and their terms of reference were set down: the members of the working group were mainly to be drawn from the Audit Bureau and the Finance Bureau, and the main purpose of the group should be to review and check economic problems. The size of the group was set at thirty members. The responsibilities and restrictions of the group were also laid down: accepting offers of hospitality was strictly forbidden and the members had to be incorruptible, unblemished and above reproach. They had to be cautious in word and deed, and immune to both flattery and insult. During their time at the factory, they were not allowed to eat in the company canteen or at any place chosen by the company. It was strictly forbidden to leak any information on issues investigated to outside parties, especially during the course of the investigation, and it was also strictly forbidden to have any private meetings with the parties concerned. If any of these conditions were broken, there would be immediate and serious repercussions.

What caused some controversy was the choice of work unit to lead the investigation. Some people thought it would be best to instruct the Discipline Inspection Department, but others felt it better to go straight to the heart of the matter with the Legal and Political Department. There were still others who said the leaders of the Municipal Party Committee should take control and form an all-inclusive large-scale working group to conduct a comprehensive investigation.

However, all these suggestions were ultimately rejected by Yang Cheng, secretary of the Municipal Party Committee.

He believed that the main purpose of assigning a working group to Zhongyang Textiles was not to make a big splash, or cause an earthquake, but to discover the details and solve the problems as soon as possible. The workers might be making trouble because they had their own opinions, but the principal problems concerned production and finance. Of course, production problems had their roots in financial problems as, when you got down to brass tacks, did all problems in the company. In truth, financial malpractice would be bound to exist in any work unit where there was corruption. Over the past few years, there had been many loss-making work units in the city, and many businesses that could not pay their workers' wages, but there were not many with troublemakers like at Zhongyang Textiles. The main reason for this probably also stemmed from financial problems. What the workers at Zhongyang Textiles were most irate about was not simply the company's inability to pay wages, but more the major financial problems that had occurred there. So, to fully resolve the problems at Zhongyang Textiles, the first thing to do was to uncover the financial problems. Only when they were cleared up would the heartfelt doubts and grievances of the employees be eliminated. Therefore, from this point of view, the best and most practical action at this time was to send a working group to concentrate on checking and auditing the company accounts for the last few years, as soon as possible. Thus, if the main task was auditing accounts, of course it would be better to appoint staff from the Audit Bureau and the Finance Bureau as the main body of the working group. This would not only facilitate the investigation, it would also be easy to manage without affecting the everyday work of Zhongyang Textiles. In particular, it would not have too much of a psychological impact on the workers and cadres at the company. Of course, the best result would be that no problems were discovered, but, if there were inconsistencies, it would not be too late to consider bringing in the Discipline Inspection Department and the Political and Legal Department as the next step.

Everyone agreed that this was completely justified, so, with Li Gaocheng's approval, the course of action was determined.

Such were the conclusions of the Standing Committee on the issue of Zhongyang Textiles.

Everyone was talking and laughing, looking very relaxed, as if they had been relieved of a great burden. The Standing Committee was over, decisions were made, minutes had been taken and soon a corresponding document would be printed out and copied to every unit, department, organisation, factory, mine, business...

As for the specific implementation, time would tell. Maybe there would be another Standing Committee meeting soon, and maybe there would be a whole new programme and a new round of wrangling...

Li Gaocheng found himself unable to settle down. He felt very vividly that the burdens the others had put down had all been heaped on his shoulders. All this was just the beginning. How was he actually going to deal with the problem of Zhongyang Textiles? How was he going to get to the crux of the matter? How deep and murky was this pool? In truth, everything was still an unknown quantity.

When he walked out of the conference room, he found Yang Cheng waiting silently outside. The man's face was giving nothing away, but his tone of voice was pretty relaxed.

"Why don't we have something to eat at my home? In any event, your wife's away and don't you want to see what I've done with the place you allocated me?"

Li Gaocheng hadn't expected this invitation, but he agreed immediately, without even thinking about it. He knew that as mayor, he couldn't refuse such an invitation from the secretary of the Municipal Party Committee.

CHAPTER SEVENTEEN

YANG CHENG'S HOUSE was a two-storey building with a courtyard. It was in a quiet location on the edge of the city.

According to his rank, Yang Cheng should have been living in the residential area allocated to provincial-level leaders. The environmental conditions in there were much better than here, and it was located in the prosperous part of town, very close to the Municipal Government. It would have been very convenient for his own work, his other family members' work and his child's school. But in the end, Yang Cheng rejected this location and gave up the house he was originally allocated to the deputy director of the Provincial People's Congress who was about to retire.

There were a lot of rumours about this at the time. Of course, there was another explanation for Yang Cheng's decision: a newly-appointed official makes bold moves to win over the hearts of the people and is willing to take a small loss to gain a big advantage...

Although it was the middle of winter, Yang Cheng's yard didn't seem to show any sign of the season at all. Several emerald-leaved evergreens acted like walls, dividing the yard into square blocks. More than a dozen pine trees swayed neutrally in the cold wind, neither imposing themselves nor shrinking back. However, two vigorous wintersweets gave Li Gaocheng a fresh feeling. Their crowns were full of sweet-smelling yellow flowers, and the colour and fragrance brought a freshness to the whole courtyard. From a distance, the yard looked somewhere between sparse and cluttered in a picturesque disorder. All this gave a clear picture of an occupant who knew how to live well and was a very calm and fulfilled person.

Li Gaocheng looked at the things in the yard in surprise, and his mood suddenly cheered up.

He had never imagined that the change in this courtyard could be so great. When Yang Cheng had first moved in, the yard was clean but barren looking. Now, in however long it had been, the place was lush with trees and bamboos, tall thickets and abundant grasses. It was very colourful, dark and sweet-smelling with crisscrossing branches. It had become a proper small garden.

"When you look at this yard, don't you immediately get the impression that the tenant is not a corrupt person but is certainly a lazy, idle fellow?" Yang Cheng asked with a self-deprecating smile.

"Not necessarily! Have you never heard what those poetic scribblers and scholars say? A man who loves flowers must be a man who loves life. But even a man who doesn't love life can still love this country of ours and can still love its people. Those poets are not entirely useless." Yang Cheng's humour had immediately communicated itself to Li Gaocheng.

"When someone engages in corruption, they inevitably have a faction who defend that corruption. Throughout history, princes and ministers have kept such groups of scholars and politicians beside them so they can listen to their excuses and flattery. They tell him the bad is good, the stinking is fragrant, the dead are living, and black is white. In fact, there are many such people with us now, making it hard for us to defend against them and difficult to tell truth from fiction." There was still a good-humoured look on Yang Cheng's face, but the tone of his words had changed.

Li Gaocheng too was still smiling, but inside he was quietly analysing Yang Cheng's words very carefully. The man was always like this; from time to time he would say or do something unexpected and intriguing. It was what made him so inscrutable and unpredictable.

"In fact, I have to say that my yard is much worse than yours," Yang Cheng said very earnestly this time. "Don't be fooled by all the gaudy, ostentatious flowers – there really aren't many serious and worthwhile flowers and plants in this yard. But I have made a serious study of your courtyard, and, at current prices I don't think I could buy what you have for less than forty or fifty thousand yuan."

"Really?" Li Gaocheng put on a disbelieving expression. "Let me see. Let's not say forty or fifty thousand. You can have the lot for ten thousand. It's my decision."

"Really?" Yang Cheng echoed, equally disbelievingly. "I put together my courtyard with my own hands, but, from what I know, you never did anything to yours yourself. I've just seen how you evaluate flowers, and I can tell that you are an amateur. I'm afraid to say you know little or nothing about the current market situation here, or the level of expertise and the deals that are done here."

Li Gaocheng laughed, neither admitting nor denying it. "Are you saying that I am afraid of my wife?"

"No, no, it would be a big mistake to say that. In fact, you love your wife very much."

At this, the two of them began to laugh uproariously.

Yang Cheng's home was in exquisite taste but not luxurious, and felt clean and relaxing. To Li Gaocheng's surprise, there were no famous paintings or pieces of calligraphy in the reception room. He had been to many leaders' homes, and what had always made an impression on him was that the higher the level of the leader, the more famous calligraphy and paintings there were in the household, and the better their quality. This seemed to have become a sign of status and identity, which imparted an impression and atmosphere of importance, nobility and elegance without any suggestion of extravagance, corruption and ostentation. It not only symbolised luxury and status, but also gave people an impression of honesty and connoisseurship. It could only be a good thing, so why not do it? Thus there were more and more works by famous painters and calligraphers in the homes of the leaders, and, naturally the higher those leaders climbed the higher the level of the art. Hardly surprisingly, paintings and calligraphy had consequently become a symbol of wealth. But ordinary people could not afford them, and the rich people who could afford them did not put them on public display in their reception rooms. So once again, it was clear that whether in wealth or status, prestige or position, it was the leaders who were superior.

So, Li Gaocheng did not hang any art in his home, or at least rarely hung any. It was not that he didn't have any, nor that no one gave him any; in fact, if he said the word, he could have whatever piece of calligraphy or painting he wanted by whatever famous artists in the city, province, and even further afield. It was not that Li Gaocheng really didn't want any of this, it was just that the cost was far too high. Generally speaking, a painting by a famous artist was not something you got for nothing. If you did accept one, the other party was extremely likely to present you with a string of demands. For example, for you to allocate him tens of thousands of yuan to hold an art exhibition, or to publish a volume of his paintings, or to give him an opportunity to go abroad, or even to get a good house for him and so on. Of course, there were also people who gave you calligraphy and paintings as part of a group or organisation, but that was never for free either. In fact, the money involved might well be even more; to build a dormitory block, for example, or an office building, or to increase a grant or fund an extracurricular event.

That was why Li Gaocheng didn't have any paintings; he didn't want to bring trouble down on himself.

So when he saw that there were no paintings on the walls of Yang Cheng's home, he felt that the two of them had drawn a little closer or, at least in some respects, their thinking and feelings were probably the same. What people called an "intimate friendship" was probably confirmed, bit by bit, from things like this.

The tea leaves that Yang Cheng produced for him were pretty good, being fresh, unadulterated Longjing, but the way he brewed them left a lot to be desired. He just put the leaves in the cup, without regard to quantity, brought over the water thermos, tipped the water in, any old how, and that was that. Yang Cheng must have been thirsty because he just thrust his lips under the leaves, which were still floating on the surface, and drank away. The water obviously wasn't too hot, as, after he finished the whole cup, the tea leaves hadn't even wilted. He immediately poured another cup and gulped it down too. It wasn't until the nanny brought in the food that he reluctantly put down the cup and invited Li Gaocheng to eat.

The dishes were pretty good and included garlic spinach, vinegared cabbage, stewed beef, pork with preserved vegetables, a large pot of stewed mutton with carrots, and two plates of delicious, light cold dishes, which served to stimulate the appetite.

The luxury was the wine: two 250cl bottles of Maotai.

"Let's take advantage of my wife being away to have a decent drink." Yang Cheng looked as though he was keen to get drinking.

"Wow! Are you hen-pecked or what?" Li Gaocheng asked laughingly.

"You and me both! Do you think I don't know it?! Would you be drinking if Wu Aizhen was home?" Yang Cheng was struggling to open the bottle, but it seemed to be giving back as good as it got, and after a long unsuccessful battle, he asked suspiciously: "Do you think it's a fake bottle?"

"Huh, what desperado would be reckless enough to give the secretary of the Party Committee a fake bottle?"

"You think? It's 1980 vintage. Were there fakes back then?"

"Let me have a go. I'm no expert but I've seen it done." Li Gaocheng took the bottle and tried to open it with a very professional air.

The result was the same, and even after some time, the bottle remained steadfastly sealed. The two men looked at each other and spontaneously burst out laughing.

In the end, the nanny came in and finally succeeded in opening the bottle by sawing away at it with a knife.

It was the real stuff all right, pure and bright with a powerful aroma that got you drunk before you had even tasted it.

With two cups inside them, both men seemed to have become immersed in the fragrance of the wine and neither said a word.

At length, Yang Cheng said with great feeling: "They say that all leaders are corrupt now, and it's true when you think about it. How many ordinary people can hope to attain this standard of living?"

"That may be true, but aren't we a bit phoney and hypocritical to be talking about it like this?" Li Gaocheng was one of those people who had an allergic reaction to alcohol and went red in the face as soon as the wine was inside him. Although it was not a very serious reaction, the alcohol did also make him very sad and emotional.

"Of course, it all depends who you are comparing it to. Sure, this standard is much higher than your average worker can hope for, but compare us to the big shots and money bags and we're practically peasants. But leaders like us really don't know what ordinary people are saying behind our backs. Things like, we have millions of yuan in savings, we're always being given stuff, we throw diamond necklaces out with the rubbish and we don't dare report a theft from our homes. Their accusations are scattergun, and for every hit they make, someone slips through the net. Public officials are in the top rank of society, and the people should want the best for them, but they accuse us of lounging in the sauna all day and playing mah-jong into the small hours of the morning... What kind of people tell these lies? There are even authors who put this stuff in their novels. Let the two of us here be honest – are all of today's leadership cadres really as honest and upright as they say they are?" Yang Cheng was clearly getting more voluble now he was several cups of wine down.

"When a single mouse can spoil a whole crock of food, it's not easy to be a leader in the Communist Party. To be blunt about it, in China now, it's not such a big deal if you find bad apples no matter what field they're in, and it's really quite understandable that they're there. The only place we can't have any is in Party and government departments. Anywhere else, one in every hundred people can be corrupt and everyone will understand and no one will think anything of it. But, in a Party or government department, if there is one bad apple in a thousand, it gets hyped up out of all proportion and you would think that every Communist Party cadre in the country is as black as sin. In fact, if I may say so, you will find this kind of evil amongst our own cadres, but I'm not talking about those cadres who have done something bad, I mean those ones who keep their own hands clean but accuse the whole team of cadres of being a disgrace. Those ones are cadres who have become dissatisfied, or who haven't achieved what they wanted to, so they ginger up the evidence, exaggerate what's being said, add fuel to the fire with a mixture of truth and invention and get the ordinary people all riled up along with them. Then the mess of gossip and speculation blackens the name of our whole team!" Li Gaocheng went even redder in the face as he said this.

"The way I see it, Lao Li, it's better to believe it's happening than not. I'm saying that not because I don't have faith in our Party spirit, and certainly not because I want to condemn our whole team of cadres." Yang Cheng's face was also beginning to redden. "First of all, I really don't believe our cadres are that bad. Secondly, I certainly don't even believe that one in a thousand of our cadres is rotten. If it was us who had gone to the bad, I certainly wouldn't think that all our cadres would do the same. Of course, if we have kept our integrity, I don't expect all our cadres to have done the same either. Take the issue of food and drink, for example – we've issued order after order and warning after warning, it has been discussed over and over, and many systems have been set up prohibiting wastefulness and extravagance with food and drink. If any cadres are found out eating and drinking just as they please, they will be severely punished. What is more, we formulated the 'four dishes one soup' rule, but how has that worked out? We leadership cadres certainly follow it, but do the lower-level cadres do the same? In particular, did the cadres you have around you follow it? Did the cadres above us? When I was in the Prefectural Committee, I once went to the lower office on an inspection. Before leaving, I repeatedly told my secretary that drinking alcohol was strictly prohibited and so were banquets. The 'four dishes and one soup' rule had to be strictly implemented. At first, I thought it was really effective. I went for a meal with a group of important leaders, and we didn't even have beer. But, as time went on, I found out that there was a problem with that. It turned out that it was all just for show! It turned out that they were all just gulling me! Later on, I even started fooling myself over this. What kind of fucking secretary of the Party Committee does that make me?" With that, Yang Cheng drained his cup at a gulp, and perhaps he drank it a little too violently, because he didn't speak again for quite a while.

"I may not be very clear about how things stand out in the countryside, but at any rate, when I was working in the textiles sector, whenever we were visited by senior leadership cadres, they were all scrupulously honest, and no one would have dared try and deceive them. If an illustrious Prefectural Party Committee secretary, such as you are, goes on an inspection visit, who would dare try anything on, especially when they know there's a crackdown on the rules?" Li Gaocheng felt himself gradually being irresistibly swept up in the power of Yang Cheng's words.

"Do you know how bold they're getting?" Yang Cheng wasn't going to drop the subject, and his anger was still simmering away. "In the dining room of the county guest house, there were four of us having a meal, including the secretary of the County Party Committee and the county magistrate, and we really did stick to four dishes and one soup. But there were a dozen or so of our entourage, including some county cadres, right under our noses in the room next door. We could even hear their voices quite clearly through the wall, and they were really spreading themselves with all kinds of delicacies and big fish and meat dishes. There were beer and spirit bottles littering the table! You ask how they dared? Well, my secretary told me afterwards that they had said that leadership cadres were all the same everywhere. The regulations were about as effective as a gust of wind, and they were all just pretending to do what they were supposed to. What is happening, in particular, is that the leaders are turning a blind eye, and even if they see what is going on, they make out they haven't. So their subordinates aren't afraid of anything. What kind of a thing is that to say, you ask? I'm just saying that if you leaders want to act like goody two-shoes, go and act like goody two-shoes. Just make sure the grown-ups have something decent to eat. They were making donkeys out of us, putting all us important leaders together in one room and giving us four dishes and one soup. It was all monkey tricks at our expense. Just think how sad it is for a leader to be in that position. If all leadership cadres are like that, what hope is there for them!"

"Ah yes! I remember now!" Li Gaocheng suddenly recalled something as he looked at Yang Cheng's furious expression. "A year or so ago, weren't two County Party Committee secretaries sacked because of something to do with food and drink? Was that your doing?"

"Actually, there were a lot of cases like that, and when I was Prefectural Party Committee secretary, there were a lot of measures taken to crack down hard on the open giving of gifts to cadres during the New Year and other festivals, and also on the giving of disguised gifts. At the time, I told my secretary and the security guards over and over that they weren't to admit anyone who came to my house carrying gifts. What was the result? No one gave me any gifts and the number of people who came to see me not for work but to try and exploit connections grew a lot less too. But I found out after a while that some of my subordinates were giving gifts to my secretary and my guards in order to get to see me. If the people close to you dare do that kind of thing, what chance have you got with people outside your immediate circle? Do you think you can spot them? Do you think you can stop them?"

Li Gaocheng let what Yang Cheng was saying sink in, and it gradually dawned on him that the man had summoned him to his home with a definite message for him. He didn't reply but sat in silence, eating, drinking... and listening.

"Sometimes, Lao Li, I think to myself that the burden on our generation of leaders is really too heavy, much too heavy. Nothing really creditable ever comes to us, but when problems arise they are heaped on us one after the other. How do we bear it?" Yang Cheng's words sounded like a complaint, but there seemed to be an accusatory note to them too. "Our predecessors came through a forest of guns and a hail of bullets, and the people they led were the common people who had come through from the old society. But it is completely different now, and even our children are sneering at us, 'Don't you know we're in the twenty-first century? What old calendar are you working from?' Sometimes, the more I think about it the more frightened I am. What do people like us who are running the country have to rely on? What do we really have to rely on? For example, if there is a problem with five out of a hundred cadres, what should we do about it? What if it's ten? Or twenty? Or thirty? Can we handle it? Can we prevent it? Do we dare take control of those cadres with problems? Can we control them? Do we have the ability? Do we have the courage? Also, do we really have the authority? The most important thing is that when the interests of the country, the Party and the individual are all put in front of us at the same time, what kind of choice do we make? Particularly in some exceptional circumstances, when you choose the interests of the Party and the country, it will likely damage your personal interests, even your position and power. In that case, what do you do?"

Although Li Gaocheng did not know exactly what Yang Cheng was implying, he felt deeply moved. He told himself he hadn't experienced anything like what Yang Cheng had been talking about, but how many things had gone against his conscience since he joined the city government? So, in fact, he thought, every one of us encounters this kind of thing almost all the time, but how many people stop to think about it that way? When absolute obedience conflicts with the fundamental interests of the Party, what should a true communist do? How about himself? What would he do?

At this point, Yang Cheng gathered the two wine glasses together, filled them both, and then offered one to Li Gaocheng, respectfully using both hands. His face was flushed, but he sounded very sincere as he said: "Lao Li, this glass of wine is my tribute to you. I have been here for more than a year now, and thanks to your support, we have been able to cooperate well together and our whole team is firmly united. Let me say though, it has not all been easy. To be honest, when I first arrived, I was really afraid that you would make trouble for me, because people said that this post of secretary of the Municipal Party Committee should have been yours. The way I have been talking today may not be in line with organisational principles, but it all comes from the heart. I'm not telling a word of a lie when I say that I am really fortunate to be working with a person like you."

"...what's going on with you, Yang Cheng? What is today all about?" Seeing Yang Cheng like this, Li Gaocheng didn't know what to say. "How could our team work effectively if it was just me in charge? Surely you are being too self-deprecating, talking like this!"

"I am speaking from my heart now, and you know that I am not one to spray compliments around willy-nilly. I know very well that you are a practical, straightforward man and you never mess around behind people's backs. You are never defensive or suspicious and are always direct. You say what you think, and you always address the problem not the people. This is what everyone says about you and what I, personally, greatly respect about you. What today is all about is getting on with our cooperation and getting things done!" When Yang Cheng finished, not bothering whether Li Gaocheng followed suit or not, he tilted his head back and drained his cup at a single gulp.

When they had drunk the wine, the two men found themselves with nothing left to say. Although Li Gaocheng had drunk quite a lot, his head was still perfectly clear. What was going on with Yang Cheng today? He had brought out the Maotai as if he was full of worries and had encouraged the two of them to drink as much as they had. Was it because of today's Standing Committee meeting? Was it because of Deputy Provincial

Committee Secretary Yan Zhen's telephone call? Or was it because of something else he still had to say to him? Or could it even be that he felt he had gone too far in their conversation yesterday and had brought him here specifically to apologise and to express his true feelings?

Unlikely. Yang Cheng wasn't that kind of person; it wasn't in his nature. The reason he had shown the depth and weight of his emotions today, emotions which he had kept bottled up inside him for so long, had to be that there was some dark secret inside there too.

What could it be? What was it that Yang Cheng wanted to say to him?

"I am quite sure you have something to say to me, Secretary Yang." Li Gaocheng cut straight to the point. "I know you didn't ask me here today just to taste your vintage wine."

Yang Cheng didn't reply for quite a while and finally said, with a startled look in his eyes: "I have already told you several times, Lao Li, that the key to whether the business with Zhongyang Textiles ends well or badly rests with you. On consideration, I think what I have just said was rather too self-centred."

"I certainly didn't have that feeling." Li Gaocheng really hadn't expected Yang's reply.

"It's not your feelings that I'm talking about, but mine." Yang Cheng said equably. "Another thing I have repeatedly told you is that, in general, there is nothing to be greatly afraid of in the problems at Zhongyang Textiles. The only real fear is that they prove to be the tip of the iceberg. I don't know if you've had time to think that through carefully for yourself, because there are some things I don't feel I can go into more detail about with you. But I have come to understand, particularly after I had that call from Secretary Yan Zhen during the Standing Committee, that there are some things I need to explain to you at this point. I can't keep you in the dark, but what I could do is tell you, with the greatest respect and deference, that it is up to you to handle the whole affair. But it would be too immoral to do that. I am, after all, still Party secretary and I'm in charge. No matter how big the matter is, I should take the main responsibility."

"Have you discovered something, or heard something?" Li

Gaocheng found himself asking as he was drawn back into the peculiar atmosphere of the occasion.

"Have you read all the materials the representatives of the staff of Zhongyang Textiles submitted today?" Yang Cheng asked unexpectedly as he poured some more wine.

"I've read them through once, and their basic meaning is clear." Li Gaocheng actually thought to himself that he had read them very carefully.

"I'm not talking about the petition calling for an investigation; I mean the list of accounts of Xinchao Co. Ltd."

"Same answer – I've had a quick look through them. I hadn't expected Zhongyang Textiles' tertiary business to have so many companies or be such a big organisation. Ah! Are you saying that's where the biggest problems are?"

"Did you bring the two documents with you? Are they in your briefcase?"

"I've got them here. Is there a problem with them?" Li Gaocheng said, taking the documents out of his briefcase.

"You can see here that there is a transport company called 'Te Gao Te' under the Xinchao Company umbrella. This company has nearly fifty large luxury limousines, and pretty well monopolises all the passenger transport business to and from the Beijing Expressway. The entire company has more than 50 million yuan in fixed assets and an annual profit of more than 10 million. It counts as one of the largest subsidiaries of Xinchao Co. Ltd and it is also one of the most profitable..."

Li Gaocheng pondered the possible problems here while watching Yang Cheng pointing to different parts of the material in front of them.

"Think how much annual profit a transport company with all those advantages should make. You can see the company was first formed in 1993 and took out a loan of 20 million yuan from Zhongyang Textiles, but didn't declare a cent of profit. In 1994, it took another loan from Zhongyang Textiles for 15 million, again without declaring a cent of profit. Before October 1995, it took up another 8 million with the same result. The location of the Te Gao Te Transport headquarters comprises an area of thirty *mu*, and it occupies more than fifteen thousand square metres of public housing, without ever paying a cent for land occupation and use. Over nearly three years, it has neither paid a penny of profit to the state nor repaid a penny of interest on the state's loans. Essentially, it is using state money for a private enterprise. Think about it! Who might it be who has the opportunity and nous to take up tens of millions of loans from the Zhongyang Textile Group without paying out a penny of profits or interest?"

Li Gaocheng began to feel the weight of Yang Cheng's words. It seemed that he hadn't been reading carefully enough and had not thought things through the way Yang Cheng had.

"Who do you think the bosses of the Te Gao Te Transport Company are? The general manager is Zhang Dewu. He doesn't have any influential backers, but he is a real expert. He understands the passenger transport business and was the deputy general manager of the old provincial transport company. The two deputy general managers are drawn from the workers and they also understand business and have good communication skills. The problem is that on this board of directors, there is a vice chairman named Wang Yiliang. Do you know who he is?" Yang Cheng looked directly at Li Gaocheng as he asked the question.

Li Gaocheng suddenly remembered who the man was: he was a former Zhongyang Textiles manager who had worked at the company for many years. When Li Gaocheng was the factory manager there, Wang Yiliang was already the vice manager. He had not thought that he could be in such an important position as vice chairman of the Te Gao Te Transport Company so soon after his retirement! No wonder the company could get its hands on so many loans! Li Gaocheng was more than a little surprised and said: "How could it be him? I really didn't expect that..."

"Don't get yourself too excited about that, there's more to come! Do you know who the chairman of the board, Chao Yuye, is?"

Li Gaocheng thought about it. The name seemed familiar but he couldn't pin it down.

"You won't recognise the name, but you definitely know who he is. He is the younger brother of Deputy Provincial Party Secretary Yan, who called both of us today on the telephone. Chao Yuye is just a pseudonym to keep his chairmanship secret – he's really Chao Wanshan, the current deputy director of the Economic

Policy Theory Research Office of the Provincial Party Committee!"

"...Ah!!" Li Gaocheng gasped and sat there, lost for words for a moment.

Secretary Yan Zhen's brother-in-law! How was that possible?

"Is that really true? Has it been investigated..." Li Gaocheng asked in a daze, after a long pause.

"I didn't believe it at the time either. They asked me to call on the spot to check, so I did, and it turned out that they weren't lying. It is all true, and this man in his forties, who holds the real power at the Te Gao Te Transport Company, this Chao Yuye, is indeed Yan Zhen's wife's younger brother, Chao Wanshan. There's no mistake – it's all true. Those staff representatives didn't tell you straight out and just wrote 'relative of a provincial party committee leader' in brackets. But they told me that was because they all knew about your relationship with Secretary Yan Zhen, and they were afraid that if you knew about it, no one would be sent to look into it. It's all true. I wouldn't try and lie to you about something this big."

Yang Cheng's voice was not loud, but every sentence hit Li Gaocheng's heart like a hammer. It was no wonder he had felt the name was somehow familiar, because he knew that Yan Zhen's wife's surname was Chao, and that wasn't a common name in the city.

If all this was true, it was no longer any surprise that Yan Zhen had called both him and Yang Cheng out of the meeting and had talked to him in the way he did!

Everything was clear now! Yan Zhen was saying that he shouldn't let anyone stick their oar into the Zhongyang Textiles business and it would be far better not to investigate it! Also, the management team should stay in place!

How righteous and upright Yan Zhen's words had sounded, how open and candid! All that stuff about needing to be wary of some people taking advantage of the situation to cause trouble, about needing to prevent people from taking advantage of the opportunity to pursue liberalisation and democratisation? And all that stuff about how there are so many people today who love to make complaints, and how many whistleblowers there are...

So that's how things stood!

But what Yan Zhen wanted was for him to take the lead in

dealing with the problems at Zhongyang Textiles. Why? Was it just because it was Yan Zhen who had promoted him, so he didn't think he would pose any threat or cause any trouble for him? And wouldn't the others in Yan Zhen's circle naturally feel more comfortable if it was him in charge?

Or did Yan Zhen think that he might still have some dirt on his hands from his dealings with the company? Even the workers at Zhongyang Textiles were suspicious of him and were reluctant to tell him the truth, so how would those leading cadres be viewing him? How would they think to handle him? Perhaps this was the real reason why no one on the Standing Committee had anything to say.

As he sat there in a daze, Yang Cheng whispered in his ear again: "There is one more thing Lao Li, but I don't know if I should tell you or not."

"What else?" a startled Li Gaocheng asked.

"I'm really afraid that you won't be able to take it..." Yang Cheng was very hesitant.

Li Gaocheng picked up his wine cup, drained it with a glugging sound, and then said, fiercely: "After all you've already said, what is there you can be afraid of telling me?" Li Gaocheng was almost stuttering with the tension now. Didn't you just say that everybody else knew this stuff and I was the only person it was being kept from? Are you deliberately trying to hurt me?!"

"All right then, I'll tell you." Yang Cheng also drained his wine cup in one go, and then went on to refill both cups as he said: "If you go to the second page of the accounts, you'll see a Green Apple Entertainment City Co. Ltd. It is also a subsidiary of Zhongyang Textiles' Xinchao Co. Ltd. The year before last year, Zhongyang Textiles invested 6 million yuan in it. It is a leisure company that covers restaurants, dance halls, karaoke halls and saunas. The business is surprisingly good. The boss of the company is known as Huizi. That is not his real name, but you'll know exactly who he is when you hear what it is. He is the son of your wife's older brother, Wu Baozhu..."

"That's nonsense!" Li Gaocheng was furious, and before Yang Cheng could finish, he slammed his fist on the table and leapt to his feet. "I don't know about all the other stuff, but I'm absolutely sure about this. Baozhu did set up a karaoke hall, but it was only a small place of about sixty square metres. I went there a few days ago. Baozhu is on duty there every day. What's all this about Green Apple Entertainment City? How could he keep a company that size secret from me? It's nonsense!"

"You really didn't know about this?" Yang Cheng seemed happy to see how angry Li Gaocheng was. "If that's the case, I've got nothing to worry about. But Lao Li, on my honour as Municipal Party secretary, I assure you that what I've said is absolutely true, and I take full legal responsibility if one word is false! There is no need for us to be at loggerheads anymore. I think you'd better go to the Green Apple Entertainment City this evening to have a look, and then you will understand everything at a glance. That's what the employee representatives told me. They said that the facts speak louder than words. As long as you are willing to go, as long as you dare to go, there is no need for us to say anything more…"

Dumbstruck, Li Gaocheng just stared at Yang Cheng. He felt that the floor beneath his feet was collapsing, and he was sinking deeper and deeper into…

CHAPTER EIGHTEEN

The Green Apple Entertainment City was done out in fine style.

The multicoloured neon signs and decorative lights made the place feel as mysterious and enchanted as a fairy castle. It was probably this atmosphere that attracted so many customers.

Its location was excellent too.

It was in the busiest area of the city, but quite a quiet part of it, and that was probably another reason it was doing such good business.

There were a lot of customers, especially for the private karaoke rooms, which were doing amazing business. At just after six o'clock, they were all booked, and there was a bunch of people waiting in the main karaoke room, so that room was doing excellent business as well. The restaurant was thriving too as it was pretty much full and there was a waiting list for the private rooms. What most surprised Li Gaocheng was that the sauna and spa, which cost several hundred yuan a time, was also doing pretty well too. That was amazing for such an expensive establishment. There were so many big-bellied, arrogant bigwigs and bosses with their gorgeously dressed wives and young women that the place looked as busy as a bustling marketplace.

However, Li Gaocheng felt an unexpected melancholy as, when he looked at this magnificent, luxurious palace of entertainment, what he was actually seeing was the rusted workshop door at Zhongyang Textiles. When he looked at those arrogant strutting men and women, what he was actually seeing was the thousands of textile workers whose salaries weren't even being paid, standing around in the snow and ice.

A lump came unbidden to his throat.

People were saying that what was fashionable now was a kind of one-stop shop: dancing, eating, sauna, singing, playing cards, starting in the afternoon and going on until the early morning. For one visit, the average expenditure per person was over a thousand yuan, more if there were "special requirements"!

This fee for one visit was almost two months' wages for an average worker! If there were ten people in a group, it meant that the fee was almost equivalent to two years' wages for one worker, or two months' wages for ten workers, or one month's wages for twenty workers.

If twenty workers toiled away for a month without eating or drinking, they would just be able to afford one visit for one person.

Was it hard work that wasn't worth money, or was it money that wasn't worth money? Where did these people get the money from?

There were so many companies and factories in the country that were borrowing and losing money! Tens of thousands of workers were unemployed and without wages! The population below the poverty line was increasing rapidly, but the amount of savings in the banks was also increasing rapidly! That is to say, there were more and more poor people and there was more and more money, so where did all the money go?

Who on earth was it, snatching away such a large amount of the wealth of the country and of the people?

Who was responsible for the development and expansion of this abnormal consumption?

Of course, this was also answering the demands of society. Development is led by social demand and only occurs when there is such a demand. This is just universally recognised common sense. But wasn't there also a more urgent social need to maintain the most basic living requirements of the workers? Weren't the genuine, high-quality, cheap domestic products of state-owned enterprises also what people expected and needed? In contrast to private enterprise, was not the extreme fairness and justice shown to workers in state-owned enterprises just what our country needed most? In particular, weren't social stability and common prosperity also demanded by the nation and the people? Isn't that a long-term need? So why was it that the response to such social demands was not increasing, indeed was actually shrinking, while provision for these new, superfluous demands was thriving and growing?

Li Gaocheng felt an indefinable awareness growing inside him. Who was he, mayor of a provincial capital with a population of several million, supposed to be asking about such things? Should he be asking other people or asking himself? Wasn't this his own figurative province? Didn't it lie within his own sphere of authority?

Then there was the most awful aspect of this business. If this magnificent place of entertainment that only catered to the wealthy was indeed built and operated by the Zhongyang Textile Group Company – the company which had stopped production, whose workers were not getting their wages, and which was millions of yuan in debt – how pitiably ironic that would be for the workers, for the business, for the country and for the mayor! And if this place for the wealthy was run by the mayor's nephew, then how pitiful it was for him as mayor – how hateful, how sinister and how hypocritical!

It would almost be reasonable to say that his own existence was the most direct cause of the slump in the company's business and the losses it was suffering.

If there was cheating and deception involved, then he was the backer of the cheat; if there were criminal offences involved, then he was the accomplice of the criminal.

If he were to claim he knew nothing about it, that would be an even greater dereliction of duty. Everyone would think he was lying and talking nonsense. Even Yang Cheng had his doubts, and if even Yang Cheng didn't believe him, how many of the ordinary people did he think would have faith in him?

Li Gaocheng stood stiffly at the entrance of the Green Apple Entertainment City. He was getting angrier and angrier the more he thought about it. And the more he thought about it, the more he hated it.

He no longer doubted the authenticity of what Yang Cheng had told him, and the only reason he had come was to confirm just how his brass-necked and shameless nephew had hidden something so big from him for such a long time. The only reason his nephew could have dared to be so bold, so presumptuous, and so reckless, was because he had a powerful backer. And that backer was his wife, Wu Aizhen!

His secretary, Wu Xingang, stood silently behind the mayor. Although Li Gaocheng hadn't told him anything, he seemed to realise that something was up.

Although singing and dancing seemed to have become a popular measure of a cadre's commitment to "opening up", Li Gaocheng had never been to a place like this before.

He was appalled.

It wasn't because he was too stuffy and unenlightened but because he simply couldn't stand the mood and atmosphere of the dance hall.

Having lived among the workers for decades, he felt an invisible and intangible bond with them. He really couldn't face the fact that the money earned by their blood, sweat and tears could have flowed out of the company like bathwater down a plughole. When the living standards of tens of millions of people were still below the poverty line, wasn't it too extravagant, too self-indulgent, too depraved even, for people who called themselves servants of the people to spend money in places like this?

He didn't have the right sort of face. As he silently went in through the main doors, the security guards, who were probably brought in from out of town, or who perhaps didn't watch much television, immediately stopped the rather ordinary-looking Li Gaocheng. It didn't help that he was wearing an old army greatcoat at the time.

"Excuse me, sir, but have you come here to eat or are you looking for someone?" one of the doormen asked politely enough, but there was a tone of icy contempt underlying the courtesy, which clearly said: "This isn't your kind of place. What are you doing here?"

"I'm looking for someone," Li Gaocheng said, his anger flaring.

"Looking for who?" The doorman seemed completely unmoved by his anger, and not the least bit put out.

"Your manager!"

"The manager's not in. Please come back later..." The doorman seemed to be playing games with him and clearly didn't want to let him in.

"Well, you just call him up now and tell him that an old bastard called Li is waiting for him and ask him to get the fuck down here in ten minutes!" Li Gaocheng exploded.

By this time, his secretary, Wu Xingang, had put himself in front of the mayor, and told the doorman to call their manager immediately. At this point, the doorman began to feel there might be something wrong; he looked at the faces of Li Gaocheng and Wu Xingang a couple of times, and then walked uneasily into the glass vestibule to make a phone call.

The call lasted five or six minutes until the doorman put the phone aside and came running out to say: "Our manager is asking what your name is."

"...tell him that when he gets here, he'll know as soon as he sees me!" Li Gaocheng was so furious he was on the point of cursing out the doorman, stupid bastard that he was!

The doorman took another three or four minutes to finish the call before he came back out. Although his attitude had improved, his tone was still rather offhand. "Our manager says that if you want to eat, you should go and eat first. If you want to have some fun, you can do that first too. He told me to arrange things for you but he can't come here just at the moment. He's going to be busy somewhere else for a while, and he'll come to see you when he's done."

Secretary Wu Xingang was about to go over and have a word with the doorman, but Li Gaocheng stopped him. "There's no point talking to him. All I want to do is have a look inside, so let's just wait for the manager for a while."

"What an arrogant shit, treating us like dirt like that!" Wu Xingang was on the point of blowing his top.

Wu Xingang's rant served to lessen Li Gaocheng's anger a bit. The way this doorman looked at him and his general attitude were really quite honest and he was being perfectly open about it all. In his eyes, this wasn't the kind of place that someone looking like him and dressed like him belonged. This is somewhere for rich people, he was thinking, so what is a scruffy pauper like you doing here? Can you afford it? See how insignificant you look, and I know you haven't got two cents to rub together. You're wearing a faded old army greatcoat below your wizened old face. You've got no style, no presence or authority! Do you really think I'm going to let you in here?!

Everyone in this world has their boss, Li Gaocheng reminded himself. The place had hired this man, so he was just doing his job and it wasn't reasonable to be angry with him. If you curse him out for getting uppity with you, someone else is going to curse you out for being too big for your boots. What kind of person wants to hang out here anyway?

Besides, didn't they do the same thing to people at the gates of the Municipal Government compound? Didn't they really give them the third degree, refuse to telephone, refuse to sign them in? So how was he ever going to be let into this place?

What was more, this doorman's attitude and behaviour had, in fact, been perfectly respectful, not to say quite gentlemanly. What he had done was really nothing compared to those guards at the government compound. But he suddenly felt that in coming here, it was as if he had come to another place and another country. This feeling might be a bit comical, but it was very real. In a public part of the city under his leadership, an establishment had suddenly popped up that he couldn't even enter. Was that the real reason he was annoyed?

Moreover, the place's boss was a family member!

After wasting ten minutes or so getting in, his first strong impression was of how many women there were in the place!

Women with all kinds of make-up; women with all kinds of clothes and jewellery; women of all shapes and sizes. Although it was the coldest time of year, they were wearing so little, and what there was, was so skimpy, and everyone was standing so close together. Shoulder to shoulder, neck to neck, those heavily made-up faces almost sticking to his, those piercing hot eyes staring relentlessly at him; even when he got out into the corridor, it was like a furnace, and a gust of moist warmth, heavy with the smell of cheap perfume, assaulted him, full in the face.

"Can I serve you, sir?"

"Do you want a girl, sir?"

"Is it two singers you are wanting, sir?"

"Sir..."

People were openly and unabashedly selling themselves. The place seemed to be devoid of shame or guilt; as long as there was money in it, youth, body, soul and conscience, you name it and it could be traded as a commodity here.

Li Gaocheng couldn't help blushing and he felt his ears burning. He was not only ashamed of these people, he was even more ashamed of himself. It was hard for him to hold his head up when such a place appeared under his jurisdiction!

"Hey! Are you going to eat or have a bit of fun?" As he was lost in these thoughts, the doorman's offhand shout made him jump.

Li Gaocheng thought for a moment, then said casually: "Wine and song first. I want a decent karaoke room, and find me some pretty young girls!"

The doorman stared at Li Gaocheng in surprise, and it took him some time to pull himself together. He was probably surprised that a scruffy old man like Li could have such healthy appetites. It just showed that you shouldn't judge a book by its cover! To borrow an expression the hostesses often used: he'd never expected there to be so much meat on those bones! His face immediately changed from cloudy to sunny and, with a smiling, obsequious expression, he asked: "Would you like cigarettes, wine and fruit in the room?"

"Of course! I want all the extras!"

"Yes sir, of course sir! Just wait a moment and I'll go set it up. It will be ready in a minute! It will be ready in a minute!" In the twinkling of an eye, the doorman had disappeared.

Li Gaocheng glanced at his secretary, Wu Xingang, who was standing there, mouth agape and speechless with astonishment, and he gestured to him. "For now, just follow my lead but don't say a word."

It wasn't long before the doorman had made arrangements for a very acceptable private karaoke room. A suite, in fact, complete with large flat screen TVs, surround-sound and its own toilet and bathroom!

Needless to say, Li Gaocheng had never seen a karaoke room like it. He had heard about them, but never actually seen one. So now he knew first-hand that such suites really did exist, bathroom, toilet and all!

All of a sudden, four girls appeared together, presumably on the instructions of the doorman, along with a male attendant in a little red hat, who said very humbly and unctuously: "Will these four girls do for you, sir?"

"No!" Li Gaocheng pulled a disapproving face after barely glancing at the girls and rejected them out of hand. "Find me some others!"

Almost immediately, another four girls appeared, but once again, Li Gaocheng rejected them. The process was repeated four times altogether, at which point, someone, who was presumably the karaoke rooms supervisor came hurrying in to try to talk him round. "Aiya, my dear old fellow! Just what kind of girl is it you're looking for?" The supervisor's words and manner were very polite, not to say enticing. "I think this is your first time here, so we don't know your tastes and preferences yet. For example, do you like tall, well-built girls or little jade-like ones? Do you want them to be quiet and refined? Or do you prefer them a bit livelier and sexier? Do you like really young ones or a bit more mature?"

"What do you think?" Li Gaocheng's face was getting longer and longer and he couldn't bring himself to look the supervisor in the eye.

"Well, old fellow, how about you just get one of each?" The supervisor's words were really quite obscene, but his expression remained perfectly polite and modest without any outward show of emotion. It was clear he was used to this kind of conversation and business transaction, and the whole process was quite routine and almost robotic.

"All right, we'll do it your way, so just get on with it." As he spoke, Li Gaocheng looked at the supervisor standing in front of him and then asked, apparently appreciatively: "So, what's your name, my lad?"

"My name is Ma. Ma Liuliu." The supervisor seemed very modest and polite.

"How old are you?" Li Gaocheng continued to question him.

"Twenty-eight."

"Are you married?"

"Yes, with two children."

"Your accent is very familiar. Where are you from?"

"I'm from Xin County."

Li Gaocheng was astonished: his wife's family home was in Xin

County. He excitedly pursued his questioning, asking: "Which Xin County?"

"The one where Wujiagou is."

Wujiagou! That was his wife's home village! He gave a groan, as if in pain. Surely this wasn't just coincidence. Finally, he went on to ask: "What did you do there?"

"I worked in the provincial textile factory, then I was sent to Zhongyang Textiles. I was a technician there for a few years, then I came here."

"You worked at Zhongyang Textiles?" Li Gaocheng exclaimed in astonishment. "When did you start there?"

"I started in 1991."

"Ah, 1991..." Little wonder the chap didn't recognise him, as he had already left the company by then. He relaxed a little, and continued: "How long did you work there?"

"Four years and seven months. I was sent here in October last year." The date seemed to be etched in the man's memory.

"Was that because Zhongyang Textiles had stopped production?"

"Yes."

"If you're a technical school graduate, wasn't it a pity to leave there?"

"With a great big company like that going under, why would it be a pity for someone like me? There were a couple of thousand university graduates there!" The lad said indifferently.

With those words, Li Gaocheng's dislike and contempt for the young man disappeared completely. He was a village boy, a graduate from a minor technical school, already married with children. What could he do for a living? Probably with this kind of money on offer, he had no choice.

"Now, sir, we've got the girls you want together. Have a look and see if they'll do." The young man's return to his self-effacing but rather hardened manner immediately brought Li Gaocheng back from his ponderings and into reality.

Several gorgeously dressed young girls with ruby lips and dazzling white teeth were suddenly standing in front of him in all their slender elegance.

"All right, they'll do," Li Gaocheng said with a wave of the hand, after glancing at them casually.

When they heard this, some of the girls fluttered over like a cloud of butterflies, to sit one on each side of Li Gaocheng and Wu Xingang. Sitting so close, the smell of their cheap perfume was overwhelming.

"Wouldn't you like something to drink?" a tall girl asked in carefully modulated tones, as she snuggled in beside Li Gaocheng. But he could tell immediately that she was definitely a local girl.

"Alcohol? Are you old enough?" Li asked in surprise, just as he realised that this girl wasn't that young, and, indeed, probably wasn't even a "girl" anymore. He could see clearly that the crow's feet at the corners of her eyes were already quite pronounced.

"It's really interesting just talking to you, but I'll have a drink if it makes you happy," the girl said, still in her mock refined voice.

"What would you like to drink?" Li Gaocheng was already very bored with the whole thing.

"XO of course! It's a bit expensive, but it's lovely to drink and makes you so relaxed. What do you think? Is that what you'd like?"

So she wanted XO! Liu Gaocheng had tried the foreign liquor on a few occasions. He had never particularly liked it, and it was eye-wateringly expensive. He hadn't expected the girls in this kind of place to want that kind of imported drink. But, thinking about it, it really wasn't that strange. This was a place people came to enjoy themselves and, just like Zhou Yu and Huang Gai,[1] if one side wanted to be beaten, the other side was quite happy to oblige! Rich people came here for their pleasure, and the girls gave them that pleasure to get their hands on their money. Everyone got what they wanted, and that's all there was to it. The girls were expensive anyway, and if you wanted more, of course you had to pay more. The more generously you spent, the more the girl's receipts and commission would be. So, in this kind of place, everything was fake apart from the money, just like the wrinkles on the girl's face. He really shouldn't be at all surprised, and he really shouldn't be angry about it either.

Li Gaocheng waved his hand and said, none too politely: "All right, XO it is then!"

In no time at all, the coffee table in the karaoke room was covered in all kinds of goodies: fruit, cigarettes, drinks, tea and, of course, two large, eye-catching bottles of XO cognac.

Li Gaocheng glanced at the bill on the table. A cup of tea was 15 yuan, a can of soft drink was 18 yuan, a hard pack of Zhonghua was 66 yuan, a hard pack of Yuxi was 88 yuan, and a pack of premium Yunyan was 169 yuan. It was 488 yuan for a bottle of dry white wine, and 3,888 yuan for a bottle of the cheapest XO! At a rough calculation, there was over 8,000 yuan's worth of stuff there! And they hadn't started the singing yet, or the drinking, and that didn't include the fees for the girls and their tips either! If you included the obligatory dinner, and there were any other extra items, it was unlikely 20,000 yuan would cover it.

What could you do with 20,000 yuan?

In the countryside, you could take a daughter-in-law, buy several dozen cows, and buy a whole year's harvest from ten *mu* of land! A hundred children could be brought back into the classroom! At Zhongyang Textiles it would pay one month's living allowance for two hundred workers!

But half a night here and it was all gone.

From one side, it was extreme extravagance, and from the other, it was extreme profiteering.

Li Gaocheng's distress returned, not because of the prices he saw tonight, but because of how deeply he was aware that the policies and regulations he had made with his own hands had failed and had no effect. What particularly distressed him was that even the law was just as invalid and ineffective here. The Municipal Government had time and time again issued countless official regulations and proclamations aimed at curbing profiteering, and the clearest of laws had been drafted to the same end. But it seemed as though, right under his very eyes, this same profiteering was both blatant and rampant! There it was, in black and white, on the bill on the table in front of him!

Who gave these people this power?

If this Green Apple Entertainment City had indeed been opened by his, the mayor's, nephew; if he, as mayor, had not asked him about it or acknowledged him; even if he, as mayor, pretended ignorance, or, as was the case here, was in genuine ignorance; even with all these provisos, the situation here was hugely different from anywhere else. Here, even if something truly dreadful happened, nothing would be done about it.

Because no one was going to believe that his own nephew could have opened such a big establishment without his support or help, and this place did not have his backing. If he said he didn't know about it, everyone would still think he was just pretending innocence! Even a three-year-old wouldn't believe him!

He shouldn't fool himself that, even if he jumped into the Yellow River, he was going to come out clean!

Several of the girls quickly and expertly opened the bottles of brandy, immediately called for some large glasses and glugged the liquor out to more than half fill them. With that, two bottles of XO cognac were pretty much gone.

"I'm so pleased to meet you, sir! This glass is in your honour!" Another of the girls put the same plummy accent on her coyly girlish tones, but Li Gaocheng could tell for sure that she too was a local girl.

The two girls who had addressed him didn't care whether he drank or not. As soon as they finished speaking, they picked up their own glasses, clinked them against his, then tilted their necks, and swallowed half the liquor in one go!

Li Gaocheng was stunned. It was like they were drinking water!

This kind of imported liquor had a high alcohol content and it needed a good head to drink it. If the two girls didn't have a huge capacity for alcohol, there could only be one reason for them drinking it like water and that was the commission they got on any drink consumed. Money again! Money was the only reason they were there, so there was no market for courtesy, decency or honour. What was more, this kind of greed for money was contagious and it was like a crowd of hungry beggars who can't help but hurl themselves, unthinking, at a fat wallet that has been dropped on the ground.

In no time at all, two bottles of XO were completely empty.

This time the girls didn't wait for instructions from Li Gaocheng but immediately ordered two more bottles. That is to say, more than 10,000 yuan had already been swallowed up in less than half an hour. With several glasses of brandy inside them, the girls were already tipsy and blurry-eyed.

"Do you want us to sing or dance now?" It wasn't clear whether she really had drunk too much or was just getting a little carried away, but the girls sitting with them were getting more and more wanton and unbridled. The two on either side of Li Gaocheng seemed to be glued to him and, as they urged him to drink, their faces rubbed up against his. Sitting next to him, Wu Xingang seemed even more baffled and exhausted by the experience and didn't have any defences against the two girls besieging him. Seeing how things stood with his secretary, Li Gaocheng said to one of the girls at his side: "Why don't you have a dance with the other gentleman?" He knew that Wu Xingang was quite a good dancer and as long as he was doing that, he'd be able to handle things. After that girl had got up to dance, he ordered the two girls who had been sitting next to Wu Xingang to stand up and sing together. In an instant, there was only one girl left beside him, and that was the same tall girl, who was perhaps not so girlish anymore, who had first talked to him.

"By the sound of your accent, you're from this city, aren't you, miss?"

"Eh?! You... how do you know?" She had clearly had a lot to drink; she was red in the face and already slurring her words a bit.

"How old are you?"

"...how old? Don't... don't you know the rules? A girl... you can't ask a girl how old she is... don't you know that?"

"Where is your family home?" Li Gaocheng was trying to keep his voice calm and not give anything away.

"I'm not going to tell you that!" The girl seemed to think that the old fellow she was sitting with really fancied her, and she became more wanton and unbridled. "If you want to do it, let's just do it... Why all the questions like you're checking my residence permit...?"

"Do what?" Li Gaocheng was getting rather alarmed.

"Do what? All you men come here to play away don't you? That's all you lot come here for, isn't it? To do it! I'll tell you what... if you want to take just me out with you, it will be this much for the night." She held up five shaky fingers and waved them in front of his face. "If you want to take two of us together... it'll be at least... this much." She waved the same hand three times in his face. "If you want... if you want to take all of us... then you'll... then you'll have to double that. If you want to do it here... this is what it costs for one time." She held out her fingers in front of him, but he couldn't tell whether she was showing him two fingers or three.

"Here!?" Li Gaocheng was really alarmed now.

This suite's got a... double so... sofa bed... it's really convenient. I... I really like you... so I've given you the lowest price... I'm not trying to cheat you." The girl was getting more and more carried away.

"How do you dare behave like this!" Li Gaocheng could actually feel his head swelling with anger and he could hardly believe his ears.

"...Look at you... You old codgers... You're all the same... You want to do it but you want to keep your reputation... You want a young girl but you're afraid there'll be trouble... Well... let me tell you, our place here... is the safest place there is... You don't have to worry about any trouble here... You don't know the kind of backing our boss has got – no one dares start anything here... They're all scared to death of him. You know who it is? The mayor! Can't you see... how good the business is here? I'm telling the truth, you've got nothing to be afraid of... Even if there was a raid, no one would get arrested... If they do take us away, all we have to do is say we're... we're workers from Zhongyang Textiles, and the Public Security Office won't say another word... They just... they just let us go..."

"So are you really from Zhongyang Textiles too?" Yet again, Li Gaocheng felt as though a great shudder had run through him.

"Me? Of course not... that's just what I tell the Public Security if they come here, but a lot... a lot of the other girls... almost all of them... come from Zhongyang Textiles... What's wrong with you, old man? Make your mind up... if you want it then... get a move on or aren't... aren't you up to it..."

At this point, Li Gaocheng stopped seeing or hearing anything and his mind just went blank.

Zhongyang's loans, Zhongyang's girl workers, Zhongyang's technicians...

How ironic this was for him as mayor and, at the same time, how shameful!

Suddenly a vision of a great colossus rose up in front of his eyes, half dead, half alive, its huge body crawling with great fat parasites all gnawing away at it, their mouths full of blood as they shook them wildly and insatiably to and fro. The colossus was wasting away, dying by inches, as the parasites grew bigger and stronger and fatter and fatter...

His demise meant their continued existence, and their strength meant his demise. He had dedicated himself to training up a group of his own gravediggers, who were defeating him and burying him by degrees with the energy he had given them!

What particularly appalled him was that, if that day came, it was very likely that no one would miss him or mourn him, because all of it was his own fault, and he deserved it!

They were turning his own hand against him to destroy his regime! This was not being alarmist, it was a cold, hard fact!

In decades to come, centuries to come, what would future generations think of him? How would he be judged?

Won't you just be a laughing stock?

Suddenly, he heard a brusque knock on the door.

In the dim light, half of a face that he desperately wanted to see, but also really didn't want to, gradually appeared round the door in front of him: so familiar, yet so unfamiliar.

Of course, it was his nephew, Wu Baozhu who had appeared at the door of the karaoke room. Wu Baozhu, who, under the name Huizi, was also the general manager of the Green Apple Entertainment City!

CHAPTER NINETEEN

The two of them just stared blankly at each other.

When something happens so suddenly and so unexpectedly, it renders you incapable of coherent thought.

For Li Gaocheng, this came as an almost unbearable shock.

He couldn't believe it, but he had to. This was the situation he was most afraid of, yet it was an iron-clad fact. His intuition had already told him that it was all true, but, when the truth appeared right in front of him like this, it was both unacceptable and unendurable.

He could never have imagined that his wife, with whom he had been in love for more than twenty years, who had lived with him for so long and with so much affection, could deceive him so completely, so deliberately and so undeniably.

He certainly didn't expect his nephew, who had always looked timid and submissive in front of him, to look so domineering and arrogant at this moment. He was drunk, smelled of alcohol, and had a cigarette in his mouth; his suit was half open, he had one hand in his pocket, and the hand of the other arm, which was draped round a girl, held a shiny new Dageda cell phone.

He was the epitome of a wastrel son of a high official.

Perhaps the Wu Baozhu that now stood in front of him was the one closest to the real Wu Baozhu, and the Wu Baozhu that usually appeared at home, like his wife's devoted affection, was just a poorly executed fake, designed specifically to fool him.

Li Gaocheng felt heartbroken.

It was as if he had been physically struck, and he sat there in mute astonishment, staring unblinkingly at the face in front of him.

Probably because of the amount he had already had to drink, after he had so arrogantly and domineeringly thrown open the door, this general manager, this so-called Huizi, initially failed to register who it really was who had brought him charging over to see him.

Even in his wildest dreams, he had probably never imagined that his uncle, the mayor, would come to his establishment, unaccompanied!

He had probably arrived at the door in a fury, wanting to teach this man a lesson for not knowing how important he was, for scolding his doorman like a dog, and for daring to speak disrespectfully about him and point the finger. Who was this wretched creature who dared to beard the lion in his den?

Perhaps he was so far in his cups that he didn't give it all that much thought, let alone consider what harm it might do to him; after all, this was his world, so what was the big deal? He just hurried across the room, his arm still casually draped over the girl.

Perhaps he just thought, as he always had, that, in this world, there weren't many real men who came to a karaoke hall looking for wine, women and song, and if it wasn't a real man he had to deal with, there wasn't much to worry about. So, he just thought he'd take a look at whoever it was, and if they wanted to play tough, he would show them he could play even tougher.

So, when he came crashing in, looking ready to have some fun at the expense of the other party, he hadn't considered at all the possibility that the "other party" might be the mayor. But there he was, his uncle, the mayor, the person he most feared in all the world.

He stood, staring blankly, and his whole body changed in an instant. His arms dropped as if they'd been hit by an electric shock, his legs bowed and his face remained in a fixed smile. The next thing he knew, his body was trembling violently all over and his voice trembled. "Uncle!" He looked as though he was about to fall to his knees.

Li Gaocheng's face was still tightly drawn as he looked at the general manager of the Green Apple Entertainment City as if he were looking at some kind of monster. From this manager's appearance, he could immediately think of some good reasons for the place to be the "Green Apple"![1]

How could he have such a nephew? This Wu Baozhu only turned twenty-five this year; he was a poor student and only got into a special technical school because strings were pulled for him. He had probably graduated less than two years ago. Even so, that freshly graduated college student had miraculously transformed into this smooth-skinned, slick-haired popinjay in charge of an entertainment complex with nearly ten million in fixed assets!

What was his support? And why him?

Just one look at his manner and bearing told Li Gaocheng all he needed to know about how he ran this entertainment complex! No wonder there were so many shady and illegal things going on there.

Who gave him the courage to do it? Who made him so lawless that he thought he could do whatever he wanted? Everyone knew quite clearly, and even this escort girl had no doubts: it was because it had the backing of the mayor! But using power and position for personal advantage was like killing the goose that laid the golden egg; the ordinary people could see straight through it, so how did he still have the effrontery to be prancing round here, making a fool of himself?

The young manager in front of him seemed to be pulling himself together, and the frozen expression his face had been frightened into gradually returned to normal and then took on a look of respectful sincerity accompanied by an obsequious smile.

"Is it really you, Uncle!? I, I really didn't think that... that stupid bastard on the door didn't make it clear to me... I really didn't know. I didn't know you were here..." Wu Baozhu babbled as he scrambled to work out what to say, presumably because he had no way of knowing what Li Gaocheng's real intentions were; it had all been a bit too sudden for him.

The whole room had suddenly descended into a suffocating silence, and someone had quietly turned off the sound system that had been booming away only moments before. Only the gyrating images on the flat screens remained.

Maybe it was the appearance of the general manager that had taken them so much by surprise, but everyone was rooted to the spot. No one was so foolish as to think that an old man who can scare a general manager with such powerful backing into such a state was just an ordinary person.

"Uncle, I've just been told that you may not have eaten yet. Look, do you want to stay here for a bit of karaoke, or would you just like to eat now?" When Li Gaocheng remained silent, he asked, in a low voice: "Uncle, why didn't you come and say hello, so that we could get everything ready for you? Where's my aunt? Why didn't my aunt come? Should I invite her too? Would you like to make a phone call now..."

Wu Baozhu was being very careful what he said, because he understood that his uncle held his fate in his hands; it was life or death, success or humiliation, and this might be the decisive moment. He could read fury and even hatred in his uncle's eyes.

"...Are you really the general manager here?" After a long pause, Li Gaocheng tried his best to speak in a normal tone. He knew that he couldn't stay silent forever.

"No, I'm just acting manager. The board of directors is going to look into it shortly, and there will be an official general manager soon. As soon as Li Gaocheng spoke, Wu Baozhu seemed to relax.

"Then who made you acting manager? Who is your agent?" Li Gaocheng could see that his nephew was clearly lying to him.

"...That, that was also a provisional decision by the board of directors. This place only started operations last year. The organisation is not firmed up yet, and, as the board of directors is only temporary too, the decision was made on the fly..." Wu Baozhu stammered.

He was interrupted in mid-flow by Li Gaocheng. "Enough! Get rid of these people for me. I have something to say to you."

Before Wu Baozhu could say anything more, the other people in the room were already scrambling for the door as if the plague god was in there. One of the girls tripped over something and almost fell. Then the karaoke room was silent as the grave.

Seeing the girls panicked like that, Li Gaocheng's heart softened, and he felt a deep sense of guilt and self-reproach. Was it fair always to condemn these escort girls out of hand? What price self-sufficiency, self-reliance, cleanliness and self-respect? Supposing they were like his own daughter and studying at a top university with a mayor for a father, would they still need so much determination and hard work? Or if they had a regular salaried job, would they still come here to sing and dance and even sell their bodies? It was the same with those twenty or so thousand workers standing on the frozen ground in the Zhongyang Textiles dormitory compound that night, faced with an idle factory and no jobs and no work. What could he expect them to do? Empty appeals weren't going to put food on their plates! Those workers had worked in the factory all their lives, given almost everything they had to the place, and had even sacrificed their sons and daughters to it. Apart from working in the factory, they did not have any other means of earning a living. There was no backing for them to take the initiative and seize the market.

And what about their children who had been brought up, pretty much from the day they were born, to accept that everything belonged to the Party and the state: the factory belonged to the Party and the state, the company belonged to the Party and the state, their family, including themselves, belonged to the Party and the state; they were to trust the Party and trust the state, and rely on the Party and the state; they were to cherish and protect the Party and the state as they did their own eyes... in return, the Party and the state would have the working masses imprinted on their hearts, they would be connected by flesh and blood, would share their very breath and their very fate. The nature of the Party and the nature of the people were as one, the big family and the little family always together. If the big river had no water, the little river would run dry, but if the big river was full, so would the little river be...

But just now, when he faced these workers of an idle factory, how could he tell them to be self-reliant, support themselves and find their own way?

And now, when he faced these female workers who had turned to escorting because they had lost their jobs, how could he blindly condemn and despise them, or attack them and punish them for their so-called turpitude?

Could he claim this was not his responsibility?

What was more, the general manager of this place was a relative of his, his nephew in fact. There was his wife too! And who was their backer? He was!

If it came down to it, he should be the one trying to escape, not these girls! Once again, he tried to calm himself down. However unpleasant the nephew might seem at the moment, however angry he might be, so angry that he never wanted to see him again for the rest of his life, he had to get the truth of the matter out of him now.

"What about that little karaoke place you opened? When did you come here?" he could feel the spontaneous tremor in his lips.

"I'm still running that little place. I'm just the temporary manager here. I only just came here not long ago, that's the truth. I actually spend most of my time at the other place…"

"Shut up!" He couldn't restrain his fury; he'd caught the man red-handed, and he was still lying to him. "Just how stupid do you think I am? You're still lying to me. I'm going to see you prosecuted, and I'm not just saying this to try to scare you. From what I've seen today, you're looking at least ten years inside at least!"

"Yes, I know that. But you need to know, Uncle, that all karaoke bars and dance halls are like this today, both for men and for women. If they weren't, they wouldn't have any customers. Sometimes the girls have to string the punters along a bit to liven up business, and sometimes the punters manhandle the girls a bit – that's all quite normal. Besides, we have to keep order in these places, and what methods are left to us if something does kick off? Even in a place like ours, we can't always make sure there's no trouble…"

"Bullshit!" Li Gaocheng would never have believed that this unmarried nephew of his could not only show so little regard for what he had to say but could also shamelessly come out with such disgusting filth himself. Remembering the way the man had had his arm round the girl just now, Li Gaocheng roared furiously: "I could tell just by looking at you, the kind of karaoke place you'd be running. If you can't keep control of the place, how do you have the nerve to call yourself general manager? And since you can't control it, we'd better get some people in to teach you some discipline yourself!"

There was something else that Li Gaocheng didn't say and that was: If I can't even keep control of a creature like you, what kind of mayor does that make me!?

"I'm telling the truth, Uncle." Li Gaocheng's anger seemed to have the opposite effect on Wu Baozhu, who appeared to be getting calmer and more confident. Based on past experience, Wu Baozhu was probably quite justified in this: he knew that the angrier his uncle got, the less trouble it really meant. For him, a beating was a form of kiss, a scolding represented love, and, generally speaking, if he was serious about dealing with his nephew, he would not be getting so angry. That explained why Li Gaocheng saw Wu Baozhu growing increasingly confident in the face of his fury. In fact his nephew went so far as to say: "You told me to tell the truth and I did, but you just criticised me again. Who would really choose to come here? Do you think I want to be here? Didn't I tell you, before I graduated, that I wanted to join the Public Security Office? That's a place where they can really control people but all I get to do here is serve people and fawn all over them, and they all get to lord it over me. What we are after is repeat custom and we don't just want people to have fun, we want them to feel safe as well. I have to check everything top to bottom and inside out, and there's bound to be trouble if I'm careless. Do you think people will keep coming here then? The only reason they made me general manager was because they had an eye on your reputation..."

"That's enough!" Li Gaocheng interrupted him again. "Just tell me this. Who is the real boss here? Who ordered you to come here? Who is on the board of directors? You just said it yourself. I want you to tell me the truth."

"I thought you knew! It's Auntie, isn't it! She told me to stop messing around in my work unit and go out and earn some money. She said I should take advantage of it while you've still got some influence and first try and set a few things up, build a base and get some experience in. Now, nothing counts anymore as the leadership is getting weaker and it's all about the market economy. And in the market economy, it's money that talks. Not long after I graduated the year before last and was given my posting, I set up a karaoke bar. It wasn't very big, but it did good business. In six months, I made several hundred thousand yuan; of course that was because Auntie had a lot of connections, we had a lot of clients, and the place was red hot. So at the beginning of last year I invested in this entertainment complex. It was originally a company office building, but the business had stopped production for more than year – its workers hadn't been paid for two years, and they had no alternative but to rent out the building to us. The rent wasn't high, just enough to cover the living expenses of the workers. It suited both sides and it took us less than five million all told and only two months to fix up this entertainment complex. To tell you the truth, Uncle, even Auntie didn't expect it. In fact no one thought that it would do such good business. Last year alone, excluding the initial capital, the net profit was more than two million. This year, we estimate we're going to make eight or nine million. I really don't know how many people there are on the board, and Auntie probably doesn't want me to know either. Besides her, there seems to be the general manager of Xinchao Co. Ltd, the deputy general manager of Zhongyang Textiles and Xinchao's accountant. That's because Xinchao are investors and they put in six million at one go, purely as an investment, not a loan. I've heard them say it will be up to them when they decide to recoup that investment, and no one else has any claim on what's open and on the books. It's just like me being general manager here – it's just a title. There are two others who are really in control of things, and they're called deputy managers. One is the son of the deputy general manager of Zhongyang Textiles, and the other is the nephew of the general manager of Xinchao Co. Ltd. People have said that our entertainment complex alone is worth as much as the whole Zhongyang Textile Group Company. This is what is known as an 'invisible industry'. In fact, there are only a few people on the staff, and the rest are all temporary workers. Auntie says that this is only the first step, and the next step is to develop a big..."

The more Li Gaocheng listened, the more unbelievable it all became, and the more he felt the chills spread all over his body.

They were all like flies swarming around a dog, or ants crawling over a piece of rotting meat! They were cruel, unscrupulous and tyrannical! He could think of no description of these awful creatures that really did them justice.

Were these the people he himself had handpicked? By what right could he still confidently call himself a good cadre?

Was this the loving wife he had lived together with for so many days and nights?

What deeds had they been hiding from him? What were they still hiding?

For some time, he had thought that the gall and greed of leadership cadres could never be as rapacious as those of crooks and gangsters, but now he realised that the cadres were even worse in every respect.

Hundreds of thousands, millions even! These were numbers to make an ordinary person's head spin, but to these people they were just chicken feed.

Could people really turn their back on everything just for the sake of money? Even give up their lives? What were they actually going to do with so much money?

Since things had already gone this far, what more was there to be said?

The only thing that mattered now was what he did next. So what should he do about this entertainment complex and about these people?

Getting angry and cursing them out would do no good. Even his nephew didn't really take him seriously, because he still had his aunt behind him, and he knew that she was his, the mayor's, wife!

His wife actually earned more than he did!

In fact, the truth was that it was he who was generating this money, yet here he was playing the fool with his temper tantrums. Who was ever going to be afraid of someone like that?

It was his wife he had to get to grips with, and that meant getting to grips with himself!

Could he do it? Was he actually able to do it? Did he dare do it?

Once again, he remembered what Yang Cheng had told him: the key to how well the problems at Zhongyang Textiles were resolved lay in his hands – no one else's, just his.

Maybe it wasn't just Yang Cheng saying that to him and maybe it wasn't just Yang Cheng who saw him like that; what he was afraid of was that the whole population of the city saw him like that and were saying the same thing!

CHAPTER TWENTY

IT WAS ALMOST NINE O'CLOCK in the evening when he left the Green Apple Entertainment City. The cold air outside immediately cleared his head. He suddenly remembered that there was an important person expecting him that night: Yan Zhen, the deputy secretary of the Provincial Party Committee, the man who had called him that noon at the Standing Committee meeting.

Yan Zhen had asked him to report to him in person at his house immediately after the meeting. He was waiting for the results of the deliberations of the Standing Committee, and he also wanted to know the specific steps and measures that had been decided on to deal with the issue of Zhongyang Textiles. Yan Zhen had said that this was a major event and a major issue affecting political and social stability. It was necessary, therefore, to be cautious and stop and think twice.

Li Gaocheng had entirely agreed with Secretary Yan's words and very much felt the same. A large enterprise with tens of thousands of workers made for a situation that was unpredictable and could prove very tricky to handle if it was not approached with great care. This made it difficult for anyone to predict with certainty what the consequences might be. So, the thing was to be cautious, then more cautious and then more cautious still.

However, now, just a few hours later, Li Gaocheng had changed his mind completely over how he viewed the affair. It was no longer just a question of whether it should be handled with caution or not, but rather that his thinking had changed completely on why Secretary Yan Zhen had said that, and why Yan Zhen cared so much about the matter.

Before he went to Green Apple Entertainment City, he had already gained a general understanding of the basic situation of the Te Gao Te Passenger Transportation Corporation from several connections. What he had learned was basically consistent with what Yang Cheng told him but was perhaps even more surprising and shocking. According to people familiar with the matter, not only Yan Zhen's brother-in-law and the former vice president of the People's Bank of China were participants in the operation of Te Gao Te, but a relative of a former vice mayor of the city and someone in charge of the Municipal Economic Commission were also involved. In particular, it transpired that Te Gao Te's business was doing much better than expected; the appearance of Te Gao Te on the market was even affecting the business the trains were doing, because where a train might take more than ten hours to get somewhere, the same journey by car only took a few hours, even though the fare for the car was several tens of yuan more than the sleeper fare by train! People want to save time and trouble, so most of them were choosing the car over the train. That was the reason for Te Gao Te's unexpected success. In 1995, the annual turnover reached nearly 30 million yuan, and the net profit exceeded 20 million! And so far, the Zhongyang Textile Group's Xinchao Co. Ltd. had not paid back a penny of its loan or distributed a penny of interest. That is to say, with the Te Gao Te Passenger Transportation Company's profits already exceeding its original charge-free capital funding, it was still sitting on this huge amount of money. That begged another question: what were they doing with all those millions? Supposing it was sitting in the bank, the interest would be hundreds of thousands per month and millions per year.

But with their power and status, they would never leave such a sum in the bank simply accruing interest! They would never be that unimaginative, that disorganised or that stupid! In their hands, one yuan of funds would easily become two or three or even ten within a year!

When money and power come together, money can be increased

multifold without any need to take risks. Even if there was an element of risk, that could be turned to advantage, as danger becomes advantage, big problems become small ones and small ones disappear or, at the very least, become meaningless.

You could say this is just one of the advantages afforded state-operated business, because power not only makes money grow but also ensures that those ever-increasing funds never suffer any loss.

But should what these people were doing be classed as state-operated business?

Yes, it should. First, because they were officials; second, because they had power and influence; and third, their enterprise did use that power and influence. Their relatives and cronies in the enterprise were just their agents! In truth it was those very people, the active leadership cadres, who were playing the decisive role in these enterprises!

This kind of behaviour had been repeatedly prohibited by the state and the central government. The wording of the regulations was very severe, as were the punishments handed down.

The question was, who should expose this kind of illegal behaviour and who should deal with it? On the one hand, there was the old adage: officials can't investigate what the people don't report. And on the other there was also the saying: don't beg for food even if you are starving, don't lay a complaint even if injustice kills you. What was going on here was the contradictory situation between ordinary people and officialdom; it was only when ordinary people were *in extremis* that they would throw caution to the wind and make a formal complaint about their local officials. Generally speaking, such matters were only resolved when an even higher authority stepped in and took them in hand.

But the situation here was quite different. The workers' evidence had been handed over to the Municipal Party Committee and the Municipal Government, that is to say, to himself and Yang Cheng, secretary of the Municipal Party Committee. According to procedure, anything to do with the city's enterprises and the city's companies should be handled by the city. However, the evidence revealed the illegal behaviour of the provincial leaders in charge of industry and finance, who were actually his own leaders and immediate superiors. In particular, here was this very senior leader, who was his own immediate boss, clearly specifying that he, as mayor, must handle the petition and complaints of the workers and that every step he took had to be reported!

What Yan Zhen was effectively saying was: "If they lay a complaint against me, you handle it, but I control you!" To put it bluntly, it was a vicious circle, both of remarkable simplicity and of extreme complexity.

Li Gaocheng understood that he found himself in just that vicious circle now.

And from that position, his opinion of his old leader, Yan Zhen, changed completely at a stroke.

Just as he found it so difficult to explain his wife's conduct, he was at a complete loss to account for Secretary Yan Zhen, who he had always previously respected.

Was it all about the money?

If it was, what was he going to do with so much money?

It was true that his salary was not high, but Yan Zhen was always telling everybody that although an official's salary was not so high, its "gold content" was. And that was true. One yuan for a respected leading cadre went much further and had many more uses than one yuan for an ordinary person. In particular, leading cadres at the provincial level like Yan Zhen did not pay for medical treatment, housing or use of a car. The had their housekeeper hired by the state, and there were dedicated personnel to carry out any home repairs. It could be said that his "very valuable salary" fundamentally didn't cost very much, and even after retirement he would still maintain his current benefits and living standards and would continue to maintain them for a hundred years if necessary.

If it really was all about the money, what on earth could he want that much for?

If all this still didn't explain what he was doing, then there was probably only one explanation for him wanting so much money: he wanted to prepare an escape route.

What kind of escape route? Again, there was probably only one explanation: if, one day, there was some enormous upheaval, such as had happened in the Soviet Union and Eastern Europe, all those in leadership positions would, at a stroke, lose all their power, position, reputation and status. Everything, absolutely everything, would be completely different from how it was before.

But if, at such a time, he had a great deal of money stashed away and also had solid holdings and a group of factories and enterprises that continued to bring him in a lot of money, then what did he have to fear?

When he needed power, he had power; when he needed money, he had money. It was the real-life equivalent of a tumbler doll, always ending the right way up. People with no foresight would find themselves in difficulties but this was real high-level foresight!

This could be a deep cover escape route or it could be a highly practical and highly secret scheme for making huge amounts of money.

Was that what Yan Zhen was thinking?

If that really was what he thought and if he really was making a lot of money by any kind of nefarious means for this purpose, then his qualifications should be re-visited as a person, as a member of the Party, and as a leading cadre!

When a member of a political party, when a leading cadre in a regime, had shown extreme distrust or even complete lack of faith in the Party and the regime in his actions, how could he continue to be a member of that Party, and continue in a leadership role in that regime?

Undoubtedly, his behaviour was enough to prove that, whenever it suited him, he would become a subversive element and a defector from the Party!

No, that wasn't right! His current behaviour had already made him an outright traitor to the Party! It also clearly demonstrated that he was actively engaged in dismantling and subverting the Party!

For any political party, this kind of behaviour was truly heinous and unforgivable!

This was the kind of person who covered things up, pretending all was fine, who abused everybody, who deceived everybody, who damaged the country and caused suffering for the people.

If such a faction was allowed to breed within a political party, then that party was in grave danger.

Was Yan Zhen that kind of person?

If not, then all well and good; everything would be the same as before and just as it should be.

But what if he was? Then what would you do, Li Gaocheng asked himself. How would he deal with him? He had no idea.

When he walked into Yan Zhen's house, Yan Zhen seemed to have been waiting for him for a long time.

Li Gaocheng had the impression that Yan Zhen hardly ever watched television, and even more rarely watched the news broadcasts. He had once said something that left a deep impression on Li: "Watching television is an expression of degeneracy. First it is a waste of time. Second, it makes people lazy. Third, the quality of television is too low. And, most importantly, television can easily make people lose their ability to think independently. Even delivering the news, what can be done in a few minutes in a newspaper can take twenty minutes or more on TV."

These words of Yan Zhen had a great effect on Li Gaocheng, so that, afterwards, he too seldom watched television and even more seldom watched television dramas. Particularly after he became mayor, he spent much less time watching television. Even when there was footage of him, he seldom watched it. He always felt that television was very contrived and turned people into posers. His wife once said to him: "Of course you don't have to watch television. Why would you, when you are the one making the news?" Indeed, how many leaders spend all day at home watching television? If they had that kind of leisure, they wouldn't be leaders.

However, the Yan Zhen he saw that evening was completely unlike anything Li Gaocheng had expected. He was reclining comfortably on the sofa, watching a rather cheesy Hong Kong or Taiwanese soap opera with great relish; so much so that when Li Gaocheng walked into the room, he was still smiling happily, loath to take his eyes off the screen.

Yan Zhen waved his hand, motioning Li to sit down. Still watching the television, he began to converse casually with him. "Was there another meeting in the afternoon? Didn't the Standing Committee end long ago?"

"There was no other meeting, so I got together with Yang Cheng," Li Gaocheng said truthfully.

"With Yang Cheng?" Yan Zhen suddenly turned to look at him,

rather suspiciously, and asked: "Did he ask you to go? Did he tell you anything?"

"I went on my own initiative. Yang Cheng is the secretary of the Municipal Party Committee and I wanted to hear more of his opinions. We mainly talked about the Zhongyang Textiles affair and discussed what to do," Li Gaocheng lied, almost subconsciously. Somehow or other, even he himself didn't know why he intentionally chose not to implicate Yang Cheng on the issue of Zhongyang Textiles.

It was at that moment that he suddenly felt a distance between himself and Yan Zhen, and that was unprecedented. If this incident had happened in the past, if Yan Zhen had asked him the same question, maybe he would have told Yan Zhen everything that Yang Cheng had said to him. For certain, everything would have been said openly, leaving nothing out, and there would never have been any feeling that anything was wrong, let alone that it was in any way mean-spirited to do so. But for some reason, when Yan Zhen asked him that question, he didn't want to tell him anything. This sense of distance stemmed mainly from distrust of his superior. But if it was someone else, what would he have done? Li Gaocheng suddenly found himself asking the question.

This was an excellent opportunity to ingratiate himself with his superior! It was also a great chance to change the course of his career! It was more useful and opportune than giving him hundreds of thousands of yuan. A few words would be enough, his defences would be stronger, the relationship between them would be stronger, and the relationship would be closer! Let alone the fact that this was one of the leaders of the Provincial Party Committee with a hugely promising future, and that leader already held him in such favour! Even if someone found out about it later, no one would denounce his conduct as shameful or despicable, betraying his friend for advancement; rather, people would say he was righteous, dutiful and honest, as a man should be. They would fully understand his actions. What was Yang Cheng to him? The secretary of the Municipal Party Committee should have been Li Gaocheng's man anyway, and Li's relationship with Yan Zhen was of long standing; if Yan Zhen hadn't been away studying at the Central Party School back then, wouldn't he himself have been the secretary of the Municipal Party Committee? How dare Yang Cheng say bad things about Yan Zhen in front of Li Gaocheng! Wasn't that just asking for trouble, like a fish throwing itself into the fisherman's net?

What was more, the people the current leadership cadres most despised were those who brought suit against their superiors. Even if your suit was justified, people would still despise you for acting with ulterior motives, for lacking righteousness, for having malicious intentions and for fishing in troubled waters. Ordinary people who brought suit were treated with understanding, but cadres and subordinates who did so were inevitably up to no good! And wasn't that what Yang Cheng was doing?

People could do what they wanted to do and say what they wanted to say. When the time came, he would attain his highest goal and receive the greatest reward in both fame and fortune. He could kill two birds with one stone, so what reason was there not to do such an excellent thing?

At this point, Li Gaocheng felt his cheeks burning as he flushed at the startled realisation he could have such despicable thoughts. It showed him the depths of depravity to which his thinking could drag him down.

He sat on the sofa and watched in silence as a very handsome face, familiar to him, played the role of the bad guy, forcing himself on a young girl, played by an actress herself no longer in the first flush of youth, trying to make her...

Yan Zhen was also watching silently, clearly still enjoying himself. Li Gaocheng suddenly felt that Yan Zhen would never really watch a soap opera like this.

He was probably doing it to show Li that he was in a very relaxed state of mind, and that he was not feeling worried or under pressure. He wasn't asking many questions, but just waiting for Li to tell him and make his report. In other words, he wanted to see where Li himself stood on the matter.

Looking again, it appeared that Yan Zhen was not quite as relaxed as he was pretending to be.

Li Gaocheng understood that since he had chosen to go there and had already agreed to make a report, it was up to him to break the deadlock and speak first.

"Should we go somewhere else, Secretary Yan?" Li Gaocheng made a show of being serious about making his report.

"Fine, fine. I thought we'd get round to that when we've finished watching this programme. We can go to my study, and I'll listen to what you have to say." Yan Zhen began to stand up as he spoke.

Yan Zhen's study was upstairs. The tall bookshelves in the room were ranged in a long row, giving a strong scholarly feeling as soon as you entered. Li Gaocheng knew that Yan Zhen rarely received guests in his study, except for a few high-level visitors. So, it was a rare honour to be received in the study of Secretary Yan Zhen. As far as Li Gaocheng knew, Yang Cheng, secretary of the Municipal Party Committee, had visited Yan Zhen's house twice, but had never been taken up to the study.

Everyone was aware that Yan Zhen had his own opinion of the Municipal Party Committee secretary. According to those really in the know, when Yang Cheng was appointed to the post, the only person opposed was Yan Zhen, who was in charge of organisation at the time.

But what Yan Zhen really thought of the municipal secretary remained a mystery. Someone once said to Li Gaocheng that when Yang Cheng was his subordinate as secretary of the Local Party Committee, he came into conflict with Yan Zhen over the promotion of cadres, and the two even had a stand-up row. That was why some people said that if Yan Zhen had been present at the time, there was no way Yang Cheng would ever have become the secretary of the Municipal Party Committee.

Li Gaocheng had never really considered these stories and rumours too carefully, as he felt that, on the whole, since it was all now a *fait accompli*, it would be asking for trouble to delve any further and stir things up.

However, as soon as he sat down in Yan Zhen's study, a thought came to him, unbidden: was the whole business with Zhongyang Textiles destined to come down to a battle between Yang Cheng and Yan Zhen? And if so, what would his role be in it?

As he saw things at the moment, at least Yang Cheng hadn't lied to him, and two things he had told him were certainly true. Moreover, Yang Cheng had been quite candid and open with his views and opinions, and Li didn't believe he was hiding anything from him. But now, what he urgently needed to know was what Yan Zhen was going to say to him and what he most especially hoped was that he would be able to give him a clear explanation of what was going on with Te Gao Te.

The question was, how to bring the topic up in a way that would allow Yan Zhen to tell the truth. Even if the truth was impossible, Li still wanted to hear Yan Zhen's explanations and justifications.

In fact, there was just one thing he wanted to hear: did Yan Zhen know about the existence of Te Gao Te, and did he also know that his brother-in-law was involved? As long as Yan Zhen admitted this, that would be enough for him.

The thing that worried Li Gaocheng most at this point was whether, as he himself had been, Yan Zhen was genuinely in ignorance of the Te Gao Te Passenger Transportation Corporation. If he really did know nothing at all about it, then, no matter how things turned out, he, Li Gaocheng, could still hold Yan Zhen in the same deep respect he had in the past, and he would still be an honourable secretary and his trusted superior, as he always had been.

Li Gaocheng thought nervously about what he should say. He understood that this matter had to be cleared up first and only then could other things be properly explained. Te Gao Te seemed to be the bridge that had to be crossed before he could see what view to take of the problems at Zhongyang Textiles and how to solve them. Otherwise, everything would surely be fake, and just a facade.

Yan Zhen was still waiting in silence. From years of past experience, Li Gaocheng knew that, under such circumstances, Yan Zhen would never be the first to speak. Yan Zhen's way of working had always been that after you had finished speaking, reporting and explaining your position and opinions, he would be voluble and eloquent in expressing his own. Everyone who knew anything about it agreed that Yan Zhen's tactic was always to wait to strike until after his opponent had struck first. Today was no different.

But what was different now was Li Gaocheng's mentality. He no longer presented all his views and opinions without reservation, as he had done in the past, but considered what to say and how to draw out the topics he wanted to know about.

"Secretary Yan, after the Standing Committee meeting finished today, I told the Municipal Party Committee secretary to come and report to you. Has he already been?" Li Gaocheng felt that these words were rather awkward, and it was not a feeling he was familiar with.

"He has." Just those two words and nothing else. Then Yan Zhen just stared directly at Li Gaocheng in silence. He was always like this when receiving guests, especially when receiving subordinates. He would just stare straight at you. Generally speaking, no one dared meet his gaze, and they would always look away. And once you looked away, you found yourself overwhelmed by his imposing presence. There was nothing you could do about it, because he was your superior and your boss: he could look at you like that, but you could not do the same to him.

"Do you already have an understanding of the basic situation, Secretary Yan?" As he looked at the solemn and dignified figure of Yan Zhen, Li Gaocheng felt himself almost incapable of speech.

"Hmmnn! Now I want to hear what you have to say." Yan Zhen looked straight at Li Gaocheng, and Li could not help but feel the pressure. Dimly, he began to realise that Yan Zhen must know something. But what did he know? Did he know that Li had already inquired about the inside story of Te Gao Te? Or did he know that he was privy to Te Gao Te's secrets? Yes, that could well be it. If someone could give him that information, someone could also give it to Yan Zhen. That was just the way things were: if you wanted to find something out, the price you pay is that it may be found out by others as well. It was just as the old saying goes: if you don't want anyone to know, do it yourself. Where there is gain, there has to be loss as well. Of course, Yan Zhen might not know anything at all yet, but that made no difference; all he could do was be straight with him.

"This is how I think things stand, Secretary Yan. Judging by the current situation at Zhongyang Textiles, the problems are indeed quite serious, and some of them are so serious that they have gone beyond anything we imagined. If we don't make up our minds and find a solution as soon as possible, the consequences will be highly unpredictable, especially as they may affect the stability of society and the deepening reform of state-owned enterprises. Therefore, after discussion in the Standing Committee, it was agreed that a larger working group should be appointed as soon as possible to look into Zhongyang Textiles and carry out a major financial audit and inventory as a first step..."

"All right, all right, I already know all that. Your general secretary has already given me a detailed report this afternoon. Isn't it just that there is a handful of workers who want to make trouble?" Yan Zhen seemed to be behaving completely out of character as he didn't wait for Li Gaocheng to reply but plunged straight in, talking incessantly. "Now, some of our leaders seem to have developed a phobia about lawsuits. All it takes is someone, no matter how important or unimportant, to come along threatening to sue, and it's as though the sky is falling on our heads, as though it's something really terrible. What's that all about? What's so terrible? Can the leaders be sued or not? In this China of ours, no matter what level they are at or what position they hold, which leader has never been sued? What do we think our work is? Our work is management. Where there is management, there will be contradictions, and where there are contradictions, there will be differing opinions and clashes and collisions. When those reach a certain point, then there will be fierce hand-to-hand fighting with neither side willing to give in. In the past, people stuck up 'big-character posters',[1] nowadays they sue officials, so what's all the fuss about?"

"The situation at Zhongyang Textiles is different, Secretary Yan. The problems are very serious." Li Gaocheng tried his best to reverse Yan Zhen's view of the affair, in particular to make him truly understand the seriousness and complexity of Zhongyang Textiles' problems. "When I was at the factory that day, ten or twenty thousand workers came out to protest. The relationship between the cadres and the people has been tense to the point of snapping. If we don't take it seriously, the consequences will be unimaginable, and things will probably deteriorate to the point of..."

"It's really alarmist and exaggerated to say that there were ten to twenty thousand workers. At best, there are only a few disgruntled troublemakers," Yan Zhen interrupted him again, his voice gradually rising. "What are the consequences of one little group trying to cause trouble? I just don't understand where this general pessimism is coming from. What is reform? Reform is revolution – it means destroying the old and building the new, it means breaking the iron rice bowl and creating a new economic order. So then, this inevitably affects the interests of many, many people, and it also affects some deep-rooted traditional influences and outdated concepts. What reform needs to change is precisely those influences and concepts. If there is a problem, this is what is at the root of it, and if we are to talk seriously, this is the ultimate seriousness. Therefore, the reform of our state-owned enterprises is bound to involve the vested interests of some people and is bound to offend those people. This is an inevitable reaction to the deepening reform of our state-owned enterprises – what might be called the labour pains of productive reform! Can reform without pain, without contradiction, without struggle truly be called reform? Isn't that the case with Zhongyang Textiles? Losses and debts, shutdowns and stoppages have forced us to step up our efforts and resolve further to deepen our reforms. This also requires our dedication, our commitment and our sacrifice. But there are also people who will take advantage of this opportunity to make trouble, to petition, or to complain, in order to achieve different goals of their own. Those who have a difficult life want money. Those who don't have a job want a job. Those who are dissatisfied with their leaders want to complain. And then there are those who want to be leaders but have not been promoted, those who want a salary increase but have not been given one, and those who have done something wrong and been punished for it. When these kinds of people all get together, of course they are going to want things to blow up, and the bigger the explosion, the better. Of course, there are indeed many workers with very poor living conditions. Because they do not know the true situation and have a low level of understanding, it is inevitable that they will become activists and troublemakers. But, just think about it, apart from those people, how many others are there who can really make trouble? Not to mention, this was all happening on their own doorstep and they had nothing else to do since production had stopped and there was no work for them. How many do you think just came out to join in the fun? Ten or twenty thousand, maybe? Isn't what you are doing just bolstering their ambitions, damaging your own reputation and scaring yourself for no good reason? Besides, even if there were that many, so what? Didn't you manage to talk them round by going there all on your own? Didn't you stop them dead in their tracks? Whatever you may say, this is still a country ruled by the Communist

Party, and the political power is all in our hands. Listen here, Lao Li, you're no youngster anymore, in fact we're the same age, you and me, and is there anything we haven't been through before? Is there anything left to scare us? The key is to think more and analyse more. You are recognised as a doer, but now you are the mayor of a city, if you remain just good at getting things done but not good at using your brains, it really will be dangerous for you. If you had been made Municipal Party Committee secretary last time, do you think we'd be in the same situation now? I can see you haven't really thought it through, but what else is behind the trouble at Zhongyang Textiles? That petition was spread all over the Municipal Government and the Provincial Government in the space of just one morning. How many workers are there who could do that? Who is all this aimed at? Have you really thought about that? Your position is different now – you need to be clear about what the politics really are now and you need to question everything..."

Li Gaocheng silently looked at Yan Zhen's expressive face, and listened to his rhythmic words, as a realisation formed inside him. Yan Zhen's performance tonight seemed to have only one meaning: that he didn't want to listen to any report, but just wanted to hear what his, Li's, attitude was and see what position he had taken up. More than anything else, Yan Zhen needed his loyalty! In fact, from what he had said, Li could be quite sure that he already knew everything about the affairs of Zhongyang Textiles, but he simply wasn't going to reveal anything himself. As executive deputy secretary of the Provincial Party Committee, he had very carefully said enough for even the stupidest person to understand his meaning. Could he, Li Gaocheng, really be such a fool as to not understand anything even after listening for so long? The problem was that in this torrent of words, he hadn't been able to extract any real information about Yan Zhen. In all these free-thinking words, so replete with depth of thinking and breadth of philosophy, he had actually wrapped himself up so tightly that Li had been unable to extract anything detrimental to him. It was as if he had fully understood all of Li Gaocheng's innermost thoughts and intentions and hadn't let slip even a hint of any of the things Li wanted to know.

Finally, Li Gaocheng said, reluctantly: "Secretary Yan, it's not that I haven't thought about it, and I have indeed come to a few understandings. I think we have a duty to verify some of the problems raised by the material in the petition. For example, some of the questions raised by Zhongyang Textiles' subsidiary, Xinchao Co. Ltd, implicate top-level municipal cadres and even top-level provincial cadres. These are serious problems and one of them..."

"So what! The company's main business is to provide a wide range of products and services to the market. Just because they involve provincial and municipal leadership cadres, does that make the problems serious? That is outrageous! In fact, some of the issues are simply specious grandstanding, so who's to say who's involved and who isn't? You can tie yourself in knots trying to figure out which connections have been used where, but will you be able to say for certain that the leadership is implicated? It all defies any explanation and is nothing more than troublemaking for the sake of it. Are you saying that even distant relatives of leadership cadres aren't allowed to do anything just because of that tenuous connection? Of course, we have always strictly prohibited leadership cadres from participating in business, and we are never lenient over that kind of thing..."

Li Gaocheng again found himself thrust into embarrassed silence; he was in absolutely no doubt that this was definitely a no-go area with Yan Zhen, and he was not casually just going to let him in. He wasn't going to talk to Li Gaocheng about it, nor was he going to let Li talk to him about it either.

Everything clearly indicated that Yan Zhen must know all about it and Yan Zhen also knew that Li Gaocheng knew this.

Also, the reason why Yan Zhen was taking such a tough line with Li was quite simply because he already knew all about him.

Te Gao Te was one thing and the Green Apple Entertainment City was another and everybody knew about everybody, so no one could do anything about anyone else. If you're full of shit yourself, how can you have the nerve to wipe anybody else's arse. In any case, I'm your superior so you can explain things to me, but I don't have to explain anything to you, nor do I need to.

Was that what Yan Zhen was thinking?

CHAPTER TWENTY-ONE

WHEN, TO HIS GREAT RELIEF, Li Gaocheng finally left Yan Zhen's house, it was already almost midnight. The cold air outside gave him a feeling of liberation and he took in deep, almost greedy breaths to try to relax himself. Primarily, Yan Zhen's stern attitude and lengthy harangue had simply exhausted him, but they had also instilled an indefinable feeling of abhorrence.

How could this be?

How could the deputy secretary of the Provincial Party Committee, a high-status senior leader, act so tough and unreasonable? How, when he was receiving the mayor of a provincial capital city who was older than him and not far from his own level, could he not even let him finish his sentences? That stern look was more like the way a father justifiably reprimands his son!

Was it just because it was Yan Zhen who had been personally responsible for his promotion?

Strictly speaking, the promotion had come from the organisation, not the individual, but isn't it so often the case that organisational principles and organisational wishes manifest themselves in an individual? And weren't there some individuals who had no hesitation in putting themselves above the organisation, and manifesting their individual wishes through the organisation? Such people had no reticence in saying: "I promoted so and so, and so and so was also promoted by me. How dare you not listen to me?"

The promotion of cadres was according to organisational need, not personal preference. When someone undertook the evaluation and promotion of cadres, they did so on the basis of that need. If that was the nature of their job, what gave them the right to point fingers and boss around the people who are promoted, and even consider they should be treated as a benefactor for the rest of their lives?

However, it was one thing to say it, and it might well be right in principle, but would anyone dare argue the case or express it openly?

If you did dare, not only would it immediately affect your promotion prospects, your character, abilities and your reputation would also be damaged. You would be looked down on, even by the general population. Even if you were opposed to the person who promoted you, you would still be considered beyond the pale!

Acting ungratefully and taking revenge for kindness was almost the same as ignoring the needs of your family and showing a complete lack of humanity. In fact, it made you less than human!

But that was Chinese culture for you and there really was nothing you could do about it.

But this also presented a very serious dilemma which required a decision to be made. It was a paradoxical choice that might have to be made at any time: this man promoted you, but both you and he work for the same organisation. When one day, on a certain issue, you have to choose between him and that organisation, do you allow yourself to be driven by responsibility to your patron or to the organisation, and how will you choose?

There was no middle way in such a matter – you had no option but to make a choice!

Maybe it was because Li Gaocheng had been giving so much thought to the matter that he hadn't said anything to Yan Zhen. He had made no kind of statement and adopted no kind of position. He didn't want to commit himself until he had made the correct decision for himself.

In fact, the meaning of everything Yan Zhen said had already been made clear by the content of that telephone call during the meeting of the Standing Committee.

Yan Zhen had spoken a lot, and Li Gaocheng had listened a lot. But in the end, neither of them had made a clear statement or adopted a position.

He had seen that Yan Zhen wasn't happy this evening, but then nor was he.

But that was the only way it could be.

It was winter weather outside, and it wasn't long after coming out of the toasty warm house that the biting cold had gnawed through to his bones.

As it was late, Li Gaocheng didn't order up a car, but walked along the road by himself. Nowadays, even though he was just a mayor, the widespread celebrity television brought had made him something of a star, more of a star than many real stars in fact, and people recognised him wherever he went. In terms of open government, this was clearly an advantage, but in another way, it wasn't necessarily a good thing. In the past, officials like county magistrates, prefects or governors were not recognised by the ordinary people. So, if they wanted to conduct any kind of opinion poll or mingle incognito with the populace, it was an easy thing to do. But now, even just walking down the street by himself was not a straightforward thing for him to do as mayor, let alone how difficult it was for higher-level officials.

It was all a bit overwhelming. The higher up you were, the less fun and freedom you had compared to an ordinary person, and all he really wanted to do was be able to walk down the street by himself. Presumably because it was winter, there were few other pedestrians out and about, but, to Li Gaocheng's surprise, there was no lessening in the number of cars and taxis, and the late-night snack restaurants were doing a roaring trade. The bigger the restaurant and the higher its standard, the more cars and taxis there were queuing outside it. Through the big restaurant windows, he could see the crowds of people. The women were all modern, fashionably dressed young ladies, but he couldn't see many young men in their early twenties.

By the look of it, it was not normal eating and drinking, and this kind of high-end late-night stuff was the preserve of the rich and fortunate.

On the street, a middle-aged woman was hunched, sheltering from the cold behind the cigarette stall outside the door of a fancy restaurant. Although she was wearing a big old army greatcoat with a turned-up collar that practically covered her head, she was blue and shivering from the cold and stamping her feet continuously. Li

Gaocheng had walked a couple of steps past her before turning to look back. He didn't know why he did it because he didn't smoke and there were plenty of cigarettes back at home anyway, but he bought a pack of "Hongtashan". Could it have been out of pity or had he felt a twinge from a guilty conscience?

"Is there still any business this late?" he asked, fishing out the money.

"Depends! Sometimes it's good, sometimes it's not." Her hands were shaking so much as she gave Li Gaocheng his change that she could barely hold the notes. "We're not allowed to set up here during the day, so we try and squeeze a few freezing yuan out at night and make the best of it."

"You've got some high-class cigarettes here," Li said, looking for something to say.

"You don't know much, do you? Who's going to smoke rubbish at a place like this?" she said, shivering even more violently.

"Why do you say that?"

"It's obvious, isn't it! What kind of people do you think you get around here in the evening? Just look at the cars! They're all officials or rich bastards. They're not going to smoke rubbish, are they! Brands like those 'Hongtashan' of yours are old news and much too common!"

"Is that so?" Li Gaocheng felt a little like old news himself and couldn't help asking: "What kind of food do they eat here this late? Is it true that late-night eating is all the rage now?"

"What food? Anyone can tell you're an old dinosaur! This is what is all the rage now – they call it 'nightlife'. You know! Singing, dancing, playing cards, that kind of thing! When they're hungry and tired and the nightclub girls have all found their companions and a nest for the night, then they come here for a bite to eat. A nightcap, you might call it. At one hundred, two hundred yuan for a midnight snack, do you think ordinary folk come here? That's how society is now, more's the pity – the rich die rich, and the poor die poor. If someone is born into poverty, he won't claw his way out of it in four or five lifetimes…"

Li Gaocheng walked silently away.

For him as mayor, what that middle-aged woman had just said

made him feel more guilty and uncomfortable than if she had cursed him to his face.

Li Gaocheng had always been very concerned about what he read about "nightlife" in the press. People seemed to have reached a consensus that the more prosperous the economy is, the more developed and open somewhere is, the more prosperous and open the nightlife should be. But if the nightlife was like what he had encountered tonight, what were the ordinary people supposed to make of such a perversion? If it was claimed that this "nightlife" was the result of reform, wouldn't that just make them more suspicious and resentful of reform? This was a really worrying, not to say scary, view of things. It could well be the most socially destabilising factor of all.

He walked past entrance after entrance until he came to his compound. The guard on the gate was going to stop him until he walked out and saw who it was. He hurriedly nodded meaningfully at Li and told him that there were quite a few people waiting for him at home. This wasn't an unusual occurrence. Sometimes, even at one o'clock in the morning, there would be people waiting for him when he got home. Normally speaking, these midnight callers wouldn't take up too much of his time. They either had something that needed immediate approval, or they might need to remind him of something they thought important, or they had some urgent personal matter. They were not usually particularly important people, but they were all people he had some connection with.

But who could these people be tonight?

When he reached the door, he froze on the spot. There was a huge crowd of people waiting in the dark outside his front door! They were standing, squatting or sitting on the ground, twenty or thirty of them! It was obvious that they had been waiting for a long time as almost everyone was shivering from the cold, but they were all waiting quietly – no one stamped their feet, and no one spoke.

When he walked over, they stood up as if they were students catching sight of their teacher, and then they all looked at him in silence. In the dim light of the streetlamp at the entrance, Li Gaocheng could not see who they were until he got very close.

"Who's there?" he asked softly.

"Is that Mayor Li?" a very old man standing in front of him asked in a slightly hoarse voice.

"I am Li Gaocheng. Where are you all from?" Li Gaocheng still didn't recognise the people in front of him.

"We are all from Zhongyang Textiles, Mayor Li. My name is Wang Dakuan..."

"Dakuan?" Li Gaocheng was astonished. "Are you the Wang Dakuan from the Number Two workshop of Zhongyang Textiles?"

"Yes, that's me, Mayor Li."

When he turned on the door's overhead light, he could make out clearly that it was indeed Wang Dakuan, who had been awarded the title of national model worker for three consecutive years in the Number Two workshop of Zhongyang Textiles. The way he remembered him, Wang Dakuan should be about the same age as himself, but the man in front of him was so old and grey! Perhaps it was because he had been out in the freezing cold too long, but he looked sixty or seventy years old.

"We have been waiting for you here for four or five hours, Mayor Li. I really didn't expect you to be so busy!" Wang Dakuan seemed rather over-excited, and he was having trouble getting his words out. "We won't disturb you long – we just want a moment to talk to you. Zhang Faqiang, Guo Baoshan and Liu Xiaodong are here too, and they all just want to see you this once."

When he heard these familiar names, Li Gaocheng was astonished all over again. All of them had been national model workers, provincial model workers and advanced workers within the national textile system at Zhongyang Textiles. They were famous and influential figures in the factory, the city and the province! It was then he realised that all the twenty or thirty people who had assembled there were the model workers, advanced workers and pacesetters of the company. They had all been respected and revered figures during Zhongyang Textiles' best years! Li Gaocheng had held a grand award ceremony almost every year in their honour.

When the celebratory meeting was over, Li Gaocheng always used to follow the old traditional form of tribute by going to the nearby villages to find several dozen fine horses, and then he personally garlanded these model workers with red flowers and walked beside them, holding the stirrups as a mark of respect. On one occasion, with Wang Dakuan on the lead horse, he walked a full ten miles along the city streets.

He had handed out awards and presented garlands to almost all of these people in front of him. Even during the time he was deputy mayor, he still insisted on going in person to an annual award ceremony to present the awards to the model workers of Zhongyang Textiles.

Back then, these people were so fine, and so respected! Their stories were in the newspapers, their voices were on the radio, and their photographs were on the bulletin boards. All the workers in the factory and the city vowed to be like them, to become national leaders and role models!

But now, only a few years later, how could these people have been reduced to what they were now?

Their clothes were so shabby, their faces were so haggard, their bodies so thin, and their expressions were so full of feeling, as all of them huddled, frozen, in front of his house. Perhaps because Li Gaocheng had just left an area with all those luxurious hotels and restaurants, he couldn't help feeling that the looks and clothing of these people in front of them were shabbier than the migrant workers who came to the city to work!

He had a lump in his throat, and tears were welling up in his eyes.

Weren't they all the cream of the workers? Hadn't they all created great wealth for the country? Hadn't they all made great contributions to the country? Even today, even a decade or a hundred years later, would they not still be society's most valuable assets and the elite talents most needed by the nation? How had they suddenly become like this?

The people we don't need have become so rich, and the people we need so badly have become so poor! Where had this gone so wrong?

Seeing him stunned into silence, the people in front of him also stood there in the same state. After a long time, he said hurriedly, as if he had suddenly recovered his senses: "Why are you standing outside on such a cold day? Hurry up and come in! Come in!" Li Gaocheng said as he pressed the doorbell, over and over.

"No, Mayor Li, no, no, no! We just want a quick meeting with you here. It's so late, we don't want to disturb you. We knew you were busy, so we have already written up a document in advance, and everything we want to say is on it. So just read it when you have time."

Wang Dakuan's voice trembled as he shivered from the cold, and the men beside him chimed in, in agreement.

"Not at all, not at all! You must come in, you must come in. You are at my door already, so of course you must come in and sit down for a while. At least have some tea to warm yourselves up a bit." Li Gaocheng kept on ringing the bell until he gave up in frustration and started banging the door with the palm of his hand.

Eventually, the front door was opened by the little nanny.

Li Gaocheng seized Wang Dakuan by the hand and tried to pull him inside, but the other man held fast to the door handle, insisting that he wouldn't go in.

"Mayor Li! Mayor Li!" Wang Dakuan was hauling himself backwards with so much force he was in danger of falling onto his backside. "We really can't come in, Mayor Li. We just wanted to see you. There's no point pulling me, Mayor Li... If we have your word, we are quite content with that..."

In the bright light of the light over the door, he saw that the heavily wrinkled, white-haired Wang Dakuan had tears streaming down his cheeks.

Li Gaocheng was stunned into silence again, with no idea what to say.

"Here is what we wrote out for you, Mayor Li." Wang Dakuan pulled a sheaf of crumpled letter paper out of his pocket and held it in front of Li Gaocheng. The words come from our hearts. Please read it when you have time."

Li Gaocheng received the papers carefully and solemnly and said, with great emotion: "I would really like to have a long talk with you people, but with things as they stand, that will have to wait till next time. It has been a long, long time since I last saw you all." As soon as the words were out of his mouth, Li Gaocheng immediately regretted them. He felt that they were both hypocritical and pretentious. If he really wanted to talk to them, he could call them at any time, and they would be sure to come. But when would he really want to talk to them? When would the next time be?

Even so, the model workers in front of him seemed to be very moved once again. Several of the old men behind Wang Dakuan could not stop wiping their eyes.

"...Mayor, we were really worried that you were at home and didn't want to see us. We didn't think you could have changed... You are still the same man..." Wang Dakuan choked out, then said no more.

"Is there nothing else you want done? No other request?" There was a lump in Li Gaocheng's throat, and he struggled to hold back his tears.

"No, there is really nothing else, Mayor Li. We are already quite satisfied with what you have said. You have put our minds at rest. We know you are busy, Mayor Li. You have been busy all day and must be tired. Go and rest. We are leaving now. Go in! Go in!..."

The hands they each held out to take their leave were all equally coarse, cracked and covered in calluses. Only decades of hard, repetitive labour could make hands like that.

Again he felt an indescribable sense of shame. It had been so long since he had last shaken a hand like that.

Li Gaocheng watched in silence until they were out of sight, and it was only then that it suddenly occurred to him that they still had twenty *li* or more ahead of them. It was so late, and the buses had already stopped running. How would they get back? Would they walk back?

Yes, of course they would. Given their current conditions, they wouldn't have spent nearly a hundred yuan on a taxi.

Thinking about this, and looking at the papers in his hand, he once more felt indescribably sad.

How could the business have collapsed when it had workers like that?

If the enterprise had collapsed despite having such good workers, there was only one possibility: it had collapsed at the hands of those wastrel cadres!

CHAPTER TWENTY-TWO

LI GAOCHENG was mentally and physically exhausted as he went into his house, but, as he did so, he stopped dead in his tracks in amazement. There were a dozen or so people of all ages sitting there!

These people who had felt entitled to enter his house were clearly not run-of-the-mill folk; the least you could say was that they were nothing like the workers who had just been waiting for hours in the freezing cold outside his door. These people felt it was all right for them to be sitting, secure in their importance, inside his house, even though it was already well into the small hours of the morning. If they hadn't had his wife's nod of approval, if their business wasn't particularly important and if they weren't of a certain status, they would certainly not be disturbing him so late.

They were all well-dressed, self-satisfied, ruddy complexioned and wearing polite, reserved expressions. Their hands were conspicuously soft and smooth. The sharp contrast between them and the workers he had just seen off outside made a powerful impression.

He suddenly remembered that, when he arrived back that evening and reached the inner gate of the compound, there was a whole fleet of luxury limousines parked outside it, most of which were makes he didn't even recognise.

His smiling wife was busily beginning to introduce the visitors, and Li Gaocheng immediately realised who they were. They were all the top bosses of the Te Gao Te Passenger Transport Corporation.

At this point, he had already recognised the short, heavy-set figure of Wang Yiliang, the recently retired vice president of the provincial bank.

The first to shake hands with him was Chao Wanshan, the chairman of Te Gao Te, who was also the brother-in-law of the deputy secretary of the Provincial Party Committee, Yan Zhen. In addition to the chairman, there were two vice-chairmen, a general manager and two deputy general managers. The rest were the director, the divisional chief, the chief accountant and two specialised clerical staff.

They all stood up to make their introductions then sat back down to continue the greetings.

Li Gaocheng silently considered what their presence there meant and what their purpose might be.

This Chao Wanshan in front of him was pale-skinned, clean and graceful. He looked to be around forty-seven or forty-eight years old. Whatever else, there was no similarity in appearance or temperament between him and Yan Zhen's wife. His presence there at that time of night immediately made Li Gaocheng think that the reason for the visit had to have something to do with Deputy Secretary Yan Zhen. Without his assent, they would never have come hurrying over here at so late an hour.

Similarly, they would never have waited so long at his house if the matter wasn't of particular urgency.

"It is very late, Mayor Li, and we don't want to disturb you any more than absolutely necessary. I think we should get down to business straightaway, make our report and then we can discuss it," Chao Wanshan said calmly and matter-of-factly. "The situation is like this, Mayor Li. It has been more than two years since the establishment of the Te Gao Te Passenger Transport Corporation. Business over that time has been comparatively good, and, the way things stand at the moment, the operations of the company are also quite stable. Of course, this situation is inseparable from the support, help and cooperation of all relevant parties, especially your own consistent interest and support. As one of the principal board members of the Te Gao Te Passenger Transport Corporation, on the occasion of the arrival of the New Year..."

"Hold on a moment!" Li Gaocheng interrupted him furiously.

He had intended to hear the man out before speaking, but when he heard this, he couldn't stay silent any longer. "What does your 'Te Gao Te' have to do with me? And what's all this about 'board members'? Before just now, I knew nothing about the operation of 'Te Gao Te'! I've never even met any of you and I have never helped you in any way. So how can you...?"

"We would be very sorry to hear you talk like that, Mayor Li," Chao Wanshan interrupted Li Gaocheng in calm and measured tones. "When Te Gao Te was established, a company like that would not have been approved so quickly without your timely approval and support. Yes indeed, this is something that everyone is aware of, especially Director Wu, who also called on a lot of connections in support of..."

Director Wu? Needless to say, this Director Wu was his wife, Wu Aizhen. So, his wife had been involved in Te Gao Te from the very beginning! If that was true, then it meant that his wife had not only hidden the Green Apple Entertainment City from him, but Te Gao Te too! Did Chao Wanshan just refer to her as one of the principal directors?

And what was this "approval" of Te Gao Te the man had referred to? Even he himself didn't know how many documents he approved every month of the year, but he certainly didn't remember anything to do with something called Te Gao Te. Moreover, when dealing with a large passenger transport company with the size of funding and organisation that Te Gao Te apparently had, generally speaking, he would only approve it after it had been studied by the Standing Committee; so why had it left no impression on him? Was it...? He suddenly remembered something that had happened two years ago, before Yang Cheng was secretary of the Municipal Party Committee. He remembered he was in hospital being given IV infusions for influenza; the Party secretary had come to see him – his wife was there too – and had produced a comment form, saying it was for some passenger transport station or other. It had provincial approval and it just needed his signature to finalise it. He also remembered that his wife had chimed in with her support, and Secretary Yan had telephoned too, saying that this was an important measure to help alleviate pressure on the rail passenger transport system; the peak

Spring Festival period was almost upon them, so he should help things along by signing without delay. Because he was ill, because the municipal secretary had brought it to him and because Secretary Yan Zhen had exhorted him, he hadn't read the thing too carefully and just added his approval. In fact, even if he hadn't been ill at the time, he would probably have approved it; after all, it was clearly a good thing, and it was a major development that was being taken very seriously from the central to the local level, not to mention that it had the unanimous approval of Secretary Yan and the Municipal Party Committee secretary.

Could it be that that signature of approval had actually been for Te Gao Te? Li Gaocheng suddenly found himself rooted to the spot, unable to speak. Because everyone was hiding things from him, he didn't know anything about the affair and so had no right to express an opinion on it. If his wife really was involved and he still insisted that he knew nothing about it, he would make himself a complete and universal laughing stock! How could he deny knowledge of a company he himself had approved and of which his wife was a principal director? How absurd and ridiculous would that be? Even a complete idiot wouldn't believe that!

He looked silently at his wife, but she avoided his gaze. He was angry and outraged in a way he had never felt before, to see her looking so charming and elegant. How could she be like this? How did she dare?

Chao Wanshan continued in the same assured and cultured tones: "In line with our forecast, throughout two years of activity and effort, we have been able to make timely summations of our learning and experience and have constantly adjusted and corrected our business activities. Because of this, in the coming year, Te Gao Te's situation will continue to improve, and we will strive to take it to the next level. We are extremely grateful to you, Mayor Li, because, as long as we have your support, we know we have something we can rely on and that gives us peace of mind. The people who have come here today are the mainstays and key business personnel of our company. There are a few who could not come, but, essentially, everyone who should be here, is here. We all wanted very much to see you so we could thank you in person. We have already discussed the details of the company's revenue for the year with Director Wu, and, because of time constraints we will not repeat them now. I think that is all, Mayor Li, so, if you don't have any other orders, we will take our leave."

At this point, everybody stood up as if by prior arrangement, and some of them were already getting ready to go.

Li Gaocheng suddenly seemed to come back to his senses and realise what was going on. An intuition told him that, on this occasion, he had to say something to make his position clear; otherwise once they walked out of his house, everything, including what he did know and what he didn't know, would be set in stone as the facts. Besides, there were so many witnesses, he couldn't run away and he couldn't deny it all even if he wanted to. He was indelibly labelled now, and even a swim in the Yellow River wouldn't wash that label off. Having got that far in his thinking, he gestured with his hand and said: "Everybody sit down and don't be in such a hurry to leave. There is still something I want to say." By the time they had all taken their seats again, he had worked out what he was going to say. "Here's how it is. I don't want to keep going round in circles with you, so please don't play dumb with me. So far, I haven't completely figured out everything you have been going on about, but I'm not an idiot and I understand the essence of what you are saying. Now, there are a few things I want you to be clear about. First of all, I really don't know anything about the fundamental situation regarding Te Gao Te. You say that I approved the company right at the start. I quite simply don't remember that. I will check it out when I go to work tomorrow. If it proves to be so, tomorrow is by no means too late for me to take an interest in the company, and I will take the initiative to come and find you. Secondly, you said that you came to me today mainly to report on and discuss the situation. That surprised me. Te Gao Te is already more than two years old, so why do you suddenly want to come and make a report now? What do you want to report? What is the real reason? I'm really not clear about any of that, but if you actually do want to make a report, then please come to my office tomorrow. Nor am I clear about what you meant when you talked about a 'principal director'. I don't care if it was me you were talking about, or whether it was a suggestion you were making, I am telling you directly now that that is not something I can ever agree to, or ever permit. Since you are keen to leave, that's fine, and I'll leave things at that for the moment. If you want to discuss anything else, then come to my office tomorrow. It is very late now so let's leave it there and you can suit yourselves what you do next."

Li Gaocheng stood up as soon as he had finished, without waiting for any reply. He waved his hand at them and made his way towards the dining room, firstly because he was very hungry and secondly because he really didn't want to say anything more to them.

He was beyond furious!

This was the first time in his long career he had felt such withering contempt directed at him by others or been treated in such a sinister and overbearing manner. Did he not have something to say about that? If not, then he should just let himself become party to it, walk into that obvious trap, spring it, then see what he could do about it!

That meant he should quite simply beat the villains at their own game and outdo them for villainy!

Was it because Chao Wanshan was the brother-in-law of the deputy secretary of the Provincial Party Committee?

Was it just because his brother-in-law was Yan Zhen, deputy secretary of the Provincial Party Committee?

Even so, did that mean that they could treat him, the mayor, as their plaything?

The nanny brought in two reheated dishes of food and a bowl of rice, which Li Gaocheng wolfed down as his thoughts ranged angrily.

There was a rush of footsteps, followed by an accusing and reproachful voice: "What was that!? What was that!? What is up with you today? Don't you know this was what Secretary Yan wanted? Who has got up your nose today?" His wife plonked herself down in front of him and began to scold him in nagging tones. "You can go against anyone else's wishes you want, but how can you go against Secretary Yan Zhen? Just think about it! Don't you owe everything you have today to him? How did you get to be deputy mayor to begin with? How did you get to be mayor? Where do you think you'd be without him? Who else took any notice of you? What happened when Secretary Yan went away for just a year at the Party Central School? You didn't get to be secretary of the Municipal Party Committee, did you? To put it bluntly, if Secretary Yan wasn't there for you, wouldn't it be like you not being there for me? Wouldn't you just be like a dog that's lost its master? Who would we turn to for support? I know what you are feeling at the moment – you don't want to get tangled up in a troublesome and complicated relationship like this, but do you really think that once you've been dragged into a circle like this you can jump out of it, just like that? If and when you die, you will die in that circle. Even if you did leave the circle and betray it completely, other people would always think you are still part of it. Besides, why should you want to betray it? If you betray this circle, who will respect you? What other circle will accept you? If you don't have a circle, who will protect you? In a position like yours, if there is no one to protect you, won't you always be made the scapegoat? I know your temperament, Gaocheng – you are too rigid and aloof. You always think that you rely only on yourself as mayor. It's true that you are a practical person, but haven't you thought about it? There are plenty of practical people in the province and the city, so why are you the only one who became the mayor? Secretary Yan is someone you can't afford to offend in this lifetime!

"Now that Secretary Yan is in trouble, there are many people knocking him behind his back, and bringing minor cases against him. At this critical time, even you are not going to protect him. Even you want to stab him in the back, do you? What will that do for your reputation in the eyes of the people? How could you go on living in this city? A person needs to be clear about their grudges and their loyalties – that's just how things are in China…"

Li Gaocheng just concentrated on eating and let his wife berate him.

He did not try to refute her charges, nor did he want to. His understanding of his wife had changed because of what had happened today. The change was so strong and so painful that he felt that, for the moment at least, there was no basis for any conversation between them. What she had just been saying, for instance, seemed so alien to him, so far from his own way of thinking.

Wu Aizhen didn't seem to notice the change in his feelings at all and went on talking, affectionately and persuasively: "...I know, you've been mad at me today. You think I lied to you about lots of things and kept you in the dark. You think I've taken a lot of bonuses and made a lot of money. It's not that I didn't want to tell you, or that I've been trying to hide it from you. It's just that there are some things that it is better for you not to know, because what good would knowing them do you? You are a mayor, so why should you be distracted by such trivial matters? Besides, it's all legal and above board. My nephew is the manager of a karaoke hall. What's wrong with that? He is educated, capable, clean, honest and has never done anything illegal. Where does it say he cannot be a manager? What rules has he broken? As for the claim that I am a director of the entertainment complex, I have never admitted that. I'm not so far gone or unaware that I can't tell right from wrong. It's true that I did invest some money, but it was all clean and above board. It was all my brother's money. You know that my brother has the contract on a coal mine in his hometown and has made some money over the past few years. If he wants to invest in the city, am I, as his sister, not allowed to help him? I only have one brother, who raised me from a child. My parents died early, and the two of us have always relied on each other. Do you think it's been easy getting where we are today?"

By this time, his wife was so choked with emotion, she couldn't even find any tears.

Li Gaocheng remained silent, not saying a word. In all their years as husband and wife, they had had numerous arguments, but, almost every time, he was defeated by his wife's tears. In normal times, he would have been deeply moved by her words. She wasn't lying to him – she was telling the truth. She did have only one brother, and it hadn't been easy for them growing up with him having to act as her father. But was that a reason for making so much money? How did he start the family's coal mine? How did that karaoke hall get opened? And how did the Green Apple Entertainment City get built? How did her brother suddenly get all those millions? How could she lie to him now? Did she really need the money that badly? Besides, he still didn't actually know how much money she'd been making all this time, and how.

Perhaps because Li Gaocheng remained silent, or because she thought her words had swayed him, Wu Aizhen continued with increasing confidence: "Yes, we have made a bit of money, but it's all clean money. We have done nothing illegal, and our conscience is clear. I have been with you for half our lives, and I know your character better than anyone. When did you ever accept a cent from anyone? This city's leadership cadres enjoy universal admiration, and, amongst them, the name of Li Gaocheng is top of the list for incorruptibility. Over all these years, have you eaten a crumb or pocketed a cent that wasn't your due? But now you are getting on for sixty, and if you don't move further up the ladder, how much longer can you stay as mayor? Your current term will be up in a couple of years, and what will happen then? Will you get another term? You have gone as far as you can as mayor, you can't become secretary, you're past the age for promotion, so, at the end of the next two years, who do you think will still really care about you? Once you stop being mayor, what is going to be left to you? We got married late, so our children are young and still at school, but once they grow up and enter society, we will have nothing to help them with. In today's society, if you don't have influence and you don't have money, what kind of support can you give your children? It seems you have regard neither for yourself nor for your children, is that right? Of course we're not going to accept any dirty money, but shouldn't we make some clean money for ourselves?"

Li Gaocheng felt impelled to say something in reply to all this but thought better of it and stopped himself. What kind of talk was that? Hoping to make money out of his being mayor? Suppose he had never made mayor? Suppose he had remained chief engineer and cadre at Zhongyang Textiles? Would she still be having those kinds of thoughts? If he had lost all the most basic safeguards of their livelihood, would he still be in any position to be thinking about making some extra, legitimate money for their children and for their later years? Didn't she realise that, as mayor, anything he earned above and beyond his official salary was bound to be dirty money? Once he couldn't expect further promotion, should he immediately change course and start making a lot of money? If all Communist Party cadres were like this, how could the people ever take them to their hearts? It was true that his children were little, but how did that make them any different from other children? Besides, both his children were at university and would have good jobs waiting for them when they graduated. Compared with the children of poor workers, with those families who couldn't even afford to send their children to school, didn't they already have things made? Was it the case that, because he was the mayor, he should only be satisfied if their children became millionaires or billionaires? Was that what it would take for him to discharge his responsibilities? Was that what was compatible with his status? Did they have these covetous thoughts and extravagant desires when they first got married? When did they start? He was having difficulty understanding all this and found it hard to believe that his own wife could have changed so much. When did it start happening?

"...since we've found ourselves talking about this stuff today, let me tell you the bottom line," his wife went on, speaking freely now. "Over the last few years, we certainly have earned a bit of money out of the mine and the karaoke hall, but it's not really that much, only two hundred thousand yuan or so if you tot it all up. There are a few investments too, but they're dead money and can only be counted in fixed assets..."

Two hundred thousand or more! The food almost got stuck in Li Gaocheng's throat and he shivered in alarm. He looked, dumbstruck, at his wife as she stood in front of him.

"I'm not trying to trick you. That's how much there is, plus a few other things which are neither here nor there, but we'll have to look at them when we're considering insurance," his wife said, honestly and confidingly. There was even the suggestion of a pout about her lips as she said: "There's no need to look at me like that, I'm being completely open with you. That money is clean as can be and not a penny of it is going to make your hands dirty. I had nothing to do with what happened tonight. It was Secretary Yan who telephoned first to say that his brother-in-law, Chao Wanshan, was coming here. His wife insisted that he must call us, so he did. On the phone, Secretary Yan kept complimenting you, saying that you were a decent, honest, and reliable person. If he hadn't liked you, he wouldn't have promoted you in the first place. After all this time, it seems that his prescience was justified. He didn't say why his brother-in-law wanted to come here today, so it was a surprise when Chao Wanshan came and said how good the profits have been over the last two years. At the end of this year, the capital investment has basically been earned back, and by next year, it will all be profit. He said that should have been the case last year, but liquidity issues had delayed it. The situation has improved this year and the company's capital is in a positive cycle, so he brought this year's dividends over. He gave them to me on the quiet, so nobody saw. It's a total of three hundred thousand this year, and last year's will be made up for next year…"

At this point, his wife pulled a lightweight attaché case from under the table and put it down on top. As she opened it, she continued: "Chao Wanshan said this is all completely legal and proper. He said, 'Te Gao Te is a limited liability public transportation company. It is privately owned, and since there are shareholders and board members, its only right they should receive dividends…'"

"Shareholders? Board members?" Once again, Li Gaocheng was astounded and dumbstruck.

"Don't worry. That doesn't concern you either. I used my brother's money to invest some of our capital." By this time, she had the attaché case open and was piling a stack of new banknotes in front of Li Gaocheng. "I haven't checked this money, but I don't think they would…"

Pushed beyond enduring, Li Gaocheng's fury finally erupted. He leapt to his feet, grabbed the case full of banknotes, lifted it high above his head then slammed it to the floor with a crash. The bank notes that were packed into it flew out as if it had exploded and scattered all over the floor.

"What exactly do you want all this money for? Do you want to buy a house? Or land? You need to take a good long look at yourself in the mirror to see if you're still human or not! Your money-grabbing ways are worse than a prostitute's. Have a good think about it and then tell me you still think this money isn't dirty. In all our years together, I never thought I would hear you talking like this. I'm blushing for you! I don't know how you got to be head of the Anti-Corruption Bureau, but I have to say, you don't deserve to be! Don't you recognise what you are doing? What you are doing is committing the most terrible of crimes…"

"Li Gaocheng! What do you think you are!? Are you still a man?" His wife also erupted angrily with furrowed brow and blazing eyes. There was a vicious edge to her words, and she seemed to regard him as something of no importance. "I'm sick of your nonsense.

After twenty years and more, I've had enough! You can think what you like and do what you like! I've got one last thing to tell you, and you can listen to it or not as you please. I'm telling you that without Yan Zhen, you would be nothing. If you're no longer mayor, you'll have nothing and be nobody! Who in this world is going to look out for you? When, in your life, have you ever been a real man? If you think this money is dirty, then make do with your clean money. Do you think you can support two children's education with your salary alone! I'm telling you, if you lose your job as mayor and just have to rely on whatever salary you can get..."

"Enough! Money, money, money! That's all you can see!" Li Gaocheng interrupted her abruptly, less and less able to restrain his fury. "Do you think just this bit of money is going to be enough to live off for the rest of your life, is going to give your children a life of ease? If all the country's cadres were like you, if the leadership of the Communist Party all thought like you, then sooner or later it will be all up for the nation, and all up for the government, and then, just like happened to the former Soviet Union, the whole ruling party will cease to exist, and what will that money of yours be worth then? Nowadays, ten thousand roubles will only buy one American dollar, so how much do you think all those millions of yuan will be worth? Several hundred dollars at most! And if nothing like that happens, with a few million to your name, you'll be able to live peacefully and comfortably just as you are now, for the rest of your life. I simply don't understand what you want so much money for. Think of the past, look at the present, compare us to the ordinary people! What have we got to be dissatisfied with? Go to the countryside, go to the factories! Think what you have to eat, what you have to wear, where you live, the furniture you have! What do the ordinary people have to eat, to wear? Where do they live? Forget about being unworthy of the people – are you worthy of yourself? Of your children? Of your conscience? One day, when you have to answer to the people, will you be able to bring yourself to say that everything you are doing today is just for this little bit of money? What about your original ideals, original ambition, original enthusiasm, and the oath you took back then? Were they all just for this little bit of money? Don't you realise that what you are doing now will not only destroy our country and destroy our reforms, but it will also destroy the future happiness of your family!? The people of this generation will never let you off the hook! When that time comes..."

He suddenly realised that there was no point in going on; his wife had already turned around and left the room, leaving him and the terrified nanny in the dining room with its floor covered in the scattered banknotes...

CHAPTER TWENTY-THREE

IN MORE THAN TWENTY YEARS, this was the first time.

The outburst was so intense, there was no room for reconciliation.

He hadn't expected his reaction to be so strong, and he knew he was going too far, but he couldn't help it.

He also had not expected his wife's reaction to be so intense or that she would speak so heartlessly.

"I'm sick of your nonsense. After twenty years and more, I've had enough!" So that's how things stood! He hadn't expected her to say anything like that.

What nonsense was she sick of? Did she mean the kind of thing he normally said? Was he too hypocritical, too arrogant, or too impersonal? Or was he too honest, too free with the truth? She had put up with him for decades though. Had she now had enough?

The pain was so great it made him moan. He bent slowly and sat down hard. As he did so, he realised that he was shaking badly.

Why was this happening? Why?

Was it because he was more than ten years older than her? Right from the beginning, what she said, went; he indulged her and then she became so spoiled she went to the bad. By then she was the boss of the whole household, and she gradually came to look down on him. Was that it?

He had hoped just to have a quiet talk with her, pleasant and reasonable, so they could get everything out in the open. He had wanted to explain to her, quite frankly, his own thinking and his opinion of hers. He had wanted to explain things to her so she would realise for herself that she had gone too far and that to continue down that road would be very dangerous. He also wanted to ask her why she had kept him in the dark about something as big as this. Wasn't he her husband, after all? She had been his wife for more than twenty years, so how could all this have been allowed to happen?

However, their fight tonight had laid everything bare. It turned out that their relationship as husband and wife over the past twenty years had been a hollow façade, shabby tat covered in a thin veneer of jade and gold. Was it all really so fragile, so vulnerable and so false? Was he contemptuous of his wife, or she of him?

When she first married him, did she take him for a fool and a dupe? No, surely not! What did he have worth having back then? Family property or rank? Money or power? What was there for her to dupe him out of? He was eleven years older than her, both of them were technical school graduates and, at the time, her post was senior to his. He was just a technician, a deputy workshop director; what had she seen in him back then?

Yes, that was the question: why had she only had eyes for him among all her other suitors at the time?

Was it not because he was honest, kind, loyal and reliable?

Other than that, what else was there? Because he was eleven years older than her? Because he was dark-skinned, ugly, thin and dried-up? Because he was a technical school graduate technician? Because he was a workshop deputy director who was always tired and reeking of oil and sweat?

Even their own children said that, to look at, they were an ill-matched couple and that judging only by outward appearance he had nothing at all to recommend him.

When he recommended her for Party membership, he had no thought that this simple, kind-hearted, beautiful, lovable, cheerful and vivacious girl might one day become his wife.

How was it that just such a simple and unsophisticated girl could, when she got married, and then became the wife of a mayor, so quickly turn into just such an unrecognisably worldly woman!?

Was it the changes in society that made her change, or was it the change in status?

Her face was still so pretty, her temperament still so refined, her voice still so pure: even amongst all the mists of confusion, his wife still seemed to him indistinguishable from the girl he married twenty years before. And for so many years it seemed to him he had been surrounded by that misty confusion. But this evening, within the last twenty minutes or so, he had been brought rudely to his senses as if by a slap in the face, only to realise that what he now saw in front of him and what he had imagined, diverged as widely as the gulf between heaven and earth.

There were bursts of uncontrollable weeping coming from his wife's bedroom, which stabbed Li Gaocheng in the heart like a knife.

This was not guilt, it was not distress, but a kind of deep rebuke aimed at him. What exactly was she crying about?

He remembered how lightly she had taken everything, how casual, self-assured and matter-of-fact she had been: "...it's not really that much, only two hundred thousand yuan or so if you tot it all up... that's how much there is, plus a few other things which are neither here nor there, but we'll have to look at them when we're considering insurance... he gave them to me on the quiet, so nobody saw. It's a total of three hundred thousand this year, and last year's will be made up for next year..."

That was a lot of money!

The amount she had mentioned was nearly three million, but what would the principal actually be that generated three hundred thousand in annual dividends. And, on top of that, there were three years' worth of dividends, as well as the hidden, uninsured assets. How much were they going to add up to?

Could there be anything else she was still hiding from him?

He was a mayor, and a married mayor at that; how long would it take a leadership cadre like him, especially one who "never accepted gifts", to build up money and assets worth eight figures?

The thought of that much money made him break out in a cold sweat.

How much money was involved that time when Chairman Mao Zedong tearfully ordered the execution of those two corrupt officials whose crime had scandalised the world?[1]

If the sum involved today was transplanted back to those days, it would be enough for him to be executed a hundred times over!

Yet she was insisting that the money was clean with not a cent of it dirty. And she was the head of the Anti-Corruption Bureau! And deputy attorney general of the Procuratorate!

Could she explain all this if the Anti-Corruption Bureau officially opened a case against her? How did she amass so much money in such a short period of time?

Had he understood all this correctly?

How could it all be clean?! Every cent of it stank of greed and other people's blood!

Huge numbers of workers were unemployed, countless state-owned enterprises were in trouble, with so many of them going bankrupt. Retired workers who had laboured for the nation and the people all their lives were not even given enough to live off. And at such a severely testing time, a leading cadre wielding state power like him had suddenly become very rich in a very short period of time? What was going on there? How would he look in the eyes of the ordinary people?

Even if he was a slippery enough customer to get away with it now, would he still be able to in ten, twenty, thirty years' time?

The ill-gotten wealth he held now would become a hidden peril and a nightmare that he wouldn't be rid of before he died.

He would never know peace and quiet ever again.

He was lost and bewildered! So lost and bewildered! It was both pitiful and nauseating!

The little nanny had gathered up all the banknotes that were scattered on the floor, put them back in the attaché case and placed that carefully on the table. Then she quietly picked up all the other papers that had also been scattered and put them down beside Li Gaocheng.

He just sat there in silence, not making a sound.

The pile of crumpled papers in front of him gradually came into focus. Weren't they the material that the model workers had given him just now?

Those model workers had said that their heartfelt words were written on those papers, and they had told him that they knew he was busy and didn't want to bother him, but could he take a look when he had the time.

In fact, what was he so busy with all day? He held all the usual crappy daily meetings, and he was always invited up to the podium, always the same routine, the same faces, the same speeches, the same atmosphere! "...we feel greatly encouraged and supported because our esteemed Mayor Li is able to attend our meeting today during his busy schedule! Now, we will invite Mayor Li to make an important speech..." Then he would pick up the pre-prepared manuscript, read what was written there, and accept the smattering of lukewarm applause which was followed by some completely vacuous declarations: "...Mayor Li has just given us some very timely and important instructions which everyone must be scrupulous in implementing when we get back." If the secretary of the Municipal Party Committee was there, then the secretary took precedence and he took second place; if the provincial governor and the secretary of the Provincial Party Committee were there, then, as mayor, he had to take the chair and it was him making the vacuous declarations: "In the midst of their hectic schedules, the provincial governor and the secretary of the Provincial Party Committee have..."; "the provincial governor and the secretary of the Provincial Party Committee have given us some very timely and important instructions..."

Day after day, month after month, year after year, and sometimes even several times a day playing catch-up with those meetings: they were all so important, they were all so essential, and they all had to be attended by leaders. As a result, the leaders were so busy day after day that they were constantly dazed and confused and rushed off their feet. Year after year the same hectic schedule of mountains of documents and oceans of meetings was repeated time after time. In fact, even they themselves couldn't keep track of how busy they were or what they were busy with! Perhaps it was precisely because of this hectic schedule forced on the leaders that unemployment was getting higher and higher, large and medium-sized enterprises were suffering greater and greater losses, unhealthy trends were spreading more and more widely, and the dissatisfaction of the ordinary people was constantly on the rise.

When was he actually going to be able to push all that nonsense to one side and get busy with the things that he really should be busy with?

The handwriting in front of him gradually came into focus:

> Mayor Li, we all know that you are really busy. How could a mayor who is responsible for millions of people not be busy? Therefore, we can hardly bear to bother you. Indeed, we have never bothered you over many, many years, but this time is different. No matter how busy you are, in the middle of your busy schedule you must concern yourself with the problems at Zhongyang Textiles. Mayor Li, in the name of all the model workers of the company, we ask you not to let the issue of Zhongyang Textiles remain unattended and be allowed to drag on indefinitely. Mayor Li, it really can't be delayed any longer, it really mustn't be delayed any longer. The situation is too serious, and the emotions of the people are too intense. If it drags on, it will be really dangerous, and everything will go terribly wrong.
>
> Mayor Li, you are our old factory manager, so you should know and understand the situation at Zhongyang Textiles. Even if you have become unfamiliar with it after all these years, as long as you come, once you get to grips with things, it will all immediately become clear. In fact, many of the problems are very obvious, and you will understand them as soon as you ask around and investigate. The workers all agree that it is not that the problems at the company cannot be managed, it is that no one is taking control of them. The size of the problems is not the worry, the worry is that they are being left unmanaged. The workers all agree that if the Communist Party doesn't concern itself with the problems of the workers, then it can no longer call itself the Communist Party. They know these are very harsh words, but all their hearts really do remain with the Communist Party!
>
> Mayor Li, please come back to us workers and get to know us properly again. Many workers have not received a penny of wages for more than a year, and no one can take it anymore. Life is really hard. Mayor Li, we model workers have all made a promise that no matter how poor we are, no matter how hard or difficult it is, we will not beg for anything from the nation. But life for those workers really is too difficult. Many families who have worked for

Zhongyang Textiles for generations can't make it through the year. Many workers can't even borrow money for medical treatment, and no matter what is wrong with them they can only take painkillers...

Mayor Li, everyone believes in you. Although many people say that you have changed and that the Li Gaocheng who is mayor now is no longer the Li Gaocheng who used to be the factory manager, we do not believe this. We believe you haven't changed. Most of the workers at Zhongyang Textiles still hold in their hearts what you said to the thousands of students who came to the gates of the factory during the turmoil in 1989...

We still remember it all clearly, and the way you looked then is still as vivid in our minds as if it had just happened...

Tears welled up in Li Gaocheng's eyes, and finally burst out to stream down his cheeks. He really hadn't expected the workers to remember that occasion and still trust him like this.

He suddenly remembered something someone had once said: in this world, only the common people still speak with a good conscience.

It seemed as though it had just happened that day.

Thousands of excited college students were crowded in front of the gates of the Zhongyang Textile Factory. Their cries and roars grew louder and louder. They wanted to rush into Zhongyang Textiles. They wanted to persuade the workers to march with them on the streets to the Municipal Party Committee and the Municipal Government.

The tightly closed iron gate was beginning to give way, and the dozens of security officers were about to be overwhelmed.

He had driven into the factory through the back gate. He asked about the situation in general, but did not hold a meeting, and did not ask anyone for advice. He understood that, given the gravity of the current situation, he had to act decisively.

Five minutes later, he came out of the office building alone and walked straight to the gate.

Many cadres and workers in the factory had tried to persuade him not to go. They said there was no talking to those college students who were so full of rage and fury. What could he hope to achieve in the face of such a large crowd of angry young people?

He thought about it for a long time and finally still went over to the main gates.

He really had no choice at the time. He told the cadres that, as long as the students were human beings and as long as they were capable, at that moment, of normal rational thought, then there had to be a way of talking them round.

He was thinner then than now, and even seemed a little shorter.

When he reached the gate, he had someone bring up a table, which he stood on. Then he ordered the gates opened.

Thousands of students immediately rushed over...

He shouted – it was only later that people told him how loud and clear that shout was. The thousands of students immediately fell silent at the sound of it.

"Comrade students! I am the director and secretary of the Party Committee of the Zhongyang Textile Factory! Please listen to me!"

Maybe they were intimidated by the strength of his presence, maybe they were attracted by his unassuming appearance which was so unlike that of a leadership cadre, or maybe they were just taken by surprise, but whatever the case, the students were stunned into silence. There was a long pause, during which none of them tried to stop him.

"...aren't your slogans all about opposing corruption and opposing 'bureaucratic profiteering'? When you come here wanting the workers to follow you out onto the streets, aren't you also asking them to 'oppose corruption and bureaucratic profiteering' alongside you?..."

Some of the students began to yell back:

"If you oppose us, you are supporting corruption and 'bureaucratic profiteering'!"

"We just have to listen to you to know you are a corrupt faction!"

"Do you dare tell us to our face and to the workers' face that you have never done anything corrupt?!"

"Down with bureaucratic profiteering! Down with corrupt factions!"

All this time, there were more and more workers coming to join in. There were thousands of students on one side, and thousands of workers on the other. Standing on the table in the middle was the short, meagre form of Li Gaocheng.

"Very well! Since that's what you think, let me first tell you all, students and workers alike, about myself!" Li Gaocheng looked calm and clear-headed. "My name is Li Gaocheng. I am forty-seven years old this year. I joined the Party at the age of seventeen, in 1975. My grandfather, father, father-in-law and grandfather-in-law were all farmers. All three generations of my ancestors were clean and honest! I have worked in the textile industry for more than twenty years – five years as a technician, and eight years as a grass-roots cadre. In 1980, I was transferred to Zhongyang Textile Factory and became the deputy manager, and in 1982 I became secretary of the Party Committee. Didn't you ask just now, 'Do you dare tell us to our face and to the workers' face that you have never done anything corrupt?' I can tell you now that I, Li Gaocheng, never have in the past, do not now, and never will in the future do anything corrupt! I have worked in this factory for ten years, and I have been the secretary of the Party Committee and the factory manager for eight years. I have never made any private arrangement to get a worker a job or to transfer a cadre! There are dozens of buildings, dozens of workshops, and dozens of branch factories in the factory. I have never approved a single piece of steel or a bag of cement in private! As for the products of the factory, I have never done a private deal for a single cotton ticket or a single foot of cloth! This factory has built dozens of office buildings, dozens of workshops and dozens of branch factories, and I have never done a private deal for so much as a steel joist or bag of cement. I have been a cadre for all these years, and I have never arranged for a relative to join the factory! My older brother, younger brother, older sister and younger sister are still farmers! My brothers-in-law and nephews on both sides of the family are also farmers! Over ten years, hundreds of non-agricultural residence permits have passed through my hands, but I can tell you with a clear conscience that I have never done a favour in that respect for any relative or any contact! I can also tell you unequivocally that in the ten years I have been a cadre, I have never pocketed a cent of public money apart from my salary! I have never given myself the biggest and best accommodation built by the factory! If you don't believe me, go ahead and ask these workers behind me! If I'm not telling the truth, if one worker says I'm lying, go ahead and trample all over me!"

The dark mass of the crowd was silent.

After a long time, a student suddenly jumped up onto the table and shouted to the workers: "He's lying! Where would you find a cadre like that these days! Don't believe him, brother workers, don't believe him! He must be..."

The student's words were suddenly cut off by a tsunami of shouting from the huge crowd of workers he was addressing:

"Secretary Li isn't lying!"

"Director Li is a great manager!"

"Show some respect for our manager!"

"We trust him! You have no right to say that about our factory manager!"

"You're talking nonsense! You don't work here, what do you know! "

The student shouted again, unwilling to believe them: "Is he really as good as he says? Is he really a good factory manager?"

There was another wave of shouting from the workers:

"He's better than he says!"

"He's a good secretary!"

"He's a great factory manager!"

The student was still reluctant to believe them: "Do you really support him?"

The workers shouts were overwhelming:

"We stand by him!"

"We support him!"

The students finally retreated amidst the uproar.

Before leaving, the student who had jumped on the table bowed deeply to him. Li Gaocheng burst into tears.

He wept because of the understanding of the students, and he wept because of the choice the workers had made.

After so many years, when he himself had almost forgotten about it, the workers still remembered it all so clearly today.

He suddenly understood a stark truth that lay in front of him: now, it was time for him to choose.

Almost immediately, he also understood what his choice had to be.

CHAPTER TWENTY-FOUR

TWO DAYS LATER, under Li Gaocheng's supervision, the Municipal Public Security Bureau began to investigate the Green Apple Entertainment City.

Three days later, with the approval of the Standing Committee of the Municipal Party Committee, the economic review working group to be sent to Zhongyang Textiles was formally established. Following Li Gaocheng's proposal, a special audit and verification team was added to investigate the subsidiary of the Zhongyang Textile Group, Xinchao Co. Ltd.

Five days later, a working party of nearly fifty people moved into the Zhongyang Textile Group. It happened to be the tenth day of the twelfth lunar month, less than twenty days before the Spring Festival. Those five days could have been the most painful and burdensome days of his life.

In fact, it was very easy for Li Gaocheng to get the Public Security Bureau to investigate the karaoke hall, convene the Standing Committee to study and approve the establishment of an economic audit and verification working group, and have the working group stationed in the Zhongyang Textile Group. For example, assigning the working group to Zhongyang Textiles after its approval by the Standing Committee was just a matter of the implementation and operation of that decision. If things like this had made the old Li

Gaocheng feel a little under pressure, then the new Li Gaocheng was practically impervious to it.

As long as no one really knew about it, the whole thing was really just a superficial matter; no one would care about what he was doing, let alone pay any special attention to him. He was just getting on with his day-to-day job.

But what could be more worrying, troublesome and disturbing than what was currently in Li Gaocheng's house?

There were three hundred thousand yuan in the house, which gave every appearance of being a bribe, and he had no idea what to do with them. His wife had not returned home once in five days, nor had she made a single telephone call, and he had no idea where she currently was.

With so many things happening around his wife, he still couldn't make up his mind what to do.

Such a major financial problem, which was directly related to Yan Zhen, the executive deputy secretary of the Provincial Party Committee, left him at a loss and unable even to start to deal with it.

What weighed particularly heavily on Li Gaocheng was that all of the above affairs demanded immediate attention, none of them could be put off and none could be shuffled off for someone else to handle.

Just think about it, if he did nothing about a three-hundred-thousand-yuan bribe lying around in his house for twenty-four hours, let alone five days, without him doing something about it, the nature of his retention of it would undergo a qualitative change.

This was simple common sense, and Li Gaocheng appreciated its weight better than most.

As a mayor, he could make decisions of his choice on anything that fell within the scope of his leadership and authority; the only thing that caused him difficulty was his inability to decide on things that related to him personally.

He could make choices for other people, but not for himself. Here, on the one hand, he had his own former superior and former boss. And on the other, there was his wife of more than twenty years and the mother of his children. This was not an ordinary kind of choice and could certainly not be described as one that had no bearing on him.

This was no routine public matter, no routine document for

approval. With things like that it was straightforward: make a speech, express an opinion, or scrawl a signature and write a comment, and that was that. Afterwards all there was to do was supervise and encourage and then wait. If the matter was handled well, you expressed your approval; if it was handled poorly, you criticised; if it was disastrous, you issued punishments.

This affair was intrinsically different. In fact, it couldn't be simpler: in dealing with his wife and Yan Zhen, he was dealing with himself; if he punished them, he was punishing himself.

What was more, the consequences of these affairs would spiral out of control, and the eventual outcome that awaited them was equally unimaginable. Li Gaocheng didn't even dare contemplate it. Just the thought of it made him shudder, filled him with a searing sorrow and left him flustered and helpless. He might as well be sending his wife and his superior to the execution ground with his own hand.

One was his wife who had been with him for more than twenty years, and the other was his old superior who had promoted him twice. Now, they would be at the mercy of his choice, or, more precisely, of his whistleblowing. The consequences would be shocking and unpredictable, and what awaited them was severe reprimand, dismissal, sentencing, imprisonment, and even...

He didn't dare to think about it anymore, because when he did he could feel a pain shoot through his trembling heart.

When the story broke, it would hit the headlines! The deputy secretary of a Provincial Party Committee and the wife of a mayor! It would cause a sensation not just across the whole of China, but perhaps even across the whole world!

What about himself? He was afraid it was all over for him too. Many people would consider him lacking in benevolence and righteousness, neither fish nor fowl; and people were also going to look askance at him from another point of view: how could he be a good cadre or a good leader when he had been promoted by a man like that and was married to a woman like that? In addition, with such a large-scale corrupt group having developed under his aegis, what were his superiors going to think of him? How could it not be seen as him dishonouring the nation and the Party? How could any of this not have anything to do with him? How could he not be responsible?

He was not a good leader, he was not a good subordinate, he was not a good husband and he was not a good father. Leaders would not approve of him, nor would the people! It would be impossible for any class of society to accept him, and impossible for any of the people to understand him. What awaited him were loneliness, isolation and people's curses and contempt. He faced a lifetime of shame and scorn!

All of this was not only possible, it was very likely!

His wife couldn't have said it more clearly: "What would you be without Yan Zhen?"

She might also have said, but didn't: "What would you be without your wife?"

There was another implicit assertion she could have made: "Who are the true foundations of your home and of the Party that supports you? They are your wife and Yan Zhen respectively, aren't they? Could it be called a home without your wife? Who would be backing you if it wasn't Yan Zhen? If his wife had actually voiced that opinion, what kind of a man would that make him, Li Gaocheng?

If he were to choose the overall interests of the Party, he would lose the support of the one man in that Party who was behind him.

That was a tragic situation for a Party cadre.

Perhaps this was the real choice that he had to make, and it was a choice that carried a huge price tag.

He hadn't had a decent night's sleep for the last few days. Often, he would be sleeping then awake with a start and not be able to drop back off for the rest of the night. He found he wasn't eating very much either, because he had lost his appetite. People thought he looked a lot thinner, and he himself felt that he had aged, and aged a lot.

But, what to do? What to do?

On many occasions he wanted to talk it all over with Municipal Party Committee Secretary Yang Cheng so he could get his take on it and consider what to do next. But he always vetoed his own impulse. If he did tell Yang Cheng everything, wouldn't he be delivering himself into the secretary's hands forever? Couldn't he just go to Yang Cheng and speak with the courage of his own convictions? But if he let just that one person in on his secret, he would be in his power from then on. Moreover, he had no real idea just what kind of a man Yang Cheng was. Supposing he told Yan Zhen everything about his, Li's, thinking on the matter, where would he be then?

Even before the real contest began, he already felt so helpless and isolated. But he knew that there was no third way he could take on this issue. He had to make a choice, and he had to make it as soon as possible. Otherwise, he would no longer have the power or opportunity to make any choice at all.

His secretary Wu Xingang's knock on the door interrupted his cogitations. As soon as he saw the thick winter clothes Wu was wearing, he began to think that he himself might be a bit underdressed. As he ordered his driver to bring him the army greatcoat he had left at home the evening before, he also told Wu Xingang to gather everyone together and be ready to leave.

Today was the day he was scheduled to visit Zhongyang Textiles to ascertain just how serious conditions were for the workers there. He was to be accompanied by the director of the Municipal Civil Affairs Bureau, the director of the Municipal Electricity Bureau, the director of the Municipal Food Bureau, the manager of the Municipal Water Company, the manager of the Municipal Coal Company, the manager of the Municipal Non-staple Food Company, the two directors of the Municipal Government Research Office, as well as the two deputy mayors in charge of industry and finance and a deputy secretary of the Municipal Party Committee in charge of organisation.

Originally, Yang Cheng, secretary of the Municipal Party Committee, was to be in the party, but he had said something had come up and he was unable to accompany them. So it seemed that the only person left to lead the group was the mayor.

This was the first time in recent years that the Municipal Party Committee and Municipal Government had offered condolences and practical relief on such a large scale to an enterprise that had stopped work and production.

It was happening because Li Gaocheng had heard about the conditions faced by the workers at Zhongyang Textiles.

The director of the Power Supply Bureau had been brought in because some of the workers could not pay their bills and had had their electricity cut off; the manager of the Municipal Water Company was there because the same had happened with some of the workers' water supply; the manager of the Municipal Coal Company was there because Zhongyang Textiles had no money to buy coal and could not afford to run a boiler, so the workers living in the dormitory block had no heating in the winter; the manager of the Municipal Non-staple Food Company had been brought in because some workers' families could not afford meat of any kind, and could not celebrate the New Year...

This was the first time in many years that food relief had been needed in the city.

For many years, people had privately accepted the fact that decades of planned economy meant that the Chinese working class had become a kind of "aristocracy" above all other classes. They possessed the "golden rice bowl" and enjoyed "iron wages"; wives, sons, houses, bills, cars, and everything in life, old age, sickness and death were all taken care of by the state. At that time, being a worker was something that many people dreamed of and were fascinated with. No one would feel that there was anything wrong or out of place if a worker fell in love with a technical secondary school student or a college student. A worker in very ordinary circumstances, even a divorced worker, could easily marry the most beautiful girl in the village. In the end, it all boiled down to one thing: the superior status of workers and their guaranteed livelihood. That was why so many people had been arguing for years that the interests of the farmers and of the country itself were being sacrificed in the name of elevating the workers; that the workers were having too much care and attention lavished on them; and that it had given them too much of a sense of their own superiority. As a result, people were worried that once the privileged position and circumstances of the workers were chipped away at, it very likely would be the same workers who would put up the most resistance, have the most to say and be the most dissatisfied. That's all there was to it; the workers had been put on too high a pedestal, had too much care lavished on them, been given too much of a sense of superiority, so their ability to withstand adversity was much weaker than that of the farmers and other classes of people. They were unlikely to be able to withstand a single blow and might even collapse at the lightest touch.

This was exactly what Yan Zhen said. For so many years, it was only the workers who had real vested interests. So, when reform touched these vested interests, it would inevitably be resisted and opposed by the workers. The implication seemed to be that the workers were the only resistance to reform.

So, what was the truth of the matter? Over the past ten years or so of reform, it was the workers who had sacrificed the most, paid the most, shown the most resilience and endured the most! When a great fanfare of publicity was given to the news that workers had become the wives of farmers, that they had become the sons-in-law of farmers, that they had become hired hands for the farmers, it ignored the starkest of facts that all the new things that were emerging in society had been brought about by the contributions and sacrifices of the workers.

Now, poverty alleviation for workers was a phenomenon, a hard fact that people did not want to admit, were unwilling to admit and dared not admit.

Before this poverty alleviation and relief campaign, many people were opposed to it, believing that it would likely cause a major social shock and have a negative impact. This action by the Municipal Party Committee and the Municipal Government essentially acknowledged an indisputable fact to society: the status and treatment of the working class, which had been the leading class for decades, had been continuously on the slide and had finally slipped to the point where poverty alleviation was necessary.

The person who gave the greatest support to the action was Yang Cheng, secretary of the Municipal Party Committee. He believed that facts were facts and uncovering them was always better than covering them up. Acknowledging the facts proved that the administration could face up to reality, that it had the sincerity and determination to solve problems, and that it had the confidence in its ability to do so. If someone falls ill but hides the problem and refuses to seek medical help, isn't he doing himself and others a disservice, which will inevitably harm the rest of the country and its people? Nor were these just empty, sententious words; indeed, having the courage to utter what may generally be considered empty words may often prove to be the mark of a hero and a genuinely exceptional person...

Yang Cheng's forthright and determined opinion shook everyone, and the action was naturally approved. But what took Li Gaocheng by surprise was that, just as everyone was about to set out to demonstrate their concern for Zhongyang Textiles, Yang Cheng suddenly found an excuse not to go so that he himself had to lead the delegation.

Try as he might, he couldn't figure out what Yang Cheng's real motives were.

Perhaps, and it was only a perhaps, he was doing it entirely for Li Gaocheng's own benefit. Good deeds like this should be the mayor's prerogative and would, indeed, stand him in good stead for his future efforts, particularly in the eyes of the workers at Zhongyang Textiles, on whom they would leave a deep and lasting impression. Of course there could be another reason: this was very much Li's problem, and as such it should be him who resolved it. With a factory that had ceased production for almost a year, and a workforce that had mostly not received any wages for a very long time, who would want to get involved in such an uncertain situation? If you want to keep your hands clean, you don't plunge them into a muddy ditch...

Li Gaocheng didn't know why he always had two differing views of Yang Cheng. Was it because he couldn't figure him out, or was it because he didn't trust him? Or was it because he listened to too many of the opinions and views expressed in society and was afraid to trust anyone? Just look at what his wife had said, and also Yan Zhen!

When had he become like this? Even though he was the mayor of a city with a population in the millions, and a high-level local government cadre, he had lost his personality, lost his edge and even lost his capacity for independent critical thinking. He had effectively lost his voice. If an author were to model a character on him, it would likely be the least individual character, the least identifiable, the least definable and almost certainly the least successful character in the novel!

What kind of man did he actually think he was? He seemed to have completely lost his roots, so what did that leave him? What had happened to his personality, his individuality, his temper, his true character, not to mention his strength and daring and his strategic decision-making? When did he lose all these things so completely? Was he still himself? When would he recover his spikiness and his eloquence? When would he dare to hate and to love, to shout and to curse again? When would he stop worrying about other people and what they might do to him?

He might be mayor, but was he even a proper human being?

When the convoy drove in with lorry loads of rice and noodles, clothes and comestibles to distribute, they did not receive the warm welcome he had expected.

In the middle of the huge dormitory compound of Zhongyang Textiles, apart from a few scattered children who had come out to watch the fun, and some nondescript idlers and layabouts, the only people there were some of the managers who had been given advance notice and some very vigilant-looking security guards.

According to the original arrangement, all the workers of the factory should have been there, just like the last time he went there, up to twenty thousand of them. Then, the needy households as identified by the factory should have been sat in rows, those most in need at the front, and the leaders of the Municipal Party Committee and Municipal Government would have distributed the goods accordingly. When it was done, it would, of course, have been down to him to make a speech. He had worked on that speech for two days. For the first time, he had ruthlessly rejected all the drafts provided by his secretary. He had never before felt that the man's work was so poor. Not only was there no elevated tone, there was no passion either; it was too dry and factual, and it was not even up to the standard of a decent general report. In the end, it was up to him to write it himself, and, after a dozen or so revisions, he eventually settled on the final version. It was his opinion that the visit should not only be one of condolence and sympathy with the deprived on a grand scale but should also be a vibrant and enthusiastic rally to mobilise the workers. He wanted to use it as an opportunity to reawaken all the energy the Zhongyang Textiles workers had shown in the past, and to put forward his ideas for the next step in the company's reconstruction and reinvigoration.

He had seen it all in his mind's eye but had never expected no one to turn up to this mass meeting! He had brought more than a dozen lorries laden with relief supplies and there was no one at all there to receive them!

Over the years, Li Gaocheng had participated in countless meetings and activities, but he had never encountered a situation like this: a meeting with no one participating, an event with no one attending! All the municipal leaders, big and small, including he himself, the mayor, were left standing there bare-arsed with nowhere to hide.

Not only had he never seen such a thing, he'd never even heard of this happening before.

Li Gaocheng looked in silence at the familiar but strangely unfamiliar faces in front of him: General Manager Guo Zhongyao, Party Secretary Chen Yongming, Deputy General Manager Feng Minjie, Deputy General Manager Wu Mingde...

They were all dazed, embarrassed, dejected and at a loss. They looked at each other but avoided each other's eyes. After a long time, Li Gaocheng finally broke the silence: "...Where are all the people? Was there no announcement? No organisation?"

"It's like this, Mayor Li... they told us in advance to tell you they didn't want you all to come... Some of the company managers discussed it and felt it would be better not to tell you..." General Manager Guo Zhongyao replied hesitantly.

"Why? Why didn't you tell us about something this important?" Li Gaocheng didn't raise his voice much, but his expression was dark and menacing.

"...Originally we thought that there would be no trouble organising the event." Guo Zhongyao was still very hesitant. "The company's main aim is to provide the best possible service to the people. No matter what some people might think of us, the event was being organised by the municipal leaders, and it was bringing sympathy and relief to the workers. There was no ulterior motive, so we didn't think it would be difficult to organise. We made several broadcasts about it on the company's cable TV channel and organised a meeting of all the company's middle-level cadres. We probably didn't pay enough attention to the whole thing because we thought it would be a no-brainer. After all, what we were doing was offering sympathy, condolences and relief to the workers. We certainly didn't expect the workers not to come...

"So where did the list of needy households you gave us come from?" Li Gaocheng asked angrily.

"The list of households was provided by the lower-level cadres, and it is understood to be quite reliable..."

"Understood? Understood by who? Understood by you or by someone else?" Li Gaocheng was relentless.

"The situation in the company has become more and more complicated, Mayor Li," Feng Minjie, the deputy general manager of the company, took over and replied. "As you know, the situation with our cadres in the factory is not very good, so these lists are provided by the grass-roots cadres. We do think the list is reliable, but that's not the problem. The problem is that the workers don't want to come. They said no one should come, so no one dared. Since the general feeling is against it, even the ones really in need don't dare come, even if they really want to. The workers aren't listening to us at all..."

"Enough!" Li Gaocheng interrupted Feng Minjie. "Then tell me why the workers don't want to come. Why are they listening to the troublemakers and not to you?"

"It was those troublemakers who told us that the workers didn't want to come to accept any relief supplies at all. They also said that went for the neediest households too..." Chen Yongming, secretary of the Party Committee of the Metallurgical Company, took over.

"Why not? Do you know why not?"

"They said that us offering them sympathy and relief was contemptuous and insulting, and it was not something they could just shrug away..."Chen Yongming stammered. "They asked when the workers of Zhongyang Textiles had ever asked for such things. They said that there are tens of thousands of workers in Zhongyang Textiles and could we really provide relief for all of them? Some of them also said that the problems at Zhongyang Textiles had nothing to do with observing the formalities, putting on a show and offering sympathy and relief. That was not what was needed now..."

Li Gaocheng was completely blindsided. He really believed he had thought of everything, but not this! He didn't know how many changes had been made in the telling, but the meaning of what the workers had said and the power of their reasons were quite clear enough. The report sounded like the true voice of the workers. Only they could talk about being true to their words, being resolute in their deeds, not being swayed by personal advantage and being constant in their loyalty.

It was at this point that Li Gaocheng realised he had made yet another big mistake. That mistake lay in him neglecting to pay attention to something that he really could not afford to ignore: once again he had chosen the wrong partners to rely on. This management team in front of him now was an object of hatred and resentment for the tens of thousands of workers of this state-owned enterprise. They had no trust in this management team, which was the same team against which there were two mountainous piles of accusations in the petition that was distributed all through the Municipal Party Committee, the Municipal Government, the Provincial Party Committee and the Provincial Government. Just a few days ago, in this very place, he had made a promise in front of tens of thousands of workers, saying that he would identify the problems at Zhongyang Textiles as soon as possible, and that, no matter who or what was turned up, he would show no leniency or tolerance and would investigate with total impartiality right through to the end! And yet, only a few days later, he had gone back on his word and was once again relying on these managers, who the workers regarded as corrupt, to organise this event. The workers believed that both their own poverty and the plight of the factory were caused by these people, and yet there he was, asking them to come and offer sympathy and relief to those same workers! Wasn't this just like piling dung on the head of the Buddha and setting a tiger to guard against itself? Was it any surprise the workers hadn't turned up or that they said the way they were being treated was both contemptuous and insulting?

Finally, Li Gaocheng asked Guo Zhongyao: "Can you get those representatives of the workers' leaders to come here?"

Which leaders? Do you mean Yuan Mingliang, Zhang Huabin and that lot?" Guo Zhongyao seemed rather confused by the request.

"Well, who would you say the leading troublemakers are?" Li Gaocheng asked, suppressing his anger and not letting it explode out of him.

"Any others, you mean? Well, apart from them there are only a few others of no great account..."

"Bullshit! It's a disgrace to you that you're still talking like that! All right then! Whoever they are, please summon them here for me. Do you hear me, you idiot? I'll repeat it for you – please summon them here for me." Li Gaocheng's anger finally erupted. He had never imagined that this general manager of a large enterprise with tens of thousands of workers, whom he had always valued, could be so slow to react! How could he be such an idiot? So much of an idiot he remained so blind to what his boss's intentions were and how angry he was!

Guo Zhongyao had never seen Li Gaocheng in such a temper in all the time they had known each other, and he was as stunned as if he had been hit on the back of the head with a cosh. For a long time, he was unable to utter a word. Eventually he stammered out: "... Mayor Li, it wasn't that we... didn't summon them... it was them who refused to come..."

"And what about you? Couldn't you get them here?" Li Gaocheng turned his sights onto Chen Yongming, secretary of the Party Committee.

"...Li, Mayor Li, this is how it stands at the moment. Right now, I don't know where they are. If I wanted to find them, I'm afraid..."

"What about you? And you? And you?"

Li Gaocheng questioned the managers in front of him one by one, but the result was always the same: no one volunteered to summon the few people in the company who they thought were the leading troublemakers.

They stood there blankly for an age, not knowing what to do next.

In the end, it was Li Gaocheng who made the decision. He gestured at the others and said: "Drive all the vehicles, big and small, into the courtyard of the Old Cadre Activity Centre to stand by! All you cadres are divided into two groups. Myself and Deputy Mayor Guo are in one group, and Deputy Secretary Zhang and Deputy Mayor Liu are in another. Use the list provided by the company to go to the employees' homes to get a good understanding of their situation. Even if you have to work on-site here, get over whatever difficulties there are to get over and solve any problems there are to be solved. If the job can't be finished today, finish it tomorrow. If we take this opportunity seriously we can get properly to grips with what the problems at Zhongyang Textiles really are..."

The two groups were quickly formed. Then Guo Zhongyao and the others asked timidly: "What about us..."

"You still have the nerve to ask!" Li Gaocheng almost swore at them. "You all have a good think for me about what to do! It's up to you! Go and do whatever you want..."

When Li Gaocheng turned around and walked away. He didn't even look back at them, but just left all the dejected managers standing there looking lost.

CHAPTER TWENTY-FIVE

THE FIRST PLACE LI GAOCHENG WENT was the house of the old factory director, Yuan Mingliang.

His original intention was not to see how poor the old factory manager's family was and how difficult their financial circumstances were, but just to hear the man's opinion and ask him what to do about this sympathy and relief programme.

However, when he walked into the old factory manager's house, he was shocked by the evidence of poverty he saw.

He had never dreamed that the family of a former manager of the Zhongyang Textile Factory, who had tens of thousands of workers under his control, could be so poor.

Yuan Mingliang was a grandfather on both sides of the family and lived with his youngest son. Together with his daughter-in-law, his granddaughter and his wife, there were five of them living in an apartment of less than fifty square metres. It was described as having two bedrooms and one living room, but, in truth, the living room was only about six square metres and was really no more than the vestibule of the apartment. There were two bedrooms, each just over ten square metres; the slightly smaller of the two housed himself and his wife, and the larger one was for his son and his wife. There was also a storeroom of about four square metres which acted as his thirteen-year-old granddaughter's room.

In fact, there were two other people who also lived in the old factory manager's apartment: two other grandchildren, a boy and a girl. They had their meals there during the day and slept there at night, except for Sundays, when their mother took them home. That meant that there were actually four people sleeping at night in the old couple's bedroom. As a consequence of all this, although he was already almost seventy, Yuan Mingliang had, every day, to keep an eye on his grandchildren, look after the household, buy food, do the washing and the cooking and see to all the other never-ending household chores.

If things at the company had been as they used to, if the company's workers had been receiving their monthly salaries and if his children had been allocated their proper accommodation, would the old factory manager still have had to live in such cramped conditions and work so hard just to get by?

What was more, if Yuan Mingliang had three hundred thousand yuan in ready cash lying around his apartment, would the old couple still be unable to live out their later years in the normal, happy peace and quiet they deserved?

This thought stopped Li Gaocheng dead in his tracks. This unexpected and somewhat absurd idea inevitably turned his thoughts to those three hundred thousand yuan of his own...

What had happened to him?

There were eight or nine people in Li Gaocheng's group, and they filled the living room to bursting. In fact some of them had to stand in the old factory manager's bedroom. An eighteen-inch colour television with only eight channel buttons, an old-fashioned one-door refrigerator, a few folding chairs and a few round dining stools without backrests comprised the furnishings of the room. There wasn't even a sofa. In fact, there wasn't actually enough space for a sofa, and there were no other decent furniture and fittings to be seen. Li Gaocheng didn't look inside the granddaughter's bedroom, but in Yuan Mingliang's room there was nothing apart from an old wooden chest and an iron bedstead on legs of the kind fashionable in the 1960s. No bedspreads, no carpets, no wall lamps, no bedside cabinets, no full-length curtains, and certainly no fashionable contemporary wardrobes, wall cabinets or anything of that kind.

Apart from the daughter-in-law who was placed in another work unit, all the family members worked at Zhongyang Textiles. The eldest son, the second son, the youngest son, the eldest daughter, the second daughter and both his nephews: how many there were of them! Almost too many to count!

Li Gaocheng looked at the apartment in silence, and suddenly felt overcome by an unbearable wave of shame and guilt.

Back when he persuaded the old factory manager to retire, he had repeatedly asked him what he needed and what he wanted done. Even then, he had thought that the man's accommodation was a little cramped and that he ought to find some way of getting him somewhere a bit bigger.

He didn't know whether it was because circumstances changed, or because he was too busy, or because he was promoted to municipal office immediately afterwards, or because he simply forgot about the matter, but whatever the cause, everything stayed the same over the decades, and the old factory manager was still living in this apartment of less than fifty square metres.

This was the best evidence to explain the extreme selfishness and self-obsession of the leading cadres who were dedicated only to their own self-interest: use the power while you have it because it doesn't last forever.

No wonder his wife kept saying he was stupid not to be looking out for his own family, not arranging things for them, not thinking about his own life after retirement and what was going to happen to him in the future!

It was no wonder that people said that if the current leadership cadres weren't corrupt and didn't make some extra money, not many of them would be able to survive on their pittance of an official salary; only a handful of those who wanted to be honest officials and support the ordinary folk would come out of it well in the end. What it came down to was that it was there for the taking if you wanted it or could get it, but if you didn't want it or you didn't try, you ended up with nothing. No one was going to admire you for not feathering your nest, and no one was going to criticise you if you did. If you retired from office and you had no assistants, no money to do anything, no car when you went and no house of your own, no one was going to sympathise with you. You had made your own bed, so you could lie in it. It served you right! What did you think you were doing when you had all the power and prestige?

Had he played his own part in creating these social conditions? The old factory manager, Yuan Mingliang, certainly wouldn't have been expecting a delegation of leadership cadres to come to his home like this, especially not one led by the mayor!

The daughter-in-law had gone to work, and the son had a temporary job as a stevedore at a company in the city, so he had left early that morning. Only the old couple and the two children were left at home. It seemed that the presence of the children made the old man less uncomfortable and flustered. He busied himself trying to seat the guests but there wasn't actually anywhere for them all to sit. What with Li Gaocheng and Deputy Mayor Guo, and the two unabashed young children grandly taking up the four folding chairs, there was no more room in the six-square-metre living room. There was a round table that appeared to serve the multiple functions of dining table, coffee table and writing desk, since arranged on it were a bottle of ink, a notebook and an ashtray of unknown age. Yuan Mingliang rummaged around for a while in a wall cupboard in the kitchen and eventually pulled out a canister of tea leaves and a half-full pack of Red River cigarettes. The pack of cigarettes was also of unknown age and the cigarettes themselves felt as hard as if they were made out of wood. It took an age to open the canister of tea, and when it was opened it became apparent that all the leaves had turned to dust. One of the two hot water flasks was empty, and the water ran out before all the cups were filled. There was no gas, so the old man hurriedly pried open the stove that had probably been sealed up to save coal. Presumably because of this stove, the room didn't feel too cold. Once all that fussing around was over and the two children had been taken into the daughter-in-law's room by their grandmother, things finally settled down in the apartment.

The two former factory managers sat facing each other, and, for a long time, were unable to speak.

What was there to say? They had both been managers of the factory, but their status, position, rank and everything else were completely different. Especially now, when one was a relief worker, and the other a relief recipient; one was a working leader of considerable seniority, and the other was a retired cadre plagued by poverty.

Li Gaocheng told himself to take a good look at himself and at his current circumstances. How had this great gulf between them come about? Who was responsible for it? Could it really be that his own contribution to the nation, to society and to the ordinary people was bigger, greater, more glorious and more distinguished than that of this weather-beaten old factory manager who had laboured and suffered all his life? The old man in front of him had worked selflessly, unquestioningly and tirelessly for decades for his country, but now he was still poor and had nothing. Faced with this, shouldn't any cadre with a conscience feel ashamed and guilty?

"Well Lao Yuan, I never imagined that you would still be living in this same apartment after so many years!" Li Gaocheng said in a voice full of regret and apology. "I am so sorry! I once promised I would fix it, I really did..."

"You mustn't talk like that, Mayor Li. I'm just so happy that you have come here today." Yuan Mingliang's eyes seemed to have some tears in them, but he quickly recovered himself. "In fact, I'm very happy to have a place like this to live in, but the truth is, Mayor Li, I am also very ashamed! Whenever I see all those workers who have nowhere to live, it is like a knife through my heart. If I had known it would come to this, and if I had been more determined when I was in the job and had found the money to build more dormitory blocks, then things wouldn't have ended up with workers who had given their lives to the company having nowhere to live. Mayor Li, even if you found me a good house, how could I have the heart to live in it? How could I keep face if I did? There are so many workers who still live in shacks with no equipment of any kind, and there are yet more who have worked here for so many years, who still live in rented peasant houses. No one knows how many workers are still single and can't get married because they don't own somewhere to live..."

At this point, the old factory manager's tears finally began to fall uncontrollably, but he hurriedly wiped them away with his heavily-veined, work-callused hand.

"Lao Yuan, the main reason we came today was not to solve the workers' housing problems..." Li Gaocheng was at a loss for what to say next to the old factory manager. He had originally intended to seek his opinion on how to carry out this relief operation, but he had not expected to find the old factory manager of such a large enterprise living in such reduced circumstances. After gathering his thoughts, Li Gaocheng continued: "This time we are here mainly to solve the living problems of a group of extremely poor households. For example, those workers' families who cannot afford rice, noodles, vegetables or anything to celebrate the New Year. Lao Yuan, you know the situation better than anyone else in the factory. How many workers like that are there in our company?"

"Mayor Li, I need to ask you at this point, whether this initiative comes from the municipal leaders or from the company management?" Yuan Mingliang asked very seriously.

"Why? What's the difference?" Li Gaocheng asked, rather puzzled.

"Well, Mayor Li, the company management has planned sympathy and relief programmes several times in the past but has never seen them through."

"What?!" Li Gaocheng was taken aback. He had no idea that the company had already planned such an operation on many previous occasions. "...none of them were seen through? Why not?"

"Because the workers were opposed to them, all of them. Even the households in the worst situations refused their help outright. They didn't view it as any kind of charitable relief but saw it as the management sending them their leftovers to humiliate them. These managers have grown fat on the blood and sweat of generations of our workers, but now they are setting themselves up as saviours, each one of them, and using the same blood and sweat of our workers to offer us relief aid! They are worse than the capitalists of the past! The capitalists knew that it was the workers who fed them, and they had some sense of shame about it. These people don't! They strut around like masters and commanders in front of the workers and, anything the workers get seems to come as their charity and alms. But if the workers are reliant on someone else for their food and living, who do the management think they are reliant on? They simply don't seem to understand this basic principle. I told them time and time again, right to their faces – you seem to take all us workers for fools! When it comes down to it, is it the workers who feed you, or you who feed the workers? Is it the workers who come to your rescue, or you who come to the workers' rescue? Don't you understand that they had only been able to climb to their current management jobs and status because of the original diligence and hard work of the workers? And once you have everything you want, and have screwed everything you can out of it, having destroyed the company without a trace of humanity or compunction, you still have the nerve to offer aid to the workers! Aren't you members of the factory staff too? But do you stop to consider what you eat, what you wear, where you live? What do your sons and daughters eat? What do they wear? Where do they live? What kind of men do you call yourselves?"

Yuan Mingliang's words shook Li Gaocheng and everyone else present very deeply. They stung Li like a whiplash across his heart. Surely those words were directed at him! Surely they were also directed at everyone else present too!

It was indeed the workers who had toiled all day long, without a word of complaint, to provide for him, and he, in turn, was now looking to enhance his reputation by coming over here with feigned benevolence and feigned righteousness and offering them relief!

After a long, long time, Li Gaocheng said softly with great sincerity: "Lao Yuan, the honest truth is that we really didn't know about all that, and we can understand your feelings. As for today's operation to come over here to offer sympathy and relief to deprived households, it is entirely the work of the Municipal Party Committee and the Municipal Government. It has nothing to do with the company management. Right now, no matter how many opinions and complaints the workers may have, how much dissatisfaction and resentment they feel, this can only be addressed step by step. Isn't the audit and verification team sent by the Municipal Party Committee and Government already stationed in the company? But a problem is a problem and life is life, so how can the state see what difficulties the workers are in and ignore it? A few days ago, more than a dozen model workers from the company came specially to my home. They said they wanted me to go and mingle with the workers, listen to what they are thinking and saying, and see for myself how hard their lives are. They said that things are really difficult for the workers, especially those who have worked at Zhongyang Textiles for generations. They haven't been paid for more than a year, and they can't even afford noodles. No matter how ill they are, they can only afford to take painkillers. Lao Yuan, I believe them. In fact, as soon as we got to your house and saw how poor the family of a former factory manager is, we understood absolutely how bad it must be for those really poor households. I didn't expect this, Lao Yuan, I really didn't expect it. I'm so sorry we came too late. I am not speaking just for myself but for the Municipal Party Committee and Municipal Government too. You are right, it is indeed the workers who have supported the country and supported the government, and it is precisely because of this that the workers' lives are now at such a point. How can the country and the government just ignore it..."

Li Gaocheng found himself unable to go on as he saw the old factory manager's eyes filling with tears and watched the work-callused hands time and time again wiping those tears from his leathery old face.

"I told those model workers not to go, but they still went..." Yuan Mingliang stuttered out, still wiping his face.

"You are a former manager, Lao Yuan, and I know everyone still listens to you. For the sake of the company and of the nation, even if you don't care about yourself, you have to think about the workers. If the staff of an enterprise are working at cross purposes and there is no cohesion, even if that enterprise does not collapse and can still be preserved somehow or other, what good is it going to be? I believe that while our generation is still around, we can neither let the company collapse, nor let people's hearts be broken. We can still rebuild the company if it is broken, but will it be so easy to repair people's hearts if they are broken? We have shared the same experience, Lao Yuan. Right from the time we joined the workforce, we have been crying out that we must rely on the working classes, that we must rely on them forever, but now that there is something we can do about it, especially at this current juncture, how can we bear watching those same working classes drifting further and further away from us? We are all members of the Communist Party. If the Communist Party has no partners to rely on, how can it continue to exist? What support do we have for our existence? Wouldn't, then, all our years of blood, sweat and toil be wasted? How would we face ourselves, our country and the people then? Besides, aren't you and I still part of the working class? If we don't take care of our own affairs, then who will?" Li Gaocheng spoke with sincerity and honesty, hiding nothing.

"The fact is, Mayor Li, that we've been down this road and been through it all before. The workers don't want relief. They simply don't want it..." Yuan Mingliang vigorously wiped the tears from his face, then stood up and said: "Since you have brought it to this point, I will take you to the poorest households to have a look around."

"This is the list of poor households they gave me just now..." Li Gaocheng wanted to get Yuan Mingliang to take a look at the list and then seek his opinion, but to his surprise, the man interrupted him without even waiting to hear what he had to say.

"I know all about that list. Only a few of them are the real thing. Some of them are in trouble, in a lot of trouble in fact, but they are not the worst cases. The ones on that list are the most timid, the ones who don't dare speak up at all, or the ones who are still able to earn a little money at the factory. They will just lie and not tell you the real truth. But if you still want to go and see them, I can take you."

CHAPTER TWENTY-SIX

A LOW, DARK SINGLE-STOREY BUILDING of twenty or so square metres had been subdivided into three sections, and those three sections housed eleven members of a three-generation household! That family had already been living there for almost thirty years!

The cooking area was almost out on the street because this so-called kitchen measured, at the very most, little more than one square metre. If it hadn't pushed out into the street a little, there wouldn't even have been room for someone to turn round in it.

One section of seven or eight square metres served as both a living room and a bedroom, and a large old wood-frame bed filled almost the whole space. What particularly caught the eye were the two large and three small bedrolls arranged on the big bed. That is to say, at night, the bed served as the sleeping place for five people, old and young!

There were four people in the room at the time: one old woman and three children. Of the children, one was a little girl of eight or nine, one a boy less than two years old, and the last a baby less than one year old. The girl was struggling to hold the baby, which was either hungry or not feeling well, as it was crying loudly. The old woman was holding the hand of the little boy who had probably only just started walking, and, at the same time stirring a pot of some kind of food for the children.

Housing like this simply wasn't designed for so many people.

Even if you could cram yourself in, there was nowhere to sit or even to stand. So, apart from Li Gaocheng, Deputy Mayor Guo and Yuan Mingliang, the others in the party went in very briefly to take a look and then came out again.

The old woman and the children just stared blankly at these uninvited guests, startled into silence. The look in the old woman's eyes was principally one of dazed incomprehension, but there was also a touch of fear and alarm there too.

Li Gaocheng immediately recognised the old woman: it was Fan Xiuzhi, who had been a model pacesetter at Zhongyang Textiles for more than thirty years!

Li Gaocheng couldn't believe how old and haggard she looked, even though she was not yet seventy. Li Gaocheng remembered her in her early sixties at the oldest. The year Li Gaocheng was transferred to Zhongyang Textiles, she was still the team leader of the spinning workshop and had been a model worker in the company for many years. In enterprises such as Zhongyang Textiles, the uppermost retirement age for female workers was no more than fifty-five years old, and there were very few who made it to that age. It was such heavy and unforgiving work, it was very hard for a woman, even in good health, to last until they were fifty-five. But when this Fan Xiuzhi was fifty-five, she was once again ranked as the number one model worker of the whole factory and the advanced pacesetter for the whole city!

When he was first transferred to Zhongyang Textiles, someone jokingly told Li Gaocheng that this woman Fan Xiuzhi had been born to be a model worker and a pacesetter! She couldn't survive without gruelling physical labour. She entered the factory at the age of nineteen and was an apprentice for three years, before becoming a regular worker at the age of twenty-two. From then on, whenever the factory selected model workers, she was always included! And every time, she was sure to get a unanimous vote!

Even during the Cultural Revolution, she never took a day off work!

In 1967, there was a so-called "violent struggle"[1] in the city, and almost all the workers at Zhongyang Textiles took to the streets. The sound of machinery was not to be heard in a single workshop in that whole huge factory. During the whole five months of the "struggle", the only worker there who didn't miss a single day's work was Fan Xiuzhi. The driver of the factory shuttle bus that took the workers to and from work said that he lost track of how many times the only person on the bus with him was Fan Xiuzhi, and she was the only person working in any of the factory workshops!

The year Fan Xiuzhi retired, Li Gaocheng commissioned a detailed survey, and, according to admittedly inaccurate statistics, in the thirty years Fan Xiuzhi was at work, altogether she had been a model worker a total of ninety-six times. She had been a national model worker once, a provincial model worker three times, an industry-wide model worker nine times, a city model worker eleven times, and a factory model worker thirty-two times! In addition, she had also collected dozens of other model labour commendations in workshops, work groups, trade unions, women's federations and so on.

She truly was the epitome of a professional model worker!

Li Gaocheng himself could not remember how many times he had presented model worker commendations to her. Back then, the Fan Xiuzhi who stood on the award stage was a radiant sight and the envy of everybody!

How could this doddering, hunch-backed old crone standing in front of him now be the same Fan Xiuzhi? Where was the mighty and heroic spirit of the old days?

How could an old model worker who had done so much for the country, the people and the company be living in a place like this that would make people weep to see it?

Could it even be considered a home? Was it really somewhere someone who had been a model worker all her life should call her home?

There was no refrigerator, no colour television, no sofa, no washing machine, no tape recorder, no decent furniture, and probably the only thing that was even a little modern was the fourteen-inch black-and-white television sitting on an old wooden table.

The old woman was still dumbstruck, and her cloudy eyes didn't seem to recognise that the person in front of her was Li Gaocheng, the old factory manager who had given her so many awards. She almost certainly didn't know either that the same Li Gaocheng was now the city mayor!

It took a while for him to realise why Fan Xiuzhi didn't recognise him: her eyes were so densely clouded that she might not be able to see anything at all. She was probably identifying people and where they were standing by sound alone.

Yuan Mingliang wanted to introduce him and tell her why he was there, but Li Gaocheng stopped him. It was better that she didn't know, as what difference would it make if she did? Besides, this way, he might even learn something closer to the truth.

It took a while to coax the crying child into silence. It was really hungry and started gobbling down something unidentifiable from a bowl.

The house suddenly seemed very quiet.

Confronted with the home situation of a model worker like Fan Xiuzhi, Li Gaocheng didn't know what to say to the old woman. What could he say? There was nothing to say; there really was nothing to say.

"We have been sent by the city to understand the situation, old lady." This time, it was Deputy Mayor Guo who spoke. He tried his best to explain the situation calmly to the old woman. "The city is very concerned about the situation at our company. You are part of the company, a former model worker, so we especially want to hear your opinion."

Fan Xiuzhi's cloudy eyes and wrinkled face still showed no expression, and she just stared blankly at the indistinct figures in front of her. It took a long time before she said: "Huh! What's the point of my opinion? It's the government that says what's what. Us workers just fall in with it. For years, we've not only listened to the government, but done everything they said, step by step. The government says what's what – we have no opinion."

"The factory is in trouble now. I'm sure you know that production has stopped there, the workers aren't getting their wages and even you retired staff cadres' livelihood isn't guaranteed. You must have some thoughts on all that, old lady. Haven't you heard what the workers have been saying about it? This factory belongs to the workers, and this whole business is so big that the workers really ought to be thinking about what to do," Deputy Mayor Guo continued to explain.

"The way you're talking makes you sound like amateurs." The old woman seemed very unimpressed by Deputy Mayor Guo. "I don't actually know who you lot really are, and I don't know if I should talk freely to you."

"Go ahead, there's no problem. We're all from round here," Yuan Mingliang said.

It was probably these words from the old factory manager that finally reassured the old woman, who let out a deep breath. "Ai! When will this factory ever belong to us workers? For so long, no one has listened to us! If they had, do you think the factory would be in this state now?" Fan Xiuzhi's face remained expressionless, and her words were flat and without emotion. Only people who have despaired of the world talk like that.

It seemed to be all she had to say. After a long silence, Li Gaocheng asked: "You worked there all your life and you were a model worker. How much is your monthly pension?"

"It's a complete mess, but if they do get it right, it's round about two hundred or so."

"Around two hundred? How can it be so little?!"

"They haven't paid it at all for five or six months, so I don't really expect it anymore."

The whole room fell silent, and Li Gaocheng didn't know what to say. After a long time, Deputy Mayor Guo asked sadly: "Now the factory has stopped production, where have all your family gone?"

"They've gone to look for work, of course! Do you think they'd let a little thing like this get the better of them?"

"And has your husband done the same??"

"Of course he has, he's got no choice. But my eyes are no good. Do you think I'd be sitting here at home if I could see properly?

"How old is your husband?"

"Still young. He has just turned seventy!" Fan Xiuzhi replied equably.

"But what can he do to earn a living at that age?"

"Whatever he can find. Two days ago he helped the family sort this place out, and for the last two days he's been selling eggs with our son and daughter-in-law."

"Selling eggs? Where has he been selling them?" Li Gaocheng was astonished. How could a seventy-year-old man be out selling eggs?"

"In the free market, of course! First they go to the chicken farm to buy the eggs and then they sell them in the market."

"But the chicken farm is out in the suburbs and a long way from the city market. Can they still make a profit?

"They can. They make ten cents on one *jin* of eggs. With him and our son on their bicycles, they can carry about a hundred *jin* each per trip. The two men do the transport and my daughter-in-law does the selling and, with a bit of effort, we can sell the whole lot, apart from the broken ones, and make twenty or thirty yuan." She made it sound as though her husband was still a young man.

"Can a man in his seventies still carry that weight of eggs?"

"Of course he can. He's very fit!" Fan Xiuzhi sounded as though she was speaking admiringly of a young lad. "He's quicker than our son on the seventy or eighty *li* trip out to the chicken farm and back. But three days ago, he had to dodge a car and almost all of two baskets of eggs got smashed. The old man came back in tears, and he kept crying for most of the night. In actual fact, he brought back most of the broken eggs in a plastic bag, and because it's winter there was no danger of them going bad. They were enough to feed a family for several days. But the old man was so upset, he cried like a little child. He said that those two baskets meant that their work over all those days was wasted. It's almost New Year and he thought he'd spoiled it for everyone. He's never cried like that in his life before…"

Fan Xiuzhi still spoke without emotion or expression, but her tears spilt one by one from those cloudy eyes.

Yuan Mingliang turned his face away quietly and wiped his face vigorously, and two lines of tears streamed unchecked from Deputy Mayor Guo's eyes.

What more was there to be said? What more could be said? Faced by such an old model worker in her declining years, what else could you possibly say?

In the end, Li Gaocheng didn't tell the old woman who he was. He just couldn't bring himself to.

"Old lady, it will soon be New Year. If you and your family have any problems, do raise them, and the city will certainly find solutions. It was the city that sent us today with food aid and emergency money, and your household undoubtedly qualifies for them," Deputy Mayor Guo told the old woman with great sincerity and great emotion.

"No need!" The old woman's tone was very tough and determined as she refused the deputy mayor's offer. "We don't have any problems. How could we, with so many family members able to earn a living? This is nothing compared to how things were in the 1960s with the Cultural Revolution. There are lots of factory households much worse off than us. If people like us start accepting aid and relief, where would it stop?! Besides, I'm a model worker appointed by the government, aren't I? I've been a model worker all my life! What a joke it would be for me to start taking aid from the state and the government now! If people were to find out, wouldn't I be shaming the state and the government? I told Manager Guo a few days ago, as long as there is a single breath in my body, you won't find this family asking for aid. I told my family that one should never forget one's roots. My life was given to me by the Communist Party. Back then, the People's Liberation Army took me from the arms of my mother, who had died of starvation. How could I possibly ask the Communist Party for aid..."

Everybody there, inside and outside the house, started to cry. Li Gaocheng tried his hardest to hold back his own tears, but they still flowed uncontrollably. Finally, he asked: "Isn't there anything you need, old lady? What about your eyes? The city could buy you the medicine to make them better. It doesn't cost very much."

"People grow old and eyes go cloudy. My eyes aren't going to get any better. Ai! But if we're talking about requests..." Fan Xiuzhi thought for a long time, then continued: "Since you've asked if I have any requests, I know you won't laugh at me for asking you to make one for me to the government."

As she was talking, she was groping in a wooden chest under the bed and finally took out what looked like a list and gave it to Li Gaocheng with trembling hands.

It took him a while to realise that it was a purchase order for a book. It read:

Comrade Fan Xiuzhi

Your deeds and photographs have been compiled into the Directory of Chinese Model Workers. This is a glory to you and your family. First of all, please accept our heartfelt congratulations to you and your family!

You have worked silently and selflessly for the cause of the Party and the people, and the people of the motherland will never forget your achievements! This book represents the brilliance and glory of your life and is the crystallisation of the hard work and sweat of yourself and your whole family!

I hope that after you receive this notice you will please send the money for the book as soon as possible in accordance with this notice of reservation and remittance, in order that you may cherish it as a precious memory.

If you have any difficulty with this, you can contact your work unit leader for reimbursement.

Her request could not have been simpler: Fan Xiuzhi did not have the less than one hundred yuan the book cost and hoped that the work unit would reimburse her.

The old woman said that she had won nearly a hundred awards in her life, and her only hope was that she might not let her children and grandchildren forget this. When she passed away one day and the younger generations of the family read this book, they would know that among their predecessors, there had been such a woman who was not an embarrassment to them. Even if this factory did indeed go bust and collapse, the younger generation would understand that it was not because of anything she had done…

Li Gaocheng put down a one-hundred-yuan note and walked out, his tears flowing uncontrollably.

Seventy-seven-year-old former worker Wang Yinglie was so strong that no one would believe that he was an old man of nearly eighty, nor that he was a disabled person with a missing leg.

His eyes were undimmed, his hearing was unaffected, his white hair stood up like crane feathers, his face was smooth and childlike, and his voice was clear as a bell. Although his waist was a little bent, he was still more than a head taller than Li Gaocheng. He recognised Li at a glance, hopped over to him, grabbed his hand, and refused to let go for a long time.

"Mayor Li, Mayor Li, look what has happened to the company! The government must take care of it, it must take care of it…" The old man was like a child, crying and talking at the same time when he saw Li Gaocheng. "Everyone has been looking forward to this all day... How could the nation not care about such a big company? We've been waiting and waiting but we never expected you to come... Everyone's been saying that the current Mayor Li is not the Factory Director Li of before, but now they will change their minds... When people think about this company of yours these days, all they think about is the market – no one thinks about the workers... I don't believe now and I'll never believe that even in a capitalist country, let alone a socialist one like ours, everyone doesn't have to rely on the workers... Doesn't the whole world of the Communist Party rely on the workers and the farmers... When, in all these years, have us workers ever been disloyal to the government... Even in the Cultural Revolution, the workers never went against them or thought about seizing power... In 1967 and 1968, when so many workers died at the factory, wasn't it all to defend Chairman Mao and the Communist Party... I told them, isn't Li Gaocheng a Communist Party mayor? Could he be mayor if he didn't support the Communist Party? What else would the Communist Party want him to do if not take care of a factory this size? If Mayor Li was the kind of person you're saying he is, would he have spoken the way he did at the factory gates in 1969? I came to this factory in 1939, so what kind of things haven't I seen and what kind of people haven't I met? If I can't tell what kind of person someone is by now, I have wasted my life..."

Wang Yinglie went on and on in this vein and there was no knowing when he would have stopped if his daughter hadn't run over and interrupted him.

Wang's wife had died when he was in his fifties and he never remarried. He was currently living with his daughter and son-in-law, along with his two youngest grandsons who were both in their late twenties. When you added in two great grandsons, there were seven people from four generations in a one-living-room, two-bedroom apartment. Truth be told though, there wasn't really even a living room where guests could be received because, in the middle of the seven- or eight-square-metre room, there was a bed where the old man slept with one of his great grandsons.

The kitchen was also very small, with no room for a dining table. So, when the family ate, they had to set up a folding table. Then half of them sat on the bed and half on stools, so that they barely had room to eat. When guests came, they also had to sit on the bed as there was not even space for them to stand.

This was the home of a four-generations family, and this was the home of an old worker who had been in the factory for more than fifty years.

Li Gaocheng felt a heart-wrenching sorrow when he saw the limping figure of Wang Yinglie.

The old man had lost his leg years before while saving the factory.

On the eve of the Liberation, the Kuomintang troops were ordered to blow up the factory as they retreated. A whole regiment of troops armed with several dozen machine guns drove all the workers out of the factory gates.

Tens of tonnes of explosives were placed in the most critical places around the workshops and connected by a detonating wire. The minutes and seconds ticked down and the time for the detonation got closer and closer.

Wang Yinglie, who was not even a Party member at the time, just an ordinary worker, along with eight other Party members from the workforce, took on the onerous burden of saving the factory. Shielded by the other workers, they concealed themselves in the workshops where the explosives were planted.

Afterwards, Wang Yinglie said that, at the time, he had no idea that the detonator he was holding was more dangerous than any landmine. The enemy had set the time for detonation at exactly six o'clock in the afternoon, but the old pocket watch Wang had with him was actually three minutes slow! In fact, he didn't even know how to read the watch – he just knew it must go past the number six on the dial. He was equally unaware that, if the thing he was carrying went off, it would be all over for the whole factory.

Originally, he wasn't the one carrying the detonator, but it was in the hands of a young worker who, he later discovered, was the secretary of the underground Party branch in the factory.

A few minutes before the time set for the detonation, they all reckoned that the Kuomintang soldiers had definitely left, but, completely unexpectedly, when the young man stood up, he was mown down by a burst of machine gun fire. The very last words the young man said to him were: "Quick, quick, take this thing and throw it outside the factory…"

Wang Yinglie took the detonator and ran for his life towards the outside. He said that, at the time, he didn't hear the machine guns and didn't realise that he had been wounded in any way.

He ran and ran, straight towards the moat that encircled the factory. He hurled the detonator with all his might, there was a flash in front of his eyes and then he knew nothing more.

In fact, it wasn't the explosion that did for his leg; it had been shorn off by the machine gun fire.

Afterwards, he discovered that, of the nine men in that team, he was the only one to survive.

It was after this that he joined the Party. Because he had lost his leg, for the next few decades he worked as the gatekeeper at the main gates of the factory.

He continued in that job until he was in his seventies, although he officially retired when he was sixty-three. Guarding the factory gates was something that he felt it was his duty to do, and, while he was there, nothing stolen ever passed through them.

In 1992, the company management finally ordered him to leave his post at the main gates. For one thing, they said, he was too old and infirm; and for another, they claimed that he was no longer thinking clearly, and an accident could happen at any moment.

"Bullshit! It's all bullshit!" the old man said when the matter was mentioned; his face went purple with fury and his whole body shook. "See for yourself, Mayor Li, whether I'm too old or not. Am I thinking clearly or not? The reason they didn't want me on the main gate anymore was that they had guilty consciences about all the wicked things they were doing. Now you're here today, Mayor Li, I'll tell you the whole story and I'll show you all the terrible things they've done. None of my children want me to speak out, but you can deal with these things, can't you, Mayor Li? Yes, I'm old now, and yes, I can't run anywhere anymore, but if I don't speak out now, in my final years, I won't be able to take another breath, not another breath..."

At this point, Wang Yinglie took an envelope from behind a New Year poster stuck on the wall, inside which there were dozens of yellowing receipts and signed purchase orders. He opened them up, one by one, and laid them out until they covered the whole double bed in the living room.

"This is all evidence, Mayor Li, ironclad evidence, and, as long as the government really is determined to take control of the situation, these men are all trapped!" The old man looked as mortified as if he had just caught a gang of thieves. "Mayor Li, look at this one first – this is the handwriting of the company's deputy general manager, Feng Minjie. Just look how shameless this management is!"

There were some lines of writing on a sheet of office paper:

To Comrade Li Jinlan:
We have been informed by the management of the company that the Hexi Textile Machinery Parts Factory in Gaocheng County has been allocated 9,200 pieces of old loom parts from our company. Please issue a certificate.
Supply Department: Wu Feipeng
The details are correct. The parts are scrap. Please issue a certificate for release. 25 September 1991.
Feng Minjie
25 September 1991

On the strength of this sheet of paper, without a single official seal, 9,200 loom components belonging to the company just vanished! Li Jinlan was the director of the security department in charge of the guards, and Wu Feipeng was the deputy director of the supply and distribution department. With a note from the deputy director of the supply and distribution department, plus a signature from the deputy general manager of the company, 9,200 loom components were simply shipped out of the factory as waste!

Li Gaocheng was stunned into silence for a long time. How could these people be so brazen? Even if they were scrap parts, how could they be transferred to a county-level textile machinery components factory? Scrap or not, they still had to go through a series of strict identification and supervision procedures. How could such a large amount of scrap be released on the strength of a single unsealed sheet of paper? Such a large amount of scrap from state-owned enterprises could only be sold to a state-designated recycling company; otherwise it was a criminal act. But here was proof that 9,200 loom components were disposed of in just that way.

It was an open-and-shut case of theft!

There was also a certificate of export from the factory which was identical in style and form to the other document. It read:

Factory Security Office:
   There is company scrap comprising 6 roving frames, 4 spinning frames, 11 drawing frames, 14 motors, 5 transformers and various motor parts. Please release all these items.
   Transport vehicle type: Dongfeng brand 10-tonne truck.
   Number of transport vehicles: 4.
   Waste recycling unit: Dayu City Machinery Factory Waste Recycling Company.
   Supply Office
   19 November 1991

Around October 1991, the state loaned 60 million yuan to Zhongyang Textiles, and the company technical transformation project was fully launched! These vermin who were infesting the company were using underhand methods to perpetrate a massive fraud and spirit away their ill-gotten gains!

There was no official seal, no signature, not even an authorising name! Anyone with a discerning eye could see the flaws at a glance: why should scrap from the municipal state-owned enterprise Zhongyang Textile Group Corporation be going to the Dayu City Machinery Factory Waste Recycling Company, hundreds of miles away, for recycling? What was more, this Dayu City Machinery Factory Waste Recycling Company was clearly an independent waste collection station!

In this regard, the state had made countless orders and issued a multitude of legislative documents: all machines and machine parts retired by state-owned enterprises had to be disposed of on the spot as waste products; distribution to the private sector was strictly prohibited, and they could not be sold to rural areas, self-employed households and township enterprises, let alone to individuals. In particular, the machines and machine parts that had been made redundant by the technical transformation project could not be bought and sold at will. Not only could they not be sold to individuals, they could not be sold to state-owned enterprises either. The legislation specifically identified the machinery and accessories of textile enterprises because once these machinery parts and accessories were lost track of, it would inevitably open the door to the proliferation of sub-standard and counterfeit products.

As the principal boss of a large state-owned enterprise, how could it be that he had been unaware of this blatantly illegal activity?

If the first few items raised Li Gaocheng's eyebrows, the next few really made him shudder.

> Received today:
> 8,500 loom components for the technical transformation project from the Gaocheng County Hexi Textile Machinery Parts Factory.
> Received by: Ma Zhenhai, second tier warehouse administrator of the fourth branch factory.
> 18 October 1991

In less than a month, a county-level textile machinery parts factory had taken away 9,200 pieces of machinery scrap from a huge state-owned enterprise, and then shipped in 8,500 pieces of finished parts for the technical transformation project! This had been done in broad daylight, in full view of the public, and no one had done anything about it!

Another note was almost identical:

> Received today:
> 6 roving machines, 4 spinning machines, 11 drawing machines, 14 motors, 4 transformers and 143 assorted other motors from the Dayu Machinery Factory.
> Received by: Liu Liqin, Company Treasurer
> 2 December 1991

The stuff was extracted on 19 November and returned on 2 December. It took less than two weeks, start to finish! The totals tallied exactly, out and in; they hadn't bothered to change a thing!

"Mayor Li, I copied this note from Ma Zhenhai and Liu Liqin. I will answer to the law if there is anything fake about it!" Wang Yinglie pointed at the papers with a trembling finger, and said indignantly: "Ma Zhenhai and Liu Liqin admitted that all these new machines that were brought in were just the old ones that we had sent away and they had brought back! They didn't even change the name plates on some of them, but just gave them a coat of paint. Mayor Li, this kind of thing is forbidden by the law of heaven. It is utterly evil, and if it had happened in the past, it would have been punished by the death of a thousand cuts! You tell me how they had the nerve to do this! If that grand old man Chairman Mao Zedong was still alive, do you think they would dare? They say it's not allowed to run campaigns these days, but if there was a real political campaign, none of these people would get away with it, not one. If there was another Cultural Revolution they would be paraded through the streets in dunce's caps, wouldn't they! What's wrong with these leaders nowadays? They don't know how to be afraid! Even the landlords and capitalists of the past were always thinking about leaving an escape route for their children and grandchildren…"

At this point, the old man pointed to another piece of paper and said: "Look at this, Mayor Li, take a good look at this. Did you ever think they would dare to…"

He was holding several different types of receipt.

Printed on the back of exit certificates there were seventeen receipts, all with the same vehicle number, the same goods, the same time, the same unit and almost the same weight.

Received today:

From the Hexi Iron and Steel Company: 10 tonnes of 14cm steel. It has been put into storage. The truck is empty. The vehicle number is 076243. It is requested that the gatekeeper let it through.

Supervisor Number 1 Company Workshop: XXXX

16 October 1991

Received today:

From the Hexi Iron and Steel Company: 10 tonnes of 14cm steel. Already in the warehouse. The truck is empty. The vehicle number is 076243. Please expedite exit.

16 October 1991

Supervisor Number 2 Company Warehouse: XXXX

Received today:

From the Hexi Iron and Steel Company: 10 tonnes of 14cm steel. Already unloaded. The vehicle number is 076243. The truck is empty. Security, please allow exit.

16 October 1991

"These bills are the reason they wouldn't let me stay on as gatekeeper!" Wang Yinglie frowned deeply and continued: "They promised me all sorts of things I wanted and all kinds of benefits. First, they said they would double my salary, then they promised me a lump sum, and finally they said they would allocate me a top apartment. How could I agree, Mayor Li? If I did, to start with, how would that have squared with giving my all to protect the factory? If I had agreed, how could I have ever held my head up in the factory again? How could I have faced the world? Besides, all those wishes they said they would grant me were just evil, empty lies and fantasies. If this factory is done for, as it is now, and the workers' wages aren't being paid, then promising me even a tenth-grade salary is about as much use as a fart in the wind. All those managers are living in fine apartments now, all right, but what use are fine apartments when they are just the same as prisons to them? What kind of life is it if you have to be surrounded by security guards even in the daytime? They act so superior, but they're like dogs looking down their muzzles at humans! When I didn't agree, they kept trying to blackmail me and threaten me, telling me what they would do to me if I ever told anyone about all this. I told them that when I was young, I saved this factory without a thought for my own life, so why should I be worried about what you might do to me now I am old? I've worked my whole life for this factory, and if anyone wants to destroy it, I'd rather die than help them do it. I wasn't afraid of dying when I was young, and now I'm reaching the end of my life, I'm quite willing to give up what remains of it! In fact, I gave up on it a long time ago! What a bunch of profligates and wastrels! They have reduced the factory to this state, and now they come snivelling back with aid for the workers! They've all grown fat and sleek on the flesh and blood of the workers. How have they got the gall to offer aid to the workers? They've eaten their fill of us and now they're just spewing it back at us…

CHAPTER TWENTY-SEVEN

EVERY HOME THEY VISITED was just the same: just as small, just as cramped, just as poverty-stricken, and just as stark and bare.

These workers were supposed to be the backbone of the nation, yet here they were, driven by weakness and vulnerability to the verge of total disaster.

Why was it like this? Why?

Even supposing the workers were willing to accept the aid, would that in itself be enough to resolve the situation? If the workers of a country's state-owned enterprises had to rely on aid to survive, what hope was there for that country? If all this was caused by reform, then what was the point of such reform?

Could it be that the final result of reform was the massive loss of state-owned assets and the descent of state-owned enterprises into empty shells full of moths and vermin? If not, how did the current situation come about?

Why were those leading cadres, who should also be the mainstay of the country, so weak and vulnerable in their inability to withstand the temptation of money?

Why was that?

The place was a real slum. Even the toilets were unchanged in more than ten years, with open-air cesspits, low dividing walls and dilapidated cementless urinals that spread a thick layer of frozen piss across the entire floor. Even in the middle of winter, the stench was so strong it almost choked you.

Beside the toilets there was a shoe-mender's street stall. A man of about thirty was sitting there, like a clay statue, braving the icy wind and the awful smell. Li Gaocheng suddenly thought he recognised him, and after he had gone quite a distance from the toilets, he couldn't resist turning to look back. That was when he realised who it was.

Hu Huizhong! One of the most outstanding senior technicians at Zhongyang Textiles! He had taken part in the National Skilled Worker Competition and actually won it twice!

It was Hu Huizhong all right. It was a memorable name because it was also that of a famous female film star in Hong Kong and Taiwan. In fact, this Hu Huizhong was a shy young man, but, as Li Gaocheng remembered him, he was quite feminine in his personality. The two of them had been transferred to Zhongyang Textiles at about the same time. The reason Li remembered him so well was that, back then, Hui had simultaneously passed the examinations for entry to technical school and been selected for a job by Zhongyang Textiles. He had chosen not to continue his studies but to join the company. This was a big news story at the time and had been a source of great pride to the workers and cadres at Zhongyang Textiles. It had also brought considerable personal kudos and clout to Li Gaocheng as factory manager. He still remembered a conversation he had had with Hu at the time:

"Why do you want to be a worker instead of going to school?" Li Gaocheng asked with Hu Huizhong's school admission notice in one hand and his work unit listing in the other.

"...Because Zhongyang Textiles is a good factory, a national enterprise, an iron rice bowl. The pay is very good and many people can't get in even through the back door..." Hu Huizhong said slowly after a long pause for thought.

"Getting into school is just the same. There are plenty who don't manage it even through the back door. Besides, after you graduate from technical school, your status changes and you'd be a cadre, not a worker. The iron of your rice bowl would be even stronger and your salary even higher. It's the kind of thing many people long for all their lives but never get!" Li Gaocheng really wanted Hu to continue his studies at the time.

"My family have been workers for three generations, and they are very well paid now. No one has ever looked down on my father or grandfather, and they've never been persecuted, even during the Cultural Revolution. This is a socialist country, and the workers are in charge. It doesn't make any difference whether you are a cadre or a worker."

"You need to think about it very carefully, my lad. I'm afraid you may regret it later."

"No, I won't, I won't regret it. I know myself very well, and I'm not cadre material. As far as the book learning goes, I can study in my spare time. What's more, if I start work when I'm still young, I'll reap the benefits when I'm young too and my parents won't have to keep working for their living when they're old. I'll never regret it if I make my own living through my skills." The young lad spoke very decisively and seemed very confident.

Li Gaocheng was, in fact, very deeply moved by what Hu Huizhong said. He was being completely honest without any kind of pretence. It really was what he thought, and it was what he ended up doing.

Later on, Li Gaocheng learned that he had joined the Party.

In 1985, Li Gaocheng personally won Hu Huizhong a place to train for one year and three months on the senior technician training course held by the Government Textile Department. As a result, he became the backbone of Zhongyang Textiles' senior technicians.

In 1986, he won first prize in the National Textile Industry Technician Competition.

In 1987, he won first prize again in the same competition.

In the same year, Hu Huizhong married a fellow worker, who was one of the most beautiful girls in the company. Li Gaocheng was invited to attend Hu Huizhong's wedding, and he even said a few words at the ceremony because he believed that Hu had chosen his own path, and that he had walked it very doggedly and successfully.

Li Gaocheng remembered very clearly the look of extraordinary happiness and satisfaction on Hu Huizhong's face as he stood beside his beautiful, charming wife.

In the first year of Hu's marriage, Li Gaocheng left the Zhongyang Textile Group to become deputy mayor.

Li Gaocheng had never seen Hu Huizhong again after that, and Hu Huizhong had never sought him out.

He certainly never expected to meet him again now, in a place like this.

He turned back and asked softly: "Is that really you, Xiao Hu? Do you remember me?" He knew it was a clumsy question, but he didn't know how else to start.

"...How could I not?!" Hu Huizhong kept his head down and hesitated for a long time before continuing: "I recognised you as soon as you went into the toilets... Mayor Li."

Silence fell. The icy wind blowing down the passageway cut like a knife.

"...How come you are doing this?" Li Gaocheng finally asked. At that time, in those circumstances, he simply had no idea what to say to this former top-level technical worker.

"...There was nothing more suitable, so I took this." Hu Huizhong kept his head down all this time and didn't look Li Gaocheng in the eye.

"Wasn't there somewhere better than here you could set up your stall?"

"All the other places were taken. There was nowhere else."

"The dormitory compound at Zhongyang Textiles is huge. Is all the space taken?"

"Everyone else got their first, and when I tried, they... There are things going on here that you don't know about, Mayor Li."

Li Gaocheng suddenly understood that even in a job like mending shoes, it wasn't just a question of doing what you wanted wherever you wanted.

"But you're still so young and you've got so many skills. Why do you have to do this? Why can't you do something else?" Li Gaocheng asked sorrowfully.

"I tried everything, but nothing worked out. I can't be too far from home because I've got to keep an eye on my daughter. She's just turned seven and she's in first grade. Once she gets back from school, I can't work."

"What about your wife? Can't you take it in turns to be at home?"

"We got divorced almost two years ago," Hu Huizhong said weakly.

"Divorced?" Li Gaocheng was astonished. "Why?"

"The factory stopped production, they couldn't pay our wages, we didn't have any savings or anywhere to live, and we didn't have any other income. It was hopeless... Anyway, it was a fair-weather marriage and when the going got tough..."

"But didn't she know the old saying, one day of marriage is worth a hundred days of grace? How could she bear to leave her husband and neglect her child just because things were a little difficult at home?"

"The divorce was my idea – nothing to do with her."

"Eh?" Li Gaocheng was quite taken aback.

"There was no option, though later I did also realise there are some women who are never going to share your suffering. I was out of work and looking everywhere for something to do. Being a shop assistant is really exhausting, it's hard being a salesman, it seemed too shaming to run a stall and I didn't have the capital to set up a restaurant or a snack bar... The truth is, what woman is looking for a man who only offers a lifetime of suffering? If the man is a hopeless failure, what can the woman do about it... She started out by working as a cabaret singer, then an escort and after that it got just too awful and shameful... That's when I said we should get divorced. There are so many like me in the company and there's nothing to be done about it. If there was anything at all I could have done, I would never have divorced her. I couldn't have borne it. Besides, there was our daughter too, so what right did I have to talk about divorce..." Hu Huizhong sat expressionlessly in the freezing wind, talking dispassionately about himself as if it was someone else.

After a long pause, Li Gaocheng said, almost unwillingly: "But you're such a skilled technician. You're not like other people... There must be somewhere that needs a high-level technician like you. It's really too sad that you're reduced to mending shoes..."

"...Mayor Li, you have been in an exalted position for the last few years, and you have probably lost touch with what has been going on down below you. Nowadays, people pay attention to money, not skills! Just look at our situation – how many of our so-called leaders here are genuinely concerned about the factory? You must forgive me for being blunt, Mayor Li, but when you came to the factory a few days ago when the workers were causing trouble, you really had no idea of what has been going on there. Things are very different these days. People have changed, their hearts have changed, and they have given up hope. They have given up all hope. No matter what support the country gives, it is no use, and no matter how much money it sends, it is just being thrown into a bottomless pit. It's like a sieve – it leaks everywhere, and there's no stopping it. In the past, as long as it was public money, no one dared to spend it indiscriminately, but none of today's cadres take the idea of the public purse seriously anymore. All they want is to eat and drink the best stuff, drive the smartest make of car and order the best dishes in the restaurant. Our company's managers were caught by the Public Security Office fooling around with prostitutes, but there were no consequences for them when they returned to the company. The teachers at the company school haven't been paid for many months and the workers' children haven't been able to have any lessons, but the sons and daughters of the company cadres can go and have their lessons at the topflight private Pacific International School for a one-off fee of 170,000 yuan. When you are management, your older brothers, younger brothers, sons and sons-in-law all become like bosses too. If that's what happens for managers and cadres, how can us workers ever be happy? There are other people like me in the company and many couples who have had no choice but to get divorced, but there are lots, too, who are nothing like me. There are people who have hung themselves, who have taken overdoses, who can't afford to buy medicines, who can't afford to be sick, who die of pain, who rob, steal and riot... Mayor Li, it's really impossible, and there's no hope at all. In the past, when I saw the management cadres behaving like that, I would get angry and curse them in the street, but I'm so used to it now, I hardly notice. What's the point in getting angry? Kicking up a fuss doesn't do any good. Short of starting a new movement or setting off major riots, there is nothing that's going to save this country..." Hu Huizhong's face, which was already ashen from the cold, showed nothing but blank despair.

"But you're still young, Xiao Hu! You shouldn't see society in such dark terms! Of course the nation and the government will deal with these evils!"

"All I've done is tell the truth, Mayor Li. It's what I really feel. You're not going to change my mind. I've thought it all through. I'm not blaming anyone. I'm just telling you how things are. I still remember how you told me back then that I had chosen my own path. But I'm at the end of that path now and it has ended with me sitting here. I started to learn to be a painter decorator, but it only paid 200 yuan a month because they said I was just an apprentice. I lasted less than two months before I refused to do it anymore. Nowadays, all these decorators make their money by cheating people. If you don't learn how to do that too, you can't get work, and if you can't get work, you can't make money. After that, I learned how to repair bicycles. I didn't have any trouble with learning, but I couldn't get a business licence. They said there were no pitches available, and I'd have to wait. I kept going back but it was always the same story. Finally, someone told me that if I gave the authorities a little 'gift', I'd get my licence. I thought about it all evening but decided I couldn't do it. For one thing, I didn't have any money, and two cartons of cigarettes and two bottles of wine would cost several hundred yuan. I just couldn't afford it. And for another thing, mending bicycles is really tiring work, and I would have been too far from home. It's busiest in the morning and evening rush hours when it's just one bike after another and you don't even have time to eat. How could I take care of my daughter like that? In the end, I thought of mending shoes – it's easy to get a licence, the work's not tiring, it's close to home, you can shut up shop when you want to and, if you're busy, you can take work home with you. I thought that this spot by the toilets was going to be too dirty, too smelly, too off-the-beaten-track and generally too unsuitable, but actually it's proved to be really good. For one thing, it's close to home because I live right beside those toilets and my daughter can see me as soon as she gets home. For another, business isn't nearly as bad as people think it is. Think about it – who doesn't use public toilets? And this is a poor district, and poor people get one pair of shoes mended over and over, so how could business not be good? For another thing, I've got no competition here so there's no one trying to bully me out of business, and, as word gets round that I'm reliable, honest and fair, people keep bringing me their shoes. What's more, I can keep doing this job until I'm sixty or seventy, so I don't have to worry about not being able to make a living in the future. My only hope at this moment is to see my daughter grow up and that she won't be ashamed of her father for mending shoes when she does..."

Li Gaocheng was reduced to silence once again, so he just stayed there quietly, squatting on his haunches. It was only when someone came along with some shoes for mending that he silently walked away from Hu Huizhong.

What was there to say? He, Li Gaocheng, was the mayor, and this was one of his townspeople. This man was now self-sufficient, supporting himself by his own efforts, and even paying taxes to the state and the government. Moreover, he was doing a job that people were really reluctant to do. Faced by such a person, what influence or power did he have as mayor? He had no control over him, and nor did the man have any interest in listening to what he had to say. This was a man who had given up everything to follow him and now he had abandoned him in the prime of his life. Because of this, Hu Huizhong had lost confidence and hope in him, and his power had lost all legitimacy and validity in the man's eyes.

It was that simple, and that simplicity scared him and chilled him to the marrow.

Li Gaocheng suddenly felt that the so-called relief and sympathy he had come there to offer was comical and absurd. How could he use such words to these people?

Li Gaocheng felt a strange realisation creep over him: it was not these people that most needed saving, it was he himself! The mayor! And the Municipal Government that he led!

He only had to look at what the enterprises, the workers and the places under his jurisdiction had become! If all the places under the jurisdiction of a city government had become like this, didn't that mean that the government he led now existed in name only?

For reasons he himself did not entirely understand, Li Gaocheng had left the others and made his way to the school for the children of the workers.

Normally, he was worried about being recognised when walking down the street, but today he no longer seemed to feel that. Whether it was because no one wanted to talk to him, or because it was so cold and he was so thickly wrapped up that people didn't recognise him, or because the area was so run down and the people here were so hopeless and downtrodden and no one wanted to look anyone else in the eye, whatever the reason, no one recognised him.

The original school gates had changed beyond all recognition; where once there had been beautiful ornamental gates with announcement boards on either side, these had now all been replaced by a row of shop fronts. There were kiosks, snack stalls, a small pharmacy, and what especially surprised Li Gaocheng right next to the school gates, a fair-sized amusement arcade!

It was still the same five-storey teaching block whose construction he had personally supervised, but what had once been the most luxurious and beautiful workers' school of its day was now looking very old and dilapidated.

It was school time, and he walked up floor by floor. He hadn't expected there to be so few students. In some classrooms, there were only a dozen or so of them! In many classrooms, there were no teachers, and the students were being allowed to fight and run riot. Quite a few of them were actually spilling out of the classrooms. He was particularly surprised that, with the students so chaotic, no teacher came out to take them in hand.

When we went into one of the teaching and research rooms, none of the three young teachers there recognised him. There was one male teacher in his early twenties and two female teachers of a similar age. The arrival of a stranger in their midst interrupted their animated conversation and horseplay, and one of the female teachers, with a smile still on her face, asked him offhandedly: "Who are you after?"

Apparently, they didn't recognise him as mayor, and it was quite likely they had never even seen the mayor before, even though he had often been on local television. According to a reliable internal survey, other than in cadre families, ordinary young people and even a considerable number of adults seldom watched the local television news. The provincial news was broadcast at seven o'clock in the evening and was followed by a city news programme. If it has nothing to do with them, people will only watch the news for a certain length of time, so, although Li Gaocheng was something of a

"TV superstar" in the city, his appeal did not extend to the younger demographic.

Li Gaocheng didn't answer the young teacher's question but asked instead: "It's class time and there are lots of students running riot in the corridors. Why has no one gone to bring them to order?"

The three teachers were momentarily stunned, then one of the girls said, with nonchalant mockery: "Oh yes? And are you the dean of students, may I ask?"

This was followed by a burst of cocky laughter, but Li Gaocheng didn't join in. He just stared at them in silence as he took a seat. It was perhaps the old army greatcoat that made the young teachers think he was unlikely to be the dean of students. Their laughter over, the teachers began to feel there might be something unusual about all this. The young man stopped smiling and asked: "So, who are you actually looking for?"

"This school is in chaos! Is there no one to take charge?" Li Gaocheng asked again.

"Listen to you! Do you think this is a good place to work? We haven't been paid for months, and there isn't even a headteacher! So who exactly is supposed to take charge of who?" one of the girls asked contemptuously.

"No headteacher?" Li Gaocheng had heard about the salaries not being paid, but had no idea there was no headteacher. "What happened to him?"

"What happened to him? He got sick and went home," the other girl said curtly.

"What about the deputy head?"

"Transferred to the city."

"Was there only one deputy head?"

"The other one was transferred too."

"So there's no one in charge here?" Li Gaocheng couldn't believe it.

"The company's in such chaos, who's going to bother about taking charge here?"

"But this is a school!"

"Well you seem to think you're the president of the country, don't you! If the city bosses can't take charge of this place, who are you to do any better?" This was said in the same dismissive, mocking tone.

"The city bosses can't take charge? Who says so?"

"Ha! So now you're the Public Security Office, are you? Who says so? I say so, he says so, they say so, the workers say so, the cadres say so..." Probably because Li Gaocheng was so thin and weedy to look at, the young teacher seemed to relax his guard and started laughing again. "The company workers held a demonstration the other day, and I hear the mayor freaked out. He didn't dare shut his eyes for a whole day and a night, and he spent all the time bowing and scraping and apologising to them. He was like a scared kid and he almost peed his pants..." The rest of his words were drowned out by a burst of raucous laughter that seemed to go on forever.

"How do you know that?" Li Gaocheng asked flatly, once the laughter had finally died down.

"It's all over the company and all over the city. Everybody knows! I've heard that the mayor is being investigated by the province. This whole thing is going to catch up with him sooner or later and he'll be done for." The young teachers had stopped talking to Li and were talking amongst themselves by this time. "The company bosses were all promoted by the mayor so there's got to be problems with him too. I've also heard that the mayor's wife has got shares in a lot of different companies and they're all being prosecuted by the province and the state. Some people are even saying that the mayor has got shares in the Pacific International School and that's why all the company bosses send their kids there..."

Li Gaocheng kept listening for a while, then walked silently away. He really didn't want to hear any more.

Until you take a clear stand and make a choice, people will always make all sorts of comments and speculations about you that you've got absolutely no control over or choice about. You might as well try to block a river as try to shut the people up.

Did he really think he had any chance of shutting down the gossip with a track record like he was supposed to have?

CHAPTER TWENTY-EIGHT

THERE WAS NO POINT in him going anywhere else; what else could he possibly want to see?

Here in front of him, hadn't he seen more than enough of the stupefying poverty that had arisen from stupefying crimes, and the mind-boggling polarisation of money-making methods that were even more mind-boggling than primitive capitalist accumulation?

The prospect of reform had originally been so beautiful and beguiling, so what was it in this large state-owned enterprise, that was, step by step, subverting, eroding and destroying the original essence and intention of that reform?

Li Gaocheng stood pondering this, as the icy wind whistled round him.

He had been thinking of going home, but some extraordinary emotion generated by this exceptional environment prompted him to go and seek out another person he found himself particularly longing to see – someone he hadn't seen for more than ten years.

Her name was Xia Yulian, a female worker at Zhongyang Textiles who had been nanny to his two children for almost six years.

She was about the same age as Li Gaocheng, so, thinking about it, somewhere around fifty-four or fifty-five, and had probably already been retired for a good while. With the company in its current state, if you left or retired you could, intermittently, still receive some kind of monthly pension and living allowance, whereas if you were still in work, with production stopped, you got nothing. What's more, if you were still fit and healthy and wanted to go back to some kind of work, as long as you went through the relevant formalities, you could pick up temporary work, which was the equivalent of getting a double income but even more secure.

Xia Yulian and his wife Wu Aizhen had children almost at the same time, but Xia Yulian was on her fourth child while Wu Aizhen was having her first.

At that time, Li Gaocheng and Xia Yulian were both working in the same workshop in the Xinhua Textile Factory. The difference was that Xia Yulian was just an ordinary female textile worker, while Li Gaocheng was already the manager of the workshop.

When his wife gave birth to their child, the procuratorate gave her more than five months of leave, but Xia Yulian appeared in the workshop less than half a month after she gave birth. She didn't have to come back to work so early, as maternity leave for female textile workers could be extended to three months. The real reason she went back was that she was a lunchtime meal supervisor in the workshop, and there was an allowance of 80 cents per day for the job. Although she had just given birth, she did not go home once during the day and, after several days of this, Li Gaocheng realised that she must have given the child away to someone else.

Then, one summer afternoon, she passed out in the workshop and didn't come to for a full three hours. Extreme fatigue, weakness and malnutrition, four children and a husband who was very sick: the burden of running such a household under those conditions had proved too much for her.

Li Gaocheng and some of the other workshop leaders went to visit her in the staff hospital.

What still surprised Li Gaocheng, even now, was that this skinny, weak, malnourished woman who was already a mother of four, should have two breasts so full and swollen with milk. She had been away from the child for almost ten days already, but the milk was still coming down and showing no sign of stopping. So much so that, when she fainted in the workshop, there was a wet patch on the top she was wearing, and during the two hours Li and the others went to visit her in the hospital, she had to wipe her chest with a towel several times.

In complete contrast, during her month of confinement, Wu Aizhen was sleek and well-nourished with a double chin on her plump face, but her breasts were shrivelled and empty and showed no sign of ever filling. She had more than her fill of chicken, duck, fish, meat, all kinds of traditional Chinese and Western medicines, but her milk just dwindled away until there was practically none at all.

Things back then were different from now when, if there is no mother's milk, there is cow's milk, and if there is no cow's milk, there is milk powder, and you can take your pick from a dazzling array of baby foods of all kinds in shops big and small. Back then, when even rice, cloth, sugar, soap and matches were all effectively on ration, a packet of milk powder was really hard to come by. Moreover, the Xinhua Textile Factory was situated in the suburbs, several dozen *li* from the city proper, and even in the city centre you had to go and queue to buy rationed milk at four o'clock in the morning. If it had sold out before it was your turn, however much you needed it, you had to come back and queue up again the next day.

Li Gaocheng did not have that kind of time, and generally speaking there was no way he could get up at three or four o'clock in the morning and go dozens of miles away to queue for milk for his children. There was no shuttle bus service back then and it was ridiculous to think of going by bicycle as the return trip would have taken as much time as a whole work shift. It wasn't that he couldn't have managed it, it just wasn't a viable proposition.

So, when Li Gaocheng saw Xia Yulian's breasts swollen and overflowing with milk, an idea immediately began to stir in him. That evening, he and his wife took a bag, brimful of nutritious foodstuffs, to her home.

The terms of the job were very simple and very easy. Xia Yulian was not to go to work during her maternity leave, but, instead, was to go every day to Li Gaocheng's home to breastfeed the baby, help with the housework a bit, and, ideally, take her meals with the family. In other words, she was to be a sort of wet nurse-cum-nanny and, needless to say, the pay was quite considerable at forty-five yuan per month, not counting meals.

This was almost as much as Xia Yulian could earn working full-time at the factory for a month and was three times the normal pay for a nanny. Fortunately, Li Gaocheng was earning good money at the time and had some savings. Wu Aizhen's own family was not badly off either, and her mother, who was still alive at the time, had secretly given Li Gaocheng three hundred yuan before her daughter gave birth. In any case, the baby not having any milk was an urgent problem, and Li was willing to do anything for the child. Wu Aizhen agreed to the plan without even thinking about it.

After two months, not only was the child plump and lively from Xia Yulian's milk, Li Gaocheng and Wu Aizhen felt as though they had been liberated and found that there was nothing for them to do around the house, even at weekends. This was because, apart from feeding the baby, nursing it and washing its nappies, Xia Yulian also did practically all the household chores. She cooked, did the laundry, bought vegetables, bought rice, bought noodles, bought coal... She did all the jobs that Wu Aizhen would normally have done and all Li Gaocheng's tasks too. On top of all this, she still had to do all the chores at her own home too. Often it would be the small hours of the next morning before she got back home...

What really surprised Li Gaocheng and what he found almost inexplicable was that, over those two months, Xia Yulian's face grew ruddy with health, her body filled out and she put on almost twenty kilos in weight.

She seemed to have been born into this world to suffer; she always seemed to choose the lowliest food and take on the heaviest tasks. Usually, no matter whether Li and his wife were home or not, she never touched the choice foods she brought back to the house. Once when the couple were away on a business trip for a week, they came back to find that not one of a tray of twenty eggs had even been moved. She would wear an item of clothing until it couldn't be mended any more, and only throw it out when it was finally too tatty to wear. She had no idea about fashionable hairdos and never wore make-up.

It was perhaps because of all this that the family seemed to be inseparable from Xia Yulian. Even after she went back to work, she was still joint head of the household. She breastfed the couple's first child for a full year and nine months, and a year later she fed their second child for nearly two years...

It was this relationship that prompted Li Gaocheng to make

every effort to get Xia Yulian's family transferred along with him when he was moved from the Xinhua Textile Factory to Zhongyang Textiles. Given his comparatively lowly status and influence at that time, it was no easy matter for him to transfer a whole family with whom he had no blood ties, from the countryside to the provincial capital. But he did it for the sake of his wife, for the sake of his child, for his own sake and out of his sense of obligation to this good, but retiring, woman.

The second year after Xia Yulian was transferred to the city, her husband, who had been plagued by ill health for many years, finally succumbed to a terminal illness, and Xia, who was in her forties by then, never remarried.

From then on, Li Gaocheng rose higher and higher in status, but Xia Yulian remained just the same, humble, ordinary worker. Li tried to get her promoted to team leader and other such positions, but, every time, after just a few days, she would step down, saying that she wasn't either leadership or advanced-model-worker material.

It was indeed true that although no one complained about her work, no one voted for her either if her name was put forward as a model worker.

She was just too normal, too ordinary; so much so that many people forgot she even existed.

In 1982, Li Gaocheng was transferred as deputy factory manager and deputy Party Committee secretary at Zhongyang Textiles. Because the company was establishing a new textile workshop and urgently needed skilled female workers, once again, Xia Yulian was transferred along with Li Gaocheng.

Later on still, as the children grew up, Li Gaocheng and Wu Aizhen also rose through the ranks and their relationship with Xia Yulian gradually began to weaken. From time to time, when they remembered to, they would send the children over with some gifts for her.

Li remembered that she had come to see him in the year he left Zhongyang Textiles. He couldn't remember exactly what it was about, but it was something to do with dividing up the family accommodation. With the children grown up and wanting to get married, they hadn't come up with any way of handling the problem and hoped that he might be able to help them find a solution.

He seemed to remember talking to her workshop manager about the matter, but he had no idea whether it had been sorted out or not or how things might have been settled.

He was too busy.

For all those years, he had always been so busy.

And now it seemed that all these painful and horrific scenes he was witnessing had stimulated his memory and raised a yearning in him to see his children's old wet nurse; indeed, she might be called his whole family's old wet nurse. With the company in its current sorry state, how were she and her family coping? Was she able to support them? Was she able to scrape a living?

Li Gaocheng looked blankly around him and felt that he had lost all sense of direction. He realised that he didn't know where to find Xia Yulian's home. He either couldn't remember because he had been there so seldom, perhaps only once, after she moved into the city from the provincial factory; or it could be that he had never actually been there at all, and only had some vague recollection that his children had told him she lived in this general vicinity. Or maybe again, the buildings in the area had changed so much, he had no chance of remembering. It certainly wouldn't be because the buildings there had got bigger or newer, but rather because they were more numerous and smaller. It was, in fact, precisely because it had remained the same for so many years that it had become what it now was: around each original single-storey building, like a brick beehive, there were now clusters of lower, smaller and narrower buildings. The original alleyways had become narrower and narrower, so you could hardly even make them out; the original houses couldn't be distinguished from subsequent buildings, and even the original courtyards had disappeared, so it was impossible to work out how to get in and out of the clusters.

Li Gaocheng couldn't help remembering how Xia Yulian had come to him for help with her family's housing situation, and he felt a sudden stab of indefinable guilt that in all those years, she had never asked him for any more help. Were her children still living in this maze of buildings? After inquiring at a succession of households, he finally worked out Xia Yulian's address.

His fears and suspicions were simultaneously confirmed: Xia Yulian's family did indeed still live there.

It was not far, just a short walk down through a small gap in the alleyway, two more turns and he was there.

As soon as he arrived, his memories all came flooding back.

That's right, he thought to himself. This was the place all right! In fact, nothing had changed, and it was all just as it had been, just the same size. Of course, like everywhere else, a honeycomb of different shapes and sizes of dwellings had also sprung out from it.

The only thing that left him puzzled was that he didn't know which one of the similar-sized doors that confronted him to knock on.

Fortunately, a woman was coming out of one of them to put out her rubbish, and Li Gaocheng hurried over to ask her.

"You're looking for my mother-in-law?" Either because of the icy wind, or because her eyes were adjusting to the light, the woman blinked rapidly for a while before replying. Her face was a bit puffy, and she was wrapped up tightly against the cold. "Where are you from? What do you want with her?"

Quite by chance, the woman he had asked turned out to be Xia Yulian's daughter-in-law.

"I'm from the city. Is she in?"

"From the city?" The woman's suspicious manner told Li Gaocheng that she either hadn't recognised him or had no idea who he was or didn't think it could possibly be him. After she had weighed him up with a look, she went on, coldly: "Has something happened? She's not here."

"Doesn't she live here, then?"

"Yes, she does, but she's at work."

"At work?" Li Gaocheng was taken aback. "What work? Where? I thought she was retired."

"Where in the city are you from?" On the receiving end of this barrage of questions, Xia Yulian's daughter-in-law gave him another doubtful and suspicious look.

"The Municipal Government. My name is Li." He felt that was the most he could say at this point.

"Ah!" The woman's expression immediately changed to one full of affability and politeness. "You must be the Master Li who lent my mother-in-law that money! She was talking about you only yesterday! It's cold out here! Come inside! Come inside and sit down!"

At first, he thought she had recognised who he was, but then he realised she had, completely unexpectedly, mistaken him for some kind of debt collector called Master Li.

The room was much smaller than he had expected and there was all manner of random stuff all over the place, with every cranny filled to bursting, so the already cramped space seemed even smaller. A little courtyard no more than two or three metres square had been pressed into service as a place to prepare food.

The lights were on in the house, even though it was full day, but the light was still surprisingly dim. For one thing, the home was too dark, and, for another, the wattage of the bulb was too low. Presumably to save power, the bulbs were only fifteen watts at most. No wonder the woman had been dazzled when she walked outside just now.

The main room appeared to have been given to the daughter-in-law, but it was still pitifully small to be called a main room. Apart from the double bed and a small selection of simple furniture, there was little space left for anything else. Xia Yulian herself lived in what was the original open-air kitchen! In fact, it was just a small gap between the two houses, only about one metre wide and less than two metres long. It was roofed with a piece of plastic sheeting. It was too cramped for anyone to get in properly and even a small man like Li Gaocheng could only enter it sideways. He saw that inside this small cell where Xia Yulian lived there was a thick layer of ice in the water cup beside the bed!

Tears began to flow down Li Gaocheng's cheeks and it was a long time before they stopped. His own children's wet nurse living in a place like this! How could such a good woman, who had lived such a hard life, live out her final years in this way?

He had never dreamed it could be so miserable; so miserable he couldn't bear even to look at it.

He sat in silence on a stool beside the daughter-in-law's double bed.

The daughter-in-law gave him a cup of hot water, telling him to warm his hands with it. He could tell how cold it was in the room from the steam rising from the cup.

It was as he was drinking his water that he discovered there was a newborn baby wrapped in a quilt on the bed. No wonder, then, that the woman herself was bundled up so tightly.

She'd just given birth!

He had just been feeling real anger towards the young couple for forcing the old lady to live in such a wretched space, but as soon as he saw the baby, his anger just evaporated.

Who could blame them? The living space proper was taken up almost to the last inch. Any grandparent in the world, let alone a woman like Xia Yulian, would have given up the only room in the house when there was a wife with a newborn baby involved.

Xia Yulian's daughter-in-law seemed very well disposed towards her mother-in-law. As she made her guest welcome, she chattered away. "My mother-in-law never stops talking about you. She says that if it wasn't for that eight hundred yuan of yours, who knows what might have happened. Originally, I didn't think I'd have to go to the city hospital. I thought I'd be fine at the company hospital – it's closer and it's cheaper. I didn't expect to be in labour for two days and nights, and after that I don't remember anything about what happened until I came to and realised I was in the city hospital. It was only later that my mother-in-law told me the deposit was five thousand yuan. She's got lots of friends, but even after borrowing money from relatives, friends and neighbours, she was still a thousand yuan short. She was worried to death and the doctor even told us afterwards that if it had been two hours later, it would have been all over for me and my baby. But it made no difference how urgent it was, you couldn't get admitted to the city hospital without that five thousand yuan deposit, not even if it was a matter of life and death! It's the same everywhere these days – it's money that counts, not people, and the hospital doesn't care about life or death. My mother-in-law said that strange things happen in emergencies, and she has no idea why she suddenly thought of you, even though she hadn't seen you for ages. She would have been happy with four or five hundred and she never expected you to say you'd give her as much as she wanted and that you'd hand over eight hundred yuan just like that! She says that she met a living Buddha in you that day and that there really are some good people left in the world! I told the rest of the family that, in a few days, I would go and visit you to thank you for saving my life and for the rest of my days…"

Li Gaocheng listened to her in silence as he contemplated the soul-shattering scene that had played out in this family.

Five thousand yuan, almost all of which Xia Yulian had borrowed from neighbours, relatives and friends, and including, of course, the family's life savings. That five thousand yuan that almost cost two lives was nothing to some people today! Just enough for a meal and an evening's karaoke!

Xia Yulian's daughter-in-law was still chattering away. "My mother-in-law said you'd be coming in the next few days and that by that time she would have scraped together pretty much all the money you lent us and she'd be sending it round to you. Actually, she would have got it back to you before, because the hospital didn't cost that much in the end, but there was a wedding in the family and she gave it to them first..."

"I'm not the Master Li you're thinking of. My name is Li Gaocheng." Li Gaocheng finally managed to interrupt her to identify himself.

"Li Gaocheng?" The face in front of him was suddenly covered with the same confusion and bewilderment as before, as if she had no idea who Li Gaocheng was. It took a while before she said: "So you're not Master Li from the city then! ...Li Gaocheng? That name seems very familiar! What do you want with my mother-in-law?"

"Hasn't she ever told you about me?"

She was about to say something but hesitated and just shook her head gently.

It seemed she still didn't recognise the name Li Gaocheng, let alone what it signified. She probably hadn't thought or made the connection that there was a mayor whose name was also Li Gaocheng. Besides, the way the man in front of her looked and was dressed must have been a long way from the picture of a mayor she had in her imagination. How could a mayor whom the eyes of the world were on and who was constantly surrounded by his own retinue possibly come to a place like this to see a poor woman like her mother-in-law?

What was more, Xia Yulian most likely had never mentioned a person called Li Gaocheng in front of her daughter-in-law.

Li Gaocheng suddenly felt a rare sense of embarrassment. He wanted to reveal his identity, but immediately stopped himself. Now he even regretted revealing his name. Wasn't it just because he wanted her to know he was the mayor? And what good would that do? Wouldn't she start by being surprised, embarrassed and alarmed that her mother-in-law had such a connection with the mayor, and then wouldn't she get her to use that connection and keep coming to pester him?

Was that why Xia Yulian hadn't told her daughter-in-law?

Yes, that would be completely in keeping with the character and conduct of a woman like Xia Yulian. Li Gaocheng felt himself wracked by ever-increasing guilt and unspeakable sadness.

"So, what do you want?" The daughter-in-law fell silent for a while, then a wary look began to spread across her face. "Does she still owe you..."

"No, no, not at all! It's me who owes her. I didn't know there had been such great upheavals in your family. How about this? I'll give you my telephone number and she can call me when she gets back." As he said this, he fished out a pen and scribbled down both his home and office telephone numbers. He also wrote down his name. As he handed them over, he asked: "Is your mother-in-law in good health?"

"Ah, well, you know, sometimes good sometimes not so good. Us youngsters can't get her to change her mind. The company is in trouble, and this family of mine needs so much food, so she's still going out to work every day. Even so, it's still the same story and she hasn't had a cent in wages for almost six months. And now we've got another mouth to feed, and we've had all that trouble and we're in a whole heap of debt but there's nothing we can do and it's all down to them. Last year and the year before they let us grow stuff on a couple of *mu* of land, which did some good and at least we didn't have to worry too much about grain and vegetables. But this year, they took all the land back and said that there were new rules and regulations and we weren't allowed to grow stuff anymore..."

"Growing stuff?" Li Gaocheng asked in amazement. "Where? What land?"

"Local farmers' land! These days lots of farmers on the outskirts of the city are getting rich from doing lots of different stuff and they don't think farming is profitable enough. They let us workers, who don't really know what we are doing, get on with it. The land was going to waste anyway, so they let us plant it and if they got a little bit out of us from it, that was fine with them. So my mother-in-law planted those two *mu*, and although it was very tiring, the grain and vegetables were just about enough for us. It might not have seemed much to other people, but it was like a huge income to us. There were lots of people from the company doing the same..."

Xia Yulian's daughter-in-law was talking quite freely now, and Li Gaocheng listened to her wide-eyed and open-mouthed. So that's how things were! He had seen news reports on this kind of thing before and it had seemed that the newspapers and television stations were trying to present this as a wonderful new development brought about by the reforms, with city girls marrying farmers, and farmers contracting their land out to workers. He had found these stories full of human interest at the time but had no idea what the real situation was!

"So, where is your mother-in-law working now?" He had the impression there was more to what the daughter-in-law had said than first seemed, and he wanted to find out what was going on with Xia Yulian.

"At her age, where *can* she go? She's earning next to nothing working more than ten hours a day, night and day, for only two or three hundred yuan a month. It's temporary work at a privately contracted branch factory, and, like all of those black economy places, most of the workers are farmers doing temporary work. Everyone knows it's a mincing machine that grinds people up and spits them out, but she won't listen to anyone, she just won't listen..."

"I thought they'd stopped production everywhere! How come there's still work at a privately contracted branch factory?"

"You're an outsider, so how could you understand? The factories that have stopped production are all the public-ownership ones. Do you really think they're going to stop in the privately contracted ones too? If those places stopped, don't you think they'd be opening up the public ones again?"

"What?!" Li Gaocheng was astonished. "Who are these contractors then?"

"Who do you think? Not us workers, that's for sure! It's all the public bosses, isn't it! They call it contracting but all they're doing is taking public property and making it their own! The way things are going now, it's all just the public bosses trampling the public into the mud!"

"Where are these branch factories?"

"There are a dozen or so of them, mostly in new-build areas in a circle round the company factory. I've heard they're doing good business..."

"Which one is your mother-in-law in?"

"I think it's... Hang on a minute, my memory's not... Oh yes, that's right, that's right, it's called something like the 'Chang Long Garment and Textile Factory'. It used to be the No. 9 branch factory. It's around one stop away from the company main gates..."

CHAPTER TWENTY-NINE

THE MAIN FACTORY WAS DEAD AS A DOORNAIL, and the little branch factories were prowling round it, fangs bared, like tigers watching their prey, or serpents sizing up an elephant.

And all because one was called public and the other private? Was that all it was?

Or was it because, for one, the burden was too heavy, the responsibility too great, the control too strict, the influence too weak, the move to new products too slow, the ideas too backward, the thinking too rigid, the ability to adapt to changing technology too weak, the market awareness too poor... and for the other, the burden was light, the outlay small, there was no responsibility, no outside controls, no rigid framework. They could do as they pleased and keep light on their feet. Just as long as they made money, they could use any tactics they liked... Wasn't it inevitable there would be two different results and two different sets of circumstances?

But, if the burden was already too heavy, how could all these bigger and heavier "parasites" keep appearing? If the responsibility was too great, who was taking on the responsibility of these so-called branch factories? If the company "stall" was too big, how could all these new stalls be appearing in an already overcrowded marketplace? If control was too strict, how come there was such chaos? If influence was too weak, how could so much be getting done? If changing to new products was too slow, how could all these thriving branch factories be doing so well? If ideas were too backward, thinking too rigid and market awareness too poor, how was it that the same people could be so limp and lifeless in one place and so nimble and sprightly in another? If technology was outdated, how was it that these branch factories, whose technology was even more primitive, could be thriving while the parent company was dying?

Could you analyse it like that? Did it make any sense?

But if it really was just a question of one being public and one being private, weren't there countless public companies and state-owned enterprises like Zhongyang Textiles and weren't they all healthy and thriving and standing proud as though they owned the world? And weren't there also countless genuine, serious private and individual enterprises, which, despite all their best efforts and despite working themselves to the point of exhaustion, were still languishing and dying? Yet there were those parasites companies, which were neither fish nor fowl, neither public nor private, which had sprung up around a state-owned enterprise, and they were all living things up in the lap of luxury!

What was his explanation for all that? Was there even an explanation?

Why had this happened? Why? What was really at the bottom of it all?

Li Gaocheng considered all the sinister branch factories that now surrounded the company like bloated bedbugs, and it left him puzzled and angry. Then he remembered what Xia Yulian's daughter-in-law had just said.

"...The factories that have stopped production are all the public-ownership group ones. Do you really think they're going to stop in the privately contracted ones too? If those places stopped, don't you think they'd be opening up the public ones again?" ... "They call it contracting but all they're doing is taking public property and making it their own! The way things are going now, it's all just the public bosses trampling the public into the mud!"

The words of this apparently poorly educated, uncultured wife of a worker were so profound, so weighty and so thought-provoking.

Almost immediately, he also remembered what Hu Huizhong, the shoe mender, had said: "Mayor Li, you have been in an exalted position for the last few years, and you have probably lost touch with what has been going on down below you. Nowadays, people pay attention to money, not skills... It's like a sieve, it leaks everywhere, and there's no stopping it."

He most certainly hadn't understood, because he was unable to understand and unable to get down to the essentials. It had all been happening in front of his very eyes and he hadn't seen a thing! What else had they been up to that he didn't know about?

Even if he had been poor but honest all his life, if this was all he had to show for it, he was no different from those corrupt senior officials and the gangsters who corrupted them!

"Chang Long Garment and Textile Factory": they were not just a handful of big, strong characters, they were actually in the calligraphy of a top departmental director!

When he thought about it, there was nothing too strange about that. It was not unusual, let alone against the law, to set up a new factory and get a bigwig to inscribe its name for it. It was so commonplace that nobody took it seriously anymore. But on the other hand, if you thought about it, it really wasn't that straightforward. For such an important official to write an inscription for a company was almost like giving it a protective talisman. The factory owners could say: "What else is there worrying you? The top brass have already given our factory their support, so if you are suspicious of us, you must be suspicious of them too. You want to investigate us? Isn't that the same as wanting to investigate them too?"

As soon as he saw that sign, he felt the weight of its significance, and he felt the intimidation inherent in its origin.

There was an aura of mystery about it, and mystery is a form of power, or symbolic of a kind of unfathomable secret power.

Presumably that was exactly what the factory owners were trying to demonstrate.

Two rather imposing guards stood to attention at the main gates. Fortunately he had his official ID with him, but, to his surprise, the guards didn't take it but just gave it a cursory glance and waved him in.

So it was all just for show!

And maybe that was all it needed to be.

A ball of donkey dung is shiny on the outside, and it's only once you break it open that you discover how foul and dirty it is!

Nevertheless, he could see that the place was busy. There were people and trucks coming and going in the open-sided shed in the yard, and there was a hustle and bustle of noise. In particular there were mountainous piles of cotton in the warehouse and there was a constant stream of fully laden lorries driving in. The mark of a good textile factory, of whether it is profitable or not, can be clearly seen in how full of cotton its warehouses are.

It called itself a garment and textile factory, but the garments were only a very small part of the business, and the word was probably only there for appearances, to make it look like it was not a branch factory of Zhongyang Textiles.

But anyone who knew how these things worked only had to walk in to see quite clearly that this so-called garment and textile factory was still an out-and-out cotton textile mill whose products were identical in every respect to those of the Zhongyang Textile Group.

What took Li Gaocheng aback was that, in this factory, all the essential workshops, that is to say the grading room, the humidification room, the blow room and the cotton loosening room, were all together in one single workshop.

Moreover, the drawing room, the roving room, the spinning room and the winding room were also all under one roof, as were the warp and weft room, the sizing room, the weaving room and the finishing room.

For anyone with a passing knowledge of textiles, this was simply unimaginable, because doing things this way would not only directly affect the quality of the product but would render some of the processes useless and impossible to perform properly. If the product quality was not to be impacted and all the processes were to be carried out fully, there was only one way under these circumstances and that was to see the working conditions and individual rights of the workers massively compromised. In other words, it meant you had totally to ignore the existence and wellbeing of the workers. To put it even more brutally, lives were sacrificed to achieve these changes in production!

When Li Gaocheng finally located Xia Yulian's workshop and lifted the filthy, faded, heavy curtain that served as a door, he was choked by the pungent, almost suffocating stench that assaulted him and he couldn't bring himself to go in.

In fact, he couldn't take another step, because he couldn't see a thing in front of him!

A few hazy, indistinct objects suspended in the air were probably the workshop lights.

Lint, dust, powder, debris and moisture were diffused through the workshop like a dense fog.

The deafening roar from the various machines was almost enough to stun him. It was impossible to make yourself heard, even at the top of your voice and from only a metre away. The only way of communicating was to poke someone to get their attention and then use gestures and "air characters".

This was the first workshop after the cotton arrived in the factory. Even in a company workshop with a single process, good ventilation and complete facilities, it was always the dirtiest in the factory. Here, with several processes combined in a single workshop with extremely poor ventilation and lacking even some of the most basic facilities, the working conditions could only be imagined.

In fact, however good your imagination, the reality when you actually saw it, was even more shocking.

Li Gaocheng stood in the doorway for a few minutes, and the interior of the workshop gradually became clearer to him.

In no time at all, his face was covered with a thick layer of lint, dust, debris and other, unidentified wet, sticky things. The effect this had on his eyes was what most concerned him. As soon as he wiped them once, he had to wipe them again immediately in order to be able to see anything at all in front of him.

What Li Gaocheng found most incomprehensible of all was that much more stringent and thorough attention was paid in the warehouse to protecting the cotton than to protecting the workers. Once it was processed, the now spotless cotton was transferred out of the workshop in a big, sealed cylinder. The clean conditions in the workshop it entered were worlds away from those in the one it had just left, like comparing heaven and hell!

After asking several workers one after another, Li Gaocheng finally found Xia Yulian, who was standing by one of the machines, sweating profusely.

She looked, to all intents and purposes, like the "White-Haired Girl"[1] from the movie, as she was covered from head to foot in long white fibres which rendered her almost unrecognisable. In fact, Li Gaocheng had to look for a long time before he was sure it was indeed Xia Yulian.

She was hard at work, and he couldn't see her face, but he could see how bent her back was, how thin her frame was, and how hard she was breathing. She was wearing a huge face mask, but, probably because of the quantity of dust in the air and the humidity of the workshop, she had found it too difficult to breathe through, and it was hanging down by her chin, leaving her nose and mouth bare. The truth of the situation was that when doing such heavy physical work in an environment like that with such heavily polluted air, it was not possible to continue if you didn't have full use of your mouth and nose to take in great lungfuls of air. It was useless trying to wear a mask. But, if you didn't wear a mask, the damage to your health would undoubtedly be extremely serious, and the consequences were too awful to consider.

Li Gaocheng tapped her on the shoulder a few times until she made a great effort to turn round. She just glanced at him, waved him away and went back to work. She had no chance of recognising who it was because Li Gaocheng too was covered from head to toe in white fibres, effectively turning him into a "White-Haired Man".

Even when he drew her out of the workshop, wiped his face clean and dusted all the white fibres off his clothes, she still didn't recognise who it was.

Maybe the light outside was too strong, maybe she had been deafened by the noise inside the workshop, maybe her eyesight was now too poor, maybe it was all too sudden, but, for whatever reason, no matter how loud Li Gaocheng shouted and how hard he tried to introduce himself, Xia Yulian just stared at him blankly, shaking her head and asking what he wanted with her.

Just then, Li Gaocheng felt something tugging violently at him from behind and he found himself turned through a hundred and eighty degrees to see, only a few inches from his nose, another face covered in white fibres. This one was staring at him fiercely, and an aggressive voice thundered in his ears: "Can't you fucking see we're trying to work? Who the fuck are you anyway? What do you want here? What the fuck do you think you're doing, dragging one of our women workers out here without a fucking word? No one tells us what to do here! You've got some nerve, you fucking..."

"What do you think you're doing?" Li Gaocheng quickly recovered his self-possession. The man's rudeness and arrogance had got to him and he said, angrily: "Who gave you the right to curse people out like that, just because you feel like it? Get the factory manager here right away! Let go of me..."

"Fuck this for a laugh, you little creep..." These were the last words Li Gaocheng seemed to hear. It could have been because of the powerful stench inside the workshop, or it could have been the piercing light outside; it could have been because of his sudden over-exertion, or it could have been because he was too exhausted and too hungry; it could have been because of the suddenness of the confrontation, or because the man who had confronted him had wrenched at him too hard... whatever the reason, all he was aware of was the sun crossing his vision in a flashing arc and then a huge black iron door crashing down on him; it seemed to be crushing him to death as the concrete floor rushed up to meet him, and then he wasn't aware of anything anymore...

When he came to again, he seemed to be in some kind of passageway.

Two men, one on either side, were dragging him up inside a building, floor by floor, as if he were a bit of baggage.

He had a hazy feeling he could be in a staff canteen, or a restaurant, or a karaoke hall, or a hotel... At any rate, he wasn't far from the factory because he could hear the rumbling of the machines in the workshops and the sound was so clear it must have come from quite close-by. He tried to stand up, but the two men were dragging him along too quickly and he was still too muddle-headed, so he couldn't manage it. He could feel something sticky on his face, and it was when he touched it and realised that his nose was bloodied and bruised that he finally came properly to his senses. It gradually dawned on him that he had been struck in the face by something.

This was the city that he was in charge of, and this was the company he had led for ten years. And yet he had been so roughly and wretchedly manhandled and thrown to the ground.

He tried again to stand up but couldn't. The two men were

holding him down so firmly, it felt as though he was being kidnapped.

When they had gone up another level, the concrete floor changed to carpet. The insulation there must have been better, because the noise of the workshops was much fainter. They seemed to have gone as high as they were going because he was now being dragged along the carpeted corridor into the interior of the building. He gradually became aware of the sound of distant but lively music, and, at the same time, he smelled a delicious fragrance of food. He was assailed by hunger but, also, either because of that hunger, or because he was being dragged along so roughly, or because of his fall, his head began to swim again.

The two men stopped at what seemed to be a padded leather door and rang the bell. Li Gaocheng was about to take the opportunity to get to his feet, when the door was abruptly opened. He was dragged inside. He suddenly realised that the two men dragging him along like this saw him as a kind of trophy and were looking for some sort of reward for meritorious service. He was about to be hauled in front of their boss.

The factory director? The manager? Or someone else? He couldn't help himself trying to guess.

One set of rooms followed by another. The carpets were thick, the sofas, tables and chairs were luxurious, the air was pure, the rooms were warm, and, in particular the soundproofing was so good that it cut off the sound from outside. It was a kind of self-contained paradise that almost defied imagination!

As the final door swung open, it was as if the floodgates had been opened on an ocean of sound and a sea of wine, as he was assailed by swirling music and giddying liquor fumes.

The two men dropped him with a thud. He felt his nose hit the floor again, and once more had the feeling of being treated as an object rather than a human being. He heard a voice that was simultaneously obsequious and boastful say, from somewhere next to him: "This is the fellow, boss. He's a nobody but he was snooping around the factory for ages, and in the end he snuck into one of the workshops and dragged out one of the woman workers. I don't know what he's up to. When we grabbed him, he said he wanted to see the factory manager. You can see from his little monkey face that he's nothing to worry about..."

Li Gaocheng felt as though his head weighed a ton, but he used his hand to raise it and look up. What he saw was an enormous round table, and across its surface, which was covered in a variety of plates and dishes, a row of faces...

He shook his head, then shook it again...

He drew his hand across his eyes...

He couldn't believe it. He quite simply couldn't believe it! How could those faces be so familiar? How could it be those particular faces?

He didn't want to look at them. He really did not want to look at them!

What he saw was practically the same bunch of people as had been in his house a day or so before: Chao Wanshan, the brother-in-law of the executive deputy secretary of the Provincial Party Committee and chairman of the 'Te Gao Te' passenger transport company. Wang Yiliang, the former deputy governor of the Provincial People's Bank and the vice chairman of the 'Te Gao Te' passenger transport company. There were also the two company directors who came that night, and the man who was apparently the chief accountant... and two unfamiliar faces, who might be the bosses of this place, whatever it was...

In addition, and there could not have been a less welcome addition, there was his wife, the woman who hadn't been home for the last five or six days: deputy chief prosecutor of the District Procuratorate and director of the Anti-Corruption Bureau, Wu Aizhen!

Was this real? Could this possibly be real?

Li Gaocheng felt a stab of piercing pain and screwed his eyes tight shut, unable to face the cruel truth in front of him. But, of course, how else could they have come by all their wealth and swagger?

It was the company's money, the state's money and the people's money and it was all being used for their own benefit. As the popular saying went: the debt was the state's and the money was theirs.

So, was this their ultimate goal? Or was there something else?

On the surface, there they were, each one of them expressing sympathy, swearing loyalty, exuding kindness and virtue, but as soon as they turned their backs they showed their blind greed, rapaciousness, corruption and lawlessness!

It was hard to believe that such a vile and shameless group of people could exist in this world.

Someone switched off the sound system, and the room fell into a suffocating silence.

Li Gaocheng opened his eyes again, and this time he saw that the faces were now as distorted by pain as his.

Li Gaocheng thought he heard someone moaning and mumbling in a shaky voice: "...Mayor Li, Mayor Li, Mayor Li..."

His wife's scream sounded to him as though she had been stabbed with a knife.

Then he saw someone at the table spring like an enraged lion at the two men standing beside him; there was the sound of blows and a burst of furious, hysterical cursing.

This was followed by the sound of the two men who had dragged him there falling to their knees beside him, protesting their innocence and pleading convulsively for mercy...

Li Gaocheng struggled halfway to his feet and finally pushed himself upright.

Some of the others at the table rushed over in a panic to help him, but he pushed them angrily away. Two of them fell to the ground, either out of sheer terror or because Li Gaocheng had shoved them so hard. They just sat there, not knowing what to do next.

Li Gaocheng tried again to wipe the blood and dirt from his face, and stood there swaying but upright, at the limit of his strength.

He squinted at the dazed, silent, panic-stricken faces in front of him and slowly spat the blood from his mouth onto the table full of food and wine.

Gasping for breath, he wiped his hand across his face and mouth again.

He wanted to turn around and walk out of the room; his feelings of hatred were so strong that he couldn't bring himself to say anything to them, and really there was nothing to say. But when he did turn round, he saw two gorgeously dressed girls coming in carrying two large plates of fancy food. A long-suppressed anger, and a bloodlust that he thought had disappeared years ago, finally erupted from him like a volcano.

Unable to control himself any longer, he impulsively snatched a plate from one of the girls' trays and slammed it with a resounding crash onto the table that was already itself full of plates.

He hurled another plate, followed by another. Then he seized one of the trays and slammed that down too. It was followed by the second tray. As he threw them, he roared like a lion: "Go on, eat! Drink! Gorge yourselves! Go on!"

When he had exhausted all the plates and trays, he kept on cursing furiously: "What's this you're eating? It's the blood of the workers! It's the flesh of the workers! You swallow it today and spit it all out tomorrow! Take a good look and see who you think is going to let you get away with it! You've already got one foot in the grave, but you still think you're in paradise! You want to take everything with you into your tombs! Look at your workers! Look at what you've got on your plates! Then look at your consciences and see if you can still bear to swallow that stuff! You are eating the flesh of the workers! You are eating the blood of the workers! Just think what's going to happen to you bunch of useless..."

Li Gaocheng finally saw with absolute clarity that it was this group of people who were subverting and destroying reform, who were turning people's enthusiasm for reform into hatred of it!

Not only were they destroying and subverting reform, but they were destroying and subverting the country, the Party, and the people's future!

They were the mortal enemies, the murderers of the whole of society and the whole of humanity!

To let them get away with it would be a sin that resonated through history!

CHAPTER THIRTY

Li Gaocheng fell ill when he got home. Seriously ill. Dizziness, headache, high fever, nausea, vomiting, stomach pains, and many other complications caused by severe influenza. The pain caused by the sudden inflammation of his cervical vertebrae left him unable to move half his body, and the swelling of his face seemed to further aggravate the condition. He originally thought he could just stay in bed at home for a while, but he only lasted one night, and was taken to the hospital by ambulance early the next morning. His condition scared the nanny half to death. He was in a semi-coma at the time, raving and shouting nonsense. He seemed temporarily to have lost his reason.

Nothing like this had happened to him for decades. He had had no idea that he was going to be so ill that he would end up unconscious and in hospital. The sedatives he was given there kept him asleep for twenty-eight hours.

When he finally woke up, he had no idea why he was there.

He strove to recall his own situation, and how the events of that day had ended...

It seemed he had walked down those five flights of stairs by himself. Yes, that was right, he was staggering, but everybody was probably too scared to go and give him a hand. Behind him there were at least a couple of dozen people, all of whom were too disturbed and frightened not to follow him...

The scene was pitiful and laughable in equal measure.

Someone must have telephoned ahead because, before he even reached the main gates, a great convoy of cars came rushing over. He didn't stop or even spare them a glance. He just walked straight ahead.

The cars all came to a halt, turned around, one by one, and followed him.

No one dared speak to him and no one dared suggest he get into one of the cars.

His secretary, Wu Xingang, was somewhere else at the time, so Li's own car was not in the convoy.

He kept walking and walking for who knows how long until Wu arrived with the car and he slowly got into it.

According to the secretary, by this time the column of cars and people following Li was more than half a kilometre long.

Wu Xingang gave him a hand towel and he slowly wiped his face. Then he told the car to stop and he sat there for a long time, eyes closed, thinking.

He felt in great pain.

His head cleared but he had no idea where his route lay or what to do next. In the current climate, there was no doubt that any so-called branch factory like that one should be shut down without a second thought.

But was that something he could do on his own? Could he really just shut it down?

What he should do was hold meeting after meeting; convene the Standing Committee over and over again; keep asking for instructions and submitting reports; seek everybody's opinion from every angle; finally, a consensus could be reached, an official document disseminated, and its implementation supervised. But if there was any kind of blockage in the process, all his efforts would be in vain, and he would achieve nothing.

Even after all the studies, instructions and documentation were completed, no one could guarantee one hundred per cent that it would be implemented. There would always be people who would not take it seriously and he would never actually get it done.

Hadn't he been through all this before? Hadn't he had enough of banging his head against brick walls?

What was more, the opponents he was facing now were much stronger and more experienced than he was, and they might well have more people than him!

Would his people stick with him or go over to the other side?

Was he really sure of himself?

Forget about how prestigious his position was supposed to be, the truth was that his current situation was exactly like the one he had just been in. If everyone turned their back on him and deserted him, those people could do whatever they wanted to him.

He really didn't have any power at all, and it was all because he himself had deserted the circles he naturally belonged in.

It was a big circle, and once you were in it, you were in it for life; to leave it was to go looking for your own death. If he tried to topple it, it would be him who lost his footing.

He suddenly felt that all the power he usually had was a sham, and that all the things he could normally get done at the click of his fingers were also a sham. Sometimes there are things you don't want to do, or dislike doing, that can be done with ease and enthusiasm, but when there is something you really want to get done, or something that is in line with the will of heaven and the will of the people, you find that you are useless, completely useless!

Take this big bunch of people sitting on his tail right now; could he just clear them out of the way? Could he really do it?

Or what about that offer of aid and sympathy today; could he change the workers' minds in the face of their deep-seated rejection?

He was useless! Totally useless!

Finally, he came to a decision.

He told his secretary, Wu Xingang, immediately to notify the Municipal Bureau of Industry and Commerce, the Municipal Taxation Bureau, and the Municipal Economic and Trade Commission, and ask them to conduct surprise inspections of all these privately contracted branch factories and small companies clustered around Zhongyang Textiles, paying particular attention to the exploitation of workers, and their safety and security. Factories like the Chang Long Garment and Textile Factory without any health and safety certification should be closed immediately, otherwise any consequences arising therefrom would be the responsibility of the leaders of the inspection units...

The dozen or so trucks of relief goods were all to be handed over to the person in charge of the Zhongyang Textile Group's Veteran Cadre Activity Centre. Then the retired cadres and workers of the company would elect representatives, who would, after careful investigation, hand over the goods to the poor families of workers who really needed relief. The workers had to be persuaded in good faith that this all came from the government and had nothing to do with the present management of the company. None of this work was to be given to the company management; they could not be allowed to provide aid to the workers, as they had lost their trust and, with it, any right to…

The audit and verification working group organised by the city that had been assigned to the company were to be notified to start work immediately. They must conduct strict inspections, clearly distinguish right from wrong, be selfless and work boldly. If evidence of dishonesty was found, inside or outside the company, it was to be dealt with seriously, and without mercy…

After some consideration, he decided that he had said everything that needed to be said. It might all prove useless in the current circumstances, but he understood he still had to say it. If he didn't, how could he begin to talk about what might come next?

These things had to be said now so that they could then discuss the next steps.

When he had finished speaking, he told Wu Xingang to stay behind on his own with authority to act on all matters; this was something that he would absolutely not normally do, but there was no alternative at this stage. This was because he was considerably uncertain, at that moment in time, who he should trust and believe.

After that, he returned alone in the car to the city. He was already beginning to feel unwell. He quietly went straight home. That was when he fell properly ill and became very confused… the next thing he remembered was waking up in hospital.

It was around five o'clock in the morning when he came to; there was no one else on the ward and all seemed very quiet. It was midwinter, so the sun would not be up for a long time and the sky was pitch black.

Even so, Li Gaocheng was well aware that a new day had begun. In this city of several million, countless people were already up and about or in the process of getting up. They were getting ready to spend another hectic day toiling away for their family, for their parents, for their children, for food and clothing, for their career, for their country, and yes, for themselves and for the tens of millions of other ordinary people.

He suddenly remembered his own home, his children, his parents and, of course, he also remembered his wife.

He thought of his father, who had been a stonemason all his life, and his grandfather, who had been a farmer all his. He was the third son of the family and, not long after he was born, the most famous fortune teller in his hometown had been consulted to tell his fortune. The man had predicted that his would be a life of toil, a life of poverty, a life of ordinariness and of no achievements; but it would also be a tranquil life with no troubles. The man said that the child had fine and delicate eyebrows that were long and up-turned, that the skin could be seen through them, that they were well situated on his brow which overhung his eyes, that they were orderly, displayed the "five colours", and had a fine complexion. This indicated he would be friendly, honest and considerate, charitable in character, intelligent and studious, warm but dignified. Under an enlightened master he would be able to turn misfortune into good fortune and sorrow into joy, and to provide a light at the end of the tunnel, and live a life of purity and nobility. The red-coloured mole between his eyebrows meant that he would have a beautiful wife and a noble son; he would live a carefree life and have a government career...

Even when he was grown up and able to think for himself, he still remembered his grandfather saying: "How's a monkey like you ever going to have a government career?"

Later on, when he passed the examinations for technical school, the villagers began to sit up a bit and take notice. When he was about to leave the village, his father said to him, still rather doubtfully: "So, that fortune teller was right after all!"

For many years, even after his grandfather and father had passed away, he often thought of the fortune teller's words, and sometimes marvelled at their accuracy. He should have been destined to live a life of constant work, of mediocrity, of general incompetence and no special talent. He had never expected to find a patron who would help him on his rapid and continuous rise to the top, to the post of mayor that he currently held. Often, when he was washing his face, he would absent-mindedly finger that unobtrusive red-coloured mole between his eyebrows, which most people didn't even notice, and wonder if it really was responsible for him, a very ordinary-looking farmer's son, being able to marry such a beautiful, smart and capable wife, who was a government official to boot. What was more, she had given him a son and a daughter who were both studious and intelligent, who had never given their parents a moment's trouble, and who had both got into university.

There was no escaping it: the patron the fortune teller had talked about, who had helped him rise to the top, was the current deputy secretary of the Provincial Party Committee, Yan Zhen; and that beautiful and virtuous wife was his current partner, Wu Aizhen.

This was how he had seen things for many years now: the fortune teller had been astonishingly accurate in everything he had predicted!

But, just in the past few days, the scales had fallen from his eyes, and he had realised that it was all an illusion. He had been living a lie all this time and not only had they been deceiving him for years, he had been deceiving himself.

He might be mayor, but he was still just a no-account mediocrity. He had let his wife deceive him for years and he had let his superiors do the same. How could anyone think of him as an outstanding leader, a clear-eyed, steady, experienced leader who understood the nature of power and change? If he was unable to act independently and take charge of his own affairs, what was the use of him being mayor, or governor, or even higher? He was as much good as a glutton or a drunkard! As much use as if he was dead!

If Yan Zhen wasn't that noble patron the fortune teller had predicted, who was? If Wu Aizhen wasn't that beautiful and intelligent wife, did he have another one?

Truthfully, could he really leave his wife?

He suddenly remembered the way Wu Aizhen had shrieked in terror at that banquet the day before, and how he had seen their decades of love as husband and wife in that face that was convulsed with pain! It was the kind of insistent, irrational love that perfused every drop of blood...

He didn't understand why, at that moment, he felt such longing and nostalgia for his wife or where this access of sympathy and affection had come from. Was it the need to cherish something he knew he was about to lose?

Did he really think he was going to lose her? Or did he know that he was going to have to lose her? Perhaps he felt that some impassable obstacle had already come between them, that the distance between them was becoming greater and greater and that ground could never be recovered. Or, at the very least, that they could never be as close again as they had once been. Could they ever rediscover their original love for each other?

In truth, they had never quarrelled, never said things that went too far, were never even that demonstrative, so why did he suddenly feel that they could never be parted? Was it because they had been in such an emotionally intimate relationship for so many years and had a tacit understanding of the boundaries that could not be crossed, that if one of those boundaries was crossed, there could never be any going back and it would be over forever?

Was this the real reason for his sudden attack of uncontrollable emotion? Were they really about to lose forever the love between husband and wife that had seen them through so many decades?

Just the thought of it made Li Gaocheng shiver uncontrollably.

Two small objects in front of him suddenly caught his eye. In the growing daylight he saw, on the bedside table, a neat little notebook with an equally neat little carbon fibre pen. His heart gave a little lurch: these were his wife's things! She was so sophisticated and fashion-conscious about even the smallest things. He stared distractedly at the notebook and pen for a long time before, eventually, reaching out and gently picking them up. He stroked them softly for a moment, then snapped on the bedside light. There was no mistaking his wife's notebook and pen.

Opening the notebook at the first page, his wife's beautiful, neat handwriting sprang to his gaze:

Gaocheng's sickbed record, by his wife, Wu Aizhen.
   3 February 1996.

It was her all right, just as she had always been: so affectionate, so considerate, so meticulous, so attentive to detail...

It was her all right, unchanged and unchanging.

She was always like that when she was at home – nothing was too much trouble. Because of this, he had long ago started feeling a kind of persistent dependence on her and a conviction that he could never be parted from her.

He suddenly felt his heart turn over. This notebook meant that she had been at his side as he was lying there asleep.

She had come back to him. She had come back to be with him.

But when? Could it have been when he was ill? Or had she followed him home from Zhongyang Textiles? How long had it been? He leafed through the notebook, checking the timings, and discovered to his surprise that it had been two whole days already. His wife had been at his side for two whole days.

What had she written in this sickbed record of hers?

3 February: Only a fortnight to Spring Festival. I hadn't thought Gaocheng would be so sick and it's all my fault. I owe him so many apologies. I have been a bad wife to him, but I hope he can forgive me.

Our daughter Meimei has written to say that she's coming home around the 7th. Our son Mingming has written to say that he is coming home around the 10th. We will be able to spend a proper New Year together as a family. Now they're grown up we don't get to spend many days all together. Thinking about the future, when there will be only us two old ones left in the house, I really don't know how we will pass the days.

If Gaocheng gets a bit better soon, I'll have to get everything ready for the New Year. We can let bygones be bygones!

...

Gaocheng's visitors today:

Deputy Party Provincial Committee Secretary Yan Zhen.

Secretary Yan brought two boxes of American ginseng and four tubes of premium tonic. He said Gaocheng was worn out and in poor health and needed building up. He also reprimanded me for not looking after Gaocheng properly. He also said that if anything happened to Gaocheng, it would be my fault. He also admitted that Gaocheng's illness came from overwork, and that was his responsibility. As he left, Secretary Yan said that I should telephone him when Gaocheng is a bit better, and he would come and see him again. Secretary Yan also called in the hospital director and secretary, and he told them to send the best doctors to take care of Mayor Li's health as soon as possible, and not to let anything get in the way. Secretary Yan was very stern and serious with them. He told them not to be lax in anything, but to examine the mayor's body all over, using the best instruments, the best equipment and the best medicines. They were not to be afraid to spend money, as the mayor's health is worth every cent! He also said that nowadays, there are too few good mayors like Li Gaocheng.

...

Guo Zhongyao, CEO of the Zhongyang Textile Group.

When Manager Guo came, he brought a big bag of fruit. He said he was also bringing Mayor Li's favourite food. I thought it would be some delicacy, but it turned out to be two Hunan pickled, smoked and salted fish. He said that when Mayor Li worked overtime at the factory back in the day, this was his favourite food. A big bowl of rice topped with a piece of salted fish was better than anything else.

It was really good of him; even I didn't remember this, but he did quite clearly. When General Manager Guo came into the ward and saw how Gaocheng looked, he wept so much that I couldn't help but join in. He said that Mayor Li's health had never been that good and he always had a bout of serious illness at some stage every year. He also said that the company's downturn in recent years had brought many grievances and complaints down on Mayor Li's head. Other people's inadequacies had brought him a lot of heartache. This undoubtedly had something to do with the mayor's illness. He also said that he had heard about yesterday's incident, and that he is cooperating with the relevant departments to investigate and deal with the matter severely. Everybody and everything connected with it would be dealt with appropriately and no leniency would be shown. He said that Mayor Li was a good man, sharp-tongued but kind-hearted. Sometimes he might show no regard for your reputation and criticise you without real grounds, but his intentions towards you were always good. He also said that Mayor Li was a man who never accepted gifts and that he would certainly refuse all these things that he had brought once he woke up. He kept asking me to promise not to tell Mayor

Li that it was him who had brought them. He wept again when he left.

...

Chao Wanshan, deputy director of the Economic Policy and Theory Research Bureau of the Provincial Party Committee.

He brought two canisters of good tea, saying that he heard from his brother-in-law, Secretary Yan, that Mayor Li does not smoke or drink alcohol, and had no other particular likes but that he did regularly enjoy a cup of tea. He said that it was a genuine celebrated tea which had been a special gift from the son of a central government bigwig at a meeting in the south of the country this year. It was what is known as "pre-Qingming and pre-rain tea"; that is to say that it is the first growth buds picked before the rains and before the Qingming Festival from specially managed hill plantations and was very expensive. In the past, it had all been given to the emperor as tribute tea and even today it never went on public sale. He said that he had given two canisters to Secretary Yan, and Secretary Yan had asked him at the time if he had any more and explained that he wanted to give two canisters to Mayor Li. If there weren't any more, then he would give Mayor Li his own...

...

Chen Yongming, secretary of the Party Committee of the Zhongyang Textile Group.

He came with his wife. When Secretary Chen saw the state Gaocheng was in, his hands trembled in distress. He said that Mayor Li had been vexed by ne'er-do-wells who just wanted to make trouble and that some people today are psychologically unbalanced. Some people are saying that it is money that we should rely on, not the working class. But that is just nonsense, as when has this country not relied on the working class? What we rely on is the real working class that listens to the word of the Party, the word of the government, and the word of its leaders, not those scoundrels who appropriate the name of the working class but are actually making trouble in their own interests. Mayor Li is an old-style leader who believes in the workers and cares about them, but he is soft-hearted and these people have taken advantage of this to kick up a fuss. It is easy to lay things at the door of the working class, but is this truly what the working class is about? Whenever there is a slight difficulty, whenever their own interests are involved, they don't care about anything else, they won't give an inch but immediately start to make trouble and take to the streets! How can they call themselves working-class people when they only care about their own gains and losses and not the interests of the country? There are thousands of laid-off workers all over the country, in Beijing, in Shanghai, in Guangzhou, in Shanxi, but are they taking to the streets to cause trouble? No, they are just as quietly respectful and dedicated as ever. Mayor Li must have angered these people somehow; it never does to be too soft-hearted towards people like that...

...

Wu Mingde, deputy general manager of the Zhongyang Textile Group.

Feng Minjie, deputy general manager of Zhongyang Textile Group.

Also two middle-level company cadres.

These people all came together. They said they had originally thought of bringing something, but then they remembered Mayor Li's temper and didn't dare. But they hadn't realised how ill Mayor Li was, and if they had, they would indeed have brought something to help restore him. Mayor Li was a good man in every way except that he was a little too inflexible and hadn't changed at all over many years. Take this question of giving gifts, for example. It was no big deal these days. Of course, giving money or jewellery or gold and silver counted as offering bribes, but how could food or drink or a bit of fruit be considered a bribe? These days, even if you went on an ordinary visit, you couldn't go empty-handed, so what was the big deal bringing their old boss a little something? It was the same with what was going on now. In the past, state officials were allowed to light fires, but the common people weren't even allowed to light a lamp. Now, it's the other way around. The ordinary people can do what they like, but if people like us get up to anything, we get reported to the central authorities on the spot. The more you want to do something, the less chance you get. Think about the famous reformers, the famous entrepreneurs, and the pioneering factory managers. Where have they all gone now? Did things end well for any of them? In fact, even if you just stand still and don't do anything at all, someone will still come along and shop you to the authorities. Look at our Mayor Li! Everyone knows he is straight as a die, but that's just what happened to him! It's the same for all of us now. There aren't many of us cadres that the common people see any good in at all...

As they went, they tried to leave a few hundred yuan to buy some tonics for Mayor Li, and it was only with great difficulty that I was able to refuse to accept.

...

Wang Lijia, executive director of the Provincial Entrepreneurs Association, former deputy editor of *Contemporary Entrepreneurs*.

Wang Lijia was Gaocheng's only classmate in the city. Gaocheng probably hadn't seen him for many years, and it was a surprise that he came. He looked at Gaocheng's face for a long time, and then said: "Yes, that's him all right. There will be fewer and fewer cadres like him in the future. It is easy to change the country but hard to change your natural character. He was like this when we were at school, and now he has grown up he is still the same. It's the only way he knows, and he's always had the same temperament. Where are the other cadres like him now? They're all part of the market economy, and they think they have a lot of power. Just because this is called a state-owned enterprise, does that make it more manageable? Over recent years, even though I haven't got involved in politics, I have read a lot, and my horizons have been broadened. What is this thing called "the market"? It is the privatisation of the economy and the marginalisation of politics. Everything revolves around the market, and everything revolves around capital. Heaven destroys those who don't look out for themselves. Our ancestors have long known this principle – it is not a modern discovery. I can only say that, as long as there is a market economy, state-owned enterprises will go bankrupt one after the other and nothing can save them. Our current leaders must keep this thought at the front of their minds – state-owned enterprise will be done for sooner or later. We mustn't think that the world is going to end if a state-owned enterprise goes bankrupt or that it is all up for the working class as a whole if some workers don't get paid. State-owned enterprises are actually a big burden to the state, and the state is actually trying to get rid of that burden by any means it can. Just look at the countryside responsibility contracting system. To put it bluntly, isn't that just the state shifting the burden onto the farmers? But what is the result? The unprecedented prosperity of the rural economy and a dramatic improvement in the livelihood of the farmers. What state leader could have managed the same, do you think? Which state leader could claim the credit? The same is true of state-owned enterprises – if the state washes its hands of them, they will get on just fine..."

...

Wang Yiliang, former deputy governor of the Provincial People's Bank.

Zhang Dewu, former deputy general manager of the Provincial Automobile Passenger Transport Corporation.

The two of them came together, carrying a lot of stuff in a variety of bags of different sizes. Since what they had brought was all fruits and nutritional supplements, and they were visiting a patient in a hospital, it wasn't easy to refuse them. They are both out-and-out businessmen who just sat here sighing deeply and saying nothing. In the end, the only thing they said was to ask me specifically to tell Mayor Li when he woke up that Mayor Li could rest assured that they had kept their noses clean all their lives so far and they were certainly not going to ruin their prospects for what remained of them...

...

Our nephew, Wu Baozhu.

He came rushing madly in at dinnertime, and as soon as he was through the door, he wouldn't stop crying. He said he hadn't known his uncle was ill and he had only just heard that he had been hospitalised. He said that as soon as he heard, he couldn't stop crying. He said that after that time his uncle had reprimanded him, he hadn't dared show his face at his uncle's house. It wasn't that he didn't want to, he was just too scared. He said his uncle was the kind of man who inspired both respect and fear. He also said that his cousins were away at university, but that he should have come to the house more often anyway. He didn't have any other relatives here and relied entirely on his uncle and aunt...

He brought with him a large lunchbox which contained shredded squid and chicken soup – a particular favourite of

Gaocheng's. He had made a huge effort to behave in a properly filial manner...

As he read, Li Gaocheng found himself swept up in an indefinable surge of emotion.

Although it was just a little notebook, its effect was overwhelming on him as though he was enmeshed in a giant, tender net woven from his wife's great love for him. Its folds were irresistible, and, almost without knowing it, yet with his willing consent, he found himself unable to escape from its sweet, beguiling embrace.

But, in truth, there wasn't anything too clever about his wife's performance, was there? Hadn't she put the notebook there just so he could read it? Hadn't she written all those things with the deliberate intention that he should read them?

It was all so obvious, so explicit, so blatant!

But stepping back and looking at the big picture, weren't heaven and earth, the mountains and the rivers, all still there with everything just the same as before? The sky was blue, the sun was shining, he was still himself, friends were still friends, superiors were still superiors, leaders were still leaders, daughters were still daughters, sons were still sons, fathers were still fathers, mothers were still mothers! Yes, everything around him was still the same: he was still the same mayor, respected by tens of thousands; his home was still a home envied and coveted by tens of thousands; it was still a home blessed with riches and honour; and the land was still a land flowing with milk and honey...

How long had it taken for him to get here? Had it been easy for him to achieve all this, or had it been hard? It is easy to pour water out, but hard to gather it back in. Was it too late to turn back?

Everything depends on the route you take and the choices you make. That was the message he was being given: his fate was in his own hands. It was all so obvious, so explicit, so blatant! Surely he must see things clearly by now, and understand what was going on!

What was wrong with him? No, really, what the hell was wrong with him? He had just been put through the wringer, mentally and physically, and he was still about to throw himself blithely into their trap!

In the past, he might have believed all that stuff was true and that life really was like that. Everyone may have their own shortcomings and their own temperament, but they also have their own merits and lovable aspects. There had to be some mutual tolerance, some give and take with people, no matter how high-level a leader he was. If he couldn't be tolerant with these people, how could he act as leader to several million others?

But recently, and not just over the last few days, everything seemed to have changed beyond recognition and been revealed in its true colours. These people had kept him in the dark, as though he was some no-account commoner, and they had sold him like a commodity. What was more, he was still funding them.

If it wasn't a trap, what was it? Why else would all the people who had come to see him be taking the same line?

Li Gaocheng's heart lurched again. What was really going on? Were all these people undertaking some kind of self-re-evaluation? Had they all somehow come to doubt themselves?

Was his wife being selective in her memory of who had come to visit him and had only recorded these people and not all the others? Was this notebook the real reason she had come rushing to his bedside?

From missing his wife, Li Gaocheng's emotions gradually shifted towards suspicion and anxiety, eventually accompanied by an indefinable sense of dread. How terrible it would be if that was how things really stood with her...

What was his wife actually after? Was she trying to isolate him from people she did not want him to see? Was she actively preventing them from coming to visit him? Or was she operating some kind of unobtrusive surveillance operation so she could keep abreast of who was spending time with him?

Had she come because she was worried about something or even afraid of it? If so, what was it that was scaring her, scaring them?

Was it the workers? Or the workers' representatives? Or those malcontent retired veteran cadres at the factory?

Or was it the other municipal leaders? Perhaps it was, perhaps it was!

But, to tell the truth, from their point of view, they really didn't have anything to worry about. As long as his position as mayor didn't change, and his viewpoint remained the same, what did the other municipal leaders matter? If a tree's roots are solid, who cares if the branches are waving around in the wind?

Even supposing the Municipal Party secretary was beginning to get ideas, what was there to be worried about or afraid of there? As far as industry and economics went, it was the mayor who had the real power, not the Party secretary. It was tantamount to exceeding his authority for a Party secretary to start interfering in industrial affairs. Mayor and Party secretary are two mutually contradictory posts and, even if they perform their respective duties correctly, there are impassable hurdles between them and obstacles that cannot be surmounted; if someone who has no business there sticks their oar in, total chaos ensues. If they were unable ever to settle the strife between themselves, how could they look after the interests of others? Even this should be no cause for concern to those people.

So, who could it be that they were worried about? It could only be one person. It had to be him. The mayor.

It was true. The person they were most worried about and most afraid of could only be him. It was quite simple: because he was the person who understood them best, who knew all their details, he was the person who was the biggest threat to them.

The sole reason they were plotting so carefully and taking such pains to lay all these traps and ambushes for him was simply to neutralise him. If they neutralised him, they neutralised everything; if they had him in their grip, they had everything.

On the other hand, because he had authority over them, he could control them. What it came down to was that he was the only person who could put a stop to all the evil, violence and crime. He was the only one who could pull it all up by the roots to serve as an example to anyone else considering such actions.

He was still the mayor!

At this moment, there was no one who could dislodge him from his position and if he really put his mind to doing something, there was no one who could stop him.

That was why he was the person they were most worried about and afraid of!

Anything they laid out to tempt him, and anything he laid out for himself was all the same. In the end, it was down to him to choose.

His fate truly was in his own hands.

Grey dawn was spreading in the east, and the sky was gradually growing brighter. He looked at his watch on the bedside table and saw it was already ten past seven. The door of the ward opened softly, and he automatically shut his eyes. Just as he couldn't face the cruel reality that confronted him, in this state and under these circumstances, he couldn't face his wife either.

CHAPTER THIRTY-ONE

"...Mayor Li, Mayor Li..." A voice called out cautiously several times before Li Gaocheng's eyes snapped open. In the dim lamplight, it was quite a while before he recognised who it was.

It was his children's wet nurse, Xia Yulian!

It was her all right, and with her was the same daughter-in-law he had met that day.

When Xia Yulian saw that Li's eyes were open, she stood staring in terrified surprise. For a long time, she had no idea what to say next. Li Gaocheng also stared at her in amazement. He had been expecting his wife, Wu Aizhen, but there was his children's old wet nurse, Xia Yulian, instead.

"Older Sister Xia! Is it really you? It's still so early..." Li Gaocheng said, momentarily at a loss.

"That's him, Ma! That's the man who came to our place looking for you..."

"Mayor Li..." Xia Yulian blinked as huge, round tears welled up in her eyes and began to roll down her cheeks. "It really was you! It really was you! I didn't recognise you..."

She swayed and almost fell. In her agitation, all the blood drained from her face, and she went deathly pale.

Her daughter-in-law had clearly anticipated this, as she caught hold of her and lowered her to sit on the sofa beside the bed. As she did so, she said to the startled Li Gaocheng: "It's nothing, it's nothing, just her old problem. She always gets dizzy when something unexpected happens. The doctor says it's because she's got low blood pressure. She'll be fine if she just lies down for a bit. Don't move, Mayor Li, you really mustn't move. It'll be all right in a moment, there's nothing to worry about."

And that is just what happened. After a couple of minutes, Xia Yulian already appeared to be back to normal. Wiping the tears from her eyes, she began to wail, remorsefully: "It's all my fault! It's all my fault! I didn't recognise you in the factory! When you said you were Li Gaocheng, I didn't imagine it was really you! Everyone says I'm a silly, muddle-headed old fool and that's what I am. None of this would have happened if I'd recognised you then! It's all my fault! It's all my fault! I've been fighting back my tears all this time! How could something like this have happened? When I thought about it, I must have had some kind of brain fog back then. How else could I not have recognised Mayor Li…"

As she tried to settle the old woman down, Xia Yulian's daughter-in-law said to Li Gaocheng: "She's been desperate to come and see you for the last few days, Mayor Li. She's been blaming herself for what happened and she's really, really sorry. She says she'd been squatting down for a long time that day when you pulled her out of the workshop, and she probably stood up too quickly. Her head was spinning, and she had no idea why she was being dragged out. She thought she must have been doing something wrong and they wanted to stop her or were taking her out to give her a talking to. The foremen in that workshop are really fierce, and because you can't hear what anybody's saying in there, if you're doing something wrong, they haul you out and curse you out. Sometimes they'll give you a bit of a beating too. The workers all say the only thing they're afraid of is being hauled out of the workshop like that when they're working. So when she got pulled out that day, Mother-in-Law went all dizzy and almost passed out. It never crossed her mind that it was Mayor Li standing in front of her. When she got home, she wouldn't eat or drink and just cried and wailed all day and night and didn't get a wink of sleep. We only heard yesterday that you'd fallen ill and been taken to hospital. We went round all the different hospitals looking for you. Luckily, you'd left your card at our house that day and we found out which ward you're in from your secretary, Wu Xingang.

We met Director Wu at the main gates of the hospital, and she said that you were really ill and weren't seeing anyone. Mother-in-law got even more agitated when she heard that and couldn't sit still. She kicked up a fuss all evening and didn't seem at all well. As soon as she shut her eyes, she started babbling and kept saying over and over again that she wanted to apologise to Mayor Li and that it was all her fault. She couldn't go back to sleep after about four o'clock this morning and nothing would do except we came to see you, Mayor Li. She said she just wanted to see you, and if she only caught a glimpse of you, she'd be able to relax. There was a nurse yesterday who saw mother-in-law waiting here to see you, not eating or drinking, and she whispered to us that if we wanted to see Mayor Li, it was best to come early, around six or seven – there probably wouldn't be anyone standing guard over you then, and we might have a chance of seeing you. We really didn't expect to get to see you and that you'd be awake. All mother-in-law was hoping for was to catch a glimpse of you, so when she saw you were awake, she couldn't even get a word out..."

"Who do you mean when you say you met Director Wu at the main gates?" Li Gaocheng didn't want to ask, but he couldn't help himself.

"Who do I mean?" the daughter-in-law asked in astonishment. "They told us it was your wife, Director Wu Aizhen!"

"And she stopped you coming in?" Li Gaocheng asked, not wanting to believe it.

"She said... she said you were so ill there was no point... she also said the hospital had rules about casual visitors and not letting people in any old how," the daughter-in-law said hesitantly. "It wasn't going to be easy for us to get in then anyway, there were so many workers and cadres from the company coming to see you. There must have been several hundred of them, and if we'd been let in too, all those people waiting outside would have been bound to have had something to say about it. There are so many people who want to come and see you, Mayor Li. I've heard that there've been a couple of thousand, counting from the first day. And those are just the official representatives. If everyone from the company came who wanted to, the hospital would probably burst at the seams..."

"Eh?" Li Gaocheng was really startled this time. Had several thousand workers and cadres really come to the hospital to see him? And all chosen representatives too! But his wife hadn't written a single word about them in that pretty little notebook of hers! She had even stopped someone like their children's old wet nurse coming to see him! And just look at who it was she had let in! Li Gaocheng became so angry at this point that his eyes blazed and his hands shook. Still reluctant to believe it all, he asked: "So, what happened? Didn't they allow any of the company cadres and workers to come in?"

"Director Wu said... she said the mayor was so ill, there was no point in going in. Director Wu also said she appreciated everybody's kindness and would tell the mayor all about it when he woke up..."

Her daughter-in-law was still talking when Xia Yulian interrupted her: "Aiya! It certainly wasn't Director Wu who was going to keep them out. She wanted to let them all in, but it was the workers and cadres themselves who didn't want to go in. They said they were afraid it might affect Mayor Li's recovery..." Xia Yulian had recovered her strength by now and she sat up straight on the sofa. "The doctors wouldn't let them in anyway. This is a hospital, isn't it? How could they let so many people in all at once, no matter who they were?"

At this point, Xia Yulian couldn't hold back her tears any longer, and as she wiped them away, she kept asking if Mayor Li was feeling a bit better or not. It was quite a while before she finally got round to talking about what was going on at the factory.

"Are you looking to shut down that factory, Mayor Li? He's already handed those two fellows over to the Public Security and fired them from the factory. He says the factory has only just been built and there are a few places where it doesn't meet government regulations but he's working as fast as he can to tighten things up and it'll all soon be set right... He told me to tell you all about it when I saw you, and to say that it hadn't been easy to set up that factory..."

"Which manager told you that?" Li Gaocheng asked angrily.

"It was... it was the manager of that factory you went to see..." Xia Yulian replied, haltingly.

"What's his name? Where's he from?"

"He's called... he's called something or other... oh, what is it... I don't know what's wrong with my memory... I can't remember..." Xia Yulian had turned very pale.

"Ai!" Li Gaocheng was very distressed to see Xia Yulian like this, but, after a moment's thought, he decided he had no option but to pursue the matter. "Why didn't he come himself instead of sending an elderly person like you. How can you speak for him if you don't even know his name? Doesn't he even have the least respect for you workers?"

"Mayor Li..." Xia Yulian seemed to be about to burst out sobbing. "I didn't have any choice. He told me to go and talk to you and I couldn't say no... I've been working there for almost three months, and they haven't paid me a cent in salary! They told me if I didn't talk Mayor Li round and Mayor Li really did close down the factory, I'd never see my money. But if you didn't touch the factory, I wouldn't have to go into work this month and they would pay me next month's salary as well..."

Li Gaocheng's anger surged. He would never have thought such a cruel and unscrupulous thing possible! Turning the screws on a retired old woman in ill health like that and shamelessly getting her to come and intercede on their behalf! What he found even more intolerable was the fact that his wife had not let their own children's old wet nurse come in to see him. And yet that same bullied, tormented old woman was still trying to defend them all and begging his indulgence for them!

Where was their conscience? Where was their humanity?

Long after Xia Yulian and her daughter-in-law had left, Li Gaocheng remained sunk in a world of pain.

Li Gaocheng had been expecting his wife to come in to see him soon, but it was after eight o'clock and she was still nowhere to be seen. The nurse came, the doctor came, his secretary came, the guards came, all of them came, but not his wife.

When the mayor woke up again, he was in good spirits, his body temperature was normal, he had no headache, no dizziness and no nausea, and the pain in his lower back caused by the osteophytes in his cervical vertebrae was much reduced. He was able to sit up and even walk around a bit and everyone heaved a sigh of relief.

One of the nurses on duty said to Li Gaocheng that Director Wu had been exhausted over the past few days and had barely had a wink of sleep for two days and nights. The nurse went on: "Director Wu is really nice. She doesn't put on airs, speaks so kindly, and is so considerate of other people. I've worked here for a long time and I've met lots of leaders' wives. None of them have been as nice as Director Wu."

Li Gaocheng didn't say anything. The nurse was probably right; his wife would indeed be very good in these circumstances. Over the years, they must have been in hundreds of similar situations together, and every time his wife had charmed almost everyone. Even he had been bewitched by her for so many years, so it wasn't surprising she had had this effect on the nurses. When Li Gaocheng asked where Director Wu had gone, the nurse said, with a confidential grin, that they had thought Director Wu was looking too tired over the last few days and, now the mayor's condition was better, they could slip her some sedatives. Director Wu had fallen asleep in one of the other wards.

For some reason, Li Gaocheng felt greatly relieved when he heard this. He had suddenly realised that it was going to be no easy thing to honestly confront his wife after they had spent so many years relying on each other. He remembered what Municipal Party Secretary Yang Cheng had said to him: "It's not that you're afraid of her, it's that you love her too much."

It was only at that moment that he felt the true weight of those words.

After he had had some breakfast and another infusion of medication, he made all the arrangements he needed to and then dismissed everybody except his secretary, Wu Xingang. Normally, Li gave his secretaries very little power and imposed a lot of constraints on them, so all the people who had held that post agreed that it was the most difficult job with the worst prospects. Normally speaking, the opposite was true and the future career opportunities for secretaries of municipal leaders like Li Gaocheng were excellent, but no secretary who worked for Li was ever further assigned to any important or influential post. This was certainly not because Li deliberately held them back, but because he never found a secretary capable of shouldering serious responsibility. It is fair to say, though, that of all the secretaries he had during his long career as mayor, Wu Xingang was the one he most respected.

First and foremost, he kept his lips tightly sealed, and had resolutely guarded himself against leaking any number of extremely confidential affairs. Secondly, he was a very meticulous person and kept very careful track of everything that Li Gaocheng said, of any promise he made however casually, and would remind Li of them so that he was never caught unawares, no matter how many years later, when even Li himself had forgotten. Li Gaocheng found this reliability very reassuring. Thirdly, Wu Xingang was a man of good character; he was not only well-educated but also very thoughtful and had particularly fine personal qualities. He had never exceeded his authority in all the time Li Gaocheng had been mayor or made any personal requests of him. These were no small things in today's materialistic world. Sometimes, when Li encountered problems or difficulties, he would talk them over informally with Wu Xingang and listen to his take on them. He was always satisfied with, and sometimes surprised by, what his secretary had to say, which was often refreshingly novel. In terms of length of service, he should already have been given a posting to allow him to gain some administrative experience at grassroots level. It was the practice of many current leaders to change secretaries as though through a revolving door, arranging a posting for the old one as the new one arrived. Since these secretaries were always solidly loyal to their former bosses, no one stood in the way of their appointment to higher office and it was just seen as the natural order of things. Besides, everyone was doing it and no one objected; it must be a good thing, so why not just do it? Although Li Gaocheng abhorred this practice of secretaries openly participating in politics or doing so under cover, that did not mean that a secretary could do anything, but only that he or she should be employed on the basis of merit, and that there should be no such generalisation. There were three reasons he had not arranged a posting for Wu Xingang: firstly, he had been too busy; secondly, he had not been able to find a suitable replacement; and thirdly, but most importantly, he was reluctant to do so.

Choosing a good cadre is not an easy task, and finding a good secretary is just as difficult.

With just the two of them in the ward, everything seemed very peaceful for the time being.

"I hope you are feeling a lot better now, Mayor Li!" Wun Xingang said with a polite smile.

"I expect you thought I cut a pretty pathetic figure that day, didn't you?" Li Gaocheng shot back unexpectedly, his gaze unwaveringly on his secretary.

"No, no, not at all!" Wu Xingang shook his head.

"So, tell me the truth. What did you feel?"

"...I thought I had never seen you like that before, Mayor Li."

"Like what?"

"Mayor Li, I don't think you yourself know what you looked like..." Wu Xingang seemed for a moment to have been transported back in time. "Truthfully, Mayor Li, I have been working for you for a long time now, and I've never seen you like that before: so individual, so imposing, so majestic and full of righteous anger. Someone who was there told me that your anger was like a divine thunderbolt and enough to scare anyone to death. There were so many people following you, and so many cars, and they were all scared rigid, terrified out of their wits. It was an extraordinary sight, Mayor Li, totally extraordinary..."

"Enough!" Li Gaocheng interrupted him angrily. "You certainly learned how to bullshit at a young age! So just cut the crap! I still don't know what I was like then – what kind of a spectacle I made of myself! I'm getting nowhere with anyone..."

"I'm telling you the truth, Mayor Li. It was just like I described!" Wu Xingang insisted, uncharacteristically. "It's not just what I think – lots of people who were there think the same. Afterwards, someone told me that some peasant of a temporary foreman hit you and then dragged you in front of the factory managers. But once you were there, Mr Mayor, you scared those managers out of their wits, and they all fell to their knees in front of you. Everyone is saying you wouldn't believe it if you read it in a novel. They're saying there's not another mayor like you, going among the people incognito and making a secret inspection of a black economy factory, then being caught by the foreman. Everyone says those two fellows must have been blind and it serves them right that the factory's run out of luck and they've bit themselves in the arse. They really met their match..."

"Is that really what people are saying?" Li Gaocheng asked, a little disbelievingly, as he had never considered this possibility.

"It's all true, it really is. I wouldn't have believed it myself if they hadn't told me. Like I say, no one's heard anything like it, even in a novel, and then they wouldn't have believed it possible. But I believed it at once. I know these things happen everywhere, no matter how important the leader is. If there is no one to protect him, there's nothing he can do if he runs up against ruffians like that. I went to the cinema with my wife the other day, and she had her purse snatched, right out in the open. I got up and gave the fellow a shove and then got beaten up by a bunch of his mates. I've still got the scars on my head."

When Wu Xingang had finished this tale, the two men were plunged into thought. After a while, Li Gaocheng asked: "What else are people saying?"

"Some of the other municipal leaders are saying that there must be some other reason you went to that factory, Mr Mayor. They think there must be more to it all, otherwise those men would never have dared to seize you and beat you up. They're saying it's a good thing that it was you who went there, not some other, lesser official, because you'll actually be able to do something about it. Now they're all watching to see what you do next. If you don't kick up a fuss, then they reckon there's no one else who'll ever get to grips with the issue of Zhongyang Textiles. There are even some people spreading malicious gossip saying that what happened to Mayor Li there was a case of the water flooding the Dragon King's temple, that neither side recognised they were going up against their own family. Just you wait, they're saying, nothing will ever come of it. The ordinary people have got lots of different opinions, but mostly they think it's going to be fun to watch how it plays out. The workers at Zhongyang Textiles are saying that they know Mayor Li is a good man, but this time things are different." Wu Xingang broke off at this point.

"What do they mean by that?"

"They are saying that good people don't get angry easily, but when they do, they get really angry, and this time Mayor Li means business."

The two men lapsed into thought again.

As Li Gaocheng saw it, the situation was that he was surrounded on all sides, being attacked from both within and without, with no way forward and no reinforcements coming. The question was what precisely should he do now and where should he do it.

"What about you? What do you think?" he asked Wu Xingang at last.

"Mayor Li, the fact is you knew very well that as soon as the problems at Zhongyang Textiles came out, you would have the eyes of the whole city on you. You are not only the mayor, but also the former manager of the company. The company management team were all promoted by you, the Zhongyang Textile Group's headquarters are located in the Dongcheng District, and the head of the District Anti-Corruption Bureau is your wife. What is more, the company really is in trouble, but even if it wasn't, ordinary people would still think there was something fishy going on."

Wu Xingang stopped and thought for a moment, before continuing: "I've been with you for a long time now, Mayor Li, and I know what kind of person you are. I know that you are determined to resolve the problems at Zhongyang Textiles, but the question now is not how determined you are, but whether you can find the best solution which resolves the problems but, at the same time, doesn't harm you yourself.

"You are a practical man, but politically very naive. You concentrate on actions, that is what you are good at, but you don't pay attention to people, as that is not your strength. But if you want to investigate and deal with a company as big as Zhongyang Textiles, it is very far from enough to concentrate only on actions. Some people say that in today's China, everyone has to be a strategist, no matter whether they are a leader or an ordinary citizen. It is particularly true for cadres – if they don't have the brains to strategise, how can they ever progress up the ladder? It's scary enough just thinking about it! None of today's leadership cadres are actually achieving anything, because they're all too busy scheming. It really can't go on, but if you don't do it too, what can you do? Look at this business with Zhongyang Textiles, Mayor Li. Have you ever considered that the problem there lies only with a few people? Aren't all the current managers there like the crafty hare with three burrows? Don't they all have several powerful backers? Haven't some of them said that they know there is a problem, but no one is looking into it, or that they know there is a problem, but they can't get to the bottom of it?

As for you, even if you do find out what the problem is, what can you do about it? Last year, the Provincial Discipline Inspection Commission investigated and dealt with corruption in a county-level auto parts factory, and as a result, more than forty leading cadres from the county, prefecture and province were singled out and the whole thing involved more than two million yuan. What was the result? The problem was discovered all right, but was it dealt with? The main culprit was sentenced to death, but the ordinary people said he was killed to keep the rest of it from coming out. And what happened in the end?

"Nothing serious came of it, except that the people investigated were either transferred or dismissed. The ordinary people had their own ideas about what was going on but didn't know the full facts. In the end, no one had a good word to say about either the investigators or the investigated. If the thing ended badly for the rotten apples, that was just as it should be, and if some of the good guys got caught up in it too, that was just the way things went. I don't have any worries about you, Mayor Li. As far as I'm concerned, you don't have any financial problems or problems with your personal style or your politics – I'm quite clear about that. You don't have any problems and you are a genuinely good cadre. What I am most worried about is that you will get to the bottom of what's wrong with Zhongyang Textiles, but you get yourself dragged into it too. Think about it, Mayor Li! When you look back, how many people who have been really serious about punishing corruption and actively correcting dishonest practice have been promoted and continued usefully in office? Fighting corruption has a price, sometimes a price you keep paying for the rest of your life. Why? Because those of today's leaders who really are corrupt have studied all this closely, and they have figured it all out and got it off pat. Even if you ferret out the problem, you'll never get to those at the top. They're all making a song and dance about fighting corruption while their wives, children, cousins, aunts, uncles, nieces and nephews are all ruthlessly engaged in every kind of corrupt practice. And if you don't get to the ones at the top, when the fuss dies down, they'll come looking for you to settle accounts, and how do you think that will end for you?

"Don't the ordinary people have a saying about this, that these days it is the rogues and slippery customers who get promoted and the honest hard workers who suffer disaster? If the leaders can keep their own superiors happy all the time, that's all that matters. They are sitting pretty, and even if there are a lot of problems, as long as they make the right strategic decisions, their future is assured. The basic principles us secretaries use when we are preparing material for our bosses are exactly the same as the leadership cadres rely on. This is how you need to talk to your superiors, how you need to jolly them along to keep them happy and not be concerned about you. If you had a problem yesterday, investigate it today and follow it up tomorrow. Even if there are problems every day, it's not a problem for you because your superiors don't have any worries about you. And in the end, aren't you just the mayor's secretary, not a leader of the Public Procuratorate, or a cadre of the Discipline Inspection Commission or the Anti-Corruption Bureau? Don't you have other things to be getting on with? Besides, if you uncover too many problems, isn't that just blackening the Party's name? Won't it affect relations between the Party and the people, between the cadres and the people? Moreover, there are always going to be people who say, do you expect us to believe you are the only honest and upright official and everyone else is corrupt? If you find out one corrupt element, you risk offending a whole host of leaders. And the ordinary people are likely as not to say that it is a major offender deliberately exposing a lesser one to shift suspicion away from himself, or that you've captured the fly, but let the tiger get away..."

"So, you are saying that I should turn a blind eye, speak duplicitously and always be looking to enhance my reputation? That as long as I can keep climbing the ladder, it doesn't matter what happens to the ordinary people?" Li Gaocheng wasn't entirely sure whether he was interrogating Wu Xingang or himself.

"That's not what I meant at all. You told me to speak honestly so I just laid out in front of you all the different things that are being said across society. You are the mayor, and the power is in your hands. The power to choose is yours too. I've told you the truth, and that's all I've done. But I am also quite sure that you are only asking me to make sure you understand everything, and that you already know what you must do," Wu Xingang said, as though he was analysing a logic problem.

"You're wrong, Xiao Wu! I really don't have any ideas at the moment, and I don't know what I ought to do." Li Gaocheng looked very serious, as though he was debating with himself. "The ordinary people are looking to me, but I still don't know what I should do."

"It's not that you don't know what to do, Mayor Li, you are just too soft-hearted."

"What?" Li Gaocheng stared at Wu Xingang uncomprehendingly.

"You want to resolve the problem but, at the same time, you don't want anyone to be harmed. You are too conscientious, Mayor Li. You are distressed by what you hear from the workers, but you are equally swayed by what the cadres are telling you."

"Is that how you see things?" Li Gaocheng's heart lurched.

"No, it's how the workers see things."

"What about you then? How do you see it?"

"I think..." Wu Xingang began, haltingly.

"What do you think?" Li Gaocheng asked resolutely.

"I think you have to decide whether this is a major investigation or a minor one, whether you should really try to get to the bottom of things or just have a cursory look."

"Eh?" Li Gaocheng's heart lurched again. "So what kind of investigation do you think it should be?"

"Do you want me to tell you the truth, Mayor Li, or do you want me to find you a way out?"

"Tell me the truth."

"As far as you're concerned, Mayor Li, there is only one way to go – a major investigation to get to the bottom of things," Wu Xingang said, his eyes shining. "In the eyes of the people, Mayor Li, you are that rare thing, an honest and upright official. In this world, everyone has their own way of living. You have chosen to dedicate your whole life to the people and to the nation. I won't try and deceive you, Mayor Li. I have read your file. You submitted thirty-six applications to join the Party. You made it very clear, in every one, that you wanted to join the Party wholeheartedly to serve the nation and the people. Your applications were very different from other people's because they didn't have so much grand language and fancy phrases. You've been true to what you said over the decades and the people recognise that and hold you in esteem. Mayor Li, you probably don't know how many workers and cadres have come to the hospital to see you over the last few days. More than anyone could possibly count! There've been several hundred representatives sent by Zhongyang Textiles alone, along with several thousand workers who came along with them. It's no easy feat for a leadership cadre to gain that kind of status. We only have a few decades in this world, and it is very difficult in that time to achieve anything praiseworthy, anything that the people will celebrate. I think the reason you are in so much pain now is simply that you don't want to stain the purity of your life. But how high do you have to climb as an official for it to be worthwhile? It's the people's approval that counts. If you don't get popular acclaim as an official, you might as well not be one. If you commit yourself to the fight against corruption, the people will never forget you, and the nation will always be grateful to you. To gain that kind of status is enough for any leadership cadre, whether they are doing it for the people or for themselves. My dad was just an ordinary worker. He died of cancer four years ago. Before he died, he said to me, 'Son, your dad has had six sons, and you are the only one who shows promise. Work hard and don't embarrass your old dad. If you do become a leader sometime in the future, just remember this one thing – as a local official you must work for the good of the local people, as a local official you must keep that locality safe.' I never showed any promise and was never even a minor official, but I still recognised those two principles. If you do become an official yourself, follow those principles and your father will bless you and watch over you from the other world..."

There were two big tears rolling down Wu Xingang's cheeks, and Li Gaocheng could not help but be deeply moved. He had never imagined Wu Xingang saw him like that, and he certainly hadn't expected him to talk like that.

CHAPTER THIRTY-TWO

It was already past eleven o'clock that morning when Wu Aizhen slipped quietly into the ward. Even though she had only just woken up, her hair was in a loose bun and her clothes were slightly dishevelled, she was still as radiant and graceful as ever. She still seemed as relaxed and easy-going, as intimate and welcoming as she always was, as if nothing had ever happened between them.

Li Gaocheng dazedly watched his wife's every move, not knowing what to say for the moment.

His wife smiled at him and sat down beside him, half leaning down, and said softly, with a kind of regret: "I've been asleep, and the nurse has only just told me that you woke up very early this morning. How are you feeling now? A little better? You have been so ill. People have been scared half to death for you..."

She stroked his head with one hand and adjusted the speed of his infusion with the other.

He drew in his wife's familiar, intoxicating scent. Her hands were still as gentle and soft as ever, and her voice was still as sweet and pleasant. He felt that he hadn't been this close to his wife for a long time; it was as if they had just been reunited after being apart for many years.

He seemed incapable of responding to this kind of behaviour from his wife. He felt as though he was at her mercy, and everything was being done according to her instructions and arrangements.

The nurse and Wu Xingang both tactfully left the room, and all was quiet for a while.

"Are you hungry? Do you want something to eat?" his wife asked solicitously. "I'll get them to make you something if you do. OK?"

"...no need," Li Gaocheng said, having finally found his voice.

"So many people have come to see you over the last two days. It's a good thing you've been asleep, or you would have been manhandled half to death by them all. They weren't the kind of people you could have turned away either, no way. Sometimes I think we were better off in the old days when we were just ordinary cadres. We just got on with our jobs and that kept us busy. Once we were off the clock, the rest of the time was our own. We could do what we liked and forget about our duties. Nowadays, everything looks very fine and grand from the outside, but, in fact, we can't call any time our own anymore... I don't know how it has seemed to you, Gaocheng, but for me, these last few days have felt like twenty years. It's all been almost too much for me, almost too much. I really can't live without you, Gaocheng, even for a moment. I'd rather lose everything, than ever lose our family, than ever lose you..."

His wife's tears rolled silently down her cheeks, one after the other. She kept wiping them away, but they just kept coming.

At that moment, Li Gaocheng found himself plunged into a maelstrom of excitement and emotion. His wife's eyes were telling him that everything she said was true, that her love for him was genuine.

"Gaocheng, I have sworn to myself that I will never make you angry again. No matter how hard life is, how tired or aggravated I am, I'll never ever make you angry again. In any event, I'm ten years younger than you, and if I make a mistake, I know you will always make allowances for me, Gaocheng, won't you? I remember you always used to tell me that in the years after we first met, after we'd just got married. You've forgotten, haven't you..."

The sighs in his wife's voice and the tears in her eyes only increased Li Gaocheng's distress.

"All right, all right, don't cry like that!" Without him realising it, his voice had begun to soften a lot and his tone became more gentle. He sounded as though he was trying to coax a little child. "A nurse or someone will think something has happened and come rushing in."

And, just like that little child, his wife stopped crying. She took out a handkerchief and wiped her face vigorously. She even managed a slightly coquettish glance at her husband, then smiled, back to being a child again.

...It's not that you don't know what to do, Mayor Li, you are just too soft-hearted... you want to resolve the problem but, at the same time, you don't want anyone to be harmed. You are too conscientious, Mayor Li. You are distressed by what you hear from the workers, but you are equally swayed by what the cadres are telling you...

Wu Xingang's words came back, unbidden, to ring in Li Gaocheng's ears. Because he was, after all, still the mayor, his secretary had couched his words in tactful, polite language, but the harsh severity of their real meaning was all too plain to him. He wanted a strong reputation as an enemy of corruption, but he didn't want to make waves or hurt anyone; he wanted to make the ordinary people happy, but keep everyone else sweet too, including those causing the problems; he wanted his horse to run fast, but he didn't want it to eat the grass; he wanted to live the life of a libertine but have a monument erected in his honour. Did he really think all the good things in the world were his by right?

Was he too clever for his own good, or too contemptible?

Thousands of workers were facing unemployment, tens of millions of yuan in capital were going down the plughole, countless workers who had spent a lifetime toiling for their country were now struggling in pain... and here he was, wracked by grief, tormenting himself over personal loss and gain, sitting in a city of sorrow with not a single idea what to do.

Was he just too insensitive or was he too incompetent?

If the people knew what he was really like at the moment, would they still be coming in their hundreds and thousands to visit him? Turning a blind eye to his conscience was just the same as cheating them and letting them down. Letting himself down was just the same as letting everybody down. The end result of letting himself down was to be held in contempt by everybody. It was as difficult to deceive the ordinary people as it was to keep them quiet and, in the end, they would always be able to tell whether something was gold or bronze or silver or pig iron. The punishment inflicted by history was actually the cruellest and most unforgiving.

Gradually, Li Gaocheng seemed to wake up, as if from a dream, and slowly returned to his senses.

"...Aizhen, is everything you just said to me true?" he asked gently.

"Do you think it's not?" his wife replied, looking at him meaningfully.

"You said that you would rather lose everything than lose our family..." Li Gaocheng continued, still in the same gentle tone. "Is that what you really think? Is that what you're really willing to do?"

"What do you think?"

"If that's the case, Aizhen, just listen to me this once – resign as the director of the Anti-Corruption Bureau, and move to another job. All right?" Li Gaocheng finished this sentence and stared straight into his wife's eyes with a look of deep expectation, eagerness, worry and apprehension.

His wife looked at him in blank astonishment, then her bright expression began to darken.

"Why?" she asked, as if she really didn't understand.

"Why?" With the change in her expression, Li Gaocheng finally realised again that his hopes were still just a fantasy, but he still said, although reluctantly: "For me, for you, for us, for the children, for our family."

"So I'm the one who pays the price, am I?" his wife asked back coldly.

"How can you say that?" The rapid change in his wife's feelings took him completely by surprise. "That's not what I meant at all. Not at all!"

"You made yourself quite clear, and you still say that's not what you mean?" There was cold contempt in his wife's eyes.

"Is being the head of the Anti-Corruption Bureau really that important to you?" Li Gaocheng asked disbelievingly. "Would giving it up be such a sacrifice?"

"So tell me, why are you doing this? Have I done such a bad job? Or have I done something wrong? Even without you as mayor, I've been in the prosecutor's office for decades, and I took my turn as a second-level deputy director. And now you want me to just give it up for no good reason? Do you think it was down to you that I got the job as bureau chief? Let's be fair about this, over the past few decades, when have you really thought about me? When have you ever tried to promote me? When have you not pressed me, and repeatedly urged me to keep a low profile? Put your hand on your heart and think about it, then tell me, in all good conscience, whether or not I have sacrificed enough for you. Don't you think you are going too far now by asking me to give up the job I love and am good at, all for your sake? Do you just think I'm such a rotten person, or have you discovered some problem with me? If you have found some problem with me, is it really down to you to deal with it? What authority do you have to talk to me like this? Something happens, and the first thing you think of is to get rid of your wife, is that it? Don't you feel a trace of guilt when you talk like this? Doesn't it make you even a little sad..."

His wife's violent reaction surprised and astonished Li Gaocheng. He waited until her anger and resentment had died down a little, and then tried a patient and gentle approach: "I have never doubted your ability, and I am not clear about what you are saying. You have sacrificed so much for this family, and I thank you from the bottom of my heart. Up to now, even though it seems that there are a lot of problems surrounding you, I still don't have any fundamental doubts about you, or want to repudiate you. To be honest, since the issue of Zhongyang Textiles first arose, you are the person who made me think most about it and who encouraged me not to let it drop. I never gave it much thought before and certainly never dared to think you might have changed. The only reason for that is that you are my wife. Sometimes, I even have the irrational thought that if my wife is indeed pure and spotless, and anyone were to make groundless remarks about her, I would never forgive them for the rest of this lifetime and into the next. I sincerely hope that my wife is clean and innocent, but the question is, who can give me a definite assurance? Can you? And even if you can, will that assurance be convincing? Will it be believable? Do you know how much talk there is about us as a couple going round society at the moment? How many people are there with their eye on us, especially at leadership level? At a time like this, I think we should be proactive, make a demonstration of some kind. And whether it involves you or me, that is going to involve some kind of sacrifice. In our case, that sacrifice is both valid and deserved. You are the anti-corruption chief in Dongcheng, and the Zhongyang Textile Group is located in Dongcheng, so under your jurisdiction. Now there are more and more workers and cadres petitioning and complaining about Zhongyang Textiles, and the workers there are getting more and more excitable. The situation is so serious it is fast becoming unmanageable. A huge state-owned enterprise has come to the brink of collapse. I am the mayor, you are the anti-corruption director, and Zhongyang Textiles is the place that brought us together. The management there were all promoted by me, and our family still has inextricable links with the company..."

"You still think it's all about you, don't you! You still think it's all about you!" His wife couldn't stop herself interrupting him. "I've told you before, what happened at Zhongyang Textiles has nothing to do with you. The first thing is, you shouldn't investigate it. The shock that is going to be caused by the reform of state-owned enterprise has only just begun, so why let it overwhelm you at the first stroke? There is one complaint about wages not being paid and you go charging in with an investigation. Do you really think that will be an end to it all? How can the management of state-owned businesses get on with their job if that's how you behave? How can they get on with reform? So what if a company stops production one day? Is that the end of the world? How could society stay stable? The second thing is, and I've told you this before too, even if there is a problem, it's nothing to do with you. When you were at Zhongyang Textiles, those management cadres were all good, honest people, weren't they? If things went wrong with them after you left, what has that got to do with you? Can you protect them all their lives? People change! Who can guarantee that someone he has employed and promoted will never go to the bad? These days, you're going to find problems with anyone you investigate. So, when you've investigated everyone else, and you are the only honest and upright official left standing, what will society do then? Are you really so spotless that if you're investigated, something won't come out? What is more, as soon as a problem appears, as soon as someone makes a complaint and starts to cause trouble, you're all over the place in a state of fear and panic, and, however big or small the problem, it seems your first thought is to get rid of your wife! I told you, I told you over and over, not to investigate, but you didn't listen. Just how high, exactly, do you rate your own abilities? So then, do you still think I shouldn't have said what I did? Once you start investigating, isn't it all going to come crashing down on your head? Nothing's even happened yet and the first thing you do is sacrifice your wife! Wait till a real problem comes out. Are you going to investigate it until you divorce your wife, scatter your children and watch your whole family destroyed? Unless you're standing weeping over their coffins, are you going to feel obliged to investigate and delve down into all your family before you turn away and give up? I really don't understand, even now, why you have to investigate Zhongyang Textiles, why you have to take charge, why you have to stick your nose in..."

As he listened, Li Gaocheng finally understood the one unalterable fact: his wife was still fighting her own corner. There was no chance of reconciling his side of the story and her side of the story, at least for the time being, and there was no sign of any coming together. There was nothing more to be said and neither side was going to talk round the other. They were like two cars running in parallel lanes and neither was going to try to pull the other one over. She was not going to give up her own views and opinions lightly. Any efforts they had made so far to act together had been futile and ineffective. It could probably truly be said of both of them that they would go to any lengths to defend their own position. Or, as his wife had put it, until they were weeping over the family's coffins.

In truth, he had made it very clear to his wife that as long as she was clean, she had nothing to fear from being investigated. If she was clean, what was anyone going to find? And, if there were no problems with her, why was it so important for her to hold onto the position of chief of the Anti-Corruption Bureau? Who was she really worried about – him or herself? Had she really not worked out that, if there was a problem with her, it was just the same as there being a problem with him? She was his wife, and if she had done something unconscionable, what would other people think of him? Who would believe that he had known nothing about it? Even a three-year-old wouldn't believe that he could be completely unaware of his wife's misdeeds. Things had gone so far, and they were so tightly bound together that it was now a matter of life and death and their fates were inextricably linked.

By now, Li Gaocheng had already lost track of everything his wife was gabbling away in his ear. Only when she had stopped talking did he ask, a little confused but still undeterred: "Aizhen, I just want to know one thing from you right now. There are only two of us in the ward, so tell me the truth. Do you have any financial problems? If so, how big are they?"

"What are you talking about?" she asked him, even more icily.

"Nothing, nothing. I just want to be mentally prepared."

Li Gaocheng looked expectantly at his wife again, but, in the end, all he saw was a kind of total exasperation.

Her icy expression gradually turned into a look of bone-deep contempt, and she said something that he never forgot for the rest of his life. "You are so selfish!" She was looking at him as if he was an ungrateful dwarf. "I really didn't think you were so selfish!"

Li Gaocheng felt his heart sink like a stone. He would never have believed his wife could say something like that to him. If it did nothing else, it sobered him up and brought him back to his senses. He had got his wife wrong for all these years. He had got her so wrong. What could he possibly say in the face of such heartbreak? Wretchedly, he said: "If that's what you think, there's nothing more for us to say."

"There's no point in trying to scare anyone by talking like that, Li Gaocheng." His wife's eyes were blazing. "Maybe you look on me as a child who's never grown up, but you're wrong. You must think I'm really stupid! If we were to swap places, I would never be talking the way you are. As soon as something happened, as soon as there was a problem that involved me, you began to make a song and dance about investigating it, about taking charge. There's nothing bold and resolute about that. There's nothing the least bit heroic. It's called being selfish. It's called being weak. It's called being cowardly. It's called being a slippery customer! Normally you are like a timid little rabbit who starts at a breath of wind in the grass and is in a panic for the rest of the day. If a single leaf falls from the sky, you're terrified it will crush you. People like you will never amount to anything! You won't take responsibility for anyone, and no one will take responsibility for you. As soon as something happens, if there is a problem with your wife, then the first thing that you think of is how you can save yourself and shake off any responsibility. And you still think you can call yourself a man? Are you even the least bit human? Well, rest assured, if I do have a problem, I'm certainly not going to involve you in it. I won't shamelessly drag you down. I haven't sunk that low yet..."

"Very well, if you really mean what you've said, I must ask you to leave." Li Gaocheng tried to keep his voice down as he said this, but it sounded very much as though he was shouting.

"As I said, I'm not going to hang around here with you, but there are a few things I still need to make clear to you. You always see everything in front of you from your own selfish viewpoint, so you think that I, the head of the Anti-Corruption Bureau, have always been a burden to you. You are wrong! It may not be long before you realise just how snobbish and hypocritical your thinking is. I have spent so much on this family, made so many sacrifices, and I have never been as selfish as you, let alone tried to keep my position like you, by being willing to discard my family and even my wife at the drop of a hat. Even now, I, the chief of the Anti-Corruption Bureau you so much want to distance yourself from, am still trying my best to protect you and help you keep your position as mayor! You are so naive that never occurred to you, did it? Why is it that people like you, with no political savvy, still think you can be heroic warriors against corruption? You're thinking is too simple and you are too easily pleased! The praying mantis may catch the cicada, but the yellow oriole is standing right behind it. Maybe you are already a prisoner before you've even taken the first step or lifted a finger..."

"Get out!" Li Gaocheng suppressed his emotions and tried to make himself sound calmer. "Get out! I want you to leave immediately!"

"I'm telling you, one day you will understand that there is only one person in this world who can save you, and that is me!"

With that, she shot Li Gaocheng a sidelong glance, then walked away, her face white and full of resentment.

CHAPTER THIRTY-THREE

IT WAS ONLY A LONG TIME AFTER HIS WIFE HAD LEFT that Li Gaocheng began to feel himself gradually being consumed by anger. And it was only when he noticed that his infusion bottle was trembling that he realised his hands were shaking. They were shaking so badly, in fact, that the whole hospital bed was rattling continuously too.

He felt his head swim again, he was short of breath, and he lapsed into a state of nervous exhaustion, verging on collapse, that went on for a long time.

What was going on with the world? Who was in the wrong – himself or his wife? Or could it be that there was no such thing as right and wrong between husband and wife on such an important matter of principle? It seemed clear that it was she who was in the wrong, who had broken the law and violated the rules, but why then was she feeling so impassioned and self-righteous? It felt like even the natural order of heaven was on her side. Instead of showing any remorse or guilt for what she had done, especially when she knew that her actions were completely illegal, she was putting all the blame on him, saying that she was not the cause of it all, that he was. It would be understandable for other people who didn't know the kind of man he was to say such things about him, but not for his wife to talk like that. Putting emotions to one side, how could she not tell the truth? Did she really have no understanding of who he was? Was he really selfish? Cowardly? A slippery customer? Did he really have no courage? Was he truly just a frightened rabbit?

Over the almost ten years he had been deputy mayor and then mayor, he had given his all for this provincial capital. No matter how difficult the circumstances, he had never backed down and certainly never been frightened off. Where this city and its several million citizens were concerned, had he ever been scared of anything?

During the years he was in charge of industry, he introduced foreign capital and deepened reforms by adopting a hard-hitting and clear-cut stance. He encouraged more than twenty hesitant and stagnating large and medium-sized state-owned enterprises to move forward nimbly and expand boldly, thus causing a violent shock in society and eliciting a strong response. Particularly during the late 1980s and early 1990s, all kinds of nonsense and tangled messes were coming out of the woodwork. People were hesitant about the policy of reform and opening up, and totally confused about the future progress of the country, especially after the fall of the Berlin Wall and the disintegration of the Soviet Union, and before and after the disintegration of Eastern Europe. At that time some extreme "leftist", dark elements and ferocious forces, clouded with fog and turbulent currents, seized hold of the banner of the Party, the country and the people, and were leading them backwards through counter-reform. All their rhetoric seemed to focus on one point: if we continue to reform like this, our regime will cease to exist, and the Communist Party's ruling position will cease to exist. The implication was that the policy of reform and opening up was the road to the destruction of the Party, and therefore must be terminated.

Li Gaocheng withstood all kinds of pressure and critical comments, but he also made a celebrated speech that attracted sustained acclaim from the ordinary people:

"As long as the people are prosperous, and as long as the people support reform, the Party's ruling position will continue. If the people continue to be poor and the country remains poor and weak, then such a Party might as well not exist! Even if it remains in power, it is already effectively disqualified from holding that power. If the choice is between the people and the status of the ruling party, a true ruling party would rather choose the former! Even if that party disappears and ceases to exist, the people will always remember it and it will live on forever in their hearts!"

Although there were many people who praised Li Gaocheng's courage and determination, there were undoubtedly also many who secretly broke out in a cold sweat because of him.

At that time, Li Gaocheng really was a bit of a go-getter, and while many people were hesitant to take the helm and even looked to retreat, not only did he not hold back at all, he actually took a big stride forward. So after Deng Xiaoping's Southern Tour in 1992, by the time some people were just coming to their senses and turning round to catch up, the reforms in Li Gaocheng's city had already left them trailing in their wake...

Even now, the direct influence and consequences of Li Gaocheng's vision were still obvious. The vast majority of state-owned large and medium-sized enterprises in the city were still operating normally and full of vitality. Compared with other provincial capitals, the rate of successful reform of state-owned enterprises in the city was much greater and their efficiency was unimpaired! When national leaders such as Jiang Zemin, Li Peng and Zhu Rongji visited the city, they all praised it and gave it full recognition. In particular, the central leaders' comments when visiting some of the large state-owned enterprises in the city were a source of delight and encouragement to the main provincial and municipal leaders. During a visit to one large enterprise, Zhu Rongji said jokingly to Li Gaocheng and other company officials: "You have done a great job with business, and everyone is really happy to see it. The bigger you grow, the more active you become. This conforms to the laws of the market as well as the laws of capital, but in our socialist country, you put us in something of a quandary..."

His advances back then were like the opening move in a game of chess, and currently the enterprises in the city, especially the state-owned ones, were maintaining steady operations with strong progressive momentum. Both in terms of the transformation of the mechanism and the reform of the system, enterprise had entered a positive cycle. Compared with other provincial capitals, the city's state-owned enterprises were in a much better state and were developing along stronger and stronger lines. Everyone, including the provincial and central leadership, was convinced by this.

When he thought of the pressure he had been under and the risks he had been taking, Li Gaocheng asked himself if anyone could say that he was selfish, cowardly and a slippery customer! Could anyone say that he had no courage and was just a timid rabbit?

In 1992, he was elected mayor and appointed deputy secretary of the Municipal Party Committee.

When he took up office, the first problem Li Gaocheng faced was that of housing. On the one hand, the average dwelling area of the general public was much lower than that of other provincial cities, and the proportion of households without homes, of dilapidated housing, and of inadequate housing was quite high; on the other hand, the phenomenon of cadres with outsized accommodation, with multiple houses and with privately constructed houses was becoming increasingly serious and there were some cadres who individually owned six or seven units. The most egregious example was one vice-departmental cadre who, in less than six years, had collected nine units because of his constant promotions and transfers, and he only had two children, one of whom had not yet graduated from university or started a family. Of the nine units, he used two himself, and, of the other seven, two were vacant and the rest were being let out at exorbitant rents. In the suburbs of the city, some county and township-level cadres had been building private houses at will, and the culture of corruption was intensifying. In five counties on the outskirts of the city, since 1983, nearly four thousand cadres had built houses that exceeded standards! Of these cadres, more than a hundred were above deputy county level, and more than seven hundred above section level! Cadres in some counties had built houses with an area of more than three hundred to four hundred square metres, and some had spent hundreds of thousands of yuan! The discrepancy between the standard of housing they built and their official income, and the sheer number of cadres who exceeded their housing allocation, was alarming in the extreme!

Before Li Gaocheng was elected mayor and was appointed as deputy secretary of the Municipal Party Committee, the Committee and Municipal Government had also investigated and dealt with the problem on several occasions, but they were very disorganised, only scratched the surface, and the whole initiative was something of an anti-climax. It was particularly apparent after each investigation and round of fines and punishment that it had actually resulted in the expansion of construction of private houses. However, this could not all be attributed to the ineffectiveness of previous city leadership. The fact that so many cadres participated in the construction of private houses and survived repeated inspections was enough to show that local influence and vested interests had deep roots. Before Li Gaocheng decided to go to war with this corruption, he made many unannounced inspections and had multiple discussions about countermeasures with many different parties. At the time, many people repeatedly advised him to act cautiously and not to come a cropper over this matter. He was continually being asked if he was aware of the power and depth of backing a cadre in a provincial capital city could have. Even if he did nothing, he was still going to have problems. If he stirred things up as soon as he took over, that was asking for real trouble. He might be mayor, but he was from an ordinary background and he had no patrons, no support and no influence. If he offended such a large and important faction immediately, how was he ever going to be able to act as an effective mayor subsequently?

But Li Gaocheng did not look back, let alone back down. With the support of the Provincial Party Committee leadership and the power of the press behind him, he made this campaign his breakthrough move as mayor and, with a great fanfare, declared all-out war against this evil faction. He first established an unambiguous system of leadership responsibility on the issue, so that, no matter whether in the city or the suburbs, at whichever level the problem was discovered, if it was not resolved, the leadership at that level bore all the responsibilities and took all the consequences. Those meriting punishment were punished, those meriting dismissal were dismissed, and anyone found guilty of covering things up were considered guilty of an additional crime. At the same time, Li Gaocheng also announced that all housing issues involving cadres at or above the county level would be handled by him personally, and he made a public statement to the effect that if he was found to have covered up anything on this issue, he would resign on the spot!

This move was widely publicised by the news media and sent a shockwave through the provincial capital. The media reported on the issue almost daily: those who voluntarily surrendered and gave an account of themselves were dealt with leniently, while those who refused to be investigated and refused to give themselves up were punished severely and without mercy. With the frequent public exposure and serious investigation of some department-level and county-level cadres, especially when some "nail households"[1] with powerful backers were removed one after another, this campaign to inspect the housing of cadres was cheered on and supported by the general public. At the same time, all cadres also expressed their support and concern. Needless to say, the final result was a historic victory for Li Gaocheng which saw his popularity reach its peak.

But Li Gaocheng secretly knew very well that he had been subjected to many overt pressures and covert attacks during those sleepless days and nights. Especially in those early days, he received threatening phone calls and slanderous letters almost every day, and some people even went far as to use human excrement to paste up insulting and slanderous couplets and small character posters on his front door. He was very well aware that anyone who could get past the twin guard posts of the main gates to the Municipal Party Committee compound and do that kind of thing, was no ordinary citizen.

He withstood all these different kinds of pressure and attack. Over a period of five months, more than four hundred people in the city had been investigated and punished, including more than thirty cadres at or above the county level; more than twenty private houses had been confiscated, more than fifty houses demolished, and more than six hundred houses were returned to farmland; more than forty people were severely dealt with, two of them were expelled from the Party, four were placed on probation, eleven were given serious warnings, and five were handed over to the judiciary; a total of nearly one million yuan in fines and compensation were levied. More than four thousand units of public housing were withdrawn from use, comprising a total area of more than two hundred thousand square meters, which was equivalent to the land needed for the construction of more than a hundred new dormitory buildings!

When those households without housing, or in dilapidated or inadequate housing, were moved into the vacant public housing, they were so excited that they burst into tears. When these astonishing pictures were brought into thousands of households by the

TV stations, they also brought tears of joy and excitement to the eyes of tens of thousands of ordinary people.

At that time, quite apart from the ordinary citizens, even among those people who detested him, there was no one who accused Li Gaocheng of being selfish or cowardly or a slippery customer. No one said that he had no courage or was as timid as a frightened rabbit.

In addition, during those years, he oversaw countless memorable major initiatives and construction projects including the construction of the second and third city ring roads, the widening of the downtown streets, the commencement of the construction of six city overpasses, and the construction of a fifty-kilometre cross-province expressway.

In this series of projects and constructions, he encountered countless unimaginable setbacks and much-unexpected resistance. During the construction of the second and third ring roads, hundreds of "nail households" refused to relocate and protested at the gates of the Provincial Party Committee, threatening to sue Li Gaocheng. The widening of the city's main street interfered with the interests of a collective enterprise, which formed a group of thousands of petitioners and staged a sit-in in front of City Hall, causing a traffic jam on the main road for nearly ten hours. When the construction of the city's overpass began, several "nail households" who refused to be relocated stopped his car in broad daylight, besieging and abusing him for several hours...

He had never flinched in the face of all this, let alone allowed himself to be intimidated; nor did he ever hold a grudge against any of these people. Deep down, he never really hated them, and neither, truly, did they hate him. Nothing ever came of any of this, because it became quite apparent that nothing he did was out of self-interest, let alone to gain any personal advantage from it. He was righteous and self-assured simply because he was genuinely upright, honest and open.

In all honesty, was there really anyone he was afraid of in his heart of hearts at that time? Did anyone ever say he was selfish, cowardly and a slippery customer? Who would have dared to say that he had no courage and was as timid as a frightened rabbit?

But now, here was his own wife calling him just those things!

He felt he could take any curses that his wife threw at him, but these words caused him real pain. It was not so much the content of the words that hurt him, but the fact that they made him feel like the complete opposite of his own perceived values and caused a total misalignment of his sense of right and wrong.

Was it now the case that it was brave and courageous, even manly, to protect wrongs and cover up crimes, while, on the other hand, it was selfish and cowardly to expose and attack such wrongs and crimes?

When you genuinely wanted to take responsibility for this country and for your family, you were wilfully misunderstood and treated as a clown or a slippery customer; but when what you were doing was intentionally or unintentionally destroying the country and destroying your family, you were applauded and even became some kind of hero and role model!

True responsibility was seen as irresponsible, while downright irresponsible behaviour was seen as some exalted, human responsibility...

What was especially distressing was that when you were a Party member and had to choose between the interests of the Party and your personal interests, the majority of people were more sympathetic to the latter...

If such people were allowed to flood the Party, what would happen to the essential conditions and foundations necessary for the Party to survive?

It was such a clear and simple truth, but how many people kept it at the forefront of their minds these days?

It was only when the nurse brought lunch that Li Gaocheng learned there were still so many workers at the gates of the hospital waiting to come in and see him. He asked the nurse to help him stand up, walked to the window and looked out. Tears welled up in his eyes. He had really not expected that there would be so many people who wanted to visit him. At a rough estimate, he thought there must be at least a thousand of them!

He understood that there was a deeper meaning to the number of workers waiting to see him. They were using their just and righteous concern to demonstrate to the government and society as a whole their moral stance and understanding of good and evil: we, the workers, support an honest mayor like Li Gaocheng. But there was also another layer of meaning which was that they hoped that he, the mayor, would stand with them, that he would stand firm and that he would not change his stance or his principles...

He shovelled in a few mouthfuls of food and then insisted on going down to see the workers. The doctors and nurses tried to dissuade him but failed. He told them that the workers had been waiting a very long time and he absolutely had to go down to them. Besides he didn't have any condition that stopped him from walking, and even if he did, he would ask to be carried down.

Since the workers had made a clear statement of their position, it was only right he should give them a clear-cut response.

Li Gaocheng realised how weak he was as he walked down; he felt tired and short of breath; his heart was hammering and he suffered bouts of dizziness and nausea. When the icy wind hit him outside, he found himself unsteady on his feet.

When he reached the hospital gates, he found there were a great many more people waiting there than he had thought. Perhaps because it was the end of the working day, there were easily three or four thousand of them.

As he entered the crowd, he discovered there were reporters from the provincial and municipal television stations conducting interviews. He hesitated and then tried to avoid them, but it was too late. "Mayor Li has come out! Mayor Li has come to see us..."

It wasn't clear who it was who shouted out, but a huge crowd immediately gathered round. One of the reporters lost no time in thrusting himself in front of him. Li Gaocheng was momentarily stunned; he hadn't expected this. With thousands of workers waiting in the biting wind to see him, the presence of provincial and municipal television reporters turning their cameras on him seemed as if it was pre-planned.

Faced with a situation he had not even considered, Li Gaocheng, who had always disapproved of leadership cadres making a spectacle of themselves, was at a loss what to do next. In normal circumstances, he would have asked someone to tell the reporters to go away but he had no way of doing that and it was simply too late to make any other move. For one thing, he didn't have his usual entourage around him; for another, he was too weak to do anything; and for a third, the situation confronting him left him no options.

Surrounded by so many familiar faces to which he could not put names, by so many sincere and unassuming workers, Li Gaocheng was swamped by a wave of emotion, and he soon forgot the existence of the TV cameras.

For the first time in all his years as a leader, he was actually unaware of the presence of the television cameras!

That night, when he saw his "performance" on the TV news, he was so moved that he couldn't help but shed a tear. What a touching and unforgettable scene it was!

There were so many hands reaching out to him in the swirling cold wind and a temperature of nearly minus twenty degrees. They were the hands of young people and the hands of old people; the hands of workers and the hands of intellectuals; the rough and calloused hands of maintenance workers who had worked in the factory for a lifetime; the thin, cracked hands of workers who had spent decades in the weaving workshops...

Every handshake made him feel so excited yet so serious, so close and so compassionate.

Words were completely superfluous; all the expressions, all the gestures, all the looks and all the emotions were so unpretentious, so sincere and so honest.

Once he was persuaded by the workers to go back inside, once the nurses had supported him away from the encircling crowd, once the television reporters had begun to interview the crowd, he was moved, time after time, by the simple and sincere words of the workers being interviewed, and, time after time, the tears came to his eyes.

Reporter: "I heard that during this time when Mayor Li has been sick, there have been workers from Zhongyang Textiles waiting out here every day, and that some of them didn't go home for two days and nights. Is that the case? I can see that you have brought a lot of gifts but I am sure Mayor Li would not and could not accept them all. Did you buy all these gifts yourselves?"

Worker: "They're all the real thing too! If we didn't buy them, who do you think would buy them for us? There are lots of fakes around these days, but there's nothing fake about any of this stuff.

Just have a walk around this crowd and look at the faces, look at the bodies covered in dirt, look at the eyes, and you'll know all right if they're the real thing or not. There may be some officials who muck the country and the people around, but when have we ordinary people ever mucked anyone around?"

Another worker: "We're not big shot cadres, and we have to be reimbursed by the work unit for any gifts we give our leaders."

Another worker: "If that was actually true, we wouldn't be here. We're more than happy to use our own money to buy things for a leader like Mayor Li."

Reporter: "Did you come here on your own or was there some kind of organisation? Did your work unit send you?"

Worker: "Do you really not know or are you pretending so you can muck us around? Would the unit send anyone for something like this? Would they be able to even if they wanted? Would they be able to arrange such real feeling? Do you think the people would come if it was for a leadership cadre they hated? Even if the leaders tried to organise it, the people wouldn't come. Even if they beat us, they wouldn't be able to beat us into coming!"

Another worker: "We've come to see our old factory manager. What do we need organising for? But if the leaders tried to organise us, we wouldn't come for sure!"

Another worker: "The bosses couldn't have organised us to come here even if they wanted to! We've come to visit our old factory manager, and the current boss probably hates us for it already!"

Another worker: "If it was organised, it was organised, but if it wasn't, there are tens of thousands of Zhongyang Textiles workers who would come here without any need for persuasion. If that wasn't so, do you think the streets would be crammed with people like this? I'm telling you, everyone here is a representative of the Zhongyang workers, sent by the Zhongyang workers..."

Another worker: "That's not true. Not everyone here is from Zhongyang Textiles – some of us aren't. But a lot of us are in the same state as the Zhongyang workers, so that's why we've come..."

Reporter: "Can you explain to us the reason why you've come here? As far as we know, for many years there has never been a situation like this in our city. Mayor Li has been ill in hospital before now, but there have never been scenes like this before. Can you tell us why?"

Worker: "Do you really need to be told? It's because there are fewer and fewer honest cadres like Mayor Li these days."

Another worker: "Please make sure you don't edit what we're saying. The reason we've come here today to see Mayor Li is that he came to see us when we were in trouble. Today's leaders all despise the poor and only like rich people. They spend all their time hanging around the kind of places rich people go. They stuff their faces with all the best food and drink and boast about how great they are! They're all in politics just for the money. As for us poor people, how many officials actually give us any thought? If all our leaders were like Mayor Li, who personally made sure he knew what was going on with us workers, even in the depths of winter, do you think we would still not be getting paid our wages?"

Another worker: "Everything is upside down these days. If we workers say we approve of a cadre like Mayor Li, all those other officials are bound to disagree. Why? Because they don't even notice him! Now is the busiest time of year for leadership cadres, and what are they busy with? They're busy giving gifts! With New Year coming, if they don't give their bosses presents, do you think they're going to be safe in their jobs? But Mayor Li is all right! When other people are busy giving gifts, he's busy bringing aid to us workers in our homes. Do you think his bosses are going to approve of a cadre like that? I'm telling you, a lot of us here are not from Zhongyang Textiles, we're here to protest about the way a good cadre like Mayor Li is being treated. How could we not come and see Mayor Li, when he took the time, with New Year round the corner, to take his cadres to go and visit the workers at a loss-making business? Even if we don't get to see Mayor Li and just end up standing here, at least it will be a mark of our appreciation. As long as we've got leaders like Mayor Li, us workers in state-owned enterprises can feel safe and secure."

Reporter: "You, sir, I can see you're getting on in years and your health isn't that good. Isn't it enough that all these young workers have come out in the freezing weather? Why have you come here yourself to wait around too? Can you tell us what you really think?"

Old master worker: "The first thing I want to tell you is that I am an engineer from Zhongyang Textiles, and I was a workshop leader for many years. I've come here to represent not only the workers, but also the intellectuals and the great mass of retired cadres and ordinary workers. What I want to tell you is that I am eighty-four years old this year and I was already retired when Mayor Li came to Zhongyang Textiles, so I never knew him! But I want you to know that I've been waiting here for three whole days ever since Mayor Li fell ill! You asked why I came here, and I'll tell you why – because I wanted to! I want to see Mayor Li! I know that the Zhongyang Textile Factory will never collapse if Mayor Li is there! Why? Because he loves this factory and he loves the workers in this factory! These days, no one seems to say that anymore. Saying that someone loves the factory like he loves his home is just like saying he is a fool. If a factory manager doesn't even love the factory he manages, how can he be a good manager? What I want to tell you is that some leading cadres today are worse than the factory managers and leaders under the Kuomintang! I worked in this factory all my life. I worked here during the Warlord Era and during the Republic of China. I'm telling you the truth. Who would have dared to act like the current director and manager of the factory manager back then? If they had, they'd have lost their heads a hundred times over! Back then the factory was also called a public company, but why didn't it collapse? Only because they were afraid of what would happen to them, and they knew that even their necks weren't too thick for the executioner's sword. If ever it came out that someone had embezzled twenty dollars or more, there'd have been no two ways about it, they'd have been for the chop..."

Another old man: "I know Mayor Li but he doesn't know me. I am not going to lie to you, I have never been much of a man during my life. I have always been very submissive, and I have never dared to say anything or do anything. But today I want to tell you openly that I have had enough! I'm so angry! If I have to watch that bunch of losers trash this factory, I won't be able to die in peace! The reason we came here to see Mayor Li is that we really really hope he won't fall down now! I'm old, I don't care about anything anymore, I've been a loser all my life and now I've got nothing more to lose. Let me tell you, when I came here, I told my wife and son that we were all coming here to let those people know they need to watch out. If anyone tries to take Mayor Li down now, I won't let them, even if it costs me my life..."

Reporter: "Have there been this many people coming to see Mayor Li every day?"

Worker: "Actually, it's got less. The first day, there were more than two thousand from the factory alone, but then some people said that wouldn't do. Such a big crowd might cause trouble for Mayor Li, so we're taking it in turns now..."

Another worker: "The workers here are not just from one company. Someone just did a count and, today alone, there are workers from twelve different companies..."

Reporter: "We've been told that Mayor Li has been unconscious for the last few days and he hasn't known that you've been here every day. Do you..."

Worker: "Do you think we only came here to let Mayor Li know we were here? You're not doing us workers justice! If we just wanted to make Mayor Li remember us, if we were just making a show, we could have gone straight to his home. Why would we bother coming here?"

Worker: "We didn't come here to let Mayor Li know we were here. We want to show how we feel. We want everyone in society to know that we workers really cherish leadership cadres like Mayor Li!"

Worker: "My wife said that if other leaders were sick and hospitalised, we would not come and visit them, but when Mayor Li was sick, we had to come and see him! Mayor Li made himself this sick for the sake of us workers, and that's why us workers in state-owned enterprises will remember him all our lives..."

CHAPTER THIRTY-FOUR

As Li Gaocheng was watching this enthralling interview on the television, tears in his eyes, the telephone suddenly shrilled at him.

He stared blankly for a moment, not taking in that it was the telephone, and then it took even longer to register that he should be answering it. It was only when his secretary Wu Xingang hurried over and said "Hello!" into the receiver, that he came back to earth. Wu Xingang turned down the sound on the television next to the phone, and asked quietly, in the characteristic tone of a secretary: "Who is it?"

The voice down the line was so loud that even Li Gaocheng could hear it clearly: "It's Yan Zhen! Please put Li Gaocheng on the phone!"

Wu Xingang obviously realised that Li Gaocheng had heard the stern and unceremonious voice at the other end. The two men stared at each other and froze for a moment.

"Secretary Yan... Mayor Li has just gone to sleep. Do you think..." Wu Xingang said softly, looking at Li Gaocheng. Li Gaocheng didn't understand why Wu Xingang had told this lie. Maybe he wanted him to give him time to gather his thoughts. Judging from Yan Zhen's tone of voice, he must have been provoked by something, although Li didn't know what.

"If he's asleep, wake him up! I have something to tell him!" Yan

Zhen's mood was so stubborn and violent he was actually yelling down the phone.

Wu Xingang froze again. "...Will you take it, Mayor Li?" he asked dazedly, covering the receiver.

Li Gaocheng nodded silently and motioned to him to hand the receiver over.

Wu Xingang stood without moving for a long moment, then slowly came over and silently handed Li Gaocheng the receiver. Then, without waiting for Li to start talking, he quietly slipped out of the room.

These few, small actions of Wu Xingang made Li Gaocheng feel both content and grateful. The young man had behaved very circumspectly and very decently, in every way as a good secretary should.

"Is that Secretary Yan?" he asked, when he was sure he was in command of himself. He knew exactly what tone he should adopt, so his voice was soft and calm, but, at the same time, carried just the right degree of respect and attention.

"Yes, this is Yan Zhen. I thought you were asleep. Are you feeling a bit better?" Yan Zhen's voice was gentler now, but there was still an undertone of uncontrollable anger.

"Much better, thank you, Secretary Yan. I'm told you came to see me the day before yesterday and have phoned several times. I'm very grateful to you, Secretary Yan," Li Gaocheng said with undoubted sincerity.

"Good, good! We're not children, the two of us, and I can do without all the polite chit-chat." Perhaps because of the other's obvious sincerity, Yan Zhen's tone seemed to have softened even more, but there was still an edge to his voice. "I thought you were still lying in your hospital bed, but I've just seen you on the television looking full of life!"

So that was it! Yan Zhen had seen him on the television! But why was he so angry and upset with him? Had that broadcast hurt him somehow? Or was there some other reason?

"It's like this, Secretary Yan," Li Gaocheng explained. "When I woke up today, I heard the nurses say that a whole load of workers had been waiting for me at the hospital gates for a very long time, so I went down to see them. I didn't know there would be TV reporters there too. You know me, Secretary Yan – I'm the last person to want to be interviewed, especially on television. I know I must have upset a lot of people with this, but today..."

"Today is different, is that what you're going to say? That the situation is different today, is that it? Today, the first thing you're going to do is give the public a statement, isn't it? Today, you want to present the people with the image of a clean and upright official, don't you?" Yan Zhen's suppressed anger seemed to have been stirred up again, and he spat the words out like a machine gun, not waiting for Li Gaocheng to finish. "To tell the truth, Gaocheng, it's not just today that I've suddenly got criticisms of your behaviour, nor am I your only critic. There is a whole lot of stuff you've done which has really exceeded your authority. You need to have some regard for your position. You're a mayor in charge of several million people, so you're not just representing yourself but a whole level of leadership. You need to have a good think about how you've come across on television. Are you the only clean official left in China today? Are you the only one who's honest? Do you understand what kind of times we are living in? Do you know why we need to talk about political stability? Are you clear about all this? After so many years as a leader, are you really still so politically naive? In the present circumstances, what do you think you are doing stirring up the emotions of so many workers? How can you allow so many people to curse the leaders, the government and the Communist Party on television? Aren't you a leader? Don't you represent the government? Aren't you a Communist Party official? How can you put yourself in opposition to the Party and the state? Don't you think about what you're doing? Are you trying to get everyone in the city to visit you in hospital? Where is your sense of the bigger picture? Where are your Party principles? Are you..."

For a while, Li Gaocheng only seemed able to listen, with no chance at all to defend himself. It was the first time in many years that Li Gaocheng could remember that Yan Zhen had lost his temper in front of him! As he listened to Yan Zhen's angry "criticism", he tried to remember if he had actually said anything on television that went too far. He racked his brains but couldn't think of anything, except that some of the things the workers had said certainly were very inflammatory, but that was all after he had left. How could he, a man lying on his sick bed in hospital, be held responsible for anything the workers had said when he wasn't there, or any questions the reporters had asked in their interviews, or anything the TV stations had seen fit to broadcast, for that matter? Besides, the workers' comments were not too out of place when you think about it. In a large state-owned enterprise that had been losing money for a long time and had not been able to pay their wages for almost a year, why shouldn't the workers, who had little to eat and no money for clothes and whose lives were becoming more impossible by the day, voice their grievances and opinions in front of journalists. And since the fact that such an enterprise was running at a loss was entirely the result of the government's ineffective measures and poor management by the company bosses, it was perfectly understandable that the workers might say a few things that went too far. Besides, if there were any real problems, the TV station would have deleted the footage long ago, and there really wouldn't be any need for all these angry words being thrown about now. In truth, wasn't what the workers were saying an expression of their profound hope and trust in their leaders, in the government and in the Party? When people talked about political stability, did they really mean that even these workers who were not getting paid, were not allowed to say what they really felt? If they were not allowed to speak from their hearts to the Party and to the country, then who could they turn to?

But thinking all this was one thing and saying it was another. However he looked at it, Yan Zhen was still his superior, he was still a member of the Standing Committee of the Provincial Party Committee, and he was still a very influential, very young and very promising deputy secretary of the Provincial Party Committee. Not only could he threaten his, Li Gaocheng's, position, the upper levels of leadership would not be able to ignore his existence and his influence either. On top of all that, Li's own status and position did not give him the strength or status to compete with him in any way. One level of seniority is enough to crush the person beneath it; this was no casual or meaningless saying in leadership circles.

It was not until Yan Zhen's tone had softened somewhat that Li Gaocheng found an opportunity to interject. "Secretary Yan, I honestly didn't know that there was a TV reporter down there waiting to interview me. All I kept thinking at the time was that there were so many workers waiting at the gate to visit me, and even if I wasn't the city mayor and was still just a factory director, even if I was just an ordinary citizen, as long as I was alive, as long as I was still conscious, as long as I could still walk, then I had to go down and meet with the workers, come what may. I told the doctors and nurses that I was going down there even if I had to be carried. It was the workers I wanted to see, not the journalists. As the mayor, I was so ashamed to be confronted by so many of the city's workers who were not being paid. Night after night, I couldn't sleep a wink when I thought of this, Secretary Yan. I felt it most when I paid a visit to Zhongyang Textiles a few days ago and I saw that there were so many old workers and old cadres who had worked there all their lives, but could not even afford to buy a colour television or a refrigerator, and still lived in tiny single-storey buildings from the 1950s, and so many workers could not even afford to buy medicine when they were sick, and their children could not afford to go to school. It cut me to the quick! Faced with these workers, I felt that I should have resigned a long time ago – even though I had not embezzled a single cent from the state, I was still guilty. And yet, when I am hospitalised, a cadre with a dismal record and inadequate abilities, and all those same workers come to visit me in the hospital, how am I supposed to feel? Why would workers come to see a leader in hospital? Surely only in the hope that their leaders can lead them better and do more for them. In all honesty, is it not an expression of trust and support for them to come and see me? I am a national cadre, a party cadre, and when they come here to see me – is it not also their expression of hope, support, care and love for the Party and for the government? I am speaking from my heart now, Secretary Yan."

"...I understand." There was a long pause before Yan Zhen seemed to react. Maybe he hadn't expected Li Gaocheng to talk like that, or maybe he thought there was more to his words than it first seemed and they were indicative of something else; in any case, he had listened in silence up till then. So when Li Gaocheng's words came to an abrupt end, Yan Zhen still seemed to be in a state of contemplation. As he emerged from that contemplation, Li Gaocheng felt that his words had not only failed to convince but had actually widened the distance between the two of them and deepened the rift. And when he did speak, Yan Zhen's real meaning became even more apparent. "I think I've finally understood you and

I can see that everything I've said has been in vain. Over the last few days, lots of people have come to see me, telling me things about you, but I didn't believe them. People should be open about their grudges and grievances, and say what you like, you would never stir up trouble for me behind my back. In any case, it was me who promoted you, wasn't it..."

"You're missing the point, Secretary Yan, it's not the same thing at all. What I mean is..." Li Gaocheng couldn't stop himself arguing back.

"Let me finish, can't you! I don't want to hear what you have to say at the moment, and I don't need you to tell me anything! I just want you to hear me out!" Yan Zhen interrupted Li Gaocheng sternly. He was clearly not willing to give an inch. When Li had finally calmed down and stopped talking, perhaps feeling that he might have gone a little too far, Yan Zhen softened his tone a little and said: "I used to think I was good at reading people, and that, whatever else might be said, it was a good thing that we had worked together as a team for a number of years. But, if you're not willing to acknowledge me as your superior, public opinion will have something to say about that, and if you don't recognise even me, how do you think you're going to get by in society? How are you going to remain in political circles? Who's going to employ you or take you in? Where are you going to find a foothold? You mustn't mind me talking like this, Gaocheng, it's just the way things are in China these days. If you're willing to sell your master out for personal advancement, you'll both end up in the same boat. Do you really think you're the only person in this society who is clean and spotless and everyone else is neck deep in the mire? Do you really think you are society's only hero, the only one who can fight corruption, the lone soldier carrying on the fight without support? Is everyone else so cowardly, so lily-livered, that they only get by, day to day, by turning a blind eye? You must know I am talking from the heart now. But you should bear in mind that you are the only person in the world I can talk like this to – there's no one else. Quite apart from anything else, I've been in the official world much longer than you and I've seen a lot more than you. What does fighting corruption mean? Do you understand? It's a campaign, a movement, isn't it! And what is that movement trying to achieve? Isn't it aimed at rectifying the cadres? Rectifying which cadres, you ask? When it comes down to it, it means rectifying dissidents and outsiders, doesn't it! So, in a word, it means using the movement to 'rectify' your opponents and bring down people who don't belong in your own circle. So, what is a movement, you ask? This is a movement! This is the real meaning of anti-corruption. Even the ordinary people understand that those fighting corruption have their own problems or that there are problems with everyone the fight is aimed at. Do you think people haven't made accusations against you? That there aren't people who want to sort you out? That there aren't people wanting to squeeze you out? Now that our relationship has reached this point, I don't want to pass judgement on your merits in front of you. If I hadn't protected you over the years, you would have fallen many times, and do you think you would have got your time as mayor then? Think about all the large-scale projects you carried out over the years. How many do you think you could have seen through if people didn't have your back. I was away at the Central School for a year, and you lost out on the post of Municipal Party Committee secretary. Didn't that tell you anything? When are you going to wise up? When are you going to grow up and show a little sophistication? You know that I am a member of the Standing Committee of the Provincial Party Committee, and I am also an executive deputy secretary. I am in charge of organisation, industry and the economy, and I am also in charge of public prosecution and the legal system. Think about how much power that gives me! To others, it looks like I can do whatever I want, but that's not the case at all. I know just how much power I have. It is easy for me to build a person up, but not so easy for me to bring someone down, even someone in a much lower position than me. Why? Although it may look like you're trying to bring down an individual, you are actually going to bring down a whole circle of people. Do you understand what I am saying? If an individual isn't part of a circle, he can be brought down at any time. I am going to ask you one last thing, Li Gaocheng – if you don't have enough people behind you, how much do you really think you are going to get done?"

Although Li Gaocheng listened to all this in silence, Yan Zhen's words hit home very hard. He had never thought Yan could talk to him in that tone or speak so bluntly and directly. In particular, he never expected him to sound so unlike what a senior provincial official should sound like.

Yan Zhen's words made Li Gaocheng feel that he was a blatant scoundrel! It made him feel shameless and abhorrent!

For so many years, Li Gaocheng had always regarded Yan Zhen as his role model. He respected him and admired him from the bottom of his heart. He believed he really was a top-level official with scarcely any flaws, and he was very glad that he had fallen in with such a good leader. Although over the short period of the last few days his reverence had begun to waver, he could not bring himself to believe that it was all true. He had always imagined that one day, sooner or later, the whole story would be revealed and that Secretary Yan Zhen would still be the same honest and unblemished Secretary Yan Zhen he always had been. He believed that the end results would prove his innocence and sincerity, that he was indeed a good cadre who had stood the test of time, and that he truly was a man of courage and integrity!

But now, faced with what Secretary Yan had just said, his illusions were shattered once and for all, and the reverential monument he had built up in his mind tumbled to the ground in pieces.

He couldn't even imagine what Yan Zhen must have looked like when he spoke those words to him. Was it really him? Could it really be him?

Li Gaocheng felt a sudden burst of indescribable anguish. How truly terrible it was that someone who was deputy secretary of the Provincial Party Committee could have spoken those words! Truly terrible! It was the greatest possible disaster for him, for his future, for his city government, for his current leadership team and for everything that was going on at that time!

If Yan Zhen really thought that way, if he really was that person, then clearly, he, Li Gaocheng, was not the only person he had talked to like that.

If you are only dealing with a leadership cadre who insists on pursuing a mistaken course or with a leadership cadre with a quick temper, there is nothing to be scared of because, as long as he is not fundamentally a bad man, once he finds out that the actions he is insisting on or the things he is getting angry about are not what he imagined, he will correct himself. He will not be a significant threat to you or cause you any serious harm. But if, as now, you suddenly find yourself confronted by a genuinely bad person, the situation you are in, and the things coming down the line at you, are vastly different. All the more so now, because the genuinely bad person involved here was no ordinary man, but a high-level leader and a leader who wielded a great deal of power and influence!

In the ordinary course of events, there was nothing to fear from someone who had simply gone to the bad or even from a criminal who had committed a heinous crime, because, no matter whether he had done something bad or something illegal, there was always a sanction and a punishment waiting for him. However, when a bad person occupied a very powerful position, and always gave the impression of being strict but impartial, it was a completely different matter, because he was not only very destructive, but also very powerful. He presented you with your biggest and most dangerous threat.

Li Gaocheng had listened in silence. He had not said a word and nor had he wanted to. What was there to say at that point?

It seemed that Yan Zhen didn't want him to say anything either. After he had said all he had to say, he continued, as if issuing Li Gaocheng his orders:

"First, since you are well enough to go outside in the freezing cold and talk to those workers, if you think you have the time and you still consider me your leader, please come to my office or my home so we can sit down together. I really want to have a proper talk with you. I particularly hope that you will not take what has been said today to heart, and if you think I have misspoken at all, please point it out to me when you come. The doors of my office and my home are always open to you.

"Second, all news reports and propaganda about your illness and the workers coming to see you will cease and you will take the initiative to inform all the relevant news work units that if there is any more news of this kind or any follow-up reports they should be quashed immediately. They would not be advantageous to your ongoing work or to the image of the government. With New Year almost upon us, stability is the priority. That is the big picture, and all work and guiding principles must follow it. They must have their origins in the big picture and that is what they must prioritise.

"Third, the investigation and clearing of accounts at Zhongyang Textiles will be concluded with all speed before the end of the year. Any negligible or superficial problems should be treated as if they are not there. Any problems for which there is insufficient or weak evidence should be treated as if they are not there. Any problems that stem from wild speculation or guesswork should be treated as if they are not there. Any problems that arise from personal grudges or preconceptions should not be included in the scope of the investigation. Any issues involving cadres at or above the director level should be reported to the relevant city or province, and the working group has no authority to deal with them. It is of particular importance to note that financial deficits or losses are not to be considered problems or evidence of corruption, and it is essential to adhere to this principle.

"Fourth, regarding the issue of Zhongyang Textiles Xin Chao Co. Ltd, it is classed as a tertiary enterprise with a wide range and broad scope of activities and has a large number of subsidiaries, many of which are joint ventures and many of which are just starting up. Therefore, all expenditure and activity that stem from its production and operation and are conducive to economic development are not to be included in the audited inventory.

"Fifth, the suspension of operation and production at the Green Apple Entertainment City and the Chang Long Garment and Textile Factory, along with the surprise inspections there, are to be lifted immediately. If we cease operation and production as soon as there is a problem, how can our economy develop? If there is a problem or a mistake, we deal with it. It is as simple as that. If we can't expect to solve everything at a stroke politically, how can we expect to do so economically? Additionally, emotional complications and conflicts should not be brought into the workplace. Mixing family problems with other problems is itself a manifestation of immaturity. Your wife is your wife and if there is a problem with her, even if she has broken the law, you cannot just shuffle it off onto society. Aren't your wife's problems your problems too? Can you really say you knew nothing about your wife's affairs? If your wife has broken state and Party law, if one day she really is dismissed and sentenced, can you just wash your hands of it all? If you do not love and protect your wife, who can you expect to do it for you? If you destroy her, you destroy yourself..."

If Li Gaocheng had been able to remain calm and collected after hearing the first part of what Yan Zhen had to say to him, the second part made his blood run cold.

In particular, there was a dangerous edge to what had been said about his wife. It was especially terrifying to hear that if he did not protect his wife, then she would be considered fair game for anyone to take down. Destroying her was tantamount to destroying himself, and the ultimate responsibility rested solely with him! In other words, they had effectively taken his wife hostage.

If that was what they really thought, then of course that was what they would really do. If that was the case, it was truly terrifying...

It was them who had brought about his wife's ruin. They had been using her all along, and when a problem arose, they made her their shield and they used her to blackmail him, to intimidate him, and even, perhaps, to bring him down, break him and get rid of him! They were killing two birds with one stone and clearly felt they had nothing to fear from him. If they had her, they had him by the vitals too. All in all, he had no option but to obey their orders and act as their shield and their mouthpiece. The other side of the coin was that he couldn't escape from her and she couldn't escape from him and they had no choice but to be the scapegoats and sacrificial lambs!

He felt an agonising stab to his heart. He was not worried about his own situation and prospects but felt indescribable pain and distress for his wife!

He was so stupid! How could he have allowed himself blindly to sign onto a pirate ship crewed by demons like these people?! It was like walking complacently into a wolf's den or falling contentedly into a tiger's mouth!

Where could she be now?

Yan Zhen must have known about their quarrel and the split between them, otherwise he would not have been talking in the way he did. That meant the first place she must have gone after leaving the hospital was straight to Yan Zhen. She was probably still there when Yan Zhen telephoned him!

He had walked into their trap! He had mistaken a thief for his father! He had served himself up on a platter to them! He was the greedy sheep that had stuck its head into a wolf's lair, all the while congratulating himself on how fortunate and secure he was.

For a time, all he could think about was the circumstances surrounding his wife and her current situation. He immediately remembered an old cautionary tale in which "the willow tree was slashed and the mulberry tree bled".[1] Sometimes people suffered through no fault of their own and it was always possible to be too clever for you own good...

CHAPTER THIRTY-FIVE

THAT NIGHT, A LITTLE BEFORE MIDNIGHT, an unexpected visitor came onto the hospital ward. Li Gaocheng was lying down but couldn't sleep, so he had just taken two Estazolam tablets. The brusque knock on the door told him this was not an ordinary visitor. Before Li could even sit up, the newcomer was standing at the bedside. In the dim lamplight, a smiling face was looking amiably down at him. It was Municipal Party Committee Secretary Yang Cheng.

Yang put his hand gently on Li Gaocheng's shoulder, indicating that he needn't get up. Then he took a nearby stool and sat down at the top of the bed.

"So, you're a bit better, are you?" Yang Cheng was so close, Li could feel the faint trace of cold he had brought in with him.

"A lot better." Li Gaocheng nodded. For some reason, these gestures of Yang Cheng stirred up his emotions and he felt as though he might be about to burst into tears.

"I saw you on television. It was great!" Yang Cheng said excitedly, with obvious sincerity. "It got a really good response, you know, especially from the ordinary people. Thousands of workers' representatives spontaneously standing in the freezing cold outside the hospital gates, waiting to see our mayor! Do you know what effect that is going to have? A coup like that is more convincing than publishing a hundred newspaper articles. You've been a huge help to me, Lao Li! This illness of yours has really had me worried for the last few days and I just didn't know what to do. Almost every day I wanted to come and see you – I was so anxious for you to get better as soon as possible. It couldn't be better! I really believe that if the workers have all been watching TV, we're not going to have any further trouble. If we go about things with a bit of care, I'm quite sure we'll be able to relax over the coming year. As Municipal Party Committee Secretary, I thank you with all my heart, Lao Li!"

Yang Cheng was practically dancing on the spot, as happy as a little child.

As he watched Yang Cheng, it dawned on Li Gaocheng that the man wasn't lying. What he was saying was the simple truth. It was then that he burst into tears. Yang Cheng seemed to understand a little of what was going on with Li, and his eyes too became moist.

After a while, Li Gaocheng said, half teasingly: "You say you came to see me every day, so how come I don't know anything about it?"

"Ah! You don't believe me, is that it?" Yang Cheng asked with mock gravity, deliberately adopting an aggrieved expression. "It's a good thing I did come – otherwise you'd have the account to settle later on. Let me tell you, when I came yesterday you didn't seem to me to be making any progress at all. If anything, your condition was more alarming than the very first day. When that secretary of yours, Wu Xingang, saw me, he broke down completely, and, to tell the truth, even I thought you might be about to cash in your chips!"

Had he really been that bad? Li Gaocheng was astounded once again. There had not been a single word about anything like that in the "diary" his wife had left for him to read. What she had done was totally incomprehensible. Quite apart from anything else, was there even a speck of human kindness in her?

Li Gaocheng couldn't help sighing, and the atmosphere in the room grew heavy again.

"Is the pressure getting too much for you?" Yang Cheng asked gently, then continued, without waiting for Li Gaocheng to answer. "I know everything that happened that day, and the relevant personnel also reported the situation to me at the time, including the preliminary results of the surprise inspection of the Chang Long Garment and Textile Factory. The problem is a lot bigger and more serious than we thought, Lao Li. When the workers came to see you this time, they really did have something to see you about. They are worried we're not up to it!"

Li Gaocheng nodded. He was about to say something but changed his mind.

"I've discounted everything else as not worth worrying about, but the one thing I really am concerned about is you, Lao Li," Yang Cheng continued. "The greatest pressure is on you now. You are in the most danger, and you may well be the one who is going to pay the highest price. I often think that in real life, for people like us, once you make the wrong choice, you are more than likely to lose a lifetime of career and reputation. If you take up the wrong position, you are stuck with it. You may still be able to get away with it in normal life, but almost certainly not in politics. Particularly for a politician, you sometimes pay the highest price for the choices you make, and you may well keep paying it for the rest of your life."

Li Gaocheng thought about this in silence and weighed Yang Cheng's words. It seemed that Yang Cheng, like Yan Zhen, understood his current state of mind and situation very well, and they only differed in their attitude and position. So, what was Yang Cheng's real meaning? In particular, how much did Yang Cheng know about what was going on with him and his household?

In particular, he was desperately worried about the huge sum of three hundred thousand yuan that was still in the house. How much did Yang Cheng know about all that kind of thing?

Of course, Yang Cheng wouldn't know all the details, but with his insight and intellect, he would be able to make some pretty good guesses. If he could get a clear picture of the situation of the Te Gao Te Passenger Transit Company and the Green Apple Entertainment City, then he would certainly know how to prise out a few family details.

The key question in the current situation was, should he turn over the whole business of the three hundred thousand yuan to Yang Cheng to deal with?

Li Gaocheng sank into deep contemplation.

Would there be any side effects to that course of action? What problems might arise? What difficulties might it put him in?

The biggest side effect, the biggest problem, and the biggest difficulty would be that, once he explained this matter in detail to Yang Cheng, he would have burned his boats. Once the matter of the money was laid bare, it was tantamount to him declaring open war on his superiors, on all the provincial Party leaders who everyone believed had promoted him and on the enormously powerful Deputy Secretary of the Standing Committee of the Provincial Party Committee. What awaited him was a life-and-death struggle, a battle with no end in sight, a bloody storm of a fight that would cost him dear even if he won. It was bound to be a battle of mutual self-destruction, fought in anger that could only ever backfire in a chaos of misfortune and desolation brought down by his own hand!

His greatest fear was that, once he opened up to Yang Cheng on this business with the money, he was putting his whole future career and his whole fate on someone else's shoulders. Life and death, success and failure, prosperity and penury, honour and disgrace, everything, absolutely everything would be in someone else's hands. If that person was trustworthy, all well and good, but if they were not, if they were a villain or a rogue, it was easy to imagine what could happen to him and how he would end up.

Perhaps this kind of thinking was too pessimistic, too desperate, even too despicable, but for some reason, he couldn't help himself. Although concrete certainty should always be the best guide, in reality, hearsay and imagination abound and often leave the strongest impression.

The question was, was he overestimating his own capabilities and allowing his own thinking to tie himself up in knots. Compared to Yan Zhen, wasn't his own power and influence too weak and ineffectual? Besides, hadn't he spent his career in economics and industry while Yan Zhen had been involved with administrative organisation? While he himself had been planning business affairs, Yan Zhen had been manoeuvring people. It had long been said in private that there was no doubt that no one in the city or the province was as powerful. Since he had been the leading organisational administrator for so many years, and then the executive deputy secretary of the Provincial Party Committee in charge of the cadre system, how many of the municipal and provincial cadres had been appointed by his hand? Seen like that, Li Gaocheng stood no chance against him, and if he were to declare war now, would that not be ample evidence that he was overestimating himself and tying himself up in knots with his own thinking?

He had always felt a little weird being constantly surrounded by an entourage. How much influence did he actually have, and did he really have the ability to project a powerful enough presence? If he thought about it now, in the cold light of day, he had nothing. Even though he was mayor, in reality, he had absolutely nothing. All his supposed power was illusory. If someone said he had it, then he had it; if someone said he didn't have it, then he didn't have it. In the normal course of events, whatever he did, whatever he said, every thought he had, every action he initiated, every move he made, every step he took, there always seemed to be people to the left and right of him, prompting him, guiding him, restraining him. He couldn't call this supervision or even control – that's not what it was at all. It was really a kind of sinister calculation, a kind of open warfare and covert manoeuvring to gain advantage. It meant that he couldn't get the things done that he both wanted and was able to do, or, at least, could not do them satisfactorily. At the same time, things he didn't want to see done, and even things that were beyond his capabilities, went through just like that with green lights all the way.

In all honesty, how much power did he really have? Where did he hold any advantage compared to Yan Zhen?

Yes, it was true that he currently had the support of large numbers of workers and of ordinary people and of a great swathe of cadres, but when it came to the crunch, particularly if it was a question of his promotion or demotion, of his staying or going, of his success or failure, of his honour or disgrace, where would all that support be? How much use would it actually prove to be?

So then, was he going to keep on covering this whole thing up and not talk to anyone else about it, and when the opportunity presented itself, give all the money back?

But what still terrified him was that if someone of his status continued to cover it up, that massive sum of three hundred thousand yuan was a deadly timebomb planted inside his very home that could go off with devastating effect at any time, leaving him shattered, with his status and reputation in ruins. Even the smoothest tongue in the world could not explain it away, and even a bathe in the Yellow River could not wash him clean. What they really wanted most was for him to go on covering it up and keeping quiet about it forever. In that way, he, the mayor, would eternally be in the hands of others and, from then on, he would never have a chance to get ahead. For three hundred thousand yuan, he was selling his power, his position, his soul and his freedom...

If so, the rest of his life would be a prison cell of torture and torment, and he would be scourged with fear and condemned by his conscience until he died!

So, now he had to find an opportunity to give it back? How easy was that going to be? Summoning a ghost was a simple enough matter, but sending it back was another thing altogether. Three hundred thousand yuan had been sent easily enough into his mayoral home, but how could he possibly send it back out and return it? And how could he do it silently, unobtrusively, unhindered and without any fuss? How easy was that going to be? How straightforward would it be? If he could manage it, would that be it? Would the whole affair just disappear at a stroke as if it had never happened? A bribe of three hundred thousand yuan was an appalling criminal act. Could it just be wished away with complete equanimity? How could his actions in any way be distinguished from a crime? How could he ever find any peace of mind?

It had been nearly ten days already. Ten days! Three hundred thousand yuan of bribe money had been sitting in his house for ten days. And he still didn't know what to do. What was the difference between this and committing a crime? Even if he'd been sick for a few days, did that make him any less responsible?

Responsibility? How could he call this responsibility?

Conversely, what if he now told Yang Cheng everything about the matter? What benefit and advantages might that bring him?

Given the current situation, it was enough that he was asking himself, for him to be clear about the answer. If he wanted to reflect on what was to him pretty much a matter of life and death, who else was he going to turn to but Yang Cheng? Firstly, he was the Municipal Party Committee Secretary and the number one operative in the city, so it was only right and proper to take the matter to him; secondly, among all the cadres at a similar level in the city, the way things stood at the time, he was the man whose thinking about the problems at Zhongyang Textiles most closely coincided with his own, and who seemed to be most resolute in his support; thirdly, to outward appearances at least, Yang Cheng had the weakest and most distant links with Secretary Yan Zhen. Also, and most crucially, throughout the past two years of dealings with Yang Cheng, he felt that Yang could be said to be essentially trustworthy and reliable. Those qualities also seemed to extend to his fundamental character and personality.

Besides, if he didn't turn to Yang Cheng, who could he turn to? Almost certainly, it would be most beneficial and advantageous to talk to him.

Now the two men had met face to face, they sat for a long time in silence. Yang Cheng almost certainly understood Li Gaocheng's complicated and contradictory feelings, so he intentionally kept quiet to create a relaxed and casual atmosphere which allowed the other more freedom to think. He waited until Li Gaocheng suddenly came to life as if taken by surprise, then he smiled faintly and said, softly, weighing his words: "There is one thing you should be clear about, Lao Li, and that is the pressures and resistance both of us are facing over the problems at Zhongyang Textiles. You do understand, don't you, that the two of us have been lashed to the same war chariot ever since that meeting of the Standing Committee. I support you, Lao Li, and I believe in you..."

"I do understand, Secretary Yang." Under Yang Cheng's luminous gaze, Li Gaocheng suddenly seemed to have found his feelings again. He also seemed to have come to a firm decision and finally become clear about what he had to do. Unable to disguise his emotion completely, he said: "Until I was taken ill like this, I had been wanting to have a heart-to-heart with you for a good few days. It is very opportune you have come like this tonight when it is quiet. I can tell you what is really on my mind..."

Yang Cheng nodded silently and then just listened quietly. From beginning to end, he appeared extraordinarily calm, and even when the sum of three hundred thousand yuan was mentioned, his expression didn't betray any surprise. When Li Gaocheng felt that he had finally said everything he needed to say, he slumped back on the bed as if he had just finished some heavy task of manual labour, and watched Yang Cheng's face in silence.

A deathly hush fell over the room.

Yang Cheng's face grew gradually more and more solemn, and, after a long while, he stood up wearily and slowly paced round the room.

Li Gaocheng remained silent too, like someone in court awaiting the verdict. After another long pause, with genuine emotion, Yang Cheng said something that Li Gaocheng would never forget as long as he lived.

"First of all, Lao Li, let me personally thank you for showing such trust in me. I genuinely thank you from the bottom of my heart."

Just those few words were enough to set the tears flowing down Li Gaocheng's cheeks like two rivers in spate. He had never expected Yang Cheng to talk the way he had or even believed that he could speak so openly and with such genuine feeling. What most moved him was the realisation that he hadn't misjudged the man and that Yang Cheng was indeed a man worthy of his trust and a totally reliable secretary. Particularly at this crucial juncture.

However, Yang Cheng immediately went on to say something else that would also remain engraved on Li's heart forever, it was so terrifying and blood-curdling.

"Lao Li, I also want to thank you for telling me the complete truth without a word of a lie and for not trying to hide anything at all from me. You should know that I already knew everything you told me two days ago. During the time you were unconscious in your hospital bed, people were already laying complaints against you with the Provincial Committee, the Municipal Committee and the Political and Legal Department and the Discipline Inspection Commission. They are accusing you of using your position greatly to enrich yourself, of misappropriating state loans to build an entertainment palace for your relatives, and of using state money to make a fortune for yourself. It is also being said that you let your wife take advantage of the opportunity to make a fortune while you were working on a case, and even that many businesses had collapsed because they couldn't afford the gifts and entertainment they were obliged to provide. The most shocking thing, they said, was that you used your position of power to ask for bribes, on one occasion of as much as three hundred thousand yuan. They also said they had cast-iron evidence and, in particular, they not only had general proof of the three hundred thousand yuan bribe, they also had a recording!"

Before Yang Cheng had even finished speaking, Li Gaocheng was sitting rigid and dumbstruck, as if he had just received a physical blow. So, they had made their first strike while he was still lying there wondering what to do. And it had come so quickly, so ferociously, so unexpectedly and so unpredictably. He had been caught completely off guard!

He had believed he had thought of everything, reasonable and unreasonable, but he hadn't anticipated this!

It was no wonder that the phone call from Yan Zhen that day had been so forceful and overbearing, and no wonder either that the man was so furious and reckless. Perhaps they hadn't expected so many workers to show such strong support for him. Perhaps they hadn't expected him, who they believed was unconscious in his hospital bed, to appear in front of the television cameras. In particular, they probably hadn't expected that despite the emotions of his wife, Wu Aizhen, and the care and concern of so many important figures, none of them had been able to make him change his mind, and the first thing he had done after coming to in the hospital was to drive his wife away and reach out a hand to the masses of the workers!

Perhaps, according to their version of things, when Li Gaocheng woke up, when he saw with his own eyes the affection of his wife and the warmth of the leaders, and then gradually learned about the complaints laid against him, his stance would change completely, he would return to his wife's embrace and to their circle, and then the situation would evolve according to their own pre-designed formula, and nothing else would happen. The easiest and most convenient explanations for all the problems would be provided for him. Corruption? There was corruption everywhere, of course, so wouldn't it do just to pick a few off, like swatting at a swarm of flies? He could have as many as he wanted with no effort at all. Why stop work and cease production? It's just the climate of the times, central government can't do anything about it, so what hope do you have? Isn't that precisely why it is being said that, over the last two or three years, the deepening of the reform of state-owned enterprises has reached a critical point? What do we mean by critical? Doesn't it mean grave and serious? What about all the unemployed workers? Isn't the government making a big effort to solve the problem? But isn't that, in fact, a problem for the enterprises themselves? What does the government have directly to do with it? How many years have we been calling out for the separation of government and enterprises? Isn't that separation designed to give enterprises and workers more autonomy? With more autonomy come more risks, isn't that right? The truth is you can't get others to do all the hard work for you, can you! Besides, isn't it normal for unemployment to occur as a result of reform? Are not these laid-off workers we keep hearing about in the newspapers and on television unemployed workers too? And when has anyone, the enterprises, the state or the government, ever said they are not a concern? The problem is that everything has to be done slowly. Reform itself is a form of revolution, not only in the life of others but also in one's own life. How can you agree with it wholeheartedly when it is someone else's turn, but, when it comes to you, start shouting, stirring things up, even petitioning and laying complaints? Surely it can't be the case that all the people who are engaged in leadership and reform have become corrupt?

So everything goes on as before, officials are still officials, people are still people; losses are losses, problems are still problems; managers are still managers, workers are still workers; the sun shines brightly, the world is as peaceful as if nothing has happened...

From his point of view, this was the least dangerous, the safest and most secure course.

From their point of view, it was the most welcome, the happiest and most hoped-for course.

As for the workers, it was just a case of taking things slowly. Even if they had grievances, they couldn't blame him and the others for them. Who actually had the ability and guts to put so many workers out of work? The state? In any case, what did it have to do with individuals? Didn't some intellectuals say that in the virtuous circle of state mechanisms, as long as everyone managed themselves well, it meant that everyone was well managed and that there was hope for the country? So from the people's point of view, the further they stayed away from government, the better...

Wasn't that the best outcome they could hope for and the most auspicious state of affairs?

A sudden shudder dragged him back to reality from the depths of his imagination and he couldn't help but be alarmed by what he had been thinking. Why was it that, at this critical juncture, his thoughts should automatically take that direction?

Was it that he felt he had gone past the point of no return? Or was it because the situation he was facing in the future was too cruel, too extreme and too unbearable, so the peace and serenity of the past now seemed particularly nostalgic and desirable?

But supposing he did want to turn back now, was that still possible? Was it achievable?

What route back was open to him? Was it even possible? Plead with them, apologise to them, beg them for their forgiveness? Everything was his own fault and they had been right. Could he countenance all that? Could he actually say it? And if he did say it, could he call himself a man anymore? Could he hold his head up in this world? If that time came, wouldn't he be shamed in front of the Party, in front of the nation, in front of the people and, indeed, in front of himself? Then again, wasn't his wife a prime example? His wife, who was so loyal to them and who still treated Yan Zhen like a father, had been sacrificed by them without mercy. He was a hostage! If they could casually crush someone like his wife like a bug to protect themselves, how did they look on him?

When the time came, his life would be worth no more than a dog's.

He lifted his head and silently looked at Municipal Party Committee Secretary Yang Cheng as he stood in front of him. He discovered that Yang Cheng was also silently gazing at himself.

Once again, he felt a strong, almost indescribable shock as their eyes met.

So, it turned out that Municipal Party Committee Secretary Yang Cheng knew everything about him, but hadn't said anything and just waited.

He had known everything and just waited for him.

When he was cudgelling his brains for ways to test his counterpart, that counterpart was already ruthlessly testing him.

Human relationships are probably always like the old saying has it: people all know that taking from others is a gain, but they do not know that giving to others is also a gain. When you take something, when you gain something, the first thing you should consider is what you are giving in return. Those in charge put dedication above intelligence. Over these last days, when he had been cooperating with Yang Cheng, had the relationship not been a little over-sophisticated, a little too slippery, a little too calculating?

It was very worrying when he thought about it. If he had delayed talking about it for a few days, if he had spent a few days overthinking it all, and waited until they had found their way to his door, had got to the bottom of things, had even begun to investigate properly, and then told the whole story over again, by that time, everything would have undergone a qualitative change and it would have been too late for regrets. By that time, it would not be a report, but a self-criticism; it would not be a disclosure, but a self-justification; it would not be a frank explanation, but a confession. By that time, if he spoke as he had done today, not only would Yang Cheng not have believed him, even a three-year-old child would never have believed him!

By that time, he would have been too clever for his own good and ended up destroying himself. If he was treated unjustly and slandered, so be it. With the ordinary people in their current mood of bitter hatred of corruption, no matter how meritorious his previous conduct might have been, he would still be cursed and vilified. He had never expected that he would become a corrupt faction. What was particularly terrifying was that countless people would draw completely the wrong lesson from his problem. The more people were named as model workers, advanced workers, trendsetters and heroes, the less they were to be trusted and the more likely they were to be up to their necks in corruption!

He looked at Yang Cheng in silence.

Yang Cheng looked back at him, equally silent.

Li Gaocheng knew that now was the time for him to speak if he had anything to say for himself. He slowly sat up from under his covers and, trembling slightly, stretched his hand out to Yang Cheng.

"Thank you, Secretary Yang. The truth is, I am the one who should be saying thank you. For you to talk to me in that way at a time like this is a good reason for me to be thankful to you for the rest of my life…"

Yang Cheng sat back down, clasped Li's hand and said, with

every evidence of being greatly moved: "Don't say that, Lao Li, I am embarrassed enough already. And please, I entreat you, from now on stop calling me Secretary Yang. How about just Yang Cheng? You are probably feeling that I have been keeping too many things from you over the last few days. You have been under enormous pressure, and I have been testing you and probing you while sitting on the sidelines, apparently indifferent to what happens. That's really not how a Municipal Party Committee Secretary and a team member should act, and it is very cruel. We have been working as a team for more than a year now, but, however you measure it, we have been very suspicious of each other all that time. Particularly at a crucial moment like this, I haven't reached out a hand to support you, to help you along, and that is no way for a secretary, for someone on the same team, to act. Just now I was worried that you would be angry with me, and I did not expect you to speak the way you did. Not only do I thank you from the bottom of my heart, but I think the entire Municipal Government and our entire leadership team should thank you too. I genuinely admire and draw comfort from your integrity, your conscience, from your generosity and your sincerity. Not just anyone could do what you have done, Lao Li. You have sacrificed everything for our country, for our Party and for our people. You have never abandoned your position and your beliefs, and that is no easy thing to do. You know full well that this choice comes at a great cost, a matter of life and death even, but you haven't budged right to the end. It is as daunting as hand-to-hand bayonet fighting and facing down loaded rifles were back in the war years..."

Li Gaocheng sat there dumbfounded for a long time before finally recovering himself. Everything was so unexpected; he had had no idea Yang Cheng would say anything like that. Faced with Yang Cheng's shame and contrition, he found himself feeling the same. In truth, perhaps we all sometimes forget the simple common-sense truth that, in human society, righteousness will always win through.

"I understood the whole situation before you were halfway through describing it, Lao Li," Yang Cheng continued with a pained certainty that also carried a tinge of indignation. "Their sole aim is to threaten you and to hit out in retaliation. At the very least they hope to muddy the waters, distract people, give the impression to outsiders that you are fighting a dirty war. They want to make you look bad in the eyes of the top-level leadership and thus make the problem go away. They can make us lose face as failures, and portray themselves as innocent victims. Recently, Lao Li, it has become more and more clear to me that the enemy inside the camp is indeed a hundred times more dangerous and frightening than the enemy outside! The reason why it is so difficult for us to fight corruption is because the corrupt people are all around us. They are leaders themselves, they even hold positions in charge of the fight against corruption, and directly control that fight. With the gun in their own hands, they are never going to turn it on themselves. Firstly, you can't oppose them, secondly, they will never let you oppose them, and thirdly, as soon as they see someone who intends to oppose them, they immediately turn their guns on him. You were just about to investigate the problems at Zhongyang Textiles, and someone immediately reported you to the Provincial Committee, the Municipal Committee and the Discipline Commission. They are the ones who are plundering the wealth of the country and the people, eating up our national strength without a care in the world, trampling on the image of the Party in a gross and arbitrary manner, and yet they all represent the Party, the nation and the people. How hateful and heartbreaking that is!

"Faced with people like them, Lao Li, I often think that if the government officials of a country have no checks and balances at the top and no supervision at the bottom, and only know how to corrupt, pervert, extort and plunder, they threaten not only the livelihood of the people but also their very existence. They will not only fail to maintain the existing means of production for society, they will also squander all the wealth accumulated by society! If all the new social functions and positive factors born out of reform and opening up are wiped out, and if these people form a bureaucratic group that hinders the development of our country and causes our society to lag behind over the long term, then what use are they to society? What use are they to the nation? What are they to the great mass of ordinary people? Would they not be doomed to be scorned and spat upon for generations to come, and eventually buried in the dust of history?"

Looking at Yang Cheng's face, which shone with excitement under the lights, Li Gaocheng could not help but be inspired. It was the first time in a long time that he had seen Yang Cheng look so impassioned and defiant. Perhaps the Yang Cheng in front of him now was the real Yang Cheng, and the previous one was another Yang Cheng altogether. When he appeared as secretary, he was so calm, steady and wise. But when he showed his true colours, he was so angry and vengeful. He continued, his teeth gritted as he contemplated the shocking corruption that was taking place before his eyes:

"It often strikes me that leaders at our level are already top-level officials in the national government and top-level cadres of the ruling party. Having attained that kind of status, be it in the Party or in the government, you have already been entrusted with the power of the Party and the survival of the nation. The Party's existence is your existence. The prosperity of the Party's cause, its honour and disgrace, its very survival, may be said to be closely related to your own, you live and you die together. In all honesty, we already have a lot of privileges compared to ordinary people! For us personally, there are no worries about food, clothing or housing. We have a car when we go out, we are not charged for medical treatment, and we have many special provisions for official and non-official purposes. However, some of our cadres, including some senior Party cadres, not only do not feel the slightest guilt or anxiety, but rather become increasingly disgruntled and dissatisfied. They seek to surround themselves with luxury everywhere and in everything; they compare themselves with those money-bag foreign businessmen; they have to outdo everyone. If they are an official, they want to be a businessman too, and if they have power, they want money as well. Their greed and selfishness mean that they can wield more and more power and gather more and more money. Why don't they understand that if the Party is eventually corrupted and destroyed by them, there will be nowhere left for them? How could they survive in today's society? What will be waiting for them when that time comes? They do not have any sense of fear or ability to recognise a crisis. Lao Li, I really don't understand how a political party such as ours can give birth to such parasites in its own body! Is it that we are too weak to prevent diseases, and fight them when we catch them, or do we simply not have the ability to do so? What is the best way to deal with all this? What should we do? Truly, what should we do?"

Yang Cheng's words to this point were half accusation, half

outpouring of pent-up emotion. Underneath his obvious resentment, there seemed to be an undertone of helplessness. The sight of him affected Li Gaocheng very deeply. Could it be that the inexpressible pain and impotent grief and anger in Yang Cheng's heart were even greater than his own? Could it be that Yang Cheng understood even more clearly than him that faced with a leadership cadre like Yan Zhen, sometimes there was nothing to be done? You know full well that he is an out-and-out bad guy, an enemy, but your hands are tied, and you are helpless against him. Not only can you not move an inch against him, you actually have to bend the knee and take orders from him. Even words such as he had just spoken with such righteous anger could not be repeated in public; they could not be repeated at all.

This was perhaps the saddest thing that could happen to a leadership cadre who was full of loyalty to his country and to the people.

In a society where it is more difficult, onerous and painful to make the wrong choice than the right one, to make the virtuous choice rather than the evil one, to make the choice that benefits the many rather than just you, perhaps that society itself is too dangerous and burdensome.

Yang Cheng's feelings of grief and helplessness were not without foundation.

He went on to tell Li Gaocheng a few things that took him completely unawares. First, the Municipal Public Security Bureau investigation that Li Gaocheng had ordered into the Green Apple Entertainment City had been terminated because both the Municipal Public Security Bureau and the Provincial Public Security Department had simultaneously received notice that the matter had been taken over by the Discipline Inspection Commission and the Judicial and Legal Departments and they were required to withdraw immediately.

Second, the relevant senior departments had also ordered the cancellation of the surprise inspection of the Chang Long Garment and Textile Factory. The reason given was that the Chang Long Factory belonged to the groundbreaking exploratory tertiary sector of industry and was also in the process of negotiating with foreign businesses and was preparing to enter into joint venture projects with such businesses. The surprise inspection was inappropriate, as it was detrimental to the image of the country, the province and the city, and not conducive to the deepening of the reform of enterprise, so it had to be stopped immediately. If it was considered that there was a genuine problem, it should be verified under the unified organisation and deployment of the Provincial Party Committee. All in all, the matter should be handled appropriately in the light of the overall situation.

Third, the working group that was conducting financial inspections at Zhongyang Textiles had also recently been frequently questioned and criticised by the leadership. They believed that some of the working group's practices had gone beyond the acceptable scope of financial inspections. Some members of the working group had even ignored the requirements of social stability and intentionally expanded and intensified the conflict between the workers and the company cadres. This had had some very irresponsible side effects and negative impacts. Because of this, in view of the approaching Spring Festival, and considering the overriding need for stability, the working group was to complete the financial audit work as soon as possible. Any problems found would be reported to the Provincial Year-End Financial Inspection and Guidance Office for handling. As long as the problems remained unconfirmed, no one was allowed to spread them openly or discuss them privately. If anyone violated that condition, they would be held entirely responsible for any consequences.

Fourth, Yan Zhen, Executive Deputy Secretary of the Provincial Party Committee, said at a recent political and legal meeting that the current petitions and complaints by some enterprises should be properly handled with the aim of finding a prudent solution to the problem. This meant accepting what is reasonable, not giving in to what is unreasonable, and, above all, abiding by principles and not betraying them. In general, the principal tools used for workers and cadres submitting petitions should be advice and persuasion. It was necessary to act with understanding but also to be clear about what was reasonable. Some actions by the masses might seem reasonable, but in fact were illegal. Equally, some of the problems with the cadres might seem unreasonable but were completely legal. This was very important, and it was essential to give the masses a clear explanation of the relationship between reasonableness and legality. It was also necessary to strive to nip unstable factors in the bud. If someone wanted to take the opportunity deliberately to exacerbate the situation, to cater to the abnormal ideological motives of some people, or to achieve their own ulterior motives, that kind of behaviour would be very dangerous, and the Party and the government should never let it go unchallenged. If such things were ignored and allowed to develop, those responsible would be strictly investigated and severely dealt with.

Fifth, almost a third of the members of the team investigating Zhongyang Textiles had taken either sick leave or personal leave. Ever since what Yan Zhen had said at the political and legal meeting had been disseminated, the work of the investigation team had effectively ground to a halt. What was particularly serious was that several members of the team, including some of the cadres, had already completely betrayed their proper responsibilities and were in the pockets of the oppressors...

Li Gaocheng stared at Yang Cheng in a daze, stunned into a long silence.

How can the decision to terminate the investigation of the Green Apple Entertainment City be taken without going through the Municipal Party Committee and the Municipal Government? Could it be that subordinates had the right to go over the heads of their superiors, but that under no circumstances could superiors bypass their subordinates? In fact, Li Gaocheng was very clear that this move represented a protective measure or, at least, an intention to protect the interests of the parties involved. In fact, fundamentally speaking, it was another warning and threat aimed at him by Yan Zhen: those who obey me prosper, those who oppose me perish. This is a place run by your brother-in-law and your nephew. From my position, I can totally protect you, but I can also destroy you just as completely!

As for the statement about the Chang Long Garment and Textile Factory, how absurd and dictatorial that was. Was it then the case that a "groundbreaking and exploratory enterprise" could violate the law and act indiscriminately? If that was the case, wasn't it just carte blanche for any company or enterprise to act recklessly and break the law? The investigation must be stopped just because the company was in negotiations with foreign businesses and it would otherwise damage the image of the country, the province and the city. Wasn't that even more bizarre? When you considered the investigation next to the horrific conditions for the workers, which was more detrimental to the image of the country, the province and the city?

It was the decision of the Standing Committee of the Municipal Party Committee to send the working party into the Zhongyang Textile Group. Which level of leadership could freely question and criticise that decision? Was it a criticism of the Municipal Party Committee and the Municipal Government, or of the working group? In this situation, who had the power to order the working group to close its investigation as soon as possible? In particular, how was it that the results of a specially established investigation team, moreover one that had been sent in by the Municipal Party Committee and the Municipal Government, should be sent to the Provincial Year-End Financial Inspection and Guidance Office? Wasn't this statement and the behaviour it represented just a big joke? Wasn't it completely reckless?

How could a provincial leader bring up the subject of commercial enterprises at a political and legal meeting? Even if there was a connection, how could he then print out his speech and distribute it across all levels of government? Even from the perspective of stability, who was it who was intentionally creating instability, deliberately exacerbating the situation, and deliberately intensifying social conflicts? Moreover, following the logic, his words were also creating new social contradictions, under which the people were acting reasonably but not legally, and the leaders were acting legally but not reasonably.

Everyone knew what was going on, and everyone could understand the reason behind it, but he still couldn't come up with a better, more effective and more powerful way to counter it, so he couldn't do anything about it.

Just look at the high-sounding and upright words they used to disguise their ugliness, and how frank and righteous their tone was.

He couldn't find any fault or flaw in the actual meaning of what they had said. Everything was for the greater good, everything was for reform, everything was subordinate to stability, everything was subordinate to the interests of the Party and the state. Yan Zhen was a senior Party cadre, so he need have no qualms about speaking on behalf of the Party.

The two men sat face to face for a long time as if there was nothing more they could say. It was only when Yang Cheng was leaving that he said softly but very forcefully: "Lao Li, this is just the beginning, but we have certainly won the first round. As far as the problem of the three hundred thousand yuan goes, as the Municipal Party Secretary, I can testify that you told me about it before the complaint was made to the Municipal Party Committee. Even if they have any recordings or other evidence, they won't get past me."

"Yang Cheng, I pledge on my Party and personal honour that I simply do not believe they have any recordings or other evidence. If I have done anything that goes against my conscience on the issue of the three hundred thousand yuan, then I am willing to accept public trial in the court of the three million people of this city!"

"Lao Li, as a Municipal Party Secretary, I ask you never to talk like that again. You and I are both the same kind of person, and we both feel things deeply. In a word, I believe in you, so please, you too should believe in me."

Once again, they clasped hands firmly.

At this moment, Li Gaocheng was clear about one undeniable fact: if Yang Cheng really testified as he had said, it would mean that he would take on himself all the responsibility, all the pressure, all the attention, and all the risks that came from Yan Zhen and the group of people around him. He would never look back, even if it meant dying a horrible death.

CHAPTER THIRTY-SIX

EARLY THE NEXT DAY, under arrangements made by Yang Cheng, Li Gaocheng was moved to a quiet comfortable place to convalesce. A week later, he was fully recovered.

His sudden reappearance in the mayor's office caused many people considerable surprise. Some had thought that he would be conveniently "sick" for a long time and that he would not return until things had calmed down and all was well again. Even if he didn't do that, he would surely never make his return in these extraordinary times. Besides, he was genuinely ill, and everyone knew it. It was a golden opportunity, especially at such a time. Surely no one would pass up on it so easily!

Certainly, not many people expected him back in the office at that particular time.

Li Gaocheng's mood seemed to have made a complete turn-around and, for the first time in many years, he felt remarkably calm and relaxed at work. Apart from a few people who saw him and went over to say hello, hardly anyone came to him to action anything or report on anything. Other than the pile of materials and documents waiting for his approval on the table, there was almost nothing urgent to be done.

But Li Gaocheng knew very well exactly what was going on in the Municipal Government those days.

On the day Li Gaocheng was discharged, Yang Cheng convened

an emergency meeting of the Municipal Committee Standing Committee. There was only one issue on the agenda, and that was how to deal with the three hundred thousand yuan bribe that Li Gao had handed in. Everything went as Yang Cheng expected, and the Standing Committee did not make any immediate resolution. Nonetheless, the real purpose of the meeting had been successfully achieved. Yang Cheng's move was to let everyone at the level of the Standing Committee of the Municipal Party Committee know what was going on: there was a company that secretly offered the mayor bribes, one of which amounted to three hundred thousand yuan! And Mayor Li Gaocheng had already handed over the three hundred thousand yuan to Yang Cheng, the secretary of the Municipal Party Committee, before he fell ill.

It was like a massive thunderclap, which shook both the Municipal Party Committee and the Municipal Government. Despite Yang Cheng's repeated exhortations that, before the matter was thoroughly investigated, it was to remain top secret within the Party, and it was strictly forbidden for anyone to spread it around outside, in the end, the news spread like wildfire, and soon everyone in society knew about it, and it was the talk of an amazed city. It was common knowledge among the people that the bribe was offered by Yan Zhen's brother-in-law and other relatives, and that it was refused by Mayor Li Gaocheng. Of course, there were other versions, both favourable to Li Gaocheng and against him.

The one thing that made Li Gaocheng feel the plan was working was that, so far, he wasn't aware of anyone sticking their oar in or making a song and dance about the affair. Maybe the other party was waiting for a suitable time and for further developments; maybe they were waiting for Li Gaocheng to reappear, to see what he did next; maybe they had been temporarily stunned by this move and the whole lot of them had been thrown into confusion and didn't yet know how to respond.

But Li Gaocheng and Yang Cheng were not left in peace for very long, because the other side were, in fact, already mounting an all-out offensive, attacking fiercely from every direction. Even the action the two of them had taken over the three hundred thousand yuan was a purely defensive tactic they had employed when under attack, and the truth was that they were constantly in protective, defensive mode, and didn't have a single offensive move. So, the problem they were faced with was how to eliminate all these negative factors so that they could carry out their pre-determined plan without disruption.

In the end, he was the one trying to deal with the problem, trying to get to the heart of it, but before he knew it, everyone's fingers were suddenly pointing at him, and there were even signs that people were beginning to look on him as both the origin and the heart of the problem. Wasn't he the one investigating corruption at Zhongyang Textiles? And didn't that investigation lead to him? Didn't the origins of that corruption lie in him? Wasn't he the most corrupt element at the heart of the problems with Zhongyang Textiles?

It wasn't just him who had problems, his wife did too and so did his subordinates. It was just as his wife had said – by investigating Zhongyang Textiles, he was investigating himself.

Wasn't that exactly what was happening?

Therefore, his priority was not how to defend himself, but how to find a way to achieve his established goal as soon as possible. In other words, to find a way to solve the issue of Zhongyang Textiles once and for all. Having made his choice, the next step was to see it carried out without delay. If he made a choice but failed to achieve his goal for whatever reason and abandoned it halfway through, or if he allowed others to take advantage of his choice, leading to its complete failure, then that choice would harm not only himself but others too! It would prove that his choice had no validity to start with!

The ring of a telephone pulled him back to reality. It was Yang Cheng's voice at the other end: "I asked my secretary to send you two documents, Lao Li. Please take a look at them as soon as possible."

Li Gaocheng was a little taken aback. He knew that, whatever else, these were not going to be run-of-the-mill documents.

When he received the documents, he did indeed find himself staring at them dumbstruck for a long time.

One was entitled "Report of the investigation into the economic problems at Zhongyang Textiles" and the other "Accepting a bribe or refusing it: the truth behind the enormous sum of three hundred thousand yuan".

The two documents were contained in two briefcases. The investigation report was very thick, and the other document was only a few pages, but had an audio tape attached.

To Li Gaocheng's surprise, both documents already carried the comments of the leadership. On the investigation report, Yan Zhen had commented: "This investigation report has been read in detail, and in general it is found to be rigorous, thorough, realistic, and very persuasive. Excellent. The solution to the problems at Zhongyang Textiles should be based on this."

The comment on the other document was written by the Provincial Party Committee Secretary Wan Yongnian: "This material has been read, and the recording has been listened to, both are shocking. Comrade Yang Cheng, please organise a small-scale investigation as quickly as possible and report the results to me as soon as possible. Additionally, if both their health permits, Comrade Yang Cheng and Comrade Li Gaocheng are to come to my office as soon as possible to discuss this."

Li Gaocheng didn't have to read the two documents to know what was in them, but the little cassette tape gave him goosebumps of alarm.

This tape had kept him on tenterhooks for several days and disturbed his sleep. He spent most of his time wondering what kind of tape it could be. What would it say? Would it be his words or someone else's? If they were his, where had it been recorded? If it wasn't him, who could it be? In the past few days, he went over his interactions with those people in recent years, and he couldn't recall anything wrong. The fact was, he hadn't had any real dealings with them, and they had hardly even talked to each other before they came to his house. How could this tape appear as evidence all of a sudden?

After much deliberation, there was only one occasion he was a little worried about: the night they actually brought the money to his house!

All he remembered about it was that it was a very busy and chaotic evening, and that, having just seen off one group of people who were waiting at his door, he had found another large group waiting inside. He couldn't even remember how many people he had met in the course of the day. By the time he got home, he was so exhausted that he couldn't recall anything that had been said, and the worst part of it was that he didn't even know, and hadn't indeed considered before, whether they had handed over the three hundred thousand yuan to his wife, Wu Aizhen, before he got home.

The question was, what did he say at the time? And could those words be used as evidence that he was asking for a bribe?

If the tape did come from that night, it would certainly complicate the situation. For, even if he had no knowledge of the three hundred thousand yuan, it was still possible that his words could have been recorded and used as evidence.

That was a terrifying thought, quite terrifying. It meant that, when they came to his house, it was already all planned out: they had lots of potential witnesses and they secretly recorded it all.

It seemed that they had already made their move at that point. He had only just begun to suspect them, but they had already turned him into the enemy. And they did it so quickly, so ruthlessly, so deviously, so viciously, that it took him completely unawares. There seemed to be only one explanation for all that, and that was that they knew everything he was doing at the time. In other words, by that time or even earlier, they already had him in their hands.

He remained frozen for a moment, then quickly asked for a tape recorder, told his secretary Wu Xingang that he would not be seeing anyone for a while, then locked himself in his office and listened tensely to the tape.

His worst fears were realised! The recording was of the events at his house that night.

There was a lot of background noise, but the tape was quite clear.

First came the sound of confused footsteps, immediately followed by a woman's voice calling out in warm and enthusiastic greeting: "Ah! It's you lot! I said my left eye had been twitching a lot and this must be why![1] Come in here at once, Xiao Lian! Make some tea!"

Xiao Lian was the family nanny.

The words were spoken in a very relaxed and familiar manner, giving the immediate impression that the relationships were very close. This impression was reinforced by the use of the old saying for good fortune: "My left eye has been twitching."

This was followed by a burst of greetings for Director Wu mixed in with the sound of his wife's happy, self-satisfied laughter.

Then there was the sound of people sitting down, chatting, pouring tea, drinking tea, as though in mid-discussion of something. Next, came something that took Li Gaocheng by surprise and terrified him.

There was the sound of people standing up and a flustered shout, followed by a warm and respectful greeting: "...Mayor Li!"

"Hello, Mayor Li!"

"Hello, Mayor Li!"

"Mayor Li, we know how busy you must be, and that it is already very late, and here we are disturbing you! I'm so sorry..."

"We originally wanted to visit you in your office, Mayor Li, but then we thought about it and about how many people you have coming to see you during the day, and how noisy the office is, we didn't think we'd be able to talk properly, so we decided it would be more convenient to visit you at home..."

This froze Li Gaocheng to the spot.

The cumulative effect of these snippets of recording was to give the distinct impression that Li Gaocheng had come out of an inner room and that he had made it clear to them in advance that he wanted to see them.

Li Gaocheng's memory of the occasion suddenly seemed to be completely restored, and there could be no doubt that cunning editing had been used to create a totally fraudulent recording. The tape had quite obviously been cobbled together with the sole intention of discrediting him.

It was already very late when he got back that night, and he later heard the nanny, Xiao Lian, say that the others had arrived at about 10 o'clock and had been sitting waiting in his home for almost two hours. However, when the two sections of the recording were spliced together, it gave people the impression that he and his wife were already together in the house and had warmly greeted their visitors. Particularly relevant was the part of the conversation where it was made clear that the office was too busy and full of people coming and going to discuss these matters there, and that was why they had come to see him so late and at home.

It was quite heart-stopping!

The same trick was subsequently repeated, and it was more than good enough to leave anyone who was not party to the ploy open-mouthed in astonishment.

"It's very late, Mayor Li, and we don't want to inconvenience you any longer than we have to, so we'll get straight down to business..."

These words should have been spoken by Yan Zhen's brother-in-law, Chao Wanshan, but they had been processed somehow so it no longer sounded like him. They had actually been said to Li Gaocheng when the group was about to leave, but they had now been put in front of something that had been said earlier: "...bring that case over here, Director Zhang." There was the sound of footsteps and then of an attaché case being opened. "...there are three hundred thousand yuan in here, please don't think anything of it, it's nothing these days..."

"Whose idea is this? ...How will you explain it if something happens?" That was his wife's voice, sounding extraordinarily calm and clearly with no real intention of rejecting the money.

"It has been ratified by the company, and, although Mayor Li is not actually named, he is a legitimate director of the company. The three hundred thousand yuan is completely justified. I hope Mayor Li will not think it is too little. The main reason is that the company only started up in the past two years, and the need for liquid funds was very great. There was nothing to be done about it, otherwise we would have sent this over sooner. I also need to make it clear that this is only your share from the year before last year. Last year's and this year's are definitely going to be more than this. When the accounts are finalised at the end of the year, as long as the situation allows, you can rest assured that we will make those two years' payments as soon as possible. Mayor Li has helped our company so much, it wouldn't still exist without him. We are a private company, so no one checks up on us. Even if they did, they wouldn't find any mention of Mayor Li..."

Following this, there was a bit of recording from when Li Gaocheng was actually present:

"...I've never been of any help. How can you do this?"

"You mustn't say that, Mayor Li, or we will lose face... Without your timely instructions and support, a company like ours would never have been approved so quickly. Everyone knows this. Director Wu, in particular, has also pulled a lot of strings for us..."

Next, it was his wife's voice again: "Ai! By the sound of what you are saying, it looks like we are only in this for the money. If you were to say that publicly, you really would be selling us down the river!"

"We would never, ever dare to say anything like that, Director Wu! If it came down to it, we would go through fire and flood, suffer the death of a thousand cuts and have our bodies trampled into tiny pieces to protect Director Wu and Mayor Li!"

"Then you are all holy martyrs!"

This was followed by a great roar of laughter.

And then there was another edit to the time when he was there.

"We are very grateful to you, Mayor Li. As long as we have your support, we feel safe and protected. Everyone who has come to your house today represents the backbone and principal business personnel of the company. Except for a few people who were otherwise occupied, everyone who could come has come. Firstly, everyone just wants to meet you, and secondly, we want to thank you in person. As for the specific situation of the company's revenue this year, we have discussed it in detail with Director Wu. Due to time constraints, we will not repeat it all now. I think that's everything, Mayor Li. If you don't have any other orders for us, we will take our leave now."

"Well, if there is anything else you need to talk to me about, come to my office tomorrow. It's getting really late now. Let's stop here, so you are not further inconvenienced."

Then there were more confused sounds of people saying goodbye and leaving. His wife's voice was particularly prominent and enthusiastic.

That was where the recording ended.

Li Gaocheng's eyes went blank after he had listened to it, and his whole body trembled.

A wave of unspeakable fear hit him, leaving him feeling suffocated and powerless.

How shameless and despicable! How lowdown and nasty! They were a bunch of poisonous scoundrels!

Wolf-hearted rogues! A real bunch of gangsters!

So ruthless, so poisonous, so black-hearted!

He hadn't thought there had been anything going on over the last few days and he certainly hadn't expected a sudden move like this.

He couldn't believe they would do such a thing.

At the time, they had quite clearly been on the receiving end of a series of severe reprimands and rejections, but the editing had turned the whole thing into evidence of him asking for bribes and accepting bribes.

They had thought it up and gone ahead and done it!

For a while, Li Gaocheng simply could not calm himself down.

What to do? What to do? Faced with this bunch of gangsters, faced with this shameless and despicable material and so-called "evidence", what should he do? Just at this moment, what could he do?

Small as it was, this little cassette tape was like an all-ensnaring net, tangling him at every turn. It was like a thunderbolt from heaven that could shatter him in an instant.

Even if he had ten thousand mouths defending him, could he explain away what was on that tape? Could he ever be clean again?

He knew all the things on the tape were lies and fake, but who was going to believe him? What better, stronger, more powerful evidence could he come up with that would prove the tape was a fraud and full of lies?

Did he have such evidence? Could he find such evidence?

In the midst of his stupefied daze, he could only think of one person: his wife.

In normal times, if their relationship was still the same as it had been before, perhaps she might have thought of a way out...

No, no she couldn't! People were now so confused about him, what could she do? Even if she would still stand by his side like in the past, she would be totally helpless. What was more, she was also among the people his enemies were after. When defending himself, wasn't he also defending her? What was the use? They were husband and wife, weren't they? Everyone would know that anything she said had no legal standing.

So, who was there who could clear his name? No one! Absolutely no one!

This little, manipulated tape could eat him alive!

Then the telephone rang.

Li Gaocheng picked it up without thinking, then found he couldn't remember what to say.

"Hello! Who's there? Hello!" The voice at the other end got louder and louder.

After a while, he seemed to wake up from the depths of his angry grief and despair, and he realised it was Yang Cheng.

"...Hello, Yang Cheng, this is Gaocheng here."

He tried his best to make his voice sound casual. Nonetheless, Yang Cheng seemed to have detected there was something wrong, and his words were clearly meant to encourage him:

"You will have read those two pieces of evidence, Lao Li!" Yang Cheng's voice was strong and resolute. "First off, I need to tell you that I have already got the Public Security Office and the Security Bureau to conduct secret tests on that tape, and there is no doubt that it has been manipulated. That is to say, the only thing the tape can be used to prove is that it has been faked, nothing else. So don't be fooled by it, let alone be concerned that it might cause you any damage. Besides, going right back to basics, even if it can't be proved that it is forged or deceitful, according to the law, this kind of recording made without notifying the person being recorded cannot be used as real evidence. Furthermore, it is illegal in itself and a violation of human rights. So from this point of view alone, there is absolutely no need to worry about it. All they are trying to do at the moment, Lao Li, is throw up smokescreens to distract people's attention, to disrupt your position, so that you will have to be constantly on guard. They want to tire you out running around defending yourself, so you are too busy to cope and too scared to think about how to clear yourself. That way they will achieve their real purpose: to turn defence into attack, to turn your own knife onto yourself, to overwhelm you so that they can turn defeat into victory and make their escape. I have to tell you a difficult truth, Lao Li. Even if we can't clear ourselves at the moment, we can't just sit still and wait for others to do it for us. Our only effective strategy is to cut a bloody path out of the siege. We have to attack, attack, attack! Do you understand? Only when we uncover the real culprits, when we pull off their masks, will they stop attacking. Their true form and colours will be revealed in the course of their self-destruction. We have to find a way to hit them where they least expect it! We have to make them leap with pain! Then, finally, we pound them into unconsciousness!"

"I understand, Yang Cheng. Thank you!" Li Gaocheng seemed to leap free from the swamp of confusion that had been sucking him down, as understanding suddenly dawned. At the same time, he couldn't help feeling like a little child, simple to the point of stupidity. What did he think he was doing? People had laid a complaint against him that was already on the desk of the secretary of the Provincial Party Committee! Things had gone that far and there he was still leaping around just trying to work out how to free himself. The whole affair was neatly wrapped up and in someone else's pocket. He'd been served up and swallowed whole, and all he was thinking about was clearing his own name. "Don't worry, I know what I have to do!" He suddenly felt supremely confident.

"I don't know if you have read that inspection report yet, Lao Li, but from anyone's point of view, it is vital stuff. The content is really important, and if we don't take measures quickly, everything we've done may prove to be in vain and we'll be finished." Yang Cheng was speaking very earnestly and urgently. "To tell the truth, I was afraid of a move like this when I instructed the inspection team. That's why I didn't dare agree to it including anyone from the Public Procuratorate and Law Department. If anyone from the Public Procuratorate had gone in and come up with a result like that, then our goose would have been well and truly cooked and there would have been no getting back from it, however hard we tried."

"I haven't had a chance to read it yet. I've only just listened to the tape..." Li Gaocheng admitted.

"To hell with the tape! To tell you the truth, Lao Li, I had that tape with me here for two or three days, but I was afraid it would upset you, so I didn't let you listen to it. If I thought it was really a problem, do you think I would have kept it from you? No matter what, you've still got me to rely on! As far as the three hundred thousand yuan goes, that tape is no fucking use at all! It's a piece of crap! So get on with it and read that report. The Provincial Committee is going to hold another meeting of the Standing Committee, and I'm going to raise the issue there if I get the opportunity. I also want to discuss it with Secretary Wan and Provincial Governor Wei. Let's put our heads together after the meeting and discuss what to do."

With that, Yang Cheng didn't ask Li Gaocheng anything more, but just hung up the telephone.

That was the first time in their long acquaintance that Li had heard Yang curse or swear. He could just imagine how Yang Cheng looked when he swore.

Yang Cheng was clearly really pissed off, just as he himself had been. But Yang Cheng's behaviour when he was angry was very different from his own. Yang Cheng's instinct was to go into full-on attack mode. But when he, Li, got angry, he became very defensive. Even now, when he knew Yang Cheng was supporting him and when he knew what he had to do, he really didn't feel that the pressure on him had eased very much at all.

He suddenly felt very inferior to Yang Cheng.

If all this had been happening to Yang Cheng, how would things have worked out then?

Li Gaocheng took almost two hours to go through the report. He understood why Yang Cheng was so angry and why he took the material so seriously.

Although the whole document was three or four hundred pages thick, if you excluded the photocopied documents and accounts, the report itself was no more than twenty pages long and could be summarised in a couple of sentences. Just like the tape, this so-called report was nothing more than a piece of clumsy, petty-minded perjury and a naked, unadorned attempt to shift the burden of guilt. It might look like an investigation report, but it was, in fact, a carefully targeted rebuttal statement. The first target was the ten thousand-signature petition and the second was the whistle-blowing material from Zhongyang Textiles' Xinchao Co. Ltd. Of course, it made it sound as though the whole case was cut and dried.

According to some people at Zhongyang Textiles, the company had serious economic problems in areas such as buying cotton, waste products, reselling old machinery, excessive hospitality, management style, and the tertiary enterprise, Xinchao Co. Ltd, and so on.

The report concluded that apart from a small number of the problems identified, which were genuine and had already been investigated and dealt with by the company, most of them were based on rumours and hearsay, with little evidence or no evidence at all. Because it had shut down production, the company had not been able to pay wages for nearly a year, so the dissatisfaction of the workers was completely understandable. But emotion cannot replace reason, dissatisfaction cannot replace the law. There was no problem with corruption, and the loss of production could not be equated to breaking the law.

On the issue of buying cotton for example, it was certain that the reports of problems were without foundation... upon investigation... the accounts were clear, all the invoices and entries were in full compliance with the financial rules and regulations, and there was no irregularity... buying cotton in the South was a last resort, under the pressure of inherent conditions, the pressure of product contracts, the pressure of financial operations, particularly the consideration that if the funds were not spent before the end of the year, the bank was likely to freeze them in accordance with relevant regulations... taking into account all aspects of the situation, it was completely understandable for the management of Zhongyang Textiles to make an urgent purchase of cotton... the price paid for the cotton by Zhongyang Textiles was quite reasonable and in accordance with general cotton prices at the time... it was classed as of lower-middle quality. It benefitted Zhongyang Textiles at the time to be able to buy cotton of that quality at that price. It should be noted that the management of Zhongyang Textiles had put in a lot of work in this regard.

It was reported by some people that the management of Zhongyang Textiles had reported the price they paid for first- and second-grade cotton but had actually bought fourth- to fifth-grade cotton, or even fifth- to sixth-grade... this had been thoroughly investigated.

Investigation showed that the allegations did not match the facts... It was true that some of the cotton was of poor quality but that was mainly due to the fact it was not possible to check all the bales individually, so some bales of low-quality cotton slipped through inspection. However, this was a very rare occurrence; all claims for compensation were actively pursued and compensation was generally built into the next purchase... claims that poor quality cotton was intentionally purchased with secret kickbacks were irresponsible and unsubstantiated.

In the matter of the disposal of waste material and the resale of machinery, there was a strong reaction among workers and cadres to the reporting by some elements at Zhongyang Textiles that the management cadres at the company were taking advantage of the state loan to carry out technical improvement projects. They dismantled the old machines and sold them as scrap, which was then bought back in at the price of new machines. A lot of money was generated by this dishonest practice.

Upon investigation... found to be pure hearsay... lack of evidence... all accounts for the purchase of new machinery, their sources and payments... completely clear, with supporting evidence and reliable accounts... the circumstances of all scrap recycling... immediate evidence of accurate accounts... no loopholes or areas of suspicion were found.

It was reported that the management cadres at Zhongyang Textiles spent so much money on lavish food and drink on a daily basis that in just a few short years they spent the equivalent of the cost of a whole new factory. Some of them bought luxury cars, luxury houses, and other luxury goods just as they pleased.

Upon investigation... measures taken by the management of Zhongyang Textiles as a whole... efficient and effective. However, it was also true that some managers and mid-level cadres were not effective in this area and they were not strict in their controls... As a state-owned enterprise, it was common practice to try to dominate the market in the context of the fierce competition within the industry, so, in a sense, such behaviour was inevitable... In the past few years, Zhongyang Textiles had dealt severely with dozens of cadres in this respect, including sixteen at department level and two at senior level... Zhongyang Textiles had been comparatively effective in this area.

It was reported that the management of Zhongyang Textiles had misappropriated and forcibly seized a large amount of funds loaned to the company by the state for the development of the tertiary sector. Particularly over the past few years, the accounts of the tertiary sector were in disarray and demonstrated serious problems. Some managers had taken advantage of the development of the tertiary sector to turn their public duties into private interests and made huge profits. This had happened to such an extent that every cadre above the deputy department level had, without exception, received a million dollars of tertiary development capital before leaving their jobs on reaching retirement age. This made a very bad impression on the public and was one of the reasons for the repeated petitions and complaints by the workers and cadres.

Upon investigation... the management was chaotic and supervision ineffective. The problems with Zhongyang Textiles' tertiary enterprise, Xinchao Co. Ltd. were indeed very severe, especially in terms of the poor management and heavy losses. In particular, some branch companies and businesses had long existed in name only, without conducting any business... In some branch companies, even the original management team and board of directors had long since ceased to exist.

Upon investigation... there were many reasons for the current situation... conditions were not ripe, the market was not fully understood, the start-up was rushed... if an enterprise starts losing money from the first day of operation, it is inevitable that it will go bankrupt and shut down... some projects were launched entirely speculatively, believing that as long as the state has approved the project, made the loan, and launched the enterprise, it would never stand by and let the project collapse... serious losses in such circumstances were inevitable.

Upon investigation... it appeared that blind investment and rolling investment were the most basic causes of losses. For example, thirteen garment companies were established despite the fact that they were inefficient, had no target market and their products were not the least bit competitive. The market had long outstripped demand for shirt factories, but four were built at one go... of the more than one hundred enterprises, only four were marginally profitable, twelve were essentially breaking even, more than sixty were losing money, and the remaining more than forty had all ceased production and gone out of business... there was no risk awareness, and, in particular, no market awareness; the businesses were plagued by rigid thinking and a lack of any sense of responsibility; their only strategy was to wait, rely on the parent company, make demands, and keep asking... a lack of technical talents was also a major contributory factor... most of the staff taken on were a combination of the children of company personnel and workers laid off during the company restructuring. Consequently, the quality of the products was poor and there was no market for them. This inevitably resulted in serious losses and bankruptcy.

Upon investigation... such large-scale losses were indeed serious and distressing. The investment of tens of millions in state loans had supported a very large number of industrial companies with heavy debts and serious losses. The lessons to be drawn were profound and the results were thought-provoking.

It was believed that, in this regard, the company's management certainly must bear some responsibility... although the company as a whole was extremely busy and the workload very heavy, and it was also true that most of the leaders of Xinchao Co. Ltd were retired managers and cadres, and a variety of reasons made it not straightforward to manage, this did not mean they could all shirk their responsibilities...

Upon investigation... there were individual cases of reckless spending and extravagance with food and drink and examples of differing degrees of financial problems... but, overall, it was not a common problem, and definitely not as serious as described in the complaint materials, which talked of using public funds for private gain and turning large profits... the problem was there, but the conclusion could not be drawn that the whole of Xinchao Co. Ltd was the same. On the principle of basing findings on fact, it was necessary first to have a clear understanding of this matter and to come to a unified view... a loss is a loss, a liability is a liability, and losses and poor business practice cannot always be regarded as the result of corruption... therefore, the statements in the complaint were both irresponsible and unrealistic... in responding to the dissatisfaction of the majority of workers in this regard, first, it was necessary to have a correct understanding of the problem; second, correct guidance had to be established... people should be convinced by reason, presented with facts, and persuaded by patient ideological work...

No wonder Yang Cheng was cursing the way he was!

The most infuriating and incomprehensible thing was that this material had actually been written by people they had appointed. Not only were their own people going completely against what they had intended, they were actively sabotaging their defences and effectively making them slap themselves in the face.

Were these investigators simply intimidated by the power of the people involved and that was the sole reason for the current situation? That was hard to believe!

But if they let this report serve as the authoritative version of the problems at Zhongyang Textiles, and it was presented as such to the Provincial Party Committee and the Provincial Government, then that would leave them absolutely no room for manoeuvre.

But wasn't this the very material they had sent the group out to investigate? If it was material that they themselves had produced, how could they have any complaint?

Besides, everyone now thought that the reason they were trying to discover problems at Zhongyang Textiles was to take advantage of them in another way. That was why people thought they were putting so much time and effort into it and would never let up. But now, a team of several dozen cadres had put in almost twenty days of hard work and had sifted through all the material, so how could they possibly say it wasn't their doing and that there were actually problems with that same material?

Going by this report, there was nothing wrong with Zhongyang Textiles at all. The problems supposedly uncovered by the workers had turned out to be all rumours and hearsay. They were false, unfounded and even irresponsible! You could almost make the case that all these problems uncovered by the workers were actually deliberate false accusations and slander against the company management.

No wonder Yan Zhen had written his approval on the "investigation report". His complacency and arrogance spoke volumes. He was killing two birds with one stone as easy as spitting! He, Li Gaocheng, was being made to slap himself in the face and he could say nothing about it. He would lose the trust of the workers and they would think he was in league with the opposition. His enemies were covered from all sides and had it easy, but he was oppressed left and right and unable to please anyone. What was particularly concerning was that Xinchao Co. Ltd, which was the most problematic and biggest of the enterprises involved, a great black hole that had swallowed up tens of millions of yuan, a place that even the other side were wary of, had been given a clean bill of health by his own investigators!

Tens of millions of yuan in losses, yet only one minor issue of responsibility was uncovered. Tens of millions of yuan in deficit, and it was classed as a routine loss!

Tens of millions of yuan! When it was nibbled away, bit by bit, swallowed up, sneaked away, embezzled, squandered and plundered, they were able to switch off their conscience and say, with perfect equanimity, that it was all normal and legal, that it was neither an economic problem nor corrupt practice.

It was particularly distressing that, even though he firmly believed there were serious problems, this was the conclusion reached by his task force after nearly twenty days of review and investigation!

So it was fair to say that he himself had turned all these alarming financial problems into perfectly legitimate and normal losses and that he had made it easy to dismiss such a serious act of corruption as a matter of generalised responsibility.

Anyone could say to him: "You did all that! You were behind it all!"

How was he going to get out of this trap? Provincial Party Committee Secretary Wan wanted to see him, didn't he? How was he going to explain it all to him?

Just look at how lightly and airily the report said: "The company's management certainly must bear some responsibility..."; "serious losses like this are inevitable"; "this inevitably resulted in serious losses and bankruptcy"; "the problem is there, but the conclusion cannot be drawn..."; "a loss is a loss, a liability is a liability, and losses and poor business practice cannot always be regarded as caused by corruption... therefore, these statements in the complaint are both irresponsible and unrealistic".

And after all that time and trouble, what remained was the single sentence: what you workers have done is reasonable but not legal; what the management cadres have done is at least legal, even if not reasonable.

Reasonable losses. With just those two words, the loss of tens of millions of yuan was quietly written off.

What kind of corruption could be more terrifying and shocking than this?

How was he going to explain it to Secretary Wan, to the Provincial Party Committee, to the Provincial Government, to the Municipal Party Committee and to the Municipal Government?

How was he going to explain it to the tens of thousands of cadres and workers in Zhongyang Textiles? And how was he to explain it to the three million plus people in the city?

No wonder Yang Cheng was cursing the way he was.

Li Gaocheng had a splitting headache. He felt as if blood was dripping from his eyes, and the investigation report in front of him seemed to have turned into a pool of red.

Yang Cheng was right – he really had to take measures quickly; otherwise, all his efforts would be in vain, and his collapse would be total.

He looked at his watch. It was not yet half past eleven. He had to find a way of calming himself down first. Only by calming down could he sort out the problems confronting him.

He poured a glass of water and drank it slowly, as he flipped through the pile of letters on the table.

He pulled out a telegram. It was from his son, Mingming.

> Mum and Dad, school ends on 8 February (20th of the twelfth lunar month). I'm going to my classmate's house, so I might be a few days late. I have tried calling you at home and at the office, but I couldn't reach you. You are probably too busy. Please take good care of your health. See you when I get back.

He sighed. His son had always been carefree like that. He suddenly found himself missing his children terribly. His daughter had come home two months ago, but he and his son hadn't seen each other for almost six months.

Then he was momentarily stunned by the sight of a letter from his daughter.

Judging by the postmark, it was from four days ago. He felt a rare excitement, and when he opened the letter, he almost tore the paper inside.

> Dad, tell me the truth! What happened at home? What has happened to you and Mum?
>
> I want you to tell me the truth! We have eight days before term ends, so please write to me now! Explain things to me now!!!
>
> Over the last few days, I have called home and the office almost

every day. Yesterday, I called home at 2.40 in the morning, but no one answered. The nanny has tried to put me off but I could tell she was lying to me!

Dad, what has happened at home? Why doesn't Mum come home?

Why have you been away from home all day all this time? What has happened?

I want you to tell me the truth!!
WRITE TO ME NOW!!! NOW!!!!!!!!!

Li Gaocheng looked in silence at the exclamation marks his daughter Meimei had written, and he suddenly realised what kind of Spring Festival was waiting for him this year!

He put his head in his hands and found himself saying to himself: "I've got nothing to hide, so bring it all on!"

CHAPTER THIRTY-SEVEN

AT NOON, Li Gaocheng was at home having lunch with his secretary, Wu Xingang.

The food in the Municipal Government dining hall was really not bad, but he was too tired and didn't want to go over there. He had had a stay in hospital, and he was also a figure of public interest. All those people wanting to say hello would be too exhausting. He was not in the mood to show his face at the moment. It might stir up a lot of unnecessary trouble, and he needed time to think. Besides, he hadn't been back to the house for many days, and he needed to go and see what was going on.

The kids were coming home soon, and he had to find some way of getting the place tidy. When the nanny, Xiao Lian, saw he was back, she was so startled she didn't know what to say. He suddenly felt that a house without a woman was really not a home. He hadn't realised that he should have phoned ahead. His wife wasn't there, so he hadn't thought to call.

Xiao Lian was a young nanny personally chosen by his wife. She was straightforward and down-to-earth, a neat worker and had a good brain. With his wife's careful training, there could be no complaints about either her cooking or her housework. In particular, her well-cooked dishes were always fulsomely praised by all their guests. Her wife had promised her that after a period of time, she would sort out her resident's permit and her work status. So she worked hard around the house and was obedient, loyal, reliable and quiet. The house was clean and orderly, even when no one was around.

He was usually busy, and his wife was in charge, so he rarely talked to the nanny. Although there were attendants and guards, she was alone in the house most of the time, and he felt rather ashamed about it when he stopped to think.

"Are you going to invite your parents over during the Spring Festival, Xiao Lian?" Li Gaocheng asked attentively as he was eating.

"No point!" Xiao Lian said in apparent surprise. "My family is very busy this year. It's the first year since my second brother got married, and my eldest sister's partner wants to visit his new family during the holiday, so he's coming to the house to pay his New Year respects sometime in the first month. There's so much going on that, much as they'd like to, my parents can't come. They both said that I should get on with things in peace here and, as long as Mayor Li and Director Wu have a happy New Year, they will have nothing to worry about." Xiao Lian sounded very sincere.

"Have there been any phone calls over the last few days?" Li Gaocheng asked, as casually as he could manage.

"Director Wu called many times a few days ago, and she called twice the day before yesterday. She hasn't called in the last two days." Xiao Lian seemed to know what Li Gaocheng was asking, and she answered clearly and directly. "Mingming and Meimei also called. Meimei calls almost every day, and she called just now, in fact."

So, his son and daughter had called, and they certainly hadn't found anyone at home. "Anybody else?" he asked.

"Lots of people! I wrote down the important ones on the notepad next to the telephone in the reception room, and I took no notice of the ones that didn't matter." Xiao Lian gave the impression of being an excellent secretary. She spoke succinctly and with a due sense of proportion. "There's also been a lot of post. I have put the letters and telegrams on your bedside table, and the rest of the stuff I've put in the reception room. You've had a lot of visitors too, and I've put all their names on the notepad."

"Well done!" Li Gaocheng was sincere in his praise. "I know you've had more to worry about with the house so empty over the last few days."

"Mayor Li…" Xiao Lian was about to say something but stopped.

"Go on!" Li Gaocheng said, then looked at her in silence.

"Mayor Li, Meimei has been really insistent on the phone these last few days, and I haven't known what to say. Mayor Li…" Xiao Lian hesitated for a long moment, before continuing, clearly with some difficulty, "…you should go and find Director Wu and get her to come home. It's been so long already, you should tell her to come home. Every time Director Wu has phoned here, she has asked after you and told me to take good care of you. Mayor Li, no matter what has happened, I am quite sure that Director Wu is worried about you. There are lots of things she's thought of that you haven't, really there are, and there's a lot of stuff that I know too and you don't. Go and tell her to come home, Mayor Li! My mum and dad squabble a lot too, but it's all fine again when the argument's over. It's not like you. When you start arguing it's really scary…"

Li Gaocheng was vaguely aware of something more lying behind Xiao Lian's stumbling words, but he didn't enquire further and Xiao Lian didn't say anything else.

Secretary Wu passed on a piece of news as they ate.

He had learned from Provincial Governor Wei's secretary that the morning meeting of the Provincial Party Committee's Standing Committee had been very intense, and it was still going on. This time the Standing Committee's main purpose was to determine the leadership of each city, and there had been some very sharp arguments. Unexpectedly, however, Executive Deputy Governor Wang Yumin brought up the issue of the three hundred thousand yuan bribe money. He said that it was already a hot topic of gossip in society, and everybody knew about it. True or not, the government had already been humiliated. The affair certainly shouldn't be suppressed any further and must be investigated as soon as possible to establish the truth. It was important to give the public an explanation of what was going on. He also said that regardless of whether the three hundred thousand yuan was going to be used as a bribe or had been received as a bribe, it was extremely suspicious for a Communist Party mayor to have three hundred thousand yuan delivered directly to his home. If the relationship between all these people was normal and above board, if they weren't very tight with each other, what were they doing sitting in the mayor's living room? How could they plonk three hundred thousand yuan down in front of him? How could they dare have three hundred thousand all in one lump sum? As soon as the rumours became rife, and the investigation closed in, they handed the money in. But supposing it hadn't been brought to light and reported? Supposing no one ever knew about it? Wouldn't it have stayed in that house forever? Wasn't that all crystal clear and self-evident? Some people were saying the tape had been faked. Even supposing it was faked or an outright forgery, wasn't it still inexcusable and unforgivable that three hundred thousand yuan was recovered from the mayor's house? That was a considerable act of corruption in itself. So Deputy Governor Wang proposed that the investigation should be carried out immediately and rigorously, and that anyone found out should be examined down to the last detail, no matter how important his backers, how powerful he himself was, or how high an official position he held. He should be dismissed from his post if that was merited, and he should be punished by the law if that too was deserved. This kind of thing should never be condoned or tolerated!

Executive Deputy Governor Wang Yumin was a vicious, extremely individualistic member of the Standing Committee of the Provincial Party Committee, and it was not uncommon for him to speak in such tones in Standing Committee meetings. But what shocked Li Gaocheng was the content of his words and the assumptions he made. If you thought about it, that really was how things were, just as the ordinary people said: these days, even if you had money, there was no way for you to give it to whoever you wanted; the only people who could, were those with real connections and real ability! Didn't the three hundred thousand yuan prove the people were right? Deputy Governor Wang had said it was so. Your weaknesses will always find you out. If there really were no problems with him, how was it that someone had brought the huge sum of three hundred thousand yuan into his house and actually got him to accept it? Could he explain even just that one aspect? It was like a prostitute selling sex. Selling it was a crime, but what about the client? If he really was all clean and above board, would any of this have happened? This wasn't any ordinary gift, it was three hundred thousand yuan! It was more money than an ordinary worker could earn in a lifetime. Pure bribery, perverting the law, trading influence for money. Otherwise, how did it get sent to his door in the first place and why did he keep it?

Wu Xingang said that after Deputy Governor Wang finished, the Provincial Party Secretary Wan Yongnian asked, poker-faced, who had sent the three hundred thousand yuan. Yang Cheng, secretary of the Municipal Party Committee, replied that it was sent by the Te Gao Te Passenger Transportation Company, which he specifically explained was a tertiary enterprise of Zhongyang Textiles. Then Secretary Wan asked when the money was sent. Yang Cheng replied that it was on the third day after it became clear the workers at Zhongyang Textiles were going to make trouble and the second day after the Standing Committee of the Municipal Party Committee decided to send a working group to solve the problem of Zhongyang Textiles once and for all. Yang Cheng then added that it was decided that Comrade Mayor Li Gaocheng would be in charge of finding that solution.

Apparently, there was then a long silence in the meeting room, with no one saying a word. Li Gaocheng understood that Yang Cheng's two comments were of particular interest, and anyone capable of joined-up thinking would be clear about their subtext. Judging by the questions asked by Secretary Wan Yongnian, he attached a great deal of importance to this case and had given it a lot of thought.

Then Secretary Wan said that, as Yang Cheng was the secretary of the Municipal Party Committee, and the problem was in his city, he should be the first to give his views. Yang Cheng said that he agreed with Deputy Governor Wang's opinion, but personally believed that it was also part of the problem with Zhongyang Textiles and therefore the question of further investigation and punishment should be considered in that context. Why did someone send huge sums of money to the person in charge as soon as the investigation of Zhongyang Textiles started? According to Comrade Gaocheng, he was not there when the money was delivered to his house, nor did he know anything at all about it. It is very often the case that when some people fail to achieve their desired goal, they go for broke and expose everything at once, saying that it is a whistle-blowing report and that there are recordings to back it up. Wasn't that an indication clear to everyone that it was all planned in advance?

What Yang Cheng said both expressed his own views, and also, very circumspectly, refuted the views of Deputy Governor Wang.

As soon as Yang Cheng had finished, he was strongly opposed by Yan Zhen, the Executive Deputy Secretary of the Provincial Party Committee. Yan Zhen believed that, firstly, today's meeting had not been called to study this issue, and it was too early to discuss it there. Secondly, it was ill-considered and inappropriate to link the issue of three hundred thousand yuan with the issue of Zhongyang Textiles. Each problem had its own aspects, and the two could not be mixed together. Thirdly, with both the question of Zhongyang Textiles and the question of the three hundred thousand yuan, the investigation and evidence collection work had been very efficiently carried out to date. The investigation of the Zhongyang Textiles issue had just been completed, and that work had come to an end. As for the recent development of the issue with the huge sum of three hundred thousand yuan, he had discussed it in detail with Secretary Wan and Governor Wei, and it was necessary to narrow the scope of that investigation as much as possible and not cause large-scale instability, especially given the situation of the past few days. Some workers were emotionally volatile, and the security situation in some places was not very stable. If these two things were linked together under the current circumstances, wasn't it obvious that this would intensify social contradictions and affect social stability? Therefore, it was essential to focus on the overall situation and proceed from that viewpoint. He further believed that everything should continue to be done according to the established plan and no attempt should be made to broaden the scope, to put an end to the artificial intensification and worsening of social contradictions.

After listening to this, Secretary Wan said he agreed with Deputy Secretary Yan that the two matters should not be linked together for the time being, but that there should be no let-up on the issue of the three hundred thousand yuan, and that if a legal case could be opened, it should be opened as soon as possible. If not, the investigation should proceed with all speed and not be delayed on any pretext. It would be best to set up a task force as soon as possible, and he should be briefed directly every step of the way. He also believed that the matter should be left in the hands of Yan Zhen to deal with. Governor Wei Zhenguo also agreed with the opinions of Secretary Wan and Yan Zhen, and at the same time, he also specifically asked:

"Didn't we just investigate the problem of Zhongyang Textiles, and hasn't the investigation report just been submitted? Why do you want to follow up on it and reinvestigate? It is inappropriate to do so. A large enterprise with several tens of thousands of employees has undergone a long investigation, so why do you want to go back to investigate it again? The mood of the cadres and the ordinary people has just calmed down a little. If you keep irritating them like this, isn't that bound to cause problems? Besides, next year, we will focus on solving the problems of state-owned enterprises and laid-off workers. If there are any unresolved issues, we will get to work on them immediately after the New Year. It is better to leave the issue of Zhongyang Textiles to one side for the time being. Deputy Secretary Yan has reported on and discussed this matter with me and Secretary Wan many times and I now think the opinions of Secretary Wan and Deputy Secretary Yan should be allowed to prevail. I also agree with the idea of putting Deputy Secretary Yan Zhen in charge of the case of the three hundred thousand yuan, as Yan Zhen and Li Gaocheng have been superior and subordinate for many years, and Yan Zhen is familiar with Li Gaocheng and knows him well. If there are any other ideas or opinions on this, we can exchange them after the meeting."

Executive Deputy Governor Wang Yumin agreed, and Yang Cheng said nothing more. With that, the discussion concluded.

At first, Li Gaocheng was going to criticise Wu Xingang's method of obtaining such confidential information, but after hearing it, he found himself mentally absorbed in the atmosphere of the meeting, and he once again found himself deeply shocked.

How could this be?

They were actually going to let Yan Zhen take responsibility for the case! Essentially, they were appointing a corrupt official to investigate corruption, letting a criminal handle a criminal case, putting the fox in charge of the hen coup!

So, this was the end result: he wanted to investigate problems with Yan Zhen, but Yan Zhen was going to end up investigating him. He wanted to prosecute the case against Yan Zhen, but Yan Zhen was going to end up prosecuting him. Yan Zhen wasn't going to wait for Li to come after him, he was going to come after Li first.

On the Standing Committee of the Provincial Party Committee, which could decide the fate of any cadre in the province or city, Yang Cheng was pretty much a lone voice.

What had gone on at the meeting did not necessarily mean that Secretary Wan and Governor Wei were siding with Yan Zhen, and certainly did not indicate that they couldn't tell black from white or right from wrong. But, at some point, status and power do make all the difference. If he couldn't even get next to the person with the power to decide his fate, and especially as there was someone standing in the way, determined to obstruct him, it was easy to imagine what his future held. Come what may, if he matched himself against someone of Yan Zhen's status, his own influence was never going to be great enough. Yan was one of the youngest and most promising executive deputy Provincial Party Committee secretaries in the country, and the weight of anything he said was likewise always going to overcome anything Li had to say. Secretary Wan and Provincial Governor Wei had made one thing clear: Yan Zhen had already submitted many reports on this matter to them, and they had discussed it on many occasions. He examined the affair from every possible angle and what it came down to was that the lies of a villain can become the truth if they are repeated enough times, let alone if that villain is the honest and dignified Deputy Secretary of the Provincial Party Committee and doesn't need to repeat his lies even once.

He couldn't help but worry about his next move. To be honest, if a case was filed for review, it meant that you were already on shaky ground. Yan could suspend him for investigation at any time or strip him of his powers. He could quite openly say that any decision was based on the investigations of the Standing Committee of the Provincial Party Committee, not his personal wishes. In other words, he was not representing himself personally in any way but was representing the Provincial Party Committee.

He was also deeply worried about Yang Cheng's situation. It was at that point that he was once again struck by the man's upright personality and conduct.

He knew that Yang Cheng would make further moves, and he

would definitely go to Secretary Wan and Governor Wei. At this point, he, like Li himself, had nowhere else to go.

The key question now was what he should do next on his own account. Time was running out and his chances were running out too. Strive for the good and keep your thoughts on the bad, just as Yang Cheng had told him. He couldn't stay there like a sitting duck and wait for others to take control. The most effective way now is to cut a bloody path out of the siege and go all out on the attack!

Yang Cheng's antennae were much more finely tuned than his on this issue. He seemed to have known the seriousness of the situation a long time ago, which was why he was able to say the things he did to the Standing Committee.

After thinking about it for a while, he felt that come what may, he should talk to the secretary of the Provincial Party Committee and the Governor immediately. The sooner the better. Yan Zhen was more sensitive and quicker than him on this issue. The truth was, all along it was as though they had been playing chess, and although it looked as though he had always had the opening move, in fact, he had always been on the defensive and had never actually had the upper hand.

Yang Cheng had made his meaning very clear: they could no longer be beaten around and bullied like this.

But what could they do? If he was a farmer or a worker, and he was backed into a corner, he could go to the Complaints Bureau to petition, go to the Justice Department to take out a case, go to various government departments to complain, or even risk everything and go out with a bag of explosives and fight them to the death! But now he was a mayor and a very important official in the eyes of the common people, and when he was genuinely wronged, he couldn't do any of the things that the common people could do.

An open attack is easy to deal with but sneak attacks are a different matter. For now, he could only fight in the dark, not in the open. In the dark he had to rely on his wits and his courage and couldn't fight with real swords and spears as he could in the open. His enemies, on the other hand, were free to act in the open. Everything they said seemed open and honest and everything they did looked to be the same. People were doing things that were almost too bad to be true, but all the time they were using such righteous language and legitimate power to fight him and drive him into his grave. Good people could not act openly, but the bad guys had no such constraints. Those who were enacting justice and serving the country faithfully could not do so out in the open, but the wrong-doers could openly do whatever they wanted with total impunity! For a leader this was perhaps the ultimate tragedy.

CHAPTER THIRTY-EIGHT

LI GAOCHENG ATE a few desultory mouthfuls of food, but really had no appetite. After he had seen Wu Xingang off, he sat by himself in the living room and began to flip through the notebook beside the telephone.

There certainly had been a lot of calls.

His daughter Meimei had called the most, almost every day. One day she had called twelve times, and the nanny Xiao Lian had made a clear note of each, recording the time, the content and the phone number for a callback. The second most frequent number was his wife's, which he recognised very well, and she too always left a number for a callback.

Seeing this, he suddenly realised his daughter must have been in touch with his wife too. What had his wife said to her? Even if she hadn't told her anything, his daughter must surely have picked up on something; otherwise, why would she have used so many exclamation marks in her letter?

There were also a lot of calls from city leaders. The secretary to Provincial Party Committee Secretary Wan Yongnian had also called several times, which meant that it was very likely that Secretary Wan had wanted to see him. There were also some cadres and workers from Zhongyang Textiles, including the old wetnurse Xia Yulian and her daughter-in-law, who called several times. What Li Gaocheng did not expect was that several senior managers from the company had called many times, saying that they wanted to make contact with him to report on the situation. It was also particularly worthy of note that Yan Zhen, deputy secretary of the Provincial Party Committee, had called him several times in a row! This happened after he was transferred to the other hospital to convalesce.

Li Gaocheng stared silently at Yan's name for a long time. What was he after at that particular time? Was he trying to reel him in one last time? He had spoken to Yan Zhen on the phone that night, and Yan had told him very sternly that he hoped to see him very soon. But he had transferred hospitals early the next morning and had not gone to see Yan Zhen. Indeed, he hadn't even called him and that was why the executive deputy secretary of the Provincial Party Committee hadn't known where he was. Did he really think Yan wouldn't be angry? Did he really think he would not take further action? The simple truth was that Yan was angry with him because he felt that he could no longer control him, and he, Li, had become a potential threat to him. He was acting against him out of fear that he was making a move against him, and he had sensed that that move was already in progress.

No matter how high and powerful Yan was now, in fact, everything he was doing only served to prove that he was worried and afraid. Maybe he too was on edge all day long, restless, sleepless and burnt out. The only possible reason for this was that he had a guilty conscience!

Many people had also come to his house looking for him.

What surprised him was that the people who had come over the past few days were mostly workers and retired cadres from Zhongyang Textiles. The old factory managers Yuan Mingliang and Li Suzhi, the old chief engineer Zhang Huabin, the old Red Army man Ding Jincun, the old model worker Fan Xiuzhi, the old worker Wang Yinglie, and even the mechanic Hu Huizhong who had become a shoe mender, had all come to see him!

A surprisingly large number of leaders from the Municipal Government had also come visiting, including Deputy Secretary Zhang, Deputy Secretary Yu, Deputy Mayor Guo, Deputy Mayor Liu, as well as representatives from the Finance Bureau, the Tax Bureau, the Grain Bureau, the Industry Bureau, the Economic

Commission, the Planning Commission, and even the leaders of the Municipal Discipline Inspection Commission, the Municipal Public Security Bureau and the Propaganda Department of the Municipal Party Committee. What most amazed him was that almost all the leaders of the Procuratorate, where his wife worked, had also actually come to the house.

With the current speed of information dissemination, it was impossible for them not to know his current situation and the pressure he was under. There might be many reasons why they still came to see him under these circumstances, but at least one thing was clear: they were at his house at this time to show, in varying degrees, their support, concern and solidarity with him. To think of coming in the first place, then to summon up the courage and come was, in itself, a statement and was also very impressive. Of course, this was not always possible for everyone as it wasn't an easy thing to do, even clandestinely.

This was an expression of right and wrong. What they had made clear by their actions was their understanding of what was right and what was wrong, of what was true and what was false, of what was good and what was evil. Of course, there were times when they were unable to express these feelings and judgements in words.

What they had done was enough.

The most surprising thing of all to Li Gaocheng was that the head of the working group in charge of the investigation at Zhongyang Textiles, the deputy director of the Municipal Finance Bureau and the director of the Municipal Audit Bureau responsible for auditing Zhongyang Textile's Xinchao Company had come to see him more than once. They had even left messages in the guestbook.

The words of the deputy secretary of the Finance Bureau read as follows:

Mayor Li:

I have come here a few times, and it is a shame that I haven't been able to see you.

In accordance with your wishes, the investigation into Zhongyang Textiles has been concluded. Everyone has breathed a sigh of relief, myself included. No major mistakes, no major trouble. I have left you a copy of the investigation report and specifically instructed the nanny, Xiao Lian, to pass it on to you as soon as possible. We also sent a copy to Secretary Yan Zhen of the Provincial Party Committee, who was very pleased to see it and praised us. He said that Mayor Li would also be pleased and that we had done a great job.

Mayor Li, these words from Secretary Yan were a great relief to me. I think Secretary Yan was speaking for you too. Therefore, I also believe that from the beginning my actions have been correct, and my instincts have also been correct, as have my understanding and appreciation of the issue.

It was not an easy task to write the investigation report in its current form. I will give you a full report on the details when we meet, but as long as you are satisfied, we will be satisfied.

I'm not going anywhere over the next few days, and I'm at your disposal for further instructions and orders.

What the director of the Audit Bureau wrote was even more interesting:

Mayor Li:

When we heard that you were ill, everyone was very concerned. I have come to your house several times and also sent people to look for you. I have not heard from you, so I am leaving this message here.

The review of Zhongyang Textiles has come to an end. Please rest assured that, following all our efforts, there is no need to worry about Xinchao anymore. By that I mean that there will be no more problems with Xinchao, and that everything has been done reasonably and legally. The investigation report is very clear. Please read it.

Secretary Yan has called a few times and I have given him a detailed report of every step we have taken. I don't think either you or Secretary Yan have to worry about this anymore. Although it was difficult and demanding, the task was successfully completed in accordance with the spirit and intentions of yourself and of the Municipal Government.

I will come back again, as I have some information to tell you in person. I also have some personal matters that I would like to talk over with you again. I would like to take this opportunity to extend my greetings. You and Director Wu must please feel free to call me.

Li Gaocheng stared at the two messages in a daze, and his mind went blank for a while.

How could this be? What was going on here?

These two people were both experts in the field of financial auditing who had always been considered by the authorities to be utterly reliable, prudent, incorruptible, competent, shrewd and certainly utterly obedient to orders. After repeated screening, it was finally decided that they would be the ones to take charge, and they led several dozen of the best and brightest operatives. One of them was in charge of investigating the financial problems at Zhongyang Textiles and the other was in charge of the problems at Zhongyang's tertiary enterprise, Xinchao Co. Ltd. From beginning to end, how many times had he spoken seriously and sincerely with them, how many times had he explained things to them! He had hoped that they would make a good job of the investigation in a realistic and meticulous manner. They had to be impartial, strict, selfless and upright, and they had to complete the task in a practical and open manner with a sense of responsibility to the Party and to the people. There had also been a number of very strict rules and regulations for all investigation staff: no unofficial meals, no private appointments, no unauthorised absences, no late arrivals or early departures...

And this was what he got in return? An investigation report that completely covered up the truth?

And all of this was supposedly done in accordance with his wishes, to reassure him and to satisfy him. It was all supposedly done with a deep understanding and appreciation of the spirit of his intentions and the intentions of the Municipal Government.

How had it come to this? How?

Had he not made himself clear? Or had the situation taken a sudden turn for the worse? Was that turn for the worse perhaps the result of Yan Zhen's intervention?

No, that didn't seem to be the case. It couldn't be.

So, were these two responsible people deliberately trying to make fools of him?

No, absolutely not! They didn't have the guts. And even if they did have some such intention, there was no need for it at all. It simply wasn't worth it.

If this was not the case, then there was only one possibility: that these people he had carefully selected, all of whom he had considered to be reliable, all of whom were his own people in the eyes of others, had completely misunderstood his "spirit" and "intent" and then acted in accordance with that misunderstanding. Although it had been "very difficult and demanding", they had done it with great effort and great diligence!

Perhaps it was because he had chosen "his own people", these "own people" had to guess how to "understand" and "comprehend" his "spirit and intentions" in every aspect when completing the tasks he set them. And if they felt that they had truly "understood and comprehended" his "spirit and intentions", they would of course do their very best fully to implement them, in order to reassure him and satisfy him that they had completed the tasks he had set them.

Perhaps that was the only plausible explanation.

But if that was the case, then, in their eyes, in their thinking and speculation, did not his "spirit and intention" coincide with Yan Zhen's original thinking on the matter?

Zhongyang Textiles was his sphere of operation, the place where he started out, and his base. Zhongyang Textile's management cadres were all promoted by him, so naturally they were all his people. It was Secretary Yan who promoted him, so naturally he was Secretary Yan's man. Now, there was a problem with Zhongyang Textiles. Someone had petitioned and demanded an investigation. As a result, under the instruction of Secretary Yan, and with his support, he had been to investigate the problem at Zhongyang Textiles. When the people ordering the investigation, the people carrying out the investigation and the people being investigated all came from the same team, how hard was it for them to "understand" and "comprehend" the "spirit and intentions"? What made Secretary Yan happy would naturally also make him happy; what satisfied him would naturally satisfy Secretary Yan; as long as Secretary Yan was relaxed about it, he must surely be relaxed about it too.

This was the only reasonable and logical way things could be. And wasn't that what was happening right then?

There was nothing too surprising or unexpected in all this when you thought about it. In truth, didn't many leading cadres work and live along these lines on a daily basis? As long as you kept your boss happy, everything would be fine. That was it precisely: if the leader is happy, everyone gets what they want. And was not this way of thinking and this way of working exactly what many of our leaders liked and what they wanted? Save your time, trouble and effort, everything will be done for you with meticulous attention to detail, people will anticipate your every whim and even think of things that haven't even occurred to you yet. Everything will be done for you everywhere and in every way to make you comfortable, happy, content and carefree. With cadres who think like this at your side to serve you, political success, prestige, glory and pleasure will all be yours. What else was there to say?

So then you are happy and content, you have a better understanding of how the whole process works, you are more familiar with it, and feel more at ease with it. Gradually and naturally, you will grow bolder in promoting it and you will begin to use it in other circumstances. Wasn't that how many of the cadres before him now had climbed the ladder? Wasn't that how they took over power, step by step? And because the truly virtuous and talented did not employ this method or disdained it, they grew more and more distant and out of reach, making themselves strangers to us "in the know". Of course, you had your say about them and anyone who didn't approach you, who didn't cluster around you, who didn't sit down at your feet, who didn't run around everywhere for you, would be rejected on the pretext that they didn't understand, that they didn't know how things work, that they were not open with you. If you distanced yourself from them, they, in their turn, would mentally abandon you as well. Thus, the wise and virtuous moved further and further away from you, and the bad elements got closer and closer. In other areas, the selection of cadres aimed to promote the good and eliminate the bad, but in his case, it had been perverted to promote the bad and eliminate the good!

So it was not the least surprising that cadres selected through this process had no trouble anticipating, understanding and appreciating the significance of an investigation report like this one.

This kind of corruption ran very deep, and it was in precisely those circumstances that things like this could happen.

So it seemed that Yan Zhen might not have had to do as much work and put in as much effort as he had imagined to mount such a fierce campaign against some of his subordinates. Judging by what was happening right then, Yan Zhen might not even have needed to pick up the phone because there were so many people constantly running up to him to report every detail of every step that was carried out. He did not need to make any specific instructions and arrangements, just a few empty words and carefully crafted falsehoods that couldn't come back to him in any way, and, just like that, all the problems simply went away. And wasn't that how he himself was supposed to feel now? He had hardly had time to do anything at all, and this unprecedented, wonderful, reassuring and gratifying report had been delivered to his door. The words of the head of the Audit Bureau in particular left Li Gaocheng not knowing whether to laugh or cry. He was so confident he had done the mayor a great service that he actually said he also had some personal matters he would like to discuss with him! The meaning there was quite clear: I have done something big for you, so you need to reward me; I have paid out for you, and you need to acknowledge it! In fact, he had already hinted on several occasions that he wanted to be a candidate for deputy mayor when the vacancy next came up. According to those in the know, he had been angling for this for a very long time...

Wasn't this just how things were?

Li Gaocheng couldn't hold back a long, deep sigh.

No wonder Yan Zhen's endorsement of the investigation report was so smug and confident. As if in a dream, he suddenly saw Yan Zhen sitting quietly, quite close, and grinning wolfishly at him.

His head was pounding, his thoughts were whirling out of control, and he found it impossible to concentrate.

He really wanted to stay at home for a while and rest, but when he walked into his bedroom, he choked up and almost began to weep. How could his lovely home have become like this?

There was a huge pile of mail on the bedside table. He didn't expect there to be anything important, and he didn't want to open it all. He just wanted to flip through it casually, and then lie down, but as he looked, a worn and tatty envelope caught his eye.

It was from Zhongyang Textiles. There was no stamp on the

envelope, and it simply read: To Uncle Li Gaocheng of the Municipal Government.

As he sat on the bed, looking at the spidery handwriting, Li Gaocheng found himself opening the envelope:

Dear Uncle Gaocheng,

How are you? I have been to the city hall several times but have not been able to get to see you. They wouldn't let me in. I said I was from Zhongyang Textiles, and I was looking for Mayor Li, but they wouldn't let me in. I couldn't reach you on the phone either, and you never seem to be at home. I have no choice but to write to you. I know you are very busy, so please forgive me for disturbing you.

I am Xia Yulian's youngest son. You probably don't remember me as I only met you when I was a child. Uncle – I hope you will allow me to call you Uncle – I still remember the glutinous rice cake you brought to our home during New Year that year. It was so fragrant. I ate a huge piece all by myself, and my mother was very cross with me.

The last time you came to our home, my wife said to me after I got back from work that she had never expected such an important person as the mayor to be so down-to-earth and unpretentious.

Thank you, Uncle Li, our family is very grateful to you for making a special trip to visit us at such a difficult time, and we will remember it for the rest of our lives.

Mother has been ill since you last saw her. She says that she has never owed anything to anyone in her whole life, except only that she now regrets that she owes you an apology and has not been able to make it. She has never stopped thinking about it, saying that you went to find her, but she didn't recognise you. It is her fault that you passed out the way you did and were taken so seriously ill.

Uncle, my mother wouldn't let us tell you, she didn't even let us phone you. But we have thought about it and we think we have to tell you. Uncle Li, mother has an incurable disease, she may only have a few days to live. After she fell ill, she was diagnosed in hospital with terminal lung cancer that has spread to the lymph system and liver.

Uncle, this is all my fault as an unfilial son! My mother has suffered all her life for the sake of our family. In our early years, when we were young, she supported the whole family on her own. When we were older, we should have been able to let her enjoy a few years of happiness, but I never expected things at the factory to be so bad. Seeing my mother's pain and suffering, I really wish I could take my own life to let my mother live a few more years.

Uncle Li, the only reason I am writing this letter is to beg you to find time in your busy schedule to visit our mother. If you came and she could see with her own eyes that you were in good health and nothing bad had happened to you, she might be able to die without regret.

As he read this, Li Gaocheng's eyes filled with tears, and he felt himself choking up with emotion.

A vision of the scene that day appeared unbidden before his eyes. In that dark and dirty workshop, in that unprotected workspace, Xia Yulian, looking like the "White Haired Girl", was breathing in the foul air through her mouth and nose, the black mask hanging uselessly from her chin...

It was only a short letter, but every word seemed to pluck at his heartstrings.

He suddenly felt so selfish and irrelevant. What could he possibly have to say when faced with these people? What did he have to worry about? What did he have to be afraid of? What did he have to hesitate over? A woman like Xia Yulian could be said to have been born into this world with nothing. She had worked hard all her life and, now she was about to leave the world, she still had nothing. But even at this most painful time, the one person she cared about, who she thought about all the time, and the one person she couldn't bear to leave behind in death, was still not herself.

She hardly even gave herself a thought.

So why was he so worried, so calculating, so preoccupied with each little step he took? Was it because he had too much? Was that why he thought about himself so much?

In the end, it came down to just one word: fear. Fear of losing his family, fear of losing his reputation, fear of losing his status, fear of losing his position. In other words, fear of losing his privileges and vested interests, fear of losing his official's hat!

What was so important to him about his official post? Had it become an inseparable part of his life and who he was? Would losing it mean losing everything about him? Had protecting his official post and retaining his official's hat become an integral part of his life and work? As long as he kept that hat on his head, was he content to let ruffians and thieves continue to rob and murder, both openly and covertly? Was he content to let thousands of ordinary people cry out in hunger and cold and suffer great pain, and turn a blind eye to it all, even to the point where he was complicit with those thieves and colluded in their crimes? Even if he still had a conscience and some degree of righteous anger, was he so afraid of harming his official life that he was willing to play deaf and dumb and turn a blind eye to it all?

Was it the sheer number of the cadres all around him who were just like that, that made the corruption and the insensitivity to it so extreme and so shocking?

If it was the case that as his status grew loftier and loftier, the ordinary people were becoming more and more distant from him, and as his official's hat grew weightier and weightier, his influence and esteem in the hearts of the people was getting lighter and lighter, then what was the point of him being an official at all? If a person was willing to be a puppet and an accomplice, to make himself a catspaw just for the sake of a position that was ultimately meaningless and worthless to him, then what kind of life was that?

If you don't act like an official when you are an official, and you don't act like a human being when you are one, what kind of creature are you?

There was also a postcard from the former chief engineer at Zhongyang Textiles, Zhang Huabin, and several other workers:

Mayor Li

We would like to send you our most profound wishes on the occasion of this New Year.

As long as you are forever at one with us workers, please believe that whatever difficulties and setbacks you may encounter, we workers will always be standing at your side.

At the same time, please rest assured that we workers cannot be fooled!

Li Gaocheng looked at the postcard silently for a while, and then suddenly stood up from the bed.

It was almost two o'clock and he had to go to work.

First, he wanted to get to see Secretary Wan and Governor Wei as soon as possible. Second, he wanted to tell Yang Cheng that he hoped to convene the Standing Committee at the earliest possible moment, that the investigation report in front of him had to be overturned, and that the whole Zhongyang Textiles issue had to be re-investigated. Third, he must go to Zhongyang Textiles as soon as he could and go to see Xia Yulian as quickly as possible. The letter from her son was written four days ago, and there could be no more delay.

Just as he stood up, he was surprised and taken aback to find, at the bottom of the pile of letters, a large envelope, bulging with tickets of all shapes and sizes.

He stood there silently, looking at it for a long time before he finally understood. It turned out that the tickets were all shopping vouchers for major shopping malls obtained by various work units. During the Spring Festival, for the sake of time and convenience, some agencies and work units distributed these vouchers to their employees. With them, when you got to the mall, you could buy whatever you wanted without having to bother anyone and with no one bothering you. It was a way of distributing benefits during the Spring Festival which had only quite recently become popular. Although the authorities had issued statement after statement about it, it had continued despite the prohibitions and seemed to be becoming more and more commonplace.

As Li Gaocheng studied the envelope full of vouchers, the truth suddenly dawned on him. Their great advantage was how convenient they were for senior personnel. These vouchers were just as good as cash, so leaders could use them to buy whatever they wanted. The gift of a gold necklace was a crime for both donor and recipient, but by using these vouchers you could effectively be giving a gold bar and it would be quite legitimate and without any comeback.

He was completely stunned when he totted up the value of the vouchers in the envelope and it came to more than twenty thousand yuan.

Twenty thousand! That was enough to put him in prison.

How could it be so much? Moreover, with the Spring Festival

fast approaching, more and more work units were going to be sending vouchers, so the total was going to keep going up. If the household kept accepting them in the same way, twenty thousand yuan was just the beginning.

If he accepted tens of thousands of yuan in shopping vouchers for just one Spring Festival, and he still considered himself an honest and upright official, how much worse would it get if he were genuinely corrupt?

The meticulous little nanny had made a record of every work unit and every person who had brought vouchers, but when Li Gaocheng looked through the list, he didn't see a single name he recognised. They all seemed to be people sent by work units to deliver the vouchers. The work units individually hadn't given huge sums. Some just gave a few hundred and the biggest amounts were a thousand or so, but in every case, the vouchers were divided into two equal halves, one for him and one for his wife. It was all honest and above board. It was the work units making the gifts and they sent their representatives to deliver them. So, essentially, he didn't have to worry about being investigated or there being any problem if he was. He could use them without a worry. But there was one thing he did have to remember and that was the names of the work units that gave the vouchers, because those work units would remember and their leadership most certainly would too.

Had his household received this much every year over the last few years?

He shuddered uncontrollably. Yes, for sure. His wife had always looked after household affairs, and, in any case, this had always been his own busiest time of year. He would always be out of the house very early in the morning and not get back until very late at night. Sometimes he wouldn't even come home for days at a time, as he would hold meetings in hotels and then eat and sleep there too. His wife took care of everything about the house, and sometimes he wouldn't even have time to put his head round the kitchen door.

The kitchen! He suddenly thought of the kitchen and wondered whether people might have brought other gifts. He stood rooted to the spot for a moment then slipped quietly into the kitchen and opened the door of the storeroom that opened off it. Once again, he was stopped dead in his tracks as he saw the cartons of luxury cigarettes, the bottles of fine wine and all the assorted exotic delicacies.

How had his wife disposed of all this stuff over the years? Just what he could see now was enough for a household like his to celebrate ten New Years and still have some left over.

So what was he supposed to do about it all now?

Give it all back? How easy would that be? Was it even possible? Could he give something back after accepting it?

Possible or not, that was what he had to find a way to do. He had to get Xiao Lian to phone around to arrange to return everything. Even if the stuff couldn't be returned, it certainly couldn't stay in the house. He had to get someone to take it all away immediately. He could have it taken to the Municipal Government general office or even the canteen. In the back of his mind, he felt that all this stuff was as uncomfortable and frightening to him as a great heap of bribes.

People could say what they liked! They could swathe themselves in fake emotion and fake righteousness, they could be as sanctimonious as they liked, that was up to them.

What was wrong with people these days? They just seemed to take this kind of thing for granted, and even ten times as much stuff would still be completely acceptable to their way of thinking. Especially at New Year, work units large and small, agencies, departments and businesses, no matter whether they were rich or poor, profit-making or running at a loss, even a huge loss, all strove equally to find ways of sending gifts to their superiors. It had become the right and proper, the reasonable thing to do and they would be considered to be at fault and failing in their obligations if they did not.

He also had to bear in mind that the person who knew the most about the family's secrets at this time was the nanny, Xiao Lian. She had been able to handle all of this so skilfully, so meticulously, so precisely, it seemed that she was quite familiar with it. As the saying goes, "Even the domestic servant in the prime minister's household is a seventh-rank official" and this little nanny was no simple little girl. He had to find time to have a good talk with Xiao Lian...

He was just about to go out when he heard someone knocking on the door. He opened the door and froze in astonishment. There was his daughter, Meimei, carrying a large suitcase.

She had come back by plane. Term had finished that morning and she was home the same afternoon. She hadn't hung around at the university for even a quarter of an hour.

The expression on her face was that combination of sadness, desolation and confusion unique to young girls.

Looking at her, Li Gaocheng felt his heart suddenly fracture...

CHAPTER THIRTY-NINE

It was only when Li Gaocheng got to the general office that he discovered that the meeting of the Standing Committee of the Provincial Party Committee was still going on. He sat at his desk in a daze, still immersed in the emotions of seeing his daughter.

The driver had been waiting, so he didn't say anything to his daughter, and she didn't ask anything of him, but it was clear that she was in a very bad mood. All she asked was: "Is Mum home?"

He said truthfully that he didn't know, that he had just been discharged from hospital and hadn't even been at home for two hours. He told her to rest for a while, then to call her mother and ask her to hurry home, telling her to say that was what Dad wanted too.

Meimei didn't say a word and then followed the nanny, who was helping with her things, into the house without looking back.

He watched his daughter's retreating back and called out after her, but Meimei still didn't look back or say anything. In fact, it was the nanny, Xiao Lian, who turned around to look, and acknowledged him with a word, as if acting on behalf of Meimei.

He wanted to go back in and talk to his daughter, but he thought better of it and walked out of the house. What was he going to say to her?

He hadn't thought about it yet, and he simply didn't know.

He knew his daughter's character and temperament. The girl he knew was stubborn and wilful, with little tolerance. She was too young, just nineteen years old, still a child really.

He would think about it and come back to it in the afternoon.

Now, sitting at his desk, his mind was a blank. Slowly, he dialled a phone number.

It was his wife's number. He wanted to talk to his wife. No matter what the differences or contradictions there were between them, he wanted to say, let's put them aside for the time being for the sake of the children. For Meimei in particular. She was still so young, and at such a beautiful and joyous time of the year, they should try to give the child as much beauty and joy as possible.

The call connected after only two rings.

"Hello!" It was a woman's voice. He froze for a moment, not sure whether or not it was his wife's voice.

"Is that the Anti-Corruption Bureau?" he asked.

"Yes, please go ahead." This time he could hear quite clearly that he was not mistaken, and it was, indeed, his wife.

"This is Li Gaocheng," he said and then hesitated.

There was silence at the other end of the line.

"Hello?" He assumed the other party had heard him clearly. But then there was a click as the call was cut off at the other end.

As he listened to the busy tone on the line, his brain went blank.

She wouldn't take his call. He considered messaging her on her beeper but thought better of it.

He'd play it her way.

It was very quiet in the office, which was in stark contrast to the usual constant phone calls and the crowd of people waiting outside the door to see him.

He only had a few optional meetings scheduled, and probably because everyone knew he was ill, no one bothered to resend the invitations.

No one came to see him, and he had no meetings to go to. For the moment, he had no idea what to do with himself. He suddenly saw how laughable he was. What he usually thought of as being busy was actually other people being busy for him. When he tried to take the initiative, he had no idea what to do.

Was this, then, the reality of his daily work as an honest and upright mayor?

Just as he was having these confused and confusing thoughts, someone burst into the office. At first, he was surprised that anyone would come into his office unannounced like that, but then he realised that his secretary, Wu Xingang, was not in yet.

The newcomer was Guo Tao, the deputy mayor in charge of industry.

Guo Tao also looked surprised, as he probably had not been expecting Li Gaocheng to be sitting quietly in the office on his own.

"...Mayor Li! Is that you there? I didn't think there was anyone in the office." Guo Tao's voice was as bright as always.

"Sit down." Li Gaocheng pointed to the sofa.

"I've been looking out for you for the last few days. How are you?" Deputy Mayor Guo was clearly a little flustered.

"I've been wanting to see you too. What's the situation with the businesses and factories in the city these days?"

"It's OK. Yesterday there were dozens of old workers from the tanneries sitting at the gate of the Municipal Party Committee and Municipal Government for ages, hoping that they could get this year's retirement pay before the year is out."

"Did you settle things with them?"

"Yes, Mayor Li, but I didn't know if you might have some new thoughts after we came back from Zhongyang Textiles. These days I have been thinking. Are we too optimistic about the reform of state-owned enterprises? What I'm worried about, Mayor Li, is that if we keep fooling around like this day after day, sooner or later we're going to end up with an almighty mess." Clearly, there was something more to Deputy Mayor Guo's words than he was saying.

"Do you mean in terms of the whole, or the individual?"

"It comes to the same thing. I think it's like a domino effect. If a big enterprise like Zhongyang Textiles collapses sometime in the future, tens of thousands of workers from our city will inevitably become a flood of migrant workers. Wherever they go, the same thing will happen, and each collapse will become part of a greater collapse. How are we going to manage if that happens? How can we stabilise the situation?"

"Have you heard something?" Li Gaocheng was astonished by Guo Tao's pessimism.

"You really don't know, Mayor Li? Or do you think it doesn't matter?"

"Know what?"

"The report on Zhongyang Textiles' application for bankruptcy has been approved by Secretary Yan, and it's about to be studied by the Standing Committee. It's a huge thing! Have you really not heard about it?"

"Oh!" Li Gaocheng was stunned.

They had filed for bankruptcy.

So that's how things stood.

Despicable! Unimaginably despicable! He hadn't thought them capable of something like that, but they had gone ahead and done it!

He had been caught off guard and made another mistake. The operations and activities of those people had not stopped for a minute. They had continued almost non-stop, one after another, without giving him a chance to catch his breath. The investigation report had been sent out here and the bankruptcy application had already been approved there. Perhaps, by the time he was fully awake, everything would already be a fait accompli. Once Zhongyang Textiles had gone bankrupt, the whole problem ceased to exist. What else could he want to investigate about Zhongyang Textiles?

Hundreds of millions in assets and tens of thousands of workers seemed to be nothing in their eyes, and with the stroke of a pen, nothing was left. As long as they could protect themselves, as long as their own interests were not damaged, without batting an eyelid, they could wipe out a huge state-owned enterprise that had been around for nearly a century.

"Did Secretary Yan not tell you, Mayor Li?" Guo Tao asked cautiously.

It seemed that, just like the others, he assumed Li Gaocheng was part of Yan Zhen's circle.

"How did Secretary Yan tell you?" Li Gaocheng enquired neutrally.

"Secretary Yan asked his secretary to send over the bankruptcy application that he had approved, and then he called and told me that he wanted to hear my opinion. He also said that he had already reported to Secretary Wan and Governor Wei, and the Standing Committee of the Provincial Party Committee should give it its immediate attention. He hoped I would read it as soon as possible, and it would be best if I could send my written opinions directly to him."

"Have you done so?" Li Gaocheng was now almost shaking with agitation.

"I thought about it for several days, Mayor Li, but I simply couldn't do it. It was quite clear what Secretary Yan was hoping for – he wanted me to agree with his opinion. But I couldn't get myself to that point, I couldn't do it! There are tens of thousands of workers involved, and if I agreed just like that, I don't think I could forgive myself for the rest of my life or be able to look those workers in the eye ever again..." Guo Tao's voice was trembling, and his eyes were suddenly red-rimmed.

"Thank you, Mayor Guo!" Li Gaocheng's own eyes were also growing red.

"Mayor Li!" Guo Tao looked at Li Gaocheng in surprise and then became as happy as a little child. "You have had me worried for the last few days. I really thought you agreed with Secretary Yan!"

The two men looked at each other excitedly.

"You are quite right, Guo Tao. If we were to commit a sin like that, we would never be able to cleanse ourselves of it."

Li Gaocheng was deeply moved, but, at the same time, he was also still immersed in a sea of pain and shock. How could this be happening? The problem was so huge and there were so many workers involved. Even if bankruptcy was inevitable, they should first investigate the problem thoroughly and understand it thoroughly, so they could give the government a precedent for future reference and give the workers a convincing explanation. They would also leave a tragic example for posterity and teach themselves a painful lesson. But who had given Yan Zhen the audacity to act like this? Who had given him such great power? As a top-ranking provincial leader, how could he be so irresponsible towards the Party and the nation? How could he be so corrupt, act like such a worm, such a profligate, such a black sheep?

"Can we stand up to them, Mayor Li?" Guo Tao's eyes showed his deep concern.

"Whether we can or not, we must! It depends on how many people are with us – if there are too few then we can't, but if there are many then we can!" Li Gaocheng said determinedly. "If Secretary Yan asks you again, then tell him I am not in agreement. If he has anything to say about that, tell him to say it directly to me. You can tell him I will come to him specifically to discuss this matter. If he asks you how I know about it all, tell him I know everything and I am quite clear about it all. I will say everything that needs to be said when I go to see him."

Guo Tao looked at Li Gaocheng in surprise, then said: "As long as that is your attitude, Mayor Li, there's no need to say all that. I will just tell him that I disagree. I didn't agree at first, and I certainly don't agree now. Letting such a large enterprise go bankrupt is not something that can be decided by a few people behind everyone's back. It is making a mockery of the country, of the workers, and of the credibility of our Party!"

By this time, Guo Tao's worries seemed to have disappeared and he was speaking from the heart.

"I think this whole thing is very wrong, Mayor Li. I think it is a kind of conspiracy. What I was most worried about before was that if you approved this report on the bankruptcy application, it would let other people plot against you. This is a municipal enterprise, and if you were to agree to let it go bankrupt, then the responsibility for it would all be yours. If something were to go wrong in the future, for example, if the powers-that-be decided to investigate, if the workers started making trouble, if it eventually turned into a major incident, then all the responsibility would be yours, and all the wrongdoing would be laid at your feet. People like Secretary Yan would get off scot-free. They'd put everything on you… Mayor Li, it doesn't matter if I can't stand up to them. You are the key. You have no alternative. You have to stand up to them, no matter what. And what is more, Mayor Li, if a huge company like Zhongyang Textiles is allowed to go bankrupt and tens of thousands of workers are let go into society, the scariest possibility is that it will have a domino effect. One by one, all the good companies will be dragged under too. No matter how you put it, Mayor Li, you have no other way out…"

Actually, there was no need for Guo Tao to say any of this as Li Gaocheng understood quite well that he had no alternative. What really moved him was that a deputy mayor in charge of industry should put himself in his shoes and show such concern for him!

Li Gaocheng had already called his driver and was about to visit Xia Yulian when Yang Cheng's call came in.

What Yang Cheng had to say was simple and generalised: the afternoon meeting of the Standing Committee had just finished, but the meeting was going to continue that evening. There had been several very heated debates on the issues of Zhongyang Textiles and Li Gaocheng himself at the Standing Committee. Secretary Wan and Governor Wei might not have any other engagements at this moment, so it might be an idea to give them a call. It would be best to meet with them as soon as possible. There was no need to talk about anything else and Li should just concentrate on his own problems and those of Zhongyang Textiles. The key to it all was the issue of Zhongyang Textiles. It would be best if he could also meet with the secretary of the Discipline Inspection Commission, Bai Weihua. Further investigation of the problems at Zhongyang Textiles was necessary if they were going to talk people round. A meeting of the Municipal Party Committee should be held as soon as possible, to see what they thought about things. There was a meeting over at the Municipal Committee which he, Yang Cheng, had to attend. Li should feel free to contact him at any time and they should meet up that evening to talk things over.

Li Gaocheng asked if Zhongyang Textiles' bankruptcy application had been discussed at the meeting. Yang Cheng told him not to concern himself with that because if he got involved in that debate, it would be all up with him.

He needed to talk to Secretary Wan, Governor Wei and Secretary Bai of the Discipline Inspection Commission about the problems at Zhongyang Textiles. He shouldn't talk about anything, just that. Also, he needed to be ready to deal with all kinds of pressure and other things. Did he understand that? He had to stand firm. With that, Yang Cheng abruptly ended the call.

The situation must be serious, or Yang Cheng wouldn't be in such a hurry. He was a very sober judge of things, so his opinion was almost certainly right. Li Gaocheng couldn't help but feel that Yang Cheng really was better than him, and that he himself was not secretary material. The first thing he did when something happened was to get flustered and confused. If it wasn't for Yang Cheng, it was hard to say how things would stand with him now.

First, he called Secretary Wan, but the line was busy. Then he tried Provincial Governor Wei, but there was no reply.

Secretary Bai of the Discipline Inspection Commission's personal secretary answered the phone when he called. He said that Secretary Bai was with guests and asked Li Gaocheng to call back in twenty minutes.

He tried Secretary Wan again, and his personal secretary asked him to wait. After a couple of minutes, he heard Wan Yongnian's voice: "Is that you, Gaocheng? Hello! What's up? With something this big brewing, I tried to find you several times over the last few days! Why didn't you come straight to me? Are you so full of yourself you think I must have already made up my mind against you? Well, let me tell you now that I haven't at all. Not at all! The Provincial Committee still trusts you, and both Governor Wei and I still do too. You mustn't have any fixed opinions, nor must you let the pressure and the responsibility get to you. I've talked things over with Yang Cheng several times, and Yan Zhen has had a lot of talks with me too. They both have a very good opinion of you and have complete faith in you."

Li Gaocheng was momentarily stunned. Yan Zhen was still expressing a high opinion of him to the Provincial Party Committee. And still trusted him just as much as before. It was obvious he was keeping his real thoughts to himself in front of the Provincial Party secretary. What a brilliant strategist the man was!

"Listen, Gaocheng, I want to talk this whole thing through with you in detail, but today and tomorrow are no good as my diary is very busy. Let's do it the day after tomorrow. I'll call you to fix a definite time, OK? But there is one thing I need to tell you now. I'm very worried about the issue with Zhongyang Textiles, very worried indeed. I don't care what other people are saying about it, you and I both have to be very sure of what we think, and you mustn't let down your guard for a moment. I've read the investigation report carefully, and I don't know what you think about it, but I'll give you my opinion now. I think it is certainly not a straightforward matter! If it was, what are those tens of thousands of workers kicking up such a fuss about? Just because they are not being paid? Or just because production has been stopped? Over the last two days, I have read in great detail the ten thousand-signature petition that the workers' representatives handed over a few days ago and what it describes are the symptoms, not the cause. It's a digression. How do you think the workers would react if they found out what kind of investigation report your lot have submitted upstairs? Listen, I'm not going to say any more on the phone, but I think the investigation of Zhongyang Textiles still needs to be carried out and carried out properly. If it isn't, it makes a nonsense of talking about all the other problems and that would be extremely irresponsible..."

Li Gaocheng had been listening quietly, barely able to say a word. In fact, he hadn't known what to say because he really hadn't expected Secretary Wan to talk like that. It was not until Wan had hung up the phone, and the phone rang again, that he realised he had burst into tears.

The call was from the personal secretary of Secretary Bai of the Discipline Inspection Commission, who said that, if Li Gaocheng had the time, Secretary Bai would like him to come over immediately as she had urgent business to discuss with him.

Bai Weihua was a female secretary who had long had the reputation of being a "strongman".

She had worked on the Youth League Committee for nearly ten years, serving as the secretary of the Youth League Prefectural Committee, the deputy secretary of the Youth League Provincial Committee, and the secretary of the Youth League Provincial Committee. She was then transferred to the local district as deputy commissioner and deputy secretary of the Prefectural Party Committee, and then on to the Provincial Discipline Inspection Commission as deputy secretary. She held that post for nearly six years until the year before, when, at the age of fifty-one, she became secretary of the Disciplinary Inspection Commission and a member of the Provincial Standing Committee. If it weren't for the fact that the bosses of the five top departments could work for an extra five years, she would have already reached retirement age.

People regarded her as a very scary leader, someone to be wary of. This was because, generally speaking, leadership cadres of that age had a tendency to become greedy and very forceful. Some people, when they reach this age, feel that, since they do not have many years left if they fail to take advantage of their situation, they will soon be on the downslope. As they can't work for more than a few years anyway, they have to take the chance to make some money before it disappears. That is why they are so often hated and feared. On the other hand, there are some cadres who, when they reach this age, are comfortable that they have done everything they wanted to and have no concerns or misgivings. Then again, they may think that they only have this one term of office left and they won't get another chance. If, later on, they want to do something for the people, they won't be able to. In that case, they may suddenly become totally fearless and think only of accomplishing some earth-shaking project to add an exclamation mark to their departure from office. These people are equally scary and difficult to deal with.

In Li Gaocheng's opinion, Bai Weihua seemed to belong more to the latter category. In addition, she was a senior female official with no background and no backing, who relied solely on her own talents. That was why your average leadership cadre, even at the provincial level, found her somewhat difficult to deal with.

She was a female Party member who it was difficult to get close to, who didn't smoke, who didn't drink, who didn't accept hospitality or gifts, who didn't mince her words, and who was the secretary of the Discipline Investigation Commission, specialising in investigating disciplinary cases! Who could say they weren't in awe of her? And who didn't watch very carefully what they said and did around her?

Bai Weihua was waiting for him. She didn't stand up as he came through the door, but shook hands sitting down, then gestured, unsmiling, to a chair and told him to take a seat. Almost before he had sat down, she got straight to the point, saying: "As for this matter of your three hundred thousand yuan, we have discussed it with Secretary Wan and Provincial Governor Wei, and we have decided to open a case. Tell me your thinking on it."

Li Gaocheng felt at a loss. He really didn't want to talk about this issue, or, at least, had hoped to avoid it. What they should be talking about was Zhongyang Textiles – that was the key issue. He hadn't expected the first question he was asked to be this one. He thought for a moment, then said: "I don't have any thinking on it. I just want to know if there will be any restrictions imposed on me while the case is being filed."

"What are you getting at?" Bai Weihua asked, her face betraying nothing.

"I mean, is it going to have any effect on my work, on my activities or my household?"

"Possibly."

"Can the filing be delayed a little?"

"Why?"

"I want to get to the bottom of the problems at Zhongyang Textiles first. I hope you can support me on this issue, Secretary Bai. It is very important to me, and I only need a month or two." Li Gaocheng sounded very keen and very sincere.

"The two things are not mutually exclusive," Bai Weihua said calmly. "The Provincial Discipline Inspection Commission has also filed a case on the Zhongyang Textiles affair. The Standing Committee of the Disciplinary Inspection Commission has studied it, and the Provincial Party Committee has given its agreement. The Standing Committee is cooperating with your Municipal Party Committee and the Municipal Government, and we are all striving to get to the root of the problems at Zhongyang Textiles as soon as possible. I have exchanged opinions with Yang Cheng on this matter, and the main responsibility for it lies with you."

"So, what you are saying is that you are investigating me, you are investigating Zhongyang Textiles, and you are going to file a joint case and investigate the two things together."

"That's right."

"The matter is already decided, isn't it, Secretary Bai?"

Bai Weihua nodded.

Li Gaocheng was perplexed. "Is that what you called me here to tell me?"

"No!" Secretary Bai seemed to hesitate, then looked directly at Li and said: "There is also the question of your wife. We have already decided to file a case against her."

These words hit Li Gaocheng like a thunderbolt and left him reeling. He had known this day might come, but now that it had, he still felt stunned and bewildered.

"I hope you can prepare yourself mentally for all this, Lao Li. Your wife's problems are very serious. Working from some of the materials we have from a whistleblower, our preliminary understanding shows that some of them are well-documented and substantial. I won't try and hide it from you, Lao Li, this is very bad for you. Speaking for myself personally, as well as for Secretary Wan and Governor Wei, the only hope we can see for you is that your hands are clean..." Bai Weihua continued in serious tones, a look of sadness and concern on her unsmiling face.

Li Gaocheng seemed not to have seen or heard anything during all this. When Secretary Bai had finished, he simply asked: "Is there any chance you can delay the process a little, Secretary Bai?"

"No," Secretary Bai said, her voice soft but her tone determined and leaving no room for doubt. "This is the decision of the Standing Committee of the Provincial Discipline Inspection Commission, and we have informed both Yang Cheng and the Municipal Discipline Inspection Commission."

So, Li Gaocheng thought to himself, it turned out that Yang Cheng had known about this all along, but he hadn't told him and had just said that he should hold firm and be mentally prepared for all kinds of pressure.

Li Gaocheng felt as though the sky was falling in on his head and he couldn't hold out anymore...

CHAPTER FORTY

It was during the height of the rush hour and almost every street in the city was crowded with cars and people. The journey from the city government offices to Zhongyang Textiles should have taken a bit over half an hour, but, at that time of day, it took twenty minutes just to get out of the city centre.

Li Gaocheng sat in his car in silence, his mind still a blank, except for one strange thought that kept niggling away at him. Just at this moment, he wanted to go off alone to some secluded place and not show his face or go home again for the next ten or twenty years.

It had only been a month, the people were all the same and his post was still the same, but everything had changed, everything had changed completely.

Secretary Bai had said that things were not looking good for him, but that was probably the least of it. If that tape recording didn't clear things up, did he have any way of explaining away those three hundred thousand yuan? Was everyone going to listen to his side of the story? Just look at the question of his wife. He knew full well there was a problem with her, but, even supposing he didn't, would his power and influence be enough to guarantee protection for her? Practically speaking, he couldn't – it just wasn't possible. From his point of view, the people who had placed himself and his wife in this position had not done so because of any problem with him or because of his influence. Yan Zhen had made it quite clear to him on this point. It was because he had no circle of supporters, or, to put it another way, he had lost his protective umbrella. How many of today's leaders, especially those in real charge, had never been sued? But what percentage of those cases were filed for investigation? What had Yan Zhen said about the definition of cleaning up corruption and rectifying the Party ethos? What exactly was meant by "cleaning up" and "rectifying"? What else but "cleaning up" and "rectifying" voices dissident from your own? Hadn't he said that without his support, he, Li, would have had multiple falls from grace and would never have become mayor? But, however great his power, which made it easy to bring down an individual, bringing down a whole circle of support was a very different matter.

Yan Zhen hadn't been saying that just to scare him, he was actually doing it! If Li Gaocheng had no problems, Yan Zhen could create some for him, and he could make any small problems become big ones. Conversely, he could make existing problems go away or turn big ones into small ones. Whatever the size and number of your problems, with Yan Zhen's protection, everything would be fine, but without him, you would be buried under problems, big and small, and if a case was opened against you, that case was sure to be followed through. Mighty rivers can drain away through a tiny ant hole, and the smallest fault can bring great mountains crashing down! Once the dike crumbles and the rocks start tumbling, a whole army can be crushed and no one can do anything about it. Li Gaocheng knew he could try and put the blame where he liked, but in the end the fault was his. Simply because he had a problem, Yan Zhen could control him as he pleased; because he had a problem, Yan Zhen could pick him off at will; and because he had a problem, Yan Zhen could summon clouds with the click of his fingers and call down the rain with a wave of his hand!

Secretary Bai Weihua had indeed put it very succinctly: "…this is very bad for you."

If there was a problem with his wife, of course he was involved too. If his wife had a problem, so did he.

This was Yan Zhen's trump card.

It might be despicable, but it was frighteningly effective.

How truly distressing it was that the Party could produce a man like this, but he, Li Gaocheng, could do nothing about it.

Yang Cheng had told him he had to hold out. He was right. It was all he could do.

But it wasn't just a question of holding out, the most important question was what he was going to do after he had weathered the storm.

Take them on! Fight them! It was dog eat dog! It was the survival of the fittest!

There was only one road for him to take; he had no other choice.

It was seven o'clock before he got to Zhongyang Textiles.

He bought some fruit from a stall on the street and told Wu Xingang to pick out some of the nutritional foods other people had brought him while he was in hospital. He had also brought three thousand yuan with him. He thought to himself that, if Xia Yulian was in a reasonable state, she would be all right to stay at home before the New Year. If things weren't so good with her, they could whip her into hospital immediately. He had already told Wu Xingang to fix things up there, so she could go in at any time.

It was only when he got to Xia Yulian's place that he discovered things were a great deal worse than he had imagined.

There was no heating in the house because they couldn't afford to pay the bill, and the same was true with the electricity. In advance of the New Year, the Electrical Supply Bureau had unified all the accounts on the grounds that the whole of Zhongyang Textiles was almost a year behind with its bills. There wasn't any water either because the whole dormitory compound was almost six months in arrears on its water bills. As there was no water to be had in the compound, people had to go to a nearby farmers' village to draw drinking water from a well.

Li Gaocheng felt a surge of uncontrollable anger. The last time he came, he had specifically brought along the director of the Municipal Electricity Supply Bureau and the manager of the Municipal Water Company, and told them that, no matter how great the difficulty, they must ensure normal and adequate supply during the Spring Festival. He had made it clear this was a political task, and there could be no ambiguity or compromise. That had only been a few days ago, so how could everything have changed so completely?

When he asked about it, Li Gaocheng discovered that it was being done on the orders of the provincial leadership. It was all because the water, heating and electricity bills owed by Zhongyang Textiles were so high and there was no sign of repayment in the near future, and because the news of the company's imminent bankruptcy had leaked out. In addition, the electricity and water supply units had their own contractual obligations – they were dealing with a large enterprise with tens of thousands of people, and a substantial amount of money, so they reported the matter to their provincial departmental leaders. In the nature of things, there was nothing the top brass could say about it. It was such a large amount, no one dared to just let the debt ride, nor would anyone take responsibility for writing it off. After studying the matter, the top brass gave responsibility for trying to get back the money owed to their subordinates by the end of the year. If they couldn't, then they'd have to work something out for themselves. In other words, the authorities were washing their hands of the matter, and, given the lack of any specific instructions, what else could be done except to cut off the electricity and water supplies?

New Year was coming up, and both at municipal and provincial level, the bosses of the energy supply bureaus seemed to have the same idea. An enterprise of this size was bound to find several million yuan, as they always did, to spend what needed to be spent and make up what needed to be made up. All they had to do was bring a little pressure to bear on the workers and the company by cutting off water and electricity supplies. That way, nothing bad would be reflected back on the top brass and there wouldn't be any great fuss. As long as companies felt the problem was urgent, they would certainly allocate funds as before, and then water, electricity and coal would be available as needed.

In the past, all work units had striven to find ways of asking their parent enterprises for money, but now it seemed that their tactics had changed, and they were doing their best to force their workers to raise petitions, make complaints and generally rebel!

How many people really thought about this nation anymore? How many felt a responsibility to the Party, and thought about the ordinary people?

What particularly infuriated Li Gaocheng was that here was a woman who had given her whole life to the company and was now suffering from an incurable disease, but not a single leadership cadre at any level had come to see what could be done for her.

He silently surveyed the scene in front of him.

It was still the same small, divided-up single-storey building, no bigger than a pigeon coop, the two-metre-long, one-metre-wide, plastic-sheeting-covered hallway, the two- or three-square metre "courtyard", the "kitchen" where half the pots and pans were sticking out into the street...

The only difference now was that the sick mother lived inside the building with her daughter-in-law who had just given birth, while the son had swapped places with his mother and lived in the hallway that was used as a "bedroom".

There was no electricity, and instead there were the kind of small paraffin lamps that had been used only in the countryside in the 1940s and 1950s. There was no water, and the "courtyard" housed an old water tank of a type that not even farmers used nowadays. A small, shallow charcoal briquette stove was used for both heating and cooking, probably to save coal, so, even in the darkness of the house, there was no light to be seen. In a corner under the eaves, there was a pile of several dozen charcoal briquettes, which didn't look nearly enough to see the household through the New Year Festival. These days, a cartload of briquettes cost nearly a hundred yuan at the very least.

It was only when you saw a place like this that you began truly to understand the value of money. It was no easy matter, no easy matter at all for a household like this to earn a hundred yuan.

The daughter-in-law had had a difficult birth and had been hospitalised for several days which had pretty much used up what little savings the household had. Honest and hard-working as he was, the son could not make a living working in the factory but didn't have the skills or the capital to do anything else. But, because he was afraid of losing his only job, he stayed on at the factory, even though he wasn't being paid. How could such a household be expected to support itself? How could it be expected to feed itself?

Forget about a hundred yuan – how was it going to earn even ten or twenty?

So this woman, who was almost sixty years old and had worked in a textile factory for almost her whole life was not even getting her meagre pension, was sick with advanced lung cancer, but still had to work her fingers to the bone for more than ten hours a day in impossibly harsh working conditions, in order to receive just five or six yuan! And those five or six yuan were probably all the household had to live off!

He stared in silence at the pale and ageing face in front of him, and, for a long time, found himself unable to speak. Xia Yulian was about the same age as him, but now she looked like an old woman on her very last legs. Her face was covered in wrinkles so deep they looked as if they had been carved into the flesh. Her hair was thin and grey, showing the evidence of her years of hard work and malnutrition. In her current state of drowsy lethargy, she looked so thin and emaciated that it was almost unbearable to see. The flickering of the dim, erratic kerosene lamp seemed to be announcing to the world that her journey along life's road was nearing its end...

No wonder it took her so long to recognise him when she saw him that day. She had said she was dizzy all the time; she had said her eyes had been blurry for such a long time; she had said she didn't dare to cross the street alone as she got dizzy when she saw cars and tractors; she had said she couldn't wear a mask because she couldn't breathe when she put one on; she had said she was getting old, older than her years; she had said her chest hurt after working only a short time; she had said she was completely useless, born to be a lady but reduced to a servant by bad luck and hard work; how different she was from before, now she had reached this great age.

She had thought of everything, except that she would end up suffering from an incurable disease, especially one that was so painful and cruel to the poor!

He looked around her and saw no nourishment, not even decent medicine. A patient with advanced lung cancer and she had only a small bag of Valium and a few dozen painkillers.

He felt as though he was standing by helplessly waiting for her to die.

How unfair it would be for a woman worker such as she had been to leave this world in such pain and suffering!

You only had to look at her face to realise that she had done nothing but toil and suffered nothing but hardship all her life. In all her long life, she had never known the leisure and pleasures of the rich. As a woman, she had never used or could even recognise all the different brands of cosmetics. Beauty creams costing hundreds or even thousands of yuan per tub were just a fantasy for her. A belt costing hundreds of dollars, a coat costing thousands of dollars, and a suit costing tens of thousands of dollars. She would never be able to understand how anyone could charge such sums for these things, let alone how anyone could afford them. Equally, she had never seen a luxury sauna or a fancy karaoke hall, and she could never imagine what went on in there. Nor could she ever imagine what a meal costing thousands or tens of thousands of yuan might be like, or how anyone could eat such a thing with a smile on their face and not a frown. She had no idea that, during the New Year festivities, when a family like hers was sweating over weighing out the five yuan worth of potatoes and ten yuan worth of cabbages, some leadership cadres were receiving tens of thousands of yuan in shopping vouchers from their subordinates. She would not have known that some people could offer bribes and gifts of as much as three hundred thousand yuan in one go. She could never have earned that much in ten lifetimes!

"...Manager Li!" Xia Yulian woke up with a start, seemingly confused, but as soon as she was properly awake, she sat up alertly and started to get out of bed. "Get a move on, Sanzi, and make Manager Li some tea!"

"Sanzi" was probably her pet name for her third son, and it must have been some kind of subconscious trick of her memory that she called Li Gaocheng "Manager Li" when she saw him on first waking up. It took Li Gaocheng quite some effort to stop her from getting out of bed and the minor tussle left Xia Yulian blue in the face and out of breath.

"Mayor Li, tell me the truth, is it... is it really all up for me this time?" Xia Yulian seemed to be fully awake now, and she looked directly at Li Gaocheng, panting slightly from shortness of breath, as she said: "Mayor Li, I am not the least bit afraid of death, and, if it weren't for my children, I could have died many times before now. I just want you to tell me the truth..."

When life is more painful than death, what is there to fear about dying? Li Gaocheng knew that she was simply being honest with him, but just at that moment, could he tell her the truth?

"Listen to me, Older Sister Xia, don't dwell on all that now. The most important thing at this moment is to recuperate in peace. Haven't I only just recovered from being ill myself? Do you know just how sick I was? Just listen to me, Older Sister. The reason I have come here today is to take you to the hospital in the city…"

"All right, all right, I can see you don't want to talk about it. I understand…" Xia Yulian interrupted him, suddenly looking a lot calmer and more settled.

"Uncle Li has been here for ages, Mum!" Xia Yulian's son interjected. "He has brought you lots of stuff, and three thousand yuan as well."

"There is one more thing, Mayor Li, and you mustn't try and hide it from me." Xia Yulian ignored her son's words and stared at Li Gaocheng. "Are you being sued by someone, and are the top brass investigating you? And has Aizhen been framed too? I've heard that you're going to be locked up soon!"

"Who did you hear that from?" Li Gaocheng asked in amazement. How could the news have spread so quickly? Even Xia Yulian in her sickbed at home had heard all about it.

"A load of people from the factory came to see me today and they told me all about it." Xia Yulian seemed to see the confirmation of the story on Li Gaocheng's face. "Why? Why are they doing this? Is it just because you listened to the workers and want to investigate the management? Is that why they've turned on you and are informing on you and Aizhen?"

"Don't worry, Older Sister Xia, nothing will happen. The provincial leaders still support our workers, and they still support me. There are some things that the workers don't understand, so don't listen to them."

"If the provincial leaders all support you, why do they still need to investigate you and Aizhen? Even if other people don't know what kind of people you two are, I do!"

"You must stop worrying and concentrate on getting better! Some of these things are very complicated, but they are not as people say or as you think. I will only tell you one thing for the moment, and that is that nothing is going to happen to me. Since you do know me so well, you can just make sure you get better and not worry about a thing."

Li Gaocheng firmly closed the topic with this and told Xia Yulian to go to the city hospital immediately.

"Now you listen to me, Mayor Li. I appreciate your kindness and I've spent all my time over the last few days thinking what a sick old woman like me can do to help you. If I was younger and still in good health, I would go back with you right now. You have such great responsibilities and are under such pressure, I could help you and Aizhen and your children by doing all the housework. But what can I do now? If I could prove your innocence by giving up my life, I would sacrifice it right now..."

Xia Yulian stopped abruptly at this and stared at Li Gaocheng for a long time, unable to say another word. Li Gaocheng was deeply moved and the room fell silent.

Finally, Li Gaocheng tried to persuade Xia Yulian to take his car into the city to go into hospital, but she said she would rather die than accept.

"I'm not going, so don't try to make me. Once I'm ga-ga and can't recognise anyone anymore, then you can take me there whenever you like. As long as my brain still works and I know what's happening with folk, I'm not going anywhere..." Xia Yulian was rock solid in her insistence and left no room for any doubt.

Li Gaocheng considered the situation and decided to leave it be. They could talk about it again another day.

As he was about to leave, Xia Yulian seemed to have something else she wanted to say to him, but, in the end, she held back and didn't speak.

CHAPTER FORTY-ONE

GO TO GUO ZHONGYAO'S HOME!

Once out of Xia Yulian's front door, this thought came to him as if from nowhere.

Was he angry? It didn't seem to him to be just that. Besides, what was the point in being angry with a cadre like Guo? And what right did he have to be angry with him anyway?

He just wanted to see, to see what kind of home the general manager of the Zhongyang Textile Group, a man he had personally promoted, was living in now.

Would he have no heating, no gas, no electricity and no water? Would he, like the workers, have neither food nor money and not be able to afford to see a doctor?

It was already around ten o'clock at night in mid-winter, and there was no electricity in the entire dormitory area. It was getting so dark he couldn't see his hand in front of his face. As soon as the car stopped and its headlights went out, he felt as though he had fallen into a cellar.

With some difficulty, Li Gaocheng groped his way into the two-storeyed building where Guo Zhongyao lived. It too had no electricity and was too dark to make out anything or anyone. The darkness of the building gave him a certain feeling of relief, as it meant that, however you looked at it, Guo Zhongyao was more or less in the same state as the workers, so he could be forgiven a little bit for his transgressions. On the surface at least, he was not so far gone in his presumption and arrogance as to have forgotten all shame.

Li Gaocheng knocked on the front door for a good long time, but no one came to open it nor was there any sound of movement from inside. How could there be no one in? Even if Guo Zhongyao himself had gone out, there surely must be someone left behind.

Li Gaocheng asked around after he had left the building, and finally found someone who told him: "Guo Zhongyao? Ah, you mean Director Guo! He wasn't going to stay here when there's no electricity, water or heating, was he? He wouldn't get a moment's peace from the factory workers. He would have had nothing but trouble if he had stayed here. Do you think production at the factory would still be stopped if he was living here? Would the workers still be causing trouble? Let me tell you, that man is like the wily rabbit that has three burrows. He has boltholes everywhere. He tells people they are his son's and daughter's homes, but actually, they belong to him. I've heard people say that, at the moment, he is in the east of the city in that luxury residential development they call "Mei Shu Ya" [Beautiful Relaxed Elegance] or some such name. I've also heard that he was the developer of the whole project, so, if you're looking for Boss Guo from Zhongyang Textiles, that's the place to ask."

On the surface at least, "Mei Shu Ya" lived up to its name.

The development was essentially divided into three grades: ultra-luxury, luxury, and general luxury. None of the three were affordable for ordinary people.

The ultra-luxury type was a small free-standing two-storey house with its own gate and courtyard, the luxury type was a small free-standing two-storey building for two households with a shared courtyard, and the general luxury type was a single-storey house of something over a hundred square metres, with a loft.

Guo Zhongyao was living in one of the ultra-luxurious single-occupancy, two-storey courtyard houses.

Li Gaocheng stood angrily in front of the gate for a long time. It was taller and wider than the house he remembered belonging to the secretary of the Provincial Party Committee! In terms of "Beautiful Relaxed Elegance", the Provincial Secretary's building couldn't hold a candle to it.

"Fuck it!" Li Gaocheng suddenly spat out the words. It was the first time in many years that he had sworn like that. In fact, he wasn't even sure who it was directed at. Himself? The house? Guo Zhongyao for living in the house?

Within three seconds of him ringing the doorbell, the door light came on, and within twenty seconds the door opened.

A little nanny about the same age as Xiao Lian looked at Li Gaocheng in some surprise and asked: "Who do you want?"

"Guo Zhongyao."

"Who are you?"

"Li Gaocheng."

"What do you want?"

"To see him."

As he spoke, Li Gaocheng began to push his way in. The little nanny tried to stop him, found she couldn't and began to yell at him. Immediately two men appeared. They looked like Public Security officers, but they lacked the shoulder flashes. As soon as Li Gaocheng saw them, he recognised them as Zhongyang Textiles security guards.

"Who are you?" one of them asked in a hectoring tone.

"Tell Guo Zhongyao to come out here!" Li Gaocheng replied equally fiercely.

"And you are… Ah! Mayor Li!" the man exclaimed in suddenly strangled tones.

"Please come in, Mayor Li, please come in! Director Guo is inside!" The other man was immediately cordiality itself.

"Director Guo, Mayor Li is here to see you!" the first man called out as he ushered Li Gaocheng inside.

Perhaps because the television was on so loud and the shout hadn't reached him, Guo Zhongyao was still sitting on the sofa when Li Gaocheng came into the living room. As soon as he saw Li striding in, Guo Zhongyao leapt to his feet as if he'd been given an electric shock. He stared at Li as if he had seen a ghost.

Once Li Gaocheng was fully in the room, he understood why Guo was looking at him like that. Sitting on the huge sofa in the centrally heated living room, there was a girl all dolled up in a fashionable and provocative outfit.

As he took in the girl's flamboyant and wanton appearance, Li Gaocheng knew immediately this was not an ordinary girl. She clearly wasn't a guest, or Guo's wife, daughter or other relative. No guest would be making herself quite so much at home, nor would she be dressed so skimpily. She would certainly not be wearing a pair of slippers only suitable for the bedroom, either, nor would she be reclining on the sofa as if she had just been asleep. His wife would not have such a cute but fundamentally disinterested expression on her face. The girl didn't seem to notice Li Gaocheng's surprised expression, or, if she did, she ignored it. A daughter or other relative would never be so heavily made-up in the presence of her seniors, nor be displaying such a wanton and uninhibited attitude.

Li Gaocheng knew quite well that Guo Zhongyao had never remarried after his divorce. Of course, he always said that he had not found a suitable woman yet, mainly because he was too busy with work to give it any attention. So, was the woman here now the one he had been looking for?

If she was, then any respect Li Gaocheng had for Guo Zhongyao would disappear in an instant. He would be no better than an animal. The girl was twenty years old at best, young enough to be his granddaughter!

And if none of these were the case, then there was the probability that this woman was one of those protégés of Guo Zhongyao who the workers were so outraged by, as reflected in the materials in the complaint.

"Get up, get up!" Guo Zhongyao looked exasperated as he shouted rather desperately at the woman on the sofa. "Mayor Li is here, and there you are still lying down!"

"Oh! Mayor Li!" The woman was busy chewing something and it took her a while to realise what was going on. She stood up and looked askance at Guo Zhongyao. "It's your fault, you didn't tell me! How was I supposed to know it was Mayor Li. If I had known he was coming, I would have greeted him at the door, wouldn't I..."

"All right, all right! Go and sit in the bedroom for now. I have something to talk to Mayor Li about. Hurry up!"

The woman looked down in annoyance, then glanced at Guo Zhongyao with a pout, and shuffled off into the bedroom.

The fact that he was consorting with a woman like that said a lot about Guo Zhongyao's status and preferences!

"This is one of my nieces, Mayor Li. She's very spoiled and ignorant and of no great account." As Guo Zhongyao made his explanations, he hurriedly cleaned up the mess on the sofa.

"Sit down, Mayor Li, sit down! Xiao Li, go and make a pot of good tea!" he shouted peremptorily at the nanny. From the look of him, as soon as the girl was out of the room, he felt his dignity and solemnity as a company director returning. Gradually, his expression became more honest, straightforward, serious and a little sad.

"Enough! What do I want with your good tea when I haven't even eaten yet!" Li Gaocheng said rather brusquely. "First find somewhere for my driver and my secretary to eat. We can talk and eat right here. I've got some things I want to ask you."

"What? Here, Mayor Li?" Guo Zhongyao asked in some embarrassment. "I don't have anything decent in the house."

"Anything will do as long as it's quick!"

In a quarter of an hour, the coffee table was laden with a selection of appetizing dishes including braised pig's trotters, spiced beef, Korean kimchi, American almonds, a pair of fragrant spicy squab pigeons, several quick-fried crabs, a pot of live "drunken shrimp" and two top-price bottles of Jiugui liquor.

It was apparent that this CEO, who was supposedly on the verge of bankruptcy, had very good taste, and nothing was too good for him at home.

"There are also a few frozen dumplings I brought back from Beijing. They are just cooking at the moment, and they'll be ready soon." Guo Zhongyao was making himself busy. "Actually, they are ready-made ones. If I was to make them, they'd be a lot better. You still know my skills, Mayor Li. After so many years without a wife, there may not be any other benefits, but my cooking has improved a lot..."

"OK, let's eat together."

"Actually, Mayor Li, I've already eaten, but since a visit from you is such a rare event, I'll drink a couple of glasses of wine with you." As he was talking, Guo Zhongyao hurriedly opened one of the bottles. He poured a generous amount into his boss's glass.

It was hard to tell whether Li was hungry or angry as he lowered his head and started eating and drinking in great mouthfuls, without looking at Guo Zhongyao. After a couple of gulps of wine, both men's faces began to turn red. Guo Zhongyao's formerly nervous expression was smoothed out by the fumes of the liquor.

"Mayor Li, I've been looking for a chance to have a chat with you for quite a few days now, but I certainly didn't expect you to come here." Guo Zhongyao now seemed to have returned to his normal sincere and respectful self. "You were sick a little while ago. I went to see you, but you slept for two days and two nights and didn't wake up at all. I sat by myself at your bedside for a long time and, to tell you the truth, as I looked at you in that state, my eyes were swollen from crying."

"Why were you crying? Were you feeling sorry for me?" Li Gaocheng took a big gulp of wine.

"Mayor Li, do you think, at this time, I feel I have any right to pity others?" Guo Zhongyao said, his eyes already bloodshot. "I felt sorry for you then, really sorry for you."

"Why?" Li Gaocheng asked, slowly raising his head to look at Guo Zhongyao.

"Do you really need me to tell you again? What can you still not be sure about?" Guo Zhongyao picked up the wine glass and took a sip of wine under Li Gaocheng's scrutiny. "I know quite well that you know everything about us. Anyone trying to hide something from you is just a fool. Even if you could be deceived about other things, nobody can hide anything from you about the textile industry."

"If that is the case, then there are some things I want to ask you. Are you brave enough to tell me the truth?"

"I've told you so much already, Mayor Li, do you think there is anything I don't dare tell you?" Guo Zhongyao seemed to be using the wine as cover to show that he didn't care about anything and was taking the opportunity to say all the things he usually wouldn't dare say. "The truth is I haven't been a good person for a long time now, Mayor Li. Isn't that what everyone is saying these days, that I'm a gangster who isn't afraid of anyone? It's a fact, isn't it, that it's the same in the business world and in the official world. When someone has gone this far, what else is there for him to be afraid of? I've already told you that with Zhongyang Textiles, if there is a superficial investigation it will only find superficial problems, if there is a major investigation, it will find major problems, and if there is no investigation at all, there will be no problems at all either. The more minor the corruption, the more people will investigate you, and the bigger the corruption, the fewer people will dare to investigate. The problems at Zhongyang Textiles are so great that no one dares investigate them. If they were to be properly looked into, so many people and such large groups of people would be implicated that no one would dare to investigate them or allow a proper investigation. I'm about to turn fifty-eight, and that is the state Zhongyang Textiles is in. Just think about it, there's no management job for me to do there and nothing else open to me, I'm not short of money to spend and I'm not afraid of your investigation. So, like I say, just think about it: what is there in the world for me to fear?"

"And this is really what you think and feel?" Li Gaocheng was looking at Guo Zhongyao as though he was some strange object. "Is this the real reason you have turned into what you are now?"

"Is what I am really so hateful to people? Do you think I am not telling you the truth?"

"So, when it is me who is the gangster, I need to be afraid of everyone, but when it's you who is the gangster, everyone is afraid of you, is that it? And no one is going to find you hateful when you are like this? If you are really not afraid of anything, why aren't you living in the factory compound? Why are you living here? If you are really not afraid of anything, why, even when you are living here, let alone when you go anywhere at all, do you need to have bodyguards clearing the way before you and guarding your back? You're living here but you still need several security guards from the factory standing guard over you. Why is that?"

"You've got things all wrong if that's how you think, Mayor Li. The only time to be afraid of the masses is when they have lost faith in the Communist Party and banded together. At the moment, most of them still believe in the Communist Party and have faith in the Party cadres, so there is no danger of them banding together against us. I am still a Party man and a Party cadre, so I give the impression of representing the Party and of representing the government. That's why the Party and the government will protect my interests and protect my image. In those circumstances, why should I fear the masses? The reason I am not going back to the factory is simply to make an impression on the leaders, to put pressure on them. A decision has to be made about the question of Zhongyang Textiles, and I say there is only one possible decision: to go bankrupt."

"I quite understand that you lot have been wanting to do that for a long time now. If the company goes bankrupt, absolutely everything gets written off doesn't it!" Li Gaocheng drained his glass at a gulp, then looked directly at Guo Zhongyao and said: "Do you really think you can write all this off at a stroke of a pen, Guo Zhongyao?"

"At least I don't feel threatened at the moment. To tell the truth, Mayor Li, I think it is you people are most worried about." Guo Zhongyao seemed to be growing in self-confidence as he spoke, and any misgivings he had also seemed to be disappearing. He poured Li Gaocheng some more wine and continued: "You are a serious talent, someone who gets things done. The truth is, our society only needs two types of people – doers and followers. I've been thinking about myself a lot over the last few days, and I think that, on the whole, I am one of the followers. Doers get to the top through their own efforts, followers scramble up behind them. Doers rely on their own ability, followers rely on brown-nosing, bribery, flattery, fawning and currying favour to keep their superiors happy and comfortably free from worry. But just because society needs these two types of people, that doesn't mean that either can feel safe and secure. Only someone who is both can do that."

"And that's what you think you are?"

"Yes, I think I am." Guo Zhongyao continued to speak openly and honestly. "My own ability to get things done can't be compared to yours, but it's there nonetheless. I don't have any great skills, so my being a follower comes at a price and I can't let you cut me loose just as you please. The truth with Zhongyang Textiles is that, over many years, I have nurtured countless people so that they could protect the company. It's just the same as rearing a dog. Why do you do it if it's not to get them to guard your gate? I'm telling you what I really believe now and I'm not deliberately trying to bad mouth other people to you. And what about Yan Zhen? I know that he has his own opinion of you at the moment and that you have yours about him. It is because I don't share either of those opinions that I can say that he is no match for you. At best, he is a reasonably intelligent dog. A big dog that I've fattened up! Although he's protecting me now, I really don't care about him at all!"

"How much have you given Yan Zhen over all these years?"

"Directly or indirectly?"

"You tell me."

"It's hard to say exactly. To give you an analogy, it's like the price of goods in the market. It's always going up. Ten years ago, how much did it cost to celebrate the New Year? How much does it cost nowadays? In the past, a leader's child's birthday would cost one thousand yuan, but now it's three to five thousand yuan, wouldn't you say? In the past, a leader's family could spend two or three thousand yuan on New Year's Eve, but could you get by with that now? In the past, a leader could go abroad for three to five thousand yuan, but now you would need ten to twenty thousand! There is also university education for their children, as well as birthdays and weddings, parents' birthdays and funerals, and expenses when leaders move house or fall ill, even for their clothes and daily necessities. All of these have to be taken care of. Of course, that doesn't even touch on the various needs of the leaders' wives. But why stop with the leadership? Don't we have to reimburse all kinds of stuff to the provincial and municipal departmental chiefs? Even the receipts for clothes and cosmetics end up here. In the end, I just thought, screw it! If we're just going to end up reimbursing you, why don't we just order it for you and get it delivered to you and be done with it? Fur coats, cashmere sweaters, merino wool suits, high-end cosmetics, they'll take whatever we give them. Mayor Li, do you have any idea how many leading cadres this company has to support? The fact is, I am nurturing them! Are they ever going to investigate Zhongyang Textiles even if they want to? Everyone knows that you have never accepted any gifts over the years, but do you know how much we have spent on your wife? Do you know what the total bill for your brother-in-law, your nephew and your wife adds up to? Do you know how much we spent in total when your mother died? Let's be clear about this, shall we? It's not just about you. How much do you reckon this has all cost us at every level and in every context?

"To be honest, we knew of Yan Zhen before we came into contact with you. Back then, Yan Zhen needed someone to make him look good, someone who could get things done, and he chose you. We knew back then that our hopes lay in the time after you left the company. Those hopes weren't for money or luxury goods and suchlike – they were that, once you left, you would rise quickly through the ranks. In fact, it was through you that we got to know Yan Zhen properly, and without him, we wouldn't be where we are today, and nor would you. The thing that you don't understand is that without us, you wouldn't be where you are today either. Perhaps you don't know, even now, how much stuff we gave Yan Zhen without your knowledge. Are you aware that, back then, Yan Zhen could have wiped out hundreds of thousands, not to say millions, of our business and profits with a casual note or telephone call? The way things look now, the fact that you became deputy mayor and then mayor was entirely down to your own abilities and prestige. It may be true that you had the trust and support of the majority of leadership cadres, but if you hadn't had Yan Zhen's vote, or he had vetoed you, would you have been promoted so quickly? Without our material support, maybe the mayor today would not be you. We support you, ostensibly for your sake, but actually for ourselves. Of course, if you become a big tree, we will enjoy the shade too. What we didn't anticipate was how big an appetite Yan Zhen would turn out to have. However much we fed him, it was never enough to satisfy him. If you want an honest estimate, since we first met Yan Zhen up to now, we must have given him, indirectly, at least a good few million!"

"It must be more than that," Li Gaocheng said coldly, without looking at him. "When you say a few million indirectly, are you just talking about the net profit? How can it be only a few million when you have hundreds of millions of yuan of the country's cash as capital?"

"You are right. What I estimated was just the money that ended up in his hands. But to get that money, to get those several million, he used these tens of thousands of workers, this enterprise that employed those workers and its many hundred million worth of state-owned assets as capital. When you get down to it, it was him who ruined the company's future and the whole huge

Zhongyang Textile Group collapsed because of the 'gifts' he was given!"

Clearly well into his cups now, Guo Zhongyao had shed his apparent indifference and wept openly. Perhaps his outpourings were indeed revealing his deepest and innermost thoughts.

Li Gaocheng felt a powerful tremor in his heart at the sight of the other man's tears. What shocked him most and what he had least expected was that, right from the beginning, it had been their money that had set him on his way. His position had been bought! And it had taken just one man, one Yan Zhen, to destroy so many cadres, to destroy such a huge enterprise and to destroy so many workers.

"What you are saying is that I owe you a lifetime's gratitude for what I am today. Is that it?" Li Gaocheng said coolly as he went on eating. "I can't see what you have to cry about – you're living in a house like this, eating and drinking only the best, you've got your bodyguards and you've even got a girl to keep you company. The landlords, rich farmers and capitalists of the old society left off where you are just starting! So, what are you crying about? Surely it must surpass your wildest dreams of comfort to have been able to use your power and ability to get to a place like this and have such wealth, so what have you got to be sad about? Do you think it's not enough? You became an official with the support of the Communist Party, and now you have made such a fortune by exploiting the weaknesses and loopholes of that same Communist Party. Are you still not satisfied? Just look at your house! Only a millionaire could live in a place like this. Who else could afford it? Tell me the truth, how much money do you have in your bank account right now? How many other houses do you have as well as this one?"

"You are wrong, Mayor Li. I am not as rotten as you seem to think. When it comes down to it, I'm just another human being, aren't I?" Guo Zhongyao vigorously wiped the tears from his eyes. "I'm only living here temporarily. The factory has no electricity, no water and no heating, and, besides, the workers have strong opinions about me. It's not safe for me to live there. That's the only reason I'm here for the moment. To be honest, the company has invested pretty much all the money it has made from outside enterprises in this residential development. At first, we thought that the real estate business was easy, and we were sure to make a lot of money, but we didn't anticipate that just as we made our investment, the price of housing would drop. We've had tens of millions of yuan bet on this place over a few years now, and we haven't seen even a third of that in returns yet. To tell you the truth, Mayor, this place pretty much finished off the company's tertiary enterprise. If we hadn't invested in real estate, we wouldn't be in the situation we're in now. You asked how much money I have in the bank, how much state money I've spirited away. Well, truthfully, out of the whole mess of six to seven hundred thousand yuan, there's probably less than four hundred thousand in the bank at the moment. That's all that is left to me after all these years and there's one thing I can guarantee you and that is that I have done the sums and, if I am ever properly investigated, I may be expelled from the Party and put in prison for a few years, but I won't be executed or given a life sentence. There's nothing to worry me there and I'm not afraid of it. People are making a fuss about me having millions or tens of millions of yuan, but I ask you, in all conscience! I haven't got that greedy! To tell you the truth, I thought at the time that, if our tertiary enterprises began to make real money, I would surely be able to find a way to revive Zhongyang Textiles. If Zhongyang Textiles goes, I will be totally done for. I'm almost sixty – what else can I do other than try and put a bit of money aside? I truly haven't forgotten about Zhongyang Textiles for a moment. I may have been saying that the best thing is to let the company go bankrupt, but if it does, I will be the first one to suffer."

"The way you tell it, the workers should be thanking you, not hating you, shouldn't they!" Li Gaocheng's face still betrayed no sign of bitterness or loathing as he spoke calmly. "So, the way you see it, you can talk about those hundreds of thousands of yuan with a clear conscience because they are a trifling sum compared to those tens of millions and hundreds of millions and you can still be considered an honest and upright official. We got it right when we made you CEO, and you are an excellent cadre worthy of our trust. You haven't brought disgrace on us but covered us in glory. Is that the story?"

"I haven't told you all this to make you think well of me. I just wanted to explain a little that it wasn't my deliberate intention that Zhongyang Textiles should be reduced to the state it is now in. I know that you are angry with me. I have brought disgrace on you, and I have implicated you, but from the very start, I really have wanted the company to prosper. Why else would I have taken such great risks in the tertiary sector? Do you think I feel good about Xinchao being tens of millions of yuan in debt? Even if no one can investigate me right now, I have been thinking about it, and sooner or later the day will come when that does happen. Even if I can escape the government, I am never going to escape the eyes of those tens of thousands of workers, am I!" Guo Zhongyao took another big gulp of wine, his expression betraying no sign of hypocrisy.

"Come off it! Are you still lying to me, even now? Supposing Xinchao does have tens of millions of debt, that is money owed to the state, you must know that! You say that it is in debt, but who knows that for sure? And what about Te Gao Te? How much is that worth? How much does it earn every year? How much is the Chang Long Garment and Textile Factory worth and how much does it earn? How much do those two earn you every year? And how much is this 'Mei Shu Ya' development you are living in worth? You said that you haven't recovered the cost yet, and maybe that is the truth, maybe you have only recovered a third of your investment, but how much is that investment in total? It's worth almost one hundred million, right? And you've already recovered a third of that? So, the fact is that you have already earned back what you should have earned back, you have made all the profit you deserve, and everything else is effectively a loan you owe back to the state. You say you don't own this house, and you are just living here temporarily, but there are plenty of places you could do that, so why do you have to live here? You might be able to fool little children with this nonsense, but even the workers know the kind of tricks you are pulling, and here you are still trying to fool me! You just said that you weren't afraid of being investigated by anyone so you would tell me the whole truth, but that is exactly what you don't dare do. It seems to me that you are still afraid, so what is it that you are afraid of? The workers? I've seen you lecturing them on the company's internal television station, and you were like a father scolding his children. It didn't look like you were afraid there. The way I see it, there is nothing for you to be afraid of at the moment. You don't seem to be bothered in the slightest by me, and I'm the mayor, so who exactly could you be afraid of? If you really were afraid, would you just bring a few security guards and come and live in a place like this?"

"Who told you all this, Mayor Li?" Although Guo Zhongyao seemed to be quite drunk, he was still taken aback by what Li Gaocheng said. Maybe he hadn't expected him to have such a clear picture of what was going on. "Everything you said has nothing at all to do with me, and what I told you really is the truth. I'm not involved in these things at all. I've got no say in them nor any part in them either."

"But you still get the benefit of them! Even if you're not stealing anything yourself, you are still feathering your nest with the proceeds!" Li Gaocheng burst out furiously but then calmed down. "Zhongyao, I really don't understand someone like you, given the position you are in. The Communist Party trusts you, and the country and the government have given you more than enough, so why do you say you still need all this money? Are you really happy living all alone in a huge house like this? You turned a big management team into a tight little bunch of cronies intent on filling their own pockets, so even if you are not afraid now, are you so confident about the future? The workers haven't reached a point of total desperation yet, but supposing the day comes when that changes, even if you aren't afraid for yourself, aren't you afraid of dragging your family into it? And what about the Communist Party? It has been very good to you, raised you to your lofty status and yet you have been secretly trashing it and undermining it. Are you not afraid it is going to want to settle accounts with you?"

"Do you think I haven't thought about all that for myself? But there's nothing I can do, there's absolutely nothing I can do!" Guo Zhongyao took another sip of the powerful wine, thought for a long time, and finally said, as if he had been relieved of a great weight: "When you were here, everyone followed your example. We worked hard every day, but we were also carefree. We put our heart and soul into our work, and no one thought of lining their own pockets! At least I know I didn't. Like you said, the Communist Party gave me this lofty official position and that was something beyond the wildest dreams of a poor boy like me from a family that had had to labour for its living for generations. Back then, I just wanted to help the factory thrive, to do right by the nation, to do right by the workers, to do right by myself and, most importantly of all, to do right by the Communist Party. But as soon as you were transferred, things started happening. At that time, people had high hopes of me. First, I was your protégé. Second, I was the deputy director, and I was the natural successor. Third, I probably considered myself a well-intentioned and reliable person. Fourth, it was actually what people seemed to want, as they felt that I was easy to talk to and easy to discuss things with. To put it bluntly, they were very suggestible and had no ideas of their own. They listened to whatever I had to say, and, like I told you just now, they were just compliant and competent flunkeys. Mayor Li, you are good at everything you do, with one failing. You lack discrimination and you are not a political person. You can't tell the difference between straightforward people and toadies. Take me for example, you got me all wrong. I'm not leadership material at all. When I was asked to follow your example in raising production and promoting business, the results were very ordinary. When I was made CEO, the boss of the whole company, I turned out to be incompetent. I simply wasn't up to it. And just look at that man, Feng Minjie! You let him become the deputy general manager in charge of supply and distribution. Back then, money was still worth something, and people didn't treat tens of thousands of yuan as if they were nothing like they do now. Do you know how much money he took out of his department in one go to get you made deputy mayor as soon as possible, all so he could climb another rung up the ladder more quickly? Four hundred thousand yuan! Four hundred thousand! I was stunned. If that was ever discovered, even if I had ten heads, they would all be cut off!"

"Four hundred thousand? And that was before I left?" Li Gaocheng looked up silently, seemingly unable to process the information.

"Of course you didn't know anything about it at the time. You were under constant inspection by the leadership, and you had a whole lot of business engagements. You must remember that you went to take part in some activity in Beijing and you were away for a full twenty days. Feng Minjie asked me at the time if I knew why the top brass were inspecting you so thoroughly if it wasn't because they wanted to give you some exposure at that level. I thought he was crazy at the time and told him he wanted to be a fucking official so badly it was doing his head in. He was asking to be fucking shot by trying to buy a post with that much money all in one go. Actually, I knew exactly what he had in mind. On the face of it, he wanted to find a way of speeding up the process of getting you made deputy mayor, but in fact he was doing it for himself. He wanted to speed things up a bit and push you out the door as soon as possible. Up till then, he had been having trouble finding an opportunity to get close to the upper echelons, but now they wanted to inspect you, he could kill two birds with one stone and ride on your coattails to make his own contact with the top brass and smooth his path. If he could establish his reputation, he wouldn't have to fear any consequences if he took a few risks. Even if something went wrong and there was an investigation, nothing could be traced back directly to him.

"I also have some observations to make about the way things were back then. First, he was thinking of you. Second, he was thinking of me. Third, his actions can't be considered a mistake. Fourth, what Secretary Yan Zhen said about it was that the money was just a temporary loan for the use of the municipal leaders and he was certainly not going to use it for any other purpose. Back then, Secretary Yan was about to go on a fact-finding tour of America, Australia and Europe and he had apparently let it slip that the Municipal Government was in need of some foreign currency and wondered whether a company with foreign connections like Zhongyang Textiles might not be able to offer a solution. It may have been said without any real intention, but someone who heard it might take it to heart. Feng Minjie certainly remembered it. The Zhongyang Textile Group didn't have any foreign currency at the time, so Feng Minjie used the money to buy thirty thousand US dollars and forty thousand Hong Kong dollars on the black market. The day after you came back from Beijing, he forced me to go with him to give the currency to Secretary Yan Zhen. To be honest, I was really scared at the time. My legs were like jelly when we went into his house. To my astonishment, he didn't say a word about the money when we put it on his desk. After chatting away inconsequentially for quite a while, he told us to report back to you that there weren't any significant issues with the results of their investigations of you and that you should go and see him in a couple of days' time. A fortnight later, your appointment as deputy mayor was announced. Feng Minjie was so angry he started cursing and swearing in front of me, saying that he was the one who had really bought you your post as deputy mayor. There is not a word of a lie in all this, Mayor Li, not a word!"

Li Gaocheng looked at Guo Zhongyao's earnest expression and found himself unable to speak for a considerable time. It seemed to him that it must all be true, and even if there were a few discrepancies, they were probably of no real consequence – the overall picture was accurate. He looked silently at the wine glass in front of him and almost felt like crying. In the end, he just said: "So, it was then that you started to change and turn into what you are now?"

"Maybe it was, I can't even say for sure myself. That time certainly had an enormous effect on me. I didn't expect it to turn out like this. Just think about it for a minute. Everything about the past is sacred and special to me because both you and I got where we are entirely through our own efforts, didn't we?"

"And are you saying that all the complaints the workers have made are true?"

"Some are, some aren't. Workers are workers, after all, and they don't know anything about anything, let alone about a huge enterprise like ours. It's only what we few say that counts. Whatever decision is reached it will be recorded in an official document and that will be that. These last few years have been completely different from when you were here, Mayor Li. Back then, you promoted whoever did a good job, but recently we have promoted anyone who did what they were told. That's the only possible way of doing it now. There are so many problems in the company, we wouldn't know what to do if anything went wrong internally. Outsiders can make any complaints they like and it won't worry us, but if there are any complaints from insiders, that would be very dangerous. For example, the Discipline Inspection Commission has to form its own team and so must the Workers' Association, not to mention the secretary of the Party Committee. To tell the truth, Mayor Li, it is like taking drugs. Once you start, you are on the road to nowhere and you shouldn't imagine there is any turning back, even if you want to. Do you really think it can work if you are the only clean one, and everybody else is dirty? Do you think everyone will agree with you? Will they tolerate you? Will they ever support you again? Will they ever listen to you again? Will you still be able to order them about? Will you still be able to hold on to your position as CEO? Are you still a stable general manager? In their eyes, what's the use of you as a leader if you are of no benefit to them? Mayor Li, the past few years have been very different from before. There is nothing I can do about it, absolutely nothing!"

"So, what you are saying is that everyone else's corruption is an active choice, but with you it is something passive and only done as a last resort. You think that a distinction should be made between the two because they are essentially two different things?"

"That may be your way of putting it, but you don't understand my real feelings. You are too intimately involved yourself to be able to see the bigger picture. Have you considered, Mayor Li, that if, in a given setting, everybody thought differently from you and acted differently from you, no matter how good a man you were, and how great your deeds, would you still be considered a good man in the eyes of the other people in that same setting? From their point of view, wouldn't everything you did be evil?"

"And that's why you could bring back thousands of tons of substandard cotton bought at high-quality prices and sell obsolete machinery as scrap, and buy them back as new products at inflated prices? There was no alternative even to such wickedness as that? Does that mean there is no difference between this and murder or arson? You commit the most heinous crimes, and you can still say you had no alternative? You gloss over all problems and responsibilities, saying they are the result of social forces, that they are caused by the system. If the topmost beam is crooked so will all the ones below it be, so if your superiors are all acting corruptly, you have no choice but to do the same. Is it that simple for you? It has nothing to do with you and who you are? Flies don't cluster round an egg that isn't cracked. If your mouth wasn't open with your tongue hanging out, do you think all these things would come your way by chance?

"I didn't come to see you at this time of night just to listen to your attempts to justify yourself. I just don't understand why you have done all this. What is really in your heart of hearts? Why are you doing this? Why? You have everything you could want, you don't lack for anything. When you are a leading cadre at this level, a serious, bureau-level cadre, what concerns could you have that would make you act like this? Tell me the truth. I simply don't understand, and I just want to hear what you honestly think." Li Gaocheng's eyes were red-rimmed and perhaps it was the drink that was making him so stubbornly insistent on getting right to the bottom of things.

"Since you insisted on asking the question, you shouldn't be angry if you don't like the answer," Guo Zhongyao replied, his eyes equally red-rimmed. "I'm still not sure, Mayor Li, whether you are as good as you make out, or whether you are pulling the wool over my eyes. Did you truly know nothing at all about what your wife was getting up to? Then again, did you really have no clue about what we were doing all those years? Was there a single New Year during all that time you were at the factory when we didn't come to your home? Was there a single time we didn't bring twenty or thirty thousand yuan? Quite apart from anything else, didn't we make a one-off gift of twenty thousand and some other goods especially for when your daughter Meimei went to university? We spent thirty or forty thousand yuan all told, making sure that she went to a decent university and got a good degree. Could you really not know about it? We always knew that it was your wife who handled it all, but we couldn't bring ourselves to believe that you never even asked about it. Did you honestly not know the real story?"

"Keep going, I'm listening!" Li Gaocheng glared at Guo Zhongyao.

"I know the kind of man you are, Mayor Li. You are a selfless man, entirely devoted to your work, but have you not changed over all the years? Are you still just the same as you used to be? Do you still have such a rosy view of society? Do you have as much confidence in it as you used to?"

"Can you be a bit more explicit about what you are getting at?" Li Gaocheng sounded very serious, but then he continued, encouragingly: "It doesn't matter, just say what you think. It's like you said, there's nothing I can do to you at this time anyway. Of course I won't be angry with you, so just go ahead and speak your mind."

"Mayor Li, you have been in such an exalted high position for so many years, have you not considered the future of this country? The future of our Party?"

"And have you already despaired of the country and the Party?"

"And you are still full of hope, then?"

"What do you think?"

"Actually, I think we are all pretending. On the surface, we are all busy and confident, but inside everyone is making their preparations. I think that everyone is waiting. Waiting for the day to come."

"...the day? What day?"

"Do you want me to spell it out for you, Mayor Li?"

"Are you saying that, sooner or later, the country and the Party are bound to collapse?"

"That's not what I mean. Neither the country nor the Party will collapse. They will survive, but their essential nature will no longer be the same."

"I understand. You are saying that superficially there will be no change, but fundamentally, everything will be completely different. The Communist Party will not be the Communist Party of the past, socialism will not be true socialism. It will be new wine in an old bottle. It will all just be a hollow pretence. That's what you mean, isn't it?"

"It is the kind of thinking that can be entertained but not expressed, is that clear enough for you? Let's leave it at that."

"And that's why you have stepped up your preparations, and why you are cramming money into your pockets as fast as you can. I guess like this, you think you can have it both ways. If you want money, you can have money and if you want power, you can have power. If the country is still socialist, you can be a government official, and if it's capitalist, you can be a capitalist plutocrat. Why should you be afraid of anything anyway, you'll always be one of the men on top. That's it, isn't it?"

"Isn't that what you think too, Mayor Li? We have to have a way out. We have to leave ourselves an escape route. Doesn't the cunning rabbit still have three burrows? Don't we have to give thought to our future?"

"Is that how you see all the leading cadres? Is that how you see everyone?"

"Not all of them of course, but quite a lot."

"So, deep down, is this one of the real reasons for your corruption? In other words, is it because you have lost faith in the Party and the country, because you have lost any hope in them that you began with your corrupt practices?"

"If almost everyone is doing the same thing, can you still call it corruption?"

"Do you think that a collective corruption like yours can give you peace of mind and leave you nothing to worry about?"

"Yes, for the moment, at least, this is how it is. If you pull up a radish you will always get a great clump of mud too and make a big hole. You could say the situation is like a bundle of explosives. It will blow up anyone who disturbs it. In those circumstances, who is going to want to stir things up by investigating? If others want to reap financial benefit from us, then they have to protect our political interests. To put it more bluntly, if I'm the one who is nurturing them and looking after them, they have to listen to me, don't they? So, we made sure people benefitted from us, and they naturally became our protectors and spokesmen.

"To tell the truth, after you left, I didn't want to make the Zhongyang Textiles such a big outfit. But when I thought about it later, it struck me that, the bigger I made it, the larger the conglomerate I turned it into, with tens of thousands of workers, the more secure it would be. With so many workers and such a large field of operations, wouldn't the banks be willing to give us loans to ensure stability? Wouldn't the government support us at every turn? Looking at it now, right from the outset it seems to have been the right decision. If our field of operations wasn't so big, if we hadn't been getting so many loans year after year, we would have been swept up long ago and never have survived until today. Why is it that the smaller the problem the more trouble it causes, and the bigger the problem the safer you are? Well, I've just explained what is one of the major reasons. In fact, haven't you already experienced this for yourself? Why have you been so timid and cautious about Zhongyang Textiles' affairs? Why has the company kept receiving huge loans despite its massive losses, if not for the sake of stability? Would you have offered such a lifeline to a small business? So, I'm not worried at all about my current situation, and I'm not worried at all about Zhongyang Textiles. If you buy stability with money, the state will definitely look after you. Even if the company goes bankrupt, the state will never let it get into real trouble, and it will have to find a way to look after the workers. If everything, including our personal affairs, is fully and openly investigated, how are you going to explain it all to the workers? At this moment, Mayor Li, I am not worried for myself, but I am really worried for you. Have you got a good explanation for those three hundred thousand yuan of yours? For your wife? For your brother-in-law? For your nephew?"

"So you know about all that, do you?"

"This is how things stand now. If you are serious about opposing corruption, your head may be the first one to roll. Then again, if you decide not to investigate the problems at Zhongyang Textiles, what will the result of that be? Won't you end up being investigated yourself? If you go on the way you are going, it is quite likely you will end up destroying yourself."

"You don't seem to be very optimistic."

"It's not a question of 'seeming' – that's how things are. In fact, what you are trying to protect is purely imaginary. I used to be like you. I used to try to fight and put up some kind of resistance, but I backed off in the end because I wasn't going to do it at my own expense. Isn't it a bit stupid to oppose others while destroying your own position? I think you will end up like me, Mayor Li, but you will only wake up to things once you are properly battered and bruised. Let me presume on my status as your former subordinate to try to persuade you once again. It is still not too late for you to turn back. As long as you listen to Yan Zhen, we can all protect you. Even if you can't respect a person like him, I urge you not to set yourself against him, because you can never beat him. Even if someone reports him to the central authorities, there is still no way to take him down. Because these people have already mastered all that Communist Party stuff, forget about all the bad things he has done, which everyone knows about anyway. If you really want to investigate him, I guarantee you won't find anything..."

"Well, thank you! I didn't know you were so kind-hearted!" Li Gaocheng drank his glass at a gulp, stood up slowly and said: "It seems that I wasn't so blind after all and my old subordinates do still want to protect me and are so selfless in what they are trying to persuade me to do! Hahaha..." Li Gaocheng's laughter was full of grief and outrage and ended with him bursting into tears.

"What's the matter, Mayor Li?" There was a look of panic on Gou Zhongyao's face when he saw the state Li was in.

"Guo Zhongyao," Li Gaocheng said leaning in confidentially, "how could a stinking piece of shit like you fool me for so long? Even if my eyes were blind, some ghost or other must have stolen my brain too! How the fuck could I not have seen what a turd you are?"

"Mayor Li... you said you couldn't be angry with me." Guo seemed to be in a state of temporary confusion.

"You think I'm angry with you? Do you think a miserable object like you is worthy of my anger? It's myself I am angry with. First I let a thing like you join the Party and then I handed my team over to you! I don't think I will ever forgive myself in this lifetime! Listen up, Guo Zhongyao. I said I wasn't going to get angry with you today, but I do have a couple more things to say to you. I may be blind, but so are you! You are even more blind than me! How can you think so badly of the Communist Party and view the future of this country so bleakly? I always thought that you lot were probably just a bunch of mediocrities, talentless, incompetent nothings, and that was why you dragged Zhongyang Textiles down so far. But I didn't expect you to be this stupid. Stupid enough to think that the Communist Party would be your protector and your spokesperson! Stupid enough to think that the Communist Party would trade corruption for stability! If the Communist Party really could be bought with money, then yes, sure, you would be in the pink, you bunch of useless objects! You even think that, as long as you have Yan Zhen as your backer, you can do anything you like, without a thought for the workers or even for the Communist Party itself. How can you be so naïve? Let me tell you, given my current standing, I only need one phone call, and within half an hour, I can set thousands of workers onto you, and they will rip you to shreds within thirty seconds. But, of course I won't do that! I wouldn't be stupid enough to do a deal with someone like you at the expense of the workers. I just wanted to warn you how much they hate people like you! Do you think that if the Communist Party no longer existed, you could still be the capitalist you see yourself as? Remember, if that day does come, you will be the first person to be punished by the workers, and the ordinary people will turn your bloated body into a pile of dung! You don't even know enough to be afraid! I also want to warn you that you may think that I will end up just like you, that all Communists will end up just like you because they will put their own interests ahead of protecting the interests of the majority and ahead of defending the interests of the Party and the nation. But you are wrong! Let me tell you straight, I would rather sacrifice myself, I would rather let myself be shattered and broken than ever change my stance! I would rather destroy myself! And, what is more, we will never let you ruin our Party. We will never let you ruin our reforms either or ruin the future of the ordinary people. This is where I am different from you! It is where all conscientious Chinese people are different from you! It is also where a real Communist is different from you..."

CHAPTER FORTY-TWO

It was after 11 o'clock at night when Li Gaocheng finally left Guo Zhongyao's house. Unusually for him, he kept urging his driver to go faster because he wanted to see Yang Cheng that same night. An increasingly clear idea was taking concrete shape in his head. The best and the most effective way of dealing with a group of scum as Guo Zhongyao and his cronies was to arrest them all immediately, put them under mandatory surveillance and search their homes. Immediately, it must be immediately! There was no time to lose. The decision had to be made immediately. There could be no more hesitation, not even a minute more!

Even if the search did not reveal any major financial irregularities, as long as the houses they were now living in were registered and made public, that bunch of gangsters would still find themselves in a very embarrassing position. This was the hard-hitting strategy he had discussed with Yang Cheng. Kick them where it hurt most, let them squirm with pain, then hit them hard and straight and knock them senseless!

He had had similar thoughts over the past few days, but they had only been fleeting ones. It wasn't that he didn't think it was a good idea, but he was too hesitant and couldn't make up his mind. Now he suddenly seemed to have found the determination. He was sober and decisive despite the amount of wine he had drunk. If he were still to harbour any illusions or hesitations about such people, it would be equivalent to taking the Devil's shilling and making himself a co-conspirator in their tyranny. He would be wallowing in the same mire they were up to their snouts in.

The car reached Yang Cheng's residence within ten minutes, but Yang Cheng hadn't got home yet. Li Gaocheng asked his family, but they didn't know where he was. Li Gaocheng thought about it and then called Yang Cheng's office. The secretary picked up after only one ring. Yang Cheng was still in the office. The secretary said that Secretary Yang had been waiting for him and wanted him to come to the office immediately. He had a very urgent matter to discuss with him.

He was taken aback for a moment, and immediately felt his heart flutter. It certainly couldn't be anything trivial, or Yang Cheng wouldn't still be waiting in the office at this time. So what was it going to turn out to be? He felt worried and even a little frightened. Had something else come up that he hadn't anticipated and that he couldn't prevent?

So, what was it that he was so worried about? What was he afraid of? As he sat in the car, he found he didn't have clear answers to those questions. Was it because the whole affair was so much dirtier than he had anticipated? Or was it the viciousness and ferocity of the attacks that his choices had provoked? Or was it because he suddenly felt himself so weak and vulnerable?

He thought it was almost as much as he could take that his own position as mayor could be considered so dirty!

He reassured himself that, of course, many factors had contributed to his promotion in the first place. He was promoted based on his personal qualifications, his outstanding achievements, his good, strong public support, the careful examination and investigation by the Provincial and Municipal Committees, the many positive recommendations by the Provincial and Municipal Governments, and his election by the National People's Congress, and so on. Could he really have been promoted and appointed just because of one man?

Of course, even saying all that, he had to admit that even if he had the approval of the majority, if there was some important person who was opposed or wanted to interfere, his promotion would likely not have happened. In particular, if someone like Yan Zhen had disapproved of him or even hadn't nominated him at all, he wouldn't have made it to director of the Textiles Department or the Light Industry Department, let alone deputy mayor. The likelihood was that he would still be working away as Party secretary and factory manager at Zhongyang Textiles. How many factory directors and managers were there in the city and province, and why was he the only one who had become mayor? Could it be that everyone else was inferior to him? If it was true that Yan Zhen had appointed and promoted him, or that Yan Zhen had, at least, played a key role in the process, then that was enough to establish that his position was dirty. It would be just as Guo Zhongyao and Feng Minjie had said: he was the mayor they had bought with their money! If that was the case, then where was the legitimacy of his mayoralty? Wouldn't it be hugely diminished? And that was not to mention all the other things there were question marks over. What about the things he had in his house, his children's education, even the flowers and trees he planted in his courtyard and so on? How did he explain those? It really was just as Jiao Da exclaimed in *The Dream of the Red Chamber*: nothing was clean in his house except for the stone lions at the entrance![1]

Was it because of all these issues that their attacks were so vicious? Were they what was making him feel so weak and vulnerable? Over the past few days, even if he had not been aware of it before or given it much thought, the concept of being part of a "circle" had now become burnt into his consciousness to an extent that shocked and amazed him. Was it because of all this that he had suddenly become aware of the subtle influence of that terrible, hateful "circle" and how, almost unconsciously, it made him feel weak and vulnerable now he was no longer part of it?

The first thing Yang Cheng said when he saw him was: "I was really afraid that you had made yourself disappear and I was going to ask my secretary to try and find you." He then went straight on to inform Li of three things. First, the Standing Committee had just finished its meeting, and it had introduced a new, ad hoc agenda to study the problems of Zhongyang Textiles and other poorly performing state-owned enterprises. The top leaders of the Provincial Party Committee and the Provincial Government were planning to visit several large and medium-sized state-owned enterprises before the Spring Festival to express condolences to the workers in the form of New Year's greetings. Zhongyang Textiles was one of them. The visits would probably be carried out immediately, but the specific timings had not yet been set. Second, the leaders wanted to hear reports on the situation before their visits. As Li Gaocheng had been continuously in charge of industry, Secretary Wan and Governor Wei wanted to hear his views and opinions. Third, Secretary Wan, Governor Wei, Executive Deputy Secretary Yan Zhen and Secretary of the Provincial Discipline Inspection Commission, Bai Weihua, were still discussing the issue of the petition from the workers at Zhongyang Textiles, especially the serious questions that were raised centred on the workers themselves. There were problems involving some people and some departments, and they were preparing to take decisive measures to deal seriously with them. So Secretary Wan wanted to meet him tonight to have a thorough conversation about it all.

"Tonight?" Li Gaocheng couldn't help being surprised. "When Secretary Wan called this afternoon, didn't he say that he didn't have time for the next two days and wanted me to contact him again the day after tomorrow?"

"Things have changed, and they have changed a lot." Yang Cheng looked at his watch, then looked at Li Gaocheng and said: "To be honest, even I didn't expect that the Provincial Party Committee would move so quickly."

"What has changed?" Li Gaocheng asked in surprise.

"We'll know when we meet Secretary Wan in a while." Yang Cheng looked at his watch again.

"Are you going too?"

"Yes." Yang Cheng nodded, and then added, "...and so is Yan Zhen."

Yan Zhen again! He was always there! He was like a great black grindstone pressing down on him all the time. He couldn't escape him however much he wanted to.

"What time are we going? It's already midnight." Li Gaocheng looked at his watch – it was 11.54pm.

"Some time after twelve. We are waiting for Secretary Wan's call." Yang Cheng also looked at his watch again and said, "You must get yourself mentally prepared, Lao Li."

That was the third time someone had said that to him today. Li

Gaocheng was more than a little taken aback. What was going on? He had talked with Yang Cheng enough times now to know that he was very close-mouthed. Although their relationship was now out of the ordinary, if the powers-that-be forbade it, no matter how important it might be, he would never divulge the least bit of information in advance.

What exactly was it that he had to be told, in person, after midnight? He glanced at Yang Cheng, who seemed to be deep in thought. Li Gaocheng decided that it was useless trying to guess. Since they were waiting for the call, he might as well take this time to tell Yang Cheng about his own thoughts, so he changed the subject and said: "Yang Cheng, I have an idea, and I hope you will support me over it."

"Eh?" Yang Cheng seemed to be quite agitated. "What idea? Hurry up and tell me."

"I've just paid a visit to Zhongyang Textiles' CEO, Guo Zhongyao, at his home."

"Guo Zhongyao? You've been to Guo Zhongyao's home? What for?"

"I paid a visit to Zhongyang Textiles this afternoon, and I discovered that there is still no water, electricity or heating there, but not one of the management team is living in the company dormitory compound. I was so angry I went to see him. Do you know where he is living at the moment? Do you know where all of the management team are living? They are all living in detached villas. They are even bigger and more spacious than where Secretary Wan and Governor Wei live! Guo Zhongyao admitted that the only reason he dares live in a place like that is because he has the right backers and protection. The implication of that is that no one can touch him at the moment, not even the mayor, the secretary of the Municipal Party Committee or even someone more important than that, no one! He seems to mean that he has seen through this society of ours, and, as long as you've got money, there is nothing you can't do. As long as you've got money, you can trample all over morality, principles, conscience and the law."

"There is nothing surprising about that. They've been doing it all along." Yang Cheng replied quite calmly this time. "I already know all about it. During those few days you were sick, someone reported it to me. Feng Minjie, deputy general manager, owns the most houses. He has six of them and he only has four children."

"But I only just found out!"

"It's not that you didn't know before, it's that you didn't want to believe it."

"It wasn't that I didn't want to believe it, I quite simply didn't believe it!" Li Gaocheng said sadly. "I never thought they would dare! How truly appalling they have become!"

"I understand your emotion. It is not an easy thing to have your feelings and understanding turned upside down."

"Yang Cheng, I have had this idea for a long time, and it was not until tonight that I made up my mind. I do hope you can support me in this. I want to send the case directly to the judicial authorities without delay. The Municipal Procuratorate can file it for trial straightaway."

"That is something I wanted to tell you about." Yang Cheng looked at his watch again. "The Municipal Procuratorate have already decided to file the case."

"What? Really?" Li Gaocheng was stunned. He hadn't expected to be behind the pace on this.

"Yes, really! The Municipal Procuratorate asked the Municipal Party Committee for instructions a few days ago, when you were still ill," Yang Cheng said carefully. "But this is all still at the confidential stage, and only a very few people know about it."

"But this is great!" Li Gaocheng was surprised and delighted and immediately continued excitedly: "Since that is the case, it is best to take action very soon so we can bring them all to trial as quickly as possible and raid their residences. I take full responsibility for this, and, when I say that, I know full well that if no problems are found, I will be removed from my post and expelled from the Party!"

"But have you stopped to think about who we are going to interrogate, who are we going to search?" Yang Cheng said calmly. "In addition to those we know are suspected of corruption, there are some others who we should interrogate, aren't there? Should their homes be searched too?"

People like his own wife! The thought struck Li Gaocheng like a thunderbolt.

If he wanted to pass judgement on others, he would certainly have to pass judgement on his wife.

Interrogating his wife would mean searching her home, and searching her home would also mean searching him!

Li Gaocheng's face suddenly turned pale as he was stunned by the implications of his idea.

If he had thought of it, of course others would think of it too!

Suddenly, the phone rang, and a shudder ran through him.

All at once, he came to his senses. What was he afraid of? What was he actually afraid of?

CHAPTER FORTY-THREE

IT WAS 12.30AM by the time they got to the Provincial Party secretary's office.

Li Gaocheng hadn't expected there to be several other people in Secretary Wan's office. Also present were Provincial Governor Wei Zhenguo, Secretary of the Disciplinary Inspection Commission Bai Weihua, Executive Deputy Governor Wang Yumin, and someone who made him feel particularly uneasy even though he was already expecting him, Deputy Executive Provincial Party Committee Secretary Yan Zhen.

Everybody looked very serious and the atmosphere in the office was extraordinarily tense.

After he and Yang Cheng entered the office, they shook hands formally with everyone. When he was shaking Yan Zhen's hand, he saw that the man's expression was very gentle and relaxed. He even smiled slightly at him.

It was a kind of smile that gave him an indefinable sense of humiliation. He felt quite clearly that it was a triumphant smile, a contemptuous smile, a smile of real mockery.

The feeling of humiliation also stirred up a vague anger inside him, and as soon as he saw that smile, he understood that the reason he had been called here late at night was that it must be something to do with himself. And it would not be an ordinary matter either. The fact that Yan Zhen was assuming this victorious attitude meant that the matter had come to a head. Tonight, in front of Secretary Wan and the others, it was a fight to the death!

There can be no reconciliation between the two of us, Yan Zhen!

This thought calmed him down and he silently contemplated what was about to happen and what he would say to Secretary Wan and the others.

After he and Yang Cheng had sat down, there was a little desultory chat between some of the others, and then the office fell silent.

Secretary Wan looked very tired, and both his eyes were bloodshot, but his voice was still powerful enough, and his expression was still resolute. He said that he had called everyone there so late because he had something very important to tell them.

The first thing was that the Provincial Party Committee and the Provincial Government had just learned that tomorrow morning, thousands of retired workers and cadres from Zhongyang Textiles were going, en masse, to the Provincial Party Committee to present a petition. There were loads of notices posted in the dormitory area of Zhongyang Textiles which read: "Tomorrow morning at seven o'clock, all retired cadres and workers will gather at the Veteran Cadre Activity Centre and go together to the Provincial Party Committee to ask the leaders to solve our problems and to give us food. The activity is voluntary, and latecomers will be left behind." It was estimated that there would be at least three or four thousand people and maybe more. Information had also been received that several dozen of the company trucks and the large minivans used for transporting the workers were all on instant standby. This time they were bypassing the Municipal Party Committee and the Municipal Government and going straight to the Provincial Government. They were assembling at seven o'clock and leaving by seven-thirty at the latest to arrive at eight o'clock at best.

"I don't need to spell it out to you – as everyone already knows, this is not really a petition, it is a demand that the Provincial Government solve their problems. Or, to put it more seriously, it is their attempt to demonstrate their influence over the Provincial Party Committee and the Provincial Government and to exert that influence." Secretary Wan was choosing his words very carefully.

"In fact, they just want to make trouble, and very big trouble at that!" Yan Zhen interjected. This time, his tone was very stern, and his attitude was very grave. "The aim of that trouble is very clear. They want to drive out the entire Zhongyang Textiles management team..."

"No, we have to make one thing very clear!" Secretary Wan interrupted Yan Zhen. "From now on, all leading cadres, whether they are at provincial or municipal level, will not call the workers' actions a disturbance. If you describe them like that, aren't you predetermining the nature of the situation? When workers take this kind of action, as top-level government, we should think more from the workers' point of view. When so many retired workers and cadres come to petition en masse, they are still looking to the leaders, the government and the Communist Party. They are not opposed to the government, nor are they hostile to the government. This shows that they still believe in the Party and the country. They made it very clear on the bulletin board that no matter how they worded it, whether they wanted food or a solution to the company's problems, they were still looking to the leaders of the Provincial Party Committee to provide them. Also, I have heard that the current conditions for the workers at Zhongyang Textiles are not good. Retired staff and cadres have not been paid for four months, and some active staff and cadres have not been paid for nearly ten months. Even now, the company has no electricity, no water and no heating, and the entire factory has no telephones! Tell me, in such circumstances wouldn't you expect the workers to have something to say about it? Are they not allowed to petition? If you call it a disturbance, then let me say that I think it is right and justified! If it was happening to you, wouldn't you make a scene? If it was happening to me, I certainly would. I couldn't live with myself if I didn't! Gaocheng, I want to hear what you have to say. Is the situation at Zhongyang Textiles really as it has been described? Do you understand the issue or not? Just how much do you understand it? Just how serious are the problems? I have heard that you were the one who solved the problem last time, and you have a lot of prestige among the workers there. Tell me, what should we think of this workers' action? What is the real problem with Zhongyang Textiles? In the end, how are we going to solve it? What are the principal and most important issues that need to be addressed at the moment?"

Li Gaocheng couldn't help but be surprised. He had thought of a hundred questions he might be asked, but he had not anticipated that the first thing he would be confronted with would be this piece of news. In particular, he hadn't expected Secretary Wan to ask so many questions. Although they were all about things he was entirely familiar with, the way Secretary Wan put his questions seemed very abrupt to him.

Perhaps because he hesitated, Governor Wei said: "There's nothing to worry about, Gaocheng. The top leaders of the province area are all here to listen to your opinions. It doesn't matter if you get things wrong, nor if you are over-emphatic. We just want to hear the real situation. Things have gone so far already that any falsehoods now really would be detrimental to the Party, the nation and the people. Finally, they would also be very harmful to you yourself. Say whatever there is to be said and if we cannot deal with the problems of a state-owned enterprise like this, then we are too incompetent to be called leadership cadres."

These few words cut Li Gaocheng to the quick. What Governor Wei had said was actually a criticism directed at him. How incompetent and inadequate must he be not only to be unable to get a grip on what was going on at a state-owned enterprise like this, but even to force so many provincial leaders to give up their sleep to come here at this time of night, worrying about him and wracking their brains over him? But, then again, what more did he actually have to worry about or be afraid of? Just look at Yan Zhen sitting there. He has already almost lost you your wife and your reputation and caused tens of thousands of workers to suffer from hunger and cold! What more did he have to fear from him? Having come this far, if he were still to cower from and be intimidated by these wolves and tigers, wouldn't he forfeit the right to call himself a Communist? Wouldn't he forfeit the right even to call himself a man?

Eventually, Li Gaocheng spoke: "Very well, since both the Party secretary and the governor have told me to, I will cast aside all my worries. I think the time has surely come for me to speak out."

He spoke slowly, trying to keep his words organised. He said that what Secretary Wan had detailed just now was no exaggeration, and in some respects, things were even worse. He talked about how he went to Zhongyang Textiles not long ago to try to solve these problems, about the anger of the staff and cadres of Zhongyang Textiles, about what he saw and heard when he went to offer condolences to the workers, and about their poor living conditions. When he talked about the sincere feelings of Wang Yinglie, the old worker who had almost sacrificed his life to protect the factory, about the request made by Fan Xiuzhi, the national model worker, about his encounter with Hu Huizhong, the national model technician, who now mended shoes by a public lavatory, and about Xia Yulian, who although already an old woman, was working through her terminal illness, he could not hold back his tears, and all the people present were deeply moved. Even Bai Weihua, secretary of the Discipline Inspection Commission, who had always been known as the Iron Woman, couldn't help crying. Then he talked about the main problems reported by the cadres and workers, and his investigation into, understanding of and opinions on these problems. After that, he focused on the shocking corruption that occurred in Zhongyang Textiles' tertiary enterprises, especially the transformation of public property into private and the appalling and illegal acts of fraud and outright theft.

"In a word, corruption is currently Zhongyang Textiles' biggest problem, and it is also the one problem that demands resolution." Li Gaocheng continued calmly and resolutely. "The workers themselves have already made it quite clear that it was these profligates who have made a state-owned enterprise the size of Zhongyang Textiles deteriorate so fast. If these profligates did not have the backing they do, protecting them, would they still dare run amok like this? The retired cadres and workers are a case in point. Over the years, whenever the problems of state-owned enterprises are mentioned, the retired workers are involved at every turn because of the size and weight of the burden imposed upon them. Leaving aside the fact that most of our retired workers are still working hard for the company, let us just consider the size of their annual retirement pension. The total number of retired workers at Zhongyang Textiles has already exceeded four thousand and may be as many as five thousand. It has been calculated that, over the five-year period from 1991 to 1995, the annual pension per person has been less than two thousand yuan. In fact, the retirement pensions of retired employees over the past two years have not even reached that average. The pensions of the vast majority of retired employees are only one or two hundred yuan per month. What with delays and procrastinations and all manner of deductions, very few actually get the full amount.

"Take Xia Yulian as an example: she retired in 1988 so that her child could take over her job sooner. When she retired, her monthly pension was only 110 yuan. In the years since then, the state has delegated the power to increase or decrease the wages of workers to the companies, subject to the relevant policies. For many years, citing recession and company losses as the reason, the company management have not increased the wages of the retired workers, and the increase in the wages of the active workers has also been very low. So, in recent years, especially last year and the year before, the total annual pension for retired cadres and workers of Zhongyang Textiles has been no more than a few million yuan. Also over the past few years, the average annual amount of funds loaned by the state to Zhongyang Textiles is more than eighty million! You can see that the total salaries of retired workers amount to no more than a few tenths of the loan amount!

"On the other hand, however, the lavishness and extravagance of the company management far exceeded this. From 1992 to 1994, the company's hospitality bill was over four million dollars! Even in 1995, when production was in the doldrums, it was still close to the same figure. When you add on the hospitality expenses of the various branches and subsidiaries, the total is close to 10 million. What an appalling figure, and that's just for hospitality! What is more, the number of cadres and other staff on work release across the company is almost equal to the entire number of retired staff cadres, yet the expenses of those people are far greater than the expenses of the retirees. Most of them have nothing to do with actual production, but they still need cars, offices, and large expense accounts. They also have to hold meetings, further their education, make visits, and even travel, including travel abroad. Excluding their wages and counting only these expenses, even in 1995, when the company was extremely sluggish, the total still amounted to more than ten million. This is why the retired cadres and workers can ask with confidence, who is the real burden on the company? Who is actually dragging the company down?"

"This kind of argument has been around for years, and it amounts to nothing less than an outright rejection of the Party's leadership!" Yan Zhen could no longer resist putting his oar in. "The argument itself doesn't surprise us, but what does surprise us is that some of us leadership cadres still endorse it because that is an action fraught with danger!"

"That is not how I see it," Li Gaocheng said, still keeping his voice down but speaking with conviction. He surprised even himself speaking out like this. It was the first time in many years that he had contradicted Yan Zhen, and in front of so many other leaders too. "In fact, this is not the case at all. If you insist that this is anti-Party, it is only so according to a handful of leadership cadres who claim to represent the Party as a whole!"

"Lao Yan, at this time we are listening to Mayor Li's report, and we are hearing about the real situation of the grassroots workers. How can this be related to being anti-Party?" Executive Deputy Governor Wang Yumin said with some disapproval. "To be honest, if the actual situation is as Mayor Li has described, I have to say that it is not the workers who are anti-Party, but these corrupt leadership cadres within the Party itself!"

"I feel the same way as Governor Wang," Yang Cheng stated unequivocally. "And I would like to emphasise one more point. The problem at Zhongyang Textiles is probably even more serious than this. In particular, I would like to highlight that the issue with Zhongyang Textiles will most likely involve some of the high-level cadres on our Provincial and Municipal Committees. This is almost certainly connected, at the very least, to the main reason why the investigation of Zhongyang Textiles has encountered so much resistance at this time."

"The greater the problem, the greater the resistance. This is a general rule." Bai Weihua, secretary of the Discipline Inspection Commission, spoke up calmly.

The office was suddenly silent. Secretary Wan seemed to be thinking nervously about something, while Governor Wei appeared still to be immersed in a state of emotional shock. It seemed that Li Gaocheng's report had shaken them so strongly that they were temporarily unable to adjust, and this had kept them pondering over the deep emotions it had stirred up.

It was a while before Secretary Wan said thoughtfully and deliberately: "Gaocheng, do you mean to say that the cause of the collapse of Zhongyang Textiles is nothing else but its own management cadres? That it is corruption that has brought down this great state-owned enterprise?"

"Yes. Judging from the current situation as we understand it, that is the case for Zhongyang Textiles at least. What makes the situation there particularly serious is that the corruption has infected not only individual cadres but has spread to almost the entire management. The problems at Zhongyang Textiles are sounding an alarm bell for all of us. It is like a fruit fly on an apple. If you don't catch it in time, its maggots will rot the whole apple, maybe the whole tree!" Li Gaocheng said without hesitation.

He knew that now was the time for him to tell the whole truth. Only the truth could save Zhongyang Textiles and could save the company's tens of thousands of workers. Only by telling the whole truth could he himself be saved.

"Over the last few days, I have spent all my time considering one question. I wanted to work out what exactly caused this unprecedented corruption in a state-owned enterprise. The lawless and recklessly corrupt cadres of Zhongyang Textiles are hateful enough, but who gave them the kind of unscrupulous power to do whatever they want? We gave it to them! Guo Zhongyao, the general manager of Zhongyang Textiles, said something that shook me. He said that he was not meant to be a general manager as he did not have the ability or the basic qualities to do the job. At the same time, he also told me that the other main leaders of Zhongyang Textiles are also incompetent. The reason they were able to become the senior management of Zhongyang Textiles was because I was wrong! He even said to my face that I had poor eyesight and could not see people for what they were. He might as well have just said that I was blind! I liked them and I recommended them highly, but now they are saying that I am blind! If they are all saying that about us, just think what the workers' opinion must be! To put it bluntly, these so-called general managers and entrepreneurs were, in fact, appointed and anointed with our approval and at our pleasure. First, we appointed them, and then we proposed the separation of government and enterprise and the decentralisation of power, thereby pretty much effectively giving them all the property rights, national assets and control of state-owned enterprises. At the same time, we told them that they could do whatever they wanted without any constraints or supervision. So, once they had such a great power, which had a direct effect on the fate of the country and the future of reform, there was no one, no power, or any institution that could supervise and restrict them. Even we ourselves don't have that kind of power!

"I hadn't intended to speak again, Gaocheng, but after hearing what you have had to say, I feel I must interject." An ashen-faced Yan Zhen finally decided to interrupt. "You have to take responsibility for what you say. Have you given any thought to the consequences of such words? What exactly is the thrust of what you are saying? Looking at things now, is there really any problem with Zhongyang Textiles, and, if so, how big is it? Everything is still an unknown. In fact, after nearly a month of the preliminary investigation, we have found no major problem. Without any evidence, how can you take it for granted that Zhongyang Textiles is a typical example of total corruption? Taking a step back, even if Zhongyang Textiles does have a serious problem, how can such a local phenomenon be taken as a general phenomenon? Are you presenting an incidental problem as an essential problem? You are a mayor, a Party cadre, and as such you should make sure you adopt the correct stance, so how can..."

"I haven't finished, Secretary Yan. Can you not let me finish what I have to say before giving us your own thoughts and opinions?" Li Gaocheng rebuffed Yan Zhen's interruption.

Yan Zhen had probably not expected Li Gaocheng to be like that, and, in the presence of so many people, he was momentarily nonplussed.

"You should continue, Gaocheng." Provincial Party Committee Secretary Wan Yongnian was clearly supportive of Li Gaocheng.

"I have given a great deal of thought to everything I have said today, and I take full responsibility for it," Li Gaocheng continued. "When I say that, it is not a mere form of words, I am determined to live up to it. The fact is, everyone knows that the Zhongyang Textiles affair involves me personally, my family and my wife. I have a responsibility there that I can never evade and never shirk. So, I am here to declare solemnly that even if I and my entire family are investigated over Zhongyang Textiles, even if I lose my family and my reputation, even if I am dismissed, sentenced and sent to gaol, I still request the Provincial Party Committee and the Provincial Government to investigate the issue of Zhongyang Textiles right to the end. I would rather resign immediately than see any corrupt elements escape and get away with it because of any problem with me. I should also like to point out that Zhongyang Textiles has reached the point of no return. Bankruptcy, merger, rectification, reinvestment, no matter what the future holds for the company, no matter what the next step for it is, it must only be carried out under the one premise and that is that its problems are thoroughly investigated. Since the main cause of this corruption lies with us, the best answer for the cadres and workers of Zhongyang Textiles and the only way to appease them is to cut out that corruption now. Only in this way can we motivate our workers to participate in the reform of state-owned enterprises on a larger and more ambitious scale, and only then can we continue our reforms in line with the wishes of the people.

"I once said something to a person who had saddened and disappointed me, and I want to say it again here now. Secretary Yan, I sincerely hope that you are able to understand what kind of person I am, and that is why I am giving you this as my answer. I would rather put myself on the line and let myself be battered and broken than relinquish the stand I have taken. I would rather destroy myself than let these corrupt people destroy our Party, our reforms and our future! I have already spoken to the secretary of the Municipal Party Committee, Yang Cheng, about my ideas, and, in my capacity as mayor, I am now proposing once again to the provincial leaders that, in the case of Zhongyang Textiles, all the leadership cadres who are suspected of corruption, no matter how high their positions or how deep their backing, should immediately be put under compulsory surveillance, both individually and at their residences. Those who are under serious suspicion should be put on trial as soon as possible and, if necessary, they should be formally arrested and their homes should be searched in accordance with the law!"

At this point, Li Gaocheng stopped abruptly, and, perhaps because everyone was shaken by his energy, the office suddenly fell back into silence. Even Executive Deputy Secretary Yan seemed unable to say anything, although the expression on his face had become uglier and uglier. Looking at Yan Zhen's furious but helpless expression, Li Gaocheng suddenly understood the fact that no matter how exalted a person's position, no matter how powerful he is and how prominent his status is, if he has done something wrong or something shameful, any appearance he assumes can only be a pretence, a hollow facade, strong on the outside but weak on the inside. Even the leader of the pack, when confronted with the fire, can only choose to put his sheep's clothing on again, or to run away with his tail between his legs!

There was a long pause before Wan Yongnian gave Li Gaocheng a meaningful look and said: "Do you have anything more to say, Gaocheng?"

"That's all for now. We'll talk in more detail another time," Li Gaocheng said after a moment's thought.

"However, I would like to ask you one more thing. How sure are you of what you are saying? What will the consequences be of doing what you say you're going to do? In other words, if, in fact things are not as you say they are, have you considered what kind of a situation that would leave us in?" Wan Yongnian's voice was not loud, but it was very serious.

"I have thought about this a lot, Secretary Wan, and I think that the key to our actions lies in our speed. Paper cannot wrap up fire and there is no such thing as a rumour-proof wall. If we move too slowly, we will just be alerting our enemies and it will end in neutralising our position," Li Gaocheng replied.

At this point, Yan Zhen appeared to have thought of something, but Wan Yongnian immediately silenced him with a wave of his hand. "You didn't answer my question, Gaocheng, you just talked about speed, and taking the initiative and not being neutralised. What I am asking you is, if everything is done as you say, but the result is not what you want, how much of a side effect will that have on us?"

Li Gaocheng couldn't help but glance at Yan Zhen when Wan Yongnian said this to him. When he saw the almost imperceptible smug sneer on the man's face, his chest suddenly burned with uncontrollable indignation, and, throwing caution to the winds, he said: "I understand what you are saying, Secretary Wan. Let's all of us, myself included, put ourselves to this severest of tests. I hope that you other leaders, including you high-ranking ones, can accept this challenge as I do. If the facts prove that we are all innocent, we can give the workers their answers from a position of strength. If there is a problem, or it turns out to prove that some of us have a problem, then we can still answer to the workers from the opposite point of view. I think as long as we do it in good time, we will have the capital with the workers to persuade them. Please rest assured, Secretary Wan, as I have already said, I have made all the necessary preparations..."

"All right, Gaocheng, you don't need to say anything more," Wan Yongnian interrupted Li Gaocheng sternly but calmly. "You have made everything clear, and we have all heard you quite clearly. What I want to tell you now is that I agree with your thinking, I agree with your views and I agree with your recommendations." With that, Wan Yongnian turned to Yang Cheng and asked: "How about you, Yang Cheng?"

"I agree," Yang Cheng replied almost without thinking.

"Weihua, what about you?" Wan Yongnian turned to the secretary of the Discipline Inspection Commission.

"Agreed." Bai Weihua's answer was equally firm and straightforward.

"Do you have anything else to say, Lao Wang?" Wan Yongnian asked Wang Yumin, the executive deputy governor.

"No, I agree too." Deputy Governor Wang's face was as grim as the atmosphere in the office.

"Governor Wei, please tell us your position." Wan Yongnian sounded as though he was following a well-worn routine.

"I think what Gaocheng has said is very genuine and very meaningful, and I completely agree." Governor Wei Zhenguo made no secret of his feelings and standpoint and seemed very excited.

"Your turn to talk, Yan Zhen." Wan Yongnian finally addressed the executive deputy Party Committee secretary.

"There is one thing I don't understand, Secretary Wan. What is the purpose of asking everyone to make such a statement now? Did you really summon us here at this late hour just to ask if we agree or disagree with this immature and extremely risky idea?" Yan Zhen said, with such a desperate expression on his face it was difficult to meet his eye. "So what I now particularly hope is that you can explain to us whether we are going to come to a decision, or whether we are just going to hold a discussion."

"It's not a discussion, it's a decision," Wan Yongnian said sternly, making no attempt to evade the question. "Do you agree or disagree that we should follow Mayor Li Gaocheng's suggestion? I just want you to answer this question now, and naturally, I will talk to you about other matters afterwards."

"I agree with what you have said."

Wan Yongnian gave Yan Zhen a searing look, then turned to face the others. "Since everyone is in agreement, we will now discuss the second matter, but not here. Please would everyone go to the multi-function conference room, and I will inform you of what I have to say when we are there."

Li Gaocheng glanced at Yan Zhen again, and when he saw how pale his face had become, he immediately realised that the real test had now arrived, and that what awaited him was a momentous decision and one that could well change his entire life!

CHAPTER FORTY-FOUR

THE MULTI-FUNCTION CONFERENCE HALL was a conference facility in the office building of the Provincial Party Committee that could accommodate nearly three hundred people.

When Li Gaocheng walked in, he was immediately stunned by the scene that confronted him.

In the huge hall, there were more than two hundred public prosecutors from the Provincial and Municipal Procuratorates and investigators from the Anti-Corruption Bureau. They filled the hall from the front, and all looked very serious. There was hardly a sound in the room, and the atmosphere was so tense it was almost suffocating.

As Li Gaocheng sat down with everyone else, he fully understood that the conversation just now in Secretary Wan's office had been a preparatory meeting of the several principal leaders of the Provincial and Municipal Party Committees, and it was just a prelude to a major action. Yang Cheng had known all about it in advance and had told him that the Municipal Procuratorate had already filed a case. What he hadn't told him at the time was that the Provincial Procuratorate had also opened a case. But at that point, there had been no need to tell him anything else. Everything was now revealed. The case of Zhongyang Textiles, the case of his wife, the case of his nephew and his brother-in-law, and of course the series of cases involving Yan Zhen and Yan Zhen's relatives, would all be decided tonight, broken down in all their detail.

There was no doubt that the Provincial and Municipal Procuratorates would take action that night. The reason why they were still sitting there was to report to the Provincial Party Committee to get its approval, and they were waiting for its decision.

There was also no doubt that that decision had already been made: the Committee gave its assent!

There was also no doubt that the provincial and municipal prosecutors would take enforcement measures against the suspects and would search their residences and offices overnight. Of course, that would include the mayor's home, his own home!

Although he had been prepared for a long time and across the various aspects, now this huge test had actually arrived, he still felt paralysed, and he was finding it difficult to stay in control.

So, this was how it was going to be!

But how had the attitude of the Provincial Party Committee changed so suddenly? When the Provincial Party Committee held its Standing Committee meeting in the afternoon, Secretary Wan and Governor Wei had given no sign of having such an intention. They had even asked Yan Zhen to investigate the bribery case around those three hundred thousand yuan! That had been only a few hours ago, so how had everything changed?

There could only be two possible explanations: one was pressure from above, and the other was pressure from below. Of course, the petition and evidence presented by ten thousand employees and cadres of Zhongyang Textiles would also have been sent to the central government. Maybe a central leader had read it and swiftly made a decision and passed on his instructions. As a result, everything had changed. So, what could the pressure from below be? Of course, it had something to do with the next day's petition from the retired workers of Zhongyang Textiles to the Provincial Party Committee, but it was very likely that that was only one aspect of the affair. Perhaps the Public Security Bureau, the Public Procuratorate and the Courts had been continuing to investigate. Indeed, as Yang Cheng had said, this kind of investigation could have been going on for several days without people knowing anything about it. The city had filed a case, so the province might well have done so too. If that was the case, then it was very likely that, over the past few days, the political and legal authorities had discovered conclusive evidence about Zhongyang Textiles and swiftly reported it. That would explain why the Provincial Party Committee had changed its attitude.

Of course, all of these things may or may not have happened, and everything that had been presented so far, including the attitudes of Secretary Wan and Governor Wei, were fake and just for show in an attempt temporarily to neutralise Yan Zhen...

He sat there silently, imagining what kind of trauma it would be for his daughter Meimei when the house was being searched. As for his wife who had been so obstinate in her wrongheadedness over these last few days and who remained so convinced of her own superiority, imagine how she would react to such a sudden search!

But what about Yan Zhen?

Li Gaocheng couldn't resist stealing another glance at Yan Zhen, but, other than being ashen-faced, he looked much the same as always.

Li Gaocheng felt something clutch at his heart. It looked as though Yan Zhen knew all about this sudden action. Perhaps he had approved it, or even planned it! Was what he had done just now just an act? Was he still trying to show Li that, even at a time like this, he was still doing his utmost to protect him?

Impossible! Absolutely not! They didn't have the power and influence to buy off all the leading cadres of the entire Provincial Party Committee!

When he glanced at Yan Zhen again, relief flooded through him. He saw that Yan Zhen's legs were shaking. Shaking very badly! That look of seriousness and solemnity was actually fake. His ashen face was genuinely terrified.

Even though Yan Zhen had always spoken with such enthusiasm about his unassailable, invincible "circle", he had also earnestly told his subordinates the day might come when that "circle" was no more, and then disaster would be unavoidable. However, Li had never expected that he would be so frightened at this moment. It turned out that his so-called "circle" was so fragile, impotent and vulnerable! It seemed that even if there was such a thing as this "circle", the people within it could not casually overstep its boundaries with impunity. Once you crossed that line, no matter what kind of "circle" it was, there would be no one who would dare to take the risk of sheltering you or covering for you! People within the "circle" would kick you out without mercy to protect it and treat you even more ruthlessly than anyone outside the "circle". But if you shunned it and lived in fear of it, how could you possibly protect yourself? The simple truth was that there was no place in such a "circle" for someone selfless. The majority of people in such "circles" all had their ulterior motives of unspeakable sordidness, so it is inevitable, by their very nature, that such "circles" can only be selfish and exceptionally cruel. The only outlook it offered was a very bleak one!

Li Gaocheng silently wiped the cold sweat from his forehead, feeling both ashamed that he had been so slow to make his choice, and grateful that that choice had not turned out to be too late.

As soon as they entered the conference hall, Wan Yongnian, secretary of the Provincial Party Committee, and Yang Cheng, secretary of the Municipal Party Committee, had a long, serious talk with the leaders of the Provincial Municipal Law Committee and the Procuratorate, and then the chief prosecutor of the Provincial Supreme People's Procuratorate made a speech from the stage.

"Comrades!" The chief prosecutor's words sounded very solemn and majestic as they rang out through the silent conference hall. "I hereby announce that our actions tonight have been reported to the Provincial and Municipal Committees and have received their approval and support!"

The hall suddenly echoed with a storm of applause, which sounded as loud as a shattering thunderclap in the quiet of the night.

"Comrades!" the chief prosecutor continued. "This operation is the largest anti-corruption operation ever conducted in our province and city. It is also the largest anti-corruption operation in our Procuratorate. Not only have we received the firm support of the Provincial Party Committee, the Provincial Discipline Inspection Commission, the Provincial Political and Legal Committee, the Municipal Party Committee, the Municipal Discipline Inspection Commission and the Municipal Legal Committee, but we have also received strong support from the relevant central departments. Thus, this action is relevant to the overall national situation and carries a great deal of responsibility! Everyone must be clear about their individual duties and responsibilities. Any omission may lead to major mistakes in our operation and cause incalculable damage. We have already talked about this in detail, and I will say it again now. All those who participate in this operation, please keep in mind at all times that every action of yours represents the Party, the people, the government, the country and the sanctity and solemnity of the law! Likewise, every mistake you make will be a crime against the country and the people and a desecration of Party discipline and state law! Therefore, I believe..."

The conference hall was so silent you could have heard a pin drop.

Li Gaocheng suddenly noticed that the blood had drained completely from Yan Zhen's face.

"Comrades!" The chief prosecutor suddenly raised his voice. "Before we take action, I now ask Secretary Wan Yongnian of the Provincial Party Committee to speak to us on behalf of the provincial and municipal leaders!"

There was another round of thunderous, excited applause, during which Wan Yongnian walked solemnly to the platform at the front of the hall.

"Comrades!" Secretary Wan's voice was equally solemn. "Now is not really the time to applaud, but we all know that everyone's applause shows the welcome and support you give our action. It also represents the trust and support you show for us. Thank you!"

More enthusiastic applause interrupted Wan Yongnian's words, and, after a long time, he continued: "The chief prosecutor has just told you a great deal of what is going on. What he said has made me very excited and I think all of you will be just as excited as I am. In fact, I have been excited for the past two days. Just a few hours ago, I spoke with the leading comrades of the central government and there are some things that I can tell you just as they told me. The leading comrades of the central government have said that we must increase the intensity of our investigation and handling of cases, especially major and important cases. We must seriously investigate and deal with cases of squandering and embezzling state property by responsible personnel of state-owned enterprises. Those who have caused the serious loss of state-owned property, and those corrupt elements who use power for personal gain, take bribes and abuse the law must be brought to justice, regardless of their position. Such people will never be tolerated! For those corrupt elements who commit heinous crimes, the Party Central Committee will, as always, do its best to eliminate evil and punish them severely! (*Prolonged enthusiastic applause*) With that said, everyone will be clear that our action has been fully approved and guided by the leading comrades of the central government. Therefore, we may have full confidence that our actions cannot be stopped by anyone!

"The attitude of the Provincial Party Committee on this issue has always been very clear. We want to carry out a major rectification, to make a big breakthrough, and to cause a big shock! The intention is to make those corrupt elements feel anxious, restless, and permanently panicked! (*Applause*) Anyone who tries to stop our anti-corruption campaign will be completely exposed, and everyone will be clear what kind of despicable object he is. He will be like a rat in the street that everyone curses and attacks! (*Applause*) From this, we can have full confidence that we will never have to allow those corrupt elements to do whatever they want just to maintain stability, as some people have said. On the contrary, only by thoroughly eliminating corruption and engaging in the building of a clean government machine can our society become more stable, our reforms be deepened, our country become more prosperous, and our people become happier! (*Applause*)

"What is the purpose of our Party? It is to serve the people. Therefore, our Party is a Party that serves the people, our government is a government that serves the people, and we are engaged in a socialist market economy. Therefore, the vital interests of the vast majority of workers who comprise the vast majority of the urban labour force will inevitably represent the interests of the Party and the government. Their difficulties are our difficulties. Their sufferings are our sufferings. Their aspirations are our aspirations. Their demands are likewise our demands! If a political party or a government, in the social order it maintains, allows some people who do not work and do not contribute anything to society to accumulate huge wealth and become millionaires or billionaires, while leaving millions of hard-working people who have worked hard all their lives to struggle on the poverty line, then sooner or later such a political party and government will be eliminated!

"Such a social system will be destroyed sooner or later! Our Party will never be such a Party, our government will never be such a government, and our social system will never be such a social system! (*Enthusiastic applause*) Over the years, for various reasons, some intolerable corruption has indeed appeared in our society. Although we have not yet found a complete cure for it, our anti-corruption actions have never ceased either. No indeed, this must be a battle, a war, a life-or-death struggle! Either corruption will wipe us out in the end, or we will eradicate corruption! It must be one or the other, there is no middle way! First, we destroyed the Japanese devils who were armed to the teeth while we had neither grain nor rifles, and then eight million Kuomintang troops with aircraft and artillery were unable to wipe us out. Today's corruption will not wipe us out either! (*Applause*) On the issue of anti-corruption, firstly we will not hesitate, secondly we will not waver, and thirdly we will show no fear. In a word, we will not be afraid! As long as we have the support of the masses, we will not be afraid of anything. As General Secretary Jiang said, we must never take it lightly, never be afraid of difficulties, never relax our fighting spirit! (*Enthusiastic applause*)

"When we talk like this now, we are not saying that today's corruption is strong enough to stand up to us. In today's China, no force can compete with our Party and government! We are a long, long way from anything like that. But this does not mean that we can take such corrupt behaviour lightly, excuse it, or even tolerate it and just let it pass. Facts have proved that the current corruption in the economy is not only corroding our society and corroding our hearts but is also corroding our power and our political parties. These people are trying by every means possible to match the corruption in the political world. The two could combine to become an open marketplace in power and money, a crazy form of business with power as capital!

"They only need a signature, a stamp, or even a phone call, and they can turn tens of thousands, millions or even tens of millions of public and state capital directly into private capital! They do not rely on legitimate funds, let alone hard work, but rely on the power conferred by the state and the people. Under the cover of this legitimate power, the property of the state and the people is plundered! Intellectuals call it an inside job, but ordinary people just call them common thieves. And it is this kind of behaviour, and the influence it exerts, that is unscrupulously interfering with our reforms and disrupting fair competition in the market. It shakes the foundations of our power and destroys our confidence in the future! So, in a sense, it is more abhorrent, more awful and more threatening than the Japanese devils and the eight million troops of the Kuomintang! This is the common mortal enemy of our entire party and of the people of the whole country! If we do not completely eliminate these people, if we do not completely eradicate them, we will never be able to lead a good life. The Communist Party will not let them go, and the common people will not let them go either! You must believe me too that I will never let them go! As long as it is the property of the state, these corrupt elements will never get away with even a single cent! (*Enthusiastic applause*)

"The common people often ask, 'Where is the blue sky?' If we Communists are not the blue sky, who is? (*Applause*) With the support of the myriads of our fellow countrymen and women, workers and peasants alike, what are we Communists afraid of? In things like this action today, the broad masses of the working class are our strongest backers. With their support and endorsement, we were able to defeat any kind of enemy in the past, and we can eliminate all kinds of corrupt elements today! (*Applause*)

"I have heard that your comrades in the Public Security Bureau, the Procuratorate and the Courts have a saying, 'We are not afraid of any kind of criminal, only of a telephone call from the leaders!' (*Applause*) Why are you applauding? Because I told the truth! (*Applause*) As the Provincial Party secretary, today, in front of your leaders, in front of the leaders of the Provincial and Municipal Committees, I promise you that I will never, for shameful purposes, ever give your leaders a single telephone call, nor send them a single note! (*Warm applause*) Nor will I ever allow anyone else to make such a telephone call or send such a note! (*Prolonged warm applause*) If there are still people who are willing to use devious means on behalf of those corrupt elements who harm the country, the people and ourselves, just think what kind of people they must be. They are even more heinous and hateful than the corrupt elements themselves, and they must be brought down! (*Applause*) Some people say that because I am seeking another term in office, I, Wan Yongnian, don't want to offend anyone, and will just muddle through, turning a blind eye and doing things on a nod and a wink. I will never do so! I haven't done so in the past, I won't do it now and I will never do it in the future! I believe most of you are the children of farmers and workers. Like everyone else, my grandfather was a farmer, my father was a worker, my wife is still a worker and I was once a worker myself. Today, as secretary of the Provincial Party Committee, I cannot ignore the Party's principles just to garner votes, I cannot allow the common people to suffer just to garner votes, I cannot abandon my conscience just to garner votes, and I cannot turn a blind eye to the root causes just to garner votes! Absolutely not! (*Warm applause*) As long as I, Wan Yongnian, still stand here on this land for a single day, I will never allow anyone to misuse their power or to act unscrupulously!" (*Prolonged warm applause*)

After the Provincial Party secretary had finished his speech, the chief prosecutor of the Supreme People's Procuratorate officially announced the night's action plan and its specific contents.

It was not until then that Li Gaocheng fully understood that this joint operation of the provincial and municipal procuratorial agencies, which had been reported to the Provincial Party Committee, had such a comprehensive plan organised under such conditions of secrecy. Until now, the prosecutors and investigators in the audience and most of the leaders present had no idea or only limited knowledge of the specifics of this operation.

How much hard work must have gone into it!

Li Gaocheng remained silent as he listened nervously to the news that his home and office were to be raided at 2am and to the list of people who would be taken in for questioning:

Secretary of the Party Committee of the Zhongyang Textile Group, Chen Yongming; deputy general manager of the Zhongyang Textile Group Company, Feng Minjie; deputy general manager of the Zhongyang Textile Group Company, Wu Mingde.

Chairman of the board of directors of Green Apple Entertainment City and former secretary of the Party Committee of the Zhongyang Textile Group, Fan Ligang.

Chairman of the Jinqiao Commercial Building, inspector of the Zhongyang Textile Group and former deputy general manager, Qi Renming.

Chairman of the board of directors of Daxin Supermarket and

general manager of the Xinchao Company of the Zhongyang Textile Group, Guo Daxin.

Chairman of the board of directors of the Chang Long Garment and Textile Factory and deputy general manager of the Xinchao Company of the Zhongyang Textile Group, Liu Haixi.

Vice chairman of the Te Gao Te Passenger Transportation Company, advisor to the Provincial People's Bank, former vice president, Wang Yiliang.

Vice chairman of the Green Apple Entertainment City, vice chairman of the Chang Long Garment and Textile Factory, director of Te Gao Te Passenger Transportation Company, deputy procurator general of Dongcheng District Procuratorate and director of the Anti-Corruption Bureau, Wu Aizhen.

Chairman of the board of directors of Te Gao Te Passenger Transportation Company, chairman of the board of directors of the Mei Shu Ya Real Estate Development Company, vice chairman of the board of directors of the Jinqiao Commercial Building, vice chairman of the board of directors of Daxin Supermarket, deputy director of the Economic Policy and Theory Research Office of the Provincial Party Committee, Cao Wanshan.

The reverberations of this list of names shivered through Li Gaocheng like a bell that had been struck. He was dumbfounded! This was followed by a feeling of indescribable hatred and anger. How could his wife have diverged from him so far without telling him a thing? How could she have two vice-chairmanships and a directorship, and he didn't know anything about it? He felt so ashamed, both for himself and for her!

What kind of people were these?

Guo Daxin, the general manager of the Xinchao Company, had actually named a multi-million dollar supermarket after himself, as if he was some kind of emperor! What lawlessness! Then there was also Yan Zhen's brother-in-law, with his two chairmanships and two vice-chairmanships. It was the height of insanity, the height of stupidity, the height of shamelessness! It was as if they thought the world belonged to them.

In the midst of extreme grief and anger, a vague idea finally began to take shape in his mind.

He could no longer be mayor, he couldn't do it anymore. He had to resign! It was the only thing he could do.

Under his stewardship, this serious problem with corruption had occurred, involving not only his old work unit and so many leading cadres he had hired but also even himself and his wife! How could he hold his head up in the city again? Could he blame his wife for what had been going on in front of his very eyes? Could he look people in the eye and say he knew nothing about it?

If he couldn't even explain this, how could he preside over cleaning up the city as mayor? He should feel good about making this decision. He had to be clear about it. Only in this way could he explain himself completely to the world and only in this way could he explain himself completely to his family and his children.

The ache in his heart intensified when he thought of his children, of his daughter Meimei, of how alone and frightened she must be in that great big house at this moment.

But Li Gaocheng understood that, just at this moment, he had effectively lost his freedom to act and, for the time being, he could only stay where he was and wait until the operation was completed.

Involuntarily, he glanced at Yan Zhen and saw that the majestic and tyrannical man of the past had changed completely and had suddenly become so weak and so old. His face was drained of blood and his body was rigid.

How vulnerable this mighty deputy secretary of the Provincial Party Committee turned out to be!

Then, out of the blue, he remembered what Guo Zhongyao had said: "Li Gaocheng, you can never beat him. Even if someone reports him to the central authorities, there is still no way to take him down. Because these people have already mastered all that Communist Party stuff. Forget about all the bad things he has done, which everyone knows about anyway – if you really want to investigate him, I guarantee you won't find anything..."

So then, was his current appearance just a pretence? Or was it, perhaps, because the Provincial Party Committee hadn't notified him in advance of such a major operation? Was he feeling annoyed and ashamed about this and was planning new countermeasures?

He turned round suddenly, startled by someone tapping lightly on his shoulder.

It was Wan Yongnian, secretary of the Provincial Party Committee, and behind him was Yang Cheng, secretary of the Municipal Party Committee. Li Gaocheng was about to say something, but Wan Yongnian was already speaking:

"Thank you, Gaocheng!" Wan Yongnian's voice was as gentle as his expression. "Everybody thanks you very much. It was you who helped us make up our minds because you told the truth!"

"You don't need to try to comfort me anymore, Secretary Wan." For some reason he did not understand, he felt himself choking up. He resisted it and held back his tears. "No matter what you say, I still have responsibilities I cannot shirk, and I cannot shift the pressure I feel inside me. I will formally offer my self-criticism to the Provincial Committee..."

"No, Gaocheng, you are wrong. This is not your responsibility alone – we all share it," Wan Yongnian said, sounding very solemn again. "You should know that the Provincial Committee received a no-strings donation towards the construction of its office building from Zhongyang Textiles, and it wasn't a small donation either. Together with the contribution for the Provincial Government office building, the total is around ten million yuan. A month or so ago, like you, I still believed the management at Zhongyang Textiles was a good team and entirely trustworthy. I also always thought that the problems of Zhongyang Textiles were common to all state-owned enterprises, which is why they have been allowed to drag on until now. But now I know that I was wrong, especially because of what you have said, which further confirmed my error. One thing you said really struck a chord with me, and that was that we must give the workers a clear, solid explanation. In a word, we must be accountable to the broad masses of the workers. To be responsible to the workers means to be responsible to reform, to the country and to our Party. Since we are talking like this, Gaocheng, my responsibility is even greater than yours, and I should be the first to offer a self-criticism."

"Secretary Wan, you must know that the problem with my wife alone is so serious, I cannot possibly shirk my..."

"You are wrong again," Wan Yongnian interrupted him again. "I told you before that the Provincial Party Committee and the Municipal Party Committee both trust you. Yang Cheng has already talked to me in detail about the question of your wife. We have also done a preliminary investigation. The way we see things at the moment, you have made every effort and fulfilled your responsibilities. Everyone trusts you, and you don't need to carry any more burdens. From what you just said to everyone, I think the facts will speak for themselves and prove your innocence."

"I hope that the Provincial Party Committee will grant me a request when this is done," Li Gaocheng said after a pause. "I cannot go on being mayor. I have thought about it very carefully. I formally request my resignation is accepted. I will make a written report soon."

"Do you know what your request should be called? It should be called weakness, compromise and fleeing the battlefield!" Wan Yongnian's voice was suddenly sharp. "When we avoid facing contradictions, struggles and corruption, avoiding them is the same as running away and running away is the same as surrendering! Surrender means the failure of our government!"

"What kind of time is this to have an idea like that, Lao Li?" Yang Cheng interjected. "The pressure on the Provincial Party Committee is great enough already and we should be sharing that pressure, not aggravating it."

"Also," Wan Yongnian's tone had softened now, "have you stopped to think whether the workers will agree if you try to do this? If you are a bad mayor, the workers will not agree, and if you are a good mayor, the workers will be even less willing to agree. I will give you an official reply to your suggestion right now. Even if it turns out that you have stood up to all our investigations, the Provincial Party Committee will not consider your quandary at least until the problem of Zhongyang Textiles is completely resolved. So, I will now give you your instructions, which also represent the decision of the Provincial Party Committee. If you are tired, take a break for a while. If you can keep going, let's discuss with Yang Cheng how to solve the problem of tomorrow's petition from the retired workers and cadres of Zhongyang Textiles. What I mean is that tomorrow, no, actually it is today already, you and Yang Cheng must arrive at Zhongyang Textiles before seven o'clock in the morning.

"First, you have to explain clearly to the workers the decision and determination of the Provincial Party Committee and the Municipal Party Committee. Second, you have to tell the workers what you did tonight and inform them that we have already taken action. Third, please tell the workers that, this afternoon, or tomorrow morning at the latest, I will definitely go to Zhongyang Textiles to offer my condolences to the workers. In fact, the other leaders of the Provincial Party Committee and I should be going with you to Zhongyang Textiles in the morning, but several days ago, we arranged to participate in another large-scale condolence activity in a disaster area on the outskirts of the city. If we get back in time in the afternoon, we will go to Zhongyang Textiles then. If not, we will go tomorrow morning.

"The reason why the Provincial Party Committee wants you to go, Gaocheng, is not only because we all trust you, but because the workers of Zhongyang Textiles also trust you. Fortunately, we have now taken a solid first step and I think this time things should go better because we have already taken action which was carefully planned a few days ago. With all that out of the way, there are two more things I would like to say to you. In respect of what has happened tonight, firstly, don't feel under pressure and, secondly, forget your worries and put down your burdens. You must stand proud! I believe what you said to me just now. In other words, if that is what you really end up doing, the organisation will still support you, and so will the people! That's all I have to say, Gaocheng. Is there anything else that you want to say?"

"I have one small request, Secretary Wan, but I don't know whether I should ask it or not..." Li Gaocheng suddenly felt a lump in his throat.

"Go ahead!" Wan Yongnian seemed to have guessed what was coming, and his voice softened a little.

"Can you get someone to call home and tell my daughter to find somewhere to keep out of the way for the time being?" Li Gaocheng's tears were falling unchecked now. "She is still very young, Secretary Wan, really very young. She is the only one who I am worried about."

"Don't worry, we have already thought of that!" Tears seemed to be coming to Wan Yongnian's eyes too. "Yang Cheng has taken your daughter into his house. The child will be fine."

"Thank you, thank you!"

Li Gaocheng burst into tears.

CHAPTER FORTY-FIVE

ALTHOUGH THE OPERATION HAD BEEN GOING ON for more than an hour, there had not yet been any news from the relevant parties.

Li Gaocheng didn't speak to Yang Cheng, who, understanding his mood, remained equally silent.

The house was quiet, and although the lights were still on, everyone was asleep.

Both secretary and driver were dismissed, and the two men sat quietly on the sofa, waiting anxiously. Li Gaocheng understood that Yang Cheng's current mood was likely to be even more solemn and anxious than his own, as, in a way, the pressure of responsibility the other man was feeling was probably greater than his own.

Sometime later, Li Gaocheng asked softly: "Do you know if Meimei is back?"

"She called me."

"What did she say to you?"

"That girl is very smart and she didn't say anything. She just asked me where you were and where her mother was."

"She hasn't been to see her mother?"

"It doesn't seem so. She said she called, and someone told her that her mother had just gone out. But after that, she couldn't get hold of her. She said she called several times, but her mother never answered. Her mobile was turned off all the time too. Has she changed her number?"

"Impossible. She may be trying to put pressure on me by not seeing the children. She knows they are coming back for the New Year."

"That's what I think too. Did you get to speak to Meimei at the time?"

"It was after two o'clock in the afternoon when she got home. I only saw her at the door, and I didn't think to tell her anything," Li Gaocheng said regretfully. "I really should have talked to her then so she could have a chance to prepare herself mentally."

"It's being said these days that the only thing people are afraid for is their children. We should cherish the things we have for the sake of our children." Yang Cheng wasn't sure whether he was talking to Li Gaocheng or himself. "But then again, this is such a huge thing, it must be pretty unbearable no matter how prepared you are. The fact that our children are the children of leading cadres is probably their biggest weak point."

Silence fell again. A while later, Li Gaocheng said: "How did you get Meimei to come here?"

"I told her to come for dinner and to wait for you here. I said you were sure to come because we had important things to discuss tonight. My wife added that since there was no one else at your house, she should come and stay here. She probably didn't want to be all alone at your place, so she came here and hasn't gone out since."

"Do you know which room she is in?" Li Gaocheng felt himself welling up again.

"Do you want to see her?" Yang Cheng asked, deliberately avoiding the other man's eyes.

"Do you know if she has slept or not?"

"My wife just told me Meimei has gone to sleep and seems to be well settled."

"She must be exhausted."

"She's got the guest bedroom to herself. Go and have a look."

The lights in the bedroom were still on, and Meimei was lying on the bed, still in her clothes, with even her shoes on. She must have been waiting and was too tired to stay awake.

Li Gaocheng gently pushed open the door and walked quietly over to Meimei's bedside. She didn't notice anything and stayed soundly asleep.

He silently stared at Meimei's delicate yet grief-stricken face. The tear stains at the corners of her eyes, which had not dried up yet, glistened slightly in the lamplight.

She was beautiful, just like her mother was when she was young. She had indeed grown up now and her features had those soft, feminine lines that held an insuppressible message of youth.

Meimei was in the prime of her life, innocent, pure and carefree. She was also in the most critical period of her life. She had just entered university, and her studies, ideals, career and love were all ahead of her. Needless to say, her family had a huge influence on her. If she remained the daughter of a mayor and of a bureau chief, she had a rosy future ahead of her. At the very least, there would be few obstacles in her way. Conversely, if she were the daughter of a worker and peasant, the daughter of an ordinary cadre, the daughter of a cadre who had made mistakes, or even the daughter of a criminal, what would the future be like for her then? What a prospect! What a huge blow it would be to her if her parents fell from grace like that! It would most likely affect her whole life and everything about her.

What a cruel awakening that would be for the child!

Yang Cheng had just said it. The thing people most fear for is their children. He now felt that should be changed to "the thing evildoers most fear for is their children".

At this thought, Li Gaocheng shivered involuntarily. Was this what happened to transgressors? Did they sink deeper and deeper into this state of mind, helplessly continuing on their downward path until they were buried completely?

His wife must know this too, and that was why she had deliberately thrust this young girl who was truly not yet grown up, his beloved daughter, directly before his eyes.

She is the most selfish of women, and also the stupidest! She could think of organising her own escape at the expense of her children, her husband and her family, exchanging his protection for her safety!

A child is innocent, and it is precisely because of that innocence that the parents who implicate it in their affairs are so grievously distressed.

He stood silently and for a long time in front of Meimei's bed, imagining how the child would face what had happened when she woke up.

If they found one thing in his house, they were more than likely to find other things too. Although he had told the nanny immediately to return or dispose of the "shopping vouchers" and the so-called "New Year's goods", she had only had one afternoon to do it, and there would surely be a lot of stuff still left behind. Maybe these things were not related to the main business, but who knew what else there was to find there?

Events had proved that many things had happened at home over the past few years that he was mostly in ignorance of. Even now, how many things were still hidden from him?

He was most worried by his wife's bedroom. He could almost count on his fingers the number of times he had been in there since he became mayor. Heaven knew what there was to find in there!

If they did find something, then even a swim in the Yellow River would never clean the stain on his reputation.

He didn't dare contemplate the possibility as he stared blankly at Meimei's face.

Just at that moment, he heard the shrilling of the telephone downstairs.

He gently took Meimei's shoes off for her, quietly turned off the light, left the room, closing the door behind him, and hurried downstairs.

Apart from his daughter, the most important thing for him at this moment was news, all the news there was about the progress of the operation.

Yang Cheng was listening to the phone with all his attention.

The call went on for a long time, and Yang Cheng hardly said anything but just listened quietly with a solemn expression.

This was the first call about the night's action, and it was of huge importance. It would settle the success or failure of the operation!

"Is there anything else?" This was Yang Cheng's first question. "Well, I won't be sleeping tonight, so please feel free to contact me anytime. I have nothing to add. You have done a great job, and I thank you on behalf of the Municipal Committee. If you really want my input, then I will only give you one piece of advice – be careful, you must be careful. The further you get into this operation, the more careful you must be, and the more vigilant you must be not to miss any clues. I know my words are probably unnecessary, but it doesn't do any harm to repeat them. Good then, I will await further news from you."

After Yang Cheng had hung up the phone, the two men looked at each other in silence for a long moment. Then Li Gaocheng saw that tears had begun to flow from Yang Cheng's eyes.

"We have won, Lao Li..." Yang Cheng's voice was trembling.

Li Gaocheng couldn't speak, but he understood what Yang Cheng meant by "won".

"Prosecutors found a large amount of cash in the safe at Chao Wanshan's house, more than 1.3 million in RMB, more than two hundred thousand in Hong Kong dollars, nearly one hundred thousand in US dollars and eight kilograms of gold bars, eleven of them! In addition, there were millions recorded in bankbooks and a large amount of jewels and jewellery that cannot be immediately accounted for." Yang Cheng was doing his best to keep himself calm. "The most important thing they found in Chao Wanshan's home was something that probably none of us had thought of. When they looked in the safe, they found that Chao Wanshan actually holds passports from three different countries and has three international credit cards with huge credit limits! You have to have hundreds of thousands of yuan as a minimum in your bank account to apply for those cards! In with all that, there were also two passports from other countries recently issued to someone else. The names are assumed identities, but the photographs are of someone we know very well. Do you know who it is?" Yang Cheng stopped for a moment, then exploded: "Yan Zhen! They are photos of Yan Zhen! The deputy secretary of our Provincial Party Committee! They are the passports of two unremarkable countries. This is an astonishing discovery. It's hugely significant. The chief prosecutor just said that these discoveries meant it was very likely they have huge amounts in overseas accounts, or they have already made huge investments overseas!"

Li Gaocheng was completely stunned. Not only was this news

astounding and hugely important, but it was also terrible, terrifying and almost unbelievable!

A senior official who could be said to embody the Communist Party was actually preparing to use a foreign country as one of his boltholes! The cunning rabbit did indeed have three burrows, and one of them was abroad!

Then in less than half an hour, three more phone calls came in.

Without exception in the homes of all the leading cadres of Zhongyang Textiles which had been searched, huge amounts of cash and property of unknown origin were found, and they all held foreign passports with long terms of validity and a large amount of foreign currency. There were all kinds of precious jewellery, luxury private residences, lingerie worth more than a thousand yuan a piece, glasses worth more than two thousand yuan a pair, leather shoes costing more than three thousand yuan a pair, leather jackets at eight thousand yuan, suits, watches and cameras costing tens of thousands of yuan, and diamond necklaces costing hundreds of thousands of yuan...

Guo Zhongyao, the general manager of Zhongyang Textiles, had a long-term mistress in each of his three alternative residences!

The three sons and one daughter of Feng Minjie, deputy general manager of Zhongyang Textiles, none of whom had yet started a family, already had many luxury houses. In a family of six people, apart from his wife, everyone had a car. The eldest son drove a Mercedes, and the second son a Lincoln!

Chen Yongming, secretary of the Party Committee of Zhongyang Textiles, had a son and a daughter. His son was just twenty-two years old, and his daughter was only nineteen. They were already managers and deputy managers at branches of Xinchao Co. Ltd!

Wang Yiliang, the recently retired deputy governor of the People's Bank of China only had his wife at home with him, as his son and daughter were overseas. However, more than 120 cashmere jackets, more than fifty high-end leather jackets, more than forty cameras, more than seventy watches of different makes, more than eighty pieces of gold and silver jewellery and more than two hundred pairs of luxury brand leather shoes were all found in his house...

That was more than enough! There was no need to hear any more.

Li Gaocheng's chest heaved, he was sweating profusely all over his body, he felt nauseous and he couldn't stop himself moaning out loud. He was intensely nervous, and the sole reason was that, so far, there had been no report on his own wife and family!

He felt that he simply couldn't take it anymore and he was about to collapse, but he didn't want to give himself away in front of Yang Cheng, so he forced himself to keep going. He kept drinking water, but his mouth was as dry as a chain-smoker's...

He jumped every time the phone rang.

The prolonged tension and fatigue left him vague and on the verge of passing out. He started again as another call came in, and he felt he was about to faint. Sure enough, this time it was news about his wife.

It was shocking news. A large amount of cash was found in the safe in his wife's office, including 210,000 yuan, twenty thousand US dollars and fifty thousand Hong Kong dollars... There were also four bankbooks, three of which were in false names, totalling more than six hundred thousand yuan... In addition, there were stocks worth about two hundred thousand yuan, and gold and silver jewellery worth more than a hundred thousand yuan...

Hearing this, Li Gaocheng calmed down a little. It seemed that his wife hadn't lied to him. She told him at the time that even when all the so-called fixed assets were counted, the full total was about two million yuan. Everything found that night roughly added up to that number. The way it looked at the moment, his wife's holdings were the lowest of all those that had been uncovered so far. So, from another perspective, his wife's role could still be seen as one of the deceived and exploited. He still remembered how she had told him at the time that the money was clean, and he could not be sullied by even a penny of it! So, now she had to explain it all to the powers-that-be, and then they would see just how clean her money was.

Now, what about their home?

Looking at Yang Cheng's equally uneasy expression, it seemed that there was still no news. Li Gaocheng understood that on this issue, Yang Cheng was possibly more stressed and anxious than he was himself. If it turned out that Li Gaocheng had nothing to do with any of this, then everything Yang Cheng had revealed about the problems at Zhongyang Textiles was undoubtedly correct. If not, however, the damage would be much greater. Especially if it turned out that Li Gaocheng actually had serious and irreparable problems. In that case, Yang Cheng, the secretary of the Municipal Party Committee, also had a responsibility that could not be shied away from, for covering up or even giving false testimony about a person with such huge problems. It would show that he had huge problems himself, or, at the very least, it was enough to show that he was incompetent. It would not only be an issue of responsibility, but also a moral issue, an issue of principle, and a big issue of right and wrong in terms of the Party.

The phone rang again.

"It's from your number, Lao Li." Yang Cheng handed over the phone.

Li Gaocheng almost couldn't believe his ears, and he just sat there stunned for a while. It was so late. How could it be his own number? Whose else could it be? He stared at Yang Cheng blankly. "Mine...?"

"Yours." Seeing how confused Li Gaocheng was looking, Yang Cheng explained: "It's Wu Xingang."

It was his secretary calling. He hurriedly took the phone. "Li Gaocheng here, what's the matter?"

"Mayor Li, it's just that Mingming has been trying to get hold of you..." Wu Xingang sounded rather embarrassed.

"Mingming!" Li Gaocheng was so surprised he was rooted to the spot for a moment. His son! His son was home!

"He's been calling me all this time, Mayor Li. I didn't know whether I should tell him where you were or not."

"When did he get back?" Li Gaocheng suddenly felt very drained. He had never dreamed that his son would be back home.

"Around 10 o'clock last evening."

"Aaah!" Li Gaocheng groaned. He had managed to avoid his daughter, but now his son had caught up with him.

He looked blankly at Yang Cheng, not knowing what to do.

"Get Wu Xingang to tell Mingming to come over here to my place," Yang Cheng said after a moment's thought.

"It's so late, and there's no car. Everything has already happened, so what is there for Mingming to see? He should stay at home," Li Gaocheng said weakly.

"Then get him to give me a call. At least I can put his mind at rest a little. There are some things I can explain to him," Yang Cheng said.

Li Gaocheng considered this for a long time, and, in the end, it seemed the best course.

Li Gaocheng passed on to Wu Xingang exactly what Yang Cheng had said, and within a minute, the phone rang.

But it was not Mingming.

It was a report from the Procuratorate about the search of his own home.

Li Gaocheng's heartstrings were so taut he thought they would snap, and he waited with bated breath as if for a verdict in court.

He simply didn't know what else could happen, and he simply didn't know what result was waiting for him.

Yang Cheng put down the phone without a word, and then stared at Li Gaocheng in silence. He didn't say a word, but he put his hand lightly on Li Gaocheng's, then squeezed tighter and tighter...

So far, no suspicious property had been found in Li Gaocheng's house, only a bankbook in Li's name showing a balance of twenty-four thousand yuan, and a small quantity of cigarettes, alcohol and luxury food. There was only one puzzling circumstance, and that was a bankbook found in the nanny's room, showing deposits in the nanny's name for as much as thirty-two thousand yuan!

Li Gaocheng was stunned again. Where did his nanny, Xiao Lian, get so much money?

He was fairly familiar with the current situation in Xiao Lian's family. She was from a poor county, and her parents were simple farmers. She had two older brothers, one older sister and one younger sister. The two older brothers were recently married. In addition, they had built a new house, were deeply in debt and in something of a mess. Xiao Lian's monthly salary of two hundred yuan was routinely sent home almost every month. So, how could she have an account with more than thirty thousand yuan in it? And where did the money come from?

Xiao Lian had only been their nanny for a little over two years. Even if she had saved all her money for the past two years, plus some extra pocket money she often got, it would still only be five or six thousand yuan. How could there be more than thirty thousand yuan?

He had to be aware that if he couldn't explain that money, no matter who was responsible, it would be enough to get him expelled from the Party, dismissed from his post, and even sentenced and put in jail!

Yang Cheng answered Li's questions quite calmly but also very alarmingly.

The little nanny said that since she was hired, she had found the money down the back of the sofa, next to the table lamps, under the telephone and in gift boxes. She did not know whose it was and nor would the family, so she didn't mention it and quietly put it aside. She also said that so many people came to the mayor's house to give gifts, there wasn't much she could do about it. Some people even gave her gifts and money to get access to Mayor Li and Director Wu.

In fact, the nanny's testimony was very beneficial to Li Gaocheng. She said that Mayor Li never accepted gifts, and the people who came never dared to give gifts directly to Mayor Li. They only gave them to Director Wu...

The nation's hard-earned wealth was dripping with blood. The words sprang unbidden into Li Gaocheng's head. The nation was pouring blood under the rape and plunder of these scum...

The telephone rang again. His son!

When he took the phone from Yang Cheng, he found that his hands were shaking badly.

"Mingming..." At first, Li Gaocheng didn't know what to say to his son.

"...Dad, Dad! Is that you? Is it really you?"

His son sounded so close, it upset him. He tried his best to suppress his feelings and emotions, and attempted to sound calm. "Yes, Son, it's me! It's your dad!"

"...Dad, Dad!" His son suddenly burst into tears. "Dad! What the hell is going on! Why did they raid our house? Why, Dad? What's going on with you? And what about Mum? What's going on with Mum? Tell me the truth, Dad! What's going on, what the hell is going on...?"

As he listened to Mingming crying, the tears sprang to Li

Gaocheng's eyes too. He tried his best to keep his speech steady, without any tremble, but he couldn't bear it any longer:

"Listen to me, Son! Now isn't the time to talk about it. What's happening at home right now is just routine, it's not a raid. Son, you have to trust your dad. Your dad's conscience is clear..."

"Dad! You are the mayor! How am I expected to believe that a mayor can allow his own home to be raided? Dad, have you stopped to think how we're supposed to behave with this massive upheaval at home? What is Mum supposed to do? If you really have a clear conscience, Dad, shouldn't you be able to protect your own home? Don't lie to me, Dad! Something must have happened! I want to see my mother. I don't want to see anyone else at the moment. I just want to see my mother..." His son seemed so fragile and upset, he couldn't stop crying down the phone.

"Listen to me, Mingming! Your dad will talk to you about your mother later..."

"Stop it, I don't believe you! What can you tell me now?" The boy's voice was growing hoarse. "I want to see my mother! You told me to see my mother right away..."

"I've told you things aren't as you imagine, Son! Wait until we meet..." Li Gaocheng tried his best to comfort his son but was interrupted by his son's crying.

"I don't want to hear any more from you! I don't want to see you at all! You're still lying to me now! I'm not your son, and you're not my father! I never want to see you again..."

"Mingming...!" Just as Li Gaocheng was about to try again to explain to his son, he suddenly felt as if he had been punched in the stomach.

There, right in front of him, halfway down the stairs, his daughter Meimei was staring at him motionless, ashen-faced and tearful!

Li Gaocheng tried to stand up, but suddenly he felt as if he had been caught up in a whirlwind, and then he didn't know anything more...

CHAPTER FORTY-SIX

Li Gaocheng woke with a violent start. The sunlight was almost too bright for him to open his eyes and it was a while before he could make out Wu Xingang standing in front of him.

"Where is this?" He struggled to remember.

"The city hospital," Wu Xingang replied.

"... hospital?" For the moment, he still couldn't recall what had happened.

"Secretary Yang Cheng brought you here. The doctors say you have been overworking and are in temporary shock."

"...Ah! What's the time?" He asked sharply as if he had been startled back to his senses.

"Quarter to nine, Mayor Li. I wasn't going to wake you and the doctors didn't want me to, but the workers at Zhongyang Textiles have really kicked off and they don't believe what Secretary Yang has told them..."

Before Wu Xingang could finish, Li Gaocheng interrupted him furiously. "Then why didn't you wake me earlier? Get the car ready at once. We're going to Zhongyang Textiles!"

Li Gaocheng sat up in bed as he spoke, but when he tried to stand up, he was felled by a sudden bout of dizziness.

Wu Xingang and two nurses hurried forward to help him back into bed, but he angrily refused their help.

"Take me to Zhongyang Textiles now, even if you have to carry me." His voice was weak, but he wasn't going to give any ground. "Quick, we don't have a minute to lose. Get the car ready and be quick about it!"

Three minutes later, Li Gaocheng was sitting in the car, and ten minutes later he knew everything that had been going on at Zhongyang Textiles from Wu Xingang's report.

It had already been past four in the morning when Li Gaocheng was sent to the hospital. Yang Cheng had stayed with him for less than an hour before leaving for Zhongyang Textiles.

At close to six o'clock, Yang Cheng and the two deputy mayors arrived at the Zhongyang Textiles dormitory compound. By that time, there were almost six or seven thousand retired and active cadres gathered there, and the cars to transport them were already sitting waiting and ready to go. The workers advanced the timetable by half an hour to leave on the dot of 7am, and arrive at the gates of the Provincial Party Committee around 7.30. They were hoping either to stop the leadership of the Committee from going in to work or to prevent them from leaving if they needed to go somewhere. The workers felt that this was the only time it would be possible for the leaders to speak out and meet with the workers.

After secretary of the Municipal Party Committee, Yang Cheng, arrived at Zhongyang Textiles, he immediately summoned the various representatives of the retired workers and cadres who had petitioned the leaders of the Municipal Party Committee the last time. He told them about the operation of the night before and about the attitude of the Provincial and Municipal Party Committees towards Zhongyang Textiles and informed them that the secretary of the Provincial Party Committee and the Provincial Governor were going to make a special trip to Zhongyang Textiles to visit the workers. He said he hoped that they would convey the news to the workers as quickly as possible. If they still felt there were any difficulties, or if they still could not convince the workers themselves, then he, Yang Cheng, would work personally with and for the workers.

He had thought that the workers would be overjoyed and enthusiastic when they heard the news, but, contrary to his expectations, when the representatives relayed the news to the workers, the reaction was just the opposite.

They believed that last night's operation was a trick designed to deceive them and the top brass were just killing people off to keep them quiet but only making things worse by trying to hide what was going on. Some of the workers said that it was all just a cover-up to protect the real corrupt elements, to pull the wool over the people's eyes, to pull a fast one and let the culprits slip away and hide. Others simply said that it was a swindle like a butcher's stall that displayed mutton and sold dog meat, that it was being made to look as though the corrupt elements had been arrested whereas, in fact, it was honest cadres who were being slandered and fitted up. It seems that they have arrested a few corrupt elements, but in reality, they are slandering and framing the real, good cadres! In the end, any corrupt elements who were arrested were irrelevant. Those who should be promoted or elevated would still be promoted or elevated. In other words, there would be a bit of a reshuffle, but everything would go on just the same. However, it would be precisely those honest cadres who genuinely enjoyed the support of the workers who would be dismissed or transferred one by one and might even be tried and sentenced for some triviality or other! Such things were not uncommon; on the contrary, the list of them was endless. The workers said they had seen it all before and there was no point in trying to pull the wool over their eyes again!

The more the workers talked, the more intense their emotions became, until, finally, they came to a consensus.:

This was all an excuse to attack Mayor Li Gaocheng, who enjoys the support of us workers!

If anyone wants to frame Mayor Li, we workers will never allow it!

We want to see Mayor Li now!

We want the secretary of the Provincial Party Committee to talk to us! We want guarantees from the secretary of the Provincial Party Committee!

We want the Provincial Party Committee to guarantee Mayor Li's safety!

Since Mayor Li's home has been searched, why not search Yan Zhen's home too? The root cause of Zhongyang Textiles' problems lies with the Provincial Party Committee, and Yan Zhen is their general behind the scenes!

If the Provincial Party Committee doesn't search Yan Zhen's

house, let us workers do it! We don't want to see anyone now, except Mayor Li!

If we can't see Mayor Li, all tens of thousands of workers at Zhongyang Textiles want someone from the Provincial Party Committee!

Even Yang Cheng had not expected feelings to be so intense among the workers. Within not much more than an hour, almost all the workers and cadres of Zhongyang Textiles, twenty to thirty thousand of them both active and retired, had assembled. They demanded to see Mayor Li within the hour, otherwise they would all take to the streets and petition the Provincial Party Committee!

When Li Gaocheng's car arrived at Zhongyang Textiles, the number of people gathered there had risen to as many as forty or fifty thousand because other workers and farmers from nearby who had heard the news had come to join in!

Li Gaocheng's car seemed to be crawling along almost at walking pace in the midst of the mighty sea of people and their earth-shattering cries and shouts. It had not even quite reached Zhongyang Textiles before it had to stop, unable to proceed any further.

Li Gaocheng looked at the commotion to the left and right of him, and immediately asked the driver to pull over. He then walked on through the crowd with Wu Xingang.

When he was about to reach the Veteran Cadre Activity Centre in the dormitory compound, he was stopped dead in his tracks by a completely unexpected scene. It was then he understood why so many people were crowded there.

A skinny, emaciated woman was standing on the very edge of the roof of the eight-storey business centre opposite the Veteran Cadre Activity Centre. She looked so wild and desperate, it was clear to anyone that she could fall or jump at any moment!

Anyone with any intelligence could see immediately that if the woman wasn't mad, at the very least she had given up on life.

When he got closer, Li Gaocheng could finally see the woman clearly: it was Xia Yulian!

He couldn't believe his eyes. He stared at her for a long time before he could convince himself it was indeed her.

It really was her, the terminally ill Xia Yulian!

How could she be standing there? How did she get up there?

And what was she doing in a place like that? The roof was so high up, and the mid-winter northwest wind was so strong that even a healthy young man standing there would be in immediate mortal danger, let alone a frail old woman like this!

Why was she standing there?

The explanation could simply be that she didn't want to live anymore. She wanted to end her life there in that place.

But why?

Why had she chosen to end her life in front of so many people at such a time, in such a place, and especially on such an occasion? Why?

And if that wasn't the explanation, what was?

Li Gaocheng struggled to squeeze forward through the crowd. His face was so pale and his body was so weak. Cold sweat almost soaked his shirt, but he still pushed and squeezed with all his strength. Several times he tripped over and fell to the ground, but, after Wu Xingang had helped him up, he kept pressing forward.

He vaguely realised that Xia Yulian being there probably had something to do with him. He had to see her as soon as possible. He had something to tell her, and she must have something to say to him.

What's up with you, Older Sister Xia? What's really going on?

I have asked someone to bring you the best new anti-cancer drugs from abroad, and I have also asked someone to find you the best traditional Chinese doctor specialising in cancer. Your life mustn't just vanish into thin air. Everyone wants you to live and is hoping for a miracle! It may be that you will come out of your misery better than ever. Doctors say that people like you, who can't afford medication and who have taken few drugs during their life, often have a much better chance of recovery. You can't let it end like this! Truly, you mustn't let it end like this!

His tears were already flowing uncontrollably, and Li Gaocheng felt more and more that it was most likely that Xia Yulian was standing there for him!

Xia Yulian might very well be sacrificing her life to protect and repay Li Gaocheng one last time!

This guess was soon confirmed, and the clear and manifest

purpose of Xia Yulian's completely unexpected action was just that. She wanted to protect Li Gaocheng with her own death!

She firmly disagreed with the workers going to the Provincial Party Committee to petition. With a woman's unique intuition, she told the workers that if they did so, they would only ensure that Mayor Li was punished more severely, and made to step down even sooner! If they made a fuss like that, the bad guys would definitely find an excuse to say that Li Gaocheng must have instructed the workers to do this behind the scenes. The bigger the trouble the workers stirred up, the greater Mayor Li's fault would be said to be, and the more Mayor Li would be screwed over!

"Besides," she went on, "many of you are still young, and the factory still needs you. Supposing you put yourselves at fault over this, what will happen to the factory in the future? I'm old, and useless now, so, if you insist on making mistakes, let me make them alone...

"If you don't listen to me, and you still insist on going to the Provincial Party Committee, then let me die! You will have to step over my corpse! As soon as the group sets off, I will jump from here immediately!

"I, Xia Yulian, have never had any ability or prospects, but I have never told a lie in my life! So, if you don't believe me, just try me!"

She would not let the workers go to the Provincial Party Committee to petition, but there was also one condition that she wanted immediate agreement to. She wanted to see Mayor Li Gaocheng at once! She wanted to see Provincial Party Secretary Wan Yongnian immediately. She had something she wanted to say to both of them to their faces.

If Mayor Li and Secretary Wan didn't come, then she had only one answer: she would jump!

She only wanted to see Mayor Li and Secretary Wan, and no one else was to come to the roof of the building. If she saw any trace of anyone else, she would jump without hesitation!

And no one was to try to put out any nets or mattresses to catch her. If she saw anything like that, she would jump immediately.

Even if they did try to set up anything to catch her or cushion her fall, if she wanted to jump, she wouldn't fall straight to the ground. She had prepared a nylon rope for herself: one end was tied in a slip knot and the other was fastened to a steel cable on the roof. If anyone tried to stop her, she would put the rope around her neck and jump. She said she would rather break her neck than let anyone stop her...

She said that she knew many people, many reporters and many TV stations would be coming there that day and if Secretary Wan and the Provincial Party Committee let all the corrupt people in the company off, made all the good cadres like Mayor Li step down, and let the factory that she had worked for all her life collapse for no good reason, she would die a good death in front of millions of people for everyone to see!

She said that she had been useless all her life, but at least she could die heroically! She had no other way of saving Zhongyang Textiles except to use her life or her death to rescue it one more time!

Li Gaocheng squeezed his way to the bottom of the building, and after he had listened to everything that Xia Yulian had to say, he realised that there he could hear the sound of weeping.

There were so many familiar faces there: the old Red Army soldier Ding Jincun, the old worker Wang Yinglie, the old factory manager Yuan Mingliang, the old chief worker Zhang Huabin, the chief worker Gao Shuangliang, the old model workers Fan Xiuzhi, Wang Dakuan, Zhang Faqiang, Guo Baoshan and Liu Xiaodong, the former deputy director Li Suzhi, technician Hu Huizhong, veteran worker Ma Decheng, and Xia Yulian's children and daughter-in-law...

It seemed that all of them were weeping quietly.

"...Mayor Li!" The hubbub all around him meant that he couldn't tell who it was who had called his name.

It took him a while to realise that now was not the time to cry.

He tried his best to master his emotions. There were several worker representatives and some Public Security officers who had come to maintain order as soon as they heard the news, standing next to him. He asked them as calmly as he could: "Where is Secretary Yang?"

"Secretary Yang is trying to call Secretary Wan. He's probably in one of the nearby public phone booths," a Public Security officer with a police rank replied.

"Who are you?" Li Gaocheng asked him.

"I'm the deputy head of the police station here. My name is Wei."

"Very good, Chief Wei, please notify the Municipal Public Security Bureau immediately, and ask them to increase the police presence to maintain order. Nothing untoward must happen here!"

"We have already seen to it that a lot of the officers from the city bureau are here. The rest will arrive soon."

Li Gaocheng looked around, and sure enough, he found that there were already a lot of police officers keeping order, and they had set up roadblocks and a human wall around the perimeter of the commercial centre building. There were more than a dozen police cars and two ambulances parked up nearby. Several Public Security officers were using hand-held loudspeakers to direct the crowd. The most striking aspect was that there was a red fire truck parked at the scene, with more than a dozen firefighters participating in the operation. They were preparing to raise the tallest specialised firefighting ladder at the top of which was the most advanced high-rise safety barrier.

There were already five or six TV stations present, and they were all concentrating on focusing their TV cameras on the scene. Two very familiar faces seemed to be hosting the broadcast. In addition to the TV cameras and microphones, countless other cameras were aimed at Xia Yulian on the eighth-floor roof.

This unexpected event seemed to have moved everyone deeply.

"Is there anything else going on we should know about?" Li Gaocheng asked again.

"We are making every effort to organise a rescue. Secretary Yang has informed the Municipal Street Lighting Administration. They are going to send two tall cranes as soon as possible in case we can use them."

"You can't do that, Mayor Li! No, no, it won't do at all!" The two old workers Zhang Huabin and Wang Yinglie clustered round him. "Xia Yulian will jump if they come anywhere near her! No, absolutely not!"

"You have to get up there quickly, Mayor Li! Only you can go!" The old factory manager Yuan Mingliang also gave his advice. "She'll only talk to you! It's you she wants to see..."

"But Secretary Wan hasn't been contacted yet. She will definitely be more suspicious if Secretary Wan isn't here," Li Suzhi, the old deputy director of the factory, said worriedly. "If Mayor Li goes up, and she only sees him but no Secretary Wan, then..."

"Mayor Li, Xia Yulian has been standing out there for more than an hour. The weather is so cold, and the wind is so strong. If there is any more delay, she won't be able to hold out," the old Red Army man Ding Jincun said mournfully. "She is so ill, Mayor Li..."

It was right at that moment that Li Gaocheng realised he knew what he had to do. He addressed the few people standing near him, speaking firmly, pretty much like giving orders: "Wu Xingang, go back immediately, and bring Meimei and Mingming here no matter what, the sooner the better, and don't waste a second!"

"Lao Wu, Lao Yuan," he said to two of the worker representatives beside him, "you assist our comrades from the Public Security Bureau to look after things down here, especially to keep the workers calm. The first priority is to save her life. Second, please tell the workers that my situation is fine, and I am still the mayor. Tell them also to trust the Provincial Party Committee and the Municipal Party Committee. They will never wrong a good person, nor let a bad person go! Third, if anyone makes any other trouble in the current circumstances, then no matter who they are, no matter what they are trying to do, they will be reviled in Zhongyang Textiles for the rest of time! Chief Wei, I will go to the top of the building right now. Please come with me to the eighth floor. I hope you can work with me. Lao Li!" Li Gaocheng turned around and spoke to Li Suzhi, the old deputy director. "You are a woman and a comrade, please go over and use the loudspeaker to shout to the top of the building to tell Older Sister Xia that I am here, and I will be up there right away. Tell her that I have a lot to say to her, and that her two older children want to see her as well, and they have a lot to say to her too..."

CHAPTER FORTY-SEVEN

It was called an eight-storey building, but it was actually ten storeys high because the first and second floors were both commercial halls, and each was as high as two floors.

There was no elevator and no lights in the corridors. After the fourth floor, the staircase became narrower and narrower. By the time Li Gaocheng reached the fifth and sixth floors, he was already exhausted and out of breath, and had to stop and rest several times before continuing upwards.

Every floor was guarded by numbers of workers and Public Security personnel who were there to prevent children or anyone else who had no official reason to be there rushing up to the top of the building and exacerbating the situation.

Director Wei explained that everything was being done as specifically instructed by Secretary Yang Cheng. The only way of keeping Xia Yulian safe was to do everything just as she wanted it.

It had been no small matter for Yang Cheng to give him the support he had, but he would have been lost without it. Over the past few days, at every difficult and critical time, it was Yang Cheng's presence and support that had enabled him to get through them. He was very aware of his own good fortune, for, if it hadn't been for Yang Cheng, it was hard to imagine that he would have been able to keep going until now. Yang Cheng was indeed an excellent secretary!

When he reached the top floor, he looked with some surprise at the steel wire frames nailed to the wall to form a ladder that reached up to the skylight access to the roof. The first wire frame was a metre and a half above the ground! It took a man like him a lot of strength to get up onto it, and he couldn't imagine how the short, skinny Xia Yulian had managed to climb up to the roof from there!

Xia Yulian was terminally ill, and her body was much weaker than his! When he had seen her the day before, she was almost unable to move, let alone walk, but now she was able to climb up a ladder like this to get to the top of such a high building all by herself!

According to the building management, the window to the roof of the building had been wired shut, and the average person would have found it impossible to open without specific tools. An analysis of the situation suggested that it was likely that Xia Yulian must have reconnoitred the situation in advance and come prepared to climb up onto the roof.

A cancer patient who was so sick that she could barely take care of herself would never have been able to climb up there without superhuman perseverance and amazing stamina, let alone do it twice.

Li Gaocheng looked down from a window on the eighth floor, and the crowd, which looked like a swarm of ants, made a sound like the tide coming in on a beach, and many people shouted, with tears in their eyes: "Don't jump! Don't jump! Don't jump…"

Someone using a loudspeaker was shouting over and over again: "…Xia Yulian! Listen! Xia Yulian! Listen! Mayor Li is here already, and he will be at the top of the building immediately. He is by himself and he says he has a lot to say to you. Listen, Xia Yulian, Mayor Li is very ill. He has come straight from the hospital! Secretary Yang said that his fever reached forty degrees last night! But as soon as he heard that something had happened to you, he came rushing over immediately! Xia Yulian, I am Li Suzhi, please listen to me. When Mayor Li gets up to you, you can take your time talking to him! Secretary Yang is contacting Secretary Wan for you, and Secretary Wan will definitely be here soon. Also, Mayor Li told me to tell you that the two children you brought up for him, Meimei and Mingming, are coming to see you soon too…"

The sound of Li Suzhi's already hoarse voice was heartbreaking.

Li Gaocheng said to Director Wei, who was standing beside him: "Listen, I will go up there alone, and no one else is allowed up without my consent, even if something terrible happens. I'm the only one going up. When my children arrive in a bit, notify me through the loudspeaker, then let them come up when I agree..."

Li Gaocheng found himself choking up again.

His intuition was telling him that Xia Yulian could not hold out much longer. She was a woman who had suffered all her life, was at the end of that life, but was still making such a huge sacrifice for others. A woman who had almost never in her life had the chance to speak out in front of others but who had managed to maintain such optimism and concern for society in such difficult circumstances! She still had a deep and abiding love for the textile factory where she had worked and suffered all her life; she had the same love for the many workers in the factory who had never heard of her, let alone known her; she also deeply loved an ungrateful mayor whose two children she had raised with her own milk and her own blood, but who had all but forgotten her for years...

She was not only using her life and her death to stop the actions of the workers, she was also saving him, the mayor! She was saving his life as he confronted both the nation and its reforms, but he had still been hesitating! He was the mayor and he had been hesitating!

At that moment, Li Gaocheng seemed once again to have remembered the true meaning of the sentiment so commonly voiced: only she and thousands of workers like her were the masters of our country! She was the backbone of our country! She was the mainstay of our era!

Another thought also struck him very strongly. Many things in this world are often so simple: only if he kept her in his heart would she keep him in hers; only if he was always concerned about her survival would she be concerned for him and be willing to sacrifice her life...

As Li Gaocheng poked his head through the skylight, a burst of pain cut across his face and he couldn't even open his eyes.

The first thing that surprised him was the strength and ferocity of the biting northwest wind in this suburban area. It was presumably because there were so few other high-rise buildings nearby and this one was so high and exposed. The icy wind was carrying swirling clouds of dust and sand, which not only forced him to keep his eyes closed but also made it difficult for him even to breathe.

He forced himself to hold on for a moment, then stood up.

Perhaps it was the wind, perhaps it was the cold, perhaps this had been going on too long and Xia Yulian was too weak, but Li Gaocheng had been standing there for quite a while without her seeming to notice him. She didn't even turn to look.

He stood there silently, not knowing what to do for the moment. He wanted to shout but felt that he shouldn't; he wanted to walk towards her, but he didn't dare. He knew that in a place like this, in circumstances like these, any mistake would have irreversible results.

The place where Xia Yulian stood was really scary and perturbing. She was standing on a brick balustrade about sixty centimetres high that ran around the perimeter of the roof. The rough-built, cracked brickwork was less than twenty centimetres wide, and her body was so thin that the wind could easily blow her off it. She stood there swaying on that meagre twenty centimetres!

The commercial centre building was actually a cheap construction that had cut corners to save money. From the side fronting the street below, it looked quite big, wide and tall, but this really was just a facade. You could see from the back that the building got narrower as it went up, and when you reached the top you discovered that the building was surprisingly small, and the area of the entire roof was no more than about two hundred square metres. So Li Gaocheng was surprised to find himself so close to the spot where Yulian was standing. It encouraged him into the risky thought that, if he took two quiet steps and then swooped, he could pull Xia Yulian back from the brink of death in only a couple of seconds…

Almost without thinking, he took a step forward and then suddenly stopped as if frozen. He had definitely heard a very weak, very hoarse but very clear voice saying: "…don't come any closer!"

Li Gaocheng stood there in astonishment and stared blankly at the woman's thin back for a moment before he hurriedly said: "Older Sister Xia! It's me! It's Li Gaocheng!"

"I know it's you, Manager Li!" Xia Yulian kept her back to him as she still stood there on that heart-stopping ledge.

Xia Yulian had not addressed him as "Mayor" this time but had used his title from when he was factory director more than ten years ago!

"Can you get down to talk to me, Older Sister Xia? That's such a dangerous place you are standing – even if you let me talk to you, how can I be clear about what I have to say to you!" Li Gaocheng tried his best to talk calmly to Xia Yulian, while desperately thinking about what he should do next. "Even if you don't come down, Older Sister Xia, why don't you just sit down and talk to me?"

"Don't try and force me, Manager Li!" It may have been the wind that made Xia Yulian's voice sound so weak. Even so, Li Gaocheng could hear her quite clearly. "You know, I only have a few days to live. You really don't have to worry about me at all. When I die, I won't be a drag on my family, on you or on everybody else anymore. I will be dead, so I won't be suffering and nor will anybody else. I found the strength to climb up here today, but I don't expect ever to go back down."

"...Older Sister Xia!" There was a lump in Li Gaocheng's throat, but his tone was angry. "How can you think like this? If you do this, don't you care about how much everyone else will suffer? Even if you aren't thinking about yourself, you should think about the children, you should think about this factory! Older Sister Xia, if you won't think about me, your old factory manager at Zhongyang Textiles, then what about Meimei? What about Mingming?"

"Enough! I've already told you, don't try and force me! I just have one thing to ask you: has something happened to you? Tell me the truth, has something happened to you?"

"...What do you mean?" Li Gaocheng was puzzled by the question.

"We have grown far apart over the years, and all I remember now is what was going on all that time ago. Back then, I was clear about you, and we were all at ease with you. I'm not asking you this now to mock you – I just want to be sure. Manager Li, are you still as clean and pure as you were then? You have been working for the public for so many years, and your official position has got higher and higher, so is it still the case that you have never taken advantage of the public and have never done anything that you are ashamed of towards our workers?"

"I understand, Older Sister Xia! I can tell you that nothing has happened to me, nothing has happened!" Li Gaocheng replied vigorously. "I was a clean and honest factory manager and a clean and honest secretary. I am still the same today. I am a mayor who is worthy of the common people! I never considered embezzling a cent from the public purse in the past nor would I consider it today! I have never done anything that I am ashamed of in the past, and I won't do anything today! Since I saw you that day, I have given my past a lot of thought. I may perhaps have done something wrong or made a mistake, but it was never, ever intentional! I know that I have a great responsibility over the problems at Zhongyang Textiles. I know that I haven't paid enough attention to the workers there in recent years, and I haven't put my mind to things here properly! But one thing I can assure you is that, in terms of my finances and my lifestyle, I have not done anything that I would have to apologise for to the people here or to the factory…"

"If that's the case, then why did the province send people to investigate you and raid your home? Is what the workers have told me true, that someone called Secretary Yan went out of his way to make trouble for you? Was he trying to take revenge on you for investigating him? Do all the provincial leaders look to him because he is their boss? Is that how it works?"

"Who told you that, Sister Xia?" Li Gaocheng hadn't expected Xia Yulian to see things that way. "What they said is wrong, it's not true. The leaders of the Provincial and Municipal Committees are on our side! On the workers' side! The corrupt managers in the company have all been arrested already…"

"Then why haven't they investigated that Yan person instead of investigating you? Why didn't they raid his house, not yours? Why? Don't you dare tell a dying woman the truth?" Xia Yulian's eloquent speech was accompanied by a stern look. She was a completely different person from the Xia Yulian of before.

Li Gaocheng was almost knocked sideways by the question, and he didn't immediately know how to answer. After a while, he continued: "Older Sister Xia, sometimes things don't happen as quickly as we would like. But don't worry, no matter who he is, if he has done anything shameful, if he has done anything unconscionable or that the people wouldn't be in agreement with, he will be punished sooner or later…"

"I understand. You don't need to say any more!" Xia Yulian swayed a little. There was a collective gasp from the people upstairs and down below, but she quickly found her balance again and continued: "Director Li, as long as you are telling the truth, then there is nothing more that I have to do..."

"No, Older Sister Xia!" Li Gaocheng exclaimed. He hadn't anticipated an answer like that from her. "You told me to tell the truth! I've told you the truth, so can't you sit down now? Let's talk about it..."

"Can you get Secretary Wan to come too, and ask him if he will answer one question from a dying old woman? I won't take up much of his time, only a minute. I've listened to what you have to say and I want to hear from him too."

"Secretary Wan went out of town early this morning, and Secretary Yang has contacted him, but he is quite a long way away. It will be a while before he can get here."

"That's OK, I can wait. As long as he's definitely coming, I think... I can wait."

"Are you sure you are strong enough? You are sick and weak. If something goes wrong, how will I explain it to Secretary Wan? How will I explain it to the workers?"

"No, I know my own body. When I climbed up here, I took three painkillers, and I know I can hold out." Xia Yulian's tone brooked no argument, and she never even turned round to look at him.

"...But Older Sister Xia!"

Li Gaocheng called out to her desperately, on the verge of rushing over to her, before he was stopped in his tracks by her shouting: "Stay where you are!" Although she had her back turned, Xia Yulian seemed to be able to see everything that was going on. "I've told you before, don't try and force me..."

"Mayor Li, Mayor Li..." Li Gaocheng heard Chief Wei calling softly from behind him, "Here is a note for you from Secretary Yang."

Li Gaocheng glanced at the note Chief Wei was poking through the skylight behind him, thought for a moment, looked at Xia Yulian's back, and then carefully bent down and took the note.

Lao Li:

I have been in touch with Secretary Wan's secretary, and he is speaking to the people in the disaster area. He said that he would

579

talk to Secretary Wan about the matter right away. He said that Secretary Wan will definitely come, and, as we know what Secretary Wan is like, we can be sure he will.

Just in case, we have prepared protective equipment under the window where Xia Yulian is standing, but we have kept it hidden, otherwise it could easily cause trouble. You must do your best to talk her down because, especially with so many people present and so many news organisations, even if we stopped her when she tried to jump, it would still be unacceptable to everyone, including ourselves of course.

You are on your own up there; that's the only way it can be and none of us can help you. You should be clear that what you are doing now is not just about saving one woman, and you are not only dealing with one person but thousands of people. What confronts you is not just the life of one person, but the hope and trust of thousands of people. It is our hope and trust too!

It is a good idea to let Meimei and Mingming come. At times like this, emotion may be the only key to the situation.

Confronted with Yang Cheng's note, Li Gaocheng suddenly seemed to realise something. He thought for a moment, then took out his pen and wrote on the back of the note:

Yang Cheng:

Is it too late to get Secretary Wan to hurry back straight away? I don't think Xia Yulian will be able to hold out otherwise. Can you think of a way to get Secretary Wan to talk to us directly? Anything will do if it saves her life. I reckon there must be radio and TV stations where Secretary Wan is, doing on-the-spot interviews. Can they transmit Secretary Wan's words directly here so Xia Yulian can hear his voice? Then he can answer her questions himself.

In less than a minute, Yang Cheng's next note was handed up.

Lao Li:

Great idea! I'll get them to do that right away. I don't think it will be a problem. Also, Meimei and Mingming are coming soon, so please be ready.

Li Gaocheng thought nervously for a moment, then turned to Xia Yulian and said: "Older Sister Xia, Secretary Yang has just told me he has contacted Secretary Wan's secretary. He said that Secretary Wan is talking to the people in the disaster area but he will answer you immediately. The trouble is that he's too far away, more than two hundred miles. Is it all right for Secretary Wan to talk to you on the phone first?" Li Gaocheng wanted to be sure Xia Yulian would agree.

"You can get Secretary Wan... to call me here? ...How can I be sure that it's Secretary Wan I'm talking to? I suppose with so many workers up here and down there to bear witness... I can know whether Secretary Wan is telling the truth or not."

Xia Yulian's speech had already become rather halting, and Li Gaocheng's heart lurched. He was very much afraid she wasn't going to be able to hold out.

"Then can we get Secretary Wan to talk to the reporters of the radio and television stations, and they can pass on his words to you? And you can do the same in reverse. How about that?"

"No, I want to hear from Secretary Wan in person, and I also want the workers, wherever they are... I want them to hear him too."

Xia Yulian's voice was very weak, but her words had a very powerful effect on Li Gaocheng.

So, that was how things stood!

She wanted the tens of thousands of workers who had gathered there to hear the voice of the Provincial Party secretary!

Li Gaocheng was stunned; he felt as though he had been hit over the head. He was amazed how far and how deeply this weak old woman in front of him had thought things through! She was not doing this just for him, but also for the sake of Zhongyang Textiles and the tens of thousands of workers there...

He suddenly felt so shallow and wretched, and that feeling in turn made him deeply ashamed.

Li Gaocheng's determination to help this woman and the tens of thousands of workers who had gathered there instantly hardened. He must carry out her wishes to the letter!

"Older Sister Xia, I will get them to do as you say right away! Not only will you hear Secretary Wan's words, but all the people here will hear them too. I want the whole city and the whole province to hear them. I'll have them broadcasting here live immediately in an instant..."

The reason Li Gaocheng was so confident in making this promise was that he had one important piece of knowledge. He had heard Secretary Wan's speech the night before, so he knew exactly where the secretary stood on the issue of Zhongyang Textiles, and he also knew exactly what he would say and do.

CHAPTER FORTY-EIGHT

LI GAOCHENG HARDLY HAD ANY WORK TO DO once Xia Yulian agreed to his suggestion. The reporters from the city radio station and the provincial TV station were there in just twenty minutes.

They had everything ready for live coverage and live broadcasts.

Almost immediately, the connection was made with Wan Yongnian, secretary of the Provincial Party Committee, and Li Gaocheng could clearly hear Yang Cheng talking to Secretary Wan on the stairs below the skylight.

From what he could hear, Wan Yongnian had interrupted Yang Cheng before he finished speaking, and, a moment later, Yang Cheng was shouting up to him: "Secretary Wan says that his secretary has already explained what is going on. As long as the safety of the female worker can be ensured, he will do anything he can! He has had his car readied and can leave in five minutes. Even if there are no accidents, it will still take several hours to reach Zhongyang Textiles! He can talk directly to Xia Yulian now, in any case."

Li Gaocheng burst into tears again. Thank you, Secretary Wan!

A minute later, the voice of Wan Yongnian, secretary of the Provincial Party Committee, came through loud and clear via the radio and TV stations, as well as through Zhongyang Textiles' own high-frequency speakers and the loudspeakers on site:

"...This is Wan Yongnian, secretary of the Provincial Party

Committee, and I am now talking directly with the workers of Zhongyang Textiles through the municipal radio station and the provincial television station, directly with the people of the whole city and the whole province, and directly with Comrade Xia Yulian!

"May I call you 'Older Sister Xia'? I know I may be older than you, but I hope you will let me, because that is what Mayor Li Gaocheng, Secretary Yang Cheng and all the workers here call you, so I think I should too! You worked long and hard for Zhongyang Textiles, for our country and for our government, and expended a lifetime of effort, blood, sweat and tears. For this alone, we should always thank you from the bottom of our hearts! That is also why you will always be our big sister. I heard that you also nursed Mayor Li's two children, Older Sister Xia, so I would like to say something of special meaning today – you were not only wet nurse to those children, but you and the thousands of workers are also the wet nurses of our country! Without your painstaking care, our country would not be where it is today!

"According to Mayor Li Gaocheng and Secretary Yang Cheng, you are not in good health, and you have been ill for a long time. Despite this, and the fact that you have been retired for many years, you still have to run around trying to earn a living and you are struggling with many hardships. When Mayor Li Gaocheng went looking for you, he found you living in extremely poor conditions and a very harsh environment! I was so sad when I heard this that I wept!

"Older Sister Xia, it is not only Mayor Li Gaocheng who feels so bad for you, it is the workers too – we are all responsible for something like this, and I, the secretary of the Provincial Party Committee, have the greatest responsibility of all! We all feel so sorry for you..."

Li Gaocheng listened in silence and wept quietly to himself. It turned out that Secretary Wan knew everything. He had told hardly anyone about going to Zhongyang Textiles to find Xia Yulian, and he certainly hadn't expected Secretary Wan to know about it in such detail!

"The Provincial Party Committee already made its decision last night," Wan Yongnian continued. "I will go to Zhongyang Textiles this afternoon or tomorrow morning to visit the workers, and there is one thing I was going to say to everyone then, but, as all this has happened, I will do it now. Problems like those at Zhongyang Textiles will never happen again in the future! We will formulate new rules and regulations as soon as possible, and resolutely prevent any damage to and erosion of workers' rights and interests!

"Sister Xia, I know your situation, and I think I know what is in your heart right now. You can't see me, but I can see you quite clearly here! People across the whole province and the city can also see you clearly. I think I know what you are going to ask me, Older Sister Xia, and I will answer you truthfully in front of the people of the whole province and the whole city!

"First of all, I want to tell you and everyone else that the Provincial Party Committee and the Municipal Party Committee are determined to resolve the problems at Zhongyang Textiles! They will never let the issue drop. They will never let the leading cadres get away! They will never lose their grip on the current predicament and future of Zhongyang Textiles! They will never lose their grip on the difficulties and demands of the workers of Zhongyang Textiles!

"The second thing I want to tell you and everyone is that last night, the Provincial Party Committee and the Municipal Party Committee took strong action on the issue of Zhongyang Textiles! In the current preliminary circumstances, I can confirm to everyone that the problems that the staff and cadres of Zhongyang Textiles have been exposing and reporting recently are all completely correct! This also demonstrates convincingly that the anti-corruption struggle of our Party and government must always rely on and mobilise the masses! Only in that way can that struggle be as thorough and effective as it needs to be! As for the corrupt actions of the management cadres at Zhongyang Textiles, the Provincial Party Committee can now assure all of you that those responsible will never escape the severe punishment of Party discipline and state law!

"The third thing I want to tell you, and everyone, is that in the course of the operation last night, we also unmasked the corruption of some other leadership cadres related to the problems at Zhongyang Textiles. The Provincial Party Committee is equally determined on this issue. We reported the preliminary results of the operation to the Party Central Committee early this morning!

"I will now turn to another issue that everyone is very concerned about. With the approval of the Central Committee, the Central

Commission for Discipline Inspection of the Communist Party of China has decided to file a case and conduct a serious review of the issue of the deputy Provincial Party secretary, Yan Zhen.

"There is another point, which I know is the issue that you and everyone are most concerned about, and that is that, because of our operation last night, we have further identified and come to understand one person in particular. That person is Comrade Li Gaocheng, who we know is deeply loved and supported by all of you! I can now tell everyone with complete confidence that Li Gaocheng is indeed a good mayor! He is a true member of the Communist Party who has been tested and absolutely withstood that test!"

During Wan Yongnian's exhilarating speech, Li Gaocheng suddenly felt someone touch him lightly on the arm. When he turned around, he saw Chief Wei gesturing twice at something behind him.

It was Meimei and Mingming!

The two children looked stunned, their faces were pale, and they were listening and watching everything that was happening in front of them in bewilderment!

He really wanted to bring the two children closer to his side, but seeing how stunned they looked and also noticing Chief Wei standing beside them, he dismissed the idea.

Provincial Party Secretary Wan Yongnian's speech would be more convincing at this moment than any of his other actions and words.

Everyone was listening in silence.

"...The so-called bribe of three hundred thousand yuan, the so-called cover-up of his wife's crime, the so-called complicity with corrupt elements and the so-called tapes used as evidence are all trumped-up charges designed to frame him!

"Just last night, we also found a tape in a safe in Li Gaocheng's wife's office. This tape not only displayed to us the despicable shamelessness of those corrupt elements but also demonstrated the honesty and righteousness of a real Communist Party member!

"I am very proud of you, Older Sister Xia! Your aim is to protect Mayor Li Gaocheng who is standing behind you at this moment. He was a good secretary and factory manager, and he is also a good mayor now!

"I have already been talking for too long, Older Sister Xia, and I think I have said all that I need to say to you! My car is already here, and I am going to get back as quickly as possible. Finally, I want to share with you this tape that I have just listened to. Everyone else can listen to it too. It was secretly recorded by her nanny on the orders of Mayor Li's wife in order to protect herself. This tape is absolutely genuine! We are fortunate that the little nanny not only recorded the shameless acts of bribery with huge sums of money but also recorded the quarrel and argument between Li Gaocheng and his wife over the matter!

"Older Sister Xia, since I asked the radio and TV stations to play this to everyone, I hope you have been able to listen to me, and I hope you will also listen to the words of our good mayor, Li Gaocheng, who has been trying so hard to persuade you. If anything bad should happen to you, everybody would be heartbroken. Also, Older Sister Xia, look behind you right now! The two children you raised are watching you with tears in their eyes! Do you have the heart to let them mourn for you for the rest of their lives..."

At that moment, Secretary Wan's speech was suddenly drowned out by a cry of alarm.

Xia Yulian, who had been standing in silence all this time, turned round, almost involuntarily. Perhaps the turn was too slow, but for whatever reason, it made her stagger on the balustrade as if she could not keep her balance any longer, and she almost fell over!

"Nanny!"

The two children shouted hoarsely at almost the same time.

"Older Sister Xia..."

Li Gaocheng also gave a heart-wrenching cry.

Then Li Gaocheng saw Xia Yulian reaching her hand out towards him and the children...

Li Gaocheng hurled himself across the roof like a madman and immediately fell to his knees with a thud, hugging Xia Yulian to him as she fell, almost in a coma.

At the same moment, he saw the children behind him and everyone else who was there also falling to their knees as if in terror.

"...Nanny!"

He heard the sobbing cries of his two children.

He also heard the earth-shattering, sky-splitting cries from all around him.

When Xia Yulian was carried down from the roof and all the way into the ambulance, Li Gaocheng realised that they were surrounded by the entire Zhongyang Textiles staff of tens of thousands of workers.

They were all looking on silently and listening, all of them with tears in their eyes.

They were listening to that recording!

Yang Cheng told him that this tape had been secretly recorded by his wife, Wu Aizhen, when they sent him three hundred thousand yuan in cash that night. Although his wife and the others had seemed to be acting together, both sides had made secret recordings! It turned out that each was on their guard against the other and neither trusted the other an inch!

Things that look dirty and shameful will always turn out to be just that – dirty and shameful!

Interestingly, the little nanny had not only recorded the whole process of the handing over of the money, but for some unknown reason, she also recorded the quarrel between Li Gaocheng and his wife. It was very likely that, for some reason or other, she forgot about the recording and left it going while the two of them argued...

For some strange reason, Li Gaocheng didn't entirely understand, his wife hadn't deleted the latter section. Perhaps, in trying to protect herself, she had imagined a day like today and thought that if that was what it came to, and there was no one to protect her, maybe if she saved her husband, it would mean she was protecting her children too. That would explain what she had said to him when he was in hospital: "There is only one person who can save you, and that is me!"

What an indescribably twisted way of thinking!

Society was so complex, and people were so complex too.

The quality of the recording was very clear, and the impact of hearing his own voice was very powerful, not to say shocking:

"...I just don't understand what you lot want so much money for! Think about the past, look at the present! What have we got to be unhappy with compared to the ordinary people? You swan around the countryside, you swan around the factory! Look at what you eat, what you wear, where you live, what car you ride in! What do the ordinary people have to eat or to wear? Where do they live? Are you saying you can live with that in the face of those people? Are you saying you can live with yourself, you can live with our children and you can live with your conscience? When the day comes and you do have to face up to the ordinary people and answer for yourself, are you going to say you did it all for the sake of this money? Were your original ideals, original ambitions, original enthusiasm and original oath all just for this little bit of money? Don't you know that what you are doing now will not only destroy our country and destroy our reforms, but it will also ruin your family's happiness and prospects for the future? And that includes you yourself! Because of your sin and greed, you will be trampled under the feet of the people for thousands of generations! You will be nailed to the pillar of shame for all time to come! The people of all the generations that follow will never forgive you..."

Li Gaocheng vaguely felt that these words could have been written for today's occasion.

Yes, there was no doubt that, in the face of the marketplace and reform, everyone was going to be confronted by severe tests and new choices!

Suddenly, cheers and applause erupted around him. He knew that the recording had ended, and he also knew that the cheers and applause were all for him.

He found that his two children were watching him silently with tears streaming down their faces.

"Dad, why didn't you tell us these things before?" His son seemed to be regretting the things he had said the night before.

"...Dad, are the things in the recording really true?" Meimei asked in sorrowful bewilderment.

Li Gaocheng didn't answer, but just gently took his daughter in his arms. Meimei could not stop sobbing.

"Dad, what is this all for? Dad, how can things be like this, how can they be like this? What is it all for? How is it possible?"

He couldn't answer Meimei, and he couldn't answer himself.

It had all come at them too fast and too hard, especially when they hadn't developed any resistance to such things...

EPILOGUE

A MONTH LATER, the on-site meeting regarding the deepening of the reform of the province's state-owned large and medium-sized enterprises was held at Zhongyang Textiles.

Three months later, the preliminary results of the investigation into the company's problems came out. The state-owned assets lost by Zhongyang Textiles, including fixed assets that had been invested abroad, illegal profits obtained over the years, and cash and goods that had been uncovered and inventoried, totalled more than 270 million yuan! Over 60 million of that was in cash.

Five months later, the Provincial Party Committee, the Provincial Government, the Municipal Party Committee and the Municipal Government made a joint decision and obtained the consent of all the cadres of the various provincial and municipal bodies. In view of the fact that when the Provincial Party Committee offices and the Municipal Government building were refurbished, they had raised a great deal of the necessary money from Zhongyang Textiles, all the leading cadres of the two Party committees and governments each donated a month's salary as the re-launch capital for Zhongyang Textiles.

Six months later, the new management team of Zhongyang Textiles was formally elected by all the staff and cadres after careful inspection by the Municipal Party Committee and the company's new Party Committee.

Seven months later, all the active and retired staff and cadres of Zhongyang Textiles, under the leadership of the new team, had raised a total of 425.68 million yuan!

Nine months later, with the full support of the Provincial Party Committee and the Provincial Government, the Municipal Party Committee and the Municipal Government, and including donations from provincial and municipal cadres, the proceeds from the investigation and the funds raised by Zhongyang Textiles employees and cadres, a total of 100 million yuan was reached along with 70 million yuan of start-up and technology improvement funds! After careful investigation, the National Bank was also prepared to continue its loan of 30 million yuan!

Ten months later, Zhongyang Textiles officially started operations again. The leaders of the Provincial Party Committee, the Provincial Government, the Municipal Party Committee and the Municipal Government held a grand opening ceremony together with the workers.

On the same day, at her repeated pleading, Xia Yulian, who had been hospitalised for several months, was carried to the construction site by the workers. When the loud rumbling of the machinery started up, Xia Yulian, who was already close to death, insisted on standing up, and asked the workers to help her over to one of the machines, where she held a ball of cotton in her own hands.

The workers said that the cries and weeping of all the people present that day, including the leaders of the province and the city, almost drowned out the noise of the machinery.

The investigation and trial of the case of Zhongyang Textiles was still ongoing...

On New Year's Day 1997, when a new project for the technological improvement of Zhongyang Textiles, a glass fibre product that had been a hot seller on the international market, was launched, the company brought in its first-ever real joint venture partner: a heating conduit company from X, a country in Eastern Europe.

The representative of the party from X was Chinese, but his secretary was the Minister of Labour of the former Eastern European Communist country of X!

The former minister's name was Barbern, and after a joint

venture was agreed upon, Li Gaocheng made a point of treating him to a meal during which he asked the man a few questions:

Li Gaocheng: "Mr Barbern, I don't mean to pry but I just want to ask you – you were once a senior government official in X and now you are a secretary in a private company. This must be a deeply emotional thing for you, mustn't it?"

Barbern: "It is."

Li Gaocheng: "Can you tell me about it?"

Barbern: "I think it is something you yourself can relate to."

Li Gaocheng: "I would like to hear the details."

Barbern: "Actually, I'm pretty calm about it now but if you had asked me at the time, it would have been a different story. It was almost too much for me. How should I put it? It seemed as though, overnight, you were suddenly nothing, nobody. You had absolutely become a penniless pauper. Can you imagine what a horrible experience that is? The house you used to live in has been confiscated, all your funds and property have been frozen, all sources of livelihood have been cut off, and you have no job, no salary and no source of income to support your family. The most frightening thing is that you have no means of survival and no ability to survive. You have lost almost everything, and you are not even able to support yourself."

Li Gaocheng: "And what happened next?"

Barbern: "There was nothing for it – I had to take temporary jobs. I worked as a porter, a stevedore, a cleaner, but I wasn't any good even at that kind of work. But that wasn't what saddened me the most. If I wasn't any good at it, I could slowly get the hang of it. If I couldn't carry the heavy stuff, I could carry the light stuff. If I couldn't earn a lot, I would earn a little. What saddened me the most was that, once they recognised me, my colleagues and fellow workers laughed out loud and pointed at me, saying that all I knew was how to hold meetings and talk all day, but now I was just the same as them. We were finally equals, and I would find out what it was like to be a worker."

Li Gaocheng: "It sounds as though you must be very sad."

Barbern: "I'm not sorry for myself, but I am for our past actions. We were in power for so many years, and all we got in return from the people was ridicule. That is what is really sad."

Li Gaocheng: "Have you analysed the main reason this happened to your country?"

Barbern: "I think you know quite well but I will still give you my opinion."

Li Gaocheng: "Thank you, I very much want to hear it."

Barbern: "To start with, there is the well-known reason. The influence of the former Soviet Union was too great, and everything we had could only follow their model, which made it impossible. Second, I didn't expect the former Soviet Union to disintegrate so quickly. When it ceased to exist, we also ceased to exist..."

Li Gaocheng: "But if you were determined to carry out immediate reforms and were determined to break free from the rigid model of the former Soviet Union, was it necessarily too late..."

Barbern: "Yes, it was too late."

Li Gaocheng: "Why?"

Barbern: "The mechanisms of state were defunct, and it no longer had the ability or strength to function. In a word, the country was too poor, and its national strength had been exhausted."

Li Gaocheng: "But surely the confidence of the people had not been lost, their enthusiasm had not been extinguished, and you still had their support..."

Barbern: "No, none of that."

Li Gaocheng: "Why not?"

Barbern: "We made them wait too long, and they were so poor..."

Silence fell.

After a long time, Li Gaocheng said slowly: "I don't think we will be in the same situation."

"I don't think so either," Barbern said thoughtfully. "Let's drink to that!"

"Cheers!"

AFTERWORD
FOREVER WRITING ON BEHALF OF THE COMMON PEOPLE

When the lawsuit was filed in Beijing over my two books *Skynet* and *Fa Han Fenxi*, several old farmers from Linfen came all the way to the capital to support me. Beijing in July is like a furnace. When they had crammed themselves onto a crowded bus and, with great difficulty, found out the address and rushed to the Fengtai Court, the public hearing had already been over for two days. Somehow or other they managed to discover the address of the Mass Publishing House and found me there. Tears welled up in my eyes when I first saw them. Their clothes were old-fashioned, their faces, dark from the sun, were creased and wrinkled with deep concern and anxiety, and their sweat seemed to be impregnated with a kind of honesty and sincerity. As soon as they saw me, they immediately enquired if I had won or lost, if the court had found in my favour or not, and then asked how they could help. They said that they had told the people at the Fengtai Court that originally all the people from their village had wanted to come, but, because they didn't know what things were like up here, they just sent this deputation to find out the news. If the judgement went against the author Zhang Ping, the whole village would come to Beijing to post placards in support of him! The ordinary people wanted to see for themselves how the law was enacted! They wanted the whole world to see that the ordinary people supported writers like Zhang Ping!

After CCTV and Beijing TV reported the news of my lawsuit,

especially after Beijing TV made it the subject of a special feature in the "Good Morning, Beijing" segment, so many people began to recognise me in the crowd. I went to one restaurant to eat where the proprietress kept looking at me over and over. Finally, she couldn't hold back anymore and asked me if I was the writer who had been put on trial. I nodded and said I was. She looked at me again and disappeared without another word. Quite soon, she came back with two large plates of food which she said she had cooked herself. She told me to sit there and eat them and they were on the house. In fact, she went on to say that, in the future, I could eat there every day for free! In those days, I was living at a friend's place in a large dormitory compound. Before the lawsuit, the old concierge was always fierce towards me with my unfamiliar face and strange accent. Sometimes, when I made a phone call and forgot to pay, he would yell at me: "Come back! Pay up!" He never gave me a friendly look, even when I apologised. To my surprise, one day when I went to make a call, he looked at me silently, but with a kind and gentle look in his eyes. When I had finished the call, he said: "You are that writer who has been accused. I didn't recognise you. Listen, young man, I'm an old man and I can't really help you much, but you can use this phone anytime, free of charge!" On another occasion, when I was on the bus, a middle-aged man in his forties leaned over and whispered to me that he had once lived on a rural commune in Shanxi, so he understood what went on there. He said that I could rest assured that the Chinese people would support me. I went to the park one day and some old people who were playing cards recognised me. They kept telling me: "You can't lose. Beijingers may not show it, but they don't miss a thing, and understand everything. If a writer like you loses, what would that do to Beijing's reputation?"

I simply can't keep track of how many times this kind of thing happened and how many people like this I met!

From the time of their publication to the conclusion of the lawsuit, *Skynet* and *Fa Han Fenxi* drew nearly two thousand letters from readers. The calls and letters just kept coming in, particularly during the actual court case. They came from Xinjiang, Sichuan, Guangdong, Heilongjiang, Yunnan... I have no idea how these readers got my address and phone number. I have received four letters with multiple signatures of more than a thousand people and twelve from more than five hundred people! A reader wrote in one letter: "Author Zhang Ping, you mustn't give an inch. Even if you lose, it doesn't matter, because in the hearts of the common people, you will always be the winner..."

In addition to finding this exhilarating, I ask myself over and over again, what is the reason for all this? What have you done to deserve so many people's concern and support as a writer who has only written a few thin books? Is it because, in your work, you portray leaders who are loved by the people, because you pay attention to social issues that the people are concerned about, and because you speak a few words of truth and justice on behalf of the ordinary people?

Therefore, I often feel fortunate in my own experiences and grateful to my own books. Where would I be in my creative career if it were not for works such as *Fa Han Fenxi*, *Skynet*, *Orphan's Tears* and *The Choice*? If my books had all been idealised fantasies and bits of trivia, if they had all been set in ivory towers of impossible purity, if they had been about the luxury and extravagance of the dance hall and the banquet table piled high with gold and flowers, if I had been experimenting on my readers with fancy new trends and techniques, would the ordinary people understand me? Would they remember me? Would they be showing me the concern and support that they do today?

Books get the readers they deserve, and readers get the books they deserve. There is a need both for highbrow literature and lowbrow trash. As a writer, the attributes of your life will inevitably determine the attributes of your works. The kind of life you are familiar with and the kind of life you yearn for will inevitably produce corresponding works. If you are familiar with the life of karaoke bars and casinos, you will write very realistically about the atmosphere and environment of such places; if you have a soft spot for the relationships between men and women, you will write very realistically about the emotions between men and women; if you live in your own lonely little world all the year round, then it is impossible for you to write vigorous, emotional, epic period literature of majesty and solemnity; if you always pay close attention to the changes in society and the lives of the common people, then it is impossible for you to write only frivolous mysteries and idle fantasies all the time. For a writer, neither life itself nor the subject matter of the book determines the quality of a work. What determines the quality of a work should be the writer's attitude towards life and his understanding of literature.

We always complain that the level of readers is too low, that they are immature, and we moan about how hard it is to find someone who understands us, so what we really want is to leave our works for people to study in the next century. Before writing, we always think about how to be up with the times, how to break through, how to surpass, how to delight the experts, how to convince our colleagues, and how to leave a mark in the history of literature. Modernism, postmodernism, post-postmodernism... deconstruction, subversion, disruption, destruction... text is a game, language is a cage, ultimate meaninglessness, reading is misreading... even going as far as anti-meaning, anti-interpretation, anti-form, anti-genre, anti-aesthetics... these are the things we are looking at, what we are studying, and what we are comparing. These pre-conceptions have become so ingrained that they take over our subconscious and control our thinking and writing all the time. When I look at my past works and aspirations, even I myself feel astonished beyond words. Why did I gradually turn a blind eye to those tens of thousands of ordinary people who still live in such poverty, both spiritually and materially? Why did I, who am so intimately connected to this land, keep looking to other places? When did I become so indifferent and dismissive of the appeals and judgments of the ordinary people? How is it that responsibilities, ideals and sense of urgency have been given up so completely and contemptuously? Why did I become like this? What made me become like this? In contrast, we seem seldom to remember that there are still tens of millions of illiterate people in our country, hundreds of millions of semi-literate people who have not completed compulsory education, and nearly one billion farmers and workers. Few of us seem to think and act on the principle that these works of ours should be written for the most ordinary people at the bottom of the heap, and for those nearly one billion peasants and workers. Faced with the temptation of the market and money, our ability to persevere is so fragile and vulnerable. We may fix our gaze on the big bucks or abandon our dignity and sense of duty, or regard the world as empty and broken; or, driven by endless resentment and impetuosity, decide that writing is only a word game... If writing does follow these tendencies, then the life of the common people will no longer seem so important: wherever there is life, there is material, so the joy and passion of playing with language will be squandered willy-nilly, and our lives and our times will become devoid of any meaning. Thus our works grow further and further away from the lives of ordinary people, and our readership gets smaller and smaller. So, at this point, we come up with the theory of "marginalisation" and "multi-polarisation" to prove that literature will always be neglected and its readership will always diminish. In the face of people's appeals, criticisms and dissatisfaction, we still remain calm and discuss whether literary works should have ideals, responsibility, conscience, justice and nobility. In the face of the country's earth-shaking and unprecedented reforms and changes, some writers who are complacent and indifferent still shut themselves in their "ivory towers", still dreaming selfish, useless literary dreams, or preening themselves for their aloofness, or reducing themselves to mere writers of meaningless ciphers. Perhaps this is the deadliest of all the reasons why literature has fallen into the abyss and cannot extricate itself.

Our era needs all kinds of literary and artistic works, but it will never need the pretentious words of a pseudo-literature full of lust and selfish desires. Writers are not saviours, but they must never let themselves become distanced from the reality of the times and the people. A writer who does not pay attention to the reality of the times, and is devoid of ideals and a sense of responsibility, may become an excellent writer, but he will never become a great writer. A simple truth is revealed by a simple question: how can the people love literature if literature does not care about the people?

Before writing *The Choice*, I interviewed dozens of state-owned large and medium-sized enterprises and private enterprises both inside and outside the province. It was a very thought-provoking experience that has given me a deeper understanding of literature from a different perspective. With factory directors, managers, bosses, big money men, chairmen of the board, as well as those senior workers, chief workers and leading cadres who may be classed as intellectuals, the higher they climb their particular ladders, the less they read any literature; they don't even watch TV dramas. They don't have time. They are too busy, they are too tired, and they socialise too much. They are intimately familiar with what writers should consider to be the most unimportant form of writing: popular songs. They can sing all the most fashionable songs, old and new, and they do so very well. Contrary to expectation, it is people at the grassroots, the most ordinary of workers, who are, in fact, most exposed to literature and art. They are still the most honest and loyal audience and readers of films, television, theatre, novels and essays! This is even more the case in the countryside. Every word of the works that some writers despise the most, such as *The Casebook of Judge Bao*, *The Casebook of Judge Shi* and *The Three Loyal Heroes and Five Righteous Gallants*, are still read with great interest by peasants. Even their children's educational reading materials are still made up of these works. Is this not a great tragedy and a great irony for our nation's contemporary literature? The works we think should be the least popular are still widely circulated, while the ones we feel should be the most popular are being weeded out and discarded at the rate of one batch every three to five years...

Is there any need to ask why?

Renewing ideas and techniques does not mean that we can renew our foundations just like that; transcending ourselves and our texts does not mean that we can transcend our times at will. I will never believe that a work that is not recognised by the people of my own country will go on to take the world by storm; I will never believe that a writer's work can have no influence during his lifetime, but go on to become an enduring classic after his death; I cannot believe that works that have no readers in the contemporary era will have a large number of admirers and researchers in the future... If I take a step back to consider, even if there could be such a situation, it is certainly not what I desire or am aiming for.

The emergence of the work *The Choice* was not accidental. Last year, when my colleagues and I interviewed large and medium-sized state-owned enterprises, we never expected that the workers would respond so strongly to the idea of being interviewed. This was the complete opposite of the factory managers who seemed to have had enough of being interviewed. When the workers heard that we wanted to interview them, and that we wanted them to tell the truth, they were so moved that they queued up to be interviewed, telling us we could ask them whatever we wanted. They said that over the years, very few people had come to interview the workers. Mostly, interviewers were looking to make some money out of the company, or the interviews were simply for show as part of an advertising campaign. They would find a few trustworthy managers who were good with words and sit them down so they could praise the brilliant achievements of the senior management; they could then blithely extol the company's bright future, take a few pictures, scoff down the free hospitality, and keep everybody happy. A quick pat on the backside and then they were off. No one had ever actually asked what the workers really thought or what they needed. Many people have asked us over and over again: "Why can't you write about us workers? Why do so many scriptwriters, directors, writers and artists focus only on the factory managers and the big money men? Aren't we workers the masters of the country, the people on whom the country depends? Why have you forgotten and abandoned us? Why can't you write something that reflects us workers and makes us want to read it?"

I feel ashamed and guilty, but I have no answer.

Can I claim that I am unfamiliar with the lives of the workers? The workers just say: "Come and visit us, have a good look around and won't that give you the familiarity and understanding you want? Are you trying to tell us that those authors who write celebratory pieces and biographies about factory managers, directors and leadership cadres are intimately familiar and have a deep understanding of their subjects? We have heard that some of you immerse yourselves in the lives of these people and even go into their companies as temporary trainees, so why can't you do the same with us workers? Could it be that you writers too abhor the poor and love the rich, and only choose to run around with the rich and powerful?"

I quite simply have no reply.

In 1995, when I went to Pingyao with the directors and scriptwriters of the Beijing Film Academy, we found a dirty, tattered copy of *Skynet* on the bed of an old farmer in a remote mountainous area. When the old farmer asked me to sign the book, I could hardly find a blank space to write. I couldn't imagine how many people must have read that copy and I had no idea what I should write. In the end, I just wrote: "Thank you, Grandfather! I will never forget the kindness and friendship you have all shown me." I was very sincere in that sentiment as it really was what I was feeling at the time. Truly, from the bottom of my heart, I am grateful to them because without them I think all my efforts, past and present, would be meaningless.

I've said it before and I'll say it again: I just keep my eye on reality, which speaks louder than anything else. Even if others are selling ginseng, I am quite happy selling my carrots. As long as my work can have some positive and meaningful impact on the democracy and freedom of our society, on the prosperity and strength of our country, and on the happiness and improvement of the lives of all people, even if no one is reading my works in three, five or ten years' time, I will still be perfectly happy and perfectly content. In a word, I admit it! If I hadn't really thought about who I was writing for before, I have really thought about it now and decided that my work is for the millions of ordinary people at the bottom of the ladder. I will always write for them!

NOTES

CHAPTER 4

1. The much-feared Japanese military police during the Sino-Japanese War

CHAPTER 18

1. A story from *Romance of the Three Kingdoms*: Zhou Yu wanted Huang Gai, his subordinate, to pretend to defect to Cao Cao's side so that Huang Gai could gain Cao Cao's trust. This allowed Huang Gai to set fire to Cao Cao's fleet during the Battle of Red Cliffs, forcing Cao Cao to retreat. Zhou Yu had Huang Gai flogged in front of Cao Cao's spies so that they would not be suspicious

CHAPTER 19

1. From the company's point of view, "Green Apple" is a bright, fresh, appealing name, but Li Gaocheng is thinking of it in its figurative sense denoting a callow, inexperienced youth

CHAPTER 20

1. Big-character posters were handwritten posters with large characters, usually mounted on walls in public spaces such as universities, factories, government departments, and sometimes directly on the streets. They were used as a means of protest, propaganda and popular communication

CHAPTER 23

1. This refers to Liu Qingshan and Zhang Zishan, two heroes of the Chinese Civil War, who exploited their resulting positions of authority to plunder economic development money. Their subsequent trial and execution was the signal case in an anti-corruption "campaign against three evils" that ended late in 1952, with the announcement that 196,000 party members and cadres had been convicted of something

CHAPTER 26

1. Violent Struggles, or Wudou (武斗), were factional conflicts (mostly among Red Guards and "rebel groups") which began in Shanghai and then spread to other areas of China in 1967. It brought the country to a state of civil war

CHAPTER 29

1. A famous Chinese opera, movie and ballet of the early Mao era in which the daughter of a tenant farmer is persecuted by her landlord, and her hair and skin turn white due to lack of sunlight and poor diet

CHAPTER 33

1. Households that refuse to sell their properties to allow development of an area. In some cases this is done out of principle but in others it is a way of forcing government and developers to pay extortionate sums to buy them out

CHAPTER 34

1. A story from Jingshi Tongyan (*Stories to Caution the World*), the second of a trilogy of widely celebrated Ming dynasty vernacular story collections, compiled and edited by Feng Menglong and published in 1624

CHAPTER 36

1. There is an old Chinese saying: "Left eye twitching, good fortune; right eye twitching, disaster."

CHAPTER 42

1. 红楼梦 *Hongloumeng*, variously translated as *The Dream of the Red Chamber*, *A Dream of Red Mansions* and *The Story of the Stone*, is one of the four great classical novels of Chinese literature. Written by Cao Xueqin in the mid-18th century, it tells the story of the fortunes of two branches of the wealthy Jia family. Jiao Da is a faithful old family retainer who gets drunk one day and starts blabbing the family secrets. He has his mouth stuffed with horse dung to shut him up

ABOUT THE AUTHOR

Zhang Ping (1953-) is an author from Shanxi Province. Known for the passionate sense of social responsibility in his works, he has served in numerous official posts such as chairman of the Shanxi Provincial Writers Association and vice chairman of the China Writers Association alongside his career as a novelist.

His prominent works include novels such as *Skynet*, *The Murderer*, *Red Snow*, *Ambush From All Sides* and *National Cadre*, as well as short story collections such as *Memorial for a Wife* and *Elder Sister*. He has also published essay collections such as *I Can Only Speak the Truth* and the documentary novel *Orphan's Tears*.

He has received numerous commendations, including the Chinese Book Award, the National Book Award, and the Five-One Project Award. The Choice won the Fifth Mao Dun Literature Prize in 2000 and was also selected as a commemorative work for the 50th anniversary of the founding of the People's Republic of China. The novel has also been adapted into a film titled *Fatal Decision*, which won Best Feature Film at the Golden Rooster Awards.

His works have been translated into many languages, including English, French, Russian, Japanese and Portuguese.

ABOUT THE TRANSLATOR

James Trapp has an honours degree in Chinese from the School of Oriental and African Studies, University of London, with special papers in pre-Han archaeology and early Buddhist sculpture. After graduating, he spent ten years as an art dealer working for companies based in London, New York and Hong Kong.

Subsequently, with the rise in interest in Mandarin in UK schools, he refocused on making Mandarin accessible to young learners. He has produced a comprehensive Programme of Study for Primary Mandarin, with a focus on the constructive use of Chinese art and culture in Mandarin teaching. He has developed this in classrooms and after-school clubs across a wide range of primary and secondary schools, as well as through his work at the British Museum.

James first visited China in 1982 and has since travelled extensively throughout the country. He has published China-related books on characters, proverbs, astrology, science and technology. His translation works include new versions of Sunzi's *The Art of War* and Laozi's *Daodejing*, and, for Sinoist Books, Wang Hongjia's *Final Witness*, Ma Pinglai's *The Elm Tree*, Su Tong's *Shadow of the Hunter* and Zhou Daxin's *Longevity Park*. When not translating, James is to be found walking his dog, Pebbles, and perfecting his versions of classic Sichuan dishes.

About **Sino**ist Books

We hope you enjoyed this story about the exploitation of working people and their fight for justice.

SINOIST BOOKS brings the best of Chinese fiction to English-speaking readers. We aim to create a greater understanding of Chinese culture and society, and provide an outlet for the ideas and creativity of the country's most talented authors.

To let us know what you thought of this book, or to learn more about the diverse range of exciting Chinese fiction in translation we publish, find us online. If you're as passionate about Chinese literature as we are, then we'd love to hear your thoughts!

sinoistbooks.com
@sinoistbooks